Wittgenstein's Place
in Twentieth-century Analytic Philosophy

Wittgenstein's Place in Twentieth-century Analytic Philosophy

P. M. S. Hacker

Fellow of St John's College · Oxford

BLACKWELL
Publishers

Copyright © P. M. S. Hacker, 1996

The right of P. M. S. Hacker to be identified as author of this work has been
asserted in accordance with the Copyright, Designs and Patents Act 1988.

First published 1996

Reprinted 1997

Blackwell Publishers Ltd
108 Cowley Road
Oxford OX4 1JF, UK

Blackwell Publishers Inc
Commerce Place, 350 Main Street,
Malden, Massachusetts 02148, USA

British Library Cataloguing in Publication Data
A CIP catalogue record for this book is available from the British Library

Library of Congress Cataloging in Publication Data
Hacker, P. M. S. (Peter Michael Stephan)
Wittgenstein's place in twentieth-century analytic philosophy /
P. M. S. Hacker.
p.   cm.
Includes index.
ISBN   0–631–20098–3 (alk. paper). — ISBN   0–631–20099–1 (pbk. :
alk. paper)
1. Wittgenstein, Ludwig, 1889–1951. 2. Analysis (Philosophy)
I. Title.
B3376.W564H245   1996   95–42004
192—dc20   CIP

Typeset in 10 on 12pt Bembo
by Graphicraft Typesetters Limited, Hong Kong
Printed and bound in Great Britain by Hartnolls Ltd, Bodmin, Cornwall

This book is printed on acid-free paper

For
Jonathan, Adam and Jocelyn

Contents

Preface

In this book I have tried to paint a picture of the evolution of analytic philosophy in the twentieth century. From the beginning of the century and for the next seventy-five years, it was, in all its various transformations, the most distinctive style of philosophical thought of our times. To the extent that the seventeenth and eighteenth centuries can be characterized as above all the age of reason and enlightenment in philosophy, and the nineteenth century as the age of historicism and historical self-consciousness, then to that extent the twentieth century can be said to have been the age of language and logic. The task of exploring the philosophical consequences of the thought that man is above all a language-using creature fell to analytic philosophy. So too did that of clarifying the significance of the unprecedentedly powerful formal logic invented at the turn of the century, and of elucidating the relations between logical calculi, language and thought. Modern analytic philosophy was born on the banks of the Cam, whence its influence spread to the Danube and the Isis, and thence to far-flung countries across the globe. Many figures played a role in its development, but none greater than that of Ludwig Wittgenstein. His impact upon successive phases of analytic philosophy is my theme. The pages that follow constitute both an epilogue to a work I began together with Gordon Baker in 1976 – a multi-volume *Analytical Commentary on the Philosophical Investigations* – and an independent historical study in its own right. To explain its peculiar status, it is simplest to relate the story of its genesis.

After completing the first draft of *Wittgenstein: Mind and Will*, the final volume of the *Analytical Commentary*, I felt loath to close simply with the exegesis of §693. Wittgenstein's book was unfinished, lacking any concluding remarks. But that seemed no good reason why the *Commentary* on it should similarly tail away. Having completed four large volumes, which are not (and were not meant to be) readily surveyable, I felt the need to round off the *Commentary* with a synoptic essay. This I envisaged differently at different times, being uncertain whether I should endeavour to write an essay which would give an overview of Wittgenstein's masterpiece, or try to articulate why it is, as I believe, the most important contribution to philosophy since Kant's *Critique of Pure Reason*, or perhaps attempt to juxtapose it synoptically with his first masterpiece, the *Tractatus Logico-Philosophicus* – for he had wished the two works to be published together in a single volume, so that the contrast between his new thoughts and his old ones could be seen. For some time, I toyed with these and other ideas. It was while I was still hovering indecisively that I had the good fortune to come upon Professor G. H. von Wright's illuminating essay 'Analytic Philosophy: A Historico-Analytic Survey' in his book *The Tree of Knowledge and Other Essays* (Brill, Leiden, 1993). This fired my imagination, and I resolved to try to give a synoptic view of Wittgenstein's role in the history of twentieth-century analytic philosophy.

I envisaged this as an epilogue to the *Commentary*, and thought to write an essay of some forty pages. After a fortnight's work, I found myself floundering. For as I tried again and again to sketch outlines and to begin drafting, the material kept threatening to get out of hand, and each effort to compress led to distortions and oversimplifications. I moaned, as is my wont, to my friend John Hyman. He cheerfully suggested that I should drop the idea of an essay and write a small book. I was horrified; it was as if, after eighteen years of scaling this interminable mountain and being, as I thought, at last within sight of the summit, I was being told that there was yet another peak to assail. A few days later, over dinner with Peter Strawson, I told him my predicament and John's advice. My heart sank as he replied enthusiastically, 'What a splendid idea!' After another week's futile struggle with the material, I came to realize that their advice was sound. To do what I wanted to do, what was necessary was a book, not a mere short essay. The still unpolished draft of Volume 4 of the *Commentary* was accordingly shelved for the duration, and I turned to the new task, determined to conclude it first.

In the course of the next few months, the project became more ambitious. For it became evident that in order to tell the tale I had in mind, I must begin in Cambridge in the 1890s, and sketch the philosophical *mise en scène* which confronted the twenty-two-year-old engineer who accosted Russell in his rooms in Trinity College on 18 October 1911. And to explain the importance and impact of the master-work that was the remote result of that meeting, it would be necessary to give a Janus-faced portrait of the *Tractatus*, to explain its reaction to the conception of logic and language which the young Wittgenstein saw in the works of Frege and Russell, as well as to explain the revolutionary, very different, conception articulated in that book, which inspired both Cambridge analysis and Viennese logical positivism in the inter-war years. So an overview of the *Tractatus* was necessary, and if so, then so too was a synoptic view of the *Investigations*, and hence also a comparison of the two fundamentally different modes of thought. Nevertheless, my main theme was the influence which Wittgenstein, in his teaching and in his two great works, had upon the development of analytic philosophy, and that required a broad canvas, populated by a multitude of figures, from Cambridge, Oxford and Vienna. And so the canvas grew larger, the landscapes depicted multiplied, and the project of a short book turned into something rather more substantial.

I have not tried to depict the whole history of twentieth-century analytic philosophy. That would have required an even larger book. My goal has been more limited in one way, more ambitious in another. I have aimed, as is patent in the prosaic if informative title, to tell the tale of Wittgenstein's influence upon that history. Accordingly, this book is concerned with only one current within it, albeit the dominant one. However, I did not want to paint this history in grisaille, but to display in vivid colours the struggle with new conceptions of philosophy which has characterized analytic philosophy in all its phases, the conflict of ideas and the passionate arguments to which they gave rise. These began with the revolt against Absolute Idealism, which, together with the work of nineteenth-century mathematicians on the principles of mathematics (in particular of the calculus), gave birth to a new conception of philosophical analysis. In due course, this initial phase of analytical philosophy took a 'linguistic turn' that led to the emergence of Cambridge analysis, then of logical positivism with its optimistic revolutionary fervour. In its last great phase after the Second World War, analytic philosophy, dominated by Oxford, underwent yet another transformation – hardly less revolutionary than logical positivism, even if in muted Anglo-Saxon mode. I have tried to depict how Wittgenstein's ideas were received, how they were both understood and misunderstood, how they were both interpreted and misinterpreted – and so too how other philosophical ideas emerged, in the Vienna Circle, in Cambridge and in Oxford. Precisely because I am not telling the tale of analytic philosophy as a whole, many of the personages whose parts in that larger plot are substantial make only a brief appearance here, and some, none at all. This does not betoken a judgement upon their historical significance, but only upon the relation between their work and Wittgenstein's philosophy.

I initially thought to bring my chronicle to a close in the Oxford of my youth, the Oxford of the 1960s, greatly influenced by Wittgenstein, to be sure, but also with a lustre and glory of its own. But my friends Oswald Hanfling, John Hyman and Avishai Margalit persuaded me otherwise. A comparison of Wittgenstein's later philosophy with that of Quine was, they urged, essential. For it was Quine's ideas, together with post-positivist philosophy in the United States, that contributed most to the waning of Wittgenstein's influence and to the decline of analytic philosophy in all but name. Having embarked upon that, it seemed natural to go further, and to clarify and evaluate some of the most influential criticisms of both Oxford philosophy and Wittgenstein, which contributed most to the change in direction and inspiration of Anglophone philosophy in the 1970s. *This* tale, however, I have not tried to recount; I merely offer some tentative reflections on how and why that change occurred.

Although this book was begun as an epilogue to the *Analytical Commentary*, it rapidly assumed a life of its own. It can be read and understood by those who have not read the *Commentary*. Whereas the *Commentary* presupposes familiarity with Wittgenstein's texts and a willingness to study them in detail, this volume makes no such demands upon the reader. But there are connections, for those who are interested in pursuing them. In discussing Wittgenstein's philosophy, I have aimed at an overview; so I have frequently given interpretations, and ascribed specific ideas to him, without evidence or argument. In all such cases, I have cited essays in the *Commentary* where the requisite evidence and arguments can be found.

The following pages bring to its conclusion a journey commenced nineteen years ago. I regret that it has taken me all this time to complete, but *ars longa* . . . However, I do not regret the journey in the least. I could not have found a more fascinating or more variegated landscape to traverse, from the deserts of the Augustinian picture of language, through the jungle of the private language arguments, to the mountain peaks of Wittgenstein's discussions of the nature of necessity. I hope that my readers will find interest, and perhaps some profit, in this record of my long trek in Wittgenstein's footsteps.

P.M.S.H.
St John's College, Oxford
1995

Acknowledgements

In the course of writing this book, I have incurred many debts to institutions, colleagues and friends, who have supported me materially, intellectually and morally. This has been heart-warming, and it gives me pleasure to acknowledge so much generosity and kindness.

The Leverhulme Foundation relieved me of teaching for three years, from 1991 to 1994. The last nine months of this period were spent composing this book, which, without that support, would not have been written. I am deeply grateful to the Foundation. My college, St John's, not only allowed me to take up the Leverhulme grant, but also gave me sabbatical leave for the academic year 1994–5, thus enabling me both to complete this work and to put the finishing touches to *Wittgenstein: Mind and Will*, the concluding volume of commentary on the *Investigations*.

Sir Isaiah Berlin, Sir Stuart Hampshire, Professor Rom Harré, Sir Peter Strawson and Professor Georg Henrik von Wright kindly allowed me to interview them, and shared with me their many memories of the great period of philosophy through which they have lived, and to which they have contributed so much. Rom Harré, Professor Avishai Margalit, Dr Stephen Mulhall, Bede Rundle, Severin Schroeder, Professor Stuart Shanker, Peter Strawson and Georg Henrik von Wright generously agreed to read the whole typescript, and gave me valuable comments on it. Professor Laurence Goldstein and Professor Herman Philipse read some of the chapters, and Professor Peter Hylton, Dr Daniel Isaacson and Dr Anat Matar read the chapter on Wittgenstein and Quine. Their criticisms were most helpful. I am also indebted to Dr Erich Ammereller for illumination on the *Tractatus*. Dr Ross McKibbin gave me the benefit of his insights into the methodology of the history of ideas. My greatest debts are to Dr Hans-Johan Glock, Professor Oswald Hanfling and Dr John Hyman, who read each chapter as it was written, discussed it with me and made numerous suggestions for improvement. To all these colleagues and friends I am most grateful, not only for their constructive criticisms, but also for their moral support and encouragement.

I have, yet again, been most fortunate to have Jean van Altena as my copy-editor. She has rectified innumerable infelicities, and made many constructive suggestions.

A shortened version of chapter 6, §3, was presented at the Kirchberg International Wittgenstein Conference in Austria in August 1994, and published in the proceedings of the conference. A much abbreviated version of chapter 7 was presented at the University of Tel Aviv in March 1995, and again at the University of Swansea in April 1995. Yet another version of that chapter will be published in

Wittgenstein and Quine, ed. R. L. Arrington and H.-J. Glock (Routledge, London, 1996). Material from chapters 1–3 was used in a paper entitled 'The Rise of Twentieth-Century Analytic Philosophy' which was presented to a conference on that subject at the University of Reading in April 1995 and will be published in *Ratio*, new series, vol. 9 (1996).

Abbreviations

1. Wittgenstein's published works

The following abbreviations are used to refer to Wittgenstein's published works. The list includes derivative primary sources and lecture notes taken by others.

AWL   *Wittgenstein's Lectures, Cambridge 1932–35, from the Notes of Alice Ambrose and Margaret Macdonald*, ed. Alice Ambrose (Blackwell, Oxford, 1979).

BB   *The Blue and Brown Books* (Blackwell, Oxford, 1958).

C   *On Certainty*, ed. G. E. M. Anscombe and G. H. von Wright, tr. D. Paul and G. E. M. Anscombe (Blackwell, Oxford, 1969).

CV   *Culture and Value*, ed. G. H. von Wright in collaboration with H. Nyman, tr. P. Winch (Blackwell, Oxford, 1980).

GB   'Remarks on Frazer's "Golden Bough" ', tr. J. Beversluis, repr. in *Ludwig Wittgenstein: Philosophical Occasions 1912–1951*, ed. J. Klagge and Alfred Nordmann (Hackett, Indianapolis and Cambridge, 1993), pp. 118–55.

LA   *Lectures and Conversations on Aesthetics, Psychology and Religious Beliefs*, ed. C. Barrett (Blackwell, Oxford, 1970).

LFM   *Wittgenstein's Lectures on the Foundations of Mathematics, Cambridge 1939*, ed. C. Diamond (Harvester, Hassocks, Sussex, 1976).

LPE   'Wittgenstein's Notes for Lectures on "Private Experience" and "Sense Data"', ed. R. Rhees, *Philosophical Review*, 77 (1968), pp. 275–320.

LW I   *Last Writings on the Philosophy of Psychology*, vol. I, ed. G. H. von Wright and H. Nyman, tr. C. G. Luckhardt and M. A. E. Aue (Blackwell, Oxford, 1982).

LW II   *Last Writings on the Philosophy of Psychology*, vol. II, ed. G. H. von Wright and H. Nyman, tr. C. G. Luckhardt and M. A. E. Aue (Blackwell, Oxford, 1992).

LWL   *Wittgenstein's Lectures, Cambridge 1930–32, from the Notes of John King and Desmond Lee*, ed. Desmond Lee (Blackwell, Oxford, 1980).

M   'Wittgenstein's Lectures in 1930–33', in G. E. Moore, *Philosophical Papers* (Allen and Unwin, London, 1959).

NB   *Notebooks 1914–16*, ed. G. H. von Wright and G. E. M. Anscombe, tr. G. E. M. Anscombe (Blackwell, Oxford, 1961).

PG   *Philosophical Grammar*, ed. R. Rhees, tr. A. J. P. Kenny (Blackwell, Oxford, 1974).

PI   *Philosophical Investigations*, ed. G. E. M. Anscombe and R. Rhees, tr. G. E. M. Anscombe, 2nd edn (Blackwell, Oxford, 1958).

PLP   *The Principles of Linguistic Philosophy*, by F. Waismann, ed. R. Harré (Macmillan, London, and St Martin's Press, New York, 1965).

PR   *Philosophical Remarks*, ed. R. Rhees, tr. R. Hargreaves and R. White (Blackwell, Oxford, 1975).

PTLP   *Proto-Tractatus – An Early Version of Tractatus Logico-Philosophicus*, ed. B. F. McGuinness, T. Nyberg and G. H. von Wright, tr. D. F. Pears and B. F. McGuinness (Routledge and Kegan Paul, London, 1971).

R   *Ludwig Wittgenstein: Letters to Russell, Keynes and Moore*, ed. G. H. von Wright (Blackwell, Oxford, 1974).

RFM   *Remarks on the Foundations of Mathematics*, ed. G. H. von Wright, R. Rhees and G. E. M. Anscombe, rev. edn (Blackwell, Oxford, 1978).

RLF   'Some Remarks on Logical Form', *Proceedings of the Aristotelian Society*, suppl. vol. 9 (1929), pp. 162–71.

RPP I   *Remarks on the Philosophy of Psychology*, vol. I, ed. G. E. M. Anscombe and G. H. von Wright, tr. G. E. M. Anscombe (Blackwell, Oxford, 1980).

RPP II   *Remarks on the Philosophy of Psychology*, vol. II, ed. G. H. von Wright and H. Nyman, tr. C. G. Luckhardt and M. A. E. Aue (Blackwell, London, 1980).

RR   *Discussions of Wittgenstein*, by R. Rhees (Routledge and Kegan Paul, London, 1970).

TLP   *Tractatus Logico-Philosophicus*, tr. D. F. Pears and B. F. McGuinness (Routledge and Kegan Paul, London, 1961).

WWK   *Ludwig Wittgenstein und der Wiener Kreis*, shorthand notes recorded by F. Waismann, ed. B. F. McGuinness (Blackwell, Oxford, 1967). The English translation, *Wittgenstein and the Vienna Circle* (Blackwell, Oxford, 1979), matches the pagination of the original edition.

Z   *Zettel*, ed. G. E. M. Anscombe and G. H. von Wright, tr. G. E. M. Anscombe (Blackwell, Oxford, 1967).

Reference style: all references to *Philosophical Investigations*, Part I, are to sections (e.g. PI §1), except those to notes below the line on various pages. References to Part II are to pages (e.g. PI p. 202). References to other printed works are either to numbered remarks (TLP) or to sections, signified '§' (RPP I and II, LW I and II, C, Z); in all other cases references are to pages (e.g. LFM 21 = LFM, page 21) or to numbered letters (R).

2. Nachlass

All references to unpublished material cited in the von Wright catalogue (G. H. von Wright, *Wittgenstein* (Blackwell, Oxford, 1982), pp. 35ff.) are by MS or TS number followed by page number. Wherever possible, the pagination entered in the original document has been used. The Cornell xeroxes in the Bodleian are defective; sometimes a dozen or more pages have been omitted. Consequently, where access to the originals or to complete xeroxes has not been possible, some errors of page reference will unavoidably have occurred. For memorability, the following special abbreviations are used:

Manuscripts

Vol. I, Vol. II, etc. refer to the eighteen large manuscript volumes (= MSS 105–22) written between 2 February 1929 and 1944. The reference style Vol. VI, 241 is to Volume VI, page 241.

Typescripts

EBT 'Early Big Typescript' (TS 211): a typescript composed from Vols. VI–X, 1932, 771 pp. All references are to page numbers.

BT   'Big Typescript' (TS 213): a rearrangement, with modifications, written additions and deletions, of TS 211, 1933, vi pp. table of contents, 768 pp. All references are to page numbers. Where the page number is followed by 'v', this indicates a handwritten addition on the reverse side of the TS page.

FW   Dictations to Friedrich Waismann, referred to by *Nachlass* number. These are about to be published, edited by G. P. Baker, under the title *Wittgenstein and Waismann: Dictations and Preparatory Studies for 'Logic, Language, and Philosophy'* (Routledge, London).

All other typescripts are referred to as 'TS', followed by the von Wright number. In transcriptions from the *Nachlass* I have followed Wittgenstein's convention of enclosing alternative draftings within double slashes (//), and have represented the wavy underlining he employed to indicate hesitation over phrasing by a broken underline.

3. Abbreviations for works by Frege

BLA   *The Basic Laws of Arithmetic*, vol. I (1893), vol. II (1903).
CN   *Conceptual Notation and Related Articles*, tr. and ed. T. W. Bynum (Clarendon Press, Oxford, 1972).
FA   *The Foundations of Arithmetic*, tr. J. L. Austin, 2nd edn (Blackwell, Oxford, 1959).

4. Abbreviations for works by Russell

OK   *Our Knowledge of the External World as a Field for Scientific Method in Philosophy* (Open Court, Chicago and London, 1914).
PM   *Principia Mathematica to *56* (Cambridge University Press, Cambridge, 1967), co-authored by A. N. Whitehead and first published in 1910.
PP   *The Problems of Philosophy* (Oxford University Press, London, 1967), first published in 1912.
PrM   *The Principles of Mathematics* (Allen and Unwin, London, 1903).
TK   *Theory of Knowledge, the 1913 Manuscript*, in *The Collected Papers of Bertrand Russell*, vol. 7 (Allen and Unwin, London, 1984).

5. Abbreviations for Works by W. V. O. Quine

AQ 'Autobiography of W. V. Quine', in *The Philosophy of W. V. Quine*, ed. L. E. Hahn and P. A. Schilpp (Open Court, La Salle, Ill., 1986).

CLT 'Carnap on Logical Truth' (1954), repr. in *The Ways of Paradox and Other Essays* (Random House, New York, 1966).

CVO 'Carnap's Views on Ontology' (1951), repr. in *The Ways of Paradox*.

EN 'Epistemology Naturalized' (1968), repr. in *Ontological Relativity and Other Essays* (Columbia University Press, New York and London, 1969).

NK 'Natural Kinds' (1969), repr. in *Ontological Relativity*.

OR 'Ontological Relativity' (1968), repr. in *Ontological Relativity*.

PL *Philosophy of Logic* (Prentice-Hall, Englewood Cliffs, N.J., 1970).

PT *Pursuit of Truth* (Harvard University Press, Cambridge, Mass., and London, 1990).

Res. 'Responses', in *Theories and Things* (Belknap Press of Harvard University Press, Cambridge, Mass., and London, 1981).

RoR *The Roots of Reference* (Open Court, La Salle, Ill., 1973).

SLS 'Mr Strawson on Logical Theory' (1953), repr. in *The Ways of Paradox*.

SLT 'The Scope and Language of Science' (1954), repr. in *The Ways of Paradox*.

TC 'Truth by Convention' (1935), repr. in *The Ways of Paradox*.

TDE 'Two Dogmas of Empiricism', repr. in *From a Logical Point of View*, first published in 1953, 2nd edn first published in 1961 (Harper and Row, New York, 1963).

TI 'Three Indeterminacies', in *Perspectives on Quine*, ed. R. Barrett and R. Gibson (Blackwell, Oxford and Cambridge, Mass., 1990).

TTPT 'Things and Their Place in Theories', repr. in *Theories and Things*.

UPM 'Use and Its Place in Meaning', repr. in *Theories and Things*.

WO *Word and Object*, first published 1960 (MIT Press, Cambridge, Mass., 1964).

WTI 'On What There Is', repr. in *From a Logical Point of View*.

6. Journals

PAS *Proceedings of the Aristotelian Society*.

PASS *Proceedings of the Aristotelian Society*, supplementary volume.

PBA *Proceedings of the British Academy*.

7. An Analytical Commentary on the Philosophical Investigations

G. P. Baker and P. M. S. Hacker, *Wittgenstein: Understanding and Meaning, Volume 1 of an Analytical Commentary on the Philosophical Investigations* (Blackwell, Oxford, 1980).

G. P. Baker and P. M. S. Hacker, *Wittgenstein: Rules, Grammar and Necessity, Volume 2 of an Analytical Commentary on the Philosophical Investigations* (Blackwell, Oxford and New York, 1985).

P. M. S. Hacker, *Wittgenstein: Meaning and Mind, Volume 3 of an Analytical Commentary on the Philosophical Investigations* (Blackwell, Oxford and Cambridge, Mass., 1990).

P. M. S. Hacker, *Wittgenstein: Mind and Will, Volume 4 of an Analytical Commentary on the Philosophical Investigations* (Blackwell, Oxford and Cambridge, Mass., 1996).

All references to these are of the form 'Volume', followed by the volume number, and the quoted title of an essay in the designated volume. References to the exegesis are flagged 'Exg.', followed by section number prefixed with '§'.

1

The Background

1. The origins of analytic philosophy

'During the period since 1914 three philosophies have successively dominated the British philosophical world', Russell wrote in 1959,[1] 'first that of Wittgenstein's *Tractatus*, second that of the Logical Positivists, and third that of Wittgenstein's *Philosophical Investigations*.' This judgement is substantially correct, and not just regarding British philosophy. Wittgenstein bestrides fifty years of twentieth-century analytic philosophy somewhat as Picasso bestrides fifty years of twentieth-century painting. Nevertheless, some qualifications and addenda to Russell's observation are necessary. It should be stressed that the primary influence of the *Tractatus* (1921) was upon the logical positivists; its initial influence in Britain was slight, confined primarily to a small group of Cambridge philosophers, and rapidly overtaken by the impact of Wittgenstein's presence in Cambridge from 1929 onwards, when he abandoned the philosophical viewpoint of the *Tractatus* and began developing his later philosophy. Although logical positivism had only a brief period of efflorescence in Britain in the 1930s, its general impact was wide and deep, both then and later. The emigration of many members of the Vienna Circle to the United States had a major influence on the post-war development of philosophy in America, second only perhaps to that of Quine, himself briefly a member of the Circle and much influenced by their views.[2] To a large extent, contemporary North American philosophy is the outcome of grafting the later ideas of members of the Circle on to the native American pragmatist stock. The impact of the later Wittgenstein's philosophy in the United States was relatively brief, and was coincident with the influence of what was popularly and misleadingly known as 'Oxford Linguistic Philosophy' or 'Ordinary Language Philosophy'. Ironically, it had to contend with the lively and flourishing post-positivist tradition which had descended, *inter alia*, from the *Tractatus*. By the mid-1960s its influence was already declining, and twenty years later it was evident that in many respects the spirit of the *Tractatus*, merged with the scientific and occasionally scientistic character of post-positivist ideas derived in part from members of the Circle, had triumphed over the spirit of the *Investigations* and its Oxonian offspring.

The history of ideas is a delicate undertaking. The first and foremost task of the historian is to give an accurate description of the ideas whose impact he intends to depict. The four volumes of *Analytical Commentary on the Philosophical Investigations* have delineated the philosophy of the later Wittgenstein as it is represented in the

Investigations (with extensive auxiliary discussion of other works from 1929 to 1951), often comparing and contrasting it with the philosophy of the *Tractatus* and to some extent with the philosophies of Russell, Frege and (occasionally) members of the Vienna Circle. The present volume is an attempt to give an overview of Wittgenstein's central innovations, and to describe their influence. This forces upon the writer the need to select and judge the relative importance of his chosen themes; other writers may reasonably make different choices. Different judgements of influence may be equally licit. For a philosopher may influence the development of his subject in various ways. He may affect the subsequent evolution of philosophy by the power, originality or truth of his insights and arguments, and his influence may lie primarily in his successors' attempts to proselytize, to expound his ideas and to persuade others of their truth. It may lie in their attempts to apply his ideas in fresh fields, often in ways undreamt of by their begetter, and perhaps even in ways which would have been anathematic to him. Equally, his ideas may be influential through distortion; those who see themselves as his successors and disciples may propound ideas which they wrongly attribute to him, but the impact and fruitfulness of these distorted ideas may be of the first importance, and they may well owe their emergence to the writings whose distortion they are. A philosopher may be influential not because his ideas, for a time, are generally accepted, but because he has placed new subjects or new approaches to old subjects in the forefront of fruitful philosophical debates for a period. Finally, a philosopher's ideas may be of historic importance not because of their widespread acceptance, but because of the reactions they stimulate, the new and different paths into which his rejected ideas induce his successors.

Each of these forms of influence has characterized the philosophy of Wittgenstein. Many of his pupils and later followers have endeavoured to explain and defend his ideas. The secondary literature on Wittgenstein's philosophy already runs to many thousands of items. His admirers have tried to apply ideas derived from his work to areas of philosophy on which he wrote little, if anything – to ethics, aesthetics, legal and political philosophy and the philosophy of religion. His influence on members of the Vienna Circle was second to none, but to a very considerable degree they misinterpreted the *Tractatus* (see chapter 3 below), and, consciously rejecting central claims made in that book, steered their thought on some crucial issues down channels inimical to both its spirit and its letter. Indeed, the forms of conventionalism propounded by the Circle were extensively anatomized and criticized by Wittgenstein himself in his later, post-*Tractatus* writings. Nevertheless, the passionate debates on verificationism as a theory of meaning and a criterion of meaningfulness and on conventionalism regarding necessary truth, which dominated analytic philosophy from the early 1930s for more than a quarter of a century, are a landmark in the history of twentieth-century philosophy. It was primarily (though not always only) because of Wittgenstein's writings that certain new subjects or long neglected subjects came, or came back, on to the agenda of philosophy this century. The discussion of the possibility of a private language, the analysis of ostensive definition, the subject of aspect perception, the prominence of family resemblance concepts, the puzzles of rule-following belong to the first category. The nature of necessary truth, the metaphilosophical debate that characterized philosophy in mid-century, the analysis of the use of words and the consequent centrality of linguistic meaning for philosophy, the revival of interest in the theory of action and analysis of intention belong to the latter category. Moreover, the so-called linguistic turn which was a hallmark of logical positivist and Anglophone philosophy from the 1920s until the decline of analytic philosophy is above all due to Wittgenstein. Finally, the particular forms in which Anglophone philosophy has evolved over the last twenty-five years have, to a considerable degree, been moulded by a reaction against Wittgenstein's animadversion to theory construction in philosophy, against his insistence that philosophy 'neither explains nor deduces anything' (PI §126), advances no theses (PI §128) and 'leaves everything [in language] as it is' (PI §124).

The influence of individual thinkers upon the stream of philosophy may be likened to that of tributaries that pour into it. Some may flow quietly into the running waters, adding to their volume and creating eddies in the persistent flow. Others may burst into the mainstream as a great fall erupts into a river, moving the very river bed, shifting the sandbanks, creating powerful new currents and undercurrents, and sweeping away familiar landmarks along the banks by their torrent and turbulence. It is then only many miles downstream that the waters of the river subside and flow calmly again. By then it may be barely possible, and perhaps of little interest, to determine which waters originated in which tributary. In this book I shall try to sketch Wittgenstein's influence upon the analytic tradition in philosophy. I shall outline the background to the *Tractatus*, its achievement and impact, first upon the Vienna Circle and then upon the Cambridge school of analysis. Subsequently, I shall delineate what seems to me the achievement of the *Investigations*, and examine its influence upon philosophy, primarily in Britain. This will be followed by a detailed comparison of Wittgenstein's later thought with an alternative paradigm which has been highly influential since the 1960s, especially in the United States: namely, the philosophy of W. V. Quine. I shall, however, say only a little about the aftermath in the last twenty-five years, during which mainstream Anglophone philosophy, partly under the influence of Quine, has increasingly moved away from Wittgenstein's ideas. That subject deserves book-length treatment in its own right. My purpose here is to give a surview from one of many possible points of view. Others would doubtless paint the scene differently, for the appearance of the landscape inevitably differs according to the position from which one depicts it.

My concern is with Wittgenstein's contribution to, and impact upon, twentieth-century analytic philosophy. The latter appellation requires clarification, since the term 'analytic philosophy' is the subject of controversy.[3] In a loose sense, one might say that all, or the bulk of, philosophy is analytic. Considered independently of their antecedents and sources of inspiration, if Austin's investigations of excuses belong to analytic philosophy, then so too do Aristotle's investigations of voluntary action; if Ryle's writings on the concept of mind are an example of analytic philosophy, so too are Aquinas's; if Strawson's writings on 'individuals' are a variety of analytic philosophy, so too are Kant's on 'objects'. If the term 'analytic philosophy' is to be useful as a classificatory term for the historian of philosophy, it must do more work than merely to distinguish mainstream Western philosophy from the reflections of philosophical sages or prophets, such as Pascal or Nietzsche, and from the obscurities of speculative metaphysicians, such as Hegel, Bradley or Heidegger.

I shall take the term 'analysis' to mean what it appears to mean: namely, the

decomposition of something into its constituents. Chemical analysis displays the composition of chemical compounds from their constituent chemical elements; micro-
physical analysis penetrates to the subatomic composition of matter, disclosing the
ultimate elements of which all substance is composed. Philosophical analysis harboured similar ambitions within the domain of ideas or concepts which are the
concern of philosophy. Accordingly, I take the endeavours of the classical British
empiricists to be a psychological form of analytic philosophy, for they sought to
analyse what they thought of as complex ideas into their simple constituents. This
method of analysis, they believed, would not only clarify problematic complex
ideas, but also shed light upon the origins of our ideas, as well as upon the sources
and limits of human knowledge.

Taking 'analysis' decompositionally, twentieth-century analytic philosophy is distinguished in its origins by its non-psychological orientation. One (Russellian) root
of this new school might be denominated 'logico-analytic philosophy', inasmuch as
its central tenet was that the new logic, introduced by Frege, Russell and Whitehead,
provided an instrument for the *logical* analysis of objective phenomena. The other
(Moorean) root might be termed 'conceptual analysis', inasmuch as it was concerned with the analysis of objective (mind-independent) concepts rather than 'ideas'
or 'impressions'. From these origins, as we shall see, other varieties grew. Russell's
Platonist pluralism, considerably influenced by the pre-war impact of the young
Wittgenstein, evolved into logical atomism. Fertilized by the *Tractatus* linguistic
turn in philosophy, and greatly influenced by the contemporary writings and teaching of Moore and Russell, Cambridge analysis of the inter-war years emerged. At
much the same time, the *Tractatus* was a primary source of the different school of
logical positivism, which arose in Vienna, was further fertilized by contact with
Wittgenstein between 1927 and 1936, and spread to Germany, Poland, Scandinavia,
Britain and the United States. In both these phases of the analytic movement,
philosophers, in rather different ways, practised and developed forms of reductive
and (its mirror image) constructive analysis. Under the influence of Wittgenstein in
Cambridge (and later, of his posthumous publications), analytic philosophy became
more syncretic, and entered yet another phase. Reductive and constructive analysis
were repudiated. Connective analysis,[4] exemplified in various forms in Oxford
after the Second World War, emerged, and, with it, therapeutic analysis.

If the term 'analytic philosophy' is to be used to characterize mainstream
Anglophone, and for a while Viennese, philosophy in this century (as well as their
influences elsewhere), it must be understood dynamically. For it is a historical
phenomenon, and, like all historical phenomena, was in a process of constant change
and evolution. It cannot, I believe, be defined by reference to a determinate number
of non-trivial doctrines or principles, all of which were embraced by every philosopher who can with justice be described as a member of the analytic movement.
Rather, it consists of different, overlapping strands, with no usefully defining fibre
or fibres running through its whole temporal length. However, it would be misleading to claim that the term 'analytic philosophy' expresses a family resemblance
concept, for so to conceive it would diminish its usefulness in characterizing a very
particular historical movement of the twentieth century. (Of course, that no more
means that analytic philosophy had no precursors than the use of the term 'the
Romantic movement' to characterize a phase in late eighteenth- and nineteenth-

century European culture implies that Romanticism had no precursors.) Nevertheless, there is a kinship with family resemblance concepts, inasmuch as each phase
in the evolution of analytic philosophy shares methodological, doctrinal and thematic features with its antecedent and subsequent phases. Since the various phases
overlapped temporally (indeed, many philosophers participated in two or three
transformations of the movement), each fructified the other by stimulus and challenge. Hence the phenomenon of analytic philosophy must not be viewed as a
simple linear development. It has a complex synchronic, as well as a diachronic,
dimension.

Twentieth-century analytic philosophy has its twofold root in Cambridge at the
turn of the century in the work of G. E. Moore[5] and Bertrand Russell.[6] Although
it later merged with, it did not arise as a modern continuation of, the classical
British empiricist tradition that runs from Hobbes and Locke to Mill. On the
contrary, when Moore and Russell initiated their revolution in philosophy, the
empiricist tradition in Britain was moribund. Since the 1860s Absolute Idealism had
dominated philosophy in British universities, being a belated assimilation of Hegelian
idealism tempered by British moderation.[7] The stale controversy between utilitarian empiricism and intuitionism (the latter originating in the Scottish 'Common
Sense' school of Reid and Stewart, and subsequently championed by Hamilton and
Mansel) was brushed aside. Kant and Hegel were thought to have dealt a death
blow to empiricism. British philosophy seemed for awhile to be rejoining 'the main
stream of European thought',[8] although, ironically, in Germany in mid-century
Hegelianism was a spent force, and the neo-Kantians were triumphant.

The seeds of Absolute Idealism were planted by the publication of J. H. Stirling's
Secret of Hegel in 1865 and W. Wallace's translation and commentary on Hegel's
smaller logic (Book 1 of the *Enzyklopädie*) in 1874. They were brought to fruition
by T. H. Green (1836–82) and F. H. Bradley (1846–1924) in Oxford and Edward
Caird in Glasgow (and later in Oxford as Master of Balliol after Jowett). In its early
phase Absolute Idealism met two needs in social and intellectual thought: it provided a defence of Christianity against threats from science (in particular, Darwinism and geology) and German biblical historical scholarship, hoping to reconcile
science and religion in a 'higher synthesis'; and it advocated an ethics of social
responsibility in opposition to both utilitarianism and social Darwinism, thus contributing to the non-Marxist, Christian socialist roots of the subsequent ideological
development of the British Labour party. Green was the most influential figure in
the first phase of the new school, both in his anti-empiricist polemic in the introduction to his (and Grote's) edition of Hume's *Treatise* and in his posthumous
Prolegomenon to Ethics (1883). He provided, it has nicely been remarked,[9] a quasi-
metaphysical backbone for evangelical liberalism. The most powerful thinker of the
movement was Bradley, whose career straddles both phases of the peculiar British
version of neo-Hegelian idealism. He shared neither the Christian enthusiasm of the
early British neo-Hegelians nor the individualism or 'personalism' of the later idealists. In his *Ethical Studies* (1876) he criticized both utilitarian and Kantian ethics
from a neo-Hegelian perspective. His *Principles of Logic* (1883) similarly had two
important targets: he exposed the psychologistic errors of the empiricists who had
thought of judgements and inferences as mental operations on ideas, conceived as
psychological objects; and he argued against Aristotelian logic, insisting that the

grammatical subject of a proposition need not be its logical subject, that universal propositions are best construed as hypotheticals, that not every proposition attributes a predicate to a subject, and that not all deductive inference is syllogistic. His major work was *Appearance and Reality* (1893), in which he propounded his own neo-Hegelian metaphysics, arguing that common-sense conceptions of reality, no less than those of science and popular religion, are severally incoherent or inadequate, misrepresenting reality by assertions that are at best only partially true. All judgements of common sense and science are only partially, or relatively, true. Absolute truth, if it is to be found at all, is to be found in metaphysics alone.

What is given in immediate experience is a unified whole within which different features may be distinguished; the object of immediate experience is not felt as constituted of distinct entities related to each other. But what is thus given is determined by things which are not given, penetrated by external relations which carry the experience beyond itself. The fact that immediate experience is, contrary to the empiricists, not discrete and self-contained is a 'contradiction', which is transcended in thought. But all thought is relational – indeed, is involved in multiple relations to other things – and relations themselves contain 'contradictions', and are therefore 'unreal'. For they imply both the distinctness of their relata and their unity in a whole. The relatedness of relata is either unintelligible or generates a vicious regress by invoking a further pair of relations to explain the relation between the relata and the relation which connects them. While all relations are unreal, internal relations are less misleading and less distorting than external ones. For they make their unreality evident: *qua* internal, they make it clear that the relata are not independent; *qua* relations, they present the relata as independent. So internal relations 'point towards a higher consummation beyond themselves'. They are to be transcended in the higher unity of the Absolute, in which the separateness of their relata and their relational nature will disappear. The 'contradictions' of immediate experience and of thought are fully overcome only in the Absolute – the one and only self-subsistent substance, constituting Reality. Since matter, space, time, causation, change, the self all involve relations, they are mere appearance. The Real, Bradley further argued, is essentially mental or spiritual, an indivisible unity, not a plurality.

A different strand in British idealism, in opposition to Bradley's, was generated by Andrew Seth (Pringle-Patterson, 1856–1931) in his *Hegelianism and Personality* (1887), which defended the uniqueness and individuality of 'selves'. It became known as 'Personal Idealism', and was taken up and fully developed by the leading Cambridge idealist J. E. McTaggart.[10] A pluralist, in opposition to Bradleian monism, he argued that reality consists of individual minds and their contents, and that space, time and matter are mere appearances. He taught both Russell and Moore, whose first philosophy was unremittingly idealist. It is noteworthy that until the 1920s idealists held nearly all the leading chairs in British philosophy departments.

The assault on idealism arose both in Oxford, with Cook Wilson (1849–1915) and his followers (see below, p. 88), and in Cambridge, where it was spearheaded by Moore, swiftly followed by Russell. Moore's revolt against idealism began with his 1898 dissertation, and was rooted not in empiricism, let alone common sense, but in Platonist realism. He insisted that relations are objective and mind-independent, and, with some qualifications, external. He rejected the monistic holism of Bradley's idealism, propounding instead an extreme form of pluralist, atomist realism.[11] His motivation was not unlike that which inspired Meinong and Brentano on the Continent. In 'The Nature of Judgement' (1899), Moore defended the anti-idealist view that concepts are not abstractions from mind-dependent ideas, but independent existences in their own right. They combine to form propositions which are mind-independent objects of thought. Indeed, reality *consists* of concepts combined in propositions. The idealist notion that the unity of a proposition depends upon the synthesizing activity of consciousness was brushed aside in favour of unrestricted Platonism.[12] A true proposition does not *correspond* with reality; it *is* (a part of) reality. Contrary to the Absolute Idealist doctrine, the truth and falsehood of propositions are absolute, not a matter of degree. Truth is a simple, unanalysable, intuitable property which some propositions have and others lack.

Having repudiated the monism of the idealists, Moore turned, in his 1903 article 'The Refutation of Idealism', to assail the idea that reality is, in some metaphysical sense, subjective, spiritual or mental. This seminal article, rather curiously, took as its target not Bradleian metaphysics, but rather the Berkeleian claim that *esse* is *percipi*, although it is evident that Moore thought he also had Kant in his target area. His purpose was to sustain the claim that no good reason has been given for the doctrine that there is no distinction between experience and its objects, or that what we perceive does not exist independently of our perception of it. More generally, he insisted that objects of knowledge (including propositions), exist independently of being known. For knowing something, whether by way of perception or by way of thought, is quite distinct from the object of that knowledge; it is a cognitive relation *external* to the object of knowledge.

In these early papers and in *Principia Ethica* (1903) Moore invoked 'analysis' – a method or approach to philosophy which was to have great influence over the next decades, despite the unclarity with which Moore explained what he meant by it. Sometimes, it seems, analysis is of properties or universals, sometimes of concepts, and sometimes of meanings of expressions. The difference is perhaps insignificant for Moore, since by and large he took a concept to be the meaning of an expression – what the expression 'stands for' – and it was natural enough from this perspective to assimilate concepts to properties. What is clear is that analysis was not conceived to be of language, but of something objective which is signified by expressions. The analysis of the meaning of 'X' was variously characterized as being: (i) specification of the constituent concepts into which the concept of X can be decomposed; (ii) specification of what one sees before one's mind when one sees the meaning of X (i.e. the concept of X) – for example, a common property which may be simple and unanalysable or analysable into constituents; (iii) specification of how a given concept is related to, and differentiated from, other concepts. Far from intending to point philosophy in the direction of scrutiny of language and its use, Moore distinguished sharply between knowing the meaning of an expression, knowing its verbal definition and knowing its use, on the one hand, and knowing the analysis of its meaning (or knowing the analysis of the concept expressed by a given verbal expression), on the other.[13] He differentiated between knowing the meaning of an expression, construed as having the concept before one's mind, and being able to analyse that meaning – that is, being able to say what its constituents are and how it is distinguished from other related concepts.[14] One may know the meaning of an expression, but not know the analysis of the concept for which it stands. Moore conceived of analysing a concept as inspecting something which lies before the mind's eye, seeing the parts of which it is composed and how they are combined, and discerning how it is related to and distinguished from other concepts. Hence his theory of analysis implied that it is possible to analyse a concept without attending to its linguistic expression. In practice, however, as might be expected from his questionable conceptions of meaning and concepts, his actual analyses – for example, his (later) celebrated discussion of existence[15] – were effected by comparing and contrasting the uses of expressions. The upshot of analysis was either the revelation that a given concept is simple and unanalysable (as in the case of 'good') or a specification of a set of concepts the combination of which is *equivalent* to the *analysandum*. The latter kind of case committed Moore to the linguistic representation of the analysis of complex concepts into their constituents by means of a paraphrastic equivalence, a conception which in practice converged on the general view of logico-linguistic analysis in the 1920s and 1930s. However, in distinguishing one concept from another in terms of similarities and differences, he did not insist on finding equivalences. This approach became common in post-Second World War British philosophy, by which time Moore's conceptual realism had rightly been rejected. 'Conceptual analysis', as practised in Britain after the war, was an heir to Moorean analysis. The term 'analysis' was retained, but its implications of decomposition into simple constituents was jettisoned. Similarly, the term 'concept' was preserved, but its Moorean realist or Platonist connotations were abandoned. 'Conceptual analysis' thus conceived amounted, roughly speaking, to giving a description, for specific philosophical purposes, of the use of a linguistic expression and of its rule-governed connections with other expressions by way of implication, exclusion, presupposition and so on. (As noted, the Strawsonian name 'connective analysis', or 'connective elucidation', may better convey this method of philosophy.) Though the expression 'analytic philosophy' continued to be widely used, its content had been transformed. To a considerable degree, post-war analytic philosophy had lost direct contact with the philosophical perspective and aspirations in which it originated.

Just how far Moore's conception of philosophical method was from the linguistic orientation which analytic philosophy subsequently assumed is evident from his later lecture 'What is Philosophy?', given at Morley College, London, in 1910, which forms the opening chapter of his book *Some Main Problems of Philosophy*.[16] The most important objective of philosophy, Moore declared, is no less than

> to give a general description of the *whole* of the Universe, mentioning all the most important things which we *know* to be in it, considering how far it is likely that there are in it important kinds of things which we do not absolutely *know* to be in it, and also considering the most important ways in which these various kinds of things are related to one another. I will call this, for short, 'Giving a general description of the *whole* Universe', and hence will say that the first and most important problem of philosophy is: To give a general description of the *whole* Universe. (Ibid., pp. 1–2)

Philosophy thus differs from physics primarily in its generality. The very general *kinds* of things which Moore enumerates (starting from common-sense beliefs) include the existence of material things and states of consciousness within a spatio-temporal framework. He further enumerates the various fundamental relationships in which things of these kinds stand to each other: for example, the mind-independence of material things and the spatial dependence of acts of consciousness on the location of the bodies whose states of consciousness they are. These metaphysical (or ontological) beliefs, which in Moore's view are part of our common-sense beliefs, have been contraverted by many philosophical theories – particularly those of the Absolute Idealists against which Moore was campaigning, and it is part of the task of philosophy to investigate the truth of these beliefs and the ways in which we can establish them to be known with certainty to be true.[17]

Although Moore led the revolt against Absolute Idealism, Russell followed swiftly in his footsteps. Although taught by J. Ward, a Kantian, G. F. Stout and H. Sidgwick, it was McTaggart who influenced him most, and his first philosophy was idealist. His reaction against idealism started in 1898 under Moore's stimulus.[18] Philosophically, the most important feature of his youthful revolt was his rejection of Bradley's doctrine of relations as unreal and reducible to properties of their relata, in consequence of which reality cannot consist in a plurality of items externally related to each other in a multitude of ways. All relations were construed by Bradley as internal – that is, as essential properties of their relata (although, even as such, they were held to be 'unreal'). Since everything is related to everything else, nothing short of the Absolute comprises the truth as such. Russell saw what he called 'the axiom of internal relations' as informing five salient doctrines of Absolute Idealism: monism, the doctrine that there exists only one substance, the Absolute; the coherence theory of truth; the doctrine of concrete universals; the ideality or spirituality of the real; and the internal relation between the mind and the objects of knowledge. One of the many consequences of this strange doctrine is that it makes it impossible to give a coherent account of mathematical thought. For asymmetric relations essential to mathematics, such as 'is greater than' or 'is the successor of', are not reducible to properties of the relata without regress.[19] The proposition 'A is larger than B' is not reducible to 'There are magnitudes x and y, such that A is x and B is y' without the addition of 'and x is larger than y'. Recognition of external relations not only liberates the philosophy of mathematics; it also abolishes the monism of the Absolute, and admits that reality consists of a plurality of things.

Russell's adoption of analysis (as opposed to the neo-Hegelian synthesis associated with Absolute Idealism) had additional roots.[20] One of his main concerns as an undergraduate had been with the foundations of the differential and integral calculus; but, as he later reminisced, 'Those who taught me the infinitesimal Calculus did not know the valid proofs of its fundamental theorems and tried to persuade me to accept the official sophistries as an act of faith.'[21] It was only after he had gone down from Cambridge that, as he indignantly remarked, he discovered what he ought to have been taught during his three years as an undergraduate.[22] Weierstrass had long since shown how to establish the calculus without infinitesimals, and, more recently, Cantor had given a precise definition of continuity, as well as overcoming venerable logical puzzles about infinite number and discovering (or inventing) transfinite arithmetic. Russell's reading of the works of Weierstrass, Dedekind and Cantor on the principles of mathematics coincided with his abandonment, under Moore's influence, of idealism, and was a potent source of his conception of philosophical analysis. The work of the German mathematicians in analysing – that is, giving rigorous, systematic definitions of – continuity, limit and so forth 'swept away great quantities of metaphysical lumber that had obstructed the foundations of mathematics ever since the time of Leibniz'.[23] In particular, it liberated Russell from Kantian and Hegelian misconstruals of arithmetic and geometry, freeing his conception from any dependence upon a priori intuitions of space and time, and enabling him to repudiate the synthetic apriority of mathematical propositions.

Russell became persuaded that the royal road to truth in philosophy was analysis, and later wrote: 'Ever since I abandoned the philosophy of Kant and Hegel, I have sought solutions of philosophical problems by means of analysis; and I remain firmly persuaded . . . that only by analysing is progress possible.'[24] Like Moore, Russell replaced Absolute Idealism not by empiricism, but by unbridled Platonist realism. Initially, his conception of analysis was Moorean. In *The Principles of Mathematics* (written largely in 1900 and published in 1903), he wrote: 'All complexity is conceptual in the sense that it is due to a whole capable of logical analysis, but is real in the sense that it has no dependence upon the mind but only on the nature of the object. Where the mind can distinguish elements, there must *be* different elements to distinguish' (PrM 466). Analysis is essentially the decomposition of conceptually complex things (of which the world supposedly consists) into their simple, unanalysable constituents. When analysis terminates in simples, or 'indefinables', the task of philosophy is

> the endeavour to see clearly, and to make others see clearly, the entities concerned, in order that the mind may have that kind of acquaintance with them which it has with redness or the taste of a pineapple. Where, as in the present case, the indefinables are obtained primarily as the necessary residue in the process of analysis, it is often easier to know that there must be such entities than actually to perceive them. (PrM p. xv)

Subsequent developments in his philosophy, however, enriched his conception of analysis, lending it a more pronounced logico-linguistic character, and giving it a reductive purpose.

In the *Principles*, inspired by Peano, Russell made his first attempt to carry out his logicist programme, attempting to show that arithmetic is reducible to purely logical notions alone.[25] Like Meinong, he accepted a referential conception of meaning: namely, that if an expression has a meaning, then there must be something which it means:

> *Being* is that which belongs to every conceivable term, to every possible object of thought – in short to everything that can possibly occur in any proposition, true or false, and to all such propositions themselves. . . . 'A is not' must always be either false or meaningless. For if A were nothing, it could not be said to be; 'A is not' implies that there is a term A whose being is being denied, and hence that A is. Thus unless 'A is not' be an empty sound, it must be false – whatever A may be, it certainly is. . . . Thus being is a general attribute of everything, and to mention anything is to show that it is. (PrM 449)

As Meinong had argued, one must have due respect for what subsists without being actual. Accordingly, Russell held that every significant expression stands for something. His ontology included not only material particulars but also spatial points, instances of time, relations, universals, classes, correlates of vacuous definite descriptions such as 'the golden mountain', logical objects for which logical expressions such as 'or' were thought to stand, not to mention Homeric gods and chimeras (ibid.).

Within a short time, however, what Russell later called his 'robust sense of reality' reasserted itself. His theory of descriptions (1905) enabled him to reduce the luxuriant growth of subsistent entities which he had hitherto admitted. But there was a price to be paid for this achievement. It created the possibility of a rift between the grammatical structure of a sentence which expresses a proposition and the logical structure of the proposition expressed. Heretofore, Russell, like Moore, had taken for granted that the linguistic expression of a proposition is a transparent medium through which to view the real subject-matter of philosophical reflection – namely, propositions. For it was propositions, not sentences, which, in his view, were the bearers of truth and falsehood, and he conceived of them, as did Moore, as mind-independent, non-linguistic objects, which contain not words but objective entities which he called 'terms' (akin to what Moore had called 'concepts'). The theory of descriptions, according to Russell, showed that the grammatical form of an expression (e.g. 'The king of France is bald', which has the subject/predicate form) may conceal the true 'logical form' of the proposition expressed. For the logical analysis of such propositions reveals the presence of quantifiers, identity and logical constants (e.g. 'There is an x such that x is king of France, and x is bald, and for all y, if y is king of France, then y is identical to x'). And 'denoting phrases', which seem to stand for something, do not do so at all, despite their occurrence as the grammatical subject of a sentence. This had far-reaching implications for his conception of philosophical analysis.[26]

First, it transformed the previous conception of analysis from piecemeal analysis of the entities which are ostensibly mentioned by expressions in a sentence into a conception which recognized the existence of what Russell called 'incomplete symbols' (of which definite descriptions are one kind). Such expressions occur in sentences, but have no meaning (do not stand for anything) on their own, although the sentences in which they occur do have a meaning – that is, express a proposition. The analysis of such propositions is to be done by the transformation of the original sentence into a sentence from which the incomplete symbol has been eliminated (as above). Consequently, and secondly, analysis becomes an instrument for the uncovering of the true logical forms of propositions, which may be altogether different from the grammatical forms of the sentences which express them. When Russell began to invoke the notion of facts, rather than propositions, as composing the world, he expressed this by distinguishing the grammatical form of a sentence from the logical form of the corresponding fact. Indeed, he argued that the primary task of philosophy is the investigation of the logical forms of the facts of the world. Thirdly, logic and its technical apparatus became the salient tools of analysis, enabling one to penetrate the misleading features of ordinary grammar and gain insight into the true logico-metaphysical structure of things. Fourthly, the theory of descriptions forced Russell to concede greater importance to the investigation of language and symbolism than heretofore, if only because it apparently revealed how misleading the symbolism of ordinary language is if taken to be a transparent medium through which to investigate the forms of propositions (or facts). Moreover, although Russell was loath to acknowledge it, the theory of descriptions exerted great pressure to consider analysis as an intra-linguistic operation of sentential paraphrase for the purpose of philosophical clarification, not a super-physical investigation of the logical structure of reality (either of facts or of propositions).

The theory of descriptions enabled Russell to pare down his ontological commitments. It strengthened his adherence to the principle of Occam's razor – that entities should not be multiplied beyond necessity. This set him on the high road to reductive analysis in various forms, later articulated in 'the supreme maxim of all scientific philosophizing': *Wherever possible, logical constructions are to be substituted for inferred entities*. Analysis made it possible to show that apparent entities are actually merely logical constructions out of familiar items of which we have direct experience. Harnessed to Russell's distinction between knowledge by description and knowledge by acquaintance, it became an apparently powerful tool in epistemological, as well as ontological, investigations.

In 1901 Russell discovered the set-theoretic paradox, which so devastated Frege.[27] In the course of his attempts to resolve it, he subsequently, in 1906, introduced his theory of types. By delimiting the range of significance (the range of possible values of the variable) – that is, the 'type' – of a given propositional function 'x is F', one could exclude certain apparent (and paradox-generating) propositions as meaningless. A function must always be of a higher type than its argument; hence, while an individual (e.g. Leo) can be or not be a member of a class (of, say, lions), a class (such as the class of lions) can neither be nor fail to be a member of anything else but a class of classes. (So, while it may or may not be true that Leo is a lion, it is neither true *nor false* that the class of lions is a lion – it is quite meaningless.) Such restrictions are, Russell thought, rooted in the nature of things; a predicate cannot take itself as its argument, because no property of objects can also be a property of properties. The theory of types distinguishes sharply between what is true or false, on the one hand, and what, although grammatically well formed, is in fact meaningless, on the other. Again, while Russell originally conceived of entities, not expressions, as being of one type or another, his theory was subsequently to be transformed and given a more markedly linguistic orientation by conceiving of type-distinctions as syntactical distinctions between kinds of expression.

Both Moore's and Russell's rather different styles of analysis inaugurated twentieth-century analytic philosophy. Though both philosophers were adamant that they were analysing phenomena, the foundations they laid were readily adaptable to logico-linguistic analysis, once the 'linguistic turn' in philosophy had been taken.

2. The problem-setting context of the *Tractatus*

To characterize the achievement of the *Tractatus* and its contribution to the analytic movement in twentieth-century philosophy, it is necessary to sketch its problem-setting context. Although the young Wittgenstein was influenced by such diverse figures as Boltzmann, Paul Ernst, Hertz and Schopenhauer, his first masterpiece was inspired by, and written in reaction to, the works of Frege[28] and Russell. By 1911, when Wittgenstein, then aged twenty-two, arrived in Cambridge, Russell's thought had evolved further, and it continued to do so during his period of contact with Wittgenstein. *Some* of this background – in particular, Russell's views on logic and language, on logical truth, and on the nature of philosophy and philosophical method – needs to be sketched.[29] Furthermore, some indication of Russell's development of analytic philosophy in the direction of constructive analysis is requisite. Similarly, an outline of some of Frege's views is necessary in order to make clear Wittgenstein's innovations.[30]

In *Principia Mathematica* (1910), Russell, together with Whitehead, had demonstrated to his satisfaction that arithmetic can be analysed into, reduced to, purely logical notions alone; or, to put the same point differently, that one can construct arithmetic out of a limited range of simple, unanalysable logical concepts. Exhausted by his years of labour on the philosophy of mathematics, Russell was relieved to be invited by Gilbert Murray to contribute an introductory book on philosophy to the Home University Library series. *The Problems of Philosophy* (1912) was not only one of Russell's most successful books; it also heralded a new phase in his work. Thenceforth his primary interest was in problems of epistemology and logical construction. His aim was to use the distinction he had drawn in 'On Denoting' between knowledge by acquaintance and knowledge by description (and to draw on the logical apparatus that had apparently been so successful in his logicist endeavours) for epistemological and ontological purposes. *The Problems of Philosophy* was, and was intended to be, a popular, non-technical book. Not so *The Theory of Knowledge*, which he began writing in 1913. The project was to analyse the data of sensation to provide the basis for the logical construction of space, time, matter and causation. This work, as a result of Wittgenstein's criticisms, in particular of Russell's new theory of judgement, was never completed. The less philosophico-logical part of the project was partly carried out in *Our Knowledge of the External World* (1914). Here, and henceforth, Russell's guide-lines were Occam's razor and the maxim that 'wherever possible, logical constructions are to be substituted for inferred entities'. In *The Problems of Philosophy*, he had conceived of material objects as inferred entities, the existence of which explain our sense-data. In the later book, by contrast, he undertook the logical construction of what he called 'the world of physics', construing spatial points as three-dimensional complexes and space as six-dimensional. Material objects, he argued, are logical constructions out of sense-data and unperceived sensibilia or appearances. For the ideas underlying this constructive analysis he was indebted to Whitehead.

In 1910 a deep change occurred in Russell's ontology and metaphysics. In the early years of the century, he had followed Moore in propounding an extreme form of Platonist realism. He had argued that the world is composed of 'terms' – things and 'concepts' (or attributes) – which are constituents of propositions. Propositions were conceived of as objective entities, neither mental nor linguistic, which had the unanalysable properties of truth or falsehood. Terms were 'contained' in, or 'constituents' of, propositions. Judgement was thought to involve a direct relation between a person and a proposition, conceived as existing independently of judgement. True propositions were facts obtaining in the world. This conception had been variously refined and qualified over the decade between 1900 and 1910, but not abandoned. In 1910 Russell abandoned the ontology of propositions and the unanalysability of truth and falsehood. This change is manifest in his essay 'On the

Nature of Truth and Falsehood'[31] and in the twelfth chapter of *The Problems of Philosophy*. He rejected his old notion of the proposition, arguing that there are no such entities as 'that Charles I died in his bed'; that is, that false propositions are not objects. And if there are no such entities, then there are no such entities as true propositions (as previously conceived) either. For it cannot be that a true belief is a dual relation between a person and a proposition, while a false one is a multiple relation between a person and the terms mentioned in the sentence expressing the judgement. For if it were, then the person making the judgement would be able to distinguish between true and false judgements without more ado – which, alas, is not something one can do. Symbols which appear to express or stand for propositions (as hitherto conceived) are incomplete symbols, which have a role in a suitable sentential context (e.g. 'A believes that p'), but do not stand for anything. Russell no longer claimed that truth is an indefinable property which some propositions have and others lack, but rather that it is a property of some judgements or beliefs, which is definable in terms of correspondence with a fact. He no longer held that judging is a two-place relation between a person and a proposition, but argued that it is a multiple relation between a person and the constituents of a (possible) fact. If Othello judged that Desdemona loved Cassio, then Othello stood in a complex relation to Desdemona, love and Cassio, not in a simple relation to the proposition that Desdemona loved Cassio. The constituents of a judgement must be objects of acquaintance, but whether one judges truly depends on whether there is a fact to which one's judgement corresponds. (He subsequently began to use the expression 'proposition' in a quite different way, to refer to a linguistic entity, which expresses the judgement that corresponds or fails to correspond to a fact.)

The multiple relation theory of judgement claimed that judging (e.g. that aRb) is a relation between the person and the constituents of his judgement (a, R and b) *and* their logical form ($x \Phi y$) – that is, the way they are united (TK 144). Otherwise there would be no way to distinguish the judgement that aRb from the judgement that bRa. The form of a judgement is identical with the form of the fact that makes it true. Forms, Russell argued, are themselves entities – wholly general facts, with which the mind is acquainted, and which it combines in a judgement with the constituents of the judgement. The form of the fact that aRb, for example, is the general fact that something is related somehow to something. Our acquaintance with forms is part of our 'logical experience', and is presupposed by all judgement. Forms are explicitly obtained by a process of generalization: if we replace all names of particulars, properties and relations in a fully analysed sentence (i.e. one from which all incomplete symbols have been eliminated) by real variables, we are left with an expression of a pure form. Judgements concerning forms are themselves wholly general (and have no 'constituents'). Russell could see no essential difference between these and judgements of logic; both appeared to concern completely general structural facts about the world.

In the course of the 1910s, Russell advocated 'the scientific method in philosophy'. Inspired by his advances in the logical analysis of number, he contended that 'Every philosophical problem, when it is subjected to the necessary analysis and purification, is found to be not really philosophical at all, or else to be, in the sense in which we are using the word, logical' (OK 33); that is, it arises out of the attempt, by analysis, to determine what kinds of facts there are and how they are related to each other. Philosophy, like science, aims to achieve knowledge – a theoretical understanding of the world. It differs from the special sciences in respect of its generality, apriority and formality. It is the science of the general. Its core, logic, consists of completely general propositions. Propositions of logic, Russell argued, include such propositions as 'Something is related somehow to something' (or 'There are dual complexes'), as well as 'If anything has a certain property, and whatever has this property has a certain other property, then the thing in question has the other property', but *not* such propositions as 'If Socrates is human, and whatever is human is mortal, then Socrates is mortal' or 'Either it is raining or it is not raining' (OK 56f.; TK 98). The latter pair he thought of as applications of propositions of logic. 'Something has some property' or 'Something is related somehow to something' he considered to be atomic propositions of pure logic (TK 177).[32] The enumeration of such propositions is a crucial part of logic (and hence of philosophy), since it is part of the task of making an inventory of logical forms – that is, of describing the most general structures of things. The enumeration and analysis of logical forms, the classification of the various types of possible facts, provides an inventory of possibilities, a repertory of abstractly tenable hypotheses.[33] For not only does this give one knowledge of the most general facts about the universe; it also makes clear the formal components of all possible judgements, since, as we have seen, according to the multiple relation theory of judgement, the form of the possible fact judged enters into the judgement. The discovery of the logical forms of facts is a *sine qua non* for the analysis of space, time, perception and so on, and is required for the enterprise of constructive analysis. Apart from atomic propositions of pure logic, logic is also concerned with propositions such as 'If anything has a certain property, and whatever has this property has a certain other property, then the thing in question has the other property'. This is an example of a perfectly general truth, which is independent of any empirical evidence, and which applies to all things and to all properties. Unlike empirical generalizations, which depend on the inductive principle of the uniformity of nature and are to that extent, at best, only highly probable, such general propositions of logic are absolutely certain.

Philosophy, or logic, is perfectly general or formal. It is concerned with all things and with such properties of all things as do not depend upon the contingencies of nature. In this sense, its concern is with what is true of any possible world, independently of facts which can only be discovered by sense experience. Hence, Russell argued, it is also a priori – that is, known independently of the knowledge of any *particular* empirical facts (ibid., p. 65). Unsurprisingly, he had no clear conception of a priori truths. He thought of the propositions of logic as being a priori, but also as the most general truths about the universe. While he thought that our knowledge of them is independent of knowledge of any specific empirical facts, he also held that all knowledge was knowledge either by acquaintance or by description (and the latter reducible on analysis to the former). So he held that logical knowledge involved *acquaintance with logical objects*, or, as he sometimes put it, 'logical experience'. To understand such logical expressions as 'relation' or 'dual complex' which are names of logical forms, as well as such words as 'or', 'not', 'all' and 'some', which are names of logical objects, we must be acquainted, by means of 'logical intuition', with the logical forms and objects for which they stand (TK 98–101).

A moving force behind Russell's philosophy was the desire to establish firm foundations for knowledge. He conceived of philosophy as being continuous with the special sciences. By contrast with the Absolute Idealists, he saw philosophy as having no special source of wisdom or insight which is not available to the sciences, and the results of philosophy as not radically different from those achievable by the sciences. It differs from the sciences primarily in its degree of generality, in its foundational (and corresponding constructive) aspirations, and in its critical examination of the principles of reasoning in science and everyday life. Like them, it is value-neutral and aims to extend our knowledge of reality – for example, by cataloguing logical forms of facts, by determining unanalysable 'primitives' that are ultimate metaphysical constituents of reality, and by elaborating the most general truths that hold of this and any other possible world. He conceived it to be one of the tasks of philosophy to ensure, by analysis and logical construction, that our putative knowledge of reality is genuine – in particular, that it is immune to doubt. Hence he thought that Cartesian methodological doubt was of the essence of philosophical criticism. His 'scientific method' in philosophy was the method of logical analysis – that is, the investigation of logical forms, which were the key to logical construction. This, he thought, would make it possible to emulate the sciences in propounding tentative hypotheses which enable piecemeal, progressive approximation to the truth, by contrast with systems of speculative metaphysics, constructed *en bloc*, and if not wholly correct, then wholly incorrect and no basis for further investigation. As the rift between the grammatical forms of sentences and the logical forms of facts grew ever wider in his analyses, he came to think that the new logic, which he and Whitehead had devised, constituted a logically perfect language which mirrored the logical forms of facts and hence revealed the logical structure of the world.

Both Russell and Frege, in their formal logical systems, had axiomatized logic. The theorems of logic are deducible from the axioms by means of stipulated laws of inference. Frege held the axioms of logic (the 'basic laws') to be certified directly by a 'logical source of knowledge'.[34] They are indemonstrable necessary truths about logical entities, unfolding the essential natures of primitive logical concepts and relations. Knowledge of the laws of logic rests ultimately on self-evident truths: 'The question why and with what right we acknowledge a law of logic to be true, logic can answer only by reducing it to another law of logic. Where that is not possible, logic can give no answer' (BLA I p. xvii; see also BLA II, appendix).

Russell wavered; in *Principia* he argued that the primitive propositions must indeed be assumed without proof. They are self-evident, or 'obvious to the instructed mind, but then so are many propositions which cannot be quite true, as being disproved by their contradictory consequences' (PM 12). The proof of a logical system is its adequacy and coherence. (Russell was here groping for the later notions of completeness and consistency proofs.) So self-evidence is no guarantee of truth. Rather, the axioms get inductive support from their consequences.

> In fact self-evidence is never more than a part of the reason for accepting an axiom, and is never indispensable. The reason for accepting an axiom, as for accepting any other proposition, is always largely inductive, namely that many propositions which are nearly indubitable can be deduced from it, and that no equally plausible way is known by which these propositions could be true if the

axiom were false, and nothing which is probably false can be deduced from it. If the axiom is apparently self-evident, that only means, practically, that it is nearly indubitable; for things have been thought self-evident and have yet turned out to be false.[35] And if the axiom itself is nearly indubitable, that merely adds to the inductive evidence derived from the fact that its consequences are nearly indubitable: it does not provide new evidence of a radically different kind. (PM 59)

By contrast, in *The Problems of Philosophy* he argued that 'it seems, however, highly probable that . . . the highest degree of self-evidence is really an infallible guarantee of truth' (PP 68). The axioms of logic are self-evident and incapable of being proved. We have intuitive knowledge of them, and they 'may be taken as quite certain' (PP 81). He repeated this view in *Theory of Knowledge* in 1913: 'every series of definitions and propositions must have a beginning, and therefore there must be undefined terms and unproven propositions. The undefined terms must be understood by means of acquaintance. The unproved propositions must be known by means of self-evidence' (TK 158). And he argued against his own earlier conception, claiming that it confused logical and epistemological premises:

It may happen that, as the inductive empiricist contends, the simplest logical premises are only rendered *probable*, not *certain*, by the self-evidence of the propositions which would be their consequences in a purely logical order. But this can afford no argument against self-evidence as the source of knowledge, since, if the whole body of propositions in question is to be accepted, self-evidence must belong to the propositions which are the epistemological premises and which give inductive support to the purely logical premises. Thus here again self-evidence remains epistemologically fundamental. (TK 159)

Frege and Russell alike thought that logical propositions are perfectly general truths. According to Frege, the 'laws of thought' which logic investigates are generalizations over propositions, judgeable contents or thoughts (CN §§1, 14ff.).[36] A proposition such as 'Either it is raining or it is not raining' he conceived as analytic – a particular instance of a logical law, but not itself a logical law or theorem of the science of logic. Laws of logic are completely general truths about concepts, judgements (or thoughts) and their logical relations. These laws govern everything thinkable, since 'Thought is in essentials the same everywhere; it is not true that there are different kinds of laws of thought to suit the different kinds of objects thought about' (FA p. iii). Hence 'The task we assign logic is only that of saying what holds with the utmost generality for all thinking, whatever its subject matter . . . Consequently logic is the science of the most general laws of truth.'[37] Although Frege distinguished his axioms from transformation rules, he tended in his discussions of his logical system to blur the distinction between rules of inference and truths of logic, for he described the axioms and theorems of his system as truths concerning logical objects and concepts, and as laws of thought which prescribe how we ought to think if we wish to achieve truth in our reasoning (BLA I pp. xv, xvii). The manifest tension between conceiving of the laws of logic as descriptive generalizations about abstract entities and conceiving of them as normative laws of thought was apparently alleviated by construing them as guiding our thought on the model of technical norms that presuppose causal generalizations (e.g. 'If you want to heat the room, you must turn on the fire'). Since the logical truth

'$p \,\&\, (p \supset q) \supset q$' is a generalization about the relations of truth-values of thoughts, then if one wants to reason correctly – that is, infer only truths from truths – one must infer in accord with the inference rule of *modus ponens*. The laws of truth are 'boundary stones set in an eternal foundation, which our thought can overflow but never displace' (BLA I p. xvi).

Frege's great achievement as a logician had been to give a complete formalization of the first-order predicate calculus with identity. He had done so by following a novel inspiration within the mainstream of logico-mathematical endeavour in the nineteenth century. Where Boole had applied algebraic techniques to the formalization of patterns of reasoning, seeking to display logic as part of arithmetic, Frege applied concepts derived from the mathematical theory of functions to logic, with the ultimate logicist goal of demonstrating the reducibility of arithmetic to pure logic alone. He generalized the notion of a mathematical function to admit not merely numbers, but any object whatever as the argument or value of a function. He construed concept-words as function-names, and first-level concepts as functions mapping objects (their arguments) on to truth-values, that is, what he called 'the True' and 'the False'. He represented quantifiers as second-level concepts (functions) taking first-level concepts (functions) as arguments and mapping them on to a truth-value. Sentences he construed as names of truth-values – they have a sense, the thought they express, and a reference (or meaning – *Bedeutung*), which is the truth-value they stand for. Thoughts – that is, what we think when we think that such-and-such is the case – he took to be abstract objects, real but not actual, which exist timelessly in a 'third realm' of Platonic entities. The two truth-values Frege held to be logical objects. Singular referring expressions and concept-words alike have both a sense and a reference. He conceived of the notions of object, concept, first- and second-level function as ultimate *summa genera*, ontological distinctions 'founded deep in the nature of things'.[38] The logical connectives he thought to be names of logical entities, namely, unary or binary first-level functions (negation being a concept mapping a truth-value on to a truth-value, and the remaining connectives being relations, i.e. binary functions mapping a pair of truth-values on to a truth-value). Logic was the science of the relations of these entities.

Russell's conception, as we have seen, was equally far removed from modern ones. Like Frege, he thought that the propositions of logic are perfectly general. Unlike him, he was prone to think of them as the most general truths about reality (rather than, as Frege believed, about relations between abstract entities, at least some of which Frege conceived to exist in a 'third realm'). Like Frege, Russell thought that the primitive axioms of logic are self-evident, indemonstrable truths, and he conceived of the system of logic developed in *Principia* as an axiomatic science. The laws of logic are general truths about the ultimate logical forms of reality. What is important about them 'is not the fact that we think in accordance with these laws, but the fact that things behave in accordance with them; in other words, the fact that when we think in accordance with them we think *truly*' (PP 40f.). Hence he shared Frege's view that the laws of thought are related to the laws of logic somewhat as technical norms are related to underlying empirical laws or generalizations. They provide an anankastic foundation for prescriptive norms of thinking. The constituents (and part of the subject-matter) of the laws of logic are pure forms, which are the *summa genera* of logic, the residue 'from a process of generalisation which has been carried to its utmost limit'. These Russell called 'logical constants' or 'logical objects', and as we have seen, he held that we understand the terms for such entities as 'particular', 'universal', 'relation' or 'dual complex' by means of *logical experience* or *logical intuition*, which is an acquaintance with logical objects (TK 97–101). Acquaintance with them is a prerequisite for understanding the propositions of logic and for the philosophical task of making inventories of logical forms.

Both Frege and Russell displayed an equivocal attitude to natural language. Of course, language is a *vehicle* for the communication of our thoughts, and is useful in countless ways for the daily tasks which it fulfils. But as a guide to the structure of the (Fregean) thoughts which it expresses, or to the ultimate structure of the (Russellian) facts which it describes, it is endlessly misleading, representing second-level predicates in the same guise as first-level predicates, properties of properties in the same form as properties, employing denoting expressions which have the grammatical form of singular referring expressions, and so forth. 'It is the business of the logician', Frege wrote, 'to conduct a ceaseless struggle against . . . those parts of language and grammar which fail to give untrammelled expression to what is logical.'[39] The logician must try to liberate us from the fetters of language,[40] to break the power of the word over the human mind, to free thought 'from that which only the nature of the linguistic means of expression attaches to it' (CN, preface). For his purpose, unlike the grammarian's, is to investigate thoughts, not sentences; to discover the laws of thoughts, not of sentences.

> It cannot be the task of logic to investigate language and determine what is contained in a linguistic expression. Someone who wants to learn logic from language is like an adult who wants to learn how to think from a child. When men created language, they were at a stage of childish pictorial thinking. Languages are not made to match logic's ruler.[41]

In logical investigation 'we need not be concerned with what linguistic usage is. Instead, we can lay down our linguistic usage in logic according to our logical needs' (ibid., p. 71). The logician investigates the laws of logic, and these do not bear the relation to thought that the laws of grammar bear to language. The norms of grammar change as human speech patterns evolve, but the laws of logic are 'boundary stones set in an eternal foundation' (BLA I p. xvi). Nevertheless, Frege, like Boole and Jevons, thought that there was an approximate general correspondence between language and thought.

> As a vehicle for the expression of thoughts, language must model itself upon what happens at the level of thought. So we may hope that we can use it as a bridge from the perceptible [i.e. signs] to the imperceptible [thoughts]. Once we have come to an understanding about what happens at the linguistic level, we may find it easier to go on and apply what we have understood to what holds at the level of thought – to what is mirrored in language.[42]

Language, though a flawed, distorting mirror, may nevertheless provide invaluable *clues* for the logician. But 'the use of language requires caution. We should not overlook the deep gulf that separates the level of language from that of thought, and which imposes certain limits on the mutual correspondence of the two levels' (ibid.). The remedy for these defects is the invention of a logically perfect language,

which Frege thought himself to have done with his concept-script. Logical investigations 'are especially difficult because in the very act of conducting them we are
easily misled by language . . . Fortunately as a result of our logical work, we have
acquired a yardstick by which we are apprised of these defects.'[43] The yardstick was
Frege's concept-script, conceived not merely as a notation, but as a language.[44]

Similar sentiments are expressed by Russell. On the one hand, natural language
'possesses no unique simplicity in representing the few simple, though highly abstract, processes and ideas arising in the deductive trains of reasoning [in *Principia*].
In fact the very abstract simplicity of the ideas of this work defeats language' (PM
2). For 'ordinary language is rooted in a certain feeling about logic, a certain feeling
that our primeval ancestors had, and as long as you keep to ordinary language you
find it very difficult to get away from the bias which is imposed upon you by
language'.[45] The remedy for the logical defects of natural language is to be found
in the invention of a logically ideal language, as exhibited in *Principia*. On the other
hand, one must admit that 'The study of grammar . . . is capable of throwing far
more light on philosophical questions than is commonly supposed by philosophers.
Although a grammatical distinction cannot be uncritically assumed to correspond
to a genuine philosophical difference, yet the one is *prima facie* evidence for the
other . . . Grammar, though not our master, will yet be taken as our guide' (PrM
42).

Both philosophers thought that natural languages were logically defective, that
ordinary grammar was a fallible guide to the real structures which, in their view,
logic and philosophy must investigate, and that the new logic provided a logically
ideal language for the purposes of philosophy. Frege's concept-script – 'a formula
language of pure thought', as he called it – was conceived to reveal the true structure of thoughts which natural languages obscure. It does not represent second-
level concepts by means of expressions which look as if they were proper names
of objects (as 'nobody' allegedly does) or names of first-level concepts (as 'exists'
allegedly does). Nor does it allow the same expression to stand sometimes for an
object, sometimes for a concept (as in the sentence 'Vienna is a metropolis, but
there is only one Vienna'). All expressions in his formula language are sharply
defined, and it is impossible to form expressions lacking reference or sentences
expressing thoughts with no truth-value. Concept-script was not an analysis of
forms of natural language, or even an instrument invented to do the same job as
natural languages, only better. Rather, on Frege's view, it stands to ordinary language as the microscope stands to the eye (CN, preface). It is a specialized instrument for specialized proof-theoretic purposes in logic and mathematics. Here it is
necessary to employ a language which, unlike natural language, accurately represents the structures of thoughts, their constituents and the entities their constituents
present. Russell, cleaving as he did to metaphysical atomism and to the correspondence between true proposition and fact, held that

> In a logically perfect language, there will be one word and no more for every
> simple object, and everything that is not simple will be expressed by a combina-
> tion of words, by a combination derived, of course, from the words for the
> simple things that enter in, one word for each simple component. A language of
> that sort will be completely analytic, and will show at a glance the logical struc-
> ture of the facts asserted or denied. The language which is set forth in *Principia*

Mathematica is intended to be a language of that sort. It is a language which has only a syntax and no vocabulary whatsoever. Barring the omission of a vocabulary I maintain that it is quite a nice language. It aims at being the sort of language that, if you add a vocabulary, would be a logically perfect language. Actual languages are not logically perfect in this sense, and they cannot possibly be, if they are to serve the purposes of daily life.[46]

It is evident, from the perspective of the late twentieth century, that, despite the great advances in formalization achieved by Frege and Russell, there was little, if any, advance in the understanding of the nature of logic and the propositions of logic. (i) There was deep confusion over the characterization of logical truths, which were conceived (as we might now put it) as generalizations of tautologies, while tautologies were thought to be instantiations of logical truths. In Russell's case, in particular, what he thought of as statements about forms were conflated with logical truths, conceived of as generalizations of tautologies. (ii) No satisfactory explanation of logical necessity was offered. Frege treated modality as merely a matter of the grounds for holding a proposition to be true, and hence as logically irrelevant (CN §3). Consequently, whether a proposition is a necessary or a contingent truth was held to make no difference to its logical form. Russell did not adequately distinguish 'completely general truths' from necessary truths of logic. (iii) It remained altogether obscure what meaning or content logical truths and their 'instantiations' had. On the one hand, they were held to describe relations between abstract entities in a 'third realm' or to be descriptions of the most general features of the structure of the world; on the other hand, their instantiations seem to say nothing, to have no content at all. (iv) The axiomatization of logic left obscure the relations between propositions of logic, demanding both that different laws of logic may follow one from the other and that different laws of logic can be independent of each other. This required that they may differ in content. Yet the employment of laws of logic in empirical reasoning requires that they be without content; otherwise the addition of a logical law to a set of empirical premises in order to display the reasoning as a valid inference would add to the content of the premises. (v) The status and epistemic grounds of the primitive axioms were patently philosophically problematic. (vi) Both philosophers were confused about the nature of the logical connectives, conceiving of them as names of logical entities – of concepts or relations (unary or binary functions) in Frege's case, of logical objects of logical experience in Russell's. (vii) The relationship between logical propositions and 'normative laws of thought' (rules of inference) was misconceived. These were the issues which the young Wittgenstein confronted and struggled with in the second decade of the century.

2

The Achievement of the
Tractatus

1. Unquestioned legacy

Wittgenstein was drawn into philosophy through an interest in the foundations debate in the philosophy of mathematics and a complementary concern with the nature of logic. The primary stimulus for him was the new logic of Frege and Russell and its philosophical underpinnings. His initial concern, evident in his correspondence with Russell and his early dictations to Russell and Moore, was with the indefinables of logic, the use of variables in the specification of the laws of logic, the analysis of negation, disjunction and generality, and with the theory of types. The focus of his concern rapidly sharpened, for he came to think that the key to the whole task before him lay in the essential nature of the proposition as such. But this, far from narrowing the scope of his investigations, extended it from the foundations of logic to the nature of the world (NB 79). The fruits of his seven years' labour were presented in his first masterpiece, the *Tractatus* (1921), which, through its impact on the Vienna Circle, changed the face of philosophy in the second quarter of the century.

Panofsky characterized the development of great artists as passing through three stages: in the first the artist defines his attitude towards tradition, in the second he originates a tradition of his own, and in the third he outgrows the tradition established by himself and attains a sphere no longer accessible to others.[1] *Mutatis mutandis*, something similar applies to Wittgenstein's work in philosophy. In the *Tractatus* he defined his attitude to the conception of logic exemplified in the works of Frege and Russell, and also brought a more general tradition in philosophy to its culmination. He did the former in his criticisms of his two predecessors, and in the different conception of logic and its relation to the world which he defended. He did the latter in giving a venerable picture of the relation of thought, language and reality its most sophisticated articulation. He propounded a form of analysis that was both *atomistic* (in the Locke/Hume tradition of reducing all complex ideas to their ultimate simple constituent ideas) and *logical* rather than psychological. In this respect, he followed Russell, but freed himself of many of Russell's deep confusions about the role of logical expressions, the characterization of the propositions of logic and the nature of logical form.[2]

To see the *Tractatus* aright, in respect of both its achievements and its flaws, it is important to locate it in its historical context. The young Wittgenstein was not well read in the history of philosophy. The problems he tackled were, to be sure, perennial – the deepest problems of logic and metaphysics. But they were presented to him primarily through the writings of Frege and Russell, and through endless conversations with Russell, and to a lesser extent with Moore, in Cambridge between October 1911 and the summer of 1913. Although he was influenced by others, in particular Hertz, Boltzmann and Schopenhauer, he approached his problems from the perspective of the Cambridge analytical revolt against Absolute Idealism, reinforced by the complementary Fregean realist revolt against German psychologism. Consequently, although he criticized both Frege and Russell, seeking to transcend their work in order to achieve a definitive solution to the problems which they presented, he accepted from them an array of suppositions which he did not, at this phase in his career, question. I shall mention here only some of these which he was *later* to repudiate as fundamentally misguided.

First, he accepted a version of metaphysical realism. The simple objects of the *Tractatus* are heir to the realist ontologies of Frege, Moore and Russell. They resemble Fregean concepts in being 'unsaturated', Fregean and Moorean concepts in being sempiternalia, Moorean and Russellian simple concepts and terms in being unanalysable and indecomposable, and all three in being conceived to be constituents of reality.[3] His conception of complexes and of facts (which are distinct from complexes) was derived from Russell, though not without modification. The metaphysics of all four philosophers admitted to reality numerous things never dreamt of as constituents of the world by the common man or, indeed, the common scientist.

Secondly, and correlatively, he accepted without question a version of what he was later to call 'Augustine's picture of language'. According to this pre-theoretical picture, the fundamental role of words is to name, and of sentences to describe. Every genuine name has a meaning, and its meaning is the object for which it stands. His sophisticated variant of this venerable *Urbild* did, to be sure, differ from those of both Frege and Russell, but the *Tractatus* everywhere displays the force of this mesmerizing picture of the essential nature of language and of the relation between language and reality. It was part of the unquestioned framework of the Fregean and Russellian philosophies, and Wittgenstein, in his confrontation with his predecessors, worked within this framework (see Volume 1, 'Augustine's picture of language: *das Wesen der Sprache*', §§4–6).

Thirdly, as a corollary of any form of the Augustinian picture, he accepted the idea that there is a *connection* between words and their meanings, conceived as the things they signify or name. Accordingly, an explanation of how that connection is established or determined is requisite. Frege invoked his apparatus of senses of expressions (conceived as abstract entities that are modes of presentation of meanings) to explain the connection between words and world, between proper names and objects, and between concept-words and concepts in the realm of meanings (*Bedeutungen*). Russell invoked acquaintance. The *Tractatus* was coy on the matter. The meaning of a simple name *is* the object in reality for which it stands. How that connection is effected was left obscure. But it is evident from the *Notebooks 1914–16* and from his later criticisms of his earlier views that he thought that the connection between names and their meanings was effected by mental acts or processes of meaning *this* ↗ object by such-and-such a name (see Volume 4, 'The mythology of meaning something', §§2–3).

(4) Fourthly, he accepted the demand for determinacy of sense. This requirement was prominent in Frege's logic as an ideal which a logically perfect language must attain, but which natural languages fall short of achieving. According to Frege, the explanation of any concept-word in a language adequate for scientific purposes must determine for every possible object whether or not it falls under that concept, whatever facts may obtain. Not only must actual vagueness (actual borderline cases of application) be excluded, but the very possibility of vagueness must be excluded likewise. Wittgenstein agreed that if a language is to be in good logical order, then sense must be determinate, otherwise the law of excluded middle would not apply to the propositions of the language, and entailments would not be settled by the structure of propositions. However, he denied that any language could be logically defective (it would not be a language at all), and hence concluded that the vagueness of ordinary language is merely a surface phenomenon, which will disappear on analysis. Any indeterminacy in ordinary language will, on analysis, be shown to be determinately indeterminate, analysable into a disjunction of determinate possibilities (see Volume 1, 'Vagueness and determinacy of sense', §2).

(5) Fifthly, he accepted the anti-psychologism of Frege, Moore and Russell. It is noteworthy that while Frege thought of psychologism (in particular B. Erdmann's theories and the early Husserl's) as among the major targets that must be eradicated if the philosophy of logic and mathematics is to make any progress,[4] Moore and Russell were able to take anti-psychologism more or less for granted. For the Absolute Idealists themselves had already mounted an assault upon the psychologism of the classical British empiricists. The primary concern of Moore and Russell was, as we have seen, to insist against the idealists that the object of judgement is independent of, externally related to, the act of judging. While the anti-psychologist criticism was justified, its consequences were deplorable, but were taken on board uncritically by the young Wittgenstein. For the main goal of the anti-psychologists was to insulate the subject-matter of logic, mathematics and, more generally, the objects of judgement from psychological contamination. Once the objectivity of logic and mathematics had been secured, once truth had been distinguished from being thought to be true, the account of understanding, of meaning something by one's words or utterances, of thinking, could, it seemed, be left to the empirical science of psychology to investigate, and accordingly brushed under the carpet in philosophy with a few apparently innocuous platitudes. Thus Frege famously wrote:

> grasping (*Erfassen*) . . . is a mental process! . . . and this process is perhaps the most mysterious of all. But just because it is mental in character we do not need to concern ourselves with it in logic. It is enough for us that we can grasp thoughts and recognize them to be true; how this takes place is an independent question.[5]

Russell was less cavalier, but hardly more illuminating, since he cleaved unshakeably to the principle that every proposition which we can understand must be composed wholly of constituents with which we are acquainted, and this committed him, as we have seen, to the mysteries of logical acquaintance with logical entities. Wittgenstein accepted the main tenets of anti-psychologism, declaring rightly (but misleadingly) that 'psychology is no more closely related to philosophy than to any other natural science' (TLP 4.1121). His study of sign language, he declared, corresponds to the study of thought processes which philosophers used to consider essential to the philosophy of logic, and he must be careful not to get entangled in inessential psychological investigations (ibid.). Taken *au pied de la lettre*, this is innocuous enough. But its consequence was that fundamental *philosophical* questions concerning understanding and the conceptual relations between understanding, meaning (*Bedeutung*) and explanation were brushed aside as irrelevant (see Volume 1, 'Meaning and understanding', §§3–7). A mythology of meaning (*meinen*) was tacitly embraced, meaning something by an expression being construed as a (mysterious) mental act or activity connecting words with the objects in the world which are what they mean, and sentences with the states of affairs which they depict (see Volume 4, 'The mythology of meaning something', §2). Moreover, since a philosophical explanation of the concepts of word-meaning, definition, sentence-meaning, proposition, logical relation, truth, assertion and so forth cannot fail to involve the concepts of understanding, following a rule, correct and incorrect use, and of the criteria of understanding, failure to address the issue directly is a virtual guarantee of unexamined and probably questionable assumptions. So it was with Frege, and so too, as Wittgenstein realized in 1929–30, with the *Tractatus*.

Sixthly, although Wittgenstein rejected the characterization of the propositions of logic in terms of complete generality, he accepted an important corollary of that conception. As we have seen, Russell conceived of logic (and hence of philosophy) as the science of the completely general. Frege's conception was similar (although he did not think that the propositions of logic described the most general facts about the world). The task of logic, he held, 'is only that of saying what holds with the utmost generality for all thinking, whatever its subject matter . . . Consequently logic is the science of the most general laws of truth.'[6] Wittgenstein denied this conception of logical truths (TLP 6.1231) – the mark of a logical proposition is not that it is an absolutely general truth, but that it is an absolutely essential, necessary one. But he did accept a corollary of the Frege/Russell conception: namely, the topic neutrality of logical operators (connectives and quantifiers). Indeed, this conception was crucial to the conception of logic which he propounded in the *Tractatus*. For he argued that all the logical constants (operators) are given together with the mere idea of the elementary proposition as such. Only in 1929, with his realization that there are logical relations (of entailment and mutual exclusion) determined by the *inner structure* of elementary propositions (in the case of, e.g., colour exclusion), did he come to realize that the alleged topic neutrality of logical operators is highly problematic.

Viewed from afar, the main achievements of the *Tractatus* can be brought under four headings: (i) its criticisms of Frege and Russell; (ii) its metaphysical picture of the relation of thought, language and reality; (iii) its positive account of the nature of the propositions of logic; (iv) its critique of metaphysics and its conception of future philosophy as analysis. In each case, as we shall see, the achievement is marred by error, which he himself was later to recognize and point out. The path to enlightenment lay through the quagmires of error; but the achievement provided the foundations for the later developments of the *Investigations*.

2. Criticisms of Frege and Russell

It would be out of place to attempt here to itemize all Wittgenstein's criticisms of his predecessors. Attention will be focused upon seven main points. (There are others, equally fundamental, but more technical.)

(i) Against Russell's multiple relation theory of judgement in particular, Wittgenstein pointed out that (a) it failed to ensure that one cannot judge a nonsense. A correct theory of judgement must show that it is impossible to judge that 'This table penholders the book' (NB 96). But mere acquaintance with the constituents of the judgement '*aRb*' and standing in the 'judging relation' to *a*, R, and *b* patently does not ensure that '*aRb*' is intelligible. Nor does it exclude the nonsensical judgements that RR*b*, or that R*ab* and so on. (b) Equally, from the proposition that A judges that *aRb*, the proposition that *aRb* ∨ ∼ *aRb* must follow directly, without the use of any other premise (R 12). For if A judges truly that *aRb*, then what is the case is that *aRb* – what A judges to be the case is precisely what *is* the case (his thought reaches right up to reality (cf. TLP 2.1511), and 'does not stop anywhere short of the fact' (cf. PI §95)). But equally, if he judges falsely that *aRb*, what he judges to be the case is precisely what is *not* the case, since what is the case is that ∼ *aRb*. But nothing in Russell's theory of judgement ensures this. (c) Although Russell had tried to budget for the logical form of what is judged by claiming that the judgement that *aRb* involves acquaintance with the constituents *a*, R, and *b*, *and* the form (*x* Φ *y*), this (even if we disregard its opacity) does not suffice to distinguish the judgement that *aRb* from the judgement that *bRa*. Distinguishing, in addition, the 'sense' or 'direction' of a relation, as Russell tried to do, was of no avail, since he continued to insist that understanding a proposition involves no more than acquaintance with its constituents and form, and the 'direction' of a relation can be neither of these. The objections shattered Russell, and, it seems, put an end to his work on *Theory of Knowledge*. Clearly, once he relinquished his previous (Moorean) conception of a proposition, the multiple relation theory of judgement was pivotal to his whole conception of truth, analysis, acquaintance and form.

(ii) Wittgenstein argued that Frege and Russell had misconstrued the relation between language and logic. They had held natural languages to be logically defective, both in containing vague terms and in failing adequately to represent the subject-matter of the truths of logic. Hence, for logical, proof-theoretic and metaphysical purposes, they should be replaced by a logically perfect language: namely, the language of *Begriffsschrift* or *Principia*. This would make sense only if the *propositions* of *Begriffsschrift* or *Principia* (i.e. logical propositions) depicted the most general facts in the universe (as Russell thought) or truths about a 'third realm' (as Frege thought); that is, only if the role of the propositions of logic is indeed to represent a certain subject-matter with maximal accuracy. But this is misconceived (see §4 below). Contrary to Frege and Russell, Wittgenstein argued that 'all the propositions of everyday language, just as they stand, are in perfect logical order' (TLP 5.5563). By this, he later explained, he meant that 'the propositions of our ordinary language are not in any way logically *less correct* or less exact or *more confused* than propositions written down, say, in Russell's symbolism or any other "Begriffsschrift". (Only it is easier for us to gather their logical form when they are expressed in an appropriate symbolism.)'[7] Logic, he claimed, is a *condition of sense*; hence there can be no such thing as an illogical language. If a sign expresses a sense at all, then it is in good logical order; if it does not, then it is just a meaningless mark, and says nothing. What Frege and Russell had achieved in their logic was a logically perspicuous (though not yet perfect) *notation*. Natural languages are defective only in their appearance.[8] (Vagueness, as we have seen, Wittgenstein held to be merely a surface feature of natural language. And the propositions of logic – that is, tautologies – he argued (see below, pp. 32–4), *have* no subject-matter.)

(iii) Both Russell and Frege had conceived of such expressions as 'object', 'concept', 'relation', 'function' and so forth as names of logical and ontological *summa genera*. On Frege's view, these distinctions are 'founded deep in the nature of things'. On Russell's, they are 'logical constants', ultimate, indefinable forms which constitute the residue 'from a process of generalization that has been carried to its utmost limit' (TK 98). Wittgenstein objected that generalizations about forms are not even propositions, let alone propositions of logic. These 'categorial' expressions ('object', 'concept', 'relation', etc.) do not name entities of any kind; they are formal concepts, which (being variables) cannot occur in a fully analysed well-formed proposition. Wittgenstein criticized this conception from the very beginning of his work with Russell: 'The propositions of logic contain only apparent variables and whatever may turn out to be the proper explanation of apparent variables, its consequence must be that there are no logical constants' (R 2). Later he sharpened his objections. Russell conceived of expressions such as '$(x, \Phi) \, \Phi x$' (or '$(\exists x, y) \, xRy$') as names (of a form and relation respectively), but he failed to explain the meaning of their negations, for example of '$\sim (\exists x, y) \, xRy$', which, by his lights, should be significant; but it is not intelligible to negate a name (NB 104). 'Russell's "complexes" ', he remarked acidly, referring specifically to Russell's conception of forms, 'were to have the useful property of being compounded, and were to combine with this the agreeable property that they could be treated like "simples"' (NB 99). For despite the internal, structural complexity of Russellian forms, these very general facts were held to have no 'constituents' – that is, to be simple. Acquaintance with them, which is a prerequisite for understanding the correlative assertion that, for example, *a* stands in relation R to *b*, is not a multiple relation but a dual relation, and so too is the judgement that there is such a form. Russell, Wittgenstein saw, was led into the confusion of thinking that forms are entities (with which we are acquainted) through his employment of free variables as signs of generality, and was thereby led to think that logic 'dealt with things which have been deprived of all properties except thinghood, and with propositions deprived of all properties except complexity' (NB, 2nd edn, 107).

(iv) Generalizations about forms, such as 'Something stands in some relation to something' or 'There are dual relations', which Russell conceived of as descriptions of the most general facts in the universe, are not propositions of logic at all. Indeed, they are not even well-formed propositions. Russell's conception of logic as the science of the completely general – that is, a science of the properties and relations of logical objects or 'constants' that are constituents of logical (completely general) propositions – bargained away the necessity of logical propositions. For completely general propositions may nevertheless be only accidentally true (TLP 6.1232). It distorted the essential truth of logical propositions in the endeavour to obtain for them a subject-matter – namely, the most general features of the world. Neither Frege nor Russell had given an adequate characterization of the propositions of logic. For these are not essentially generalizations, and it was a mistake to think that real (free) variables occur in their formulation. Both thought the propositions of logic to have a subject-matter, to be true descriptions of how things stand in a given domain – the realm of abstract entities in Frege's view, the most general facts of the world in Russell's. They thought that these propositions had a sense or content, and that they express truths. Neither had ventured an intelligible explanation of their essential truth, of the fact that they are *necessarily* true.

(v) Both Frege and Russell misconstrued the essential nature of the proposition. Frege conceived of propositions (sentences with a sense) as names of truth-values, Russell as names of complexes (facts). But it makes no sense to negate a name (as we can negate a proposition), and what can be signified by a name cannot be true or false. A proposition is *essentially* either true or false. It is of the nature of a proposition to be capable of being true *and* capable of being false; that is, it must be *bipolar*. Although both Frege and Russell had related the concept of a proposition to the concepts of truth and falsehood, they had not done so correctly. Frege had conceived of the True and the False as a pair of logical objects named by propositions; on his account there is no *essential* connection between them. For suppose that the thought that F*a* is true; then the sense of the formula 'F*a*' is that the True is the value of the function F(ξ) for the argument *a*. But what relation does this thought have to the False? It does not designate the False, because the False is a different object from the True; but that no more demonstrates an essential connection between that true thought and the False than it demonstrates an essential connection between the thought that F*a* and Julius Caesar, who is also a different object from the True. Of course, by the definition of negation, '~ F*a*' expresses a false thought if 'F*a*' expresses a true one. But that no more demonstrates an internal connection between the true thought that F*a* and the False than the fact that 'the number of *x*'s moons' takes the value 1 for the argument 'the Earth' shows that there is an internal relation between the function x^2 for the argument 1 and the planet Earth. Thus conceived, it is sheer accident that the True and the False are co-ordinate and exhaust the range of possible entities named by propositions (sentences with a sense). Russell had argued (in his Meinong articles in *Mind* in 1904) that 'Some propositions are true and some false, just as some roses are red and some white',[9] as if 'true' and 'false' signified two properties among others. But then it ought to be a remarkable fact that every proposition possesses one or the other of these properties (TLP 6.111). This is precisely to fail to apprehend the essential connection between the concept of a proposition and truth and falsity.[10]

(vi) Both Frege and Russell conceived of the logical connectives as names of logical entities. Frege construed them as function-names which name functions mapping truth-values on to truth-values, negation being conceived to be a concept (unary function), and the others to be relations (binary functions). Russell construed them as naming functions from propositions to propositions. This conception was linked to their idea that propositions are names of truth-values (Frege) or complexes (Russell). But it is a dire error to think that '$p \lor q$' has the same logical form as 'aRb'. Wittgenstein argued that the connectives are no more function-names than propositions are names. Against Frege, he noted that if the True and the

False were objects, and were the arguments of molecular propositions such as '~ *p*',
'then Frege's method of determining the sense of [for example] "~" would leave it
absolutely undetermined' (TLP 4.431). For if '~' were a name of a genuine function
the argument of which is one of the two truth-values, then, provided that '*p*' has
the same truth-value as '*q*', '~ *p*' would have the same sense as '~ *q*'; for each such
molecular proposition expresses the thought that a given truth-value falls under the
concept of negation. But that is absurd by Frege's own lights, since '~ *p*' has the
same sense as '~ *q*' if and only if '*p*' has the same sense as '*q*'. The logical connectives
are not function-names at all. These 'primitive signs of logic' are in fact interdefinable,
and this suffices to show that they are not primitive signs (TLP 5.42). '*p* ⊃ *q*' is the
same truth-function of *p* and *q* as '~ *p* ∨ *q*', which shows that the binary connectives
are not names of relations (TLP 5.41–2). If '~' were a name, then '~ ~ *p*' would say
something different from '*p*', since the former would be about ~ and the latter
would not (TLP 5.44). The logical constants, in short, are an altogether different
kind of symbol from function-names.

   (vii) Russell's view of philosophy was simply 'a retrogression from the method
of physics' (NB 44), Wittgenstein observed, criticizing Russell's conception of 'scientific method in philosophy'. It is the task of physics to construct theories about
reality, which may be tentative, enabling greater or lesser approximation to the
truth in the hypothetico-deductive consequences deduced from them. But logic,
being a condition of sense, can allow no hypotheses. If philosophy were a description of logical form, as Russell supposed, there could be nothing piecemeal or
merely probably correct about it. For what would be a mere approximation to the
truth in science would be nonsense in philosophy. And if it is not a description of
logical form, as Wittgenstein argued, but rather the activity of elucidation of propositions by analysis, then it is equally misguided to think that it can gradually approximate to a correct analysis, since a mere approximation to a correct analysis is
an incorrect, nonsensical analysis (as a mere approximation to a correct inference is
an invalid inference). It is inconceivable that philosophy should share in the methods of the natural sciences (see Volume 1, 'The nature of philosophy', §§2–3).

3. The metaphysical picture of the relation of thought, language and reality

The *Tractatus* delineated a conception of the relation between thought and language
and between language and reality which crystallized a host of leitmotifs that run
through European philosophy, culminating, in *different* ways, in the philosophies of
Frege and Russell. Arguably, it not only conforms to the philosophical syndrome
of the Augustinian picture of language; it gives that philosophical *Urbild* its most
articulate, sophisticated expression.[11] It propounded a conception of language according to which its fundamental function is to communicate thoughts by giving
them expression in perceptible form. The fundamental role of propositions, sentences with a sense, is to describe states of affairs. Propositions are composed of
expressions. Logical expressions apart, the constituent expressions in a proposition
are either analysable, definable by an analytic definition or contextual paraphrase,

or unanalysable simple names. The simple names are representative of objects in reality which are their meanings. Hence, names link language with reality, pinning the network of language to the world. The elementary proposition is a concatenation of names in accordance with logical syntax, which does not *name* anything, but *says* that things are thus-and-so. It asserts the existence of a (possible) state of affairs (TLP 4.21) that is isomorphic to it, given the rules of projection. For the names in the fully analysed elementary proposition must possess the same combinatorial possibilities in logical syntax as the metaphysical combinatorial possibilities of the objects in reality that are the constituents of the state of affairs represented. Representation and what is represented must share the same logico-mathematical multiplicity. In this sense, the logical syntax of language, of any possible language, mirrors the logico-metaphysical structure of the world. Hence language is necessarily 'heteronomous', for the depth grammar, the logical syntax, of any possible language is inevitably, and ineffably, answerable to the logical structure of the world as a condition of sense.[12]

The metaphysics of the *Tractatus* was pluralist and atomist. It was atomist in a twofold sense. First, elementary states of affairs are essentially independent ('atomic' rather than 'molecular'); that is, a given elementary state of affairs may obtain or fail to obtain while all other existing elementary states of affairs remain the same. This is reflected by the logical independence of the elementary proposition. Secondly, the constituents of elementary states of affairs are metaphysically simple, indecomposable, sempiternal constituents of reality. This is reflected by the logical simplicity, the unanalysability, of the names of which they are the meanings. Objects cannot be said either to exist or not to exist. They are constituents of states of affairs, and 'exist' only as such. This is reflected in the fact that '*a* exists' ('$(\exists x)(x = a)$') does not express a proposition if '*a*' is a simple name; for in that case it is not bipolar inasmuch as its negation '*a* does not exist' must be nonsense. Objects have an essential form, consisting of their internal properties – that is, their combinatorial possibilities with other objects (they are, in this respect, akin to chemical ions with a given valency). The metaphysical form of an object is mirrored by the logico-syntactical form of the name of which it is the meaning; that is, by the licit logico-syntactical combinatorial possibilities of the name in a sentence. That it is of the essence of an elementary state of affairs that it either obtains or does not obtain is reflected in the essential bipolarity of the elementary proposition.

The ontology of the *Tractatus* was realist (rather than nominalist), in the sense that simple properties and relations[13] counted among the 'objects' of reality (LWL 120).[14] Objects were conceived to be concatenated (like links in a chain) to form states of affairs, without the need for any relations to link them. (Hence Bradleian and Russellian (TK 80f., 88) worries about the regress of relations were simply brushed aside as absurd.) A spatio-temporal point may concatenate with a property to form the state of affairs that such-and-such point has such-and-such property, and these two 'objects' need no relation to bind them together.

The metaphysics of experience of the *Tractatus* was not realist, but arguably a form of idealism. More specifically, it apparently defended a Kant-like conjunction of empirical realism and a transcendental solipsism.[15]

The picture of language and the world was accompanied by a variant of a venerable conception of thought and understanding. Sentences are expressions of

thoughts. But thought is itself a kind of language, composed of thought-constituents. The form of a thought must mirror the form of what it depicts no less than
must a sentence. Natural language is necessary for the communication of thoughts,
but not for thinking, the latter being effected in 'the language of thought'. Indeed,
it is mental processes of <u>thinking</u> and <u>meaning</u> that inject content into the bare
logico-syntactical forms of language. <u>What pins a name to an entity in the world
is an act of meaning *that* object by the name.</u> What differentiates a mere concatenation
of signs from the living expression of a thought is the employment of the method
of projection, which is thinking the sense of the sentence (TLP 3.11) – that is,
meaning by the sentence '*p*' the state of affairs that *p* (i.e. what is the case if what
one has said is true) which is its sense. For it is concurrent processes of meaning by
one's utterance that such-and-such is thus-and-so that give the sentence its 'life'.
The intentionality of signs is parasitic on the intentionality of thought. The intentionality of thought is intrinsic (or, alternatively, dependent on the volitional, non-
phenomenal activities of the 'metaphysical subject' engaged in acts of meaning (see
Volume 3, 'Thinking: the soul of language', §1, and Volume 4, 'Intentionality',
§2)). Parallel to this mythology of acts and processes of thinking and meaning is
a mythology of understanding. Understanding is a mental state or process that consists in interpreting the sounds heard and assigning to them the same content as the
speaker. The upshot of understanding is that the hearer has the same thought before
his mind as did the speaker.

   The account of the intentionality of thought and language which is elaborated in
the *Tractatus* is informed by a <u>fundamental insight</u>: namely, that <u>thought and proposition alike</u> are *internally related* to the state of affairs that makes them true. The
thought that *p* is the very thought that is made true by the existence of the state of
affairs that *p*, and so too, the proposition that *p* is the very proposition that is made
true by the existence of the state of affairs that *p*. What one thinks, when one thinks
that *p*, is precisely what is the case if one's thought is true. <u>In this sense, one's
thought reaches right up to reality</u> (TLP 2.1511), for what one thinks is *that things
are thus-and-so*, not something else – for example, a proposition or Fregean *Gedanke*,
which stands in some obscure relation to how things are. By the same token, what
one thinks if one's thought is false, is how things are *not*. This insight into the
internal relation between thought and reality constitutes a fundamental advance
over the reflections on intentionality to be found among Wittgenstein's predecessors, who typically failed to see that the relation between thought and reality is
internal, and who characteristically interposed some third thing, a mental image,
representation or proposition between thought and the reality that makes it true. It
also made it possible to reformulate a puzzle about the intentionality of thought that
goes back to Plato: namely, <u>how it is possible to think what is not the case.</u> For if
what one thinks is identical with what is the case if one's thought is true, how can
one be thinking anything at all if one's thought is false? For if what one thinks is
not the case, the state of affairs in question does not exist. Yet one thinks something
for all that.

   The <u>picture theory of thought</u> and proposition constitutes an elaborate logico-
metaphysical explanation of how it is possible for thought and its linguistic expression to satisfy the demands made by the undeniable internal relation between thought,
language and reality. It is an attempt to explain (a) how it is possible for a thought

to anticipate reality; that is, how it is possible for a thought to determine what state of affairs in reality will make it true; (b) how it is possible for a thought to be both identical with what is the case if it is true and to have a content even if it is false; (c) how it is possible that one can read off from a thought, in advance of the facts, what will make it true; (d) how it is possible for the 'mere' signs of language to be intentional; that is, for a name to reach up to the very object itself of which the name is the name, and for the sentence to describe the very state of affairs (which may not obtain) the existence of which will make true the proposition expressed. The logico-metaphysical explanation ventured was predicated on the assumption that what has to be explained is the possibility of an internal relation between two domains: namely, thought on the one hand, which is essentially a mental phenomenon, and reality on the other. The explanation involved an elaborate ontology of simple objects, states of affairs and facts, and correlative to it an elaborate account of the analysability of the expressions of every possible language into simple names belonging to different categories, governed by rules of logical syntax – a universal depth grammar of any possible language.

The importance of this metaphysical picture and of the correlative conception of analysis lies in the fact that it articulates perennial temptations of thought. Once laid bare, as Wittgenstein laid them bare in his later philosophy, the work of demolition, of demythologizing, can begin. But it is noteworthy that the insight into the internal relations between thought, language and reality, construed not as a relation between distinct ontological domains but rather as intra-grammatical relations between concepts, is no less pivotal for Wittgenstein's later treatment of the problems of intentionality than it was for the *Tractatus*. It was not for nothing that Wittgenstein later remarked that the *Tractatus* was not *all* wrong: it was not like a bag of junk professing to be a clock, but like a clock that does not work.[16]

4. The positive account of the propositions of logic

From very early on, Wittgenstein saw that the correct explanation of the propositions of logic must assign them a unique status. They are neither about 'logical entities' nor about logical forms – in fact, they are not *about* anything. They are not essentially *general* ('Either it is raining or it is not raining' is no less a logical proposition than a completely general logical truth), but rather essentially *true*. '(p) (p ∨ ~ p)' is not a proposition of logic, but a pseudo-proposition specifying a formal property of the formal concept of a proposition (Wittgenstein would later characterize this as a 'grammatical proposition', viz. that every proposition is either true or false). By contrast, 'p ∨ ~ p' is a logical proposition (or rather, representative of a whole class of logical propositions, the sentence-letter being a dummy sentence with a sense), and, like all logical propositions, it says nothing at all. It is an empty tautology – a limiting case of a proposition with sense. For in a proposition of logic, the constituent propositions have been so combined that no matter what their truth-value, the resultant proposition will be true. Its truth is unconditional, independent of how things are in reality, and this explains its 'necessity'. So too, no matter what the sense of the constituent propositions, their mode of combination ensures that whatever information they convey is cancelled out. The propositions of logic are senseless (but not nonsense – they have, in a manner of speaking, 'zero sense'). Hence recognizing a tautology gives one no knowledge, either about the world or about a 'third realm'.

All tautologies say the same: namely, nothing. But different tautologies neverthe-less differ, for every tautology is *a form of a proof*, and different tautologies reveal different forms of proof. *That* a given symbol – for example, 'p & $(p \supset q) \supset q$' – *is a tautology* shows that 'q' may be inferred from 'p' and '$p \supset q$'. Once this is realized, then it seems obviously superfluous to lay down rules of inference, as Frege and Russell did, to *justify* inferences (TLP 5.132). If one proposition is deducible from another, then they are internally related; the sense of one is contained in that of the other, the truth-grounds of the one are contained in the truth-grounds of the other. No further addition of a rule of inference is necessary to cement together an internal relation. All entailment, Wittgenstein then thought, is dependent upon the internal complexity (the truth-functional composition) of the related propositions, and that is something that would be perspicuous in an adequate notation.[17]

[margin note: INTERNAL RELATION B/T TWO PROPOSITIONS IF ONE IS DERIVED OR INFERRED DIRECTLY FROM THE OTHER]

It is a mark of the propositions of logic, Wittgenstein held, that in a suitable notation they can be recognized as such from the symbol alone. This showed the nature of the propositions of logic, as well as their categorial difference from em-pirical propositions. He invented a special notation to display this, his T/F notation for propositions. Instead of writing molecular propositions by means of symbols for logical connectives, he used truth-tables *as propositional signs* (TLP 5.101).[18] In this notation, it is immediately perspicuous from the sign alone whether a pro-position is a tautology, and if it is, it is visibly evident that it *cannot* be false. It is equally evident whether one proposition follows from another, whether the truth-grounds of one are contained within those of the other. The significance of this is not *qua* decision procedure, but rather as a demonstration of the nature of logical truth. The fact that it did not provide a decision procedure for the predicate calculus was obvious (one cannot write down an infinite conjunction or disjunction) and fully appreciated (TLP 6.1203), but detracted not one whit from its philosophical significance. (The quantifiers were construed as operators generating logical sums or products. They operate not upon a list of propositions but upon a propositional function or variable (such as 'fx'), which is a logical prototype, collecting all propo-sitions of a certain form, whose values are all those propositions obtained by sub-stituting a name for the variable (i.e. fa, fb, fc, etc.). This makes it perspicuous why it is a logical truth that $(x)fx \supset fa$.

All the propositions of logic are *given* with the mere idea of the elementary (logically independent) proposition as such. For the logical connectives are reduc-ible to the operation of joint negation (the Sheffer stroke) – that is, to conjunction and negation. Since it is of the essence of the proposition to be both bipolar and assertible, the notions of negation and conjunction are given by the mere fact that every proposition can be either true or false, and any pair of propositions can be conjunctively asserted. For 'It is false that p' is equivalent to '$\sim p$', and the successive assertion of 'p' and 'q' is equivalent to the assertion of 'p & q'. Hence every possible truth-function of elementary propositions can be generated by the successive appli-cation of the operation of joint negation to elementary propositions. Every finite truth-function of elementary propositions can be displayed in T/F notation without recourse to logical connectives at all. The possibility of T/F notation is founded in the essential nature of the elementary proposition, and the nature of the propositions of logic is made perspicuous by it.[19]

This conception of logical propositions made clear how misleading the Frege/ Russell axiomatization of logic, with its appeal to self-evidence for the axioms or basic laws chosen, was. Their axioms are not privileged by their special self-evidence or indemonstrability. They are tautologies no less than the theorems. They are not essentially primitive, nor are the theorems essentially derived propositions (TLP 6.127); for 'all the propositions of logic are of equal status', namely tautologies. If so, they all have the same sense, namely none. Hence the idea that proof *in* logic (i.e. proving a logical proposition) is equipollent with proof *by* logic (i.e. deducing an empirical proposition from given premises) is deeply mistaken (TLP 6.1263). For a proof *in* logic merely derives a senseless tautology from a proposition with the same sense – that is, another senseless tautology. It does not so much prove its *truth* as prove *that it is a logical proposition*, that is, *a tautology*. It tells one that by a series of transformations upon a tautology one can derive a further tautology. The proof tells one something about the *nature* of the proposition derived. For a logical proposition is itself *a form* of a proof,[20] and its proof shows that it *is* a form of a proof, and not a truth about anything. Consequently, the laws of logic do not constitute the *foundations* for the elaboration of technical norms of human thinking. Since the propositions of logic, unlike those of physics, are not descriptions of the properties and relations of objects in a certain domain, since they are senseless, they cannot constitute a genuine anankastic foundation for prescriptive norms of thinking.

This conception of the nature of logic and logical truth was a colossal advance over nineteenth-century thought and over the philosophical ideas of Frege and Russell. It was still far from the whole truth; nor was it wholly true, but it had taken great strides in the right direction, liberating the philosophy of logic from its antecedent failure to differentiate adequately the truths of logic from empirical, psychological or putative Platonist generalizations. It emphasized the *unique* status of the propositions of logic. While Wittgenstein accepted the topic neutrality of the logic operators and laws of logic, he rejected Frege's conception that 'the laws of thought are everywhere the same', inasmuch as he denied that the application of logic to logic itself and to mathematics, which consist respectively of senseless and nonsensical propositions, is the same as the application of logic in reasoning from empirical propositions. He denied that inference *in* logic (from one empty tautology to another) is the same as inference *by* logic from non-logical propositions that have a sense. So too, he denied the logical homogeneity of physics, geometry, arithmetic and logic, which Frege had conceived to differ only in their subject-matter and to lend themselves equally to axiomatization. Wittgenstein's new conception of logic illuminated the essential nature of the propositions of logic (even though distortions remained), and it shed light on their role. It dispensed with the apparent necessity to axiomatize logic (on the model of geometry or mechanics), and therewith to invoke self-evidence as the epistemological foundation of the 'primitive laws' of logic. It cleared up deep confusions concerning the relations between logical truths and 'laws of thought'. And it paved the way for Wittgenstein's own subsequent advances.

   The flaws in the *Tractatus* conception of logic lay in its metaphysical roots, in
particular in the following points, all of which Wittgenstein was later to jettison
(see ch. 4, §3): (i) the conception of a general propositional form common to
everything that can be called 'a proposition' – namely, 'This is how things stand'
– which assigned to the proposition the essential role of describing states of affairs;
(ii) the claim that bipolarity is the essence of the proposition; (iii) the contention
that propositions are facts; (iv) the independence thesis for elementary propositions;
(v) the claim that every proposition is a truth-function of elementary propositions
(the thesis of extensionality), which was built into the formal characterization of the
general propositional form: $[\bar{p}, \bar{\xi}, N, (\bar{\xi})]$, which says that every proposition is a
result of successive applications to elementary propositions of the operation of joint
negation $(N(\bar{\xi}))$; (vi) the insistence that the logical operators have no meaning (this
was rooted in a misuse of the concept of meaning; jettisoning that, however, did
not necessitate reversion to the Fregean and Russellian confusions), and that they
are all replaceable by T/F notation (a thesis wholly dependent upon the independence thesis for elementary propositions); (vii) the thesis that the logical connectives
and the propositions of logic are given by the essential nature of the proposition as
such, and hence by the essential nature of any language (this too relied upon the
independence thesis). His later philosophy cut his conception of logic and language
free from the dogmatism of *Wesensschau* (e.g. bipolarity as the essence of the proposition, the general propositional form, the independence thesis for elementary propositions) and from metaphysical foundations (e.g. that the proposition is a fact, that
simple objects can only be named not described), without necessitating reversion to
the theses he had combatted in the *Tractatus*.[21]

5. The critique of metaphysics and the conception of future philosophy as analysis

From the very beginning, Wittgenstein insisted upon a sharp distinction between
philosophy and science. In neither its method nor its product is philosophy akin to
the sciences. There can be no hypotheses in philosophy, or tentative approximations
to the truth. The task of philosophy is not to describe the most general truths about
the universe – that is the province of physics. Nor is it to describe the workings of
the human mind – that is the province of psychology. It does not investigate the
metaphysical nature of things and report its findings in special philosophical, synthetic, a priori propositions, for there are no such things. Traditionally, the goal of
metaphysics was to uncover non-trivial necessary truths about reality, to disclose
the essence of the world. But this is not possible, for the only form of expressible
necessity is logical necessity, and logical necessity consists in empty tautologies.
According to the *Tractatus*, there are indeed metaphysical truths, many of which
have been paraded in the book. But any attempt to state them, including that of the
Tractatus, is doomed to transgress the bounds of sense, to employ formal concepts
as if they were material concepts, and to propound apparent propositions which are
neither tautologies nor bipolar but are ill-formed (since they contain real variables).
Hence the propositions of the *Tractatus* are *stricto sensu* nonsense – violations of the

bounds of sense (TLP 6.54). What metaphysics strove to say is ineffably shown by the well-formed propositions of language, by the fact that meaningful names are the values of such-and-such variables, which manifest the forms of the objects that are their meanings. That R is an unanalysable colour, that one is a number, cannot be expressed by a well-formed proposition, since 'colour' and 'number' are formal concepts. But these ineffable truths are shown by such propositions as '*a* is R' or 'One F is located at such-and-such a point' – that is, by the logico-syntactical form of the relevant name or expression.

Hence, what is, strictly, the correct method in philosophy (TLP 6.53) is *not* the method practised in the *Tractatus* itself. The *Tractatus* was intended to be the swan-song of metaphysics. Its method is to be discarded, and its propositions transcended and rejected, like a ladder which is to be thrown away after one has climbed up it (TLP 6.54). For the insight it has attained into the logical structure of the world, into the essential nature of the substance of the world, is not knowledge of any facts, and is not expressible in propositions. Philosophy, as it should be practised henceforth, will construct no theories, propound no doctrines, attain no new knowledge of facts. Rather, it will be an activity of logical clarification (TLP 4.112). Philosophy, unlike the sciences, is not a cognitive discipline. It contributes not to human knowledge, but, by means of logical clarification, to human understanding. This revolutionary, non-cognitive conception of philosophy, unprecedented in the history of the subject, marks a break in the early development of analytic philosophy in this century. It was to exert great influence upon the Vienna Circle, shaping the conception of philosophy that characterized logical positivism. It also paved the way for Wittgenstein's later, much richer account of the nature and limits of philosophy.

'All philosophy', Wittgenstein declared in a remark which heralds the 'linguistic turn' characteristic of subsequent twentieth-century analytic philosophy, 'is a "critique" of language' (TLP 4.0031). Its task is to eliminate misunderstandings, resolve unclarities, and dissolve philosophical problems that arise out of confusing features of the surface grammar of natural language. This is to be done by *analysis*. He articulated this vision perspicuously only later, in 'Some Remarks on Logical Form' (1929); but what he then wrote sheds light on the programme of the *Tractatus*:

> The idea is to express in an appropriate symbolism what in ordinary language leads to endless misunderstandings. That is to say, where ordinary language disguises logical structure, where it allows the formation of pseudo-propositions, where it uses one term in an infinity of different meanings, we must replace it by a symbolism which gives a clear picture of the logical structure, excludes pseudo-propositions, and uses its terms unambiguously. (RLF 163)

The need for analysis arises from unclarities in the propositions or crypto-pseudo-propositions of natural language. The possibility of analysis was held to be established by the putative insights that all propositions are truth-functions of logically independent elementary propositions, and that elementary propositions consist of names of simple entities in the world (with which, arguably, we are acquainted). Whether in the practice of analysis one will need to penetrate to the level of elementary propositions and simple names will depend, presumably, upon whether the difficulties that need to be resolved can be eliminated at a higher level than that of the ultimate analysis. The results of philosophy are not 'philosophical propositions', but, rather, clarifications of non-philosophical propositions (TLP 4.112). Analysis, thus conceived, consists in finding perspicuous paraphrases of problematic sentences, which will lay bare their logical structure and remove misunderstandings.

The conception of analysis which the *Tractatus* advocated was *atomistic* and *logical*. Unlike Moorean conceptual analysis, it was *linguistic*. It was an analysis not of ideas (as was classical empiricist analysis) or of concepts (conceived as objective entities that one can 'hold before the mind' and inspect), but of propositions – *sentences in their projective relation to the world* (TLP 3.12). It was to be conducted by analysing propositions into their constituent elementary propositions and displaying their truth-functional mode of combination, and by analysing names of complexes into an appropriate combination of simple names. Definable expressions would be replaced by their *definienda*, and such names of complexes as definite descriptions would be replaced by their *analysans* in accordance with a version of Russell's theory of descriptions. The ultimate analysis would yield an array of logically independent elementary (atomic) propositions truth-functionally combined. Such elementary propositions would be composed only of simple indefinable names, the meanings of which were conceived to be metaphysically simple constituents of reality. The elucidation of philosophically problematic 'scientific' (i.e. empirical) propositions would display their logical structure and constituents in a perspicuous manner.[22]

In addition to its task as clarifier of sense, philosophy has a more negative task. Whenever someone wants to make a metaphysical statement, the philosopher must show him that he has given no meaning to certain signs in his proposition (TLP 6.53). If someone, trying to describe essences, uses 'is a number' or 'is an object' as predicate expressions, it must be pointed out to him that, as such, these expressions have been given no meanings. They are signs for real variables, and are not names, but formal concepts, which cannot occur in a well-formed proposition. This may seem unsatisfactory to the person whose puzzlement we are resolving and whose metaphysical pronouncements we are demolishing. For, in philosophizing thus, we say nothing metaphysical about the essence of the world, and present no doctrine of logical form about the essence of language. But this method is the only strictly correct one. Metaphysical truths cannot be stated in language, but only shown.

This conception of the philosophy of the future, which Wittgenstein was in due course to repudiate in all but its negative aspects, was destined to inspire the doctrine of analysis prominent in the Vienna Circle and elsewhere in the late 1920s and 1930s. In six different respects, the *Tractatus* introduced the 'linguistic turn' in analytic philosophy, marking a break with the conception (though not obviously with much of the practice) of analysis as advocated by Moore and Russell.[23] First, although the declared aim of the book was to set the limits of thought, it proposed to do so by setting the limits of language – by determining the bounds between sense and nonsense. This put language, its forms and structure, at the centre of its philosophical investigations. Secondly, the positive programme for future philosophy was committed to logico-linguistic analysis of propositions – sentences with a sense. The task of philosophy is the logical clarification of thoughts, which is to be effected by the clarification of propositions (TLP 4.112). Thirdly, the negative programme for future philosophy was to demonstrate the illegitimacy of meta-physical assertions. This was to be done by clarifying the ways in which attempts to say something metaphysical transgress the bounds of language, by endeavouring to say something which, by the intrinsic nature of *language*, cannot be said (TLP 6.53). Fourthly, the key to Wittgenstein's endeavours was held to lie in his clarification of the essential nature of the propositional *sign* (TLP 3.1431). That was achieved by elucidating the general propositional form – that is, by giving 'a description of the propositions of *any* sign-language *whatsoever* in such a way that every possible sense can be expressed by a symbol satisfying the description, and every symbol satisfying the description can express a sense, provided that the meanings of names are suitably chosen' (TLP 4.5). Fifthly, the logical investigation of 'phenomena', the unfolding of their logical forms, is to be effected (as he made explicit in 'Some Remarks on Logical Form') by logical analysis of the linguistic descriptions of the phenomena. For the logical syntax of language is (and must be) perfectly isomorphic with the logical structure of reality. Sixthly, the greatest achievement of the book, at least as viewed by its most influential readers, was the elucidation of the nature of logical truth. This was patently achieved by an investigation of *symbolism*. The 'peculiar mark of logical propositions [is] that one can recognize that they are true from the symbol alone, and this fact contains in itself the whole philosophy of logic' (TLP 6.113). Although the *Tractatus* was rooted in a misconceived metaphysics of symbolism (that only simple names can represent simple things, only relations can represent relations, only facts can represent facts, etc.), it gave analytic philosophy a linguistic orientation it had not had before, far removed from the conceptions of philosophy and philosophical method of Frege, Russell and Moore.

3

The Impact of the *Tractatus*:
The Vienna Circle

1. The Vienna Circle

The primary influence of the *Tractatus* was upon a group of philosophers gathered in Vienna around Moritz Schlick (1882–1936), who held the chair of the history and philosophy of the inductive sciences at the University of Vienna.[1] Schlick had trained as a physicist in Berlin, where he wrote a doctorate on theoretical optics under Max Planck, but then resolved to pursue a career in philosophy. His *Space and Time in Contemporary Physics* (1917) was an early interpretation of relativity theory and its philosophical implications. In 1918 he published his *General Theory of Knowledge*, defending an empiricist epistemology and a Hilbertian form of conventionalism with regard to necessary truth. He came to Vienna in 1922, having previously taught at the universities of Rostock and Kiel. From 1924 Schlick gathered around him a group of distinguished intellectuals, many of them trained physicists or mathematicians, who met weekly for philosophical discussion. Initial members included Friedrich Waismann,[2] Herbert Feigl,[3] Hans Hahn,[4] Otto Neurath[5] and his wife Olga Hahn, Felix Kaufmann,[6] Victor Kraft and Kurt Reidemeister. In due course they adopted the name 'the Vienna Circle'.[7] The Vienna Circle constituted the fountain-head of the post-First World War wave of analytic philosophy, which became known as 'logical positivism',[8] and was coincident with the Cambridge school of 'logical atomism' (or, as atomism waned, simply 'Cambridge analysis'; see ch. 4 below). Over the years in which the Circle flourished, membership of the group came to include Gustav Bergmann, Rudolf Carnap,[9] Philipp Frank, Kurt Gödel, Bela Juhos, Richard von Mises, Karl Menger and Edgar Zilsel. Similar, scientifically minded philosophical groups existed in other Central European universities, such as Berlin, Prague, Warsaw and Lemberg (Lvov), and extensive contacts with them were fostered. The Berlin group was particularly noteworthy. Hans Reichenbach[10] was appointed lecturer at the University of Berlin in 1926, where he established the Society for Scientific Philosophy. Members included von Mises (from Vienna), Kurt Grelling, Walter Dubislav, Alexander Herzberg and, later, Reichenbach's students Carl Hempel and Olaf Helmer. Because of close friendships, there were strong links between the Berlin group and the Vienna Circle. Visitors and associates of the group included A. Tarski and K. Ajdukiewicz from Poland; E. Kaila, J. Jörgensen, A. Naess and A. Petzäll from Scandinavia; W. V. Quine from the United States; and A. J. Ayer from Britain.

The movement rapidly gained momentum, and became widely known. In 1930 a periodical was started – *Erkenntnis*, edited by Carnap and Reichenbach. Various series of publications were established: Schlick and Frank edited *Schriften zur wissenschaftlichen Weltauffassung*; and Neurath, Carnap, Frank and Hahn established *Einheitswissenschaft*. In 1938 these were supplemented by the Library of Unified Science series and Neurath's *International Encyclopaedia of Unified Science*. Among these were distinguished, historically significant publications. International congresses were held in Prague (1929 and 1934), Königsberg (1930), Paris (1935 and 1937), Copenhagen (1936), Cambridge (1938) and at Harvard (1939).

Unlike the Cambridge school of analysis, the Vienna Circle had firm empiricist roots – in the late nineteenth-century philosophical works of Ernst Mach (1838–1916) and R. Avenarius (1843–96). Hence, unlike Moore and Russell (in their early phases), its members were well-disposed to the classical empiricist (idealist) tradition of Hume, and lacked sympathy for realist (Platonist or conceptualist) analysis. Hence they harnessed logical analysis to reductive empiricism.[11] With the Vienna Circle, as we shall see, the 'linguistic turn' in analytic philosophy came to full fruition.

Members of the Circle viewed themselves as heirs of the Enlightenment.[12] As they saw it, the First World War had swept away the old order, and made room for new ideas, as well as for a transformation of society. They conceived of science as the embodiment of rationality and the vehicle of intellectual, moral and social progress, and metaphysics and theology as residues of the Dark Ages. Clarity was to be striven for, and 'dark distances and unfathomable depths rejected . . . Everything is accessible to man', they proudly declared; 'man is the measure of all things.'[13] With tragically unwarranted faith in the future, they claimed to discern that 'the spirit of enlightenment and *anti-metaphysical factual research* is growing stronger to-day, in that it is becoming conscious of its existence and task' (Manifesto, p. 3). This progressive, optimistic spirit was nicely articulated by Carnap in his preface to *Der logische Aufbau der Welt*:

> We feel that there is an inner kinship between the attitude on which our philosophical work is founded and the intellectual attitude which presently manifests itself in entirely different walks of life; we feel this orientation in artistic movements, especially in architecture, and in movements which strive for meaningful forms of personal and collective life, of education, and of external organisation in general. We feel around us the same basic orientation, the same style of thinking and doing. It is an orientation which demands clarity everywhere, but which realizes that the fabric of life can never quite be comprehended. It makes us pay careful attention to detail and at the same time recognizes the great lines that run through the whole. It is an orientation which acknowledges the bonds that tie men together, but at the same time strives for the free development of the individual. Our work is carried by the faith that this attitude will win the future.[14]

Schlick read the *Tractatus*, and was overwhelmingly impressed by it. 'This book', he later wrote, 'in my unshakeable conviction is the most significant philosophical work of our time. . . . The scope of these ideas is in truth immeasurable: anyone who reads them with understanding must thereafter be a changed man from a philosophical point of view. The new insights are absolutely crucial to the destiny of philosophy.'[15] He met Wittgenstein in 1927, and was no less impressed by the man. Later he said to Kaila that Wittgenstein was 'the greatest genius of all time in logic' (the philosophy of logic).[16] Although Wittgenstein refused to attend meetings of the Circle, he agreed to regular meetings with Schlick, Waismann, Carnap and Feigl. The last two were subsequently excluded from these meetings, but he continued to meet and communicate his new ideas to Schlick and Waismann, who transmitted them to the Circle.[17]

In 1924, apparently at the instigation of Reidemeister (possibly at Schlick's and Hahn's request), and again in 1926, the *Tractatus* was read line by line and discussed at the weekly meetings of the Circle. Jörgensen, in his history of the Circle, later wrote that these ideas 'have on essential points determined the view of the Circle on philosophy and its relation to the special sciences'; 'the book . . . contributed essentially to the formation of logical positivism and provoked both agreement and disagreement'.[18] Victor Kraft, in his survey of the Circle, pointed out that, quite aside from the new logic, 'A common starting point was provided also by the philosophy of language which Ludwig Wittgenstein had developed. It was through critical examination of his ideas, leading partly to their further development, partly to their transformation, partly to their abandonment, that the work of the Vienna Circle unfolded to a great extent.'[19] What was abandoned was the picture theory of the proposition, the doctrine of showing and saying, and the bulk of the metaphysics of logical atomism. But what was embraced was perceived to be of the greatest importance: the account of the nature and limits of philosophy, the conception of logic and logical necessity, and the idea of logical analysis of language. These ideas, duly interpreted and to a degree misinterpreted, were to exercise the greatest influence upon the Circle. Hahn, one of the founding members, said in 1927 that the *Tractatus* 'probably represented the most important contribution to philosophy since the publication of Russell's basic writings'. 'To me', he added, 'the *Tractatus* has explained the role of logic.'[20] Carnap later wrote: 'For me personally, Wittgenstein was perhaps the philosopher who, besides Russell and Frege, had the greatest influence on my thinking.'[21] Ayer, who attended meetings of the Circle in 1932–3 and introduced logical positivism in to Britain with *Language, Truth and Logic* (1936), opened that dramatic book with the sentence 'The views which are here put forward derive from the doctrines of Bertrand Russell and Ludwig Wittgenstein'.[22]

At Schlick's suggestion, Waismann was commissioned to write a book entitled *Logik, Sprache, Philosophie* in collaboration with Wittgenstein, which would present a clear account of the main doctrines of the *Tractatus*.[23] It was intended and advertised as the first volume of the series of publications entitled *Schriften zur wissenschaftlichen Weltauffassung*. Its goal was to give 'the clearest expression to the spirit, programme and aim'[24] of the scientific world-view which was to be propagated by the Circle in the projected series. It is small wonder that in the Manifesto of the Circle, *The Scientific Conception of the World: The Vienna Circle* (1929), published in Schlick's honour by the Verein Ernst Mach, of which he was president, and composed by Neurath, Carnap, Feigl and Waismann (with a preface signed by Hahn, Neurath and Carnap), Wittgenstein is cited, together with Einstein and Russell, as one of the three leading representatives of the scientific world-view.

In surveying the impact of the *Tractatus* upon the Circle, it will be convenient to distinguish five themes: (i) the conception of philosophy, analysis and the scientific world-view; (ii) the demolition of metaphysics; (iii) necessary truth and conventionalism; (iv) the principle of verification; and (v) the unity of science.

2. Philosophy, analysis, and the scientific world-view

It is characteristic of philosophy that it should, at least periodically, call itself into question. The *Tractatus* repudiated the three main prevailing conceptions of philosophy: namely, as a mental science which studies the cognitive workings of the mind,[25] as an extension of the non-psychological, empirical sciences, differentiated from them primarily by its generality,[26] and as a metaphysical investigation.[27] In their place Wittgenstein advocated an unprecedented, radical, non-cognitive conception of philosophy. According to his view, as we have seen, the task of philosophy is to analyse the propositions of science (by which expression Wittgenstein misleadingly included the totality of empirical propositions (TLP 4.11)) and to expose the pseudo-propositions of metaphysics. This conception was deeply appealing to the Vienna Circle. The *Tractatus* put metaphilosophical questions at the heart of the agenda of the Circle. Not since Kant's *Critique of Pure Reason* had the nature and limits of philosophy been so extensively discussed as they were throughout the inter-war years, both in the Vienna Circle and in England.[28] Moreover, the debate was to be given renewed impetus after the Second World War with the publication of Wittgenstein's later views on the nature of philosophy (see below, pp. 110–17). Wittgenstein inaugurated almost half a century of philosophical self-consciousness.

Schlick saw the *Tractatus* as opening a new era in philosophy, in which the subject had at last reached maturity. Philosophy had reached a turning-point, at which the interminable disagreements which have dogged it throughout the ages can finally be settled by the new paths that have been discovered. 'The paths have their origin in logic. Leibniz dimly saw their beginning. Bertrand Russell and Gottlob Frege have opened up stretches in the last decades, but Ludwig Wittgenstein (in his *Tractatus Logico-Philosophicus*) is the first to have pushed forward to the decisive turning point.'[29] Philosophy, he argued, elucidates propositions; science verifies them. The latter is concerned with the truth of propositions, the former only with what they mean. Philosophy is not a 'system of cognitions', but a system of acts; it is the activity through which the meaning of statements is revealed or determined (ibid., p. 56). Thus conceived, one may legitimately hope that 'all so-called philosophical disputes [can be settled] in an absolutely final and ultimate manner'. Indeed, the new insight seemed to Schlick to herald the end of philosophy. He announced to the seventh International Congress of Philosophy in Oxford in 1930 that 'The fate of all "philosophical problems" is this: Some of them will disappear by being shown to be mistakes and misunderstandings of our language and others will be found to be ordinary scientific questions in disguise. There remarks, I think, determine the whole future of philosophy.'[30]

Carnap concurred, although with a difference. He too held that traditional philosophy was at an end. All factual statements that assert anything at all belong to the province of science. What is left over for philosophy is neither statements nor theory, but only a *method*, the method of logical analysis. Its negative application is to eliminate metaphysical pseudo-statements. Its positive use is to clarify meaningful concepts and propositions, and to lay the logical foundations for science and mathematics.[31] The latter task loomed large in Carnap's philosophy, and evolved into the doctrine that traditional philosophy was to be replaced by the investigation of the logical syntax of the language of science. '*The logic of science takes the place of the inextricable tangle of problems which is known as philosophy*',[32] and the 'logic of science' is the logical syntax of the language of science. Although this conception was derived from the *Tractatus*, it is important to realize that Carnap's conception of logical syntax differed fundamentally from Wittgenstein's. For Wittgenstein had argued that *all* possible languages share, and *must* share, an essential, unalterable logical syntax, which is isomorphic with the logical forms of what can be represented by a language. Carnap, however, thought that different languages may have a quite different logical syntax – indeed, that we are free to construct our languages and their logical syntax as we please. Beginning with *Der logische Aufbau der Welt* (written before he came to Vienna), Carnap pursued foundationalist objectives in the form of systematic logical construction.

The Manifesto of the Circle articulated the shared view clearly: 'The scientific world-conception knows *no unsolvable riddle*. Clarification of the traditional philosophical problems leads us partly to unmask them as pseudo-problems, and partly to transform them into empirical problems and thereby to subject them to the judgement of experimental science. The task of philosophical work lies in this clarification of problems and assertions, not in the propounding of special "philosophical" pronouncements' (Manifesto, p. 8).[33]

The method of the new philosophy was conceived to be logical analysis as advocated by Russell and especially by Wittgenstein, who had given such analysis an explicitly linguistic orientation. *Principia* had developed a logically perspicuous notation as a tool for foundational studies in mathematics. The Circle, following Wittgenstein's programme for future philosophy, intended to put it to use for the 'logical analysis of science in general'. The proper domain of the 'logic of science' is the linguistic analysis of scientific propositions,[34] a claim that seemed licensed by Wittgenstein's assertion that philosophy is not a body of doctrine, but an activity of elucidating propositions, of the logical clarification of thoughts (TLP 4.112). It is the method of logical analysis, the Manifesto announced, that distinguishes the new empiricism and positivism from nineteenth-century positivism, which was more 'biological-psychological' in orientation (Manifesto, p. 8). The Circle accepted, *inter alia*, three salient doctrines from the *Tractatus*: that all propositions are analysable into elementary propositions; that all propositions are truth-functions of elementary propositions (the thesis of extensionality); and that every elementary proposition represents a state of affairs.[35] A language was conceived to have the structure of a calculus – a system of expressions interrelated by definitions and formation and transformation rules. The network of concepts thus constituted was thought to be given content by correlating the indefinable primitive names of the system with entities in the world. This was effected by what Schlick called 'concrete definitions', which later became known by W. E. Johnson's term 'ostensive definitions'.[36] (As we shall see, this made the principle of verification seem an obvious corollary, since the undefined terms of the calculus of language must, it seemed, be given content by being connected to items given in experience.)

The 'scientific world-view' was explicitly characterized by a method, an attitude to problems, a goal and a negative crusade. The method was logical analysis of language. The attitude towards problems was declared to be 'specifically scientific'.

This had two aspects: first, unqualified empiricism, which was thought to be at least implicit in the *Tractatus*; second, a 'scientific' approach to disagreement – namely, that 'what can be said can be said clearly' (here the Manifesto explicitly quoted the *Tractatus*), that any difference of opinion can ultimately be resolved – hence interminable disagreements in philosophy will be a thing of the past. This was tantamount to placing the same faith in the programme and method of analysis as the empirical scientist places in experiment. The goal was *unified science* (see below, pp. 59–62). The negative crusade was the demolition of metaphysics (and theology). The name which the Ernst Mach Society had chosen – namely, 'The Scientific World-View' – encapsulated their orientation, namely 'science free of metaphysics' (Manifesto, p. 7).

3. The demolition of metaphysics

The Manifesto boldly declared that the representatives of the scientific world-view 'resolutely stand on the ground of simple human experience'. The negative side of this empiricist stance was the task 'of removing the metaphysical and theological debris of millennia' (Manifesto, p. 19), a task members of the Circle approached with zest and confidence. Three kinds of explanation were ventured for the aberrations of metaphysics: psychological, sociological and logical. Freudian psychology would shed light on the first, while the Marxist account of ideological superstructures would contribute to the second. But the third, it was argued in the Manifesto, had already come to fruition in the work of Russell and Wittgenstein. According to the Manifesto, two kinds of logical mistake underlie metaphysical theory. The first is the error of hypostatization, due to excessive reliance upon the misleading forms of natural languages and on the idea that every substantive stands for some entity. This error had been exposed by Russell's account of 'denoting phrases' in general and definite descriptions in particular. Second is the belief that pure reason alone can yield knowledge of reality from its own resources. Wittgenstein's logical investigations had shown, however, that all reasoning is merely tautological transformation of symbolism, and can yield no knowledge (Manifesto, p. 9). His insight that sentences of metaphysics are pseudo-sentences devoid of cognitive content strengthened the conviction of members of the Circle, rendering it 'more definite and radical'.[37]

Interestingly, Wittgenstein was scornful of this aspect of the Circle's ideology. On the one hand, as he remarked in criticism of the Manifesto, there was nothing new about 'abolishing metaphysics'.[38] On the other hand, one may presume, what had seemed to him original in his anti-metaphysical remarks in the *Tractatus* was disregarded by the Circle. For he had argued that there are indeed metaphysical truths about the essential nature of the world. What he had claimed, however, was that they are *essentially ineffable*, that they are shown (and must be shown) by the depth structure (which will be revealed by analysis) of any possible language. The typical reaction of the Circle is exemplified by Neurath's response to the concluding line of the *Tractatus*: 'Whereof one cannot speak, thereof one must be silent' – namely, that one should indeed be silent, but not *about* anything.[39] For there are no

ineffable metaphysical truths. The preferred line of attack among members of
the Circle was to argue that putative metaphysical sentences (and here they were
thinking largely of theological assertions, vitalist claims about entelechy, Kantian
claims about noumenal reality, neo-Hegelian utterances about the Absolute, and
Heideggerian assertions about Being and Nothingness) do not pass the test of verifiability, conceived as a criterion of meaningfulness. Such sentences as 'only the
Absolute contains the truth as such', 'There is a God' or 'There is an entelechy
which is the leading principle in living beings' are not analysable into elementary
sentences concerning what is 'immediately given' in experience. They contain words
which have not been given a coherent meaning (e.g. 'entelechy', 'noumena', 'inher-
ence', 'the Absolute') or words which do have a meaning, but are employed in
illegitimate syntactical constructions (as in 'We know the Nothing' or 'the Being of
being'). This, it was argued, shows that metaphysical sentences which employ such
words or syntactical constructions are devoid of 'cognitive meaning'.

Carnap attempted to circumvent Wittgenstein's insistence that the forms of language are indescribable by distinguishing between an object language and a metalanguage, and between the 'formal' and 'material' modes of discourse. In *The Logical
Syntax of Language*, he argued that instead of the prohibited 'metaphysical' pseudo-
proposition '*A* is an object', one can capture the only truth that is thereby expressed
by saying ' "*A*" is a thing-word'. In so far as this is conceived to be a *contingent* truth
about the use of a sign in English, Carnap was mistaken to think that the *Tractatus*
laid any prohibition on such remarks (unless 'thing-word' counts as a formal concept). But of course such contingent propositions about signs fail to capture the
essential truths which they displace. Wittgenstein was later to argue that such sentences as '*A* is an object' express perfectly respectable propositions, but they are
grammatical propositions, rules for the use of the constituent expressions, misleadingly expressed in the form of empirical propositions. They license, for example,
the inference from '*A* is on the table' to 'An object is on the table'. Carnap failed to
see that the prohibited atomic necessary truths are in effect norms of representation.

4. Necessary propositions, conventionalism and consistent empiricism

Part of the goal of the Circle's crusade against metaphysics was to uphold what they
thought of as 'consistent empiricism'. The major flaw in traditional empiricism was
the difficulty in accounting for our knowledge of necessary truths. These fall into
four categories: putative metaphysical truths, truths of logic, truths of arithmetic
and geometry, and moral truths. Members of the Circle thought that the first had
been definitively shown to fail to meet the criterion of meaningfulness given by the
principle of verification: the most one could glean from these barren fields were
statements in the formal mode about the logical syntax of expressions in a language
(e.g. that 'red' is a colour-word or that 'one' is a number-word). The category of
moral 'truths' was denied to have any cognitive content, being emotive or tacitly
imperatival. The propositions of logic and mathematics, by contrast, constituted a
more formidable problem.

Schlick's *General Theory of Knowledge* (1918) had already defended a form of conventionalism regarding necessary truths.[40] Its primary target was the Kantian notion of synthetic a priori truths: that is, necessary truths which have a cognitive content, apply to reality, and can be determined independently of experience. Schlick's inspiration was Hilbert's *Foundations of Geometry*, in which it was argued that the axioms of geometry are implicit definitions (i.e. conventions of symbolism) of the constituent expressions. These were conceived to be purely syntactical. They are arbitrary, and different conventions are possible, as is evident from the discovery of alternative geometries. But they are subject to the constraint of consistency. The 'truth' of the theorems of pure geometry is merely a matter of their describing the relations between the concepts introduced by the implicit definitions of the system. The network of concepts allegedly determined by implicit definitions is given a content by an interpretation, which links the network to reality. The result of such an interpretation, however, is, no longer a system of a priori truths, but an empirical theory, typically a theory about space. This (highly problematic[41]) conception seemed capable of generalization. Logic (Aristotelian logic), Schlick suggested, could likewise be treated as a system of implicit definitions (e.g. of the logical terms 'all', 'some', 'not') and their consequences (the theorems), thus relieving one of the need to appeal to self-evidence or logical intuition, although an explanation of why no alternative logics seemed possible was necessary.[42] As a result of reading the *Tractatus*, Schlick abandoned his earlier view that all logical inference is syllogistic. The claim that all the propositions of logic are tautologies and that all reasoning is merely the tautological transformation of symbols seemed to him a revelation of the true nature of logic. It confirmed his antecedent conviction that there are no synthetic a priori truths and that pure reason alone can yield no knowledge.

Although in some respects Schlick's account of necessary truths anticipated the Circle's conventionalism, members of the Circle uniformly viewed the *Tractatus* as the real inspiration for their view. As they saw it, the propositions of logic and mathematics constituted the major objection to consistent empiricism: one had either to abandon empiricism or to give a distorted account of logic and mathematics. Hahn wrote: 'Only the elucidation of the place of logic and mathematics . . . made consistent empiricism possible.' And it was 'Wittgenstein who recognized the tautological character of logic and emphasized that there was nothing in the world corresponding to the so-called logical constants'.[43] Schlick characterized Wittgenstein's insight into the nature of logic and its relation to reality and experience as 'the most important step in philosophy'.[44] And Carnap later wrote:

> The most important insight I gained from his work was the conception that the truth of logical statements is based only on their logical structure and on the meaning of the terms. Logical statements are true under all conceivable circumstances; thus their truth is independent of the contingent facts of the world. On the other hand, it follows that these statements do not say anything about the world and thus have no factual content.[45]

As they understood the *Tractatus*, it had shown that logical propositions are senseless tautologies that say nothing, and that logical deduction (a priori reasoning) is nothing but the tautological transformation of symbols. It had liberated the philosophy of logic from the incoherent idea that logical truth rests on an array of privileged self-evident axioms known by intuition, thereby showing that the axiomatization of logic is needless. 'The usual distinction between fundamental and derived sentences is arbitrary. It is immaterial whether a logical sentence is derived from other sentences. Its validity can be recognised from its form.'[46] It also showed that, *contra* Frege and Russell, there are no logical objects; that is, that the logical operators do not symbolize entities of any kind. And it rendered obsolete the idea that the propositions of logic consist of generalizations about logical entities, forms or the most general facts in the universe. Truths of logic, unlike those of pure geometry, are not conventions of symbolism (implicit definitions); nor are they true in virtue of describing the relations between the concepts thus implicitly defined. 'There is only *one* kind of truth, and only the structures of [a priori and empirical] propositions differ . . . What distinguishes an a priori from an empirical proposition is the structure of the proposition-*combination*, not the *quality* of its truth.'[47] A tautology is unconditionally true, being a truth based only on its logical structure. This conception represented a great advance over the attempt to generalize Hilbert's conception of geometry over propositions of logic. For logical propositions are not related to logical axioms (e.g. of *Principia*) as the theorems of a geometrical calculus are related to geometrical axioms. Being tautologies, they can be shown to be true independently of any axioms. Unlike the propositions of pure geometry, logical propositions are not conventions of symbolism at all. But wittingly or unwittingly, members of the Circle modified Wittgenstein's account in crucial, and arguably catastrophic, ways.

On their view, truths of logic are true in virtue of the meanings of the logical operators. They held, and attributed to Wittgenstein the view, that the truth of a tautology follows from the truth-tabular definitions of the logical connectives. Disregarding Wittgenstein's use of T/F *notation* to eliminate the logical connectives and to give a visible display of the tautologous nature of logical propositions, they viewed the truth-tables as a method for calculating whether a proposition is a tautology. A logical truth was therefore conceived to be the logical consequence of conventions (definitions). They construed Wittgenstein as having shown that the truth of a proposition depends upon a factual component and a linguistic component, and that what is distinctive of logical propositions is that the factual component in them cancels out. So what *makes* a logical truth true is a convention or conventions of symbolism. The cognitive non-triviality of logic (and mathematics) they attributed to human frailty; that is, to the limitations on our power to see immediately what are the consequences of the conventions we lay down. An omniscient being would have no need of mathematics or logic, Hahn argued,[48] but would 'at once know everything that is implicitly contained in the assertion of a few propositions' (i.e. the definitions or conventions of the system). We, on the other hand, have to make ourselves conscious of these logical consequences of our conventions by successive tautological transformations.

It is ironic that although the Circle's conventionalism was inspired by the *Tractatus*, and was rooted in Wittgenstein's explanation of the tautologous character of the propositions of logic and of their essential senselessness, the conception of the Circle is in fact far removed from what Wittgenstein was advocating. Where the members of the Circle thought that the logical constants of the calculus are arbitrary symbols introduced to form molecular propositions, he had argued that all the logical constants are given together with the mere idea of an elementary proposition as such (since the idea of negation is given together with bipolarity, which belongs to the essence of a proposition; and the idea of conjunction is given with the mere possibility of successive assertion). Where they argued that logical propositions are consequences of conventions, he had argued that they are given by the very nature of language. They flow, not from arbitrary conventions, but from the essential bipolarity of the proposition, and they reflect the logical structure of the world (TLP 6.124). Logic, far from being determined by conventions, is transcendental (TLP 6.13).

With respect to geometry, the Circle tended to cleave to the Hilbertian picture. As far as arithmetic was concerned, they thought that Russell's logicism had shown, barring technical difficulties that would surely be overcome, that arithmetic is derivable from pure logic alone. Surprisingly, they thought that the *Tractatus* had shown that arithmetical propositions are tautologies[49] (whereas Wittgenstein had argued that arithmetical propositions are, technically speaking, nonsense – equations, hence pseudo-propositions, not tautologies). Aware of the controversies between logicists, Hilbertian formalists and Brouwerian intuitionists, the Manifesto optimistically surmised 'that essential features of all three will come closer in the course of future development and probably, using the far-reaching ideas of Wittgenstein, will be united in the ultimate solution' (p. 13). Nothing could have been further from the truth, as far as Wittgenstein was concerned. He had rejected logicism in the *Tractatus*, and at the very time at which the Manifesto was being written, he had started developing his objections to formalism and intuitionism. In due course he was to reject all three, and indeed to dispute their shared understanding of the foundations crisis that had led to their formulation.

The Circle's conventionalism was deeply defective. In the endeavour to insulate 'consistent empiricism' from any taint of the synthetic a priori, members of the Circle had erected an inconsistent philosophy of logic. The requirement of consistency among any set of conventions was left as a non-conventional constituent in their thinking which they could not dispense with. So too was the law of identity, to which appeal had unavoidably to be made to license substitution in the demonstration of the analyticity of analytic propositions. The suggestion that *truths* can intelligibly be said to *follow* from conventions was problematic (since a proposition can *follow* only from a proposition), as was the idea that a convention can *make* a proposition true (for the only proposition which a convention can make true is one of the form 'There is a convention which . . .'). Similarly, the notion that a rule can determine the meaning of an expression and that we may then investigate *the logical consequences* of that meaning is incoherent. It is rooted in the misguided *Bedeutungskörper* conception[50] (which Wittgenstein later anatomized (see Exg. §138 and Volume 2, 'Grammar and necessity', pp. 312–18)), which distorts the notions of meaning, understanding and following a rule. The logical equivalence of ' $\sim \sim p$' with 'p' does not *follow* from the meaning of '$\sim$' as defined by its truth-table, but is *constitutive* of its meaning. The idea that a proof in logic or mathematics verifies that a proposition does indeed follow from conventions of symbolism, and is therefore the a priori equivalent of the verification of an empirical proposition, is misconceived. For proof *within* the a priori sciences is categorially distinct from proof *by means* of the propositions of the a priori sciences.

While the Circle learnt from Wittgenstein that the propositions of logic are not conventions, that they are true but nevertheless senseless, its members failed to address the question of the *role* – in particular, the *extra*-logical role – of the propositions of logic, or indeed of humble analytic propositions. They tended to view them, as it were, as veritive danglers, unavoidable but harmless excrescences upon the body of language. Wittgenstein was later to argue that the propositions of logic are correlates of rules of inference, and that rules of inference are grammatical rules which are partly constitutive of the meanings of logical operators. Different tautologies, though all saying the same, namely nothing, are correlates of different rules of inference; a tautology is not a rule, but *that* a certain formula *is a tautology* is a rule. For 'p & $(p \supset q) \supset q$' does not say that q *follows* from p & $p \supset q$ (indeed, being a tautology, it says nothing); but to say *that* 'p & $(p \supset q) \supset q$' *is a tautology* is to say that q follows from p & $(p \supset q)$ (LFM 277; AWL 137f.). Analytic propositions such as 'Bachelors are unmarried', on the other hand, are, despite the fact that we talk of them as being true, rules in the misleading guise of statements (as, indeed, we say that it is true that the chess king moves only one square at a time). 'Bachelors are unmarried' is the expression of a rule which licenses the inference from 'A is a bachelor' to 'A is unmarried'. While it was part of the programme of the Circle to show that all necessary truths are true 'by convention' or are 'consequences of conventions', its members restricted themselves to propositions of logic, analytic truths that can be displayed as such by the substitution of *definiens* for *definiendum* (given by formal definitions), and propositions of mathematics. This left a lacuna when it came to propositions such as 'Nothing can be red and green all over' or 'Red is darker than pink'. For these are not reducible to logical truths and analytic definitions. That the struggles with such propositions proved unsuccessful was in part a consequence of the fact that members of the Circle misconstrued ostensive definitions as forging a link between language and reality (and even when Waismann brought them the fruits of Wittgenstein's subsequent reflections on ostensive definition, they failed to grasp their implications). Consequently, they did not realize that the object pointed at in giving an ostensive definition of, say, 'red' is functioning as a sample which belongs to the means of representation, and that an ordered pair of red and pink samples can also be used as a sample to define the relation of 'darker than'. 'Red is darker than pink', therefore, is a rule (a grammatical proposition) that licenses the inference from 'A is red' and 'B is pink' to 'A is darker than B'. It is not a truth that *follows from* a convention, but is itself a further convention (see Volume 1, 'Ostensive definition and its ramifications', §§3–5).

The discovery of alternative logical calculi, such as Brouwer's intuitionistic logic, was problematic. One could either respond, as Schlick was prone to do, that they are not really 'logic'. But such a response lacked any firm rationale. Or one could introduce a 'principle of tolerance' in logic, as Carnap did in response to Menger's urging,[51] allowing one to choose which logic to use according to convenience, as, it was thought, one could choose which geometry to adopt for purposes of physics. But this solution fails to budget for the way in which central features of standard logic are built into, and held in place by, our concepts of thinking, inferring, reasoning, argument, contradiction and so forth, and the roles of these concepts in human life (see Volume 2, 'Grammar and necessity', pp. 317f.). So it makes no sense to talk of *choosing* an alternative logic, as Carnap suggested, any more than it makes sense to talk of choosing alternative concepts of inference, contradiction, argument, thinking or reasoning. (To this extent, Schlick was right, but failed to see why he was.)

The Hilbertian conception of geometry which was adopted by the Circle was vitiated by a misconception of ostensive definition as forging a connection between an uninterpreted calculus (syntax) and reality. It further misconstrued 'applied geometry' as an empirical theory of space, whereas a geometry, Wittgenstein argued (WWK 62f.; RR 123ff., 149ff.), is a grammar of space and spatial relations (see Volume 2, 'Grammar and necessity', §3). Alternative geometries are not alternative theories of space, but rather determine alternative concepts of space and spatial relations.

Despite these interpretations and misinterpretations of the *Tractatus*, and the further confusion engendered by the fragmentary insights into Wittgenstein's constantly evolving ideas communicated to the Circle by Waismann, there is no question but that Wittgenstein's conception of logic and logical propositions moulded the Circle's theorizing. The subject of the nature of necessity and the character of logical truths was firmly placed centre-stage in philosophical debate, and remained there for the next three or four decades.

5. The principle of verification

The hallmark of logical positivism was the principle of verification: namely, that the meaning of a proposition is its method of verification.[52] It was the basis for the Circle's criterion of meaningfulness: namely, verifiability. Accordingly, a sentence or proposition (and it was problematic which of these was in question) is meaningless if there is no method for verifying it. This criterion played a major role in the Circle's anti-metaphysical polemics (in contradistinction to Wittgenstein's strategy in the *Tractatus*, where he argued that there can be no expressible atomic necessary truths, and that any attempt to express such would involve illicitly employing a formal concept). The principle was attributed to Wittgenstein. Carnap, in his 'Intellectual Autobiography', wrote of 'Wittgenstein's principle of verifiability' (p. 45).[53] Juhos similarly referred to 'Wittgenstein's "verification thesis"',[54] and Kraft remarks that 'This formula ["The meaning of a proposition is determined by its method of verification"] is due to Wittgenstein, whose "Tractatus Logico-philosophicus" has been the starting point for the Vienna Circle's theory of meaning and meaninglessness'.[55] Given that there is no statement of the principle in the *Tractatus*, this may seem surprising. And doubts about the attribution were strengthened by Wittgenstein's later remark 'I used at one time to say that, in order to get clear how a certain sentence is used, it was a good idea to ask oneself the question: How would one try to verify such an assertion? But that's just one way of getting clear about the use of a word or sentence. . . . Some people have turned this suggestion about asking for the verification into a dogma – as if I had been advancing a *theory* about meaning.'[56] Some light can be shed on the sources of the principle and on Wittgenstein's later disclaimer by scrutiny of the available texts.

The principle of verification first appeared in print in Waismann's 'A Logical

Analysis of the Concept of Probability' (1930–1). He acknowledged on the opening page that he was 'using Wittgenstein's ideas'. On the second he explained, 'If there is no way of telling when a proposition is true, then the proposition has no sense whatever; for the sense of a proposition is its method of verification. In fact, whoever utters a proposition must know under what conditions he will call the proposition true or false; if he cannot tell this, then he does not know what he has said.'[57] This seems to be derived from Waismann's 'Thesen', first composed in 1930 (a slightly later version of which is published as Appendix B in *Ludwig Wittgenstein and the Vienna Circle*) and circulated among members of the group. It was an attempt to epitomize of Wittgenstein's philosophy, and supplemented the *Tractatus* with new ideas derived from Waismann's meetings with him. In section 6, entitled 'Verification', Waismann wrote:

> A person who utters a proposition must know under what conditions the proposition is to be called true or false; if he is not able to specify that, he also does not know what he has said.
>
> To understand a proposition means to know how things stand if the proposition is true.
>
> One can understand a proposition without knowing *whether* it is true.
>
> In order to get an idea of the sense of a proposition, it is necessary to become clear about the procedure leading to the determination of its truth. If one does not know that procedure, one cannot understand the proposition either.
>
> A proposition cannot say more than is established by means of the method of its verification . . .
>
> *The sense of a proposition is the way it is verified.* . . .
>
> A proposition that cannot be verified in any way has no sense. (WWK 243ff.)

In the sequel, Waismann connected the principle of verification with the conception of ostensive definition as linking language and reality, giving the syntactical structure of a language content by 'pinning' it to entities in the world:

> There are two ways of giving a sign a meaning: 1. By means of ostension (*Aufweisung*) . . . 2. By means of definition . . .
>
> . . . Ostension steps outside language and connects signs with reality. . . .
>
> If we analyse the signs in a statement, replacing them by other signs in accordance with their definitions and replacing those by yet other signs, etc., the verification-path becomes visible step by step.
>
> *Definitions are signposts. They show the path leading to verification,* . . . a verification-path cannot lead to infinity . . . but ultimately we must reach propositions that . . . point to reality . . .
>
> If it were otherwise . . . there would be no connection between language and the world.
>
> The propositions that deal with reality immediately are called *elementary propositions* (WWK 246ff.)

Members of the Circle saw these claims as merely making explicit what they thought was implicit in the *Tractatus* (and it is by no means obvious that they were *altogether* wrong). The principle of verification, in its simplest form, was, as far as they were concerned, a reasonable corollary of the fact that the syntactical network of language, as Wittgenstein had described it in his book, had to be connected with reality by projecting the indefinable simple names on to objects in the world. (The only novelty was the conception (or misconception) of ostensive definition, for there was no account of ostensive definition in the *Tractatus*; at that stage Wittgenstein thought that names are pinned to reality by mental acts of meaning.) Schlick was quite explicit about this:

> It is clear that in order to understand a verbal definition we must know the significance of the explaining words beforehand, and that the only explanation which can work without any previous knowledge is the ostensive definition. We conclude that there is no way of understanding any meaning without ultimate reference to ostensive definitions, and this means, in an obvious sense, reference to 'experience' or 'possibility of verification'.[58]

These ideas chimed with the empiricist orientation of the Circle, and quickly spread. Carnap wrote: 'The meaning of a word is determined by its criterion of application (in other words: by the relations of deducibility entered into by its elementary sentence-form [i.e. its simplest propositional function, such as '*x* is a stone' for the word 'stone'], by its truth-conditions, by the method of its verification).'[59] It is noteworthy that members of the Circle saw no incongruity in thus claiming that the meaning of a sentence is given by its truth-conditions, by its method of verification, and by the conditions of its application (its use). Carnap was by no means the only one to take this apparently eclectic view. Schlick wrote:

> Whenever we ask about a sentence, 'What does it mean?', what we expect is instruction as to the circumstances in which the sentence is to be used; we want a description of the conditions under which the sentence will form a *true* proposition, and of those which will make it *false*. The meaning of a word or a combination of words is, in this way, determined by a set of rules which regulate their use and which, following Wittgenstein, we may call the rules of their *grammar* . . .
>   Stating the meaning of a sentence amounts to stating the rules according to which the sentence is to be used, and this is the same as stating the way in which it can be verified (or falsified). The meaning of a proposition is the method of its verification.[60]

With the hindsight of decades, it may seem bizarre that members of the Circle could roll together such apparently incompatible conceptions of language and meaning as truth-conditional semantics, verificationism and an account of meaning in terms of use.[61] For philosophers from the 1970s onwards were prone to claim that the *Tractatus* is a paradigm of truth-conditional semantics and, as such, a form of 'realism'. It was thought that verificationism followed a quite different paradigm: namely, a form of 'anti-realism'. And the claim that meaning is use was conceived to belong to Wittgenstein's later, and in the view of some philosophers, bewilderingly anti-theoretical conception of meaning.[62]

This is misconceived and anachronistic. The *Tractatus* did indeed give a truth-conditional account of the sense of molecular propositions. *Given the sense of the constituent elementary propositions,* the sense of a molecular proposition is given by the conditions (the distribution of truth-values among its constituents) under which it comes out true in its truth-table. But an elementary proposition no more has *truth-conditions* than does a tautology or a contradiction. Given what the term 'truth-condition' means in the *Tractatus*, namely, a *condition which a proposition must satisfy*, the very idea that a non-molecular proposition could have truth-conditions is confused, conflating the truth-*conditions* of a proposition with the truth-*grounds* of a proposition (TLP 5.101–5.121). The sense of an elementary proposition is a function of its constituent expressions (their meanings and their forms), and consists in its agreement and disagreement with possibilities of existence and non-existence of states of affairs (TLP 4.2). It agrees with the existence of the possibility – the state of affairs – it presents, and disagrees with its non-existence. The existence of the state of affairs presented is the truth-ground of the proposition. The canonical Tarskian formulation ' "*p*" is true iff *p*' does not, by the lights of the *Tractatus*, specify a *condition* which an elementary proposition '*p*' must satisfy in order to be true (whereas ' "*p* & *q*" is true if and only if both "*p*" and "*q*" are true' does). One must beware of reading post-Tarskian developments and shifts in the *concept* of a truth-condition into the *Tractatus*.[63] But it is, of course, correct that a proposition is true if we use it to say that things stand in a certain way, and they do (TLP 4.062).

Nor should one be surprised that members of the Circle invoked the notion of use. After all, the *Tractatus* had remarked, quite innocuously, that 'In order to recognize a symbol by its sign we must observe how it is used with a sense' (TLP 3.326), and to observe the different ways in which different propositions are compared with reality (verified) is to do just that. The very different account of meaning that we find in the *Investigations* is not determined simply by the dictum 'The meaning of an expression is its use'. Only in the context of an overall picture delineating a network of internal relations between the concepts of language, proposition, name, meaning, explanation, understanding, use, truth and so on does this dictum assume a determinate significance.

How did the *Tractatus* stand on the matter of verification and its relation to meaning? There is some reason for thinking that in so far as Wittgenstein had any conception of what simple objects and elementary propositions might be, he thought of the former as objects of acquaintance (though not as sense-data) and of the latter as descriptions of states of affairs that are objects of possible experience. To know whether an elementary proposition is true or false, one must verify it, compare it with reality (TLP 2.223). The proposition is like a yardstick, to be held against reality for a Yes/No reading (cf. TLP 2.1512f.). It seems likely that the idea of an *elementary* proposition which is not verifiable would not have been intelligible to him. *If* simple objects are objects of acquaintance, which presumably they must be *if* names are attached to the objects that are their meanings by a mental act or process of *meaning* by a name one uses *this ↗ object*, and if understanding an elementary proposition means knowing what must be the case if it is true – that is that such-and-such objects are concatenated thus-and-so (that things are as the elementary proposition says they are) – then to understand such a proposition *is* to know what experience would 'verify' it, what experience one must have in order to know whether it is true. (Of course, a multitude of problems lie concealed here, of which Wittgenstein only later became aware.) If so, then implicit in the *Tractatus* was a commitment to verifiability as a criterion of empirical meaningfulness for elementary propositions, although not a verificationist *definition* of meaning in terms of the method of verification.

When he returned to philosophy in 1929, he realized that the independence thesis for elementary propositions could not be upheld. Incompatibility relations, hence entailments, between propositions attributing a determinate of a determinable to a given object are not reducible to the entailments of a logical sum or product of logically independent elementary propositions. Although he tried briefly to budget for this (in 'Some Remarks on Logical Form' (PAS 1929)), he rapidly came to see that the collapse of the independence thesis implied the collapse of the *Tractatus* picture of the essence of logic and of logical relations between propositions. For it is no longer possible to argue that the mere bipolarity of the elementary proposition and the possibility of the joint assertion of any pair of such propositions suffices to determine every possible truth-function of elementary propositions. For 'A is red' and 'A is green' do not yield as a possible combination 'A is red & A is green'. 'A is red $\supset$ A is green' is *not* a possibility (hence the truth-table for implication must be adjusted for such cases, since it allows as a possibility something which is excluded, viz. the truth of both antecedent and consequent). If logical relations can be determined by the inner structure of propositions that are not molecular, then the whole conception of logical relations defended in the *Tractatus* is undermined. Tautologies and contradictions emerge which are not simply the result of a degenerate case of combination of independent propositions: for example, 'A is red $\supset$ ~ (A is green)' and 'A is red & A is green'. So it is not true that all the propositions of logic are given in the logical syntax of any sign language (TLP 6.124), if that claim is understood as confined to the combinatorics of elementary propositions.

With the collapse of the independence thesis, Wittgenstein introduced the notion of 'propositional systems' (*Satzsysteme*) into which propositions concerned with determinates of a determinable are organized. He adjusted his metaphor for comparing the proposition with reality. A proposition is indeed like a yardstick held against reality, but the *whole scale* of the yardstick gives a set of interdependent readings; for example, if A is 1 foot long, then it is not 2 feet long, not 3 feet long and so forth, and if A is red, then it is not green, not yellow and so on. At much the same time, he relinquished the metaphysics of facts and objects that informed the *Tractatus* and the conception of simple names the meanings of which are simple objects. He came to realize that in the *Tractatus* he had been confused about ostensive definition and analysis (WWK 209f.), in thinking that there was a 'connection between language and reality'. He now saw that one must not confuse the use of a sentence of the form 'This $\nearrow$ is A' to make a statement with its use to give an ostensive definition (PR 54), a confusion arguably embedded in *Tractatus* 3.263.[64] Further, he saw that it is misguided to think, as Schlick and Waismann did, that an ostensive definition leads out of language, connecting words and world. The object pointed at, in the ostensive definition of a colour-word, for example, is best conceived as a sample belonging to the method of representation. Of course, that object may also be described – but then it is no longer being used as a sample. For whether an object is a sample is a function not of its intrinsic nature but of the use we make of it. The *Tractatus* simples were, in effect, samples seen through a glass darkly.

His interest shifted not only to propositional systems, but also to the method of comparing propositions with reality. In the *Tractatus*, it seems, he had seen no problem about how one compares an elementary proposition (one understands) with reality. All one need do, apparently, is see whether the objects that are the meanings of the names are concatenated as the proposition says they are. But if, as

he realized by late 1929, it was misguided to think of the world as consisting of
facts, if facts do not consist of objects, if the meanings of (some) simple names are
explained by reference to samples that belong to the method of representation, then
the way we compare a proposition (which contains expressions defined in terms of
samples) with reality must be pertinent to its meaning. The method of comparing
a sample with reality must be internally related to the meaning of the proposition
in question. In *Philosophical Remarks*, he wrote:

> I should like to say: for any question there is always a corresponding *method* of
> finding.
>   Or you might say, a question *denotes* a method of searching.
>   You can only search in *a space* [i.e. in visual space for shapes and colours,
> auditory space for tones, tactile space for textures, etc.]. For only in space do you
> stand in relation to where you are not.
>   To understand the sense of a proposition means to know how the issue of its
> truth or falsity is to be decided. . . .
>   You must find the way from where you are to where the issue is decided.
>   You cannot search wrongly; you *cannot* look for a visual impression with your
> sense of touch.
>   You cannot compare a picture with reality unless you can set it against it as a
> yardstick.
>   You must be able to fit the proposition on to reality. (PR 77)

Given that the metaphysical picture of the relation between a proposition and the
fact that makes it true is misconceived, then to say that one understands a proposition when one knows what is the case if it is true is to say virtually nothing. For,
with only minor qualifications, '*p*' is equivalent to 'It is true that *p*'. Of course, if
I understand the proposition that snow is white, then I know that if it is true that
snow is white, then snow *is* white.[65] But if the theses of isomorphism between
language and reality are a mythology, then we need a fresh account (from case to
case) of what it *is* for the fact that *p* to obtain, of what *counts* as the proposition that
p's being true, of what *counts* as knowing that things are as the proposition that *p*
says they are. For we can no longer explain what it is for it to be the case that *p*
in terms of a concatenation of the constituent *meanings* of '*p*' in reality. Meanings,
thus understood, are now 'obsolete' (M 258). Meanings of expressions are explained
by explanations of meaning, and remain 'within language'. Some explanations of
expressions are given by ostensive definitions which involve samples, which are
elements of representation. How a proposition is compared with reality, therefore,
is (in such cases at any rate) a feature of its meaning. ('A is red' is compared with
the *visual* field, not the auditory field.) Wittgenstein now expressed this by the
claim that the meaning of a proposition is its method of verification. For, it now
seemed clear, 'To understand a proposition means to know how the issue of its
truth or falsity is to be decided.' Indeed, it is the verification which gives the
grammar of the proposition, and so answers the question '*What would it be like for
it to be true?*' (AWL 20). If the meaning of 'red', for example, were an object in
reality, then to know the meaning of red would already be to know how 'A is red'
is to be compared with reality. But if the meaning of 'red' is given by an ostensive
definition by reference to a sample, then in order to know what 'A is red' means,
one must know how to 'lay the proposition alongside reality', how to verify it.

Wittgenstein communicated his new ideas to Waismann and Schlick in 1929. On 22 December he expounded his verificationism to them. The sense of a proposition is its verification. He demanded *complete* or *conclusive* verification: 'If I can never verify the sense of a proposition completely, then I cannot have meant anything by the proposition . . . In order to determine the sense of a proposition, I should have to know a very specific procedure for when to count the proposition as verified' (WWK 47). Three days later, he elaborated further. Difference of verification indicates a difference in meaning (WWK 53). If one lays two propositions alongside reality in different ways, then they have different meanings. He propounded similar ideas in his lectures at Cambridge in 1930–1 (M 266; LWL 66).

By this time, Wittgenstein had abandoned his earlier thought that the formal concept of a proposition signifies a single general form: namely, the general propositional form exemplified by every proposition whatsoever. At this stage he distinguished between three essentially different kinds of structures that we call 'propositions'. (Later he was to go even further, claiming that the concept of a proposition is a family resemblance concept, displaying countless different varieties (PI §23), interconnected in many different ways (PI §65).) First, there are 'genuine propositions', which are conclusively verified or falsified by comparison with reality. These are propositions describing immediate experience – that is, sense-datum statements. For them, there is no gap between appearance and reality, no distinction between seeming and being. They concern what he called 'primary experience'. Secondly, there are 'hypotheses' (PR 282ff.). These are not conclusively verifiable by reference to experience. Propositions about objective particulars (as opposed to propositions about one's own immediate experience), about the past or future, about other people's mental states, universal generalizations, laws of nature and so forth are hypotheses. They are not propositions in the same sense as descriptions of immediate experience, but are altogether different kinds of logical structures. They cannot be said to be true or false (WWK 101; PR 283), or at any rate not in the same sense (PR 285). To say that a hypothesis is not conclusively verifiable is not to say that there is a verification of it which, through human frailty, we can only approximate but never fully attain. Rather, a hypothesis has a different formal relation to reality from that of a conclusively verifiable proposition (WWK 210; PR 284ff.). One can conceive of it as a law (or rule) for constructing propositions in the sense in which the equation of a curve gives a law for determining the ordinates if one cuts the curve at different abscissae. Analogously, genuinely verifiable observation statements are cuts through the connected structure of a hypothesis (WWK 100, 159; PR 284ff.). The relation between a hypothesis and the 'genuine propositions' that support it is therefore a priori. A proposition which gives support to a hypothesis Wittgenstein called 'a symptom' (WWK 159). A hypothesis is a rule for deriving symptoms ('a law for forming expectations' (PR 285)), and a symptom provides confirmation for a hypothesis. The probability of a hypothesis is a measure of how much evidence is needed to make it worthwhile to reject the hypothesis (PR 286).[66] The third kind of proposition Wittgenstein distinguished was the mathematical proposition, which cannot be compared with reality at all, and neither agrees nor disagrees with reality. The sense of a mathematical proposition is given by its proof. But, he warned, 'Nothing is more fatal to philosophical understanding than the notion of proof and experience as two different but comparable methods of verification' (PG 361). For what a mathematical proof proves is *a grammatical construction*, a *rule of representation*, not a truth about the world, let alone about a world of abstract objects.

There can be no doubt that Wittgenstein espoused verificationism in 1929–30, or that the members of the Circle derived their principle, and their criterion of meaninglessness, from him. But how can his later insistence that he had never advanced verificationism as a theory of meaning, but only as 'one way of getting clear about the use of a word or sentence', be explained? It was not, I think, wholly disingenuous. It is doubtful whether even in 1929–30 he would have thought of his verificationism as a *theory* of meaning. A clue to what may have been his position is to be found in Schlick's 'Positivism and Realism': 'It would be quite mistaken to see, somehow, in what we have said a "theory of meaning" (in Anglo-Saxon countries this insight, that the meaning of a proposition is determined wholly and alone by its verification in the given, is often called the "experimental theory of meaning"). What precedes every formulation of a theory cannot itself be a theory.'[67] It is plausible to suppose that this was a point Wittgenstein was eager to emphasize. In the much later paper 'Meaning and Verification' (1936), just after having stated that his remarks stem from conversations with Wittgenstein, Schlick reverts to this caveat:

> This view has been called the 'experimental theory of meaning'; but it certainly is no theory at all, for the term 'Theory' is used for a set of hypotheses about a certain subject-matter, and there are no hypotheses involved in our view, which proposes to be nothing but a simple statement of the way in which meaning is actually assigned to propositions, both in everyday life and in science. There has never been any other way, and it would be a grave error to suppose that we believe we have discovered a new conception of meaning which is contrary to common opinion and which we want to introduce into philosophy.[68]

It is noteworthy that in a conversation with Waismann on dogmatism in philosophy in December 1931, Wittgenstein compared dogmatic and undogmatic invocations of the principle of verification. These remarks strongly suggest that it would be very misleading to characterize his view as a 'theory' of any kind (and this *may* explain his later observation):

> First I shall speak dogmatically, and then undogmatically. Thus I say, if a proposition is verified in two different ways, then it has two different senses in these two cases. That still sounds odd and could give rise to objections. For someone might say, I do not see at all why a proposition should have different senses in that case and why it should not be possible to verify the same proposition in two entirely different ways. Now, however, I shall express myself undogmatically and simply draw attention to the following point: the verification of a proposition can itself only be given by means of a description. Thus the fact of the matter is that we have two propositions. The second proposition describes the verification of the first one. What, then, am I going to do? I simply lay it down as a rule of grammar that the first proposition is to follow from the second one. Thus I do not talk of sense and what sense is at all; I remain entirely within grammar. If you now say that one sentence has two different verifications, then I will point out that these verifications are described by different propositions; thus, in deriving the same proposition, we *proceeded according to different rules; and I did not want to say anything more than that.*

> Thus I simply draw the other person's attention to what he is really doing and refrain from any assertions. Everything is to go on within grammar. (WWK 186)

Over the next two decades, the members of the Circle and their heirs and supporters struggled to formulate the principle of verification in a manner that would render it foolproof to intuitive counter-examples, to include all and only scientifically respectable propositions, and to exclude all propositions tainted, in the view of the Circle, by metaphysics. The difficulties proved formidable. There was disagreement over whether there were 'ultimate verifiers' or 'protocol sentences' – that is, basic propositions of a given class which were conclusively verifiable and from which all other meaningful propositions could be constructed (see below, pp. 59–62). If so, were they material object statements or sense-datum statements? There was controversy as to whether verification was to be taken as verification 'in principle' or 'in practice', and as to what might count as a method of verification that was possible in principle but not in practice. There was disagreement over whether conclusive verifiability was demanded, or whether a weaker form of the criterion of meaningfulness was sufficient. Controversy broke out over the status of the principle of verification. Was it an empirical statement or an analytic truth? Or was it merely a recommendation that we adopt a certain usage of the words 'meaning' and 'meaningless'? The analysis of general statements, of statements about past and future, about other people's states of mind, all proved highly problematic. And after a decade and more of struggle, the bold confidence of the early days of verficationism evaporated. The principle of verification as the key to meaning proved incapable of unlocking all and only the doors the Vienna Circle wished it to. Equally, the criterion of verifiability as the litmus paper for distinguishing sense from nonsense excluded either too much or too little.

Wittgenstein's adherence to verificationism was short-lived. He rapidly abandoned his distinction between 'genuine propositions' and 'hypotheses'. By 1932–3, as is evident from Moore's lecture notes (M 266), he had realized that what he had earlier conceived of as genuine propositions admitting of conclusive verification – namely, expressions (*Äusserungen*) of immediate experience – are precisely propositions which admit of no verification and involve no comparison with reality. It makes no sense to ask 'How do you know that you have a pain?' or 'How do you know that A looks red to you?' (see Volume 3, 'Avowals and descriptions'). His conception of a hypothesis disappeared equally rapidly. It was a mistake to conceive of material object statements as hypotheses which are rendered probable to a greater or lesser degree by 'symptoms', which are immediately verified experiential statements. And it was misguided to think of statements about other minds as hypotheses which cannot be conclusively confirmed, and of others' experiences as logical constructions out of behavioural symptoms (see Volume 3, 'Behaviour and behaviourism', §§1–3).[69] He realized that one must distinguish between empirical, inductive evidence and a priori evidence (which, in the case of statements about other people's mental states, he called 'criteria'). Reading in the newspaper that Cambridge won the boat-race may be how I learn of that event, but it can hardly be thought of as part of the grammar of the proposition. At best, such statements 'only go a very little way towards explaining the meaning of "boat-race"' (M 266; arguably, even this is going too far). The claim that in giving the verification of a proposition, one is giving its meaning, was far too sweeping, for in fact it is, he now declared, just a 'rule of thumb' (ibid.). For 'verification' means different things. 'How far is giving the verification of a proposition a grammatical statement about it?', he remarked in 1932–3; 'So far as it is, it can explain the meaning of its terms. In so far as it is a matter of experience, as when one names a symptom [inductive evidence], the meaning is not explained' (AWL 31). In essence, this very modest claim was the one to which Wittgenstein continued to adhere. In the *Investigations* §353, in what may be taken to be his final view of the matter, he repeated a remark written in the early 1930s: 'Asking whether and how a proposition can be verified is only a particular way of asking "How d'you mean?" The answer is a contribution to the grammar of the proposition.' (See Exg. §353.)

6. The unity of science

A major plank in the logical positivists' platform was the programme of 'the unity of science'. This phrase was originally introduced by Neurath to mark opposition to the view that there are different kinds of science with radically different methodologies and logical structures. In particular, he opposed the view, originating in modern times with Dilthey's school, that there is a sharp methodological and logical difference between the physical and the psychological and social sciences (history or, closer to Neurath's heart, sociology and economics), or between the natural and the normative sciences. (Kelsen, who was associated with the Circle, was to defend the autonomy of the 'normative science' of law.) Neurath's hope was to initiate a great encyclopaedic work, akin to Diderot's *Encyclopédie*, to be known as *The Encyclopaedia of Unified Science*, which was planned as a set of twenty-six volumes, each comprising ten monographs, written by scientists and philosophers, emphasizing the unity of all science.

The philosophical thesis of the unity of science was a particular form of radical empiricism. It was committed to a reductionist programme of displaying all cognitively significant propositions as deducible from an array of basic propositions that constitute 'the given'. What precisely constitutes 'the given', whether the basic 'protocol sentences' are descriptions of sense-data or physical object statements, was a matter of heated controversy within the Circle. The Manifesto was clearly committed to the former view:

> The aim of scientific effort is to reach the goal, unified science, by applying logical analysis to the empirical material. Since the meaning of every statement of science must be statable by reduction to the given, likewise the meaning of every concept, whatever branch of science it may belong to, must be statable by step-wise reduction to other concepts, down to the concepts of the lowest level which refer directly to the given. If such an analysis were carried through for all concepts, they would thus be ordered into a reductive system, a 'constitutive system'. Investigations towards such a constitutive system, the 'constitutive theory', thus form the framework within which logical analysis is applied by the scientific world-view. . . . Investigations into constitutive theory show that the lowest layers of the constitutive system contain concepts of the experience and qualities of the individual psyche; in the layer above are physical objects; from these are constituted

other minds and lastly the objects of the social sciences. . . . With the proof of the possibility and the outline of the shape of the total system of concepts, the relation of all statements to the given and with it the general structure of *unified science* become recognisable too. (Manifesto, p. 11)

This clearly shows Carnap's imprint. For in *Der logische Aufbau der Welt*,[70] he had attempted precisely such a 'rational reconstruction' of knowledge. His goal was to synthesize the insights of empiricism and rationalism. Both these great philosophical schools had agreed that all concepts and judgements require the co-operation of experience and reason. The senses provide the materials for knowledge, whereas reason synthesizes them to form a system of knowledge. Empiricism rightly stressed the contribution of the senses, but underestimated the role of logical and mathematical forms. Rationalism was all too aware of the contribution of reason, but erred in thinking that reason alone could yield not only forms of knowledge, but also fundamental content – namely, synthetic a priori truths. Inspired by Frege and Russell, Carnap tried to articulate a defensible synthesis, one that would do justice to the forms of knowledge without succumbing to the temptations of rationalism. Although he acknowledged the possibility of physicalist constructionism, with the choice of elementary particles (or space-time points of the four-dimensional space-time continuum, or 'world-lines' of physical points) as basic particulars, such constructional systems, he argued, would not reflect the *epistemic* order of things.[71] His central thesis in *Der logische Aufbau* was that it is in principle possible to reduce all concepts to 'the given'. His basic elements were 'elementary experiences', construed as unanalysable and epistemically primary, and the basic relation was that of recollected similarity. On this 'auto-psychological' basis, he tried to 'construct' first the domain of physical objects, conceived, roughly speaking, as logical constructions out of experiences, then the domain of the 'hetero-psychological', conceived as second-order logical constructions. *Der logische Aufbau* signals the thoroughgoing systematic transformation of logical analysis into its 'logical constructionist' phase, far surpassing Russell's earlier moves in that direction.

   This enterprise was conducted independently of any contact with Wittgenstein, although Carnap had evidently read the *Tractatus*. It is striking that in 1929, Wittgenstein himself, quite independently of Carnap, was moving along similar lines. For, in his *Philosophical Remarks*, he propounded the view that the basic propositions are experiential ones; that material object statements are hypotheses, which are, in a loose sense, logical constructions out of experiences; and that statements about other people's mental states are second-order logical constructions out of observable behaviour. This strategy, like Carnap's, committed him to a form of methodological solipsism. For the only 'experiences' recognized by the two philosophers are, in effect, one's own; that is, the only experiential, non-constructed propositions that can be cashed in terms of immediate, conclusive verification are abstractions from first-person, present-tense psychological propositions, in which the first-person pronoun is redundant. Propositions about the experiences of others are, on such an account, constructed out of propositions about their behaviour (see Volume 3, 'Behaviour and behaviourism', §§1–2).

   Given the impact which the *Tractatus* had had upon the Circle, it is hardly surprising that the general programme should have been appealing. Although the

Tractatus had not specifically discussed the thesis of the unity of science (and it is not easy to see how its schematic remarks about scientific theories fit into the overall picture of language delineated in the book), it was committed to the reducibility of all empirical propositions to elementary propositions and their truth-functional combinations. *All* propositions were held to be truth-functions of elementary propositions. Non-extensional contexts were held to be reducible to extensional ones. And these claims provided a logical basis for the thesis of the unity of science.

By 1931, under pressure from Neurath, Carnap abandoned his programme of reducing all empirical statements of any science whatever to an auto-psychological base. He adopted instead what he and Neurath called 'physicalism' – a similar reductivist programme, but committed to the choice of physical things as the basic elements for the construction, and to concepts of observable properties and relations of physical things as the basic concepts. This had the advantage of intersubjective agreement, unlike the auto-psychological base of the *Aufbau*, and physicalist language was supposed to be the language which scientists employ in their pre-systematic communications about their work. Carnap now argued that propositions of physics, biology, psychology and the social sciences are all reducible to propositions couched in the 'thing-language' which we use 'in speaking about the properties of the observable (inorganic) things surrounding us'.[72] Carnap and Neurath propounded their new views in a series of articles in *Erkenntnis* between 1931 and 1934. They were committed to a form of logical behaviourism, arguing that not only are propositions about others' mental states reducible to propositions about their behaviour, but also that first-person, present-tense propositions about one's own mental states are to be construed as reducible to propositions about one's own behaviour.

The shift to physicalism heralded an important change in logical empiricism, and also in analytic philosophy. Although the commitment to analysis was no less fervent than before, the attempt to reduce all sentences to an elementary, unanalysable level was abandoned. While members of the Circle had not accepted the rigorous (and unfathomable) atomism of the *Tractatus*, they had initially opted for what seemed the next best thing: namely, dropping the independence requirement for elementary propositions and interpreting elementary propositions as propositions concerning what is 'immediately given in experience'. This appeared to be licensed by Wittgenstein's evolving views, in so far as they were correctly represented by Waismann's 'Theses', §§7–8 (WWK 246–60). With the shift to physicalism, however, came a liberalism in the choice of the basis for reduction, in what is to count as reduction, and a corresponding principle of tolerance in logic. The task, as Carnap and Neurath saw it, was to give a rational reconstruction of 'the language of science', and the philosopher should be free to construct languages without dogmatic constraints. The choice of the reduction base was optional, and it was pragmatic considerations that dictated the choice of the 'thing-language'. Moreover, Carnap no longer demanded of reduction that it meet the stringent condition of simple definitional substitutability of equivalent statements, but introduced conditional definitions in the form of 'reduction statements' (e.g. the reduction statement for 'x has an electric charge at time t' is 'If a light body y is placed near x at t, then: x has an electric charge at t iff y is attracted by x at t'). This tolerance was even extended to logic itself. 'In logic', Carnap declared in 1934, 'there are no morals. Everyone is at liberty to build up his own logic, i.e. his own form of language, as he wishes.'[73] Whether classical logic, intuitionist logic or many-valued logic is chosen is a matter of convenience, constrained only by the cogency and fruitfulness of the resulting constructional system. Further diversification and lively internal controversy arose within the Circle when Neurath and Carnap rejected the correspondence theory of truth in favour of a coherence theory.

By this time, opinion within the Circle had polarized. In particular, Schlick and Waismann, who maintained contact with Wittgenstein and read his manuscripts, were perceived to be at odds with the 'orthodox' world-scientific view that was evolving primarily at the hands of Carnap and Neurath. 'The Wittgenstein period', Neurath later wrote to Waismann, 'took you (and to some extent Schlick too) away from our common task.'[74] This was hardly surprising, since Wittgenstein, in the early 1930s was moving off in very different directions, repudiating much of what he had argued in the *Tractatus* and what he had propounded in 1929–30 during his brief verificationist, constructionist phase. What sympathy he once had for reductive programmes of analysis evaporated as he demanded ever greater particularity, context-sensitivity and language-game relativity in his descriptions of the logic or 'grammar' of segments of our language (while denying the intelligibility of alternative logics for *a language*) and in his appreciation of the indefinite multiplicity of language-games. To the extent that Schlick and Waismann followed in his tracks, they could not but become doctrinally alienated from the other defenders of the 'world-scientific view'.

It should be noted that despite the invitation to reductionism implicit in the *Tractatus* conception of the elementary proposition and thesis of extensionality, and explicit in 'Some Remarks on Logical Form', Wittgenstein had little sympathy for the scientific spirit of the Circle. He did not think that the sole task of philosophy was the construction of the logical syntax of the language of science as Carnap and his followers interpreted that phrase. The programme for future philosophy which he had delineated in the concluding remarks of the *Tractatus* was more negative than that envisaged by Carnap and Neurath (and was the ancestor of his later therapeutic conception of philosophy). The primary role for future philosophy was to curb metaphysics and restrain one, by the method of analysis, from transgressing the bounds of sense. But, according to the *Tractatus*, this was because metaphysics is inexpressible, not because there are no metaphysical insights to be gained. On the contrary, they are shown by a perspicuous notation which reveals the logical forms of facts. Ethics, aesthetics and religion are inexpressible, not mere illusion. To be sure, Wittgenstein abandoned his doctrine of what cannot be said but only shown in the early 1930s, rejected the metaphysics and ontology of logical atomism, and repudiated his idea of a universal logical syntax necessarily common to all possible languages. However, this did not bring him any closer to the views of the Circle, either on metaphysical utterances or on ethics, aesthetics and religion, let alone on philosophy of language and logic.

Furthermore, Wittgenstein did not conceive of either himself or his work as heir to the spirit of the Enlightenment. He did not see scientific progress as the vanguard of moral, social and cultural improvement. Nor did he share the Circle's optimism regarding historical development. Although the Manifesto hailed him, along with Einstein and Russell, as a leading representative of the scientific world-view, this was not done with his consent. And it would be difficult to be more misleading than to so characterize his apocalyptic vision of the development of Western civilization. It has been suggested that the draft for a foreword to a book which he wrote in 1930 (one version of which has been printed as the preface to the *Philosophical Remarks*) was intended for the projected book of which the 'Big Type-script' was the draft, and that it was written in part as a response to Carnap's preface to *Der logische Aufbau der Welt* (part of which was quoted above, p. 40).[75] It is instructive to juxtapose the two. Carnap's preface included the following declaration of alliance between the new philosophy and science:

> The new type of philosophy has arisen in close contact with the work of the special sciences, especially mathematics and physics. Consequently they have taken the strict and responsible orientation of the scientific investigator as their guideline for philosophical work. . . . This new attitude not only changes the style of thinking but also the type of problem that is posed. The individual no longer undertakes to erect in one bold stroke an entire system of philosophy. Rather each works at his special place within one unified science . . . in slow careful construction insight after insight will be won. . . . Thus stone will be added to stone and a safe building will be erected at which each following generation can continue to work.[76]

This conception is characteristic of Russell's 'Scientific Method in Philosophy', and is altogether unlike what Wittgenstein had essayed in the *Tractatus*. Wittgenstein had repudiated Russell's methodological programme as a 'retrogression from the methods of physics' (NB 44), and he had indeed undertaken 'to erect in one bold stroke an entire system of philosophy'. Although he subsequently rejected his earlier conception and accepted the possibility of piecemeal advances (BB 44f.), he did not take the methodology of the empirical sciences as his model. In his 'Sketch for a Foreword' he remarked that the spirit in which he writes is not

> the spirit of the main current of European and American civilization. The spirit of this civilization makes itself manifest in the industry, architecture and music of our time, in its fascism and socialism, and it is alien and uncongenial to the author. . . .
> It is all one to me whether or not the typical Western scientist understands or appreciates my work, since he will not in any case understand the spirit in which I write. Our civilization is characterized by the word 'progress'. Progress is its form rather than making progress being one of its features. Typically it constructs. It is occupied with building an ever more complicated structure. And even clarity is sought only as a means to this end, not as an end in itself. For me on the contrary clarity, perspicuity are valuable in themselves.
> I am not interested in constructing a building, so much as in having a perspicuous view of the foundations of possible buildings.
> So I am not aiming at the same target as the scientists and my way of thinking is different from theirs. (CV 6f.)

As his ideas developed during the early 1930s, he came to see ever deeper flaws in the attempt to import scientific method into philosophy. Not only does it misconstrue the nature of philosophical investigation, as he had already objected with regard to Russell's conception, but it is itself a source of further metaphysical confusion (see below, pp. 117–23).

Logical positivism in its 'classic', Viennese phase collapsed under both internal and external criticism. The central shared doctrines proved to be unsustainable.

(i) The reductivist base, the nature of protocol sentences, was a bone of contention among members of the Circle, at least once Carnap and Neurath adopted physicalism. Some members cleaved to the original empiricist inspiration that demanded reduction to what is 'given' in experience, conceived as reports of subjective experience, while others accepted the physicalist programme. Despite great efforts over the years, no one, irrespective of whether they stuck to the original programme or adopted the physicalist thesis, succeeded in producing a convincing reductive account of any general domain of discourse.

(ii) The reductivism committed orthodox logical positivism to either methodological solipsism (as in Carnap's *Logischer Aufbau*) or radical behaviourism (as in Carnap's *Logical Syntax*). (Carnap envisaged neurophysiological reductivism too, but did not pursue it.) Neither of these options was to prove acceptable.

(iii) The thesis of extensionality proved exceedingly difficult to defend. No convincing method was found for analysing the large range of sentence-types incorporating intentional verbs which take propositional clauses as their grammatical object without being truth-functions of them.

(iv) Neither the principle of verification nor verifiability as a criterion of meaningfulness were capable of watertight formulation.

(v) The conventionalism regarding necessary truth was shown to be inadequate; it was internally incoherent, relying for its explanation upon appeal to principles which could not, by its own lights, be accounted for as conventions; its explanation of logical truth depended upon a misguided notion of truths as following from meanings; its account of mathematical truth proved unacceptable.

(vi) Substantial problems lay buried beneath the acceptance of classical logic as the basis for logical analysis of language or for the rational reconstruction of the language of science. (The problems were extensively explored by Oxford philosophers in the post-war period.) It is far from obvious that the logical operators as defined in the propositional and predicate calculus correctly represent the ordinary use of their natural language correlates (whether that matters is still debated). It is evident that the formation rules of the calculus of logic with topic-neutral quantifiers license structures that are nonsensical in natural language (e.g. 'There is a circle in the square' makes sense, but 'All circles are in the square' does not (PG 266); 'Write down some numbers' is an intelligible order, but 'Write down all numbers' is not; 'Some of the rules are sometimes broken when playing chess' is a genuine proposition, but 'All of the rules are always broken when playing chess' is not). For our concepts of generality are not topic-neutral. Moreover, it is evident that the inference patterns licensed by the predicate calculus do not exhaust the forms of licit inference we employ (e.g. determinate exclusion). The view, advocated by Carnap in the form of his 'principle of tolerance', that a philosopher is free to choose whichever logic he pleases for the purposes of rational reconstruction of 'the language of science' not only fails to address the problem posed by the deviation of the classical calculus of logic from our forms of thought and reasoning; it proposes an alternative of dubious intelligibility.

(vii) The thesis of the unity of science came under attack from two different directions. First, philosophers questioned the putative monolithic character of the empirical sciences themselves. It is not obvious that there is 'only one science', or only one 'language of science', in Carnap's sense. It is by no means clear that the 'languages' or concepts of physics (and its various branches), botany, entomology, zoology, meteorology, geology, palaeontology, physiology, psychology, history, sociology, law, economics and so on are all reducible to what Carnap called 'the thing-language'. Secondly, the fundamental thought informing the conception of the unity of science was a denial that psychology, history and the social sciences are methodologically different from the physical sciences. This itself is highly questionable. The challenge came in the post-war period as a result of the revival of hermeneutics, on the one hand, and of Wittgenstein's later philosophy, on the other.

(viii) The conception of philosophy and of analysis was, at the very least, too narrow. If the whole of philosophy is characterized as the logical analysis of the language of science, this evidently precludes large areas of thought and discourse from the province of philosophy. Moral, political and legal discourse can hardly be characterized as part of the 'language of science'; nor, for that matter, can aesthetics. The superficiality of the logical positivists' brief forays into ethics was all too evident, and a reaction against their emotivism duly set in after the Second World War. Legal and political philosophy slowly reasserted themselves.

(ix) The equation of 'the language of science' with the whole domain of empirical discourse was, at best, misleading. Our ordinary concepts of 'medium-sized dry goods', as Austin later put it, and our concepts of their properties and relations are not scientific (let alone theoretical) concepts. And our rich vocabulary of common-or-garden mental or psychological expressions are not 'scientific' either. There is no reason to expect, and every reason not to expect, either that these two huge domains of language lend themselves to a uniform style of analysis, or that the myriad concepts within these two domains have a structurally similar form or forms.

(x) Whether analysis is conceived as a matter of strict translation or as a matter of the production of reduction statements, it proves to be far too restrictive for purposes of philosophical clarification. This became clear with the liberalization of the notion of analysis that characterized the mainstream British post-war movement in philosophy. Analytic philosophy, both in its initial phase and in its later constructive phase (whether in Vienna or among philosophers of the Cambridge school of analysis), did not fulfil the high expectations harboured by its originators.

That the radical empiricist programme failed, however, was a lesson worth learning. And it is greatly to the credit of the Circle that so much of the criticism of its doctrines came from its own members. By the mid-1930s the original unity of the Circle began to disintegrate for reasons other than doctrinal disagreement. By 1933, Carnap and Frank had accepted chairs at the University of Prague. Hahn died in 1934, and in 1936 Schlick was murdered. With the rising tide of Nazism, most members of the Circle fled. Feigl had already gone to the United States in 1931. Carnap went there in 1936. Other members or associates of the Circle followed them. Waismann came to Britain in 1937, and Neurath escaped from Holland to England in 1940. However, flourishing schools of analytic philosophy had been established in the Scandinavian countries, where they survived the war. The forced exile of so many analytic philosophers in the United States, where there was already a significant logical empiricist following (Morris, Nagel, Quine, Goodman), had an immeasurable impact upon philosophy in that country, giving it a logico-analytic and scientific orientation which it has retained to be present day. This will be examined in chapter 7.

4

The Inter-war Years:
Cambridge and Oxford

1. Cambridge between the wars

The impact of the *Tractatus* in Britain was less dramatic and more localized than among the ever wider-spreading waves of the Vienna Circle. It was primarily upon Russell (who by then was no longer teaching at Cambridge) and upon the younger generation of Cambridge philosophers. Consequently its influence was very different in Britain, merging, as it did, with the Cambridge styles of analysis, in contrast with the Machian heritage of the philosophers of the Vienna Circle. It constituted one of the main sources of logical atomism which flourished from the end of the war until the mid-1930s.

After the war, the main representatives of the older generation at Cambridge were McTaggart, who continued teaching there until 1923, still defending his peculiar brand of neo-Hegelian idealism, and W. E. Johnson,[1] who had briefly, but unsuccessfully, tried to teach Wittgenstein in 1912, and whose lectures and supervisions on philosophical logic were both respected and influential. Moore, by now a well-established figure, was the leading proponent of 'analysis' in philosophy. Though he published relatively little, his influence was paramount. McTaggart's successor was C. D. Broad,[2] who had come up to Trinity College in 1906 with a science scholarship, but subsequently switched from the natural sciences to philosophy. His scientific training prepared him for his later extensive writings in the philosophy of science. He had, prior to coming up to university, been imbued with Schopenhauerian idealism. At Trinity his teachers were McTaggart, Russell, Moore and Johnson. Russell's *The Principles of Mathematics* was a major influence upon his thinking, teaching him *inter alia*, 'not to *welcome* contradictions as proofs that such and such features in the apparent world are unreal',[3] but rather to suspect that it may be the argument of the philosopher that is at fault. Though he greatly admired McTaggart's endeavour to construct a system of speculative, deductive metaphysics, he disagreed with it, and in due course dedicated a three-volume work, *Examination of McTaggart's Philosophy* (1933–8), to a critical study of its arguments. Moore's 'Refutation of Idealism' (1903) knocked the bottom out of his youthful subjective idealism, and Moore's lectures induced an abiding interest in perception. Johnson inspired his preoccupation with the problems of induction and probability.

Broad identified with the new-style analytic philosophy pioneered by Moore and Russell, being sympathetic to Russell's boldness in producing ever new systems of philosophy and to Moore's meticulous accuracy.[4] He distinguished between

'Critical' and 'Speculative' Philosophy. Critical Philosophy, he argued, tries to analyse and define the very general concepts which are used in daily life and in the special sciences – for example, substance, cause, person and so on. It investigates general propositions – for example, that every event has a cause – and principles of reasoning, such as laws of logical inference or the principle of the uniformity of nature, and subjects them to criticism. Within Critical Philosophy he distinguished three methods or principles: (a) The Principle of the Extreme Case, according to which, if one wants to analyse a term, it is useful to consider its application to abnormal cases, which may make one aware that the term is more complex than it appears; (b) The Principle of Pickwickian Senses, according to which one should distinguish between the common use of a term and its more precise analysis – we can continue to use a term in philosophy in a Pickwickian sense, knowing that its 'inner meaning' is very different from its common use, as in the case of 'matter' or 'self'; and (c) The Transcendental Method – roughly Kant's critical method, but without the peculiar applications Kant made of it.[5] He classified propositions into a priori, empirical and postulated ones. A priori propositions he construed as propositions that are necessary and recognized by us as such. They may be inferred or uninferred. The uninferred are either premises (e.g. that colour cannot exist without extension, which expresses a connection between universals which is seen to be necessary by reflection upon instances) or principles (such as principles of inference). Inferred a priori propositions are those that are deducible from the uninferred. Empirical propositions are uninferred (e.g. introspective and perceptual ones) or inferred (either purely inductively or partly deductively). Postulates are such as the principle of the uniformity of nature or that every event has a cause. This was the style of philosophy which Broad advocated and practised – far removed from the spirit of the *Tractatus*, let alone the later Wittgensteinian conception. Nevertheless, he furthered Cambridge analytic philosophy, and contributed to its concern, stemming from Moore, with the analysis of perception in terms of 'sensa' or 'sense-data'. The characteristic Cantabrigean interest in induction and probability was given a stimulus by the publication in 1921 of John Maynard Keynes's *A Treatise on Probability*, and in the ensuing debate Broad played a role. Neither at this stage, nor later, was he in the slightest bit influenced by Wittgenstein's ideas.

   Prominent members of the younger generation were F. P. Ramsey, R. B. Braithwaite and A. J. T. D. Wisdom. The philosophical milieu in which they were educated was described by Braithwaite a decade and a half later: 'In 1919 and for the next few years philosophic thought in Cambridge was dominated by the work of Bertrand Russell. After his expulsion from Trinity College in 1916 he did not choose to return to Cambridge; but his books and articles in which he developed his ever changing philosophy were eagerly devoured and formed the subject of detailed commentary and criticism in the lectures of G. E. Moore and W. E. Johnson. Russell's statements on the various topics of philosophy were . . . the orthodoxy . . .'[6] Russell's philosophy from 1912 until the mid-1920s evolved to a considerable degree under the influence of Wittgenstein. This came in two waves, first the pre-war impact of conversations with Wittgenstein and the typescript 'Notes on Logic' of 1913. We have already noted Wittgenstein's criticism of Russell's multiple relation theory of judgement and Russell's consequent abandonment of his projected *Theory of Knowledge*. In 1916 he wrote to Lady Ottoline Morrell: 'His criticism, tho' I don't think you realised it at the time, was an event of first-rate importance in my life, and affected everything I have done since. I saw he was right, and I saw that I could not hope ever again to do fundamental work in philosophy. My impulse was shattered, like a wave dashed to pieces against a breakwater.'[7] He did, to be sure, recover from this set-back, and over the next decade he tried to assimilate what he could grasp and accept of the young Wittgenstein's ideas. In his prefatory note to his lectures on 'The Philosophy of Logical Atomism' (1918), Russell wrote that this work is 'very largely concerned with explaining ideas which I learnt from my friend and former pupil Ludwig Wittgenstein. I have had no opportunity of know-ing his views since August 1914, and I do not even know whether he is alive or dead. He has therefore no responsibility for what is said in these lectures beyond that of having originally supplied many of the theories contained in them.'[8] Russell's logical atomist phase was the result of grafting what he had understood from Wittgenstein's early ideas on to the philosophical conception of analysis that he had been evolving in the early 1910s. He continued to believe that ordinary and scien-tific thought alike are epistemically defective in their reliance upon unproved as-sumptions and upon postulated or inferred entities, and that it was the task of philosophical analysis to reduce hostages to fortune by replacing inferred entities by logical constructions. Cartesian doubt was invoked to attain the hard data of indu-bitable certainties – namely, sense-data, sensibilia and universals – from which the task of logical construction can begin.

He accepted from Wittgenstein the distinction between names and propositions, and now denied that propositions are names of facts, since both 'p' and '$\sim p$' cor-respond to the same fact (which makes the one true and the other false), the non-obtaining of which does not deprive 'p' of meaning (whereas a name, on his view, as on Wittgenstein's, either corresponds to a particular or is meaningless). He ac-cepted the reducibility of the logical connectives to the Sheffer stroke, and their eliminability in T/F notation. Consequently, he now denied that the connectives are names of logical objects. He attributed to Wittgenstein the insight that the logical form of belief is unique, and that it is a function of the logical form of what is believed (cf. TLP 5.542). In *Introduction to Mathematical Philosophy* (1919), he claimed that logical propositions are characterized by being tautologies, but admit-ted that he did not know how to define 'tautology'. The insight into the importance of the concept of tautology for the definition of mathematics he attributed to Wittgenstein.[9]

In 1919, Russell received the manuscript of the *Tractatus* from Wittgenstein, who was then languishing in a prisoner of war camp at Monte Cassino. The introduction which he wrote for it in 1920, after extensive discussions with Wittgenstein in the Hague, displays his admiration for the work, his penetration of some of its mys-teries, as well as his failure to grasp the overall nature of Wittgenstein's project.[10] Certainly it shattered his faith in the substantiality of logical truths, for he thence-forth accepted that they are vacuous tautologies, not descriptions of the most gen-eral features of the world.[11] One deep misapprehension runs through Russell's introduction: namely, that Wittgenstein was concerned with elaborating the condi-tions for a logically perfect language. This was no trivial misunderstanding, since the point of the book was to elaborate the logico-metaphysical conditions for any possible language. It was a treatise on the essential nature of any form of representation whatsoever – a metaphysics of symbolism. Almost equally grievous was Russell's failure to comprehend Wittgenstein's reasons for his doctrine of the limits of language, of what cannot be said in language but only shown. Russell disagreed with the doctrine (and indeed Wittgenstein was later to repudiate it), but the reasons for his disagreement showed that his understanding of the argument of the book was defective. He suggested, as Carnap later did, that what Wittgenstein conceived to be unsayable could in fact be said by ascent into a metalanguage. At the time, and for the next few years, Russell accepted the *Tractatus* doctrine of structural isomorphism between a proposition and the fact it depicts, the thesis of extensionality and the independence of atomic facts. These substantially affected his attempt (of which Wittgenstein disapproved) to revise *Principia* in the second edition of 1925 – trying to show that, *pace* the *Tractatus* (whose analysis of identity he rejected), mathematical equations are reducible to tautologies.

One subject with which Russell was unable to come to terms was the *Tractatus* account of the nature of philosophy itself. His 1924 paper 'Logical Atomism' was written for Muirhead's *Contemporary British Philosophy* as a survey of his philosophical views and their development. In it he expressed his indebtedness to Wittgenstein,[12] but continued to argue in favour of 'scientific method in philosophy', expressing doubts about 'whether philosophy, as a study distinct from science and possessed of a method of its own, is anything more than an unfortunate legacy from theology' (p. 361). The essential task of philosophy is logical analysis, followed by logical synthesis (i.e. construction). 'Philosophy should be bold in suggesting hypotheses as to the universe which science is not yet in the position to confirm or confute' (p. 379). In this respect, Russell was rapidly left behind by the younger generation.

The *Tractatus* was published in English in 1922, the translation having been made by C. K. Ogden together with F. P. Ramsey. Its impact in Cambridge was described by John Maynard Keynes in a letter to Wittgenstein: 'I still don't know what to say about your book, except that I feel certain that it is a work of extraordinary importance and genius. Right or wrong, it dominates all fundamental discussions at Cambridge since it was written' (R 116). Broad, no friend of Wittgenstein, remarked acidly on 'the philosophical gambols of my younger friends as they dance to the highly syncopated pipings of Herr Wittgenstein's flute'.[13] Among those younger friends was Frank Ramsey,[14] who wrote the most important review of the book (*Mind*, 32 (1923)), before he met Wittgenstein (later that year) in Puchberg. In it he rectified Russell's misinterpretation of the *Tractatus* theory of symbolism. Ramsey accepted Wittgenstein's conception of logical truths as tautologies. To him, as to others of his generation, this clarification came as a liberation, rather than as a sad disappointment of Platonist longings for a timeless world of pure forms. However, he sided against Wittgenstein in defending logicism. In his 'Foundations of Mathematics' (1925), he tried to use Wittgenstein's new conception of logic to reconstruct mathematics as a system of tautologies without recourse to the flawed Russell/Whitehead axioms of reducibility and infinity. He wrote: 'I hold that mathematics is part of logic . . . I have therefore taken *Principia Mathematica* as a basis for discussion and amendment; and believe myself to have discovered how, by using the work of Mr Ludwig Wittgenstein, it can be rendered free from the serious objections which have caused its rejection by the majority of German authorities.'[15]

Interestingly, Braithwaite reports that at the time of his death in 1930, Ramsey was coming to agree with Wittgenstein that the system was irremediably flawed.[16]

During his all too brief philosophical career, Ramsey tackled problems inherited from Russell and Wittgenstein, as well as from Keynes's book on probability and induction. In 'Facts and Propositions' (1927) he wrote: 'I must emphasize my indebtedness to Mr Wittgenstein, from whom my view of logic is derived. Everything I have said is due to him, except the parts which have a pragmatic tendency [and the suggestion that the notion of an atomic proposition may be relative to a language (fn.)] . . . his conception of formal logic seems to me indubitably an enormous advance on that of any previous thinker.'[17] His pragmatic tendency, he said, was derived from Russell (presumably Russell's *Analysis of Mind* (1921)). It is manifest in his analysis of probability, in his account of belief and disbelief, which he differentiated in terms of their causes and effects – in particular, by reference to behavioural dispositions – and in his repudiation of the *Tractatus* claim that induction is not rational (TLP 6.363–6.36311) in favour of a pragmatic justification of induction. He came to reject Wittgenstein's account of general propositions in terms of infinite conjunctions of atomic propositions ('General Propositions and Causality' (1929)). He suggested instead that propositions such as 'All men are mortal' (which he referred to as 'causal laws') are rules rather than genuine propositions.[18] It is plausible to suppose that he imparted this idea to Wittgenstein, who adopted it in his distinction in 1929 between 'genuine propositions' and 'hypotheses'. Ramsey seized upon the *Tractatus* insight that a proposition is true if we use it to say that things stand in a certain way and they do (TLP 4.062), and gave it fresh elaboration, independently of the logico-metaphysical apparatus of that book. He argued that 'there is really no separate problem of truth but merely a linguistic muddle'.[19] According to Ramsey, 'It is true that *p*' means no more than '*p*'; 'Whatever he says is true' means 'For all *p*, if he says that *p*, then *p*'; and other locutions will involve perhaps more complex, but still essentially similar, forms of paraphrase. Wittgenstein himself advocated much the same view (PG 123f.; PI §136).

R. B. Braithwaite,[20] another influential member of the younger Cambridge generation, was proficient in mathematics and the natural sciences, and was later to write extensively on the philosophy of science. A contemporary and close friend of Ramsey's, he shared his interest in, and ultimately his opposition to, J. M. Keynes's *Treatise on Probability*, as well as his excitement about the *Tractatus*. Viewing the Cambridge scene from the vantage-point of 1933, Braithwaite thought of the various streams of analytic philosophy as gradually merging. He rejected Russell's scientific conception of philosophy, but saw Broad's notion of 'critical philosophy' as pointing the way to the future. 'Most of the work done at Cambridge during the last fifteen years', he wrote, '. . . counts . . . as "critical philosophy".'[21] Its hallmark was the analysis of propositions, and the most satisfactory approach to it was exemplified by Moore, who insisted that the business of philosophy is to accept the propositions of common sense and then to analyse their meanings.[22] For Moore, Braithwaite reported, philosophy answers the question of what the analysis is of those 'common-sense' propositions which we all agree to be true. This, to be sure, was a far cry from Russell, who held no brief for common sense. The Cambridge preoccupation with the analysis of material object statements had various sources, including Moore's and Russell's interest in the subject; but it was further stimulated by the advent of the theory of relativity, which seemed to show that the space of perception and the space of physics differ, and hence to make 'exceedingly unplausible the most naïve form of realism, – that physical objects are literally the things which we directly perceive and have the properties they appear to have'.[23] Additional stimulus was provided by Whitehead's Tarner Lectures (1919), which were a preliminary draft of his *The Concept of Nature* (1920), in which he argued that the basic particulars of reality are events – a line of argument which Russell also exploited in his Tarner Lectures in 1926, published as *The Analysis of Matter*. The lively debate about induction and probability centred on Keynes's book, which had been written largely before the war, and bore the hallmark of the first (Platonist) phase of Cambridge analysis. The primary participants in the debate were Broad, Johnson, Ramsey, D. M. Wrench and H. Jeffreys. The discussion of the philosophy of mathematics centred on *Principia* and on Russell's and Ramsey's different efforts to save the logicist thesis. Wittgenstein's explanation of logical truths as vacuous tautologies was generally accepted, although, as in the Vienna Circle, the background metaphysical apparatus was either not noticed or quietly jettisoned.

Wittgenstein's return to Cambridge in 1929 and his subsequent lectures dominated the Cambridge philosophical scene until his early retirement in 1947. This will be discussed in more detail later. Writing in 1933, Braithwaite conceived of Wittgenstein's overall account of necessary truths, including his explanations of seemingly metaphysical necessities (e.g. that red is a colour, that nothing can be red and green all over) as 'grammatical propositions' (i.e. rules for the use of the constituent expressions) as the death-knell for the older style of Cambridge metaphysics against which Moore and Russell had fought. It precluded the possibility of a deductive metaphysical system to which experience must conform, hence 'we can be certain beforehand that a system professing to derive by logically necessary implications from logically necessary premises interesting empirical propositions is wrong somewhere. We in Cambridge have been fortunate in having *The Nature of Existence* of J. E. McTaggart as an awful example.'[24] The aim of philosophy, as seen from Cambridge in 1933, was, Braithwaite claimed, the logical clarification of thoughts (TLP 4.112), the analytic elucidation of the meanings of words. It is not an investigation into the nature of the world, no matter whether metaphysical or proto-scientific, but the clarification of the correct use of words in order to resolve intellectual confusion. Moore and Wittgenstein were seen as the major contributors to this endeavour.[25]

A. J. T. D. Wisdom (1904–93) read philosophy at Cambridge from 1921 to 1924, where he was taught by both Broad and Moore. He lectured at St Andrew's from 1929 until his return to Cambridge in 1934, where he was elected a Fellow of Trinity a year later. The major early influences upon him were Moore, Russell and the *Tractatus*. His first book displays his adherence to Russellian analysis. *Interpretation and Analysis in Relation to Bentham's Theory of Definition* (1931) brought to readers' attention the fact that Russell's theory of incomplete symbols had been anticipated by Bentham's theory of logical fictions. In subsequent papers, in particular, 'Logical Constructions', five long, convoluted essays in *Mind* 1931–3, Wisdom pushed the analytic programme of logical atomism, crossed with Moorean analysis, to its limits (and arguably well beyond). With a plethora of technical terminology, Wisdom argued that the task of philosophy was the analysis of the facts to which ordinary statements correspond. Drawing on Russell's conception of logical construction, on Moore's idea of analysis of meanings, and on Wittgenstein's picture theory of the proposition, Wisdom tried to articulate *in concreto* what such logical analysis amounted to. The purpose of philosophy, he argued, is not to acquire knowledge of new facts, but rather to acquire new knowledge of familiar facts, in particular, knowledge of their constituents and ultimate structure. Analysis was supposed to reveal that nations are logical constructions out of individuals, that propositions are logical constructions out of sentences, and that material objects are logical constructions out of sense-data. The project was further pursued in 'Osten-tation' (*Psyche*, 13 (1933)) and 'Is Analysis a Useful Method in Philosophy?' (PASS, 13 (1934)). There he distinguished between 'material analysis' – namely, the defi-nitions of terms in science – and 'formal analysis', as exemplified in Russell's theory of descriptions. These are both denominated 'same-level analysis' inasmuch as they do not carry analysis to ontologically more fundamental levels. 'New-level analy-sis', however, replaces what is 'less ultimate' by what is 'more ultimate' – namely, nations by individuals, individuals by sense-data and mental states, and so forth. The general outline of the programme was not far removed from that of the Vienna Circle, although it lacked the latter's preoccupation with verificationism as a theory of meaning and verifiability as a criterion of meaningfulness, with the logical syntax of the language of science and with the logical reconstruction of scientific theory, and it cleaved, as logical positivism did not, to the metaphysics of logical atomism. From his return to Cambridge in 1934 until 1937, Wisdom attended Wittgenstein's lectures. These converted him to a variant of Wittgenstein's later methods of phi-losophizing, of which he became for a while a leading proponent, and no more was heard from him about the logical atomist analysis of facts into their constituents. The change in his views was heralded by his influential papers 'Philosophical Per-plexity' (PAS, 16 (1936)) and 'Metaphysics and Verification' (*Mind*, 47 (1938)).[26]

Susan Stebbing (1885–1943) studied philosophy at Cambridge from 1906 to 1909, just missing both Moore (who was away from Cambridge from 1904 to 1911) and Russell (who resumed teaching in Cambridge only in 1910). She was a pupil of Johnson's, but acknowledged Moore, whom she later came to know, as the main influence upon her work. After leaving Cambridge, she became a lecture first at King's and later at Bedford College, London, where she was elected to the chair in philosophy in 1933. Like Wisdom, she participated in the lively logical analysts' debate throughout the 1930s about the nature of philosophy and of philosophical analysis in particular. She was well-informed about and interested in the develop-ments of logical positivism in Vienna, and it was she who first invited Carnap to lecture in Britain in 1934.[27] In 'The Method of Analysis in Philosophy' (PAS, 33 (1932–3)), she represented the task of philosophy as being the metaphysical analysis of propositions. Like Moore, she held that fundamental deliverances of common sense are known to be true, but that their analysis is opaque. Although we under-stand such propositions as 'Here is a pen', we do not know how to analyse them, and in that sense, do not know what their constituents are. Following the logical atomism of Russell and Wittgenstein, she held that the world consists of facts. To know precisely what a given fact is, is to know the elements which make up that fact and their mode of combination. Analytic metaphysics, which stands in contrast to deductive metaphysics as exemplified by McTaggart, aims to disclose the 'basic

facts' and their elementary constituents which make up the familiar facts we encounter in experience. Complete analysis will display isomorphism between an
analysed proposition and the basic fact to which it refers. Analysis proceeds in
stages, from the more to the less complex, from the less to the more ultimate, and
is consequently denominated 'directional analysis'. In 'Logical Positivism and Analysis' (PBA, 19 (1933)) she distinguished four different forms of analysis: (i) analytic
definition of a symbolic expression, as in Russell's theory of descriptions; (ii) analytic clarification of a concept in science, as exemplified by Einstein's analysis of
simultaneity; (iii) postulational analysis, as exhibited in mathematicians' definitions
of terms; and (iv) directional analysis of sentences, which will reveal the form and
the elements, as well as their mode of combination, of the fact expressed by the
sentence. The latter, 'new-level analysis' in Wisdom's terminology, is the distinctive task of philosophy.

The analytic, reductive fervour of logical atomism declined throughout the 1930s.
The programme was not matched by performance. It was one thing to paraphrase
propositions about the average man's properties, quite another to paraphrase propositions about nations into propositions about individuals, let alone to exhibit an
even remotely convincing reduction of material objects to sense-data. Secondly,
logical positivism gradually made inroads into the British philosophical scene. With
Ayer's *Language, Truth and Logic* (1936), the tiger was within the gates. With it came
a new preoccupation with linguistic meaning and the criteria of meaningfulness,
which had hitherto been confined largely (though not exclusively) to Wittgenstein's
circle in Cambridge. The positivists' anti-metaphysical fervour displayed a side of
the *Tractatus* which had been neglected in Britain, and it militated against the
metaphysics of logical atomism no less than against the metaphysics of Absolute
Idealism. The ontology of facts and their elementary constituents and the problems
of the relation between a proposition or belief and the fact 'in the world' that makes
it true gradually crumbled. Thirdly, Wittgenstein's new philosophy, inimical to the
whole idea of logical atomist analysis, slowly spread via his pupils' writings and
teaching, and through the circulation of the typescript of the *Blue Book*. By 1942,
Stebbing had lost all confidence in the reductive analytic programme of logical
atomism. In her essay 'Moore's influence', written for Schilpp's volume in the
Library of Living Philosophers, *The Philosophy of G. E. Moore*, she continued to
adhere to Moore's defence of common sense. But she abandoned her earlier belief
in 'directional' or 'new-level' analysis and in the existence of 'basic facts' to which
it was committed. The notion of basic facts, she declared, 'is a hang-over from the
days when "the problem of the external world" was envisaged as primarily a problem of justifying common sense beliefs, although it is Moore himself who has
clearly shown us that these beliefs do not stand in need of justification but only of
analysis. Consequently, sense-data should not be regarded as having an essential and
absolute priority, logically, epistemologically, or metaphysically' (p. 527). The way
ahead, she suggested, lay in 'same-level' analysis – that is, the analytic definition of
expressions and the analytic clarification of concepts. Indeed, she wrote:

> Moore has himself achieved results of first-rate and lasting importance in his
> analysis of 'material implication and entailment', 'reality', and 'descriptive phrases'.
> In his discussion of these problems, as in his treatment of the common sense view

of the world, Moore has laid the greatest stress upon taking words in their ordinary meanings. He has shown that many problems which have genuinely puzzled philosophers turn out on examination to be merely nonsense questions; in formulating these questions we have put together expressions which are in disagreement with ordinary usages through which alone these expressions have meaning. The steady application of this method, which involves the constant demand for *instances* of the usages in question, does result in an extraordinary clarification of problems. This procedure has, I make no doubt, been carried further by Professor Wittgenstein, although his only published work suffers from his having accepted the Moore–Russell view of absolutely specific facts. (pp. 528–9)

Max Black (1900–88), another Cambridge man who came under Wittgenstein's sway, read mathematics at Queen's College, Cambridge, and attended Wittgenstein's classes in the early 1930s. He took up a teaching post at the Institute of Education, University of London (1936–40), after which he emigrated to the United States (see below, p. 146). In his address to the Fourth International Congress for the Unity of Science at Cambridge in 1938, 'Relations between Logical Positivism and the Cambridge School of Analysis' (*Erkenntnis*, 8 (1939–40)), he emphasized the change that was coming over Cambridge analysis. Russell's scientific method in philosophy, in some respects congenial to the Vienna Circle's 'scientific world-view', was rejected by the younger generation at Cambridge. Moore's appeal to elementary common-sense beliefs which we all know to be true was thought to be an effective bulwark against metaphysics, in particular against the Absolute Idealists' denial of the reality of space, time, matter and the self. The indubitability of these beliefs, Black argued, was to be established by appeal to correct linguistic usage. This appeal to ordinary language, he asserted, had made English 'analysts' suspicious of Russellian or Carnapian 'ideal languages'.

Norman Malcolm,[28] who studied at Cambridge with Moore and Wittgenstein from 1938 to 1940, took a similar view of Moore's philosophical method. In his contribution to Schilpp's volume on Moore, Malcolm wrote: 'The essence of Moore's technique of refuting philosophical statements consists in pointing out that these statements *go against ordinary language*.'[29] That this misrepresents Moore is true, but not to the point. What is important is that Stebbing, Braithwaite, Black and Malcolm, well-informed philosophers of a younger generation, understood him thus. It was Moore's practice, as opposed to his official doctrine, which made it almost inevitable that he should be co-opted, rather against his will, to the defence of the emerging forms of conceptual analysis that were to characterize the post-war phase of analytic philosophy, which was dominated by Oxford philosophers.

By the end of the 1930s, logical atomism, and the style of analysis which characterized it, was in retreat. Analytic philosophy was cutting itself loose from its decompositional inspiration and from its constructionist aspirations, and was about to move into its next phase – 'connective analysis'. In this transformation, as in the antecedent rise of logical atomism and logical positivism alike, Wittgenstein played a leading role.

2. Wittgenstein in Cambridge

Wittgenstein came to Cambridge in January 1929, in the hope of returning to philosophical work. In the years since completing the *Tractatus* he had done none. In 1923 he had enjoyed conversations with Ramsey, who visited him in Puchberg, where he was teaching at a primary school, and later, in 1927, they exchanged philosophical correspondence on identity; in the course of 1927–8, he met some members of the Vienna Circle (Schlick, Waismann, Carnap and Feigl) for conversations, not always about philosophy, and in Vienna in 1928, he attended a lecture by L. E. J. Brouwer, founder of intuitionistic mathematics, which aroused both his interest and his opposition. His initial intention in returning to Cambridge, as he wrote to Schlick, was to work on problems concerning 'visual space and other things'. During his first year in Cambridge, he did no teaching. He submitted the *Tractatus* as a doctoral dissertation, and was awarded the degree in June 1929. His post-*Tractatus* philosophical writings, in large manuscript notebooks, begin from February of that year. It is evident from the early notebooks that the transformation of his views was by no means immediate. On the contrary, his early efforts were to a large extent further developments of the conception of analysis advocated in the *Tractatus*. The lecture he prepared for the Joint Session of the Mind Association and the Aristotelian Society in Nottingham in July 1929, 'Some Remarks on Logical Form' (which, in the event, he did not deliver, choosing instead to talk on generality and infinity in mathematics), gives some idea of what analysis, as conceived programmatically in the *Tractatus*, might look like.

In this paper, he continued to argue that the propositions of natural language are misleading, inasmuch as they conceal their true logical form, and that they are analysable into atomic propositions, the constituents of which are the material out of which all else is constructed. To display this, we need a perspicuous notation, which will give a clear picture of the internal logical structure of atomic propositions. We can arrive at such analyses only by the logical investigation of the phenomena (of experience) themselves – that is, in a sense, a posteriori – and not by conjecturing about a priori possibilities. It is this which differentiates such analyses from the logical analysis of molecular propositions which had been completed in the *Tractatus*. Given the independence postulate for atomic propositions and the thesis of extensionality, the latter task could be carried out, as had been done in the *Tractatus*, wholly a priori. But logic cannot anticipate its application by saying what elementary propositions there are (TLP 5.557) – for that, experience is necessary. For logic cannot anticipate whether the world is multi-coloured or colourless, noisy or soundless. When we come to an actual analysis of experiential propositions,

> we find logical forms which have very little similarity with the norms of ordinary language. We meet with the forms of space and time with the whole manifold of spatial and temporal objects, as colours, sounds, etc., etc.,[30] with their gradations, continuous transitions, and combinations in various proportions, all of which we cannot seize by our ordinary means of expression. (RLF 165)

He suggested that for the representation of actual, perceptual phenomena, rational and irrational numbers must enter into the structure of atomic propositions themselves in order that the representation have the logical multiplicity of properties which admit of gradation – for example, the pitch of a tone or the brightness or hue of a shade of colour. Here he grappled with the problem of determinate exclusion, realizing, as he had not done in the *Tractatus*,[31] that there are logical relations (of exclusion and implication) which are determined not by truth-functional composition, but by the inner structure of atomic propositions. At this stage, he suggested that this be budgeted for by abandoning the topic neutrality of the logical connectives and drawing up truth-tables specific to the 'propositional system' (*Satzsystem*) to which the atomic proposition belongs (viz. the 'system' of determinates of a given determinable). Thus, in the case of colour exclusion, the conjunction of 'A is red' (A being a given spatio-temporal point) with 'A is blue' (i.e. the truth-tabular assignment 'TT') is nonsense, giving the proposition greater logical multiplicity than the phenomena admit of, and must be excluded by rules of syntax. This concession, as he realized shortly thereafter, spelled the death-knell for the philosophy of logical atomism, and struck at the heart of the metaphysics and the conception of logic which he had advocated in the *Tractatus* (see below).

In the course of his first year back in Cambridge, Wittgenstein had extensive, stimulating conversations with Ramsey. In the preface to the *Investigations*, written sixteen years later, he acknowledges these conversations and Ramsey's criticisms as having helped him to recognize the grave mistakes in the *Tractatus*. This fruitful exchange of ideas was brought to an end by Ramsey's premature death at the age of twenty-six in January 1930. In November 1929, Wittgenstein gave a lecture on ethics to the Heretics, a Cambridge undergraduate society. This lecture too is evidently an elaboration of ideas already mooted in the *Tractatus*. From January 1930 Wittgenstein began teaching classes at Cambridge, which he continued to do each term until his retirement in 1947, save when he was on leave or away during the war.

Among those who attended Wittgenstein's classes from 1930 until 1935 were Alice Ambrose,[32] Black, Braithwaite[33] and his wife Margaret Masterman, Karl Britton, Maurice Cornforth, R. L. Goodstein,[34] A. Duncan-Jones,[35] Margaret Macdonald, Moore and Wisdom. Among his students in the period 1935 to 1939 were J. N. Findlay, D. A. T. Gasking, Casimir Lewy, Norman Malcolm, G. A. Paul,[36] Rush Rhees,[37] A. M. Turing the mathematician and G. H. von Wright.[38] 'From this jealously preserved little pond', Ryle later wrote, 'there have spread waves over the philosophical thinking of much of the English-speaking world.'[39] Ambrose, Black and Malcolm were the main transmitters of Wittgenstein's thought and methods of philosophizing to the United States (see below, pp. 146–8). Paul and Gasking introduced Wittgenstein's philosophy to Australia, where John Anderson had hitherto been the dominant voice, and von Wright did the same in Helsinki.

During the years 1929–33, Wittgenstein's ideas went through rapid transformation, evident in his manuscript volumes I–X (MSS 105–14), and in his lectures as reported by Moore, who took detailed notes of them from 1930 to 1933, and Desmond Lee (*Wittgenstein's Lectures, Cambridge 1930–32*). The published volume we now have under the title *Philosophical Remarks* (1964) is a hasty typescript compilation from volumes I–IV (MSS 105–8), forced upon him by the need to obtain a Research Fellowship at Trinity, which he was duly awarded in December 1930. But his major efforts went into the composition of a projected book based on dictations from his manuscript volumes V–X (MSS 109–14). The closest he came to completing a draft is the so-called Big Typescript (1933) of 768 pages, together with an annotated table of contents (unique in his corpus of unfinished works). The chapter headings give an idea of the wide range of topics covered: 'Understanding', 'Meaning', 'The Proposition and its Sense', 'Instantaneous Understanding, etc.', 'The Nature of Language', 'Thought and Thinking', 'Grammar', 'Intention and Depiction', 'Logical Inference', 'Generality', 'Expecting, Wishing, etc.', 'Philosophy', 'Phenomenology', 'Idealism, etc.', 'The Foundations of Mathematics', 'On Cardinal Numbers', 'Inductive Proofs and Periodicity', 'Infinity in Mathematics'. By the time he had composed this, a major transformation in his thought had occurred.

Determinate exclusion definitively undermined the independence of the atomic proposition as conceived in the *Tractatus*. But the thesis of independence was the linchpin of the whole system of his logical atomism. Without it, the thought that the logic of propositions depends only upon the essential bipolarity of the elementary proposition collapses. And like a row of dominoes, the central theses of the account of logic in the *Tractatus* collapse too. The significance of T/F notation as a revelation of the essential nature of logical propositions and relations evaporates, since there are logical relations which are dependent upon the inner structure of propositions.[40] Not all logical relations are determined by truth-functional combination, since A's being red implies that A is not green, not yellow, not orange and so forth. The logical operators are not topic-neutral, since one cannot conjoin 'A is 2 foot long' with 'A is three foot long'. The idea that there is a single general propositional form likewise collapses, since the very idea of a general propositional form was tailored for logically independent propositions. The best one could now claim was that the propositional form of sets of propositions belonging to the same propositional system – for example, colour-ascribing propositions or length-attributing propositions – is shared. So separate truth-tables would have to be drawn up for each such propositional system. If the idea of the logical independence of elementary propositions must go, then so too must the ideas that generality can be analyzed into logical sums or products and that the quantifiers can be given a uniform, topic-neutral analysis. For the account of the quantifiers as operators on sets of propositions of a common form patently depended upon the thought that the propositions are independent. 'All primary colours . . .' or 'All the days of the week . . .' are analysable as logical products, but not 'All men . . .', let alone 'All numbers . . .'. It makes sense to say 'Write down any cardinal number', but not to say 'Write down all cardinal numbers'. 'There is a circle in the square' [$(\exists x). fx$] makes sense, but not '$\sim \exists x. \sim fx$' – that is, 'All circles are in the square'. And so on (PG 266).

As the logical theory of the *Tractatus* collapsed, Wittgenstein assailed the associated metaphysics of logical atomism. The world does not consist of facts rather than things; rather, a description of the world consists of statements of facts, not an enumeration of things. But a statement of a fact is just a true statement, not a description of a configuration of objects concatenated like links in a chain. Facts are not concatenations of objects in reality, for one cannot point at a fact, only point out a fact. Unlike concatenations of objects, facts have no spatio-temporal location. And to point out a fact is to point out that things are thus-and-so – that is, to make a true assertion. It may be a fact that this circle is red, but it is confused to suppose that this fact is composed of circularity and redness concatenated together. Facts (and states of affairs) are not composed of anything, and do not have objects as 'constituents' ('elements' or 'components'), as Wittgenstein had supposed in the *Tractatus*.[41] To say that the proposition that *p* is made true by the fact that *p* is misleading, for it looks like 'Telling lies makes one unpopular', but is actually like 'Telling lies makes one a liar'.[42] It simply means that the proposition that *p* is true if, in fact, things are as it says they are. The atomist notion of simple, indecomposable, sempiternal objects was equally confused; simple and complex are relative notions, not absolute ones, and standards of complexity and simplicity must be laid down for each kind of thing of which we want to predicate such terms. It is a misuse of language to call unanalysable shades of colours, spatio-temporal points and relations like *being on* 'objects'.[43] What had appeared to be objects which *had* to exist were in fact (for the most part) samples employed in the grammar of our language (see Volume 1, 'Ostensive definition and its ramifications', §7).

With the collapse of the metaphysics of logical atomism, the picture theory of the proposition fell too, and with it the thesis of isomorphism between language and reality, and the very idea of logical form as previously conceived. What had seemed like an internal relation between proposition and the fact that makes it true was no more than the shadow cast upon reality by the intra-grammatical relation between the expressions 'the proposition that *p*' and 'the proposition which the fact that *p* makes true' – that is, a relation constituted by the grammatical rule according to which these expressions are intersubstitutable. It was perfectly correct to claim that there is an internal relation here. The error was to think of this internal relation as holding between thought and reality, and to construct an elaborate metaphysics about the essential structure of reality *and* the correlative essential structure of every possible language to explain how this can (and indeed must) be. It is noteworthy that Wittgenstein's detailed criticism of the picture theory was conducted by way of an investigation of intentionality – namely, of the relation between an expectation and its fulfilment, a belief and what makes it true, a command and what constitutes compliance with it (see Volume 4, 'Intentionality'). In all these cases, what appears to be an internal relation between proposition and fact, expectation and the event that fulfils it, desire and the state of affairs that satisfies it, command and the act which complies with it – that is, between thought (expectation, desire, wish) and reality – is merely the shadow of a grammatical relation between expressions. For the expectation that it will be the case that *p* IS the expectation that is satisfied by its being the case that *p*; that is, these are simply alternative specifications of that expectation, just as 'the command that N. shut the door' = 'the command which is obeyed by N.'s shutting the door'. 'Like everything metaphysical the harmony between thought and reality is to be found in the grammar of the language' (PG 162). (See Volume 4, 'Intentionality'.)

With the collapse of the thesis of isomorphism, the whole conception of the proposition and of the relation between a proposition and what it describes was undermined. The claim that an elementary proposition consists of simple names, combined according to the necessary rules of the logical syntax of language, connected to the objects in reality which are their meanings by being projected on to them by mental acts of meaning, and which, thus combined, represent in virtue of the fact *that* they are thus combined, was itself a mythology of symbolism. Names

may be connected by an ostensive definition to the samples which provide standards of comparison for their correct application. But the samples that thus define
them are not their meanings. The meaning of an expression is not an object of any
kind, neither a mundane, perishable one nor a sempiternal one. And defining samples are best conceived as instruments of grammar, and so as belonging to the
means of representation. In the sense in which the *Tractatus* held that language *must
be* connected to reality – by names as it were being pinned on to the objects that
are their meanings – there is in fact *no* connection between language and reality.[44]
It was mistaken to claim that a proposition is a fact (that only facts can represent
facts) or that only 'simple names' can represent simple objects. It is not *the fact* that
the constituent words are combined thus-and-so that makes it possible for the
resultant sentence to mean what it does, but rather that *this* combination is given
this use by the rules of our language. Far from the logical syntax of any possible
language having to mirror the logical structure of the world, the rules of a language
are autonomous. They owe no homage to reality. They do not reflect metaphysical
possibilities, determined by the essential nature of objects represented, but rather
themselves determine logical possibilities – that is, what it makes sense to say. And
different languages may be constituted of different rules, constrained only by human interests and needs, human discriminatory capacities, shared abilities and reactive propensities, and by the limits of what we call 'a language' (see Volume 4, 'The
arbitrariness of grammar and the bounds of sense').

It was equally mistaken to suppose that bipolarity is the essence of the proposition, an essence which mirrors the metaphysical nature of facts,[45] namely, that it is
of their essence that they either obtain or fail to obtain (FW 55, 'Satzkalkül'; PLP
374). It is true that a fact may obtain or fail to obtain, but that plumbs no metaphysical depths; it signifies only that what we call a fact is what we also say either
is or is not the case, obtains or does not obtain. Similarly, although it is not true
that all propositions are bipolar, it is correct that truth and falsehood belong to our
concept of a proposition. But that has no metaphysical roots; it means only that
what we call a proposition is what we also say is either true or false (see Exg.
§§136f.). Innumerable propositions are indeed bipolar, for their truth characteristically *excludes* a possibility. But this is not uniformly the case, and where bipolarity
is absent, then an investigation is called for to reveal the character and role of the
proposition in question.

As the metaphysics of symbolism was swept away, and with it the metaphysics
of logical atomism, of simple objects, states of affairs and facts, the pivotal notion
of logical form disintegrated too. For the very idea that a philosophical investigation can uncover the logical structure of the world, the logical forms of facts and
of their constituents, was predicated upon the assumption that the propositions of
a language must reflect the nature of things, and that the logico-metaphysical nature
of things is objective and language-independent. Frege and Russell had held that
natural languages are defective in this respect, and are only partial guides to the
objective logical structures of reality (of a third realm, or of the world), whereas the
Tractatus had argued that *every* possible language *must*, as a condition of sense,
mirror (on analysis) the logical forms of what is represented. When the metaphysics
of logical atomism fell apart, it became clear that the very idea of logical form
amounted to no more than the grammar of expressions, the rules for their use – in

particular, their combinatorial possibilities and the circumstances that license their employment. 'Logical form' does not reveal the objective *logical* structure of things, since they have no such structure. They can be said to have a nature or essence, but that is *determined* by grammar, by the rules for the use of the expressions in question, which lay down what it makes sense to say, and is not answerable to reality for truth or correctness (see Exg. §§371–3; Volume 2, 'Grammar and necessity'; Volume 4, 'The arbitrariness of grammar and the bounds of sense').

So much for 'clearing the ground of houses of cards'. This destructive work was the fruit of prolonged struggle. To arrive at this stage took some years, in the course of which Wittgenstein went through a brief verificationist phase (see ch. 3, pp. 50–9), coupled with a form of phenomenalism and methodological solipsism. However, much – though not all – of the above critical material was in place by the time he composed the 'Big Typescript'. It would, nevertheless, be misleading to suggest that the sole result of this endeavour was destructive. Indeed, it would be wrong to think that nothing of the philosophy of the *Tractatus* survived this critical onslaught. The large part of the criticism of Frege and Russell still stood intact. The insights that 'Logic must turn out to be a *totally* different kind than any other science' (R 2), that there are no 'logical constants' (that the logical connectives and quantifiers are not names of logical entities, and that categorial expressions are not names of forms), that logical truths are senseless tautologies that say nothing, but display forms of proof, that inference *in* logic (the derivation of one logical truth from another) is categorially different from inference *by* logic (the derivation of an empirical proposition from empirical premises by means of logic), that a proposition is internally related to the state of affairs that makes it true – all this could be retained. But it had to be severed from its original logical foundations in the bipolarity of the elementary proposition and the independence thesis and from its metaphysical foundations in the ontology of logical atomism, in particular from the idea that logic is 'a mirror-image of the world' (TLP 6.13). In cutting these earlier fundamental insights free from their original support, Wittgenstein was, as he himself later wrote, rotating the axis of reference of his investigation about the fixed point of our real need (PI §108). Instead of 'referring' to the putative metaphysical structure of the world, the axis of reference was now pointing inwards, to the autonomous rules of grammar. The propositions of logic do not follow from the essential nature of the elementary proposition as such (bipolarity and independence), but are partly constitutive of that nature. Our concept of a proposition is interwoven with the concepts of truth and falsehood, since what we call 'a proposition' is also what we say is either true or false; with the concepts of assertion and denial, since what we assert or deny is *that* things are thus-and-so; with the concepts of negation, alternation, conjunction and implication, since what we call 'propositions' are that to which we apply (with qualifications) the calculus of truth-functions; with the concepts of rules of inference, of knowledge and belief, proof and evidence, supposition and judgement. This large network of concepts does not, as a metaphysical necessity, reflect the 'logical structure of the world', but is free-floating; it neither has nor needs any extraneous justification, ineffable or expressible. For grammar is autonomous – yet it informs our lives, and determines what we call thinking, inferring and reasoning. As the system of the *Tractatus* collapsed, Wittgenstein bent his mind to clarifying the ramifying reticulations of this array of interconnected concepts from this new perspective. This endeavour ultimately bore fruit in the *Philosophical Investigations*.

It is not surprising, given this transformation, that Wittgenstein turned against the *de jure* conception of future philosophy advocated in the *Tractatus*, and against the Cambridge style of analysis to which it had contributed. Talk of analysing facts and propositions involves a misleading metaphor. Analysis in science – in chemistry, for example – reveals new facts. But this is not the case in philosophy. *Pace* the *Tractatus* programme for future philosophy (and its exemplification in 'Some Remarks on Logical Form'), analysis does not tell us anything new, which we did not know before, such as the logical forms of the simple objects constituting the substance of the world. And if it did give us any new, genuine piece of information, it would not interest us (LWL 34f.). It was wrong to have supposed that atomic propositions will emerge from future analysis. 'We can talk of atomic propositions if we mean those which on their face do not contain "and", "or", etc., or those which in accord with methods of analysis laid down [e.g. Russell's theory of descriptions] do not contain these. There are no hidden atomic propositions' (AWL 11). Logical analysis is not a discovery of the real meanings of terms, of which competent users of the language were previously unaware. It is a paraphrastic antidote, the importance of which is to halt the confusions which we get into when reflecting on words (as in Meinongian cases (AWL 21)). Moore's idea that only logical analysis can explain to us what we mean by the propositions of ordinary language (i.e. give us an 'analysis of its meaning' as Moore conceived of meaning) is misconceived. It is absurd to suppose that when people say 'Today the sky is clearer than yesterday', they do not know what they mean – whether they are talking about sense-data or even more recherché entities (WWK 129). Analysis in logic means giving the grammatical rules for the use of the expression in question; and that, in effect, was all that Russell was doing in his theory of descriptions (even though he thought that he was doing much more).[46] This conception patently involved the abandonment of the programme of Russellian and Moorean analysis alike, a rejection of 'new-level analysis' as envisaged by logical atomists. Instead, Wittgenstein now, in effect, defended 'same-level analysis', and even this became progressively more flexible as his conception of explanation of meaning became more elastic. For meaning, as he now used the term, is not what a name 'stands for', but rather what is given by an explanation of meaning – which is itself a rule for the use of the expression explained. Explanations of meaning come in numerous different humdrum forms, since an explanation is adequate if it fulfils its role of providing a standard for the correct use of a term – if it is adequate for understanding. And understanding is exhibited in using an expression correctly, as well as in explaining what one means by it.

He had been right to insist, against Frege and Russell, that 'all the propositions of our everyday language, just as they stand, are in perfect logical order' (TLP 5.5563; cf. PI §98). But he had been misguided to suppose that that order was something *hidden*, to be revealed by analysis. Being 'in perfect logical order' is a condition of sense; but that is ensured not by a metalogical relation between names and the objects that are their meanings and between propositions and the states of affairs whose existence makes them true, but by the fact that expressions have a use in the life of a linguistic community. The order of language is in full view – in the use and the rules of use (exhibited in explanations of meaning) of the expressions of a language. That common-or-garden use is what has to be described in order to resolve philosophical problems, not by giving new information or depth analysis, but by arranging what we already know, yet overlook or misinterpret when we are in the grip of conceptual confusion. Hence, he observed in the 'Big Typescript': 'All reflections can be carried out in a much more homespun manner than I used to do. And no new words have to be used in philosophy [such as "pictorial form", "representational form", "logical form", "pictorial relationship", etc.], but rather the old common words of language are sufficient' (BT 420). Analysis, if the term is to be retained at all, is simply the clarification of the use (the rules for the use) of expressions, which displays their logical connections with related concepts for the purpose of the resolution and dissolution of philosophical difficulties. In this respect, there can be little doubt that Wittgenstein's lectures in Cambridge during the 1930s played a major role in the demise of the logical atomist phase of Cambridge analysis and in the emergence of connective analysis.

However, unlike Stebbing, Black and Malcolm, Wittgenstein dissociated his new style of philosophy from Moore's defence of 'common sense' and from the invocation of ordinary use in defence of allegedly common-sense views. One cannot refute idealism or solipsism simply by appeal to what we do or do not say, let alone by insisting on what we really know. Such naïve realism does not solve, but skips, the difficulties which his adversaries see (BB 48):

> You must not try to avoid a philosophical problem by appealing to common sense; instead, present it as it arises with most power. You must allow yourself to be dragged into the mire, and get out of it. Philosophy can be said to consist of three activities: to see the common-sense answer, to get yourself so deeply into the problem that the common-sense answer is unbearable, and to get from that situation back to the common-sense answer. But the common-sense answer in itself is no solution; everyone knows it. One must not in philosophy attempt to short-circuit problems. (AWL 109)

One can get out of the mire not by the emphatic assertion of what we all know, but by showing that sceptical claims transgress the bounds of sense, that metaphysical assertions are at best expressions of grammatical rules in the misleading guise of descriptions or recommendations that we adopt a new notation, recommendations that are distorted by being presented as if they were insights into the real nature of things (BB 57; see Volume 2, 'Grammar and necessity', §§2–3; and Exg. §402).[47]

In his lectures in 1930–1 Wittgenstein emphasized that philosophy as he was now doing it was 'a new subject', not merely a stage in a 'continuous development', that there was now a 'kink' in the development of human thought, comparable to that which occurred when Galileo invented dynamics. A new method had been discovered, as had happened when chemistry emerged from alchemy, and for the first time it was now possible for there to be 'skilful' philosophers, who would apply this method (M 322). He did not, apparently, say expressly what his new method was, although the hints he dropped indicate that it involved, on the one hand, the transformation of the conception of what philosophy is and what can be hoped for from it, and, on the other hand, the description of the use of expressions with which we are all familiar. The skill lies in the rearrangement of such familiar facts, which will unravel the knots in our thinking.

From the very beginning of his career, he had insisted that philosophy is not one of the natural sciences, that it gives us no true or false pictures of reality, and can neither confirm nor confute scientific investigations (NB 93; TLP 4.112). In philosophy there are no deductions, or any more or less probable hypotheses; hence he condemned Russell's advocacy of 'scientific method in philosophy' as 'a retrogression from the method of physics' (NB 44). On this negative judgement, Wittgenstein never changed his mind. In 1913 he had held that philosophy is the doctrine of the logical form of propositions (NB 93), both 'scientific' (i.e. empirical) and 'primitive' propositions (i.e. the axioms of *Principia*). By the time he wrote the *Tractatus*, he had rejected the latter claim, maintaining that philosophy is not a body of doctrine, for there are no 'philosophical propositions' at all. *De jure*, philosophy is an activity, which results not in philosophical knowledge expressed in propositions, but in elucidations of problematic propositions by logical analysis. The task of philosophy is to clarify such propositions by displaying their truth-functional composition, or, in the case of metaphysical pronouncements, to reveal their illegitimacy (TLP 4.112, 6.53). The analysis of elementary propositions (essayed only in 'Some Remarks on Logical Form') would involve digging deep into their hidden depth grammar to disclose logico-syntactical structures with which we are *not* familiar – for example, the occurrence of real numbers in the analysis of propositions ascribing perceptual qualities. The *de facto* practice of the *Tractatus* was different. His analysis of logical propositions purported to disclose their real logical form (generality, for example, was held to conceal infinite logical sums or products). The metaphysical pronouncements of the book, admittedly transgressing the bounds of sense in trying to say what can only be shown, were held to be insights into the metaphysical structure of the world which resulted from reflection on the logico-metaphysical conditions for the possibility of representation. In this respect the *Tractatus* was the culmination of the high metaphysical tradition in philosophy. All this now fell away as illusion – a phantasmagoria of reason ensnared in the web of grammar. The *de facto* practice of philosophy in the *Tractatus* was 'the symptom of a disease' (as he wrote in Schlick's copy of the book); the *de jure* recommendation for future philosophy was flawed by its commitment to 'analysis'.

Philosophy, as Wittgenstein now conceived of it, consists in the dissolution of philosophical problems (BT 421). All philosophy can do is to destroy idols (and that includes not creating new ones, such as 'the absence of an idol' (BT 413)). One of the greatest impediments for philosophy is the expectation of new, deep, hitherto unheard of information or explanation (BT 419). Philosophy produces no new knowledge, but only grammatical elucidations – reminders of how we use words – which unravel the knotted skein of our philosophical reflections. But the activity of presenting these elucidations is as complicated as the knots it unravels (BT 422). According to the old conception of the great Western philosophers (and of the *Tractatus* too), there are two kinds of problem in the field of knowledge: the essential, great, universal ones, with which philosophy deals (the ultimate nature of reality, the most general facts about the universe, the characterization of the substance of all possible worlds), and the inessential, quasi-accidental ones, which are the province of the empirical sciences. But on his new conception, there is no such thing as a great, essential problem, in the sense in which there are problems in the field of knowledge (BT 409).

What he was now doing was very different from what Plato or Berkeley had done.[48] Why should it still be called 'philosophy'? Because one might feel that it *takes the place* of traditional philosophical enquiry (AWL 28), as the question of whether one can solve a general cubic equation with square roots takes the place of the question of whether one can trisect an angle with a compass and rule (see Exg. §334). For here too, one might say, after exposure to Wittgenstein's manner of dissolving a philosophical question by clarification of the rules for the use of the relevant terms and by explaining the entanglement of rules that generates nonsense, 'Yes, that was what I had in mind' (see M 322; LFM 87f.; PLP 400). His philosophical method 'removes mental discomforts the old [activity of philosophizing] was supposed to' (AWL 28). Like traditional philosophy, Wittgenstein's investigations are fundamental to ordinary life and to the sciences, while being independent of any special results of the sciences (M 323). They are a priori, conceptual investigations into what does and what does not make sense, with the purpose of resolving philosophical puzzles.

It is striking that Wittgenstein later (1938) remarked that if he were asked what is the main mistake made by philosophers of the present generation, including Moore, his answer would be that it is that when language is looked at, what is looked at is a form of words, not the use made of the form of words (LA 2). It is true that the grammatical forms of words are endlessly misleading in contexts of philosophical reflection. But what grammatical forms conceal is not a hidden logical form that is to be dug out by means of logical analysis, but rather the diversity *of use* of expressions. In 1929, when his new method was just dawning, he wrote: 'The classifications made by philosophers and psychologists are as if one were to try to classify clouds by their shape' (cf. Z §462); that is, they focus upon form, rather than use. He added in cipher: 'I still find my way of philosophizing new, and am so struck by its novelty that I must frequently repeat myself. For another generation it will have become part of their very being and the repetitions will seem boring; for me they are essential. This method is basically the transition from the question of truth to the question of meaning' (Vol. I (MS 105), 46).

With this shift, Wittgenstein had, as it were, completed the 'linguistic turn' which had begun with the *Tractatus*. Although he did not subscribe to the view that language is the subject-matter of philosophy, he did claim that the description of language and the rules for the use of expressions is a central *method* of philosophy, since one great source of philosophical problems lies in the false analogies between grammatically similar forms of expression which nevertheless have altogether different uses. Beginning with the 'Big Typescript' and continuing until completion of the *Philosophical Investigations* in 1945, Wittgenstein turned to the elucidation, by means of his new method, of a wide range of philosophical problems, which include most of the central themes he had tackled in the *Tractatus*, as well as the hidden philosophico-psychological presuppositions which he had previously swept under the carpet as belonging to psychology. His main concerns in the 'Big Typescript' were with the pivotal trio of internally related concepts of meaning, understanding and explanation of meaning (see below, pp. 125–8). He assailed the notion of ostensive definition as forging a connection between language and reality, and clarified the idea of the autonomy of grammar. He made some first steps towards elucidating the concept of thinking, and repudiated the conception of thinking that was implicit in the *Tractatus*. By means of an investigation of intentionality, he demystified the 'harmony between thought and reality' which lay at the heart of the picture theory of representation. And he articulated, in fairly polished form, his new conception of philosophy.[49] Approximately one-third of the 'Big Typescript' was concerned with the philosophy of mathematics; indeed, it should not be forgotten that in the years between 1929 and 1944 about half Wittgenstein's writings were on this subject.[50]

No sooner had Wittgenstein completed the 'Big Typescript' than he became dissatisfied with it. He revised the first 350 pages with extensive manuscript alterations, deletions and additions. In 1933–4 he began an *Umarbeitung*, a new manuscript revision of most of the first half of the typescript in notebook volumes X and XI (MSS 114–15). Dissatisfied with this, he began a *Zweite Umarbeitung* (MS 140, also known as the 'Grosses Format'), in which he revised the first 56 pages of the *Umarbeitung* (1934). This was not the last of the 'Big Typescript', for in the autumn of 1937, he began yet again to work it over, selecting remarks he thought salvageable (Vol. XII (MS 116), 1–135). Although he never managed to mould this material into a book, it is noteworthy that more than 200 of the remarks in the *Investigations* already occur in the 'Big Typescript' or its revisions. It should be borne in mind that a fair proportion of the ideas in these texts were communicated to his pupils in his lectures, and through them influenced the development of analytic philosophy long before the publication of the *Investigations*.

In 1933 Wittgenstein dictated the *Blue Book* to five of his pupils.[51] This was duplicated, and circulated among his students. Duly copied again, the *Blue Book* circulated well beyond the confines of Cambridge, and was, until the posthumous publication of the *Investigations*, the primary source in England[52] of Wittgenstein's new ideas for all those who did not belong to the privileged circle of his pupils and friends. It was through the *Blue Book* that the concepts of a language-game, of criteria (roughly, logically good evidence) for the application of an expression, and of family resemblance concepts first entered circulation – and with them, the explicit repudiation of the demand for determinacy of sense and the rejection of the idea that a language is *au fond* a calculus of sharply defined rules. Here too was a detailed discussion of his new method of philosophizing, and its application to the problems of the relation between experiential propositions and material object propositions. A preliminary discussion of the problem of 'other minds' anticipates the later, more elaborate discussion in the *Investigations* of the relations between the 'inner' and the 'outer'. The detailed discussion of the problem of solipsism and personal identity gives quietus both to the mysterious transcendental solipsism of the *Tractatus* and to the methodological solipsism of the *Philosophical Remarks*.

In 1934–5 he dictated the *Brown Book* to Skinner and Ambrose. Unlike the *Blue Book*, this was not intended for widespread circulation among his students. It did enter circulation, however, although on a smaller scale than the *Blue Book*. In it he exploited, arguably to excess, the language-game method. He made a German translation and revision of it in 1936 (Vol. XI (MS 115), 118–292, posthumously published as *Eine Philosophische Betrachtung*), but subsequently abandoned it as worthless. Between 1934 and 1936 he wrote extensively on private experience and sense-data in preparation for lectures which he delivered in 1936.[53] They signal the deepening of his interest in the battery of related problems which crystallized in the great 'private language' arguments of the *Investigations* §§243–315. In the academic year 1936–7 he went to Norway, where, after a futile attempt to redraft and expand the *Brown Book*, he wrote the first part of the first version of what was to become the *Philosophical Investigations* (MS 142). The typescript (TS 220) made from this covers roughly §§1–189(a) of the final version, but with many differences. Initially, Wittgenstein intended to continue this in the direction of the philosophy of mathematics, and a version of Part I of the *Remarks on the Foundations of Mathematics* (viz. TS 221) continued smoothly from the end of TS 220.[54] In the summer of 1938, Wittgenstein offered this to Cambridge University Press for publication, but withdrew it a month later. He did, however, have the first part translated by Rhees, and, although he was disappointed with the translation, revised it hastily in order to show it to Keynes, who was one of the electors for the chair in philosophy which Moore had vacated on his retirement and for which Wittgenstein was now applying. In February 1939, he was elected to the chair. That year he delivered a series of lectures on the philosophy of mathematics, since published as *Wittgenstein's Lectures on the Foundations of Mathematics, Cambridge, 1939*. These are the most accessible of his reflections on the subject, rendered all the more fascinating by the fact that Alan Turing attended the lectures and by the lively exchanges between him and Wittgenstein, who clearly viewed Turing as a representative of the very conception of mathematics which he was trying to extirpate.

By the end of the 1930s, Wittgenstein's later philosophy had matured. Although much remained to be done before he would complete his second great masterpiece, all the major breakthroughs had been made. And much of this was communicated to his pupils, through whom these ideas, sometimes in mangled form, entered general circulation. Analytic philosophy was poised for yet another transformation, which was to come, not so much in Cambridge, but in Oxford, although by no means independently of Wittgenstein's influence (see ch. 6). It is to the background of that subsequent transformation that we must now turn.

3. Oxford between the wars

Although the stream of philosophy that flowed from Cambridge does not compare in volume with the torrent from the Vienna Circle, it flowed powerfully, and its impact upon the development of analytic philosophy in Britain between the wars was substantial. In Oxford, however, the story was very different. After the great days of Absolute Idealism at full flood, Oxford philosophy declined to a trickle, its pools and rivulets muddied by parochial strife between the remaining Oxford idealists and their local opponents, the Oxford realists. Little was published, and what was published has by and large not stood the test of time. Not until the mid-1930s, when a new generation was replacing the survivors from pre-war days, were there marked signs of revival. That revival was stemmed by the Second World War, and it was only after 1945 that the dam broke, releasing a flood of energy and creativity in philosophy such as had not been seen at Oxford since the Middle Ages. The post-1945 story will be told in due course (see ch. 6); for the moment, we must lay the groundwork for it by surveying the inter-war years at Oxford, where the leading figures of what was to become known as 'Oxford Philosophy' or 'Oxford Linguistic Philosophy' were maturing in the backwaters. Wittgenstein's impact there was insignificant save upon two pivotal figures, Gilbert Ryle and his pupil A. J. Ayer.

Prior to the First World War, the philosophy of Bradley and, to a lesser extent, of Bosanquet was dominant, either as a model to follow or as a target to attack. H. H. Joachim (1868–1938), whose defence of the coherence theory of truth (and hence of the idea of relative and partial truth) in *The Nature of Truth* (1906) had been the object of Russell's criticism in his paper 'The Nature of Truth' (PAS, 7 (1906–7)), was a staunch defender of neo-Hegelian thought. Initial resistance to the idealists had come from Thomas Case, who was Professor of Metaphysics and Morals from 1899 until 1910 and President of Corpus Christi College until 1924. The leading spirit of the realist revolt, however, was J. Cook Wilson, who held the Chair of Logic from 1899 until his death in 1915. Unlike the majority of Cambridge philosophers, the Oxford realists were not trained mathematicians or scientists. They had read Literae Humaniores, and were, in the venerable Oxford tradition, predominantly Aristotelian scholars. This gave them a philological and linguistic interest typically lacking in Cambridge, which they passed on to the next generation of Oxford philosophers.[55] Cook Wilson had been taught by Green and Jowett at Balliol, but soon rebelled against the doctrines of his teachers. He published little during his lifetime, and his main book, the posthumous *Statement and Inference* (1926), consists of lectures, papers and correspondence. Nevertheless, through his teaching and lectures, he inspired the next generation of Oxford realists, or 'Cook-Wilsonians'. His attack on idealism was rooted in respect for ordinary language and ordinary usage of terms. Distinctions current in language, he insisted, can never be ignored. Indeed, it is the business of the student of logic to determine the normal use of an expression, for which a multiplicity of examples is necessary. In so far as there was any long-term Cook-Wilsonian legacy at Oxford, it lies here. Against the idealists, he argued for the distinctness of knowledge from its objects, for the reality of relations, and for the claim that the subject-matter of logic is not judgements, conceived as the expression of mental acts of judging, but statements, which may be the expression of diverse 'acts of mind' (knowing, believing, supposing, inferring). Although critical of traditional subject/predicate logic, he was contemptuous of contemporary mathematical logic, whether Boolean or Russellian. He adopted a realist account of knowledge, but insisted that knowledge was simple and indefinable, a *sui generis* activity of consciousness, exemplified paradigmatically (but not only) by mathematical knowledge. It is the fundamental form of thought, which is presupposed by opining, believing, wondering, and so forth, inasmuch as they rest on evidence. As far as perception was concerned, he held that we have direct awareness of the primary qualities of objects, but he took a Lockean view of secondary qualities. Cook Wilson's most influential follower was H. A. Prichard.[56] His primary interests were epistemology, in which he was a 'Cook-Wilsonian', and ethics, in which he was one of the main protagonists of Oxford ethical intuitionism (together with W. D. Ross, J. L. Stocks and E. F. Carritt). Though he published little, the tenacity of his argument and his meticulous, painstaking scrutiny of distinctions made him a provocative, impressive teacher. Despite being mocked by Collingwood as a 'minute philosopher', his rigour and attention to detail were admired by others, including, in the 1930s, by the young J. L. Austin. He was, however, indifferent to Cantabrigean developments. Another locally important Cook-Wilsonian was H. W. B. Joseph, tutor at New College.[57]

The remaining neo-Hegelians were not the only idealists at Oxford. J. A. Smith (1863–1939), who held the Chair of Moral and Metaphysical Philosophy from 1910 until 1935, derived his idealism from Croce and Gentile. This interest in Italian idealism was shared with three other Oxford figures who survived the war: J. L. Stocks (1882–1937) at St John's (until 1924), H. J. Paton at Queen's (until 1927) and R. G. Collingwood (1889–1943) at Pembroke (until he was elected to the Chair of Metaphysics in 1934). Collingwood was arguably the most significant philosophical figure at Oxford in the inter-war years. Contemptuous of the Cook-Wilsonians, he held himself aloof, and pursued his own brand of historicist idealism. He had no interest in the emergence of the new style of analytic philosophy.

As a result of the slaughter of the war, most of the surviving teachers of philosophy were separated from the next generation of young tutors by a gap of twenty to forty years. Few had lived to bridge the generation gap, the exceptions being Collingwood, Paton and Stocks. Oxford philosophy after the war was 'completely inbred',[58] lacking any contact with Cambridge, let alone anywhere else.[59] Joachim was elected to the Chair in Logic (1919–35), and kept idealism more or less alive; but in the 1920s he simply ignored the developments in philosophy outside Oxford. J. A. Smith, according to Mabbott,[60] 'provided the one breath of fresh air among our seniors'. In his autobiographical memoir, Ryle[61] gives a depressing picture of the state of the subject in Oxford:

> During my time as an undergraduate and during my first few years as a teacher, the philosophical kettle in Oxford was barely lukewarm. I think it would have been stone cold but for Prichard, who did bring into his chosen and rather narrow arenas vehemence, tenacity, unceremoniousness, and a perverse consistency that made our hackles rise, as nothing else did at the time. The Bradleians were not yet extinct, but they did not come out into the open. I cannot recollect hearing one referring mention of the Absolute. The Cook-Wilsonians were hankering to gainsay the Bradleians and the Croceans, but were given few openings.[62]

A contemporary of Ryle was H. H. Price (1899–1984), who had studied Literae Humaniores. He was taught by Prichard, and came under the Cook-Wilsonian influence. After graduating, 'with heroic sang froid, [he] migrated for a postgraduate spell to the university of Moore, Russell and Broad. He thus made himself our first personal and doctrinal link with "the other place", and launched the idea that young Oxford could and should learn from Cambridge. Soon Oxford's hermetically conserved atmosphere began to smell stuffy even to ourselves' (ibid.). Appointed to a Fellowship at Trinity in 1924 (which he held until 1935, when he was elected to the Chair of Logic (1935–59)), Price brought back to Oxford the Cambridge preoccupation with sense-datum theories of perception. His major book, *Perception* (1932), was a detailed investigation of, and defence of one variant of, sense-datum theory. The subject remained at the centre of Oxford preoccupations until it crumbled under the successive blows of G. A. Paul's seminal paper 'Is There a Problem about Sense-Data?', Ryle's *Concept of Mind*, Wittgenstein's *Investigations* and Austin's *Sense and Sensibilia*. Price's main interests remained in epistemology, and his teaching brought a freshness and novelty to Oxford philosophy that had long been missing.[63]

The senior philosophers at Oxford had an institution called 'The Philosophers' Teas', to which juniors were likewise invited for weekly meetings. But the generation gap was too great to bridge, and Ryle and Mabbott founded their own discussion group, which they punningly named 'The Wee Teas'.[64] They restricted their number to six, the founding members being Ryle, Mabbott, Price, W. F. R. Hardie, T. D. Weldon and C. S. Lewis (who soon abandoned philosophy for English literature). Those who resigned (mostly due to departure from Oxford) were replaced, and over the years subsequent members included M. B. Foster, W. G. Maclagan, W. C. Kneale, Oliver Franks and H. M. Cox. Through this small group, centred around Ryle, 'Oxford Philosophy' revived.

Ryle's early preoccupations were two. The first concerned the nature of philosophy. 'I must have been near my middle twenties', he later wrote, 'when good-humoured fraternal scepticisms about the existence of my subject showed me that it really was part of my business to be able to tell people, including myself, what philosophy is. Perhaps it was this brotherly tail-twisting that awakened me rather early to the plot of Wittgenstein's *Tractatus*.'[65] Vehement anti-psychologism was taken for granted in Oxford;[66] hence, Ryle later reminisced:

> No longer could we pretend that philosophy differed from physics, chemistry and biology by studying mental as opposed to material phenomena. We could no longer boast or confess that we were unexperimental psychologists. Hence we were beset by the temptation to look for non-mental, non-material objects – or Objects – which should be for philosophy what beetles and butterflies were for entomology. Platonic Forms, propositions, Intentional Objects, Logical Objects, perhaps even Sense-Data, were recruited to appease our professional hankerings to have a subject matter of our own.[67]

His list of entities or pseudo-entities here reflects his early reading of Bolzano, Brentano, Frege, Husserl, Meinong, Moore and Russell (in particular his *Principles of Mathematics*). This second preoccupation, with the pros and cons of realism about what is thinkable, linked up with the first, and was likewise influenced by the *Tractatus*. 'So far', he wrote, 'my motivation was that of a would-be antibiotic epistemologist. "Fidgety Cook-Wilsonian" would, so-far, have been a fair title for me. But – and here I can't tell you why – I was, from a very early stage, in the 1920s, hooked by the twin notions of meaning and the meaningless. Though grossly misunderstanding the whole thing, I spotted in very early days that the *Tractatus* had this pair of notions for its focus.'[68]

Ryle had what he later called 'an Occamizing zeal', manifest in all his early papers. He did not want Price and Moore to have their immediate acquaintance with sense-data; nor did he wish to concede to Meinong, Russell or the early Wittgenstein 'their trout-like apprehendings of universals, objectives, propositions or constituents of propositions. What was wanted was (a) Realism without additional entities to apprehend or (b) Realism without fabricated apprehendings' (ibid.). Despite disagreements with the *Tractatus* logical atomist ontology of simple objects and with the picture theory, what he learned from that book was crucial. He accepted from it that 'no specifications of a proprietary subject-matter could yield the right answer, or even the right sort of answer to the original question "What is Philosophy?"' – a conception which lent his natural 'Occamizings' a positive purpose. Philosophical problems, he concluded, are problems of a special sort, not problems of an ordinary sort about special entities. He discerned in the *Tractatus*, as few had, a central concern with the Russellian (type-theoretic) distinction between nonsense and the true-or-false which was carried far beyond anything Russell had envisaged. Ryle's subsequent concern with category distinctions in language, both in his papers of the 1930s and in his later, mature writings, has its origins here.[69] In 1929, at the Joint Session of the Mind Association and the Aristotelian Society in Nottingham, Ryle first met, and struck up a friendship with, Wittgenstein,[70] which substantially affected his subsequent philosophy.

Among Ryle's early 'Occamizing' papers, the most influential was 'Systematically Misleading Expressions' (PAS, 32 (1932)). He opened with the remark, startling to the older generation, that philosophical arguments 'have always largely, if not entirely, consisted in attempts to thrash out "what it means to say so and so"'. To say, as Moore did, that philosophers are analysing 'concepts' is only a gaseous way of saying that they are trying to discover what is meant by the general terms contained in sentences, since 'is a concept' is itself a systematically misleading expression. However, this posed a problem, since ordinary users of an expression know what they mean, and do not need the aid of philosophers to understand what they are saying (for Wittgenstein's similar response to Moore, see above, p. 82). So in what non-trivial sense can philosophers discover what is meant by expressions? Ryle's answer was that our language is replete with systematically misleading expressions, expressions which are harmlessly used in non-philosophical discourse, but which are misleading in philosophical reflection. For such expressions are couched in grammatical or syntactical forms which are demonstrably *improper* to the states of affairs which they record. They are systematically misleading, inasmuch as they suggest that the states of affairs they record are quite different from the ones they are. They task of philosophy is to recast them in forms that are syntactically proper to the facts recorded. Ryle picked out four classes of such expressions.

(i) Quasi-ontological statements containing expressions such as 'exists', 'is an existent', 'is an entity', 'has being', 'is real', is a substance', 'is an actual object' and so forth and their negative counterparts 'is a non-entity', 'is unreal', 'is a fiction', 'is a logical construction' and so on misleadingly suggest that a characteristic is being ascribed or denied to a subject. 'Satan is not a reality' looks like 'Capone is not a philosopher', and 'Mr Pickwick is a fiction' appears to be like 'Mr Baldwin is a statesman'. But the fact that the first member of each of these two pairs records is quite different from the fact that the second member records. They can be paraphrased in a form more appropriate to the fact recorded – for example, by saying that there is no one both called 'Satan' and who is infinitely malevolent.

(ii) Quasi-Platonic statements such as 'Unpunctuality is reprehensible' misleadingly suggest that among the objects in reality are universals, such as Unpunctuality, which have certain properties, on the model of 'Jack is reprehensible'. But the fact recorded is simply that whoever is unpunctual deserves reproof.

(iii) Descriptive and quasi-descriptive phrases, such as 'the eldest son of Jones', misleadingly suggest that they are referential phrases, whereas, as Russell had shown, their 'proper' form reveals that they are condensed predicative phrases.

(iv) Quasi-referential phrases, such as 'the top of the tree' or 'hates the thought that', misleadingly suggest the existence of *entities* such as tops of trees or thoughts, whereas they transmute into 'higher than any other part of the tree' and 'feels distressed whenever he thinks that'.

In all these kinds of cases, Ryle argued, the paraphrase exhibits the logical form of the fact it records. Is the propriety of a given grammatical form to logical form *natural* or *conventional*? Ryle hesitated, settling for the unhappy half-way house that 'it is more nearly conventional than natural'. The task of philosophy, he held, is 'the detection of the sources in linguistic idioms of recurrent misconstructions and absurd theories' and to paraphrase systematically misleading statements by transmutation of syntax. This is what philosophical analysis is, and this, Ryle concluded, is the sole and whole function of philosophy. Therapeutic analysis was emerging from the *Tractatus* programme for future philosophy (TLP 6.53), although the umbilical cord connecting it with the logical atomist ontology of facts still remained to be cut.[71] Ryle's article signalled the emergence of young Oxford from the shadow of the previous generation. Its adherence to the logical atomists' conception of objective logical forms of facts, a notion that was rapidly to become defunct over the next decade or so, was nevertheless in tune with the winds blowing from Cambridge at the time. As late as 1951, Ryle's paper was described as 'the first powerful plain manifesto' of the 'modern movement in British philosophy'. His claim concerning the task of philosophy, and Wittgenstein's claim in the *Tractatus* that all philosophy is a critique of language, were held to be 'expressing in their very different ways what was substantially the same insight . . . it is from this central and fundamental discovery that all the other characteristic doctrines and assumptions of modern British philosophy have been developed and founded'.[72]

By the time he wrote 'Categories' in 1938, Ryle had abandoned the nexus with logical atomism that is marked in 'Systematically Misleading Expressions', while retaining his concern for the philosophical examination of kinds of absurdities which stem from inattention to logico-grammatical differences between kinds of expression. He now argued, still in the spirit of the previous paper, that all philosophers' propositions are category-propositions which assert something about the logical type of a proposition-factor (a sentence from which expressions have been removed, leaving gaps). He associated the notion of the logical type or category of a factor with that of the logical form of the proposition in which it occurs. For to know all about the logical form of a proposition – that is, its logical powers or 'liaisons' – is to know all about the logical types of its factors. (Ryle's notion of 'logical form' is *not* that of formal logicians, who abstract from all non-logical proposition-factors, hence from all category differences of the subject-matter of propositions. It is, rather, akin to, though not the same as, that of the *Tractatus*, according to which the logical form of a proposition is what it has in common with what it depicts. It is even closer to that of 'Some Remarks on Logical Form', from which the *Tractatus* independence postulate for atomic propositions has been dropped, and according to which propositions belonging to different propositional systems have a different logical form.) Two proposition-factors are of different types or categories if there are sentence-frames such that when the expressions for those factors are imported as alternative complements to the same gap-signs, the resultant sentences are significant in one case and absurd in the other.[73] Characteristic philosophical antinomies and puzzlements stem, Ryle now argued, from failure to apprehend category differences between expressions. The conception of a category mistake was to loom large in Ryle's post-war writings (see below, pp. 149f., 168f.). It is noteworthy that his criterion of category difference was inadequate, since importing, for example, first '27' and then '37' into the gap-sign in 'She is over . . . and under 33 years old' will show them to belong to different categories.[74] Moreover, Ryle did not clarify, but only gave examples of, the kind of absurdities that result from category mistakes. And it is evident that not every kind of *reductio ad absurdum* involves category mistakes, as indeed formal contradictions do not.

Fresh winds wafted in from the Continent too. At the international congress of philosophy at Oxford in 1930, Ryle met Schlick, and was much impressed with him. He kept in touch with developments in the Vienna Circle, and later wrote: 'In the 1930s the Vienna Circle made a big impact on my generation and the next generation of philosophers. Most of us took fairly untragically its demolition of metaphysics. After all, we never met anyone engaged in committing any metaphysics; our copies of *Appearance and Reality* were dusty; and most of us[75] had never seen a copy of *Sein und Zeit*.' He recognized the importance, and the inadequacy, of the principle of verification, and noticed that it made it even more pressing to attain a satisfactory answer to the question of what status to attribute to philosophical assertions, including those of the positivists. The dichotomy of 'Nonsense or Science' seemed, he wrote, to contain too few 'ors'. Nevertheless, it was apparently a desire for closer contacts with Vienna that led Ryle to recommend to his most able pupil, the young A. J. Ayer (1910–89), that he spend a year in Vienna after his graduation.

Ayer read Greats at Christchurch. Ryle introduced him to the writings of Russell, Moore, Ramsey, Broad, Nicod and Poincaré and, in his final year, to the *Tractatus*, of which Ayer later wrote, 'Among all these influences, that which the *Tractatus* had upon me was the strongest'.[76] His paper on it, delivered to the Jowett Society in 1932 (to which his contemporary Isaiah Berlin[77] replied) was the first public discussion of Wittgenstein's work in Oxford, and 'was the opening shot in the great positivist campaign'[78] in revolt against the entire traditional conception of philosophy as a source of knowledge. Although he was unsympathetic to the picture theory of the proposition and to the doctrines of showing and saying, he accepted (the Vienna Circle interpretation) that all significant propositions are either tautologies (propositions of logic and, as the Circle argued, of mathematics) or empirically verifiable. He took for granted that atomic propositions are experiential, referring to observable states of affairs. And he accepted the view that the sole task of philosophy is analysis. He was, in short, a logical positivist in the making. After he graduated, Ryle drove him to Cambridge in order to introduce him to Wittgenstein, who thereafter, for a number of years (until he gave offence by a remark in a broadcast in 1946), treated him as a protégé.[79] Elected to a two-year lectureship at Christchurch, with an initial leave of absence for two terms, Ayer was at first inclined to go to Cambridge to work with Wittgenstein. However, Ryle persuaded him to spend his leave in Vienna and learn as much as he could about the work of the Vienna Circle. He attended meetings of the Circle in 1932–3.[80] On his return to Oxford in the summer of 1933, he gave the first course of lectures in Oxford on the *Tractatus*. The annual summer joint sessions of the Mind Association and the

Aristotelian Society enabled him to meet Moore and other younger philosophers from Cambridge and elsewhere. It was at the 1933 session that *Analysis* was founded, to provide a mouthpiece for the younger generation of analytic philosophers. Through Stebbing, he first met Carnap, when he came to lecture at Bedford College, London, in 1934.

Such was his enthusiasm for the Vienna Circle and its principles that his friend Isaiah Berlin persuaded him to write up these avant-garde ideas, which he commenced doing in 1934. His advocacy of logical positivism irritated his seniors, however, and when he applied for a five-year Research Studentship at Christchurch in 1935, he obtained it (in the face of considerable opposition) partly due to the enthusiastic support he received from Whitehead, to whom the manuscript of his book was referred.[81] In 1936 he published the highly polemical *Language, Truth and Logic*, which fluttered the dovecotes of Oxford.[82] Eschewing all the technical apparatus characteristic of Carnap's writing, Ayer's book was written in a pugnacious, luminous style. It enjoyed a minor *succés de scandale* before the war, and, gradually gaining in popularity, became the primary English text of logical positivism. In it he synthesized, in so far as it was possible, the Cambridge analysis of Russell, Moore, Ramsey and early Wittgenstein with the central tenets of logical positivism – namely, the principle of verification and identification of meaningfulness with verifiability, the dismissal of metaphysics as nonsense, the reduction of all empirical propositions to subjective experience, an account of necessity as conventional and analytic, and ethical non-cognitivism (emotivism). Like the Viennese positivists, Ayer rejected the metaphysics of logical atomism. Like them, he argued that philosophical analysis is essentially linguistic. Its role is to devise forms of paraphrase of philosophically problematic propositions which will display their ultimate verification in experience. Sympathetic to the classical British empiricism of Hume, and influenced by Price's work on perception, he sided with Schlick and Waismann against Carnap and Neurath on the question of whether protocol sentences are sense-datum or physicalist sentences. By contrast with the Vienna Circle, Ayer's logical positivism displayed greater interest in traditional epistemological issues than in the logic of science and the foundations of mathematics. It would be no exaggeration to say that he recast Humean empiricism in logical and linguistic materials extracted from Russell, the *Tractatus* and the Circle. He continued to defend phenomenalist analyses in his subsequent writings – for example, *The Foundations of Empirical Knowledge* (1940) – arguing that analysis of material object propositions into a sense-datum language makes clear the epistemic grounds for our assertions about material things. In 'Verification and Experience' (PAS, 37 (1936–7)) he refuted Carnap's and Neurath's defence of the coherence theory of truth. Although the *Tractatus* was a major influence upon his philosophy, Wittgenstein's later work made no impact upon him at all (see below, pp. 153f.).

Belonging to a younger generation than the Wee Teas, Ayer was invited to join a different philosophers' discussion group, at All Souls College, which was formed by Isaiah Berlin and J. L. Austin[83] in 1936–7. Berlin and Austin had been Prize Fellows at All Souls together from 1933 to 1935, and had enjoyed almost daily conversations about philosophy. In 1936 they had together given the first class in Oxford on a contemporary philosophical text: namely, C. I. Lewis's *Mind and the World Order*. This class, in which Austin displayed his formidable powers, marked 'the true beginning of Austin's career as an independent thinker'.[84] At Austin's suggestion, he and Berlin invited Ayer, D. G. C. MacNabb and A. D. Woozley to join a discussion group for weekly meetings. Stuart Hampshire, newly elected to a Prize Fellowship at All Souls also joined, as did Donald McKinnon, who was a Fellow at Keble. The principal topics discussed give one an idea of the preoccupations of young Oxford in the late 1930s. They were phenomenalism and the verification theory of meaning, on both of which Ayer defended his logical positivist approach; a priori truths which are not analytic, such as the proposition that blue is more like green than like yellow, a topic which emerged from Berlin's and Austin's visit to the Moral Sciences Club at Cambridge to hear Russell's paper on 'The Limits of Empiricism' (PAS, 36 (1935–6), see esp. p. 148); the verification of counterfactuals; and problems about personal identity and other minds. Here the next generation of Oxford philosophy was born. Austin and Ayer, Berlin reports, 'gradually became the protagonists of two irreconcilable points of view. Austin's particular philosophical position was developed . . . during those Thursday evenings, in continuous contrast with, and in opposition to, the positivism and reductionism of Ayer and his supporters. . . . there was no crystallization into permanent factions: views changed from week to week, save that Ayer and Austin were seldom, if ever, in agreement about anything.'[85]

The two living philosophers whom Austin most admired were Russell and Prichard, the former for his independence of mind and powers of exposition, the latter because of his rigour, tenacity, rejection of obscurity and meticulous attention to detail.[86] Even at this early stage of his philosophical career, Austin assailed sense-datum theories of perception, which were being propounded not only by Ayer in the group, but by Moore and Broad at Cambridge and by Price at Oxford. These early suspicions bore fruit in his posthumous *Sense and Sensibilia* (1962). He was sceptical about the value of rigid philosophical dichotomies, such as that between universals and particulars (which he discussed in his first published paper 'Are there A Priori Concepts?', (PASS, 18 (1939)), descriptive and emotive language, empirical and logical truths, verifiable and unverifiable propositions, corrigible and incorrigible expressions and so forth. Such putative clear, exhaustive contrasts seemed to him to distort rather than illuminate our thought and language. Scepticism about clear-cut philosophical dichotomies was to characterize all his work, including his last *How to do Things with Words* (1962). Now, as later, he held that ordinary language was a better guide to philosophical clarification than distinctions drawn up by philosophers with a view to defending one or another theory. Berlin observes that Austin's implicit rejection of the notion of an ideal language which was a reflection of the structure of reality sprang from a philosophical vision not dissimilar to Wittgenstein's. Nevertheless, neither his early work nor his post-war writings owe anything to Wittgenstein, save perhaps indirectly, via Wisdom's articles on 'Logical Constructions', which he had read and admired.

It is no surprise that when Paton returned to Oxford to take up the White's Professorship in Moral Philosophy in 1937 (following Prichard's retirement), he found the philosophical climate 'greatly altered'. 'The change was more obvious to me', he wrote, 'because of my ten years absence [he had held a chair at Glasgow since 1927], and the transition had no doubt been gradual. Because of the direct personal connection between teacher and pupil there is in the old universities a real continuity under surface differences; and men like H. H. Price . . . W. C. Kneale, J. D. Mabbott and Gilbert Ryle appeared to be equally at home in the old world and the new. But the Cam was flowing into the Isis, and it seemed to me that a fresh era had begun.'[87] Ryle, more than any of the other Wee Teas, not only made the transition from the old to the new philosophical world; he led the way in Oxford in the immediate post-war years. And Kneale[88] brought to Oxford a competence in, and an encyclopaedic knowledge of the history of, formal logic that had hitherto been conspicuously missing. But the future lay above all in the hands of the next generation. For, apart from the Berlin–Austin circle, other young figures were coming on the scene, who would in due course produce the Golden Age of Oxford philosophy. H. P. Grice (1913–88), who read Greats at Corpus with W. F. R. Hardie and started teaching at St John's College in 1938, was to make a major post-war contribution to analytic philosophy in Oxford (and later in California), as was one of his first pupils, P. F. Strawson (b. 1919), who read Philosophy, Politics and Economics at St John's (1938–40). An important influx from the Danube via the Cam came with Friedrich Waismann's arrival in Oxford in 1940 (see below, p. 153). Although there was by now a rift between Wittgenstein and Waismann, he nevertheless had a more substantial knowledge of Wittgenstein's later philosophy than anyone else in Oxford, and, quite apart from his own important work over the next two decades, constituted a conduit whereby Wittgenstein's ideas could flow into nascent Oxford philosophy. The contribution of these figures to analytic philosophy will be discussed in chapter 6. At the end of the 1930s, the scene was set. 'And then', as Grice put it, 'everything was more or less brought to a halt by the war.'[89]

5

The Achievement of the
Investigations

1. The hedgehog and the fox

The *Investigations* (Part I) was in effect completed by late 1945 or early 1946, although Wittgenstein continued to make minor manuscript emendations and additions to the typescript. What is now Part II of the *Investigations* was written between 1945 and 1949. The decision to publish this material in a single volume together with Part I was made by the editors. Opinions differ as to whether it was seriously intended to be incorporated in the same book (see preface to Volume 4 of the *Commentary*) or whether Part I is to all intents and purposes complete (or, at least, as complete as Wittgenstein could make it). What is clear, however, is that of his later writings from 1929 until his death in 1951, only the *Investigations* reached, or neared, completion. His other two great projects concerned the philosophy of mathematics, on which he laboured between 1929 and 1944, and the philosophy of psychology, which dominated his last years after the war.[1] Had he lived to complete his labours, and had he been able to bring together the huge mass of materials on these two themes, we would, I believe, have had not one but three complementary master-works.[2]

In the following I shall attempt to give a synoptic view of what seem to me to be the major achievements of the *Investigations*. But I shall allow myself to draw on some of his other works too, in order to illuminate his innovations. I shall say little about his philosophy of mathematics (for reasons already given) or his post-*Tractatus* philosophy of logic (which has been discussed above, ch. 3 *passim* and pp. 78–84, and in greater detail in Volume 2, in the essay 'Grammar and necessity'). The detailed arguments associated with Wittgenstein's surviews of the grammatical domains he investigated are to be found in the four volumes of the *Analytical Commentary*, as is the supporting evidence for the interpretations I advance. My purpose here is to present a view of the whole, to disregard the detail in order to display the unity of thought which informs it. For although the *Investigations* is written in brief and often apparently disconnected remarks, although it frequently jumps from topic to topic without indicating the reasons for such sudden transitions, and although it has seemed to many readers to be a philosophy that revels in lack of systematicity, it is in fact – as should be evident from the previous volumes of the *Analytical Commentary* – a highly systematic, integrated work, and anything but a haphazard collection of *aperçus*. I shall revert to this point below.

It is noteworthy that in 1943, when Wittgenstein was reading the *Tractatus* with his friend, the Russian philologist Nicholas Bachtin, he decided to publish his new book (the modified 1943 version of the *Investigations*) in a single volume together with the *Tractatus*. As he wrote in the 1945 preface: 'It suddenly seemed to me that I should publish those old thoughts and the new ones together: that the latter could be seen in the right light only by contrast with and against the background of my old way of thinking.' Although this intention was not fulfilled in the original pub- lication, the intended contrast should be borne in mind when reading the *Investiga- tions* and when trying to see it aright. Some explanation should be ventured of the significance of this intended juxtaposition.

It is true that parts of the *Investigations* – for example, the discussion of logically proper names and simple objects, of determinacy of sense, of the general propositional form – are propounded explicitly in opposition to doctrines of the *Tractatus*. Other parts are evidently directed implicitly against the early conception – for example, the discussion of intentionality (which is, in effect, his reply to the 'picture theory of the proposition') and of meaning something (which constitutes his repudiation of what he had earlier conceived of as the mechanism 'connecting language and reality'). But what is much more important is that the *Investigations* as a whole stands opposed to the philosophical *spirit* of the *Tractatus* – hence Wittgenstein's desire that the two books be published together in a single volume.[3] These two masterpieces represent diametrically contrasting philosophical *Weltanschauungen*, the one characterized by a striving for a sublime *Wesensschau*, the other by 'a quiet weighing of linguistic facts' (Z §447) in order to disentangle the knots in our understanding; the one possessed by a vision of the crystalline purity of the logical forms of thought, language and the world, the other imbued with a heightened awareness of the motley of spatial and temporal phenomena of language (PI §108), the deceptive forms of which lead us into conceptual confusion; the one obsessed by a craving for the revelation of the hidden essences of things, placing its faith in depth analysis, the other demanding for the purposes of philosophical elucidation no more than the description and arrangement of what is simple and familiar, 'hidden' only because it is always before one's eyes and so goes unnoticed (PI §129).

Isaiah Berlin took the mysterious line from the Greek poet Archilochus: 'The fox knows many things, but the hedgehog knows one big thing', and, giving it a figurative interpretation, invoked it to mark a deep difference dividing writers and thinkers.[4] On the one hand, there are those, the hedgehogs, who are possessed by a single central vision, by a more or less coherent unifying system to which every- thing is related, a single organizing universal principle in terms of which all may be understood. On the other hand, there are those, the foxes, whose ideas are centri- fugal rather than centripetal, whose thought moves upon many levels, who are aware of the prodigious multiplicity, diversity and inexhaustible richness of things, and who describe the nature of a vast variety of phenomena for what they are in themselves, without seeking to fit them into one, all-embracing unitary vision. Berlin employed this duality to illuminate the thought and art of Tolstoy, who was, Berlin argued, a fox by nature, but a hedgehog by conviction. The Archilochean duality can, I think, also be used to shed light on Wittgenstein. He was by nature a hedgehog, but after 1929 transformed himself, by great intellectual and imagina- tive endeavour, into a paradigmatic fox.

The *Tractatus*, as much as any great work of metaphysics in the history of

philosophy, is characterized by a single unifying vision. The insight into the essen- *SINGLE UNIFYING*
tial nature of the elementary proposition was held to yield a comprehensive account *VISION OF THE TRACTATUS*
of the nature of logic and of the metaphysical structure of the world. From the
essential bipolarity of the proposition, all the logical constants, hence all the combinatorial possibilities of propositions, flow, and with them all the propositions of
logic. If elementary propositions are given, then at the same time *all* elementary
propositions are given (TLP 5.524), and therewith the limits of language and description. If objects are given, then at the same time we are given *all* objects (TLP
5.524). If all objects are given, all possible states of affairs are given (TLP 2.0124),
and therewith all possible worlds. The general propositional form – 'This is how
things stand' – gives the essence of a proposition. To give the essence of a proposition is to give the essence of all description, and hence the essence of the world
(TLP 5.471–5.4711). This sublime vision is shattered by the *Investigations*. The
proposition has no essence as conceived in the *Tractatus*; although 'we too are
interested in the essence of the proposition' (PI §93), what we call 'a proposition'
is a family of structures more or less related to each other (PI §108). What appeared
to be the general propositional form was merely an illusion generated by the use of
a sentence schema for purposes of anaphoric reference (PI §134) and the dogmatic
commitment to the view that the essence of the proposition is to describe how
things are. There are no 'simple objects', as understood in the *Tractatus*, for 'simple'
and 'complex' are relative, not absolute notions, and what was legitimate about the
apparent need to postulate sempiternal simples is satisfied by the use of samples
in various language-games. It was an illusion that what is peculiar, profound and
essential in philosophical investigation lies in its trying to grasp the incomparable
essence of language, the order existing between the concepts of proposition, word,
proof, truth, experience and so forth – a super-order existing between super (i.e.
categorial or formal) concepts (PI §97). For if the words 'language', 'proposition',
'name', 'experience' and so on have a use, it must be as humble a one as that of the
words 'table', 'lamp' and 'door'. And now those uses, with all their manifold overlapping similarities and interconnections, must be described. Relative to the problems with which he dealt in the *Investigations*, this is indeed what Wittgenstein set
out to do. He aimed to 'teach us differences' – to resist the urge to seek for underlying uniformities misleadingly suggested by the common grammatical forms of
different expressions, to beware of the homogenizing effects of translation into
canonical logical notations, and to attend to the innumerable differences that spring
into view once we are reminded of the multifarious uses of expressions with common grammatical forms, of the distinct purposes of grammatically similar utterances, of the quite different roles which syntactically identical sentences fulfil.[5] His
negative task was to destroy the houses of cards which philosophers erect, and to
clear up the ground of language on which they stand (PI §118). In so doing, he
described the sources of error, the roots of philosophical confusion, the temptations
of metaphysical illusion, the irresistible allure of apparently sublime logical insight,
with a depth of understanding and richness of detail unparalleled in the history of
the subject. This he was able to do precisely because he was, by temperament,
inclined to that very vision, because he had himself erected precisely such castles in
the air, because he knew the hedgehog's vision, knew what it is to be in the grip
of an illusion of a single, great, unifying form of *Wesensschau*.

The *Tractatus* brought a whole tradition of philosophy to its culmination. As we have seen, it was rooted in the problems posed by the works of Frege and Russell concerning the nature of logic, the limits of thought and language, and the relations between language, thought and reality; and it ranged from an investigation of the essence of the proposition to that of the nature of the world. Although it concluded that metaphysics is impossible, that any attempt to state metaphysical truths must transgress the bounds of sense, the book itself belongs to the high metaphysical tradition of European philosophy. By contrast, the *Investigations* has 'no ancestors in the history of thought'.[6] It constitutes a fundamental break with the tradition of philosophy, a 'kink' in the development of the subject, as Wittgenstein himself put it (see above, p. 83). The conception of philosophy it propounds has no precedent (save in mangled form in the doctrines of the Vienna Circle, themselves derived to a considerable extent from Wittgenstein himself, either from the *Tractatus* programme for future philosophy or from his reported conversations with Waismann and Schlick in the early 1930s). Its philosophy of language is equally without ancestors: it propounds neither a form of idealist telementational linguistic theory (on the model of the classical empiricists or on the more recent model of de Saussure) nor a form of behaviourist linguistic theory (which was common among linguists in the inter-war years, and survives in Quine's philosophy of language); it defends neither a form of the 'realist' truth-conditional semantics which grew out of the attempted synthesis of Frege and the *Tractatus*, on the one hand, and Tarski's formal semantics, on the other, nor a form of 'anti-realist semantics', which (though claiming Viennese ancestry[7]) was no more than a notional Oxonian brain-child of the 1960s and 1970s. The philosophy of mind of the *Investigations* eschews any form of dualism or mentalism, on the one hand, and repudiates behaviourism and reductive materialism in all its forms, on the other. Small wonder that the *Investigations* has been so frequently misinterpreted and so often misunderstood. Attempts to locate it on the received maps of philosophical possibilities inevitably led to distortion, as did attempts to extend the maps into *terra incognita*, as in the case of 'full-blooded conventionalism' (see below, pp. 255–64). Some explanation of this phenomenon too is called for.

In a profound methodological remark, Frank Ramsey observed that, when opposing philosophical views confront each other over centuries without being conclusively resolved either way, 'it is a heuristic maxim that the truth lies not in one of the two disputed views but in some third possibility which has not yet been thought of, which we can only discover by rejecting something assumed as obvious by both the disputants'.[8] I do not know whether Wittgenstein ever read this remark, but his practice in philosophy conforms with striking fidelity to Ramsey's maxim. This can be demonstrated again and again with respect to all the great subjects with which Wittgenstein engaged.

(a) In the philosophy of language, it was generally agreed that words and sentences are able to represent what they represent in virtue of their connection with reality. The idealists (from Locke onwards) argued that words are connected to the world by the mediation of ideas derived from experience; Frege argued that they are connected to 'the real' by the mediation of the senses to which they are attached; and behaviourists held that they are connected to reality by causal links between stimulus and verbal response. Wittgenstein sided with none of these great schools of thought; *in the relevant sense invoked,* words are not *connected* with the world at all. The meaning of a word is not an object in reality. It is not an abstract object (a Fregean 'sense') which, by means of an ethereal mechanism, determines an entity in reality as its reference. Nor is it a psychological object (an idea in the mind) which resembles an entity or possible entity in reality. Rather it is, or is determined by, the use of the word, and it is given by an explanation of meaning, which is a rule for the use of that word. Ostensive definition, which appears to connect the network of language to reality, actually connects a word with a sample, which itself belongs to the method of representation and is an instrument of the language, not something represented by the ostensive definition. So language remains self-contained and autonomous. Of course, this does not mean that we do not refer to objects in the world by our uses of language, that we are not really talking about a language-independent reality. However, the intentionality of language is attributable not to connections between words and world, but to intra-grammatical connections, to explanations of meaning and of what we mean by the words we utter.

(b) In the philosophy of logic, as we have seen, Frege held that the propositions of logic are descriptions of relations between abstract entities, whereas Russell argued that they are descriptions of the most general structural features of the universe, and the psycho-logicians held that they are descriptions of the laws of human thinking. The common ground between the disputants was that propositions of logic are descriptions of something. Given that they are truths – indeed, necessary truths – it seemed that they must be descriptions. The moot questions seem to be: *What* do they describe? What is the *source* of their necessity? How can we *recognize* their necessity? Wittgenstein agreed that logical propositions are among what we *call* 'necessary truths', but denied that they describe anything at all. They are degenerate propositions that say nothing. The fruitful questions are: Why is it that they say nothing? How can they be both true and vacuous? How can one proposition of logic differ from another, given that they all say the same – namely, nothing? Rather than pursuing the question of the 'source' of their necessity in the nature of the entities allegedly described or in the alleged structure of the human mind or in the meanings of words, Wittgenstein explored what it is for propositions of logic to *be* 'necessary propositions', what function they fulfil in our conceptual economy. Instead of investigating how we can recognize their necessity – by perception of relations between universals, or by the intuitive powers of our logical faculties, or by recognition of our decisions and intentions – he investigated the roles of such propositions in our linguistic transactions. Once these questions have been properly investigated, the received questions simply evaporate, since their presuppositions are undercut.

(c) In metaphysics, defenders of the metaphysical enterprise conceived of true metaphysical propositions as descriptions of necessary, essential relations between simple natures, or Platonic Ideas, or Universals. Metaphysics was conceived as a super-physical investigation of the most general features of the universe and its ultimate constituents, which would yield a description of the necessary structural features not merely of this world but of any possible world. Unlike truths of physics, metaphysical truths were held to be descriptions not of contingent facts about reality, but of necessities (including transcendent necessary truths about God and the immortality of the soul). Kant's Copernican revolution attributed the deliverances of metaphysics to insight not into mind-independent necessities, but rather into necessities of thought, structural features which the mind imposes upon the raw data of intuition in the process of yielding conceptualized experience. Kant rejected transcendent metaphysics, limiting metaphysical knowledge to synthetic a priori truths which describe the conditions of the possibility of experience. Wittgenstein rejected the common assumption that what are conceived of as metaphysical truths are descriptions of anything, that the 'necessary truths' of metaphysics are descriptions of objective necessities in nature – that the 'truths' of metaphysics are truths about objects in reality at all. Rather, what we conceive of as true metaphysical propositions are norms of representation, rules for the use of expressions in the misleading guise of descriptions of objects and relations. They are not synthetic a priori truths about the conditions of possible experience (as Kant argued), but rules of grammar; not nonsense (as Hume argued), but conventions for the description of things.

(d) In epistemology, sceptics since antiquity have agreed that we know how things subjectively appear to us to be, but have denied that our knowledge of our own perceptual experiences can provide us with adequate grounds for knowledge claims about objects. Representationalists argued that our knowledge of subjective experience constitutes an adequate basis for an inference to the best explanation of the regular course of our experience. Idealists disagreed, concluding that our knowledge claims about objects are no more than claims about the coherence and regularity of actual and possible experiences, and phenomenalists argued that material objects are merely logical constructions out of actual and possible sense-data. Wittgenstein characteristically questioned the agreed presupposition of the debate: namely, that we *know* that we are having such-and-such a perceptual experience – not because he thought that this might be something of which we could be ignorant, but precisely because in the normal use of 'It appears thus-and-so to me' *there is no such thing as not knowing*, and, by the same token, no such thing as knowing, finding out, being right or wrong about, confirming or disconfirming, being certain or doubting how things appear to me (see Volume 3, 'Avowals and descriptions'). If such utterances are not expressions of secure knowledge, then they are *a fortiori* not *evidence* for assertions about objects, hence do not constitute the foundations of empirical knowledge. The role of such forms of words as 'It looks thus-and-so to me', 'It appears to me just as if. . .', 'It seems to me that . . .' is altogether different from that attributed to it by the foundationalist tradition in epistemology.

(e) The debate on induction, which had raged since Hume, concentrated on finding a justification for induction. Some had sought such a justification by reference to frequency theories of probability; others had appealed to pragmatic justification; yet others had invoked the alleged transcendental conditions of the possibility of experience. It was generally agreed that if scepticism was to be refuted, there must be some way to justify inductive reasoning. This was precisely what Wittgenstein denied. One cannot give a justification of induction, neither because it is beyond our limited cognitive powers, nor because the sceptic is right, but rather because the very demand for justification is senseless (see Volume 4, 'Inductive reasoning').

(f) In philosophical psychology, Wittgenstein did not *participate* in the debate between mentalists, who conceive of psychological propositions as descriptions of a domain to which the subject has privileged access (akin to a private world), and behaviourists, who repudiate the idea of privileged access and construe such propositions as descriptions of behaviour and dispositions to behave. Rather, he *undercut* it (see Volume 3, 'The private language arguments'). Both sides of the dispute agreed that first- and third-person psychological propositions in the present tense – for example, 'I am in pain' and 'He is in pain' – have the same 'logical form', are uniformly descriptions of states of affairs, and that those states of affairs are severally objects of possible knowledge. It was these shared presuppositions that Wittgenstein challenged. Typical first-person, present-tense psychological utterances are not descriptions of a private domain accessible to the subject alone; nor are they descriptions of a public domain accessible to all, on a par with corresponding third-person propositions, since they are not descriptions at all. Nor are they typically expressions of self-knowledge. They are commonly avowals, manifestations or expressions (*Äusserungen*) of experience, not assertions based on evidence or observation. Their third-person counterparts, however, are descriptions for which there are public behavioural criteria for their assertion. What they describe can be known, believed or supposed to be so.

Given this disposition to reject the shared presuppositions of the traditional debates on the central questions of philosophy, it is no wonder that Wittgenstein's philosophical stance on these questions has so often been misunderstood. The temptation to construe his philosophy as a form of crypto-behaviourism, or as implicit verificationism, or as a defence of assertion-conditions semantics, or as propounding a form of anti-realism, stems from failure to see that he undercuts the questions to which these philosophical theories or conceptions provide answers. His philosophy can no more be located on the received maps of philosophical possibilities than the North Star can be located on maps of the globe.

In what follows, I shall attempt to survey the achievement of the *Investigations* under five main headings: (i) its repudiation of philosophical analysis (reductive and constructive) as previously conceived and its espousal of connective analysis or elucidation; (ii) its conception of philosophy and of therapeutic analysis; (iii) its critique of metaphysics; (iv) its philosophy of language and conception of meaning as use; (v) its philosophical psychology and repudiation of the 'inner'/'outer' conception of the mental.[9]

2. The repudiation of analysis

The conception of analysis which informed the first phases of analytic philosophy was rooted in a pluralist Platonist ontology, which flowered into the metaphysics of logical atomism. Correlative with this metaphysical picture was a conception of language and logic. Language was conceived as a calculus of strict rules, of which speakers allegedly had 'tacit knowledge'. Expressions in a language were thought to be either definable by analytic definition or indefinable. Indefinable expressions were conceived to be linked to their meanings in reality by mental acts of meaning by such-and-such a word *this* ↗ object. The objects to which they were thus linked were thought to be the ultimate constituents of facts. The propositions of logic were thought (by Russell) to be descriptions of the most general, structural features of reality, or (by the *Tractatus*) to be the mirror of the logical structure of the world. The task of philosophy was the clarification of propositions (TLP 4.112). This task was to be carried out by analysis, which would lay bare the logical forms of propositions, and therewith the logical structure of the facts that make them true. Such analysis would also reveal the illegitimacy of certain kinds of philosophically problematic pseudo-propositions.

Wittgenstein's criticisms of the ontology of logical atomism have already been discussed, as have his criticisms of the conception of logic which informed that doctrine. It is further erroneous to assume that the meaning of an expression must be given either by an analytic or by an ostensive definition, and equally erroneous to assume that these are exclusive. We explain the use of expressions also by means of examples, together with a similarity rider, which function in such contexts as rules (e.g. in the case of family resemblance concepts), by contextual paraphrase or contrastive paraphrase, by exemplification and by gesture, and so on (see Volume 1, 'Explanation'). It is mistaken to think that an ostensive definition links language to reality (for a sample belongs to grammar), that the object pointed at is the meaning of the *definiendum* (since the meaning of a word is not a kind of object), that ostensive definition is unambiguous (since no explanation can guarantee understanding, and an ostensive definition presupposes the grammar of the *definiendum*) and gives an 'interpretation' to the bare bones of the syntax of language. Ostensive definition is *a* form of explanation of meaning, but no more privileged than any other, and does not form the foundation of a language (see Volume 1, 'Ostensive definition and its ramifications'). The idea that there are simple, indefinable names linked to objects in reality by mental acts of meaning involves a fundamental misconception of names and of what is involved in meaning something by a word (see below; see also Volume 1, 'Logically proper names' and 'Proper names', and Volume 4, 'The mythology of meaning something').

The conception of analysis which the *Tractatus* inherited from Frege and Russell involved a commitment to a bogus ideal of determinacy of sense (motivated by requirements consequent upon treating quantifiers as second-level function-names) and a misguided demand for completeness of definition. According to the *Tractatus*, what is meant by a sentence and what is understood when an utterance of a sentence is understood must, it seemed, be 'sharp'. Analysis must be unique, since any proposition is a truth-function of atomic propositions. The existence of simple objects, which are the meanings of simple names the logical syntax of which reflects the combinatorial possibilities of these objects, seemed to guarantee determinacy of sense. This ensured bivalence, the proposition accordingly dividing logical space precisely in two, eliminating any possibility of truth-value gaps, and securing the requirement that all entailments be determined by truth-functional combinations of propositions.

This mythology of symbolism was now rejected. The idea that the sense of a sentence is a function of the meanings of its constituents and their mode of combination was a distorted statement of the platitude that if one does not understand the words of a sentence or their mode of combination, then one will not understand the sentence. The notion that what a sentence means follows from explanations of what its constituent words mean, together with a specification of its structure, is a form of compositionalism which errs with respect to both meaning and under-standing. The idea that the meaning or sense of a sentence is composed of the meanings or senses of its constituents (as Frege supposed) is as absurd as the idea that a fact is composed of constituent objects. Furthermore, compositionalism mistakenly assumes that distinctions between sense and nonsense are drawn once and for all by reference to circumstance-invariant features of type-sentences, rather than being, in many *different* ways, circumstance-dependent.[10] And it disregards the very different *uses* to which sentences of the same form may be put (e.g. first-/third-person asymmetries in the use of psychological verbs, or performative, de-scriptive and frequentative uses of a sentence). It is a piece of psychological super-stition to suppose that understanding is a process of *deriving* the meaning of an utterance from the known meanings of its constituents and their mode of com-bination (see Volume 1, 'Only in the context of a sentence', §§4–7, and 'Under-standing and ability').

It is wrong to suppose that understanding consists in knowing a set of necessary and sufficient conditions for the application of an expression. For numerous expres-sions (among which are family resemblance concepts) are not explained by speci-fication of necessary and sufficient conditions for their application (see Volume 1, 'Family resemblance'). The equation of determinacy of sense with the elimination of any *possibility* of doubt or disagreement about the application of an expression not only placed an incoherent demand upon any symbolism whatsoever; it also distorted the ordinary concept of vagueness. Vagueness is not absence of determinacy of sense, since there is no such thing (see below, pp. 164f.). Its characterization is relative to explanations of meanings, and to what (if anything) has been laid down as a complete, exact specification of meaning. But 'No *single* ideal of exactness has been laid down; we do not know what we should be supposed to imagine under this head – unless you yourself lay down what is to be so called. But you will find it difficult to hit upon such a convention; at least any that satisfies you' (PI §88). Vagueness is not necessarily a defect (PI §§88, 100), and its occurrence is not logi-cally 'contagious' (see Volume 1, 'Vagueness and determinacy of sense'). The de-mand for completeness of definition was equally confused, resting on the assumption that we have an absolute conception of completeness. But the concepts of complete and incomplete are both relative and correlative (see Volume 1, 'Explanation', §4). A complete explanation of the meaning of an expression is an explanation which may legitimately be invoked as a standard of correctness for the application of that expression in normal contexts. Relative to that standard, explanations can be judged to be incomplete (as is Cephalus's explanation of 'just' in Plato's *Republic*). But it is, *pace* Frege (FA §56), no defect of incompleteness in an explanation of the concept of number that it does not distinguish Julius Caesar from a number.

The thought that analysis will reveal the 'logical structure of the world' rested on the misconceived idea that the world consists of facts, that facts have a logical structure, and that the substance of the world consists of sempiternal objects with language-independent combinatorial possibilities. Once these metaphysical confu-sions are swept away, the idea of *the logical forms* of propositions as reflections of reality collapses. What may remain of the notion of logical form is the supposition that the forms of the predicate calculus (with appropriate enrichment) display not the logical structure of the world, but the common depth structure of any possible language. (This conception became the leitmotif of philosophy of language in the 1970s and 1980s, deriving apparent support from the new theoretical linguistics advocated by Chomsky.) But, Wittgenstein argued, the idea that languages have a common essence is misconceived, since the concept of a language is a family resemblance concept. One can imagine a language consisting only of orders and reports in a battle, or only of questions and expressions for answering yes and no (PI §19). One can imagine a language in which all 'sentences' are one-word sentences, or a language in which all statements have the form and tone of rhetorical questions, or one in which all commands have the form of questions – e.g. 'Would you like to . . . ?' (PI §21). Embedded in an appropriate form of life, all these (and much else too) would rightly and unhesitatingly be deemed languages. But only dogmatic commitment to a form of representation would incline one even to attempt to squeeze such Protean forms into the Procrustean bed of the predicate calculus.

More important, the very idea that human languages have a hidden, function-theoretic depth structure (first uncovered by Frege, Russell and Whitehead's discovery (or, more precisely, invention) of the predicate calculus) is misconceived. For the structure that is alleged to characterize a language is a *normative structure*, a structure governed by rules. But it makes no sense to suppose that human beings *follow* rules (as opposed to merely acting *in accord with* rules) with which they are unacquainted. For to *follow* rules is to *use* rules as guides to behaviour, to employ them in teaching others how to engage in the relevant rule-guided practice, to invoke them in criticizing deviant behaviour or in explaining and justifying behaviour; and speakers of natural languages are normally unacquainted with the rules of function-theoretic logical calculi (see Volume 2, 'Rules and grammar'). The most that can intelligibly be claimed is that one can map a certain form of rule-governed behaviour on to a different system of *possible* rules. But these will not be the rules which participants in the relevant practice are following.[11] Moreover, any disparity between the rule-governed practices of language use and the system of possible rules cast in the form of a calculus of logic will reveal the shortcomings of the calculus, not those of the logic of our language. The Frege–Russell calculus is just another calculus – a different (and more powerful) formal mode of representation from the Aristotelian syllogistic calculus. In philosophy, it may be a useful *object of comparison* for certain purposes – for example, to highlight ambiguities in sentences involving multiple generality, which can be perspicuously disambiguated in the notation of quantification theory, or to illuminate muddles concerning negative existential statements, or to make clear how ascriptions of number differ from ascriptions of qualities and so forth. It may make certain kinds of inferences and chains of argument more readily surveyable than they would otherwise be. But, like the older subject/predicate form of syllogistic, the forms of the function-theoretic calculus misleadingly assimilate numerous different kinds of expression with very different roles (PG 202–7). The following array of sentences have a misleadingly similar grammatical form: 'Socrates is human', 'Socrates is Greek', 'Socrates is dead', 'Socrates is virtuous'; so do 'Snow is white' and 'Pleasure is desirable'; or 'Thrasymachus is a knave', 'Red is a colour', 'Two is a number'; or again, 'I have a pain', 'He has a pain', 'I have a penny', 'I have a foot', not to mention 'I have a body', and so on. To represent these uniformly in the logico-mathematical garb of the function-theoretic calculus is no less misleading than to represent them in the old-fashioned clothing of syllogistic. Moreover, the rules for the use of the logical connectives in the calculus do not match the rules for the expressions 'and', 'or', 'if . . . , then . . .'; the topic neutrality of the quantifiers in the calculus is not matched by any topic neutrality of 'some' and 'all'; the formation rules of the calculus would make nonsense if applied uncritically and without restriction to natural languages; and so on.[12] So much the worse for our logical calculi *if they are meant to reveal the logic of our language.*

What, then, remains of philosophical analysis as previously conceived? Very little. Philosophical problems are misunderstandings, caused, among other things, by analogies between forms of expression with different uses. 'Some of them can be removed by substituting one form of an expression for another; this may be called an "analysis" of our forms of expression, for the process is sometimes like one of taking a thing apart' (PI §90). Russell's paraphrastic method of eliminating definite descriptions may help to clarify certain philosophical puzzlements, but the theory of descriptions conceived (as Ramsey conceived it) as 'a paradigm of philosophy', with grandiose claims to *see through phenomena* (PI §90), to 'see to the bottom of things' (PI §89), is an illusion. And it was an illusion to suppose that there is 'something like a final analysis of our forms of language, and so a *single* completely resolved form of every expression. That is, as if our usual forms of expression were, essentially, unanalysed; as if there were something hidden in them that had to be brought to light' (PI §91).

What replaces analysis? Descriptions of the ways in which we use words, which will shed light upon philosophical confusions (PI §109), and a rearrangement of familiar rules for the use of expressions that will make the grammar of the relevant expressions surveyable (PI §92). For the main source of philosophical puzzlement and of misconceived philosophical theories is our failure to command a clear view of the use of words (PI §122). The grammar of our language is lacking in surveyability, inasmuch as expressions with very different uses have similar surface grammars. 'I meant' has a similar surface grammar to 'I pointed'; 'I have a pain' looks like 'I have a pin'; 'He is thinking' resembles 'He is talking'; 'to have a mind' has the same grammatical form as 'to have a brain', and so forth (cf. PI §664). Such features (and many other factors) lead us, in our philosophical reflections, to conceive of meaning something as a mental act or activity whereby we attach words to the world, to construe pain as a kind of object similar to a pin, only mental and private (see Volume 3, 'The private language arguments' and 'Private ostensive definition'), to imagine that thinking is a mental activity that accompanies speech and renders it thoughtful (see Volume 3, 'Thinking: the soul of language'), to think that the mind is identical with the brain, and so on. It is only by a careful description of the grammatical reticulations of such philosophically confusing expressions that we can attain a perspicuous representation of the field of interconnected concepts that is the locus of our problems. Connective and therapeutic analysis replace both reductive and constructive analysis.[13]

CONNECTIVE ANALYSIS

A perspicuous representation of segments of the grammar of our language which constitute the locus of philosophical problems is what one strives for in philosophy. It produces precisely the kind of understanding which dispels philosophical confusion, for it enables us to see differences between concepts which are obscured by the misleadingly similar grammatical forms of expressions, the use of which is fundamentally different, and connections between concepts and sentences in use which superficially appear to be quite different (cf. PI §122). Such a perspicuous representation is not to be obtained by depth analysis as previously conceived. To the philosopher who is gripped by the ideal of logical analysis, the strict, clear rules of the logical structure of propositions appear to be something hidden in the medium of the understanding; for, to be sure, one understands the proposition, knows how to use it to say what one wants to say (PI §102). They must, it seems, be extracted by logical analysis, which will reveal hitherto unknown or unanticipated logical structures – the presence of real numbers in propositions ascribing degrees of a quality to an object, or the presence of quantifiers, an identity sign and logical connectives in definite descriptions. But this conception was a mythology of symbolism. *For nothing is hidden* (PI §§126, 435) – even if there is much which one needs to be reminded of (PI §127) and much that is perfectly familiar but which does not strike one unless it is drawn to one's attention. Such features are 'hidden' only in the sense in which one fails to notice something which is always before one's eyes (PI §129). It was a deep confusion to suppose that in philosophy one can, in this sense, hit upon something hitherto unknown, that one can *discover* something new. 'The truth of the matter is that we have already got everything, and we have got it actually *present*; we need not wait for anything. We make our moves in the realm of the grammar of our ordinary language, and this grammar is already there. Thus we have already got everything and need not wait for the future' (WWK 183). One might say that 'A sentence is completely logically analysed when its grammar is laid out completely clearly' (BT 417). But to lay out its grammar clearly involves neither new discoveries nor new logical or grammatical forms. Rather, it involves describing the ways in which we use expressions, ways with which every speaker of the language is already fully familiar.

What is necessary is to assemble reminders for the purpose of philosophical elucidation, for the resolution and dissolution of philosophical problems (cf. PI §127). To be sure, such reminders of familiar rules of our language need to be *arranged* to yield a perspicuous representation (*übersichtliche Darstellung*) which will resolve the difficulties in question (cf. PI §109). 'The aim is a synoptic comparative account [*übersichtliche, vergleichende Darstellung*] of all the applications, illustrations, conceptions of [the domain in question].[14] The complete survey [*Übersicht*] of everything that may produce unclarity. And this survey must extend over a wide domain, for the roots of our ideas reach a long way' (Z §273). If we are beset by conceptual problems regarding sensations – for example, pain – and are inclined to think that a pain is an object, like a pin, only mental and private, then we must arrange the grammatical rules for the use of the word 'pain' in juxtaposition with the rules for the use of the word 'pin'. For we are prone to be taken in by the superficial grammatical similarities between 'I have a pain' and 'I have a pin', between 'I feel a pain' and 'I feel a pin', and between 'My pain is just like yours' and 'My pin is just like yours'. Deluded by these similarities, we are inclined to project the grammar of ownership ('I *have* a pin') on to the grammar of sensation, to conceive of the sufferer as being a possessor of pain and of the pain possessed as having the peculiarity of being inalienable. Similarly, we project the grammar of 'feeling a pin' on to the grammar of 'feeling a pain', and argue that to feel a pain is to *perceive* a pain (as to feel a pin is to perceive a pin), and that we know that we are in pain *because* we can perceive the pain (as we know that there is a pin here because we can perceive it). In short, we project the grammar of perceptible objects on to the grammar of sensations, and, having done so, infer that 'mental objects' like pain have further startling properties: they are inalienable, for it seems that another person cannot have my pain, but only a pain that is qualitatively similar to it; they are epistemically private, for another person cannot know what my pain is like in the way in which I can; and so on (see Volume 3, 'Privacy'). But this is illusion and confusion, which can be dissipated by careful comparison of the familiar rules for the use of sensation-words such as 'pain' with the rules for the use of material object words like 'pin'.

'To feel a pain' can be replaced by 'to have a pain' – there is no difference here – but 'to feel a pin' is not the same as 'to have a pin'. One may think that one feels a pin, but be wrong (if it is a thorn); but it makes no sense to think that one feels a pain and be wrong. One may wonder whether it is a pin one feels, and look to see or feel again; but it makes no sense to wonder whether it is a pain one feels, and to look to see or feel again. To feel a pin is to perceive a pin, but to feel a pain is no more a form of perception than is to feel cheerful or to feel like a walk. To have a pin is to possess a pin, which one can give away, whereas to have a pain is no more to possess anything than is to have a train to catch or to have a birthday next week, and it makes no sense to talk of giving one's pains away. If my pain is just like yours, then we both have the same pain (the fact that yours is in your head and mine is in my head does not mean that we have different headaches[15] – if we both have a dull, throbbing pain in the temples, then we have the same headache; similarly, the fact that 'yours is yours and mine is mine' does not mean that we have different pains, since the subject of a pain is not a property of the pain). But your pin may be just like mine, even though it is a different pin, or it may be the same pin as I had, if I gave it to you. For the distinction between qualitative and numerical identity applies to pins, but has no application to pains. And so on. The patient accumulation and arrangement of such grammatical differences will yield a perspicuous representation of the grammar of 'pain' (and similar sensation-words) and of the grammar of 'pin' (and similar words for material objects), and will enable us to resist the temptation to project the grammar of the latter upon the former, and to desist from the absurd ideas that pains are privately owned and epistemically private (see Volume 3, 'Privacy').

The point of such a description of use is not that of the grammarian, who aims, for example, at a systematic description of the syntax of a language. The order in which the philosopher arranges familiar grammatical facts is not the order that would be chosen by the grammarian. Indeed, the rules which the philosopher tabulates and arranges will typically be rules which the grammarian would overlook, even though they are, in a perfectly ordinary sense of the term, rules of language (see Volume 2, 'Rules and grammar'). The philosopher's description derives its point from the philosophical problems with which he struggles. The order in the rules of language which he strives to establish has as its end the attainment of complete clarity concerning conceptual articulations (which is far removed from the grammarian's purposes), a clarity which will dissolve the philosophical problems completely (PI §§132f.). For a philosophical problem is symptomatic of a disorder in our concepts – that is, a disorder in our *reflective* mastery of them – and it can be solved by ordering our concepts so that we can find our way around in the grammatical network without stumbling into conceptual confusion. In philosophy, unlike the sciences, all the information we need is already at hand – in our ordinary knowledge of how to use the expressions of our language. And the problems of philosophy, unlike those of the sciences, are completely solvable. Failure to solve them, therefore, is due to philosophers' failure to arrange the grammatical facts in such a manner that the problems disappear – dissolve, like a lump of sugar in water (BT 421).

3. The nature of philosophy

The idea of a perspicuous representation is crucial to the replacement of logical by connective analysis. It is also central to Wittgenstein's later conception of the task of philosophy, a conception which is at odds with, and, as we have seen, can best be described as the legitimate heir of, what used to be called 'philosophy'. If one had to choose one single fundamental insight from the whole corpus of Wittgenstein's later work, it might well be argued that it should be the insight that philosophy contributes not to human knowledge, but to human understanding; that there is not, and cannot be, a body of established philosophical propositions, a corpus of philosophical truths to which successive generations may add to constitute a body of ever growing philosophical knowledge on the model of the empirical sciences. But, of course, this insight would not be understood without the practice of philosophizing exemplified in Wittgenstein's work. Indeed, even with that context, it has proved difficult for philosophers to grasp. It has been even more difficult for them to accept that so much of the intellectual endeavour of two and a half millennia rested on fundamental conceptual confusion, a confusion which assigned to philosophy a cognitive role comparable to (though more elevated than) that of the sciences.[16]

Although the *Tractatus* programme for future philosophy formally propounded a non-cognitive conception of philosophy, denying that there can be any philosophical propositions, *a fortiori* any philosophical knowledge, there was, as previously noted, something disingenuous about the claim. For while it is true that the philosophical analysis advocated would not *state* any metaphysical truths, it was nevertheless held to *show* them. For analysis was conceived to reveal the logical forms of reality (RLF), and was so understood by the Cambridge analysts, as well as by Ryle. With the transformation of his philosophy in the 1930s, Wittgenstein came to repudiate this conception. The *Investigations* delineates a purified non-cognitive conception of philosophy. It is indeed the case that there are no philosophical truths; what appear as such are grammatical propositions which are familiar rules for the use of words in the misleading guise of statements. They neither say nor show anything about the logical forms of phenomena, for the very idea that phenomena *have* a logical form was chimerical. There is no philosophical *knowledge*. Indeed, if anyone were to advance (acceptable) theses in philosophy, everyone would agree with them (PI §128): Can one step into the same river twice? – Yes. Do things continue to exist unperceived? – Usually yes, but sometimes, as in the case of a soap-bubble, they may disappear before one can look again. How is it possible to know of the existence of material things? – By the use of one's eyes, hands and ears. There is no news from the Transcendental Times, and logic is no Transcendental Mirror. It was true to say that philosophy investigates the limits of language. But when philosophers, such as Kant or the author of the *Tractatus*, declare that at such-and-such a point we have arrived at the limits of language, it sounds as if resignation were necessary ('*This* cannot be said'); and in believing that they see the 'limit of human understanding', of course they believe that they can see beyond it ('but it can be shown' (BT 423, 425)). But in fact no intellectual resignation is necessary, for there is nothing that cannot be said, and there is nothing beyond the bounds of sense save nonsense.[17]

There are two primary aspects to Wittgenstein's later conception of philosophy. On the one hand, philosophy is characterized as a quest for a surveyable representation of the grammar of a given problematic domain, which will enable us to find our way around when we encounter philosophical difficulties.[18] On the other hand, philosophy is characterized as a cure for diseases of the understanding. These different aspects correspond to the difference between connective analysis and therapeutic analysis, but they are perfectly compatible.

The conception of philosophy as therapeutic is a leitmotif in Wittgenstein's later work. 'The philosopher's treatment of a question is like the treatment of an illness' (PI §255). He should not try to *terminate* a disease of thought, for slow cure is all-important (Z §382). There are different philosophical methods, like different therapies (PI §133). What mathematicians are inclined to say about the reality and objectivity of mathematical facts is itself something for philosophical treatment (PI §254). Wittgenstein sometimes compared his methods of philosophical clarification with psychoanalysis (see Exg. §255). Philosophical theories are latent, concealed nonsense; the task of philosophy is to transform them into patent nonsense (PI §524). Mathematicians have been trained to avoid conceptual questions of the kind Wittgenstein raises – indeed, have acquired a revulsion to them as to what is infantile – whereas Wittgenstein, in his philosophy of mathematics, encourages us to bring out such repressed doubts and questions (PG 381f.), for only then can the task of therapy begin. The task of the philosophical therapist is not to lay down rules of language (PI §124) but to elicit them from the mind of the bewildered (WWK 186), for it is conflicts in the latter's use of words that generate his seemingly insoluble philosophical problems. Hence the exact anatomy of error in the individual mind is crucial, and the 'patient's' recognition of it *as* the correct expression of what he thinks is the first step towards realization that the bounds of sense have been transgressed (BT 410; WWK 183f.). It is not the task of philosophy to resolve contradictions in mathematics, but rather to make clear the route to the contradiction, to render surveyable the entanglement in the rules that led to it (PI §125). Like the therapist, the philosopher aims to give the afflicted *insight* into their own understanding and misunderstanding.

Some of the sources of philosophical confusion have been discussed above. However, there is also such a thing as the will to illusion. Often the difficulty of an important subject is attributable to the contrast between the understanding of the subject and what most people *want* to see (BT 407). We find solace, or perverse satisfaction, in certain misconceived philosophical pictures. The Platonist in mathematics finds solace in the vision of a timeless domain of absolute certainty, 'where pure thought can dwell as in its natural home, and where one, at least, of our nobler impulses can escape from the dreary exile of the actual world'; for mathematics, thus conceived, takes us 'into the region of absolute necessity, to which not only the actual world, but every possible world must conform; and even here it builds a habitation, or rather finds a habitation eternally standing, where our ideals are fully satisfied and our best hopes not thwarted'.[19] The psychological hedonist or egotist finds satisfaction in what appears to be a hard-headed but realistic vision of human motivation, embracing a fallacious argument with alacrity, in part precisely because the resultant picture is repulsive. Incompatibilist determinism may give one a certain relief, coupling an apparently rational recognition of the hard truths of science with the solace that in the last analysis we cannot be held responsible for our lives. One of the greatest impediments for philosophy is the expectation of new, deep revelations (BT 419). For the human craving for the arcane is present in philosophy no less than in other walks of life, manifesting itself in the *desire* for hitherto undreamt-of mysteries about the mind, thought and language. But in philosophy there are no mysteries, only the mesmerizing confusions engendered *inter alia* by our entanglement in grammar. Here too, as in psychoanalysis, there is often an underlying tacit *motive* for cleaving to error and illusion. Hence, 'If you find yourself stumped trying to convince someone of something and not getting anywhere, tell yourself that it is the *will* and not the intellect that you're up against' (MS 158, 35). Work on philosophy is often more a work on oneself, on the way one sees things and what one demands of them (BT 407). It leads one to abandon certain combinations of words as senseless, and that involves a kind of resignation, not of intellect but of feeling. For it can be as difficult not to use an expression as to hold back tears (BT 406) – hence Wittgenstein's daunting remark that every philosophical error is the mark of a character failing.

The idea that philosophy is therapeutic analysis has, to many, seemed a depressingly negative conception of the subject, depriving philosophy of its depth. That impression is strengthened by some of Wittgenstein's own remarks. Philosophy, as he practised it, seems only to destroy all that is great and important (PI §118): that is, what we thought to be insights into the objective nature of things, into the essential structure of the human mind, into the conditions of the possibility of experience, or of language and thought. But, Wittgenstein replied, these were nothing but houses of cards; what philosophy does is to dispel illusion. Not only can there be no theses or theories in philosophy, there can be no explanations either (PI §126). This seems to imply that all philosophy can do is to describe the use of words in order to cure philosophical illnesses. But that would be misleading.

(i) The descriptive method of philosophy is accompanied by extensive *argument*, which demonstrates, from case to case, how the errors we commit in our philosophical reasoning lead from the high roads of good sense to the marshlands of contradiction and incoherence. 'Philosophizing is: rejecting false arguments' (BT 409).

(ii) The results of philosophy are not, or not merely, descriptions of the use of words; that is the primary (but not the only) *method* of philosophy. The results of philosophy are clarity and an articulate understanding of conceptual connections.

(iii) There can be no pathology of the intellect without a corresponding physiology. The physiology is given by the perspicuous representation of the grammar of philosophically problematic expressions. When we attain such a perspicuous representation – which is indeed a description (or, perhaps more happily, a statement) *and arrangement* of familiar rules for the use of expressions – we know our way around in the bewildering network of our grammar or, if one prefers a more august description, of our conceptual scheme – which amounts to the same thing. We have a 'map', which will help us find our way (although, of course, we must know how to read it). This is a positive achievement.

(iv) It is true that the depth traditionally associated with philosophy is an illusion. The supposition of such depth rests on the misguided assumption that philosophy aims to penetrate to the language-independent nature of all things, to uncover 'the basis, or essence, of everything empirical' (PI §89), to disclose not the physical but the metaphysical structure of the world. But although that is chimerical, the illusion of such a possibility is itself anything but trivial. The philosophical problems arising from the misinterpretation of our forms of language 'are deep disquietudes; their roots are as deep in us as the forms of our language, and their significance is as great as the importance of our language' (PI §111). The depth and impressiveness of the metaphysical vision now retreat to the illusions (PI §110). Eradicating these illusions involves digging down to the sources of our most deeply embedded habits of thought (BT 423).

(v) Although the quest for the language-independent essences of things rested upon deep misconceptions, what is genuinely intelligible about philosophical questions concerning the *nature* of thought, imagination and so on is in fact answered fully by descriptions (surveyable representations) of the uses of the relevant expressions and of their place within the network of related concepts. 'One ought to ask, not what images are or what happens when one imagines anything, but how the word "imagination" is used. But that does not mean that I want to talk only about words. For the question as to the nature of the imagination is as much about the word "imagination" as my question is. . . . The first question also asks for a word to be explained; but it makes us expect a wrong kind of answer' (PI §370). The connective analysis, or elucidation, which complements therapeutic analysis therefore leads to the understanding which philosophers have characteristically craved, even though they were typically unclear about their own questions and the methods of resolving them.

(vi) Although 'explanation' is 'on the Index' in philosophy, its exclusion does not preclude, but invites, elucidation and clarification. The contention that there are no explanations in philosophy is on a par with the claim that there are no theories. Wittgenstein took science as the paradigm of theory construction. Scientific theories enable the prediction of events and the hypothetico-deductive explanation of phenomena. They often involve idealization (as in mechanics); they are testable in experience; they may be falsified by the discovery of new phenomena. They may involve successive approximations to the truth, making possible progress in the understanding of the phenomena. But idealization in philosophy, unless it is for the purpose of constructing an object for comparison, is distortion, replacing our concepts, which give rise to philosophical puzzlement, by different concepts. This ensures that we shall not get to the bottom of the trouble which afflicts our understanding, for the trouble is rooted in our lack of a perspicuous representation of the concepts we have, not of different concepts that we might have. Philosophy can make no claims that are testable in experience or subject to falsification by the discovery of new facts. New facts may lead to the formation of new scientific theories, which may in turn involve new conceptual articulations which give rise to philosophical puzzlement (e.g. in quantum mechanics); that is grist for the philosopher's mill, not a verification or falsification of anything he may legitimately assert. Scientific theory may yield predictions which approximate the truth, but philosophy makes no predictions, and, in so far as philosophy characterizes the bounds of sense, mere approximation to sense is one form or another of nonsense. If the paradigm of theory is scientific theory, then there are no theories in philosophy. If the paradigm of explanation is scientific explanation, then there are no explanations in philosophy either. Every explanation, in this sense, is a hypothesis (GB 123). But there are no hypotheses in philosophy: if philosophy is a conceptual investigation, then there can be nothing hypothetical about it. It cannot be a *hypothesis* of mine that I am using a word to mean such-and-such. There cannot be any hypothetical rules for the use of expressions of a language. An anthropologist may hypothesize that the activity he is observing is conducted according to such-and-such rules, but the qualified participants in the activity are the authorities on the rules they follow (though not on their best codification). In this sense of 'explanation', Wittgenstein offers us no explanations.

Nevertheless, there are forms of explanation other than scientific, hypothetico-deductive explanation. The danger against which Wittgenstein warned is the use of the word 'explanation' in logic (philosophy) in a sense that is derived from physics (BT 418). The fatal thing about the scientific way of thinking, which the whole world employs nowadays, he remarked, is that it wants to produce an explanation in answer to each anxiety. But 'explanation' in aesthetics (if we are to continue to use this expression, as Wittgenstein sometimes did (LA 18)), is typically quite different in kind.[20] So is explanation of myth and ritual.[21] Indeed, so is explanation of human action by reference to reasons and motives. In a perfectly legitimate sense of 'explanation' (i.e. to render something intelligible), Wittgenstein explained in rich detail the manifold confusions and illusions of philosophers in the domains in which he was interested. *This* kind of explanation we might characterize as 'explanation by description' (see Volume 1, 'The nature of philosophy').

Can there be any progress in philosophy? If the model of progress is the advance of science over the last four centuries, the accumulation of knowledge and the construction of hierarchies of theories, then the answer is clearly negative. But perspicuous representations of the grammar of philosophically problematic expressions can be achieved. Expressions that belong together can be correctly located together, and expressions that only appear to belong together can be rightly separated (cf. BB 44f.). The former may have to be relocated together in the face of new problems and difficulties, which cannot be anticipated in advance; but the realization of conceptual affinities and differences is a definite achievement (though not a cure-all). One can construct a map of the conceptual terrain, but one cannot foresee future earthquakes and redrawings of administrative boundaries. One cannot anticipate all future sources of conceptual confusion (as one could not foresee, e.g. the invention of computers, which was to exercise a mesmerizing force upon psychologists, neurophysiologists and philosophers, or the invention of the powerful predicate calculus, which was to bewitch philosophers for the best part of a century). One cannot anticipate the future diseases of the intellect which will infect mankind. One can only provide the means and methods for their cure. The application of those methods to fresh infections is a matter which each generation must handle for itself. 'But in that case we never get to the end of our work! – Of course not, for it has no end' (Z §447).

Philosophical theories in the central domains which Wittgenstein investigated[22] are not so much false as nonsense. In attempting to plot the bounds of sense, they transgress them. In trying to delineate conceptual necessities, which are wrongly conceived to be derived from the metaphysical nature of things or the essential nature of the mind or the transcendental conditions of the possibility of experience, such theories typically generate 'conceptual impossibilities' – that is, nonsense. For 'conceptual necessities' are reflections of (or disguised statements of) arbitrary rules of grammar, which are not answerable to any reality for their correctness (but at most for their utility). And a misstatement of a grammatical proposition (a rule for the use of its constituent expressions in the guise of a description) is not a false grammatical rule, but a nonsense (see below and Volume 2, 'Grammar and necessity', §3; Volume 4, 'The arbitrariness of grammar and the bounds of sense'). Philosophical theories are not so much mistakes (the negation of which is a truth) as superstitions or myths. They cannot be combatted by denying them, let alone by defending their denial with argument (for the negation of a nonsense is a nonsense), but only by delving into the sources of confusion and demonstrating the confusions by argument.

The primary source of philosophical confusion and superstition is language itself. So we must struggle against the bewitchment of our understanding by means of language (PI §109), against grammatical illusions, and against the misinterpretation of our forms of language. This applies to the technical language of mathematicians, physicists and psychologists no less than to ordinary language. Forms of questions misleadingly suggest forms of answers: 'What is (an) X?' demands an answer of the form '(An) X is a . . .'. Such forms of answer are appropriate for many kinds of stuffs and substances, but not – or not usefully – for questions concerning intentions, desires, beliefs, numbers and so forth. Forms of expression suggest, because they often have, certain stock kinds of interpretation: the verb form linked to the designation of a person suggests that an act or activity is signified, but this is often deceptive, as in the case of wanting, intending or meaning something. Substantives suggest a correlative substance, but in the case of 'proposition', 'number', 'thought', this leads philosophers to think that such expressions signify 'abstract objects', which, as Frege held, are just like concrete objects, only neither material nor spatio-temporal. But to say that an expression signifies an abstract object is just to say that, being a substantive, it has the grammatical appearance of a name of a concrete object, but is not such. In the case of the word 'mind', philosophers (and others) have been inclined to take it for granted that it designates some thing – perhaps an immaterial substance or, if not an immaterial substance, then a physical one, such as the brain. Adjectives deceptively suggest that they signify qualities, as colour-adjectives do (*pace* representational metaphysicians); but this is altogether misleading when it comes to such adjectives as 'good' (which Moore famously held to signify a simple, indefinable, non-natural quality) or 'real'. In all such cases, we are led to assimilate dissimilar concepts, to ask questions appropriate to one concept but wholly misleading to another. We are unaware of the prodigious diversity of our concepts, for it is concealed by the limited range of grammatical forms in our language, and can be brought into view only when we are reminded of the differences in the use of grammatically similar forms. We generate philosophical bafflement when we transpose a concept from one domain to another, unwittingly assuming that the logical connections which hold in the one domain will hold in the other too (as if the queen in draughts must be just like the queen in chess – after all, it has the same name, and is placed on the same board!). So logicists, such as Frege and Russell, assume that the concept of 1:1 correlation does not change when it is transposed from the domain of finite sets to the infinite domain of numbers, and philosophers of mind assume that the transposition of the concepts of act, activity, process, event, object, state and so on from the physical domain to the mental involves no shift in meaning (see Volume 4, 'Methodology in philosophical psychology', §§3 and 5).

The philosophically misleading features of language are not the only source of problems in philosophy. We are prone to become mesmerized by paradigms, and to seek to assimilate disparate phenomena to our favoured paradigm. Explanation of word-meaning by an analytic definition has obsessed philosophers from Plato onwards, and they have wrongly viewed other forms of explanation as defective – mere provisional expedients until an appropriate analytic definition is *discovered*. Hence Frege thought it a scandal to mathematics that a sharp definition even of 'one' was unavailable, and came up with a hitherto undreamt-of definition which supposedly fixed once and for all what the number-word 'one' means – as if mankind had been using the word since time immemorial without knowing what it meant. So mesmerized are philosophers with a paradigm of knowledge as resting on secure foundations, that Descartes thought he needed to prove an indubitable existential truth (viz. that he existed) before he could go on to reconstruct human knowledge in general on firm foundations, and Kant thought it a scandal to philosophy that no proof of the existence of the external world had yet been found. But we should question whether it even makes sense to prove what they purported to prove, whether it makes sense to talk of knowing what they thought they had proved, and, indeed, whether everything that we can be said to know must rest on solid foundations of proof or evidence. For that is not how the word 'know' is used.

In philosophical reflection we are prone to be captivated by pictures – of the mind as a private space, of thinking as a process in the mind or head, of remembering as a process of reading the past off a stored picture, of the 'inner' and the 'outer', of numbers as abstract entities existing in a non-spatial, timeless realm, of language as linked to reality by its 'indefinables', and so forth. The roots of such pictures are manifold; some grow from otherwise harmless metaphors and figures of speech, some from phenomenological features, while others spring from analogies. These pictures come naturally to us; it is no coincidence that the *Investigations* opens with the quotation from St Augustine's autobiography, for Augustine's picture of language is an altogether natural one. But what is natural in philosophy is to err, and the task of the philosophical therapist is to disclose the sources of such pictures and to show how we are led into confusion by them.

It is characteristic of philosophers to strive for the most general characterizations they can attain, and nowhere was that tendency more strikingly instantiated than in the *Tractatus*. Nevertheless, the craving for generality is a source of philosophical confusions (BB 17–20). For, in pursuit of this ideal, we are prone to generalize a striking or favoured case to *all* cases. Hence it had seemed natural to Wittgenstein to extrapolate from simple cases, in which a proposition seems comparable to a picture, to all cases: 'If *one* proposition is a picture, then every proposition must be a picture, because they must all share a common essence' (TS 220, 92). We are inclined to think that to understand a general term is to grasp the common characteristics of *everything* that falls under it, failing to see that many general terms are not used thus, that we do not always explain them by citing common characteristics of their extension, and that our explanations are not therefore defective. So it is, not only with family resemblance concepts, but also with numerous concepts of sensible qualities – for example, colour concepts.

[margin note: UNIVERSALS? ↳FAMILY RESEMBLANCE]

The success of the scientific enterprise of explaining and predicting natural phenomena has been so great, and the inclination to think of philosophy as a cognitive discipline like science (only with a different subject-matter), or even as continuous with science itself, so strong, that it is hardly surprising that philosophy should become entrapped in scientism. A great source of philosophical confusion is the temptation to think that philosophy should answer questions, construct theories and strive for explanations on the model of the sciences. But, Wittgenstein insisted, 'This tendency is the real source of metaphysics, and leads the philosopher into complete darkness' (BB 18).

Although the therapeutic conception of philosophy is counterbalanced by the conception of philosophy as a quest for a perspicuous representation, and the destructive features of Wittgenstein's later philosophy are complemented by (scattered) surviews of the grammar of problematic expressions, it is nevertheless true that philosophy, as he conceived it, has fallen from grace. It is philosophy grown to the age of disillusionment – no longer the Queen of the Sciences, with a claim to insights into the metaphysical structure of the world, the necessary structure of the mind, the foundations of mathematics or of empirical knowledge. The wonderful conclusions of so much traditional philosophy are akin to the regalia of gold encrusted with diamonds, rubies and emeralds which are to be found in magical caverns in fairy-tales. The task of philosophy now is not to discover more such treasures. It is to remove them from the magical cavern into the cold light of day, where they can be seen to be no more than rusty metal and heaps of old stones (cf. CV 11). Where philosophers once sought the map of Treasure Island in order to find such treasures, philosophers who have outgrown such tales seek only the map, knowing that the map itself is the treasure.

4. Metaphysics

Metaphysics was traditionally thought to be the jewel in the crown of philosophy, the deepest investigation into the nature of things of which we are capable, an investigation which transcends science in order to study, not the contingent features of reality, but its necessary features.[23] Hume had already mounted a fierce attack on the pretensions of metaphysics. Kant had limited metaphysics to the description of the synthetic a priori conditions for the possibility of experience. The *Tractatus* had argued that any attempt to articulate metaphysical propositions must unavoidably transgress the bounds of sense – all metaphysical assertions are nonsense. This negative claim was a guiding light for the Vienna Circle's anti-metaphysical crusade. But just as Kant had drawn the bounds of knowledge to make room for faith, so too Wittgenstein had drawn the bounds of language to make room for ineffable metaphysics, which is shown by the forms of language, but cannot be said. With the collapse of his first philosophy, he joined the repudiators of metaphysics, rejecting traditional metaphysics, the Kantian project and the ineffable metaphysics of the *Tractatus* alike.[24] The line he pursued, however, was idiosyncratic, and unparalleled in the history of philosophy. Hume's critique of metaphysics had relied upon the empiricist thesis that all ideas must be derived from experience – a confused principle at best. Kant condemned transcendent metaphysics on the grounds that it wrongly attempted to apply the categories beyond the bounds of possible experience, but took synthetic a priori truths to be descriptions of the conditions of possible experience – true of the world, but antecedent to experience and derivable from reflection alone. The Vienna Circle condemned transcendent metaphysical assertions on the grounds of their unverifiability, and held mundane necessary propositions to be analytic truths – true by virtue of the meanings of words. Wittgenstein took none of these paths. Metaphysical questions are indeed misleading, for they express an unclarity about the grammar of words (e.g. of the use of 'I', 'mind', 'space' and 'time') in the form of a scientific question (BB 35). Unsurprisingly, the typical metaphysical answer appears to specify a putative truth about the world. The only gold one can extract from such ore is in the form of rules for the use of words.[25] But most of metaphysics is dross, to be discarded as nonsense. Wittgenstein's account made it clear, as most previous critics of metaphysics had not, why metaphysical assertions – that is, assertions about the world which seem to be necessarily true – are so compelling, and what modest grammatical truths lurk behind them.[26]

Putative metaphysical assertions are often cast in modal form, characterizing what is necessarily so, what is possible or impossible. Hence it is said that what is coloured *must* be extended, that nothing *can* be red and green all over, or that one *cannot* travel back in time. Since such modal forms of sentences have empirical uses in describing, for example, causal connections or in making practical statements ('If you want to cool the room, you must open the window'), we are inclined to construe such 'metaphysical propositions' as descriptions too. Consequently, the distinction between factual and conceptual investigation is obliterated (Z §458). Of course, we are prone to think that metaphysical propositions assert connections which are not causal, but stricter, harder, more rigid – indeed, necessary ones. Such connections, Wittgenstein argued, are always connections *in grammar* (RFM 88). They are laid down in the rules for the use of the constituent expressions. For it is not the property of an object that is ever 'essential', but the mark of a concept (RFM 64). The 'necessary proposition' that red is more like orange than it is like yellow is not a description of a property of red, but a licence to describe any red object as more akin in colour to any orange object than to any yellow one. It is not a truth which *follows* from the meaning of the word 'red', but is partly constitutive of its meaning, for it is the expression of a rule for the use of that word.

The apparent certainty of such 'metaphysical' propositions is a reflection of the role which such rules fulfil in our linguistic practices, and of our determination to employ the relevant expressions in accord with these rules which are misleadingly expressed in the form of assertions about reality (cf. RFM 170). The 'necessity' which we ascribe to such 'truths' is the mark not of 'a necessary fact' (since there is no such thing), but of our commitment to these concepts, of our inflexibility in employing these expressions in accord with these rules. We would not say that something is red without also being willing to say that it is coloured; we would not grant that something is pink unless it is also granted that it is lighter than something red. The 'hardness of the logical "must"' indicates our inability or refusal to depart from a concept (RFM 238). Just as the 'inexorability' of the laws of logic is our inexorability in applying them in inferring, thinking, reasoning, so the inexorability of putative metaphysical propositions of the kind in question is our inexorability in employing the constituent concepts in accord with these rules (cf. RFM 82).

Metaphysics has traditionally been cast in the role of an investigation of essences. Physics studies the contingent properties of objects, whereas metaphysics investigates their essential properties, seemingly giving philosophy a subject-matter of its own. But this is illusion. Essence is expressed by grammar (PI §371). But in so doing, grammar is not reflecting the nature of things, but determining it – by laying down what is *to count* as such-and-such a thing. Essences are reflections of forms of representation, marks of concepts, made and not found, stipulated and not discovered. It is a discovery that water is composed of two parts hydrogen and one part oxygen. We can stipulate that nothing will count as water unless it is so constituted, thus transforming a symptom of water (an inductive correlation) into a criterion for something's being water (a defining feature); but that is not a discovery – it is a decision, which changes the concept. All talk of essences is talk of conventions, and what seems to be the depth of the essences is actually the depth of our need for the conventions (RFM 65).

'Nothing can be red and green all over' and 'Pink is lighter than red' look as if they state truths about the world, but necessary rather than contingent ones. One can disabuse oneself of this illusion by querying their role. Unlike empirical propositions, they do not exclude a possibility. For to say that it is impossible that something be both red and green all over simultaneously is not to say that a certain possibility is impossible. It is rather to say that a certain form of words does not describe a possibility, that it is excluded from our true/false language-games (see Volume 4, 'The arbitrariness of grammar and the bounds of sense'). Rather than taking such propositions to describe how things 'necessarily are', and then racking our brains over the source and nature of this necessity, we should note that their role is not descriptive at all, but normative. Apparently metaphysical propositions about colours are no more than expressions of rules – that is, grammatical propositions – for the use of colour-words. For we lay it down that *this* ↗ is red, and an object is red all over if it is this colour all over; and *this* ↗ is green, and an object is green all over if it is this colour all over; and since *this* ↗ is not called 'the same (colour)' as *this* ↗, nothing *counts* as being both red and green all over. The only import of the putative metaphysical proposition that nothing can be both red and green all over is to license the inference, in advance of experience, that if something is red all over, then it is not also green all over. The legitimacy of the inference is partly constitutive of the meanings of the colour-words, just as the inference from '~ ~ p' to 'p' is partly constitutive of the meaning of negation.

The negation of a grammatical proposition is not a grammatical proposition, but a nonsense. 'Pink is not lighter than red' is not a true or false empirical proposition. Nor is it a rule for the use of the words 'pink', 'lighter than' and 'red' in our language. Were we to adopt this as a rule, it would determine different concepts from ours, licensing different inferences. It is mischaracterized as 'a necessary false-hood'. It is a nonsense, a form of words with no role in our language. There is no such thing as something pink being darker than something red, just as there is no such thing as checkmate in draughts (see Volume 2, 'Grammar and necessity').

Modal terms in putative metaphysical propositions mask a rule for the use of words. 'You cannot travel back in time' or 'You cannot count through all the cardinal numbers' looks like 'An iron nail cannot scratch glass', but it is not. For in the latter case, one can say, 'Experience teaches that iron *doesn't* scratch glass'; but it is not experience which teaches that one cannot travel back in time, it is grammar that stipulates that there is no such thing, that nothing counts as 'travelling back-wards in time'. 'Cannot' in metaphysics is not about human frailty, but an expression of a convention for the use of words (BB 54). Like 'There is no goal in an endurance race', 'You cannot count through all the cardinal numbers' is an expression of a grammatical rule which excludes the use of the phrase 'counting through all the cardinal numbers'. It does not say that there is something we cannot do; it says that there is no such thing to do. The task of the philosopher is to destroy the outward similarity between a metaphysical proposition and an experiential one, and to show that the metaphysical one hides a grammatical rule (BB 55). So too, more generally, with assertions that things *must* be thus-and-so. When Hertz says that an irregular planetary motion *must* have its cause in the proximity of a mass, if not a visible one, then an invisible one, *he is using a norm of representation* (AWL 16). In general, necessities in the world are merely shadows cast by grammar.

The great metaphysicians of the past, including the author of the *Tractatus*, were, however, in pursuit of more exotic quarry than 'Red is a colour' and 'Nothing can be red and green all over'.[27] They aimed to reveal the true nature of reality, whether it is mental or material, whether appearances are or are not a reliable guide to it, whether we can achieve knowledge of it or not, and so forth. They typically came up with startling news: that the world is really mental or spiritual, that space and time are unreal, that the mind is a fiction, that the world consists of facts, not things, and so on. In general, Wittgenstein argued, although such metaphysicians thought that they were describing the nature of reality, they were actually confus-edly objecting to our form of representation. When the solipsist insists that only his pain is real, he is not advocating the abolition of the National Health Service; when the Absolute Idealist insists that time is unreal, he does not mean that it isn't really time for tea; and when the scientifically minded metaphysician insists that tables are not really solid, he does not mean that we should not put our teacups on them.

Such metaphysicians were typically not aware that they were in effect recom-mending no more than a change in notation. One reason for this is that many metaphysical sentences have the spurious appearance of statements of fact. In so far as Lichtenberg, in Humean reaction to Cartesianism, argued that, instead of saying

'I think', we should say 'It thinks', *for this would be a more accurate representation of the facts,* he was confused. When idealists (representational or dogmatic) insist that instead of saying 'I see a chair', we should say 'I have a visual idea (or sense-datum) of a chair', since this is all one is epistemically entitled to assert, they too are confused. For they are in effect attacking the normal form of an expression as if *the form of an expression* could be true or false, whereas it is what is asserted by an expression with a given form that can be true or false. The form of an expression cannot say something false when the proposition itself says something true (PI §402). Hence it is misguided of realists, such as Dr Johnson or G. E. Moore, to insist that, contrary to the metaphysicians, *they* think ('it' does not think 'in them') or that they do perceive material things. This is in effect merely to defend the normal form of our expression; but it is to do so under the illusion that a statement of fact is being defended. The metaphysician thought that he was producing a more correct picture of reality, a conception of the world which is true to the facts. But that is wrong. There is no such thing as justifying a *notation* or a *language* as *true to the facts*. What a notation makes possible is statements that are either true to the facts or not true to the facts. Saying 'There is a pain' is not *more accurate* than saying 'I have a pain'. The solipsist has a blurred insight, which he only imperfectly grasps: namely, that 'I have a pain' has a very different use from 'He has a pain' (PI §403). We could adopt a new notation if we wished, but a new notation cannot change the facts, only the manner of stating them (BB 57).[28]

It is noteworthy that while the metaphysician in effect recommends a different notation, he typically fails to carry through the shift of grammar consistently. If the methodological solipsist insists on saying 'There is pain' instead of 'I have a pain', and 'A behaves as *this* body (pointing at his own body) behaves when there is pain' instead of 'A is in pain', he cannot go on to say 'Only my pain is real'. For 'my pain' belongs to the same grammatical system as 'his pain', and neither belong to the notation with 'There is pain'. If the representationalist insists that instead of saying that grass is green, we should say that it looks green to the normal observer under normal observational conditions, he cannot also go on to say that grass 'is not really (in and of itself) green'. For 'is not green' belongs to the same system as 'is green' – indeed, to the system in which 'is not (in and of itself) coloured' is the same as being colourless and transparent. But only what *can* be coloured can be colourless. In the mouth of the metaphysician, the concepts of sensation, colour, solidity and so forth shift; but the claim he makes is not that a new notation would be preferable to ours – it purports to be a statement of fact. Thus construed, the metaphysician invokes our ordinary concepts of sensation, colour, solidity and so on *without a contrast,* and hence contrary to the normal meaning of the expressions (BB 46). For pain stands in contrast to absence of pain, being coloured to being colourless and transparent, being solid to being hollow (or to being penetrable without breakage or distortion, or perhaps to being porous).

Ontology was considered to be a branch of metaphysics. The metaphysician, like the scientist, was thought to be investigating what really exists, what the universe really consists of, whether one kind of entity or substance can be reduced to another, what the basic particulars in the cosmos are, and so on. Wittgenstein repudiated ontology. The determination of what there is belongs to the province of experience and science. Realists argue that universals exist. After all, if the colour red did not exist, how could we talk about it (PI §58)? If the colour brown did not exist, then to have an idea of brown would be to have an idea of nothing (PG 137)! Nominalists deny that universals exist, insisting that number-words, quality-words and abstract nouns do not stand for anything – only particulars really exist. But this is a grammatical confusion, rooted in the misconception that all words are names, which either name something or name nothing. The realist is right to insist that numbers are not numerals, that abstract nouns or adjectives of quality are not empty words. The nominalists are right to insist that there are no *objects* corresponding to numerals, abstract nouns and adjectives of quality. The moot question is what is meant by saying that universals exist or do not exist, that numbers do or do not exist. To say that red exists is no more than to say that there are red things. To say that numbers exist is not to say that numbers are just like concrete objects, only abstract; but someone who insists that there are so-and-so many primes between *m* and *n* may well have said something true, and what he has said does not mean the same as saying that there are so-and-so many numerals of a certain kind between '*m*' and '*n*'. There is no such thing as ontology as conceived by traditional metaphysicians, but there is such a thing as clarifying, from case to case, what (if anything) is meant by saying 'There are Xs' or 'X exists'.

As noted, Wittgenstein identified the philosophical tendency to ape the methods of science as 'the real source of metaphysics', which 'leads philosophers into complete darkness' (BB 18). One favoured method of science has been to reduce one phenomenon to another, to explain the behaviour of stuffs in terms of the behaviour of molecules, to explain this in terms of the behaviour of ions, and so on. Metaphysicians have tried to mimic this, to reduce material object statements to statements about sense-data, to reduce psychological statements to statements about behaviour and dispositions to behave, to reduce dispositional statements to statements about structures, and so on. This Wittgenstein thought to be misconceived: 'It can never be our job to reduce anything to anything, or to explain anything' (BB 18). Rather, 'everything is what it is, and not another thing'.[29]

Since Galileo, scientists have been prone to argue that the world, as it is independently of our perception of it, is colourless, soundless and odourless, that it consists merely of particles with primary qualities alone. As the atomic theory of matter became well established, they argued that solid objects are not really solid at all. With the development of neurophysiological psychology, scientists have argued that it is the brain which sees, or that the brain receives information from the sensory system and constructs 'maps' of objects in the visual field, or that it is the brain that thinks, remembers, believes and so forth. With the invention of computers, scientists have been prone to conceive of the mind, or the brain, or (in recent misconceived jargon) 'the mind/brain', as a biological computer, which calculates, computes and so on; or to argue that computers can – or that the next generation of computers will – think. And philosophers have been eager to incorporate such astounding news in their theories or metaphysical systems. There can be no doubt that Wittgenstein thought such claims to be deeply confused (see Volume 3, 'Men, minds and machines'). In this sense, too, science in the modern era is a great source of metaphysics.

It is ironic that many readers of the *Investigations*, including Russell, have understood it to be committed to the idea that philosophy is impotent, insulated from any relevance to the rest of intellectual life, 'at best, a slight help to lexicographers, and at worst, an idle tea-table amusement'.[30] Nothing could be further from the truth. It is true that Wittgenstein remarked that 'philosophy leaves everything as it is' (PI §124; see Exg.), but 'everything' in this context refers to the use of language; that is, it is the task of philosophy not to *reform* the grammar of our language (whether ordinary parlance or the technical language of science or mathematics), but only to lay bare the grammatical sources of conceptual confusion. But this, far from being quietist, gives philosophy, for the first time in its history, a well-founded title to criticize other disciplines, if and when they transgress the bounds of sense. Philosophy may not interfere with the mathematics of mathematicians, but it can and should 'make it possible for us to get a clear view of the state of mathematics that troubles us' (PI §125). It is the task of philosophy to examine critically the prose with which mathematicians surround their mathematics, the interpretations they put upon their 'discoveries'. That, however, will prune mathematics: 'Philosophical clarity will have the same effect on the growth of mathematics as sunlight has on the growth of potato shoots. (In a dark cellar they grow yards long.)' (PG 381).[31] So too in psychology: 'The confusion and barrenness of psychology is not to be explained by calling it a "young science":[32] its state is not comparable with that of physics, for instance, in its beginnings. (Rather with that of certain branches of mathematics. Set theory.) For in psychology there are experimental methods and *conceptual confusion*. (As in the other case conceptual confusion and methods of proof.)' (PI p. 232). The task of philosophy is not to instruct scientists about how to do their experiments, but to audit the account books of *sense*. And there is no doubt that psychologists and physicists too, no less than mathematicians, in their interpretations of their results, generate conceptual confusion and metaphysical mystery-mongering, which philosophy can and should expose.[33]

In the days of the Enlightenment, science was rightly seen as being in the forefront of the struggle against religious mystification, superstition and dogma. Today science has replaced religion as the source and authority of truth. Every source of truth must, in the nature of things, also be a source of falsehoods, against which it must itself struggle. But it may also be a source of intellectual mythology, against which it is typically powerless. One great and barely recognized source of such mythology in our age is science itself. The unmasking of scientific mythology (which is to be distinguished from scientific error) is one of the tasks of philosophy. For philosophy is not the under-labourer of the sciences, but rather their tribunal; it adjudicates not the truth of scientific theorizing, but the sense of scientific propositions. Its aim is neither to engage in nor to abjure science, but to restrain it within the bounds of sense, to curb the metaphysical impulse that is released by misinterpretations of the significance of scientific discoveries, to restrain scientists and philosophers who have been beguiled by their myth-making from metaphysical nonsense.[34]

5. Philosophy of language and the unity of the *Investigations*

Although the *Investigations* deals with a very large range of subjects – the nature of philosophy, the alleged privacy of experience, the relation between the 'inner' and the 'outer', understanding, thinking, imagining, remembering, consciousness, intentionality, inductive reasoning, intending, meaning something – it is dominated by one central theme and its ramifications: language and linguistic meaning. In this respect it is similar to the *Tractatus*, although, unlike the earlier book, the nature of logic and logical propositions plays only a minor role here. That great theme was originally to have been dealt with in the sequel to *Investigations* §189 (see Volume 2, 'Two fruits upon one tree'), but was subsequently allocated to a separate projected book the unfinished fragments of which we now have in the form of *Remarks on the Foundations of Mathematics*. It occurs in the *Investigations* only as a barely audible but recurrent refrain to the main development.

The multiplicity and diversity of subjects and the occasionally abrupt jumps from topic to topic, as well as the *Bemerkungen* style of writing, give the book the appearance of a collection of *aperçus* on a variety of sometimes related, sometimes apparently wholly independent themes. This is misleading. The book has a twofold unity, methodological and thematic. The methodological unity is obvious: the book is informed by a consistent vision of the character of philosophical problems and of the methods for dealing with them. The thematic unity is given by the concern with the nature of language and linguistic representation. The investigations of subjects in philosophical psychology are largely (though not exclusively) strategic and tactical moves within a grand strategy. Autonomous investigations of philosophical psychology were, as conjectured above, to be allocated to a separate projected book, fragments of which we have in the four volumes of *Remarks on Philosophical Psychology* and *Last Writings*.

The fact that the *Investigations* opens with the quotation from St Augustine is of primary importance. Implicit in that unselfconscious autobiographical tale, Wittgenstein found an *Urbild* (proto-picture) which constitutes the pre-philosophical roots of misconceptions about language and meaning. The Augustinian picture of language is characterized by reference to the idea that naming and describing constitute the essence of language (see above, p. 23). Philosophical theories of meaning elaborate this proto-picture in increasingly sophisticated forms (see Volume 1, 'Augustine's picture of language: *das Wesen der Sprache*', §§3–6). Reliance upon these presuppositions infects the philosophical construal of psychological concepts which inform reflection upon the nature of language and its relation to experience – namely, the concepts of thought, understanding, imagination, memory, recognition, intention and meaning something. Hence misconceptions about such words as 'pain' (conceived as the name of a 'private' psychological object), 'thinking' (conceived as the name of a mental activity), 'understanding' (as the name of a mental state), 'remembering' (as the name of an inner process), 'willing', 'intending' or 'meaning something' (as names of inner acts or events) constitute a continuous theme which reverberates throughout the *Investigations*. Similarly, the idea that the role of sentences is uniformly to describe is under constant assault. Grammatical propositions look like descriptions, but are in fact expressions of rules. 'Now I understand' is not a report of an inner event; 'I have a pain' is typically an utterance of pain, not a description or self-ascription of a private object; 'I was about to say . . .' is not the description of a recollected event of intending; 'When I said ". . .", I meant . . .' is not a description of an act which accompanied saying; and so on. The resistance to the field of force of the Augustinian picture of language is manifest from the beginning to the end of the book.

Some of the sophisticated theories which are rooted in Augustine's picture of language are examined in §§1–88, the primary focus being Frege, Russell and logical atomism. Here misconceptions about word-meaning, names and naming, about sentence-meaning and the multifarious uses of sentences, about the divisibility of every sentence into a descriptive component (the sentence-radical) and 'force-indicator', about ostensive definition and samples, about family resemblance concepts and the diversity of explanations of word-meaning, about vagueness and determinacy of sense, are assailed. The critical destructive work is counterbalanced by the constructive account. In place of the conception of language as a calculus of rules, we are offered a conception of a language as a motley of language-games. Language is indeed rule-governed – in the more or less loose manner in which games are rule-governed. Indeed, speaking a language is comparable to playing a game, and a language to a motley of language-games. The use of language is interwoven with the life and practice of language-users. Speaking a language is part of an activity, which is partly constitutive of a form of life. Training and, later, teaching underpin the mastery of a language, and these presuppose shared reactive and behavioural propensities within a linguistic community. Words are comparable to tools, and the diversity of their employment is as great as that of different tools – hence masked by conceiving of their essential function as naming. Even declarative sentences are used for endlessly diverse purposes, of which describing is only one, and non-declarative sentences are misrepresented by conceiving of them as containing a force-indicator and a descriptive, truth-value-bearing sentence-radical. Moreover, the concept of describing is itself not uniform; for describing a scene is (grammatically or logically) altogether unlike describing a dream, describing the impression something made is quite different from describing the thing that made the impression, describing what ought to be done is unlike describing what was done.

The meaning of an expression is variously characterized as (i) being, or being determined by, its use; (ii) being what is explained by an explanation of its meaning, which in turn is said to be a rule for its use; and (iii) being what is understood when an expression is understood. These three truisms are the warp upon which Wittgenstein wove his philosophy of language.

(i) The correlation between meaning and use is propounded in opposition to the notion that the meaning of an expression is an 'object' of some kind for which an expression stands. 'Realists' like the early Russell or the young Wittgenstein had identified meanings with objects in the world. 'Idealists' had conceived of the meanings of expressions as entities in the mind of the speaker – ideas or images. These misconceptions are swept away by the realization that questions about meaning are questions about the use of words in a linguistic practice. Meanings of words are neither physical nor psychological entities; nor is anything gained by supposing them to be abstract entities (senses of expressions) which mediate between words and world. For meanings are not entities of any kind. It would be wrong to *identify* the meaning of an expression with its use, since we do not generally use the expression 'the meaning of a word' in the same way as we use the expression 'the use of a word'. Not every difference in use is tantamount to a difference in meaning.[35] Our notions of concept identity and difference are not so sharp as to determine, in advance of the context and purpose of the question, every difference in use as a difference in meaning (PI §§554–7). However, every difference in meaning *is* a difference in use. Hence an investigation into the meaning of an expression is to be pursued by examining its use.

The notion of use invoked is multi-faceted. The slogan that the meaning of a word is its place in grammar (PG 59) points to the licit combinatorial possibilities of a word in grammar, to 'the multitude of familiar paths leading off in every direction' (PI §534) which connect the use of a word in a sentence with other grammatically related sentences. Although Wittgenstein does not eschew the ideas of categorial similarity and difference, he abandons the *Tractatus* conception of sharply defined categories – that is, formal concepts which are in effect variables representing the constant form of all their values. Categorial concepts (loosely construed) have a perfectly legitimate use in our language, and they are typically not sharply defined (e.g. 'object', 'event', 'state'). Concepts which we would naturally allocate to the same category (e.g. 'red' and 'black') may nevertheless display somewhat different combinatorial possibilities ('The light shone red' makes sense, but not 'The light shone black'). First-/third-person asymmetry of present-tense psychological utterances are crucial features of the use of psychological verbs, and are partly constitutive of their meaning. The uses of such sentences differ, the first-person utterance commonly being an *expression* of the inner, the third-person proposition a description. Similarly, the 'paths' that lead off from the first-person utterance differ from those characteristic of the third-person case; thus, it makes sense to ask how I know that he is in pain, but not to ask how I know that I am in pain. Tokens of the same type-sentence may be put to very different use, and accordingly have a different meaning. So 'This is red' (or 'The Prime Minister reports to the President each Friday') may be used to make a statement or to specify a rule. Whether a proposition is used to express a rule is a feature of its employment, not, or not only, of its form. Mathematical propositions do not have the typical form of rules, but they are used as rules, most importantly (though not only) as rules for the transformation of empirical propositions about magnitudes or quantities of things or stuffs, and so on, and this use can teach us their meaning. How a proposition is verified may be part of its grammar, an aspect of its meaning or use. But, of course, there are many kinds of proposition of which it makes no sense to ask for their verification (e.g. 'I have a pain', 'I'm going to London', 'The world has existed for a long time'). The rules for the use of an expression include the various forms of context dependence to which it is subject, and which affect its meaning and the meaning (or meaninglessness) of the utterances in which it occurs. Indexicality is one well-known form of such dependence, but not the only one. For various forms of contextual presupposition characterize the use of certain psychological verbs (e.g. 'recognize', 'conscious of'). Other forms of context dependence are displayed by other psychological expressions: hope or expectation is embedded in the situation from which it arises; an intention is typically bound up with human institutions and practices; independently of an antecedent context and history, the use of such expressions on a given occasion would be senseless. More generally, expressions have a meaning only in the stream of human life.

(ii) The meaning of an expression is given by an explanation of its meaning. Explanations of meaning are diverse, and none occupies a privileged position independently of purpose and context; in particular, analytic (*Merkmal*) definition is not in general an ideal compared with which other forms are inferior, and ostensive definition is not privileged in linking language to reality or in constituting the foundations of language. The role of an explanation of meaning is not to correlate a word with its meaning, since the meaning of a word is not an entity that might be correlated with something. Ostensive definition appears to effect such a correlation, but the appearance is deceptive. Ostensive explanation of a proper name points at the bearer of the name, but the bearer of the name is not a meaning.[36] To say that an expression has a meaning is not to say anything about the correlation of the word with something extra-linguistic, for every explanation of the meaning of a word explains what it means in terms of other words and symbols, and so remains within language (see Volume 4, 'The arbitrariness of grammar and the bounds of sense', §4). The role of an explanation of meaning is to give a rule for the use of the expression, a standard against which its application may be adjudged correct or incorrect.

Explanations of meaning are rules, but one must beware of subliming and hence mystifying the normative character of language and its use. Since rules cannot 'act at a distance', there can be no such thing as following (as opposed to acting in accordance with) rules with which one is unacquainted. Hence, too, there is no such thing as *discovering* the 'real rules' which give the meaning of familiar expressions. Something is a rule only if it is used as a standard of correctness by participants in the practice which it determines – there is no such thing as using something with which one is unacquainted as a standard of correctness for one's behaviour (see Volume 2, 'Rules and grammar' and 'Accord with a rule'). Explanations of meaning are far more homespun than was envisaged by philosophers mesmerized by the false ideal of analytic definitions; they include explanation by examples, by paraphrase and contrastive paraphrase, by exemplification or gesture, and so on. These need not be defective explanations accepted in default of better ones. No rule is foolproof against misinterpretation or misunderstanding. An explanation is adequate if it serves its purpose as a standard of correct use in normal circumstances (PI §87), and it is not necessary or even possible for an explanation of meaning to budget for every possible circumstance or to settle every possible doubt. Although the use of words is rule-governed, it is not *everywhere* circumscribed by rules (PI §68). Some concepts just *are* vague, and often, *pace* Frege, they suit our purposes better than if they were not. There are no rules to budget for abnormal, hitherto unthought-of, cases; or for figurative and metaphorical uses. Extensions of language into secondary uses are not determined in advance by linguistic rules. And language is none the worse for that.

(iii) The meaning of an expression is the correlate of understanding. It is what one understands or knows when one understands or knows what the expression means. Three salient misconceptions about understanding are brought to light: (a) that understanding is an inner state from which the behavioural manifestations of understanding flow; (b) that following a rule with understanding is a special mental process of being guided by the rule or of deriving the required behaviour from the rule; and (c) that sudden understanding is a special mental event. Rather, understanding is akin to an ability. Understanding a language is the mastery of a technique. That a person is following a rule does not consist in any mental events or processes that accompany his behaviour, but is manifest in the reasons he gives for acting as he has, in his appeal to the rule to justify his behaviour, in his use of the rule in evaluating behaviour as correct or incorrect, and so forth. Utterances of sudden understanding are not reports of mental events, but signals of understanding (see Volume 1, 'Understanding and ability').

Viewing explanations of meaning as rules for the use of words, the use of words in utterances as rule-following behaviour, and understanding words and utterances as mastery of a technique requires that these concepts be tightly interlocked. There is an internal relation between a rule and what counts as compliance with it, which is manifest not only in the interpretations one may give of the rule, but above all in the practice of acting in accordance with it. There is no such thing as following a rule which no one else could in principle follow, for there would then be no criterion to distinguish between following the rule and merely thinking that one was following it. Using an expression correctly is both a criterion for understanding it and a criterion for understanding its explanation. Understanding has multiple criteria. It is exhibited in the use one makes of an expression – that is, whether one uses it in accord with its explanation – and also in the explanation one offers of what it means or what one means by it, as well as in the responses one makes to others' uses of it. Absence of disagreement about what accords with a rule is part of the framework of speaking a shared language. The possibility of communication presupposes agreement not only in definitions but also in judgements, for application is a criterion of understanding, and agreement in application is a criterion of shared understanding (§§185–242).

By this point in the book, the main contour lines of Wittgenstein's philosophy of language have been drawn. It stands in dramatic contrast to philosophical theories of language rooted in the Augustinian picture, hence with traditional idealist conceptions inspired by Locke, with the realist conception which informed Russell's early philosophy and, in a different way, the *Tractatus*, as well as with Frege's conception of sense and meaning. It is equally opposed to behaviourist conceptions. It reorients reflection upon language away from the model of correlation, prizes it free from the lure of mythical mental processes of imagining or of language-independent activities of thinking. It repudiates conceptions of language as a calculus of definite rules on the model of the predicate calculus, rejecting the idea that speaking and understanding are activities of operating a calculus of such 'tacitly known' rules. Its focus is the use of language as a form of behaviour in accordance with public rules of correct use, which are visible in normative activities of teaching and explaining the meanings of expressions, correcting misuses and clarifying misunderstandings. It presents our linguistic activities as inextricably interwoven with the tapestry of human life.

It would be quite wrong, however, to suppose that at this point Wittgenstein turns away from his primary preoccupation to investigate an array of interesting, but only tangentially connected, topics in philosophy of mind. Almost all the themes in the remaining half of Part I are integrally connected with the central theme of the nature of language and meaning, and with the baneful effect of the Augustinian conception of meaning. It is worth trying to make this clear before moving on to delineate his innovations in philosophical psychology.

The private language arguments (§§243–315) are motivated primarily by the need to eradicate a fundamental misconception which has dogged philosophy for centuries: namely, that language has its foundations in subjective experience. To many philosophers and linguists it had seemed altogether natural to suppose that words acquire meaning by being associated with ideas in the mind of the speaker, and that communication consists in uttering words that will generate the same ideas in the mind of the hearer as obtain in the mind of the speaker (hence the use of language is conceived to be a kind of telementation). Many were aware that this raised the ghost of scepticism about communication – for how could one know that the ideas bound up with, say, the word 'red' in the mind of the speaker are the same as those associated with that word in the mind of the hearer? Various questionable explanations were ventured to lay that spectre. It was characteristic of Wittgenstein's genius to question the intelligibility of this conception of language, not because such a private language could not be understood by others, but rather because it could not be understood even by its speaker. The confusion about the foundations of language in subjective experience is bound up with further ramifying misconceptions about the logical character of experience, which has typically been conceived to be 'privately owned' and epistemically 'private'. That, in turn, is interwoven with a distorted conception of the relation between the inner and the outer, the mental and behaviour.

The subsequent examination of the concept of thinking is motivated primarily by the fact that we are prone to misconstrue thought as antecedent to and independent of its linguistic expression, as if language were necessary only for the purposes of communicating one's thoughts, and as if it were thought which endows language with 'life', rendering dead signs significant. But the possibility and limits of thought are determined by the possibility and limits of its expression. Speech is not a *translation* of language-independent thoughts. Only one who has mastered the techniques of language can have thoughts, the only expression of which is linguistic. What gives 'life' to language is its use in the practices of living beings. Imagining is investigated primarily because of the venerable temptation to conceive of the meaning of an expression to be, or to be determined by, the images that accompany or may accompany its use. But associated mental imagery is neither necessary nor sufficient for a word to have a meaning. Intentionality is examined in order to elucidate how it is possible for words to refer to or be about things, how propositions can describe reality, how they can be false yet meaningful. Negatively, it is meant to undermine the idea that there is an extra-linguistic nexus between a proposition and the fact that makes it true, between desire and its satisfaction, or between expectation and its fulfilment. The *Tractatus* picture theory had rightly apprehended that these relations are internal, but had postulated a metaphysical pre-established harmony between language and reality in order to account for it. Russell had tried to explain these relations in empiricist terms, but at the cost of transforming an internal relation into an external one. Wittgenstein now elucidates the intentionality of thought and language in intra-linguistic terms. Expectation and its fulfilment make contact *in language*, in the grammatical relation between the expressions 'the expectation that p' and 'the expectation that is fulfilled by the event that p' (see above, p. 79). This resolution of the problems and puzzles of intentionality leads naturally to the investigation of the autonomy of grammar: grammar is not answerable to reality for its correctness. It determines the limits of what is logically possible, by laying down what makes sense (see Volume 4, 'Intentionality' and 'The arbitrariness of grammar and the bounds of sense').

The final topics tackled in the book all lie in the domain of psychological concepts (§§571–693). But again, the primary motivation stems from misconceptions about language and linguistic meaning. The concepts of expecting, recognizing, believing are all distorted when they are allowed, unreflectively, to lie in the force field of one or other variant of the Augustinian picture of language. For then *expressions* of expectation, recognition or belief will appear to be *descriptions* of mental states, and the question of *how one knows them to be true* will illegitimately arise. Clarity can be achieved only by careful scrutiny of the manifold uses of these expressions. The demystification of the idea of acts of will and the clarification of intending exemplify confusions which shed light on the concluding theme, the mythology of acts of meaning as forging the connection between words and world.

It would be misleading to suggest that Wittgenstein's trajectory is always linear. On the contrary, as he wrote in the preface, the nature of the investigation compelled him to travel over a wide field of thought criss-cross in every direction, approaching the same or similar points afresh from different directions. It is also true that at some junctures he pursues paths that veer away from his central themes, or follows misleading routes until it is evident that they are dead ends, or moves on to parallel tracks in order to illuminate the main route by way of similarities and differences. Yet, the *Investigations* is anything but a haphazard collection of remarks. On the contrary, it deals with its chosen field of problems with extraordinary thoroughness and with a systematicity which, though not immediately evident, nevertheless informs almost every move that is made. The argumentative strategy of the book is an exemplary manifestation of the 'indirect approach', informed by the well-grounded belief that the received direct approaches have so muddied the tracks as to be impassable, and that a direct approach will inevitably encounter deeply rooted preconceptions and prejudices which cannot be directly assailed but only indirectly undermined.

6. Philosophical psychology

Philosophical psychology in the modern era has been dominated by the dualist paradigm and by reactive opposition to it. Dualism represented man as a conjunction of causally connected substances, the mind and the body. Side by side with the conception of the mind as an immaterial substance was a picture of the mind as an immaterial 'world' in which mental objects exist, mental events take place, mental processes go on. The histories enacted on the mental stage were thought to be accessible to the 'self' by means of introspection, conceived as 'inner sense'. On the basis of introspection, the subject was held to know how things are with him, what he is feeling, thinking, imagining and so on. Self-knowledge, thus conceived, was held to be more certain, because 'direct' and non-inferential, than knowledge of extra-mental reality. The mind was conceived to be causally connected to the body, and the subject was thought to be capable of affecting the movements of his body by means of acts of will. Human behaviour was characterized as mere 'bodily movement'. The mental states and so on of other people were thought to be inferred from their behaviour on the basis of analogy with one's own case. The body was conceived to be the 'outer', the mind 'inner'– to which the subject had direct, privileged access. The inner was represented as hidden behind the outer. This committed one to the view that predicates ascribed to human beings are, on analysis, ascribed either to their bodies or to their minds. Personal pronouns were conceived to refer either to the body ('I am six feet tall') or to the mind ('I am thinking').

This picture set the parameters of the debate for three centuries. The substantiality of the mind was disputed. Rather, the mind was conceived to be a bundle of 'perceptions', sometimes thought to be bound together only by relations between members of the bundle, sometimes by association with the brain and body of the subject. Alternatively, the mind and the mental were thought to be epiphenomenal relative to the causally efficacious mechanisms of the brain, or to be contingently identical with the brain and neural states, events and processes. With the rise of logical behaviourism, the mind was argued to be a logical construction out of behaviour and dispositions to behave. The relation of mind to body was extensively and inconclusively debated, a degree of consensus gathering in the late twentieth century around the notion of causal interaction between the mental, conceived as 'realized' in the brain, and the body. Idealist and behaviourist reduction apart, the 'inner'/'outer' picture was barely questioned. Similarly, with the exception of the behaviourists, the conception of self-knowledge was not challenged; the debate turned only on whether introspection was or was not infallible or certain. The picture of knowledge of others' mental states was likewise unquestioned, the debate turning primarily on the question of whether the inference from behaviour to inner state was analogical or an inference to the best explanation of the observable phenomena (akin to scientific inferences concerning unobservables), or whether the mental states of others were logical constructions out of their behaviour. Most strikingly, many twentieth-century materialists, vehemently repudiating the Cartesian conception of the mind as a spiritual substance, retained the fundamental logical structures attributed to psychological concepts by the dualist picture, simply substituting the brain for mental substance, grey glutinous matter for ethereal stuff.

Wittgenstein's originality manifested itself here with no less vividness than in the domains of philosophy of logic, language and mathematics. Here, too, he questioned the framework of the centuries-old debate, holding that philosophers do not place the question-marks deep enough down (cf. CV 62). What should be challenged is the inner/outer picture of the mind, the conception of the mental as a 'world' accessible to its subject by introspection, the conception of introspection as an analogue of perception, the idea that the capacity to say how things are with us is a form of knowledge, the notion that human behaviour is 'bare bodily movement', the thought that voluntary action is bodily movement caused by acts of will, the supposition that explanation of human behaviour in terms of reasons and motives is causal, and the pervasive influence of the Augustinian picture of language which inclines us to think that psychological expressions are uniformly or typically names of mental objects, states, events and processes. In the *Investigations* and in subsequent writings, Wittgenstein painstakingly dismantled the very structure of received thought about philosophical psychology, reassembling the familiar components constituted by our manifold uses of psychological expressions in a surveyable representation of the grammar of the mental and its behavioural expression.

The picture of the 'inner' and the 'outer' is not groundless. It is true that one can think something and not say what one thinks, feel something and not manifest one's feelings; and if that is so, it may well be that another will not know what one is thinking or feeling. It is also true that *sometimes* dissimulation and deceit are possible, although one should bear in mind that what is possible some of the time is not, in this case, possible all of the time. Moreover, the first-person expression of the 'inner' does not rest on the grounds characteristic of third-person ascriptions of the 'inner'. Nevertheless, the picture is fundamentally misleading. When someone falls and screams in pain, his pain is not hidden behind his behaviour, but manifest in it; when someone says what he thinks, his thoughts are not concealed behind his words (unless he is lying), but expressed in them; when someone smiles in amusement or friendship, his amusement or friendliness is not veiled from sight, but exhibited in full view. 'We must get clear about how the metaphor of revealing (outside and inside) is actually applied by us; otherwise we shall be tempted to look for an inside behind that which in our metaphor is the inside' (LPE 280). When someone confesses his thoughts, one cannot say that one *directly* apprehends only his words or that he still keeps his thoughts to himself. Although one may not exhibit a twinge of pain, it does not follow that the pain is *in* one's mind, hidden from view; and when one blushes in shame, the shame is revealed, not concealed, by the blush. The 'inner' does not stand *behind* the 'outer', it *infuses* it – unless one is pretending (see Volume 3, 'The inner and the outer').

Concepts of the mental are not names of entities which are directly observable only by the subject, and expressions of the inner are not descriptions of something visible only *in foro interno*. The idea that they are has multiple roots, including the Augustinian picture of language. If one thinks of words as names, one will be prone to think of psychological expressions as names of psychological objects, events, processes or states. That thought drags in its wake the notion that the meaning of such expressions is fixed for each person by association or private ostensive definition. The centre-piece of the private language arguments (PI §§243–315) is the demonstration of the incoherence of the idea of private ostensive definition. Associating a name with a *nominatum* does not suffice to endow a sign with a use. There is no private analogue of public ostensive definition. For sensations cannot fulfil the role of samples. Concentrating one's attention upon one's sensation is not a form of pointing. The recollection of a sensation cannot function as an object of comparison for the application of a sensation-word. There is no such thing as applying an expression in accordance with a rule which is in principle incommunicable to anyone else (see Volume 3, 'Private ostensive definition').

It is equally erroneous to suppose that characteristic first-person, present-tense psychological utterances are descriptions of objects and events on a private stage. Rather, they are typically expressions or manifestations, rather than descriptions, of the 'inner'. They are characteristically groundlessly asserted, as a cry of pain, a giggle of amusement, or a sigh of relief rests on no evidence. Sometimes they are learnt as linguistic extensions of natural expressive behaviour, as one learns to say 'It hurts' and later 'I have a pain' instead of groaning in pain. Sometimes the peg upon which they hang is incipient behaviour, as when one learns to say 'I intend . . .' before acting, or 'I want . . .' instead of trying to get. First-person uses of epistemic verbs do not function to describe mental states or processes, but to indicate the reliability of the information they introduce, to indicate how one came by it, or to suggest the degree of one's confidence in it, and so on. Introspection is not typically the source of one's knowledge that things are thus-and-so with one; indeed, introspection is not an analogue of sense perception at all, and the ability to say how things are with one, to say what one thinks or believes, that one wants a drink or hopes for a good dinner, whether one is in pain, whether one hears or sees such-and-such, is misrepresented as a form of self-knowledge. There is such a thing as introspection, but it is not a form of inner perception. Rather, it is largely a matter of recollection, imagination and reflection in which one engages when one probes one's motives or examines one's emotional attitudes and dispositions.

Far from the inner being a paradigmatic field of certain empirical knowledge possessed by the subject, which is better known than, and provides the foundation for, all other kinds of empirical knowledge, first-person, present-tense psychological utterances are not normally expressions of knowledge at all. It is misleading to suggest that when one is in pain, one knows that one is; the truth of the matter is that it makes no sense to be ignorant here or to doubt or wonder whether one is. One's expression or manifestation of intention, of expectation, of anger or fear, of an opinion or supposition, has no evidential grounds, is not based on observation, and involves no recognition or identification. It is true that in such cases it makes no sense for one to doubt, be uncertain or ignorant, save where indecision is in question. But it does not follow that one knows, is well informed about, has verified or is certain about anything. Rather, when one is in pain, is feeling cheerful, is thirsty and so forth, it makes no sense to doubt whether one is. But by the same token, it makes no sense to be certain that one is either. It makes no sense to suppose that one might be in pain but be ignorant of the fact that one is; and, by the same token, it makes no sense to suppose that one might be in pain and know that one is. Ignorance, doubt, mistake, misidentification, misrecognition are ruled out by grammar – we have no use for such forms of words as 'I may be in pain or I may not – I am not sure, I must find out', 'I thought I was in pain, but I was mistaken', or 'Either I intend to *V* or I do not, but I wonder which it is'. But for precisely this reason, knowledge, certainty, identification, recognition are ruled out too (see Volume 3, 'Avowals and descriptions'). We misconstrue the concept of self-knowledge if we suppose it to consist in the ability to say truthfully that one is in pain, wants a drink, feels tired. Far from the subject having uniquely reliable self-knowledge *stricto sensu*, others often know the person much better than he does himself, understand his motives, emotional reactions and character, the suppressed hopes, longings and fears that inform his responses to the circumstances of life. Self-knowledge does not come automatically with one's aches and pains, hopes and desires; it is a hard-won prize which few achieve to any significant depth.

The mind is not a substance, neither an ethereal one nor a grey glutinous one. Nor is it a 'space' in which mental objects, events, processes and states are disclosed to introspective vision. The third-person pronoun refers neither to a mind nor to a body, but to a living human being – a person. The first-person pronoun, however, functions quite differently from paradigmatic referring expressions. Here reference failure, misidentification, misrecognition or indeterminacy of reference have no place. In using the first-person pronoun, one is not typically singling out a person. When I groan 'I am in pain', exclaim 'I'm tired', or snarl 'I'm furious', I am not selecting or picking out one person from among others. When I say 'I think N.N. did it' or 'I believe N.N. went home', the person singled out is N.N., not *me* (I do the pointing, but what I point *at* is not me). When I say 'I am six foot tall', I am, of course *talking about* myself, but not usually singling myself out from among others (though that is possible in certain circumstances). I single myself out from among others when I confess, volunteer or admit that I, rather than others, have done or will do something. But here one would *not* say that one was referring to oneself or speaking about oneself. One might say that 'I' is a degenerate, limiting case of a referring expression, as a tautology is a degenerate case of a proposition (PI §§404–11; see Volume 3, 'I and myself').

Psychological predicates are not predicable of the body or its parts; it makes no sense to say that the brain thinks, remembers, sees, hears or feels pain. Nor are they predicable of the mind, save metonymically. It is the living being who thinks or acts precipitously without thought, feels or is untouched by emotion, perceives or fails to notice, and desires or is indifferent to something; and the grounds for ascribing such things to a living being are the behaviour of such a being in appropriate circumstances (PI §281). Hence, too, it makes *no sense* to ascribe thought or thoughtlessness, understanding, misunderstanding or failure to understand to machines. Philosophers and scientists who think that it does make sense to attribute cognitive functions to computers do so, *inter alia*, because of misconceptions about the nature of the agency presupposed by such attributions (viz. they fail to see that it makes sense to ascribe thought only to a being that also exhibits sentience, affections and will) and misconceptions about behaviour. Like Turing, they fail to apprehend that flashing inscriptions on to a screen is not a form of behaviour which could be a ground for ascribing thought to a being; at most, it might be the *consequences* of such behaviour (e.g. if a human being is typing the message into the computer). Thought is essentially bound up with the sentient, affective and conative functions of a being that has a good (welfare and ill fare), is capable of desiring and suffering, can set itself goals and pursue them, and hope to succeed or fear to fail in the pursuit of its purposes (see Volume 3, 'Men, minds and machines').

Similarly, the pervasive conception of behaviour that has informed philosophical psychology for the last three centuries has misrepresented human behaviour as 'bare bodily movement', from which it is supposed we infer, by analogy or inference to the best explanation, the inner state and so on from which the behaviour might be thought to arise. This is a distortion comparable to the idea that we do not see objects in our environment, but only shapes and patches of colour, from which we must infer the presence of chairs and tables; or the idea that what we hear when we hear human speech is mere noises, which we must then interpret as significant words and utterances. But we *see* the pain in a person's face, hear the glee in his chortles, perceive the affection in the looks and gestures of lovers. We discern the amused, sarcastic, ironic or cruel smile, and do not *infer* the amusement, sarcasm, irony or cruelty from minute movements of facial muscles which we could not even describe. It is wrong to claim that we do not see people *acting*, but only their bare bodily movement, which we then *interpret* as action. We see and hear others scolding or praising, asking questions and answering them; we see them act intentionally, in pursuit of patent goals, engaged in rule-governed behaviour – stopping at traffic lights, checkmating their opponent, signing cheques or contracts, scoring goals, buying and selling goods, and so on and so forth in the myriad actions of such social creatures as ourselves. Our judgements about the thoughts, feelings and intentions of others rest on their behaviour, which constitutes, in appropriate circumstances, the criteria for such ascriptions. But the behaviour that constitutes such criteria is not 'bare bodily movement', and is not typically describable save in terms of the rich vocabulary of the 'inner' (see Volume 3, 'Behaviour and behaviourism', §4).

Human action is misrepresented as movement caused by acts of will. There are such things as acts of will, but they are not causal antecedents of action. There is such a thing as will-power, but will-power is not the psychic analogue of muscle power. And it is a fiction that all voluntary action manifests will-power or involves an act of will. What characterize voluntary action are not any psychological, causal antecedents which initiate bodily movements. 'Wanting' (or 'willing') is neither the name of a mental phenomenon that happens within one, nor the name of a mental act one performs. 'He *V*'d because he wanted to' does not explain his action by reference to an antecedent mental event. Voluntary action is action for which it makes sense to ask the agent's reasons for acting; but reasons are not causes, nor is explanation of action in terms of an agent's reasons a species of causal, nomic explanation. Though not all voluntary actions are intentional, intentional actions are characteristically voluntary (exceptions being cases of duress and of being obliged by circumstances). Voluntary actions are actions which, in appropriate settings, one can decide to perform, try to execute, or be ordered to do. They are typically marked by one's lack of surprise, and one can be held responsible for them (see Volume 4, 'Willing and the nature of voluntary action').

The history of philosophical psychology exemplifies again and again a tendency to mystify the mental, to project the entanglement of concepts which occurs in philosophical reflection on to the mind, and then to conclude that the mind just is very mysterious. The mind appears to be a queer kind of medium, and we imagine that the mechanism of the mind, the nature of which, it seems, we don't quite understand, can bring about effects which no material mechanism could (BB 3). In our confusion we are inclined to find the nature of consciousness baffling, to declare it an unfathomable mystery that the phenomena of consciousness can 'emerge' from mere matter. Similarly, being puzzled by the intentionality of language, we are inclined to try to explain it by reference to the 'intrinsic intentionality' of the mental, that being taken to be a brute datum which is beyond the powers of the human mind to explain. This is mere illusion. One could characterize Wittgenstein's philosophy of psychology as informed by the slogan 'There are no mysteries'. The appearance of mystery is the product of our own misunderstanding and disposition to mystify. The task of philosophy is not to explain what seems inexplicable, but to demystify, to show that what appeared to demand a theoretical explanation was in fact a misunderstanding, which can be laid to rest by a description of the use (and misuse) of the relevant psychological expressions.

The *Philosophical Investigations* ploughed up the fields of philosophical thought afresh. On virtually every subject with which Wittgenstein engaged, he broke new ground. He was characteristically pessimistic about the impact of his work, writing in the preface that 'It is not impossible that it should fall to the lot of this work, in its poverty and in the darkness of this time, to bring light into one brain or another – but, of course, it is not likely'. Towards the end of his life he remarked to a friend, 'My type of thinking is not wanted in this present age, I have to swim so strongly against the tide. Perhaps in a hundred years people will really want what I am writing.'[37] His pessimism was in part justified, in part not. The *Investigations* was immediately hailed as a work of genius. It stimulated a flood of writing as philosophers struggled to come to grips with its ideas. It had a very great impact on analytical philosophy for the next quarter of a century. It put new themes on the philosophical agenda, and revitalized old ones. For a while, at least, it held a variety of philosophical diseases at bay – until they erupted again in new, virulent forms. But it was also widely misunderstood and misinterpreted. These misinterpretations often gave rise to further philosophical theories, defended in Wittgenstein's name but inimical to his work. And, as Wittgenstein knew, his philosophy was not in tune with the spirit of the late twentieth century, with its narrow, monistic conception of understanding modelled upon scientific understanding, its craving for explanatory theories and its intoxication with scientific progress. If, for a while, the *Investigations* directed the stream of analytic philosophy into fresh channels, it is also true that twenty years later the flow had begun to lose the momentum Wittgenstein had given it, and in the 1970s and 1980s the waters became increasingly muddied with the silt of misunderstood science and misconceived scientism.

6

Wittgenstein's Impact upon Post-war Analytic Philosophy

The impact of Wittgenstein's later thought upon philosophers working within the analytic tradition was so widespread as to be unsurveyable within a reasonable compass. The concentric waves of his influence, emanating first from Cambridge and later from Oxford in particular, spread throughout the English-speaking world and the Scandinavian lands, and, much later, to the rest of the continent of Europe. The number of philosophers who wrote upon his work is legion, and the number who used his ideas in their own work is great. To give an account of even a reasonable selection of these would be a task of encyclopaedic proportions. Different waves of Wittgensteinian ideas successively broke upon philosophers. Debates about meaning and use fired the philosophical imagination for a while; the concept of a criterion was much discussed; the idea of family resemblance was seized upon and put to use in a variety of philosophical domains; the subject of 'private languages' was debated for three decades; various themes in the philosophy of mind inspired by his writings were brought on to centre-stage – for example, the relation of behaviour to the mental, the concept of a person, the analysis of intentions and intentional action, and dreaming; the explanation of action in terms of reasons and motives, and its relation to causal explanation became a central theme of philosophical controversy. And so on.

Rather than trying to survey this tangled, ramifying net, I shall, in this chapter, confine myself to a more limited task. I shall first survey the history of Wittgenstein's posthumous publications and the influence of some of his pupils, who both helped to spread and clarify his ideas and drew on them in their own philosophical work. I shall then resume the tale of philosophy at Oxford, which was broken off at the outbreak of the Second World War. The years immediately following the war saw Oxford transformed into the leading centre for analytic philosophy in the world, a position it enjoyed for a quarter of a century. This period also coincided with the zenith of Wittgenstein's influence, and nowhere was that influence more marked than in Oxford. Because the general character of analytic philosophy at Oxford during these years has been much misunderstood and distorted, I shall first try to delineate its wealth and variety, and only then outline the influence of Wittgenstein's later philosophy upon what was the main fountain-head of connective analysis in the decades following the war.

1. Publications and pupils

Wittgenstein succeeded Moore in the Professorship in Philosophy at Cambridge in 1939. With the outbreak of the war, he continued teaching in Cambridge (somewhat against his will) throughout the academic years of 1939–40 and 1940–1. Eager to be involved in the war effort, he obtained a job in autumn 1941, initially as a dispensary porter and later as a pharmacy technician, at Guy's Hospital in London. During this period he returned to Cambridge at weekends to teach, and continued to write philosophy. His notebooks from this time concern the philosophy of mathematics. In 1943 he went to Newcastle to work as a technician in a medical research project investigating wound shock, where he was too busy to write.[1] He left Newcastle in early 1944, but did not return to Cambridge until the autumn. He stayed in Swansea, where his friend Rhees was teaching, and worked on the continuation of the draft of the *Investigations*. This resulted in the 'Intermediate Version', running from §189 to §421, which replaced the mathematical continuation of the 'Proto-Philosophical Investigations' (i.e. a version of the *Remarks on the Foundations of Mathematics*, Part I) with the private language arguments and their sequel. On returning to Cambridge, he lectured for the next three years primarily on themes in the philosophy of psychology. The final sections of the *Investigations* (Part I), §§422–693, were grafted on to the 1944 'Intermediate Version' in 1945–6. His last course of lectures, in 1946–7, has since been published in the form of notes taken by three of his students, P. T. Geach, K. J. Shah and A. C. Jackson (*Wittgenstein's Lectures on Philosophical Psychology, 1946–47*). In 1947 he resigned his chair, believing himself to be doing more harm than good by his teaching, and wishing to dedicate himself to writing. Among those who attended his lectures and classes in the period 1939–47 were G. E. M. Anscombe,[2] P. T. Geach,[3] A. C. Jackson, G. Kreisel, C. Lewy, C. A. Mace, Malcolm, S. E. Toulmin,[4] and von Wright.

In the few remaining years of his life, Wittgenstein continued to work primarily on problems in the philosophy of psychology. His notes on this theme have been published as *Remarks on the Philosophy of Psychology*, volumes I and II, and *Last Writings on the Philosophy of Psychology*, volumes I and II. From this material he extracted what is now published as Part II of the *Investigations*. In addition he wrote briefly on colour (*Remarks on Colour*), and at greater length on epistemology (*On Certainty*), stimulated by conversations with Norman Malcolm on Moore's essays 'Proof of the External World' and 'Defence of Common Sense'. At his death on 29 April 1951, he left the onerous task of sifting and editing his voluminous *Nachlass* of some 30,000 pages to three literary executors, Anscombe, Rhees and von Wright, instructing them to 'publish as many of my unpublished writing as they think fit'.

Over the next forty years, the literary executors strove to fulfil his wishes. The *Investigations*, the *chef d'œuvre* of his later philosophy, was published in 1953. Strawson's penetrating review characterized the book as 'a treatment, by a philosopher of genius, of a number of intricate problems, intricately connected'.[5] Strawson later paid further tribute to Wittgenstein: 'He has an extraordinary, almost unique, power of dispelling philosophical illusion, of helping us to get a clear view of how our language, and hence our thought, *actually works*. . . . it would be hard to mention another twentieth-century philosopher who is likely to have such a profound and lasting influence.'[6] Ryle, in an obituary notice in *Analysis* in 1951 (prior to the publication of the *Investigations*), remarked on the great influence Wittgenstein had had: 'Philosophers who never met him – and few of us did meet him – can be heard talking philosophy in his tones of voice; and students who can barely spell his name now wrinkle up their noses at things which had a bad smell for him.' Ryle queried what difference Wittgenstein had made to philosophy, and responded: 'Wittgenstein has made our generation of philosophers self-conscious about philosophy itself. . . . Wittgenstein's demolition of the idea that philosophy is a sort of science has at least made us vigilant about our tools. We no longer try to use for our problems the methods of arguing which are the right ones for demonstrating theorems or establishing hypotheses. In particular we have learnt to pay deliberate attention to what can and cannot be said.'[7] In a subsequent review essay written in 1956, he elaborated:

> It comes natural to us now – as it did not thirty years ago – to differentiate logic from science much as Wittgenstein did; it comes natural to us not to class philosophers as scientists or *a fortiori* as super-scientists; it comes natural to us to think of both logic and philosophy as concerned not with any ordinary or extraordinary kinds of *things*, but with the meanings of the expressions of our thoughts and knowledge; and it is beginning to come natural to us, when we reflect about sense vs. nonsense, to take as the units of sense what is conveyed by full sentences, and not what is meant by isolated words, that is, with what is *said*, and not with what is, for example, *named*.

He added: 'I do not think that anybody could read the *Philosophical Investigations* without feeling that its author had his finger on the pulse of the activity of philosophizing.'[8] These remarks, from the last leading representative of Oxford's Golden Age of philosophy and from the primary originator of that age, attest to the impact Wittgenstein had in the main post-war centre of analytic philosophy (see §3 below). Russell, however, found the book 'completely unintelligible': 'I have not found in Wittgenstein's *Investigations* anything that seemed to me interesting and I do not understand why a whole school finds important wisdom in its pages. . . . if it is true, philosophy is, at best, a slight help to lexicographers, and at worst, an idle tea-table amusement.'[9] The reasons for Russell's bemusement and anger, which came to be shared by others, require scrutiny (see pp. 228f., 232–44).

The *Investigations* fertilized philosophical debate for the subsequent decades. The fate of the next of Wittgenstein's posthumous publications was very different. *Remarks on the Foundations of Mathematics* was published in 1956. This was a selection from Wittgenstein's writings on the philosophy of mathematics during the years 1937–44. The editors noted: 'It will perhaps later appear desirable to publish what is omitted here, or part of it. We believe, however, that it was not our business to anticipate such a demand for the publication of more extensive material' (RFM, 1st edn, p. viii). This was perhaps an unfortunate decision. The book was not well received, being met with a mixture of bafflement, incredulity and disdain. Alan Ross Anderson wrote: 'It is hard to avoid the conclusion that Wittgenstein failed to understand clearly the problems with which workers in the foundations have been concerned,' and that 'It is very doubtful whether this application of his method to questions in the foundations of mathematics will contribute substantially to his reputation as a philosopher.'[10] Michael Dummett claimed (wrongly) that 'Neither it [the book] nor any of these notebooks [from which the *Remarks* was extracted] was intended by its author as a book'.[11] Accordingly, he found it 'disappointing', claiming that 'Many of the thoughts are expressed in a manner which the author recognized as inaccurate or obscure; some passages contradict others; some are quite inconclusive; . . . other passages again, particularly those on consistency and on Gödel's theorem, are of poor quality or contain definite errors'.[12] And Paul Bernays asserted that 'Wittgenstein writes as though mathematics existed almost solely for the purposes of housekeeping', and that he restricts freedom of the mind 'through a mental asceticism for the benefit of an irrationality whose goal is quite undetermined'.[13] Part of the explanation for this almost uniformly negative reaction from philosophers of mathematics can perhaps be attributed to the fragmentary character of the *Remarks* (even though *parts* of it were highly polished). This was somewhat ameliorated by the publication of the considerably extended revised edition in 1978, although that too, regrettably, contained much that was an editorial selection from extensive manuscripts. Similarly, it was unfortunate that the *Remarks* was published before Wittgenstein's earlier writings on the philosophy of mathematics, in particular Part 2 of the *Philosophical Grammar* (and a large part of the *Philosophical Remarks*). These would perhaps have made clear the evolution of Wittgenstein's philosophy of mathematics. Since he there discusses in some detail such issues as Cantorean transfinite number theory and the continuum problem, Skolem's recursion proof and Hilbert's attempts to construct a consistency proof, it might also have alleviated fears that he thought that mathematics existed only for housekeeping or that he lacked technical competence. It might also have led his critics to reflect carefully on *why* he restricted his later writings on the philosophy of mathematics, of which the *Remarks* is representative, largely to problems that arise within elementary arithmetic.[14] However, the main reason for the adverse reception was arguably the radical – indeed, revolutionary – character of his thought in this domain. A rough outline of his equally radical views in more central areas of philosophy had long been in circulation in the form of typescripts of *The Blue and Brown Books*, lecture notes taken by his pupils, and the writings of his ex-pupils and followers, such as Ambrose, Black, Malcolm, Paul, Waismann and Wisdom, who had done their best to recount his views and to build on them. There had been no comparable 'preview' of his work in the philosophy of mathematics,[15] and the novelty and radical nature of his conception proved too great to be assimilated or indeed usefully discussed. Despite considerable efforts to clarify his ideas and reopen the debate,[16] Wittgenstein's philosophy of mathematics remains the least appreciated and, I venture to say, the most extensively misunderstood part of his philosophy.

  The Blue and Brown Books was published in 1958. It made some features of Wittgenstein's later philosophy more accessible to the philosophical public. The *Blue Book* in particular was dictated in 1933 for the benefit of his students, and was meant to be circulated among them. Consequently, its style was more expansive, and its consecutive prose more graspable than the *Bemerkungen* mode of composition of the *Investigations*. Of the whole Wittgenstein *œuvre*, it remains in many respects the most readily intelligible introduction to his later philosophy. It also contains his most extensive treatment of the puzzles associated with solipsism and the self and of metaphysics.

The 1960s saw a steady stream of publications from the *Nachlass*. The *Notebooks 1914–16* (1961) shed invaluable light upon the *Tractatus*, and contributed to the growing efforts to fathom that obscure master-work. It also revealed just how many of the themes in the *Investigations* were, at least in part, rooted in Wittgenstein's own early work in philosophy. The two appendices ('Notes on Logic' and 'Notes Dictated to Moore') in particular are indispensable for a proper grasp of his early criticism of Frege and Russell, although it was to be many years before this was fully clarified.[17] The *Philosophische Bemerkungen* (1964, translated only in 1975) showed that the later philosophy did not emerge suddenly with Wittgenstein's return to philosophy in 1929. It made it clear that he had indeed gone through a verificationist phase, that he had briefly espoused a form of methodological solipsism, that the insolubility of the colour exclusion problem had led to the dismantling of the *Tractatus* conception of the logically independent elementary proposition, that his realization that he had been confused about ostensive definition and the 'connection between language and reality' had led him to a wholly novel conception of ostensive explanation of symbols, to the allocation of samples to the means of representation and thence to the dismantling of the bulk of the *Tractatus* metaphysics. It also provided the first glimpse of his struggles with the problems of intentionality, in which he both refuted the Russellian empiricist account (in *Analysis of Mind*) and began the task of resolving the problem of the pictoriality of the proposition (the apparent 'pre-established harmony' between language and reality) to which the picture theory of the proposition in the *Tractatus* had been an attempted, and now rejected, answer (see Volume 4, 'Intentionality'). Further light was shed upon these early developments by the publication of *Ludwig Wittgenstein und der Wiener Kreis* (1967, translated only in 1979), consisting of Waismann's shorthand notes of conversations with Wittgenstein between 1929 and 1932, and by the *Philosophische Grammatik* (1969, translated only in 1974).

The *Grammar*, however, was an unfortunate *mélange*. It consisted of a combination of parts of the 'Big Typescript', the most complete typescript (apart from the *Investigations* (Part I)) which Wittgenstein ever composed, upon which the editor superimposed two of the later revisions of the opening sections (the *Umarbeitung* and the *Zweite Umarbeitung*, or 'Grosses Format'). In addition, he excised three chapters, including the important chapter on philosophy, the longest consecutive series of Wittgenstein's remarks on the subject. The decision not to print the 'Big Typescript' as it stood was, in my opinion, misguided. Nevertheless, the *Grammar* gave an invaluable insight into the emergence of Wittgenstein's later philosophy of language around 1932–3, much of which was subsequently worked into the *Investigations*. It was here that he first firmly linked meaning, understanding and explanation, gave a comprehensive account of ostensive definition, and resolved the puzzles of intentionality, therewith definitively repudiating the picture theory of the *Tractatus* and defending the autonomy of grammar (although, again, it took some years before this was clearly realized). While these works illuminated the transitional phase of Wittgenstein's thought, the publication of *Zettel* (1967) and the 'Lectures on "Private Experience" and "Sense Data"' (1968) shed much light on the later phases of his philosophy, in particular on the manifold issues embedded in the private language arguments. The publication of his last notes, *On Certainty* (1969), revealed a fresh topic to which he had turned his hand. They constitute a fragmentary, critical examination of aspects of foundationalism in epistemology, of certainty and its justification. This volume had only a modest impact on Anglophone philosophy, but was, and continues to be, extensively debated in Germany.

By the mid-1970s, interest in Wittgenstein's work was waning. The publications of students' lecture notes, *Wittgenstein's Lectures on the Foundations of Mathematics, Cambridge, 1939* (1976), *Wittgenstein's Lectures, Cambridge 1932–35* (1979) and *Wittgenstein's Lectures, Cambridge 1930–32* (1980), were invaluable for Wittgenstein scholarship, but did nothing to stem the tide of science-emulating, theory-constructing philosophy that was displacing the connective analysis characteristic of the post-war period in Britain (and, to a lesser degree in the United States, where post-positivist philosophy was the predominant trend (see below, ch. 7)). Descriptive, or connective, philosophy of language was displaced by the quest for a theory of meaning for a natural language, which seemed an a priori complement to the theoretical, empirical linguistics pioneered by Chomsky and his followers. By the time the last four volumes on the philosophy of psychology were published (*Remarks on the Philosophy of Psychology*, volumes I and II (1980) and the *Last Writings*, volumes I and II (1982 and 1992)), philosophy of mind had undergone a sea change. Central state materialism had been followed by functionalism, which was succeeded by forms of eliminative materalism, varieties of 'cognitive science' and connectionist 'neurophilosophy' (see below, ch. 8). The methodology and the wealth of insights into philosophical psychology which are to be found in Wittgenstein's last writings were incompatible with these forms of investigation, and were brushed aside as pre-scientific 'ordinary language philosophy' and a form of 'logical behaviourism'.

The fact that Wittgenstein chose not to publish any of his later works during his lifetime meant that misinterpretations of his thought could not be rectified by him. And, over the next decades, there were misinterpretations galore. The brief discussion of a 'sentence-radical' (PI §22 and p. 11n) was thought to be a defence of a semantic theory based on the distinction between a mood operator (or 'force-indicator') and a sentence-radical, rather than a criticism of that conception. The introduction of the notion of family resemblance concepts was held to invite the invention of logics of vagueness, as if what was needed was to obtain a reliable formal representation of the logical depth structure of our language by adding a 'smudge-operator' to classical logic. The fragmentary discussion of proper names was interpreted as advocating a 'cluster theory of names'. The discussion of ostensive definition was read as a demonstration of the inferiority of ostensive definition relative to analytic definitions. The core of the private language argument was held to depend upon an untenable form of scepticism about memory, or upon tacit appeal to the verification principle, or upon a Humean 'sceptical' answer to a form of scepticism about following a rule. The account of the grammar of sensation-words was understood to be claiming that sensations cannot be named. The examination of the relation between behaviour that manifests an 'inner state' and the state it manifests was variously misunderstood: some took it to be advocating a form behaviourism or a kind of operationalism regarding the application and confirmation of psychological predications; others understood it to be defending a criterial theory of meaning. The concept of a criterion was thought to be an essential component of an anti-realist theory of meaning which was intended to replace the alleged truth-conditional semantics of the *Tractatus* with an assertion-conditions semantics. The 'logical core' of the picture theory of meaning was argued to persist in his later philosophy. And so on. That these are serious misinterpretations has been argued, from case to case, in the four volumes of *Analytical Commentary*. The clarification of these matters by various Wittgenstein scholars took years, and was dependent upon the unfortunately long-drawn-out publication of further volumes of his works. Indeed, in many cases it only became possible when microfilms (and later photocopies) of the Wittgenstein *Nachlass* were made available through Cornell University in the late 1960s. Wittgenstein scholarship gradually improved and flourished, and a clearer grasp of his philosophy has emerged over the last forty years. However, the damage inflicted by misguided accusations and misinterpretations on the practice of philosophy which builds upon his great insights was far from negligible. In some circles, Wittgenstein is still conceived of as a logical behaviourist, a crypto-verificationist, an anti-realist or, in a reprehensible sense, an 'ordinary language philosopher', and endeavours to follow his guide-lines are accordingly condemned. Some of these misinterpretations will be examined in chapter 8.

The impact of Wittgenstein's philosophy, and of philosophy done under the guidance of his work, was greatly furthered by writings and teaching of his pupils, many of whom came to occupy chairs in philosophy departments throughout the world. They transmitted to the next generation much of what they had learnt from Wittgenstein, not merely by their lectures and writings on his philosophy, but by their own creative work, which, in different ways and to different degrees, bore the hallmark of his influence. In turn, many of their pupils contributed both to the furtherance of Wittgenstein studies and to the development of what may be termed 'Wittgensteinian philosophy'. The caution given in the opening pages of this book (pp. 1–3) should be borne in mind in the sequel: influence may take many forms. It may be manifest in the understanding of a work and the furthering of that understanding, both in exposition and in construction (in the latter case, the building may take a shape wholly different from anything envisaged by the originator of the ideas constituting the foundations). It may take the form of misunderstandings, which are nevertheless influential and even fruitful in their own right. Or it may take the form of reactive criticism, which leads the critic on to paths which he would not otherwise have trodden.

   After Wittgenstein's retirement, his successor to the professorship at Cambridge was G. H. von Wright. Although he held the chair for only three and a half years before returning to Finland, his subsequent contribution to Wittgenstein scholarship and to Wittgensteinian philosophy was great. It was he who drew up the definitive list of the Wittgenstein *Nachlass*, determining the dating of, and relationship between, the numerous different manuscript volumes, notebooks, typescripts and dictations; and he who traced the complex tales of the composition of the *Tractatus* and of the *Investigations*. Together with Heikki Nyman, he edited the 'Early Version' of the *Investigations* (the 'Proto-Philosophical Investigations'), reconstructed the 'Intermediate Version', edited the final typescript, and took the first steps in tracking down the remarks in the *Investigations* and *Zettel* to their numerous manuscript sources.[18] His many essays on Wittgenstein have shed much light on his work.[19] Of all the Wittgenstein pupils whose work can be said to be significantly inspired by their teacher, von Wright is the most independent-minded. His magisterial, austere, luminous writing is wholly free of Wittgenstein's jargon and style. During his period in Cambridge he continued to work on induction, wrote on problems in the philosophy of logic, and began his lifelong work on deontic logic, which he virtually invented. Unlike the later Wittgenstein, he has made extensive use of formal logic to illuminate the conceptual structures he has investigated, especially in his work on the logic of preference, the logic of norms and the theory of action. Nevertheless, he has remarked that of the three teachers who had a formative influence upon him (Kaila, Moore and Wittgenstein), he learnt the most from Wittgenstein, who moulded his conception of philosophy, and made him 'appreciate the conceptual multiplicity of the situations with which the philosopher has to cope'.[20] However, the influence of Wittgenstein's *later* philosophy is not evident in von Wright's early writings. It was not until his great work on axiology, *The Varieties of Goodness* (1963), that one could discern a Wittgensteinian awareness of 'conceptual multiplicity' and a striving for a systematic surveyable representation of a large and complex conceptual field, even though the subject-matter was far from Wittgenstein's preoccupations.[21] The book is an exemplary case of subtle, sophisticated connective analysis, exhibiting as never before the rich, tightly woven threads of what von Wright called 'the varieties' of goodness – namely, instrumental and technical goodness, the beneficial and the useful, the goodness of faculties and organs, the hedonic, welfare and happiness, the goodness of acts, intentions and character traits, and the derivative character of ethical goodness. There is a trace of Wittgensteinian ideas in his treatment of the asymmetry between first- and third-person hedonic and eudaemonic value-judgements.

Von Wright has observed that it was not until he had worked his way independently to the neighbourhood of Wittgenstein's thinking that he could become aware of, and exploit, his influence. That influence became more evident in his extensive writings on the explanation of human action, beginning with *Explanation and Understanding* (1971).[22] These investigations were rooted in his earlier attempts to develop a logic of action in *Norm and Action* (1963), and were stimulated by Anscombe's *Intention* (1957, see below) and Charles Taylor's *The Explanation of Behaviour* (1964). Here von Wright gave an account of action and its forms of explanation in terms of intentions, reasons and motives which is recognizably a development of Wittgenstein's fragmentary work in this domain. Von Wright's conception stands in opposition to theories which explain action by reference to 'agent-causation' (a conception originating with Aristotle, whose main contemporary proponent is R. Chisholm) and theories which construe action as movement caused by wants and desires (a conception advocated by classical empiricists, most luminously and systematically by Bentham, whose main contemporary proponent is D. Davidson). Von Wright defended the autonomy of intentionalist explanation, denying that the intention in the act is separable from the behaviour in the act. His work on this subject led him to challenge the received neo-Humean accounts of causation (a challenge which he further developed in *Causality and Determinism* (1973) and 'On Causal Knowledge' (1983)), a line of argument that is in conformity with Wittgenstein's few, but instructive, notes on causation.[23] These monographs and articles contributed greatly to the criticism of the methodological monism in the philosophy of psychology and social sciences characteristic of the Vienna Circle and their contemporary heirs, and to the clarification of the logical character of the distinctive forms of explanation of human action. They also effected a rapprochement between neo-Wittgensteinian thought on these subjects and the Continental hermeneutical tradition derived from Dilthey.

In 1952, John Wisdom succeeded von Wright in Wittgenstein's erstwhile chair at Cambridge, which he held until 1969, when he accepted an appointment at the University of Oregon. His writings throughout the late 1930s and 1940s, especially his sequence of papers on 'Other Minds' (*Mind*, 1940–3), republished in a book of that name in 1952, gave philosophers who were outside the circle of Wittgenstein's pupils *some* idea of what the later Wittgenstein was doing. Admittedly, Wisdom's conception of the nature of philosophical questions and of methods of tackling them was different from Wittgenstein's (and indeed incurred Wittgenstein's wrath, apparently for what he saw as the excessive emphasis upon the analogy between philosophical treatment of conceptual problems and psychoanalysis[24]). Wisdom's characteristic, deliberate equivocations, his insistence that philosophical questions have no clear-cut answers, that philosophical understanding consists in holding a balance between competing analogies, that philosophical puzzlement is typically a manifestation of a need for a conceptual *decision*, his sympathy for metaphysical paradox and its putative insights, were arguably closer (in some respects) to the ideas which Waismann was simultaneously developing in Oxford (see pp. 163–7). Although his most important writings preceded his assumption of the chair,[25] his teaching at Cambridge perpetuated a certain 'Wittgensteinian' philosophical approach.

Wisdom was succeeded in 1970 by another of Wittgenstein's pupils, Elizabeth Anscombe, who had been at Somerville College, Oxford, since 1946, where she played a major role in transmitting Wittgenstein's ideas to Oxford. It was during her period there that she wrote her first book, *Intention* (1957), which revived interest in the analysis of intention and intentional action. She was the first to realize (and to capitalize upon the fact) that, buried among Wittgenstein's few and sometimes opaque remarks on intentions and reasons for action (see Volume 4, 'Intending', 'The will and the nature of voluntary action' and 'Inductive reasoning', §2), are a wealth of insights suggesting the futility of attempts to reduce explanation of action in terms of reasons to a form of causal, nomological explanation. In harnessing her investigations of intentions, reasons and action to the Aristotelian discussion of practical reasoning, she inaugurated a lively debate which continues to this day. Her subsequent volume, *An Introduction to Wittgenstein's Tractatus* (1959), though flawed by many misinterpretations, stimulated the growing renewal of interest in Wittgenstein's first masterpiece. Many of her numerous papers cultivated seeds scattered among Wittgenstein's writings to undermine received philosophical views and to offer constructive alternative analyses. Particularly noteworthy were her papers on sensation (especially 'The Intentionality of Sensation: A Grammatical Feature' (1965)), on the use of the first-person pronoun ('The First Person' (1975)) and on causality (in particular her Cambridge inaugural lecture 'Causality and Determination' (1971)), all of which generated extensive debate. Like von Wright, she challenged neo-Humean nomological accounts of causation, and cast doubt upon the intelligibility of received conceptions of determinism. With Anscombe's retirement in 1986, the 'Wittgenstein line' in Cambridge came to an end.

Rhees, who already before the war had left Cambridge to teach at Swansea (see

ch. 4, n. 37), contributed substantially to the transformation of the Swansea department of philosophy into a noteworthy centre for the development of Wittgensteinian
ideas, especially in the philosophy of religion (e.g. the writings of D. Z. Phillips),
ethics and psychoanalysis (see, in particular, the trilogy on Freud's thought by I.
Dilman, a pupil of Wisdom's much influenced by Rhees). He published little,[26] but
his teaching was influential. His knowledge of the Wittgenstein *Nachlass* was of
great assistance to numerous Wittgenstein scholars and translators. He retired in
1966, and left Swansea in 1970 in order to live in London, where for a while he gave
seminars together with his distinguished pupil Peter Winch. The journal *Philosophical Investigations*, edited by D. Z. Phillips together with other members of the
Swansea department, has, for the last fifteen years, provided a platform for Wittgenstein studies.

The personal transmission of Wittgenstein's, or at least of Wittgensteinian, ideas
to Oxford prior to the publication of the posthumous works owed much to Ryle,
but more to Waismann, whose work will be examined below, and Anscombe.
Stephen Toulmin and George Paul also played a role. Toulmin lectured on the
philosophy of science at Oxford from 1949 to 1955. His *The Place of Reason in Ethics*
(1950), written while he was still at Cambridge, took one of the early steps away
from the crudities of emotivism, emphasizing, against the logical positivists, the
variability of canons of reasoning in different domains of discourse, and exploring
the role of morals and moral reasoning in social life. His later *The Philosophy of
Science* (1953) similarly ventured into a subject on which Wittgenstein had not
written (save briefly in the *Tractatus*). Nevertheless, both books owe something to
his teaching. Paul came to Oxford after the war, and held a Fellowship at University College. As Ryle remarked, he did know for himself, and not merely by
hearsay, 'the philosophical voices of Wittgenstein's Cambridge'.[27] However he wrote
little, and what influence he had was by way of teaching and discussion.[28]

In the United States after the war, Black and Malcolm transformed the Cornell
philosophy department into one of the premier philosophy schools in America and
into its leading centre for Wittgenstein scholarship and the development of
Wittgensteinian philosophy. Black's *A Companion to Wittgenstein's Tractatus* (1964)
was a significant contribution to the study of that work. His numerous essays on
philosophy of language, analysis, metaphor, vagueness and induction exhibit something of Wittgenstein's influence. They were, he wrote, 'intended to show how
linguistic considerations are relevant to some philosophical problems' and 'to *use*
ideas about language' in the clarification of those problems.[29]

Malcolm, however, was, without question, the leading Wittgensteinian philosopher in the United States. His writings, renowned for their clarity and simplicity
of expression, were primarily in epistemology and philosophical psychology.
Numerous illuminating papers were devoted to the clarification of Wittgenstein's
ideas, especially upon issues pertaining to the private language arguments (e.g. 'The
Privacy of Experience' (1967)), 'Wittgenstein on the Nature of Mind' (1970), both
reprinted in his volume of essays *Thought and Knowledge* (1977). *Dreaming* (1959),
inspired by a couple of Wittgenstein's remarks (PI pp. 184 and 222), was an attempt
to show the senselessness of the Cartesian sceptical argument. He reasoned that it
is senseless to suppose that one can think or make judgements during sleep (as
opposed to dreaming that one does), hence absurd to suppose that one might judge

falsely that one was awake. The book provoked a long, vehement controversy about the criteria for dreaming, and about the relation between criteria, verification and meaning. His book *Memory and Mind* (1977), drawing heavily upon Wittgenstein's ideas, is nevertheless an original and comprehensive work on a subject upon which Wittgenstein himself had only touched *en passant*. His targets are classical empiricist imagist theories of memory (conceived as a 'storehouse of ideas') and remembering (conceived as reading the past off a present imagist 'representation') and modern causal, neurological theories, which cast a hypothesized 'engram' in a similar role to the 'stored image' of the older tradition. The book is, to my mind, the best study so far written upon this contentious theme. A similar remark could be made about his monograph *Consciousness and Causality* (1984). His biographical essay *Ludwig Wittgenstein: A Memoir* (1958) was recognized as a classic of its genre, but it was not until 1986 that he wrote a book on Wittgenstein's work. *Nothing is Hidden: Wittgenstein's Criticism of his Early Thought* examined in detail Wittgenstein's own criticisms of the *Tractatus*, and was a substantial contribution to the continuing controversy on the relationship between Wittgenstein's two major works. In his later essays he was an indefatigable critic of reductive materialism in philosophy of mind, of 'functionalism', of Chomsky's philosophical ideas (see, in particular, Malcolm's 'The Myth of Cognitive Processes and Structures' (1971)[30] and 'Wittgenstein: The Relation of Language to Instinctive Behaviour' (1981)[31]) and of the so-called cognitive scientists who emerged, under Chomsky's aegis, in the 1970s and 1980s. They seemed to Malcolm 'a new tribe of philosophic savages',[32] imbued with the scientistic spirit of the times, which he abhorred. Malcolm retired from Cornell in 1978, and emigrated to Britain. He was appointed to a Visiting Professorship at King's College, London, where he continued to teach, in what became renowned and influential graduate seminars, until his death in 1990.

Others of Wittgenstein's circle exerted a lesser, but noteworthy, influence in the United States. O. K. Bouwsma,[33] although not a pupil of Wittgenstein's, had enjoyed numerous conversations with him when Wittgenstein visited Malcolm at Cornell in 1949 and again when Bouwsma was in Oxford in 1950–1. These transformed his philosophical views. Through his teaching at the universities of Nebraska and Texas, as well as his essays (*Philosophical Essays* (1965)), he transmitted a Wittgenstein-inspired approach to philosophy to his pupils. The conception of philosophy he derived from Wittgenstein was in some respects more akin to the later work of Wisdom and Waismann than to Wittgenstein's. He denied that there are any arguments, let alone conclusive arguments, in philosophy as advocated by Wittgenstein, that there are any refutations or rectifications of mistakes, and he made much – arguably, too much – of Wittgenstein's analogy between philosophy as he practised it and psychoanalysis (see Exg. §255).[34]

Ambrose, at Smith College, together with her husband Morris Lazerowitz (who had studied with Bouwsma), was another pupil who contributed to the discussion and elucidation of Wittgenstein's ideas in the United States. Her writings upon his philosophy of mathematics, some of which are reprinted in *Essays in Analysis* (1966) and *Essays in the Unknown Wittgenstein* (1984, co-authored with Lazerowitz), were the first successful attempts to elucidate some aspects of his baffling reflections on mathematics. Her edition of *Wittgenstein's Lectures: Cambridge 1932–35* added valuable insight into the development of Wittgenstein's thought in the early to mid-1930s. Lazerowitz's numerous papers did much to clarify Wittgenstein's treatment of metaphysics and necessary truths, although he too, like Wisdom and Bouwsma, made much of the 'therapeutic' aspect of Wittgenstein's philosophy and of the psychoanalytic analogy.[35]

Other pupils exerted a lesser influence or worked in a less Wittgensteinian direction. In Britain, Geach's work in the philosophy of logic and language was undoubtedly influential, but was arguably inspired more by Frege than by Wittgenstein, and attempted, I believe misguidedly, to graft Wittgenstein's ideas on to a Fregean stock. His book *Mental Acts* (1957), on the other hand, has recognizable Wittgensteinian affinities, and provided a salutary antidote to the abstractionist theory of concept acquisition, which venerable doctrine had been advocated recently by Price (*Thinking and Experience* (1953)). Goodstein's work in the philosophy of mathematics was much influenced by Wittgenstein.[36] His only paper on Wittgenstein's philosophy of mathematics[37] reveals that, like Ambrose, and unlike most philosophers of mathematics who had reviewed the *Remarks on the Foundations of Mathematics*, he had some understanding of the character and direction of Wittgenstein's revolutionary reflections. Some of Wittgenstein's pupils repudiated or rejected altogether what he had tried to teach them (e.g. Findlay and Kreisel).

Wittgenstein considered Oxford 'an influenza area', and only once gave a talk there (to the Jowett Society in 1947). As noted in chapter 4, in the 1930s Wittgenstein's influence in Oxford was confined to Ryle and to the young Ayer's interest in the *Tractatus* and in logical positivism. A decade later, the scene was transformed (see §3 below). It is to the tale of Oxford's period of greatness in philosophy this century that we must now turn, both because the next phase in the development of analytic philosophy lay primarily there and because the fate of Wittgensteinian philosophy became interwoven with the fate of what became misleadingly known as '(Oxford) Ordinary Language Philosophy'.[38] Because of the widespread misconceptions now current about philosophy in Oxford after the war, I shall first attempt to survey the main figures and their writings, and defer discussion of the manner in which Wittgenstein's philosophy was assimilated there until the following section. For it is, unfortunately, necessary first to make clear not merely the richness of post-war philosophy in Oxford, but also its heterogeneity, a feature masked by the misleading label that was popularly affixed to it.

2. Philosophy at Oxford, 1945–70

In 1939 philosophy at Oxford was poised for a renaissance. This was delayed by the war. However, the creative abilities dammed by six years away from academia then flowed all the more powerfully when university life revived. The younger generation returned to philosophical work matured by their years at war, and post-war Oxford saw a spectacular philosophical flowering.

By 1945, Ayer later wrote, 'the philosophical climate had undergone a drastic change. It was not just that the older men had died or retired; their outlook had vanished with them.'[39] Leading members of the 'Wee Teas' (by now virtually the senior generation) and of the Berlin–Austin group, together with an influx of newly appointed fellows and lecturers, some from Wittgenstein's circle (Waismann, Paul, Anscombe, Toulmin), some of pre-war vintage (H. L. A. Hart, J. O. Urmson, Strawson), some of immediate post-war provenance (R. M. Hare, D. F. Pears, G. J. Warnock), transformed philosophy in Britain and affected the practice of philosophy throughout the English-speaking world.

Ryle, who was appointed to the Waynflete Chair in 1945 (Collingwood having died in 1943) and took over the editorship of *Mind* (1947–71) from Moore, was 'the brilliant and benevolent leader of Oxford philosophy in the post-war period. The development and flourishing of the subject here owed an immense amount to his vision and enterprise.'[40] The institution of the postgraduate B.Phil. degree in philosophy played a major role in making Oxford a great international centre for the study of philosophy, and ensured a stream, if not a flood, of graduate students from abroad, who spread the new philosophical ideas they learnt at Oxford throughout the world.[41] Ryle 'was already making, in the work that led up to *The Concept of Mind*, what was perhaps the first systematic and really large-scale application of the new philosophical style to large traditional problems'.[42] It was evident in his inaugural lecture (as, indeed, it had already been in his 1938 paper 'Categories') that he had jettisoned the remnants of the logical analysis – the investigation of the logical forms of facts – characteristic of the 1930s (see above, pp. 91f.). 'Philosophical Arguments' (1945) was, in effect, a fresh declaration of principles, replacing 'Systematically Misleading Expressions' and developing further the ideas in 'Categories'. The task of philosophy, he declared, is 'the charting of the logical powers of ideas'. In a metaphor reminiscent of the *Blue Book* (BB 57; cf. AWL 43; LFM 44), he observed that 'People often know their way about a locality while being unable to describe the distances or directions between different parts of it or between it and other familiar localities . . . Our workaday knowledge of the geography of our ideas is in similar case.'[43] Philosophical problems are generated by type-confusions (or category mistakes – a phrase he did *not* use in the lecture, but which is, as it were, omnipresent in the background). These involve misattributing to ideas or concepts logical powers which are appropriate only to ideas or concepts which belong to a different type or category. This results in absurdity and paradox. Philosophy can dissolve these paradoxes and defuse these absurdities by methodically mapping the 'logical powers' of the ideas involved, and showing how and where nonsense is generated. 'Like a geographical survey, a philosophical survey is necessarily synoptic. Philosophical problems cannot be posed or solved piecemeal' (ibid., p. 202). What has to be done is to determine the cross-bearings of all of a galaxy of ideas belonging to the same or contiguous fields. The primary tool in the activity of identifying category mistakes or type-confusions is the *reductio ad absurdum* argument. 'The discovery of the logical type to which a puzzle-generating idea belongs is the discovery of the rules governing the valid arguments in which propositions embodying that idea (or any other idea of the same type) can enter as premises or conclusions. It is also the discovery of the general reasons why specific fallacies result from misattributions of it to specific types' (pp. 204f.). This conception of the role of philosophy and of one kind of philosophical argument (Ryle did not claim that there were no others) set the stage for the methodology of *The Concept of Mind* (1949).

This book was a landmark in the history of twentieth-century philosophical psychology. Juxtaposing it with Russell's *Analysis of Mind* (1921) or James's *The Principles of Psychology* (1891) immediately reveals how far philosophy had moved in half a century, and how innovative and illuminating Ryle's work was. His target was what he called the 'Cartesian myth' of 'the ghost in the machine': namely, that a human being is a combination of a non-spatial, immaterial soul-substance and a physical body, which causally interact. The mind, according to the myth, is 'private', its owner alone enjoying privileged access to it by means of introspection, consciousness and self-consciousness. The introspectible contents of the mind enjoy an immaterial existence, and the objects, events and states that exist, occur or obtain within this private theatre are described by the nouns, verbs and adjectives with which we characterize our intellectual, affective and conative life. The Cartesian myth, Ryle argued, rested on a persistent and ramifying category mistake or series of category mistakes, representing the facts of mental life as if they belonged to one logical type or category when they actually belong to another. The logical type or category of a concept is the set of ways in which it is logically legitimate to operate with it – its logical articulations with related concepts. The myth of the ghost in the machine mistakenly construes our mental vocabulary as fulfilling a role analogous to the vocabulary with which we describe the material world, with the difference that the objects, events and states it describes are immaterial. Ryle's purpose was to explode this myth, replacing category habits by category disciplines, and plotting the logical geography of mental concepts. Further aspects of this book will be discussed below. Together with the *Investigations*, published four years later, it heralded a renaissance in philosophy of mind that lasted over a quarter of a century.

His Tarner Lectures at Cambridge, *Dilemmas* (1954), examined a series of traditional philosophical paradox-generating conflicts, such as that between antecedent truth and free action, that between the physical description of the constitution of objects and the perceptual description of the same objects, and that between the neurophysiological theory of perceptual mechanisms and the thought that we perceive objects and qualities 'outside us' (and not in our heads or minds). As in *The Concept of Mind*, though less trenchantly, the notion of a category mistake was invoked to shed light on the problems addressed. The dilemmas examined, he suggested, can be characterized by saying that 'the two sides are, at certain points, hinging their arguments upon concepts of different categories, though they suppose themselves to be hinging them upon different concepts of the same category, or vice versa'. And with his customary skill, elegance and wit, he disentangled the knots that generate the appearance of conflict and paradox. Over the following two decades he wrote a large number of important papers, on philosophy of language ('Ordinary Language' (1953), 'The Theory of Meaning' (1957), 'Use, Usage and Meaning' (1961)) and on themes in philosophy of mind ('Pleasure' (1954), 'Sensation' (1956), and, in particular, aware of deficiencies in his treatment of the subject in *The Concept of Mind*, on thinking, which was the topic of more than a dozen papers.[44]

If Ryle led the 'Revolution in Philosophy' (the title of a volume of a series of BBC broadcasts given in 1956) in Oxford, Austin guided the younger generation of 'revolutionaries' along compatible but different paths. He resumed his Fellowship at Magdalen, where he remained until appointed to the White's Chair in Moral Philosophy on Paton's retirement in 1952. By the 1950s his was the greatest influence in Oxford, partly through his famous 'Saturday Morning Meetings', the (by now) legendary classes which he organized and led for his contemporary and junior non-professorial Fellows in the sub-faculty. These were conducted for the intellectual stimulation of all concerned, to convey and apply his methods, to convince all that there was profit in getting away from the familiar moves of age-old controversies and focusing instead upon issues which careful work could settle. The results of such enquiries are, Austin held, of independent interest, and they may have the further benefit of exploding familiar dichotomies such as fact and value, appearance and reality, descriptive and evaluative utterances, sense-data and material things, which in turn might free the log-jam in traditional debates about 'central questions of philosophy'. Among those who attended his 'Saturday Mornings' over the years were Marcus Dick, Grice, Hampshire, Hare, Hart, P. H. Nowell-Smith, Paul, Pears, Strawson, Urmson, Warnock and A. D. Woozley. The subjects discussed ranged far and wide, including texts such as Aristotle's *Ethics*, Frege's *Foundations of Arithmetic* (which Austin had translated),[45] Chomsky's *Syntactic Structures* (which he much admired) and the *Philosophical Investigations*.[46] The general topics handled were equally diverse, including a term spent discussing rules of games (with an eye to questions about meaning and rules for the use of words), as preparation for which each member of the group was given a book of rules to study;[47] and aesthetics, for which an illustrated handbook of industrial design containing pronouncements on the design of humble artefacts was scrutinized in order to find out what people *actually* say in aesthetic appraisal when the topic is not too grand to inhibit good sense. Time was spent investigating dispositional concepts (in response to Ryle's extensive use of the term 'disposition' in *The Concept of Mind*), for which 'disposition', 'trait', 'propensity', 'characteristic', 'habit', 'inclination', 'susceptibility', 'tendency' and so on were carefully anatomized, compared and contrasted. Apropos Wittgenstein's comparison of words to tools, the expressions 'tool', 'instrument', 'implement', 'utensil', 'appliance', 'equipment', 'apparatus', 'gear', 'kit', 'device' and 'gimmick' were examined in patient detail (were kitchen scissors, garden shears, dress-making scissors, surgeon's scissors utensils, tools or implements?) with a view to determining the most helpful analogy.

There can be no doubt that Austin's 'Saturday Mornings' greatly influenced the participants, and through them the course of philosophy at Oxford and elsewhere. 'His Saturday morning sessions with his coevals and juniors', Ryle reminisced later, 'were soon engendering not indeed unanimities, but zeals and scruples which almost justified, if anything could justify, the invention by some non-insider of the labels "Oxford philosophy" or the "Oxford school of philosophy".'[48] To outsiders, Austin's meetings seemed indeed to be the hot-bed of what became called 'Oxford Ordinary Language Philosophy', and was derided as such. This opprobrium was misplaced. Among the Oxford philosophers who were concerned with the examination of the use of words, there were those who gravitated towards Ryle or Wittgenstein rather than towards Austin, and the differences between them were far from trivial. Even within the group there was much diversity of opinion and approach, as is evident from the subsequent writings of such figures as Grice, Strawson, Hampshire, Hart, Hare, Pears and Warnock. Grice later wrote:

> There was no 'School'; there were no dogmas which united us, in the way, for example, that an unflinching (or *almost* unflinching) opposition to abstract entities

unified and inspired what I might call the American School of Latter-day Nominalists, or that an unrelenting (or *almost* unrelenting) determination to allow significance only to what is verifiable united the School of Logical Positivism.[49]

It was sometimes thought that 'Oxford Philosophy' had a dogmatic commitment
to the avoidance of any technical terminology in philosophy. A mere glance at *How
to do Things with Words* (1962) suffices to show that Austin had no objection to the
introduction of technical terminology where and when it is useful; and other members of the group, such as Strawson, Hart and Grice, did not hesitate to introduce
their own technical terminology in their writings. The objection was against the
premature introduction of *ill-defined* or *unnecessary* technical jargon. 'In fact', Grice
observed, 'the only position which to my mind would have commanded universal
assent was that a careful examination of the detailed features of ordinary discourse
is required as a foundation for philosophical thinking; and even here the enthusiasm
of the assent would have varied from person to person, as would the precise view
taken (if any was taken) about the relationship between linguistic phenomena and
philosophical theses.'[50]

Austin published only seven papers during his lifetime, of which 'Other Minds'
(1946), 'Ifs and Cans' (1956) and 'A Plea for Excuses' (1956) were the finest and
most influential, the latter containing his most detailed methodological reflections
(see below, pp. 174f.). His only books were *Sense and Sensibilia* (1962) and *How to
do Things with Words* (1962), both published posthumously from lecture notes. The
former was a savage, witty attack on sense-datum theories of perception, the principal target being Ayer's *Foundations of Empirical Knowledge*. He reduced to rubble
the views that what we 'immediately perceive' are sense-data, and that propositions
about sense-data constitute the foundations of empirical knowledge.[51] In the course
of his destructive criticism he also shed a great deal of light on a host of perceptual
and perception-related concepts: on the differences between deception, illusion and
hallucination; between how something looks, appears or seems; between 'direct'
and 'indirect', 'veridical' and 'delusive' perception; and on the concept of a 'real'
('true', 'proper', 'genuine') *x* and its manifold opposites ('artificial', 'fake', 'false',
'bogus', 'dummy', etc.). *How to do Things with Words* is, by contrast, constructive.
Beginning with an investigation of performative utterances, he elaborated, classified and anatomized the hosts of things we do in and by uttering words, laying the
groundwork for a comprehensive theory of speech-acts, the presuppositions and
conditions for their successful performance, and the variety of infelicities and mis-
fires to which they are subject. Ryle suggested that Austin probably thought of his
'almost botanical classifications of locution-types much less as contributions to
philosophy than as elements for a future *Principia Grammatica*'.[52] Certainly, in these
unfinished lecture notes Austin did not get around to reaping the philosophical pay-
off of his Linnaean classifications.[53] Nevertheless, they stimulated extensive discussion of the topic of speech-acts over the next decade. Austin's methods and what
was, on the whole wrongly, taken to be his general conception of philosophy (see
below, pp. 174f.) drew a great deal of critical flak to Oxford philosophy, especially
after his premature death in 1960 at the age of only forty-eight.

Ryle and Austin were the most influential figures in Oxford for the first decade
and a half after the war. Their philosophical interests differed, and, as Ryle later

wrote, there was not much 'overlap between his thoughts and mine – or much conflict either'.[54] There were, however, many other eminent figures, some belonging to the older generation and some newcomers upon the scene. Kneale returned to Exeter, where he remained until he was appointed to the White's Chair on Austin's death in 1960. His *Probability and Induction* (1949) contributed a seemingly old-fashioned defence of natural necessity to the lively post-war debate on inductive reasoning.[55] He was the leading historian of logic in Oxford, his work finally coming to fruition in *The Development of Logic* (1962), which he wrote together with his wife Martha Kneale. It remains a classic in its field. Price, who held the Wykham Chair of Logic, and was, like Kneale, a member of the 'Wee Teas', was unable to match Ryle in making the transition from the philosophical style of thought of the 1920s. His *Thinking and Experience* (1953), when placed alongside its contemporaries, *The Concept of Mind* and the *Investigations*, patently looks like the last survivor from another era.

Friedrich Waismann had come to Oxford in 1940, after two years in Cambridge, where his relationship with Wittgenstein had been strained and unhappy.[56] He remained in Oxford until his death in 1959. He obtained a post, as lecturer in the philosophy of mathematics, only in 1945, becoming reader in the philosophy of mathematics in 1950, and later reader in the philosophy of science (1955–9). Although by this stage there was a deep personal rift between him and Wittgenstein, and he was now developing his own independent philosophy, he constituted a major source of Wittgensteinian ideas in Oxford. His papers 'Verifiability' (1945), 'Language Strata' (1946/1953), the series of articles 'Analytic-synthetic' (1949–53) and 'How I see Philosophy' (1956) were influential (see §3 below).

Ayer, who was elected to a Fellowship at Wadham in 1945, remained in Oxford for only a year, before taking up the Grote Chair at University College, London. While there, he transformed UCL into one of the leading philosophy schools in Britain, recruiting (among others) Hampshire (who was there from 1947 to 1950, returning again to succeed Ayer in the chair from 1960 to 1963) and Richard Wollheim. Ayer's *The Problems of Knowledge* (1956) put philosophical scepticism back on the agenda of British analytic philosophy. In it he defended, under the title of 'descriptive analysis', a conventionalist riposte to scepticism. He conceded to the sceptic that the inferences by which we allegedly reason to conclusions about material objects, or about others' mental states, or about the past, are neither deductive nor inductive. Nevertheless, he argued, they are none the worse for that, since the sceptic's qualms stem from pitching his evidential standards unrealistically high. But, it seemed, nothing more than epistemic mores vindicate our standards rather than the sceptic's. This form of epistemic conventionalism was subsequently displaced by Strawson's revival of a form of transcendental argument demonstrating the incoherence of the sceptic's stance and Wittgenstein-inspired criticisms of the intelligibility of scepticism and foundationalism alike. Ayer returned to Oxford as Wykham Professor of Logic on Price's retirement in 1959, motivated partly by a desire to combat Austin's influence. By this stage of his career, he had abandoned many of the tenets of logical positivism, including the conception of philosophy characteristic of the Vienna Circle, and was veering towards a neo-Russellian position.[57] In his inaugural lecture 'Philosophy and Language' (1960) he was critical of the view that philosophy is, in some special sense, an enquiry into language (not that Austin or Ryle ever thought it was), or a second-order discipline which neither describes nor explains the world. He ascribed to Ryle and Wittgenstein a method of determining what a given sentence says by taking a new look at the facts (about intelligent acting, e.g. or about reading (PI §§156–78)), trying to see the phenomena as they are, without preconceptions which may lead us to distort the facts. But, he argued, no record of the facts can be free of interpretation, and hence of theory. Consequently, *pace* Ryle and Wittgenstein, the method of 'ordinary language philosophy' leads unavoidably to theories about the nature of things. Until his retirement in 1979, Ayer was the leading spokesman for neoclassical empiricism in Oxford (a role subsequently assumed by J. L. Mackie, primarily in epistemology, philosophical logic and ethics, and by Pears in philosophy of mind). Ayer was a lively critic not only of Austin, but also of Wittgenstein ('Can there be a Private Language?' (1954) and 'Privacy' (1959)) and later of Strawson's neo-Kantian transcendental arguments ('The Concept of a Person, (1963)). He too founded a fruitful philosophical discussion group, members of which included Strawson, Pears, Dummett, B. F. McGuinness, O. P. Wood, P. Gardiner, A. M. Quinton, D. Wiggins and J. Thomson; later recruits (in the period of our concern) included Mackie, P. Foot, Grice, Warnock and Hart.

Grice became a prominent Oxford figure through his lectures and seminars. His classes on topics in philosophical logic with his erstwhile pupil Peter Strawson, who returned to an appointment at University College in 1947, were famous in their day. Their joint paper 'In Defence of a Dogma' (1956), in reply to Quine's attack on the viability of the analytic/synthetic distinction (in 'Two Dogmas of Empiricism'), did much to stem the influence of Quine's holistic empiricism in Britain (see below, pp. 203, 211 and 321 nn. 31 and 32). Grice's rare papers were exceedingly influential, the most noteworthy of this period being 'Meaning' (1957) – the first of a series of papers connecting the concepts of linguistic meaning with speaker's intentions – and 'The Causal Theory of Perception' (PASS, 35 (1961)), in which he attempted to rehabilitate the causal theory by detaching it from representationalism. In the latter paper, he also made the first move in his subsequently famous development of pragmatic principles of discourse and 'conversational implicature'. He contended, in opposition to Strawson, that despite apparent deviations between the use of the sentential connectives and the logical connectives of the calculus, our natural language sentential connectives are truth-functional. The differences in use, he argued, are attributable to pragmatic principles of conversation, not to differences between the *meanings* of 'and' and '&', 'if . . . , then . . .' and '⊃', and so on. His arguments, here and elsewhere, do, if correct, drive a wedge between the alleged semantic and pragmatic features of the use of an expression, and exclude the latter aspects of its use from its meaning (for critical evaluation of this view, see ch. 8, §2 (ii)). Accordingly, the ground-consequent relation seemingly involved in 'if . . . , then . . .' is attributable not to the meaning of the conditional, which is exhausted by its truth-functional explanation (its equivalence with '$\sim (p \ \& \ \sim q)$'), but to conversational conventions. Grice's defence of the causal theory was taken up, refined and elaborated by Strawson in 'Causation in Perception' (1974)[58] and 'Perception and its Objects' (1981).[59] It engendered a debate which continues to this day. His defence of the truth-functionality of 'if' was in turn criticized by Strawson in '"If" and "⊃"' (1986).[60] Grice left Oxford for Berkeley in 1968.

Strawson rapidly established himself as a leading Oxford philosopher, challeng-
ing orthodoxy (in the form of Russell's theory of descriptions) with his renowned
paper 'On Referring' (1950) and Austin in a famous symposium on truth ('Truth',
PASS, 24 (1950)). Austin defended a correspondence theory between proposition
and fact (rather surprisingly, given the demise of logical atomism and 'Cambridge
analysis' of the 1930s), and was duly criticized by Strawson, who elaborated a
Ramsey-inspired account of truth. *Introduction to Logical Theory* (1952) examined the
relations between formal logical calculi and natural language. Strawson drew attention to extensive differences between the meaning of the logical operators of the
calculus and their natural language counterparts. The ensuing debate between the
'truth-functionalists' (such as Grice) and their opponents is not yet over (see below,
p. 322 n. 37). The concluding chapter demonstrated the incoherence of demands for
the justification of induction, along lines parallel to, but independent of, Wittgenstein's
often obscure treatment of the issue in *Investigations* §§466–90 (see Volume 4, 'Inductive reasoning'). Strawson's master-work *Individuals* (1959) introduced the term
'descriptive metaphysics' into the philosophical lexicon, and revived a modified
form of Kantian transcendental argument. From considerations pertaining to identifying reference, re-identification and predication, he argued that the basic particulars of any conceptual scheme in which we can describe our experience and its
objects must be material bodies and persons. His anti-Cartesian treatment of the
concept of a person as 'primitive' – that is, not analysable as an animated body or
embodied anima – and his conception of a person as one two-sided thing rather
than a combination of two one-sided things started a debate which still continues.
The book was a landmark in post-war Oxford philosophy, being wider in scope
and more ambitious in its striving for generality than anything that had been
produced in Oxford in the previous decades. (It will be discussed in more detail
below.)

His British Academy lecture 'Freedom and Resentment' (1962) brought to bear
upon the discussion of determinism and free will consideration of our natural reactive attitudes to good, indifferent or ill will – attitudes of resentment, gratitude
and forgiveness (in the case of the conduct of others towards ourselves), of indig-
nation or approbation (in vicarious cases), and of guilt, remorse or obligation (in
self-reflexive cases). These reactive attitudes are not *irrational*; or rational either. Our
commitment to them is 'part of the general framework of human life', part of what
Wittgenstein (whom Strawson did not invoke, but might well have done) called our
'form of life'.[61] Just as our commitment to the primacy of material objects and
persons is, *pace* Carnap or Ayer, not a matter of choosing a language, so too our
commitment to such human attitudes is constitutive of human relations and human
society. This is not something that could come up for review. And if, *per impossibile*,
we had any choice in the matter, the truth or falsity of determinism would have no
bearing upon the rationality of such a choice. For we could choose rationally only
in the light of an assessment of the enrichment or impoverishment of human life
consequent upon the choice. It would not necessarily be rational to choose to be
more purely 'rational' – that is, ratiocinative – than we are.

The Kantian features of *Individuals* led Strawson to his much-acclaimed full-scale
study of Kant's metaphysics, *The Bounds of Sense* (1966). This book systematically
separated Kant's transcendental psychology and metaphysics from his analytic or

descriptive metaphysics, yielding a transformed picture of the Kantian enterprise. It stimulated a new interest in Kant on the part of philosophers working in the analytical tradition. On Ryle's retirement in 1968, Strawson was appointed to the Waynflete Chair of Metaphysics, which he occupied until 1987.

Hampshire returned to Oxford in 1950 (first New College and then from 1955 to 1960 All Souls). His *Thought and Action*, published in the same year as *Individuals*, made 1959 something of a turning-point. Hampshire's book, like Strawson's, aspires to great generality, and takes as its point of departure considerations pertaining to reference and identification. More schematic than Strawson's, with a preponderance of assertion over argument, its scope is even greater, ranging from an examination of the nature of language and its use to the investigation of intentional action, freedom of the will and value. Hampshire emphasized, more than any other of his contemporaries in Britain, the implications of the simple fact that we are embodied, active agents in a material world and conscious of ourselves as such, that perception is not a matter merely of passive receptivity but of active interaction with our environment. Handling and manipulating things are no less action than perception, and these are necessarily complementary. We could not be observers unless we were sometimes experimenters, and could not be experimenters unless we were sometimes observers. Contrary to the empiricist tradition, he maintained that the language of sensation is parasitic on the language used to describe and identify external objects, including other persons. Hampshire gave the concept of intention a pivotal role in his analysis; for, he argued, it is essentially involved in any explanation of the will, of action and the relation of thought and action, of the relation between mind and body, and of the difference between mere habit and rule-governed action. Like Wittgenstein, he emphasized the asymmetry between first- and third-person knowledge of intentions, and explored the relation between prediction and intention in the first-person case. That we are essentially symbol-using animals, he suggested, is but a special case of the fact that we are intentional animals.

H. L. A. Hart (1907–92) abandoned a career in law to take up a Fellowship at New College in 1945.[62] He was elected to the Chair in Jurisprudence in 1952. His inaugural lecture, 'Definition and Theory in Jurisprudence' (1953), repudiated the search for analytic definitions of central jurisprudential concepts, suggesting instead that they are best illuminated by forms of contextual elucidation. In so doing, he applied lessons learnt from contemporary reflections in the philosophy of language, in particular from Austin, Wisdom (especially his *Interpretation and Analysis in Relation to Benham's Theory of Definition*), Wittgenstein and Waismann, to jurisprudential questions. This enabled him to illuminate the flaws of the triangulated log-jam of American Legal Realist, Scandinavian Realist and 'metaphysical' analyses of legal obligations, rights, corporate bodies and so forth and to point the way forward to more enlightening elucidations of the role of legal concepts. Over the next two decades, he revolutionized legal philosophy, and contributed greatly to the revival of political philosophy. The first part of *Causation in the Law* (1959), co-authored by A. M. Honoré, contained a comprehensive examination of the concept of causation as employed in ordinary and legal discourse. *The Concept of Law* (1961) steered a course between imperative theories of law and moralistic theories, defending a modified positivism. Laws are essentially rules of different types, belonging to a system of rules, which guides its own creation, application and enforcement. The existence of a legal system is a form of social fact, dependent upon the shared understanding of legal officials, buttressed by the social force of what Hart called 'the internal point of view', and constrained by the necessary 'minimum content of natural law'. The book became, and has remained, one of the most renowned jurisprudential works of the century. Hart's essays in *Punishment and Responsibility* (1968) were major contributions not only to the theory of punishment, but also to wider philosophical topics in the theory of action and responsibility. His papers on rights (e.g. 'Are There Any Natural Rights?' (1955), 'Legal Rights' (1973), 'Between Utility and Rights' (1973)) were a primary source of the extensive discussion of these subjects in legal and political theory which continues to this day.

The revival of political philosophy in Oxford from a moribund state in the immediate aftermath of the war to its later flourishing condition was due not only to Hart, but also to Isaiah Berlin. Having abandoned philosophy during the war, Berlin's interests turned to the history of social and political thought. He was elected to the chair in political philosophy in 1957. His writings in the philosophy of history (e.g. 'Historical Inevitability' (1954)) added to the growing revival of interest in that subject, to which Patrick Gardiner had earlier contributed *The Nature of Historical Explanation* (1952), criticizing Collingwood's posthumously published idealist theory of history (*The Idea of History* (1946)). In his inaugural lecture 'Two Concepts of Liberty' (1958), Berlin drew the now famous distinction between positive and negative liberty. It stimulated a long-lasting debate on liberal political values, to which Hart also contributed in his response to Lord Justice Devlin, *Law, Liberty and Morality* (1964), in which he defended a liberal view of the relationship between law and morality (occasioned by the Wolfenden Report on homosexuality).

In the inter-war years the dominant trend in moral philosophy in Oxford was a form of intuitionism. This had been given a rude shock by the crude emotivism of Ayer's *Language, Truth and Logic*. A more careful emotivism was elaborated in the United States by Charles Stevenson in his *Ethics and Language* (1945).[63] Further developments of a moral philosophy which shared the emotivist repudiation of intuitionism and naturalism alike took place in Oxford. Hare's *The Language of Morals* (1952) was the first of his series of highly influential books and articles. In it he defended a meta-ethical doctrine of non-cognitivist, universalizable prescriptivism. This later evolved into a form of (non-cognitive) utilitarianism (*Moral Thinking* (1981)). Nowell-Smith's *Ethics* (1954) contributed further to the debate in the 1950s. Hare's work stimulated extensive discussion, and provoked trenchant naturalist or quasi-naturalist reactions – in Oxford primarily from Philippa Foot in numerous influential papers written over many years (collected in her *Virtues and Vices* (1978)) and from G. J. Warnock (e.g. *The Object of Morality* (1971)). Iris Murdoch's three distinguished essays, written in the 1960s and collected in *The Sovereignty of the Good* (1970), had little impact, however.

Philosophy of science never had the prominence at Oxford which it enjoyed at Cambridge. However, both Toulmin, for the short number of years he spent at Oxford, and Rom Harré, over four decades, introduced a form of philosophy of science which eschewed both Popperian and Carnapian rational reconstruction. They did not share the Vienna Circle's belief that the predicate calculus and the deductive-nomological pattern of reasoning provide the backbone for the elucidation of the language of science and of scientific theory. (In this respect, and others, they were indebted to Wittgenstein, to whom Toulmin payed tribute in the preface to his *The Philosophy of Science* (1953), and as acknowledged by Harré and manifest especially in his later work in the philosophy of the social sciences.) Eager to remain faithful to scientific practice and reasoning, they, like Mary Hesse in Cambridge, emphasized the role of models in scientific theory and explanation, and investigated non-Humean conceptions of causality. Harré's *The Principles of Scientific Thinking* (1970) was a systematic and exhaustive examination of the former theme, whereas *Causal Powers* (1975), co-authored by E. H. Madden, explored the latter.

This schematic survey of some of the works of philosophers at Oxford indicates the extraordinary flowering of the subject at that university in the twenty-five years after the war, and traces some of the many currents that flowed in the broad stream of post-war connective analytic philosophy. Paton, not altogether sympathetic to the new trends manifest by his younger colleagues, wrote in 1956:

> Whatever may be thought of post-war philosophy, there can be no doubt that it is very much alive. Its missionaries have gone out to the ends of the earth, some of them with almost too much evangelical zeal. Critics have found it narrow and inhuman, as if it had become at best a game and at worst a logomachy. Against such views may be set the almost lyrical remark once made to me by Richard Robinson in the Turl at Oxford on a summer's day. 'Never has there been such a blooming of philosophy in the whole history of the world.'[64]

That was charming hyperbole, no doubt. But the feeling that philosophy was undergoing a radical transformation – indeed, a revolution – was widespread. The survey of the work that was done in Oxford demonstrates the richness and diversity of the achievement. Many works and names have, of course, been omitted. In particular, few of the younger figures who were reaching maturity only in the late 1960s have been mentioned. I do not mean to imply that their early works were insignificant, but only that their main contributions to philosophy post-date the period which is my concern. Nor does the exclusive focus upon philosophy at Oxford imply that there were not important figures outside Oxford (both in Britain and especially in the United States) producing influential work, but only that Oxford was *the* philosophical centre of analytic philosophy in this period, and that Wittgenstein's influence was intimately bound up with it.

This extraordinary concentration of talent in one university turned out to involve a high price. For before long, outsiders were referring to 'Oxford Philosophy', as if that label picked out a doctrine, or to 'the Oxford School of Philosophy', as if that title signified a doctrinally united group of philosophers. And only a little later the expression 'Oxford Ordinary Language Philosophy' came into vogue, occasionally and, over the years, increasingly as a term of abuse. But it should be clear from the above survey that there was great diversity in the manner and matter of philosophizing current in Oxford in the quarter of a century after the war. Austin's brilliance at discerning subtleties of difference in ordinary idiom, and in employing them to break down crude philosophical dichotomies, to criticize philosophical misuses of language, and to shed light upon philosophical problems pertaining to excuses or to perception was not emulated by all (few shared his talent), nor were his methods generally thought to be the only correct way to tackle philosophical problems. This is evident from even a mere glance at the writings of Strawson and Hampshire, not to mention Ayer, and would have been evident from brief attendance at Grice's seminars. Neoclassical empiricism was championed from 1959 by Ayer, and he found able support from Quinton, Pears and, later, Mackie, and equally able opposition from Strawson's neo-Kantian descriptive metaphysics, Hampshire's trenchant repudiation of the whole empiricist conception of experience, and from the neo-Wittgensteinians. Wittgenstein's conception of philosophy and Wittgensteinian methods of analysis were defended and furthered, implicitly and with qualifications by Ryle and explicitly by Anscombe, whose influential *Intention* (1957) has already been mentioned, and from the early 1960s onwards by her pupil A. J. P. Kenny, whose *Action, Emotion, and the Will* (1963) was the first of his many distinguished contributions to philosophy of mind. Ethical prescriptivism was advocated by Hare, and controverted by Foot and Warnock, as well as by Hampshire, Anscombe and Iris Murdoch. Not only was there no doctrinal uniformity, but the fiercest criticisms of the writings of Oxford philosophers often stemmed from Oxford itself. Ryle's *Concept of Mind* was criticized (somewhat unfairly, to my mind) by Hampshire (in his 'Critical Notice' in *Mind*, 59 (1950)), and his conception of categories by Strawson (see pp. 93, 298 n. 74). Ayer was savaged by Austin in *Sense and Sensibilia*, and Austin was criticized by Strawson in the debate on truth. Ayer in turn replied to Austin's criticism, and argued against Strawson's account of the concept of a person. And so on.

Nevertheless, the appearance to outsiders of a common 'school' was not *wholly* illusory. Most, though not all, of the philosophers who have been mentioned would have agreed on some common principles, and shared some common aversions. There was a general belief in clarity of expression and perspicuity of argument – that even if 'clarity [was] not enough',[65] it is a step in the right direction. As already noted, there was an aversion to the introduction of unnecessary or ill-defined technical terminology. There was general consensus that formal logic is not an 'ideal language', or even the bare syntax of an 'ideal language', which uniquely mirrors the logical structure of the world. Indeed, the whole conception of the world as having a 'logical structure' was by and large rejected as an aberration of the logical analysts of the 1920s and 1930s. There was a broad consensus that philosophy is not continuous with the empirical sciences, and that its methods and goals differ from those of science. And there was general agreement that the predicate calculus is not a representation of the depth structure of any possible language. Hence most philosophers writing in Oxford eschewed appeal to the calculus as a key to philosophical analysis. Reductive and constructive analysis were generally rejected, and, as remarked earlier, although the terms 'analysis' and 'analytic philosophy' continued to be widely used, they were cut loose from their original moorings (and Russellings) and transformed. Ryle's charting of the 'logical geography' of concepts was the first major work in Oxford of what Strawson later called 'connective analysis'. It was not only the metaphysics of logical atomism that was rejected. Old-style metaphysics, conceived as a super-science giving special insights into the ultimate nature of reality, was generally repudiated. To be sure, Strawson revived the term 'metaphysics' in *Individuals* but, as he was at pains to emphasize in the introduction, descriptive metaphysics does not differ from philosophical or conceptual analysis save in its scope and generality. It aims to lay bare not the most general features of reality, but rather the most general features of our conceptual scheme.

What, if anything, merited the epithet 'linguistic philosophy' or 'ordinary language philosophy'? As Grice noted (see above, p. 152), the modest claim that a careful examination of the detailed features of ordinary discourse is indispensable as a foundation for philosophical thinking would have commanded assent, assuming, one should add, that the philosophical thinking concerned concepts which belong to ordinary (common, non-technical) discourse. One must distinguish, as Ryle pointed out already in 1953,[66] between the use of ordinary language and the ordinary use of language, neither of which is the same as ordinary linguistic usage (there can be misuses, but no misusages, any more than there can be miscustoms or misvogues). 'Ordinary (or common) language' or 'ordinary (or common) expressions of a language' are to be contrasted with technical, esoteric or archaic language or expressions of a language. There is no sharp boundary between what is common and uncommon, technical and non-technical, current and old-fashioned (is 'purl' on the lips of Everyman, or only on the lips of Everywoman?, Ryle queried). But it is obvious enough that 'see', 'think', 'believe', 'know', or 'mind' and 'body' lie on one side, and 'transfinite cardinal', 'entailment' and 'existential quantifier' on the other. 'Ordinary (or 'natural') language' may also be contrasted with 'formal' or 'notational' language. The ordinary (stock, standard) use of language or of an expression, on the other hand, stands in contrast to its non-standard, figurative or metaphorical use. No one in Oxford would have claimed that a philosophical investigation of such concepts as transfinite cardinal should begin with an examination of the use of *ordinary expressions*. But it would have been generally agreed that any investigation should be preceded by an examination of the *ordinary use* of the relevant expressions, whether ordinary or highly technical.[67] (And an examination of mathematicians' use of 'transfinite cardinal' does indeed reap rich dividends.) This methodological commitment, though exhibited at Oxford to a hitherto uncommon degree perhaps, and sometimes with uncommon skill, is as old as philosophy itself. Its legitimacy and fruitfulness in competent hands are surely in no way diminished by its discernible affinity, as Grice pointed out, with the professions and practice of Aristotle in relation to τὰ λεγόμενα ('what is said'). There would also have been fair consensus that neither 'explication' or 'rational reconstruction' on Carnap's model[68] nor translation into the 'canonical notation' of a logical calculus is in general a promising line of attack on the problems that were at the forefront of debates at the time.[69]

It was sometimes thought that 'Oxford Philosophy' was committed to the view that the subject-matter of philosophy is ordinary language. I doubt whether anyone at Oxford held that view, and it is certainly not the case that everyone held it. Alternatively, it was understood that Oxford philosophers agreed that the examination of ordinary language (and it is noteworthy that no distinction was drawn here between uses of ordinary language and ordinary uses of language) is the *sole* method of philosophy. Austin himself, whose methodological views will be further examined below, held that proceeding from 'ordinary language' *in the study of excuses* is *one* philosophical method, a particularly fruitful one *in this field*, 'where ordinary language is rich and subtle' (by contrast with investigations into concepts pertaining to time).[70] And he was quick to warn against 'the snag of Loose (or Divergent or Alternative) Usage', which, rightly handled, may be illuminating (see below, pp. 174f.) and 'the crux of the Last Word', where he immediately conceded that 'ordinary language has no claim to be the last word', while insisting that 'it *is* the *first* word'. Strawson argued as follows:

> Up to a point, the reliance upon a close examination of the actual use of words is the best, and indeed the only sure, way in philosophy. But the discriminations we can make, and the connections we can establish, in this way, are not general enough and not far-reaching enough to meet the full demand for under-standing . . . [hence the descriptive metaphysician] must abandon his only sure guide when the guide cannot take him as far as he wishes to go.[71]

Hampshire conceded that *at certain points* 'linguistic analysis, the detailed study of a whole range of idioms together with their normal contexts, is of the greatest value in philosophy';[72] however, 'the philosopher may find 'that the vocabulary that he has accepted without question rests on a central distinction that he cannot in detail sustain. Then he will be compelled to adapt the vocabulary to his own purposes and to find new uses for some familiar expressions' (ibid., p. 254). Ayer was altogether out of sympathy with what *he* understood by 'linguistic' or 'ordinary language' philosophy. Ryle, to be sure, held that philosophy has *something* to do with the use of expressions, for that is to say no more than that *conceptual discussions* are the concern of philosophy.[73] For to talk about the concept of, say, causation just *is* to talk of the *use* of the expression 'cause' (and related ergative verbs), a use which is shared (with at most minor deviations) by numerous different languages. The job done with the English word 'cause' is not an English job, and more than the job done with 'Ursache' is a Continental job.

> Putting the stress on the word 'use' helps to bring out the important fact that the enquiry is an enquiry not into the other features or properties of the word . . . , but only into what is done with it, or with anything else with which we can do the same thing. That is why it is so misleading to classify philosophical questions as linguistic questions – or as non-linguistic questions. (Ibid., p. 305)

One merit, Ryle stressed, of the new idiom of talking about investigating the use of expressions, as opposed to talking about investigating ideas or concepts, was that the old idiom lent itself to Platonist or psychologist illusions about the status (tran-scendent intuitables or private introspectables) and provenance of these entities (in-nate, derived from experience or part of the structure of the mind). Talk of 'use' also had advantages over talk of 'meanings', given the misconceptions about mean-ing and meanings that had dogged the first half of the century, when 'meanings' were misguidedly thought to be entities for which words stood.

Whether there was a generally agreed methodology or not and, whether the various methodological remarks made by different figures at Oxford were severally defensible are further questions. What is clear is that there was no generally held Oxford 'doctrine' that the description of ordinary linguistic use is the sole method of philosophy or that the subject-matter of philosophy is language, let alone ordin-ary (as opposed to technical) language. Nor did anyone suggest that ordinary lan-guage (as opposed to the ordinary use of language, whether common or technical) has any privilege over technical language in the appropriate technical domain of a first-order discipline or in philosophical reflection upon such a discipline (e.g. the philosophy of mathematics or the philosophy of logic proper).

3. Wittgenstein and post-war philosophy at Oxford

So far we have sketched the development of analytic philosophy at Oxford in the post-war years, with scant mention of the impact of Wittgenstein's later philosophy. It is to this that we must now turn, but with a sharp awareness of the fact that any attempt to trace the impact of ideas, even ideas as striking and original as Wittgenstein's, is rendered doubly difficult when those ideas fall, in two successive waves, upon what might be called a flourishing philosophical culture. Between 1945 and 1953, when the *Investigations* was published, most philosophers at Oxford knew of Wittgenstein's work through what they had heard from philosophers who had known him or been members of his circle and what they had read in their writings, or, in some cases, from the typescripts of the *Blue Book*, the *Brown Book* and lecture notes made by his students. These undoubtedly made a substantial impact, as is evident from both contemporary and later remarks of members of the Oxford philosophy sub-faculty. However, these works are not comparable in depth and scope to the *Investigations* or to the subsequent stream of Wittgenstein's posthumous publications. And by 1953, philosophy at Oxford was thriving as never before, greatly coloured by Wittgensteinian ideas, to be sure, but nevertheless with a distinctive profile of its own. Consequently, when the major works appeared, they were not like seeds falling upon fertile but relatively uncultivated soil, but were more akin to fresh nutrients for an already flourishing garden which had absorbed an initial impact of Wittgensteinian ideas, partly transmitted by his followers. Moreover, as has just been made clear, that garden did not cultivate a single crop, but produced a wide range of fruits. Trying to determine the impact of Wittgenstein's philosophy at Oxford is unavoidably an impressionistic endeavour, and a description of it in reasonable compass must perforce be selective.

Von Wright, an outsider, remarked on the great difference between pre- and post-war Oxford thus:

> I had visited Oxford shortly before the war, when the tradition of idealism was still strong there. Alfred Ayer, whom I met for the first time, seemed an unfamiliar local bird. Wittgenstein was next to a mythical figure; Russell and Moore had made but little impact at Oxford. When I returned to the place eight years later, I was confronted with a completely changed situation. Wittgenstein's name was on everybody's lips. Not as author of the *Tractatus*, however, but of the Blue and Brown Books and as an influential teacher whose lectures at Cambridge some privileged people had attended.[74]

The impact of the typescripts of *The Blue and Brown Books* upon the younger generation is well attested. Strawson reminisced: 'When, in the early 1950s, I first saw a typescript of Wittgenstein's *Blue Book* I felt that I was, for the first time, seeing thought *naked*, as it were. And this sense of his quality stays with one – or stays with me – as one reads more of the work of his later period.'[75] Dummett, who was an undergraduate in his final year in 1950, relates:

> It is difficult to convey the excitement of reading these works for the first time. Wittgenstein was a distant presence of which we were all intensely aware, but an utterly enigmatic presence. . . . we believed that he was probably a great genius, revealing to those fortunate enough to be admitted to his lectures a dazzling and

completely original treatment of philosophical questions: but we did not know what it was he said. There were, indeed, disciples of his, like Wisdom, whose writings we read, and Miss Anscombe, whose lectures we heard; but we could not be sure how faithfully they represented their teacher. And then suddenly, by what channel I never knew, these works arrived, smuggled into Oxford from that city that had been as closed to us as Lhasa. On me, at least, their impact was tremendous.[76]

Just how pervasive Wittgenstein's influence had become even prior to the publication of the *Investigations* is evident in the once famous collection of papers *Logic and Language* (1st series, 1951) edited by A. G. N. Flew, then a young lecturer at Christ Church, Oxford. The aim of the collection was to present a picture of the modern movement in British philosophy, and one of the criteria for selection was that the collection should contain the maximum number of articles which were constantly being recommended by tutors to their pupils. Of the nine papers included, seven were by writers who had studied under Wittgenstein or were acquainted with him: namely, Ryle, Findlay, Margaret Macdonald, Paul, Waismann and Wisdom.[77] And Herbert Hart, the author of the eighth paper ('The Ascription of Responsibility and Rights'), had been much influenced by Waismann. Flew, in his introduction, attributed the origins of the 'modern movement' in British philosophy to Wittgenstein's *Tractatus* and Ryle's 'Systematically Misleading Expressions'. He concluded with the remark:

> [W]e think that all who have been associated with this book and with the philosophic developments which it tries to represent would wish to acknowledge their debt to the genius of one man above all. Though his name is almost unknown outside the world of academic philosophy, everyone who belongs to that world will see throughout this volume marks of the enormous influence, direct and indirect, of the oral teachings of Professor Wittgenstein.[78]

The extent of Oxford's professed assimilation of Wittgensteinian ideas throughout the next decade can be gauged from remarks made by other eminent Oxonians. Warnock wrote in 1956 that 'the most powerful and pervasive influence upon the practice of philosophy in this country today has been that of Ludwig Wittgenstein'.[79] Urmson, at the Royaumont colloquium in 1958, observed that 'if you read the works of these philosophers [of Oxford], you will find the pervasive influence of Wittgenstein'.[80] Hart was moved to rare hyperbole in remarking of the *Investigations* in 1956 'This is our Bible',[81] and reported his reaction to Waismann's neo-Wittgensteinian 'How I See Philosophy' (1956) by saying: 'It was as if the scales fell from my eyes.'[82] Nevertheless, the influence was *assimilated*. There was no Oxford *school* of Wittgensteinians; rather, the figures we have been examining, or at least some of them, seized upon ideas they found – or thought they found – in Wittgenstein's writings, and put them to their own use. His ideas fertilized their thoughts, but did not replace them.

Among those who transmitted Wittgensteinian ideas to Oxford after 1939, Waismann was locally the most influential as far as members of the faculty were concerned. He had worked very closely with Wittgenstein between 1929 and 1936 on the ill-fated project *Logik, Sprache, Philosophie*, and was shown the 'Proto-Philosophical Investigations' in 1938. The former book had been completed by 1937, and had it been published then, as Waismann intended (it had reached proof stage in a German edition, but the plates were destroyed during the bombing of Rotterdam in 1940[83]) or immediately after the war, it might have made a substantial impact. For it gives a carefully organized, lucid picture (not always accurate) of Wittgenstein's thought on the philosophy of language and logic and on philosophical method as it stood in the mid-1930s. Although Waismann showed the typescript to some of his friends in Oxford (e.g. Hampshire, perhaps Ryle and possibly Hart), the book was published only posthumously, in 1965, edited by Rom Harré, under the title *The Principles of Linguistic Philosophy*. At that stage, unfortunately, no one appears to have been aware of its origins (i.e. that it was in effect largely Wittgenstein's work, carefully processed and organized by Waismann) or its original purpose (i.e. that it had been intended as volume 1 of the Vienna Circle's publications *Schriften zur wissenschaftlichen Weltauffassung*). Its impact was negligible. Waismann's presence in Oxford, however, was important; for, although his own ideas were evolving away from Wittgenstein's, he was well informed about Wittgenstein's philosophy in the 1930s, and transmitted this knowledge in his lectures and classes. His conversations and joint seminar with Kneale may have left some mark on the Kneales's *The Development of Logic*, perhaps on the discussion of the concept of number (ch. 6, §2). A joint seminar with Hampshire on the concept of intention in the mid-1950s contributed to the development of Hampshire's ideas, which came to fruition in *Thought and Action*.[84] Certainly Hart was deeply influenced by his conversations with Waismann.[85]

Waismann's papers 'Verifiability' (1945) and 'Language Strata' (Part 1, 1946; Part 2, 1953) were critical of the *Tractatus* conception of the analysability of all propositions into elementary propositions, as well of the positivist and behaviourist attempts to reduce propositions of one kind – for example, psychological propositions or material object propositions – to propositions of another kind – for example, behavioural ones or observational ones. Instead, he proposed a conception of language as stratified into 'layers': for example, sense-datum statements, material object statements, statements of laws of nature. Each stratum, he argued, is characterized by a different kind of logic; for the distributive law breaks down for quantum mechanics, the logic of sense impressions requires treating not just a single proposition as the primitive unit, but a whole propositional system (*Satzsystem*). Each stratum is subject to different standards of completeness of description, the sense of 'complete' and 'incomplete' varying from one stratum to another, descriptions within some strata being incomplete in principle. *Open texture* (a term coined by Kneale for Waismann's *Porosität der Begriffe*) – that is, not vagueness but the possibility of vagueness – characterizes most empirical concepts.[86] Accordingly, their application is never completely verifiable, but only more or less probable: 'So long as we move amongst material object statements, verification has no natural end but refers continually to ever new statements.'[87] Different concepts of truth apply in different strata, for the sense in which a statement of a subjective impression is true differs from the sense in which a material object statement is true, and that in turn differs from the sense in which a statement of a law of physics is true. And what, *if anything*, counts as verification of a proposition similarly varies. The conceptual relations between propositions belonging to different strata are looser than entailment, and do not permit the reduction of members of one stratum to those of another. It should be clear that this conception was far removed from Wittgenstein's later philosophy. In fact, it was rooted in Wittgenstein's conception of a hypothesis as adumbrated in the early 1930s, with which Waismann was familiar, but which Wittgenstein had come to reject by the time he composed the *Blue Book*. Open texture is the correlate of the claim that a hypothesis can only be made more or less probable by any relevant evidence (see Exg. §81), and its opposite is determinacy of sense as understood in the *Tractatus* (and 'completeness of definition' as understood by Frege). According to the later Wittgenstein, there is no such thing as a complete explanation of the meaning of an expression *if* that means an explanation which excludes not only vagueness, but the very possibility of vagueness – that is, every *possible* doubt about its application in every *conceivable* circumstance (PI §87). If there is no such property as being determinate in sense thus construed, then there is no such thing as lacking this 'property' either – that is, as being open-textured. The concept of open texture, from Wittgenstein's perspective, misrepresents what it is for an explanation of meaning to be complete or incomplete. Furthermore, the loose relation of propositions of different strata which Waismann envisaged is heir to the symptom/hypothesis relation, which Wittgenstein had abandoned by 1932. He came to repudiate the view that sense-datum statements are the evidence for material object statements, and to deny that material object statements are always merely probable. Nevertheless, Waismann's paper was influential. Hart seized upon the notion of open texture, and put it to use in *The Concept of Law*, to combat both legal formalism and rule-scepticism in jurisprudence.

Waismann was indeed eager to distance himself from Wittgenstein,[88] as is evident in his 1956 paper 'How I See Philosophy'. Though it could have been written only by someone deeply imbued with Wittgenstein's ideas, it nevertheless defends a strikingly different conception of the subject, one which, as remarked above, has affinities with Wisdom's. The goal of philosophy, according to Waismann, is not, *pace* Wittgenstein, the attainment of clarity, but rather *insight*. 'At the heart of any philosophy worth the name is vision, and it is from there it springs and takes its visible shape . . . What is characteristic of philosophy is the piercing of that dead crust of tradition and convention, the breaking of those fetters which bind us to inherited preconceptions, so as to attain a new and broader way of looking at things. . . . What is decisive is a new way of seeing.'[89] It is anything but showing flies the way out of fly-bottles (ibid., p. 32); rather, it is 'seeing a new aspect' (e.g. as Descartes did in the discovery of co-ordinate geometry, or Einstein in his reformulation of the concept of simultaneity). There are no questions which can be decided Yes or No (p. 1). There are no conclusive arguments or refutations in philosophy; however forceful an argument may be, it never forces. Rather, by argument, the philosopher builds up a case against a given theory (by *reductio* and infinite regress (cf. Ryle), which, though inconclusive, do nevertheless point 'to a knot in thought'), and offers one *a new way of looking at things* (p. 30). What philosophy does is quietly and patiently undermine our categories over the whole field of thought (p. 21). To say that metaphysics is nonsense, Waismann proclaimed, is nonsense (p. 38). Metaphysicians, like artists, are the antennae of their time: they have a flair for feeling which way the spirit is moving; they are visionaries who anticipate the movements in the thought of their culture. To ask whether some metaphysical vision of the world is right or wrong is almost like asking whether Gothic art is true or false.[90]

This conception of the subject is (intentionally) different from that of Wittgenstein, who argued that for him clarity was an end in itself, that his interest was not in constructing a building, but in having a perspicuous view of the foundations of possible buildings (CV 7). He aimed at *complete clarity*, the achievement of which will mean the complete disappearance of the philosophical problem (PI §133). For Wittgenstein problems are *solved* by looking into the workings of our language (PI §109); indeed, they must be *completely* solvable (BT 421). The *correct answers* to philosophical questions are ordinary and trivial – the man who said that one cannot step into the same river twice said something *wrong*; one *can* step into the same river twice. (The triviality of these answers does not matter, provided one looks at them in the proper spirit (BT 412).) The results of philosophy are not 'alternative visions', but the uncovering of one or another piece of plain nonsense (PI §119); it is these which philosophy must expose and extirpate. For its task is to destroy idols (BT 413), not to cultivate polytheism. The aim of philosophy is to *erect a wall* at the point where language stops anyway (BT 425), not to open new doors in the wall. It does so by argument, and 'we mustn't give any arguments which are not absolutely conclusive' (MS 161, 3). Its task is not to *undermine* our categories of thought but to *clarify* them, and to keep us from philosophical temptations to misconstrue them. Metaphysics obliterates the distinction between factual and conceptual investigation (Z §458); hence, too, it *misuses words*, characteristically employing them without an antithesis (BB 46),[91] and the task of philosophy is to bring words back from their metaphysical use to their *correct* (BT 412), *everyday* use (PI §116). Metaphysics, far from being 'visionary', expresses an unclarity about grammar in the form of a scientific question (BB 35), and then tries to answer that question in the way science does, leading philosophers *into complete darkness* (BB 18).

Similarly, in 'The Linguistic Technique',[92] Waismann objected to Wittgenstein's claim that 'We are not analysing a phenomenon (e.g. thought) but a concept (e.g. that of thinking), and therefore the use of a word' (PI §383). He argued that to see how a word is used, and when it is used correctly, we have to visualize some situations in which it would be proper to use it – that is, pay heed *to the phenomenon of thinking*. Moreover, analysing the use of words may not get us far enough, to the rationale behind their use, which may be hidden; which is why (*pace* Wittgenstein) it is possible *to make discoveries in philosophy*. Usage, he claimed, need not bind us. The 'linguistic approach' rests on the assumption that ordinary language is adequate, which Waismann questioned. But to see whether language is adequate or not, one has to 'look with a fresh eye at the phenomena and see how far language fits the facts'. This conception was echoed by Ayer in his inaugural lecture (see above, pp. 153f.), and resembles one of Austin's remarks in 'A Plea for Excuses' (see below, p. 174). It is misguided. Waismann made no attempt to counter Wittgenstein's explicit case against such a conception. For the idea that 'in order to get clear about the meaning of the word "think"' we should 'watch ourselves while we think', and that what we then observe 'will be what the word means' is misconceived; the word 'think' is not used like that (PI §316; see Exg.). Although there are phenomena of thinking, thinking is not itself a phenomenon (Z §417; RPP II §§31ff.); what *goes on* in thinking almost never interests us (Z §88), for a report of any 'inner' goings-on (typically a Joycean 'stream of consciousness' babble and perhaps the occurrence of mental images) is hardly ever a report of what one thought; thinking is not an experience, and to report one's thoughts is not to describe an experience (see Volume 3, 'Thinking: methodological muddles and conceptual confusions'). There are no *discoveries* in philosophy (PI §126), since something unknown can play no *normative* role in the practice of speaking a language. But there may be reminders of familiar facts, and one may come to see that there are affinities and differences between familiar uses of expressions which one had not noticed (PI §129). Our language is, to be sure, 'in order as it is' (PI §98); but what that means is that there is nothing logically awry with it which demands the invention of an ideal language to replace it. A reform of language for practical purposes, an improvement of terminology designed to prevent misunderstandings in practice, is perfectly possible (PI §132), but these are not the cases with which philosophy is concerned. Its task is to disentangle the conceptual confusions that arise from *the language we have*, not to sweep them under the carpet by giving a Carnapian 'explication' or 'rational reconstruction'. Moreover, the assumption that an 'improved language' will *not* give rise to any conceptual confusions is chimerical – they will be different confusions, to be sure, but no less confused. Finally, the thought that we can examine the facts in order to see how well language 'fits' them is misconceived, for 'the facts' are not something that we can 'look at' independently of language. They are not objects in the world (or anywhere else), and language neither fits them nor fails to fit them – none of which implies that for specialized purposes, specialists should not evolve a specialized vocabulary.

Waismann distanced himself from Wittgenstein not only in his writings on methodology, but also in his lectures on the philosophy of mathematics. In the mid-1950s he was propounding a curious form of constructive Platonism. In explicit opposition to Wittgenstein, he argued that although it is we who make the number series, we have no choice to proceed in any other way. Wittgenstein, Waismann argued, made it appear as if the generating principle of arithmetic (the step from n to $n+1$) were nothing but proceeding in accord with an optional rule. But the endlessness of the number series, far from being the result of adopting an arbitrary convention, is one of the most significant *discoveries* made right at the beginning of mathematics. It is based on the *insight* that there is an open, endless possibility of going on. We generate the numbers, yet we have *no choice* to proceed otherwise. There is already something that guides us. So we both make and do not make the numbers. We cannot control the process. The creation is stronger than the creator.[93] He similarly castigated Wittgenstein for his account of mathematical conjectures, arguing that if we did not understand, say, Goldbach's conjecture before a method for resolving it were found, how could we recognize a proof as a proof of that conjecture? What Wittgenstein's view amounts to is that only when one solves such a problem does one discover *what* the problem was. Surprisingly, Waismann seems to have forgotten, or not to have known, that Wittgenstein had discussed the issue and answered this objection (see Volume 2, 'Grammar and necessity', pp. 297–301).

Waismann was indeed a significant conveyor of Wittgenstein's ideas, especially from the period 1929–35, to Oxford. But he was not always a reliable one, and certainly not an uncritical one. His conception of philosophy and its application in his philosophical practice differed from Wittgenstein's, as did Wisdom's. But, like Wisdom's, it was to a very large extent derived from Wittgenstein, and Waismann was, for a while, an influential figure in his own right in Oxford. The other main personal source for Wittgenstein's ideas, especially from the post-war period, was Anscombe, who lectured and taught at Oxford from 1946 until 1970. After Waismann's death in 1959, she was the leading Wittgensteinian philosopher at Oxford. Her work has been discussed briefly above.

Ryle had learnt much from Wittgenstein, though what he learnt, he made his own, resolved, as he put it, 'to avoid being one monoglot's echo, even though he was a genius and a friend'.[94] His central preoccupation with the boundary between sense and nonsense, and with its transgression, originated with his reading of the *Tractatus*, but was arguably much enriched by his contact with Wittgenstein during the 1930s. Certainly the distance he travelled, with or without Wittgenstein's assistance, from 'Systematically Misleading Expressions' (1932) through 'Philosophical Arguments' (1945) to *Dilemmas* (1954) was very great. The conception of philosophy which he propounded in his inaugural lecture and exemplified in *The Concept of Mind* – namely, as charting the 'logical geography' and 'cross-bearings' of concepts – bears a recognizable affinity with Wittgenstein's quest for a perspicuous, surveyable representation of our use of words in a given domain of discourse. His insistence that philosophy contains arguments and refutations but no theorems proved from incontrovertible philosophical premises ('Proofs in Philosophy' (1954)) is not one with which Wittgenstein would have quarrelled. Was there any deep difference between the two philosophers' conception of the subject? There was perhaps a difference of depth, but no deep difference. When Ryle was asked this very question, he replied that the 'essential difference' was that he repudiated the therapeutic aspect of Wittgenstein's conception of philosophy. He did not think that philosophical problems were symptoms of a sickness of which the patient must be cured. Hence, he said, 'I use a language which is, so to speak, less clinical than Wittgenstein's, and I am less inclined than he to practice surgery.'[95] He did not share Wittgenstein's animadversion to characterizing some of the things philosophers say as true or false. To say that a philosophical proposition is true and to say that a scientific proposition is true, Ryle objected, does not entail that the two propositions are of the same order. Similarly, he did not object to talking about 'theories' in philosophy, without, to be sure, holding that a philosophical theory is at all like a scientific one. These differences are, I think, superficial. But they do betoken a superficiality in Ryle's failure to probe the reasons for Wittgenstein's animadversions. For if we are to characterize a philosophical proposition as true, we must also give an account of what it would be for it to be false. If we deny that it *could* be false, we must explain why that is so. Wittgenstein's explanation was that it is the expression of a rule for the use of its constituent expressions – and he was, of course, willing to characterize it as a 'grammatical proposition', for which there is no intelligible negation. For a 'false' grammatical proposition is not a grammatical proposition at all, since it is *not* the expression of a rule for the use of its constituent words (see Volume 2, 'Grammar and necessity', §3), and it is not a false empirical proposition either. For Wittgenstein, the matter ramifies further into the question of the autonomy of grammar, an issue upon which Ryle never touched.

Ryle's excessive reliance, especially in *The Concept of Mind*, upon the idea of a category mistake displayed a lack of caution, as well as unclarity (see pp. 92f., 149f.). Indeed, his claim that the root error underlying the Cartesian conception of the mind was 'one big category mistake' was, as Austin pointed out,[96] an oversimplification both of the sources of the Cartesian myth and of Ryle's own scintillating refutations of innumerable confusions embedded in that misconceived picture. Ryle's conception of a category, as he later realized,[97] was too ill-defined to bear the weight he put upon it. Nevertheless, as Austin emphasized, in practice Ryle did 'not confine himself to any single technique or method of argument, nor is the book one whit the worse for that'. Although Wittgenstein, in his notes, occasionally invoked the concepts of a category and of confusion of categories, he never made much of the idea, being, if anything, hypersensitive to the fact that what we are inclined to take as categorial concepts (e.g. experience, event, process, state, something, fact, description) have 'an extremely blurred meaning'. They 'relate in practice to innumerable special cases, but that does not make them any *solider*; no, rather it makes them more fluid' (RPP I §648). Moreover, most of the psychological concepts that interest us have numerous different uses, which fall sometimes in one rough category, sometimes in another (see Volume 4, 'Methodology in philosophical psychology', pp. 435f.). He did not invoke the general notion of a category mistake, but demonstrated, from case to case, how philosophical confusion is engendered by projecting the grammar of one concept on to that of another. Nevertheless, Ryle's and Wittgenstein's detailed methods of displaying conceptual differences where previous philosophers had unthinkingly assumed or consciously postulated uniformities are often very similar.

It is interesting to discover that Wittgenstein did at least look at *The Concept of Mind*. His only recorded remark on it is that 'all the magic has vanished',[98] presumably meaning that Ryle's characterization of the 'Cartesian myth' is altogether too superficial, failing to do justice to the temptations to cleave to that picture, to their mesmerizing quality and bewitching power. Certainly, Ryle did not share Wittgenstein's preoccupation with the *manifold* roots of the hedgehog's homogenizing vision. His frequent, all too swift dismissal of one or another feature of the Cartesian myth betrays an impatience, and sometimes a superficiality, which one does not find in Wittgenstein. (On the other hand, the occasional bewilderingly truncated arguments and consequent opacity of Wittgenstein's counter-moves to his opponent's is not something one would find in Ryle.)

The Concept of Mind broke new ground in a radical manner, unprecedented in philosophical psychology. Its attack on the Cartesian myth went far beyond anything previously written, both in depth and in scope. Ryle's numerous distinctions, between knowing how and knowing that, between episodic and dispositional verbs, achievement and task verbs, dispositional, semi-dispositional and mongrel-categorical statements, between avowals and reports, tendencies and agitations, and later (in 'Thinking and Language' (1951)) between polymorphous and non-polymorphous verbs, entered the philosophical lexicon, stimulating extensive debate and further refinements and modifications. There are numerous parallels between Ryle's treatment of problems and Wittgenstein's – for example, the discussion of intelligent performances and the repudiation of the dual-process conception of thoughtful, intelligent activity; the analysis of understanding, partial understanding and misunderstanding; the attack on the myth of volitions; and the repudiation of the traditional picture of self-knowledge and introspection. To what extent Ryle's thoughts on these themes were inspired by Wittgenstein is impossible to determine; but what is evident is that in each and every case he developed, expounded and

applied these ideas in his own inimitable and brilliant way, even though he lacked
Wittgenstein's depth and subtlety.

What are the central differences between Ryle's philosophy of mind and Wittgenstein's? The private language argument, with its multiple ramifications, does
not appear in Ryle. Although Ryle distinguished between avowal and report along
lines similar to Wittgenstein's distinction between *Äusserung* and description, he did
not handle the issues involved with Wittgenstein's delicacy of touch (see Volume
3, 'Avowals and descriptions') or develop the idea of *expressions* of the inner. He
made next to nothing of Wittgenstein's non-cognitive account of *Äusserungen*. Nor
did he invoke anything like the notion of a criterion,[99] or explore in detail the
asymmetry between first- and third-person, present-tense psychological utterances
in terms of the absence of criteria in the first-person case and the need for criteria
in the third-person case. Ryle's tendency to drift incautiously towards a behaviourist position (see below) is not a fault which can justly be imputed to Wittgenstein.
Of course, there were also thematic differences. Ryle dealt with some topics which
Wittgenstein neglected. His discussion of pleasure and enjoyment[100] defended a
neo-Aristotelian conception of pleasure, and stimulated a lively debate which, at
least for a time, put an end to the crudities of utilitarian empiricism. His writings
on perception, in *The Concept of Mind, Dilemmas* and his paper 'Sensation' (1956),
went beyond anything Wittgenstein had written on the theme, and, as Quinton
later wrote, 'At a time when Austin, in the lectures eventually published as *Sense
and Sensibilia*, was carrying out his brilliant but unsystematic guerrilla intrusions
into the territory of the sense-datum theory, Ryle was engaged on the larger and
more serious task of mounting an invasion in full force.'[101] Conversely, Wittgenstein
had preoccupations in philosophical psychology not shared by Ryle (e.g. aspect
perception).

Ryle certainly mishandled some topics – for example, motive, imagination, voluntary action and belief. His discussions invited, and received, criticism – but also
constructive rectification and improvement. His positive characterization of motivated action as behaviour instantiating a generalization was criticized by Anscombe
(*Intention*, pp. 18–23), who pointed out that Ryle's account precluded someone's
acting from a given motive just once or someone's acting out of character for a
given motive. She distinguished three classes of motives: those which are equivalent to intentions, backward-looking motives which involve a past or present reason for acting (gratitude, revenge), and interpretative motives which place the action
in a certain light (friendship, curiosity). This classification was further refined by
Kenny in *Action, Emotion and the Will* (ch. 4), where he differentiated intentions and
backward-looking reasons in general from motives. He construed the latter as
characterizing an action in terms of its instantiating a *pattern* of reasons (e.g. to act
out of fear is, in the simplest case, to exemplify the pattern: A is in danger of x –
A acts – A is out of danger of x, where being in danger is undesirable, and being
out of danger desirable to A).[102] Ryle's account of imagination had as its primary
target the idea that imagining is not a matter of seeing or hearing a mental image,
that seeing something in one's mind's eye is not an instance of seeing, only with
a special, private object. His negative arguments were indeed persuasive, but his
positive account, which assimilated seeing something in the mind's eye, or visual-
izing something, to imagining that one sees, and assimilated imagining to a species

of supposing or pretending, was flawed. This misconception was immediately criticized by J. M. Shorter ('Imagination', *Mind*, 61 (1952)), and, much later, was anatomized in detail by A. R. White in the best treatment hitherto of the topic (*The Language of the Imagination* (1990)).[103] Pretending to *V* is a mock performance, but imagining that one *V*s is not; nor is imagining that *p* the same as imagining that one is perceiving that *p*. Someone who is good at pretending is a good actor, but someone who is good at imagining is good at conceiving or envisaging; one can pretend that things are thus-and-so without imagining them to be so, and when one imagines something, one does not normally engage in any pretence (see Volume 3, 'Images and the imagination'). Ryle's assault on the myth of volitions may lack the depth of Wittgenstein's more subtle mining and undermining operations (see Volume 4, 'Willing and the nature of voluntary action'), but it gave a salutary jolt to a still current view. However, his account of voluntary and involuntary action rightly drew fire, for he suggested that these adjectives apply only to actions which ought not to be done, that the question of voluntariness arises only in the case of faults, which are excused in the event that the act was involuntary. This too was quickly seen to be mistaken, for intentional action in general is voluntary, unless done under duress or because one is obliged by circumstances. Similarly, his explanation of belief as a behavioural disposition was rightly criticized: irascibility or credulity are dispositional concepts, believing that *p* is not. One may believe that *p* without being disposed to say so or to act on one's belief; and if someone is disposed to say that *p* when asked whether *p*, that disposition manifests his belief that *p* only if he says that *p* because *he believes that p*, and not because he thinks that that is what his interlocutor wants to hear. Though one may act on one's belief that *p*, *how* one acts depends on what one intends, so that the belief that *p* need not be associated with any type-act, tokens of which one is disposed to perform. I may find out that I am credulous or irascible by noting my behaviour, but I do not find out what I believe by noting what I do. And so on.[104]

The Concept of Mind was widely viewed as a defence of a form of logical behaviourism. This was unjust, for Ryle did not deny that nouns such as 'pain', 'twinge', or 'tickle' signify sensations, or affirm that they are reducible to dispositions to behave. He did not, save in incautious moments, deny that words for various kinds of 'agitation' (e.g. the shock of surprise, throb of compassion, thrill of anticipation) signify episodes which have phenomenological features, or claim that they connote merely dispositions and susceptibilities. He did not deny that people have after-images, visualize things and picture things to themselves or have tunes running through their heads, but only that there are mental pictures or mental tunes which only their subject can see or hear. And he asserted that some of our thinking is conducted in internal monologue, which we can keep to ourselves. Nevertheless, the accusation was not wholly groundless, for Ryle was sometimes incautious, allowing himself to be swept away by his own anti-Cartesian zeal.[105] He arguably overworked the dispositionality of many psychological expressions (e.g. belief, motive). He failed to give due attention to the detailed analysis of the concept of disposition itself and to the differences and similarities between disposition, habit, tendency, inclination, susceptibility, liability and so forth. What was, above all, misleading was the very characterization of the cause for which he fought: namely, 'Exorcize the ghost in the machine'. For that slogan encouraged the idea that he was

defending the view that *all* mental predicates signify behaviour, behavioural dispositions, tendencies or inclinations (not to mention the view, which he did *not*
suggest, that the body is a machine!). This was a strategic error, which led to
misinterpretation. Similarly, his primary official weapon, the idea of a category
mistake, was not only blunter than he thought, it was also double-edged. His
insistence that the Cartesian myth was 'one big category mistake' could all too
easily be read as arguing that the mistake was to construe psychological predications
as categorial ascriptions to one substance, namely the mind, whereas they are hypothetical ascriptions to a different substance, namely the body – which was not what
he meant at all.

If Ryle, among the leading Oxford figures, had learnt the most from Wittgenstein,
Austin was the least influenced. 'Some people like Witters', he remarked, 'but
Moore is *my* man.'[106] Austin's impact upon Oxford coincided with Wittgenstein's.
How could these two disparate currents be simultaneously assimilated into the mainstream of connective analytic philosophy? Although Austin's conception of philosophy, *in so far as he had one*, was very different from Wittgenstein's, his practice did
not conflict with Wittgenstein's. Austin was, as von Wright nicely characterized
him, 'the *doctor subtilis*' of post-war Oxford analytic philosophy, 'the unrivalled
master in detecting conceptual shades of linguistic usage – superior in this art even
to Wittgenstein'.[107] Philosophers at Oxford may have been diverted by Austin into
close examination of linguistic minutiae which Wittgenstein would have passed by,
but when it came to the application of such results to specific philosophical questions,
there was often little discernible difference between their tactical moves. In practice,
both could be assimilated.

The common ground is clear enough. Both believed that the reductive and constructive forms of analysis which characterized philosophy in the 1920s and 1930s
were futile, and both repudiated the notion that a natural language is *au fond* a
calculus of rules or that it has a 'deep structure' which is perspicuously representable
by means of the predicate calculus. They were in agreement that analytic definitions
are rarely obtainable in the puzzling domains of thought with which philosophy is
concerned and, even when obtainable, are of little use in resolving philosophical
difficulties. Neither prohibited the introduction of technical or quasi-technical terms
in philosophy, if it is useful. Both would have agreed that the investigation of the
use of words is at any rate *a* primary key to the resolution of philosophical problems, and that sensitivity to the context of the use of expressions is of great importance. Although they were prone to focus upon different aspects of the use of
linguistic expressions, they were in agreement that attention to the function and
point of features of the use of words sheds more light on philosophical problems
than attention to their grammatical form, which is often misleading. They shared
a similar wariness of generalization, a respect for the particular case, and a suspicion
of traditional crude dichotomies.

There are equally obvious superficial differences. Austin's interest in language
was not motivated solely by the desire to resolve philosophical questions. He found
linguistic investigations of interest in their own right, and delighted in uncovering
subtle, unnoticed differences in linguistic idiom. (Why 'very' allows the substitution of 'highly' in some cases ('very unusual') but not in others ('very depressed' or
'very wicked')[108] is not a question which is likely to have interested Wittgenstein.)

Unlike Wittgenstein, he had relatively little interest in the pathology of the intellect – in the explanation of the manifold sources of philosophical confusion. In so far as he had any view of the matter, it seems that he would have attributed it simply to carelessness, impatience, over-hasty generalization and lack of attention to detailed linguistic facts. He craved progress in settling things permanently, believing this to be possible by patient investigations of linguistic use, in which agreement could be achieved on specific points (even if they were minute), which would gradually accumulate.[109] Where Wittgenstein held that there were 'countless kinds [of sentence]; countless different kinds of use of what we call "symbols", "words", "sentences"' (PI §23), Austin (apart from objecting to the apparent failure to distinguish kinds of sentence from kinds of use of sentences) would have thought that patience and industry might well lead to the solid conclusion that there are, according to such-and-such a classification, no less than 417 kinds of use of sentences.[110] He did not share Wittgenstein's animadversion to theory construction in a suitably modest sense of the term, at least in his own favourite domain of linguistic investigation – namely, the study of speech-acts – but insisted on having recourse to theory only after an exhaustive examination of the linguistic data has been completed. He craved a general theory of naming and describing. He seems to have wanted a reform of grammatical categories – for example, a systematic classification of types of conditional. He thought that his techniques might lead to a new science of language, a *Principia Grammatica* as Ryle put it, for one branch of which *How to do Things with Words* was a prolegomenon. And he believed, as Wittgenstein never would have done, that co-operative teamwork was both possible and desirable.

Deeper differences lie at the methodological (or 'metaphilosophical') level. Austin did not emphasize, as Wittgenstein did, the uniqueness of philosophy or its categorial difference from science (nor did he deny it). Like James and Russell, he claimed that

> in the history of human inquiry, philosophy has the place of the initial central sun, seminal and tumultuous: from time to time it throws off some portion of itself to take station as a science, a planet, cool and well-regulated, progressing steadily towards a distant final state. This happened long ago at the birth of mathematics, and again at the birth of physics: only in the last century we have witnessed the same process again, slow and at the same time almost imperceptible, in the birth of the science of mathematical logic, through the joint labours of philosophers and mathematicians. Is it not possible that the next century may see the birth, through the joint labours of philosophers, grammarians and numerous other students of language, of a true and comprehensive *science of language*? Then we shall have rid ourselves of one more part of philosophy (there will still be plenty left) in the only way we ever can get rid of philosophy, by kicking it upstairs.[111]

No one would deny the fact that some sciences have emerged from what was once called 'philosophy'. Nevertheless, the picture is misguided. The autonomy of mathematics, physics and mathematical logic has not meant the withering away of philosophy of mathematics, philosophy of physics or philosophy of logic. And if a future 'comprehensive science of language' is born in the next century, it will not lead to the demise of philosophy of language. The progeny of philosophy show no sign of reaching a 'steady state', and they do not cease to plague their parent with conceptual problems, despite having achieved independence. Austin did not go as far as Russell, who argued that 'as soon as definite knowledge concerning any subject becomes possible, this subject ceases to be called philosophy, and becomes a separate science', and that 'the uncertainty of philosophy is more apparent than real: those questions which are capable of definite answers are placed in the sciences, while those to which, at present, no definite answer can be given, remain to form the residue which is called philosophy'.[112] Such a view involves a profound misconception of the nature of conceptual problems, and of the differences between conceptual and empirical questions and between conceptual and theoretical difficulties.

Austin's most extensive, and most quoted, methodological reflections occur in 'A Plea for Excuses'. They are misleading, it is true; but quoting them out of context is unfair to Austin. The field of excuses commends itself, Austin argued, both because of its relevance to ethics (to the subject of freedom and responsibility) and because it is methodologically attractive if we are to proceed from 'ordinary language', 'by examining *what we should say when*, and so why and what we should mean by it'. For this is a field in which ordinary language can be expected to be rich and subtle. *If* we are going to proceed from ordinary language (which is, he stressed, *one* philosophical method), then given that words are our tools, we should use clean tools – that is, know what we mean and what we do not. Furthermore,

> words are not (except in their own little corner) facts or things; we need therefore to prise them off the world, to hold them apart from and against it, so that we can realize their inadequacies and arbitrariness, and can relook at the world without blinkers . . . our common stock of words embodies all the distinctions men have found worth drawing, and the connections they have found worth marking, in the lifetime of many generations. . . .
>
> In view of the prevalence of the slogan 'ordinary language', and of such names as 'linguistic' or 'analytic' philosophy or 'the analysis of language', one thing needs specially emphasizing to counter misunderstandings. When we examine what we should say when, what words we should use in what situations, we are looking again not *merely* at words (or 'meanings', whatever they may be) but also at the realities we use words to talk about; we are using a sharpened awareness of words to sharpen our perception of, though not as the final arbiter of, the phenomena. (Ibid., p. 130)

This was incautious. Nevertheless, to impute to Austin the view that ordinary language contains all the distinctions anyone will ever need is unjust. Not even in the field of excuses, which is what was under discussion, did he claim that ordinary language contains all the distinctions we might need (in law, for example). What he claimed was that 'If a distinction works well for practical purposes in ordinary life . . . , then there is sure to be something in it, it will not mark nothing'; on the other hand,

> this is likely enough to be not the best way of arranging things if our interests are more extensive or intellectual than ordinary. And again, that experience has been derived only from the sources available to ordinary men throughout most of civilized history: it has not been fed from the resources of the microscope and its successors. And it must be added, too, that superstition and error and fantasy of all kinds do become incorporated in ordinary language. . . . Certainly, then, ordinary language is *not* the last word: in principle it can everywhere be supplemented and improved upon and superseded. Only remember, it *is* the *first* word. (Ibid., p. 133)

The qualification is meet, for ordinary language may indeed be superseded by a technical vocabulary for specialized purposes. But the only sense in which superstition, error and fantasy become incorporated in ordinary language is by the introduction of vacuous concepts ('witch', 'phlogiston' 'hobgoblin', 'fairy', etc.), not by the embodiment of falsehoods. For concepts are neither true nor false, only more or less useful.

Similarly, to impute to Austin the view that we should 'prise words off the world', and look at the world independently of any concepts in terms of which we might articulate what we there perceive, is unfair. What he said may well be poorly expressed, but it is not evident that he meant anything more than the innocuous claim that we should examine the words we use, become aware of, for example, their vagueness, ambiguity, context-dependence, purpose-specificity (if they have these properties), *and then* 'look at the world', without being blinkered by failure to realize these limitations. It was doubtless misleading to say that we are looking 'not *merely* at words . . . but also at the realities we use words to talk about', for, taken out of context, this suggests a view of philosophy as an empirical investigation. But in context it is arguable that all he meant was that in the examination of excuses, sharpening our awareness of differences between, say, accident and mistake, negligence and recklessness, excuse, justification and mitigation, and so on will enable us to examine actual cases in the law, for example, and to draw sharper distinctions.

What conception did Austin have of philosophy and philosophical methodology? It seems to me that, apart from points already mentioned, he had *no* general conception and *no* general methodological views, other than the negative ones already discussed. He was aware that what had been deemed philosophy in the past incorporated a large variety of heterogeneous problems, some of which had in the course of history become detached from philosophy. But he saw no a priori reason to think that what was left was significantly less heterogeneous than before. He was apparently content to tackle the problems which attracted him, with the methods he felt appropriate, and refrained from any systematic general pronouncements about the nature of philosophy. As for method, we have already noted the qualified manner in which he introduced the method of 'proceeding from ordinary language'. It is noteworthy that among his papers was a sheet of notes for a lecture on his own methods, which bore the title 'Something about One Way of Possibly Doing One Part of Philosophy'.

It is, therefore, not at all surprising that philosophers could assimilate lessons learnt from both Austin and Wittgenstein without any sense of conflict or incongruity. Both sources flowed into the stream of post-war connective analytic philosophy and intermingled.

The last major figure to be examined is Strawson. With respect to Wittgenstein's influence, Strawson lies somewhere between Ryle and Austin. He acknowledges Aristotle, Hume, Kant and Wittgenstein as the primary inspirers of his thought. But in each case, what he learnt from these great forebears is thoroughly integrated into his own austere, abstract, elegant style of argument and reflection. Unlike both Austin and Wittgenstein, Strawson shared, and admired, Kant's striving for maximum generality. Though by no means succumbing to 'contempt for the particular case', his main works are characterized by the search for general structural features of our thought which are not visible in the motley of the ordinary use of language, but must be detected by reflection on fundamental functions of discourse, in particular on identifying reference, re-identification and predication. Examination of the most general conditions under which such essential functions can intelligibly be performed was a task he undertook in his most influential book, *Individuals*. Its subtitle, 'An Essay in Descriptive Metaphysics', introduced a central theme of the book, and (perhaps misleadingly) made the term 'metaphysics' respectable again after some decades 'on the Index'. 'Perhaps misleadingly', because, as previously noted, 'descriptive metaphysics', as Strawson introduced the term, does not purport to describe the most general facts about the world, let alone attain to transcendent truths. What it purports to do is to describe the most general features of our thought about the world, or, in Strawsonian idiom, of our conceptual scheme.[113] Hence it differs from the conceptual, or connective, analysis characteristic of post-war British analytic philosophy only in its scope and generality. Eschewing Collingwood's historical metaphysics, according to which metaphysics is the attempt to elicit the 'absolute presuppositions' of the science of a particular historical epoch, Strawson argued that

> there is a massive central core of human thinking which has no history – or none recorded in histories of thought; there are categories and concepts which, in their most fundamental character, change not at all. Obviously these are not the specialities of the most refined thinking. They are the commonplaces of the least refined thinking; and are yet the indispensable core of the conceptual equipment of the most sophisticated human beings. It is with these, their interconnections, and the structure they form, that a descriptive metaphysics will be primarily concerned. (Ibid., p. 10)

This structure is revealed by examination of the general conditions of identifying reference to and re-identification of particulars. What is thus revealed is the necessary primacy in our conceptual scheme – indeed, in *any* conceptual scheme capable of describing experience and its objects – of basic particulars belonging to two general types, material bodies and persons, located in a unified spatio-temporal framework.[114] Correlatively, the fundamental functions involved in the expression of thought are reference and predication, primary reference being to basic particulars identifiable within the spatio-temporal framework, secondary reference to dependent particulars, the identification of which is, in various ways, dependent upon the identification of some basic particular or particulars. And, to complete the picture, the fundamental expressions in our language with which these basic functions are performed are definite singular terms and predicates. Out of this sparse equipment, Strawson weaves a richly patterned fabric delineating the general character and forms of identifiability-dependence of kinds of non-basic particular, the nature of less fundamental functions and the grammatical modes of generation of derivative types of expression.

Where, if at all, can one discern a Wittgensteinian influence or, if not an influence, then a convergence of view? Not, to be sure, in the dazzling generality of the enterprise. But a difference of temperament, and of interest, need not betoken a conflict of judgements. Strawson's very general 'metaphysical' claims, if correct, are, from a Wittgensteinian perspective, very general descriptions of the 'grammatical' connections between expressions or types of expressions within our language – or indeed any language in which it is possible to describe experience and its objects (which is *not* to say any language). For 'descriptive metaphysics' is an investigation into the conceptual articulations and roles of general categories of expression – for example, material object names and person-referring expressions, referential and predicative expressions – and of such fundamental functions, and hence of the concepts of such functions, as identifying, describing, and so on. And, viewed from a Wittgensteinian perspective, the upshot of Strawson's investigation is a description of the grammatical web of interlocking concepts that are woven around, and partly constitutive of, our use of the expressions 'experience', 'subject of experience', 'object of experience', 'mentioning something', 'saying something about what is mentioned' and their congeners.[115]

Like Wittgenstein, and unlike traditional metaphysicians, Strawson aspires to give us a reflective understanding of what we know, indeed, of what 'is always before our eyes' (PI §129): namely, of our familiar conceptual equipment for referring to, identifying and re-identifying familiar objects of discourse. Moreover, the claim that there is 'a massive central core of human thinking which has no history' bears at least a kinship to Wittgenstein's late characterization of our 'world picture' as 'the river-bed of thought', the bank of which 'consists partly of hard rock, subject to no alteration or only to an imperceptible one' (C §99).

Though Strawson, like Ryle, has little sympathy with what he sees as Wittgenstein's excessive emphasis on therapeutic analysis, he is sympathetic to the claim that philosophy is a quest for a surveyable representation of our language or, as he would put it, of our conceptual scheme. Like Wittgenstein, Strawson repudiates the idea that philosophy is continuous with science, or that it can yield new knowledge of the world. Its goal is understanding, not knowledge. Where he differs from Wittgenstein, at this level of generality, is in the generality of his aspirations, which are 'to establish the connections between the major structural features or elements of our conceptual scheme – to exhibit it, not as a rigorous deductive system, but as a coherent whole whose parts are mutually supportive and mutually dependent, interlocking in an intelligible way'.[116] This, he claims, is 'the proper, or at least the major, task of analytic philosophy'. Like Ryle, and unlike Wittgenstein, he has no qualms about characterizing his descriptions of these connections as truths. Nor does he share Wittgenstein's aversion to the use of the term 'theory' in relation to philosophical descriptions of our conceptual scheme, though he insists that a 'theory' in philosophy is not made to the model of scientific theories. At a superficial level, this is merely a matter of terminological difference, and a distaste for provocation. At a deeper level, however, more is at stake.

The Strawsonian enterprise is to determine the fundamental structure of any conception of experience such as we can make intelligible to ourselves. Its successful upshot is the disclosure of an array of propositions which characterize this structure. 'Whether or not we choose to entitle the propositions of that structure "synthetic *a priori*"', Strawson wrote, 'it is clear that they have a distinctive character or status' (ibid., p. 44). They purport to be true propositions, though not empirical ones. They cannot illuminatingly be characterized as 'synthetic a priori', since Strawson rightly holds that Kantian category to be too unclear to be of any use.[117] But if such descriptions are neither empirical nor analytic, but rather a priori and, in some sense, *necessary*, we surely crave further elucidation. With respect to spatio-temporal unity, the determinate spatio-temporal relatedness of every event to every other event, Strawson rightly remarks that 'we are dealing here with something that conditions our whole way of talking and thinking'. But that by itself does not, *pace* Strawson, provide a *perspicuous* reason why 'we feel it to be non-contingent'.[118] Nor does the fact that spatio-temporal unity conditions our whole way of thinking explain *what it means* to claim these features to be non-contingent. The mere pervasiveness of a conditioning feature of our thought and talk does not elucidate the peculiar status of the propositions of descriptive metaphysics. Moreover, we may sense a certain conflict between the claim that such propositions are truths which we can come to know (or to realize as implicitly known) by philosophical reflection and Strawson's intimated approval of the radical Wittgensteinian view that philosophy is *not* a cognitive discipline with a subject-matter of its own, the results of which are true philosophical propositions.

Rather surprisingly, Strawson sees 'no reason why any high doctrine at all should be necessary here'. This, it seems to me, is disappointing – not because Strawson eschews the Kantian category, nor because we crave a 'high doctrine', but because he leaves us in a threefold quandary. We are left with a logical unease regarding the status of these apparently necessary propositions, which are neither truths of logic nor analytic trivialities. What is to be made of their putative necessity? Similarly, we may have epistemological qualms regarding the status of our knowledge of such propositions. It is, to be sure, a priori; but, to echo Kant, how is that possible? And what is its subject-matter? This, in turn, may leave us with 'metaphilosophical' qualms. For if these descriptions are true propositions, concerned with a certain subject-matter, then is philosophy after all a cognitive discipline, which adds to the sum of human knowledge? Are we to be thrown back to the Moorean view that its role is to describe a special domain of concepts and their relations? That is surely far removed from Strawson's vision.

If these qualms are justified, then evidently *one* way out of the quandary, which Strawson did not explore, was Wittgenstein's: namely, to treat the propositions which describe the conceptual connections between the major structural features of our conceptual scheme as expressions of 'norms of representation' or, more mundanely, as rules of grammar, in a suitably stretched sense of 'grammar'. Taken thus, their 'truth' is innocuous: it is not that they 'correspond with reality' or describe how things, in fact, are; rather, they specify rules for the use of their constituent expressions, and their 'truth' consists in the fact that they *are* the rules (just as it is true that the chess king moves one square at a time). The rejectability – if not, indeed, the unintelligibility – of their negation is perspicuous, since the negation of such a proposition is *not* a rule for the use of its constituent expressions. Indeed, it is incompatible with the rules for their use. That every spatio-temporal particular is uniquely related to every other such particular in a single unified spatio-temporal framework is partly constitutive of our concepts of spatio-temporal particular, space and time. Were someone to assert that a thing of a certain kind exists and undergoes changes, but is nowhere related to any spatial object and bears no temporal relation to any temporal event, we should conclude that the thing in question did not really exist, and that the events in question did not really happen.[119] The 'necessity' of the propositions of descriptive metaphysics merely reflects their role as norms of representation, that is, as the rules partly constitutive of the meanings of the relevant constituent expressions, and also as constituting criteria for their application or non-application. Our knowledge of them is neither knowledge about the empirical world nor knowledge about a fancied Platonic world of concepts, but merely knowledge, articulated at a high level of generality, of the rules of language by which we proceed in our linguistic transactions. The thesis of the *essential* primacy of material objects and persons in a unified spatio-temporal framework is an epitome of Strawson's reflections on the conceptual articulations of any language in which a distinction is drawn between experience and its objects. In that sense it is also an epitome of the grammar (as Wittgenstein would put it) of any such language. For a language which lacked the appropriate referential devices and characterizing expressions is one any use of which we would refuse to acknowledge as distinguishing between an object of experience and the experience of that object. This Wittgensteinian construal does not, of course, imply that philosophy is a branch of linguistics, but rather that philosophical problems are to be resolved, *inter alia*, by being reminded of, or being brought to realize, certain very general features of our linguistic practices.

Turning to Strawson's influential discussion of the concept of a person in chapter 3 of *Individuals*, we find both convergence and incompatibility with Wittgenstein. At the grand-strategic level, Strawson's attack on the Cartesian conception of a person and his defence of the primitiveness or irreducibility of our concept of a person must surely be congenial to a Wittgensteinian philosophy of psychology. At the strategic level of Strawson's refutation of scepticism about other minds, there is an affinity and a difference. The strategy is to sustain the view that 'it is a necessary condition of one's ascribing states of consciousness, experiences, to oneself, in the way one does, that one should also ascribe them, or be prepared to ascribe them, to others who are not oneself' (ibid., p. 99). This implies that a self-ascribed experiential predicate is used in exactly the same sense when it is ascribed to another. Moreover, a necessary condition of states of consciousness being ascribed at all is that they should be ascribed to the very same things: namely, persons, as certain corporeal characteristics. Further, ascription of states of consciousness to others rests not on behavioural *signs* (or, in Wittgenstein's jargon, 'symptoms'), but on *criteria* of a logically adequate kind. This conclusion follows, Strawson argued in a crucial passage,

> from a consideration of the conditions necessary for any ascription of states of consciousness to anything. The point is not that we must accept this conclusion in order to avoid scepticism, but that we must accept it in order to explain the existence of the conceptual scheme in terms of which the sceptical problem is stated. But once the conclusion is accepted, the sceptical problem does not arise. So with many sceptical problems: their statement involves the pretended acceptance of a conceptual scheme and at the same time the silent repudiation of one of the conditions of its existence. (Ibid., p. 106)

Thus Strawson's revival, and transformation, of Kantian transcendental argument. Finally, an important class of psychological predicates – for example, 'feel tired', 'am depressed', 'am in pain' – are self-ascribed 'on an entirely adequate basis', which is nevertheless 'quite distinct from those on which one ascribes the predicate to another' (p. 107; cf. p. 110). This duality, this difference between self- and other-ascription of a central group of psychological predicates, is constitutive of the unified kind of meaning they have.

The univocity of psychological predicates, their ascription to others on the basis of logically adequate criteria, the anti-Cartesian claim that they apply to one and the same subject as appropriate corporeal predicates, and the contention that scepticism is not false but incoherent constitute common ground with, and perhaps betoken some influence of, Wittgenstein. Strawson's ingenious development of the latter point, by way of a form of transcendental argument, moves in a different direction from Wittgenstein.[120] But a difference does not imply disagreement or incompatibility. However, a hint of disagreement is evident in Strawson's claim that first-person *self-ascriptions* of psychological predicates rest on *an entirely adequate basis*.[121] That this reaches deep becomes evident when we descend to the tactical level.

On Strawson's view, first-person psychological or experiential propositions involve the *self-ascription* on an *adequate basis* of a *dependent particular* – namely, an experience – to a subject, *referringly identified* by means of the first-person pronoun, who stands to the experience in question *in a relation of logically non-transferable ownership*. The identity of the experiences as particulars is logically dependent upon the identity of the person whose experiences they are. 'From this it follows immediately that if they can be identified as particular states or experiences at all, they must be possessed or ascribed . . . in such a way that it is logically impossible that a particular or experience in fact possessed by someone should have been possessed by anyone else' (ibid., p. 97). This disagreement *is* fundamental, and manifests Strawson's lack of sympathy for Wittgenstein's treatment of *Äusserungen* as *expressions* or *manifestations* of the 'inner', of the first-person pronoun and of the identity of experiences.

An utterance such as 'I am in pain' or 'I'm going to London' is, according to Wittgenstein, commonly a *manifestation* of pain or intention, not a description (although it may, in certain circumstances be a report, and there is such a thing as describing one's pain or intention, and as reporting oneself as having a pain or intention (see Volume 3, 'Avowals and descriptions')). To characterize such utterances as 'self-ascriptions' is misleading in as much as it over-emphasizes their affinity with the third-person case, and blurs the distinction between expressions (manifestations) and descriptions of the inner. A person who gives expression to his pain, avows his intention, manifests his anger or pleasure, expresses or confesses his thoughts, and so on does so without *any* 'basis' (or criterion). The first-person pronoun, in Wittgenstein's view, is at best a degenerate case of reference (see above, pp. 133f., and, in more detail, Volume 3, 'I and my self'), since its characteristic role is not to single oneself out from others, but to index one's utterance for others. Strawson's characterization of experiences as owned or possessed by the subject of those experiences, of the identity of experiences as dependent upon the identity of their 'owner', and of the 'ownership' of experiences as logically inalienable is fundamentally at odds with Wittgenstein's. To have an experience is no more to own anything, logically or otherwise, than to have a train to catch. More important, it is not a relationship, not even an *essential, identity-determining relationship*, between a basic particular (a person) and an identifiability-dependent particular (an experience). The identity of an experience is *not* dependent upon the identity of the subject of that experience. For to identify *whose* experience a given experience is, is not to identify the experience. And to identify *what* experience someone may enjoy or undergo is not to identify its subject, for the subject of an experience is not an individuating property of the experience. A pain is identified as a splitting headache, an intention as the intention to go to London tomorrow; they are not further *identified* by specification of whose pain or intention they are, any more than a colour, identified as red, is further *identified* by specification of which chairs are or have (but hardly 'own') that colour. Strawson's consequent commitment to the logical inalienability of experiences further commits him to the view, combatted by Wittgenstein (see PI §253 and Exg.), that two people cannot have exactly the same pain (or intention or thought). For if experiences are logically inalienable, then *my* experience can at best be only qualitatively, not numerically, identical with yours, for 'mine is mine and yours is yours'. But this transforms the subject of an experience into an individuating property of the experience. This is an incoherence comparable to the claim that the very same colour cannot be instantiated by two different substances, since *this* red is the colour of *this* chair, and *that* red is the colour of *that* chair. But the chair or chairs which are red are not individuating features of the colour they have. The chairs are numerically distinct, but, if they belong to the same set, may be qualitatively identical. The quality the red chairs have is neither numerically nor qualitatively the same, but just the same – if they are both the same red. The distinction between numerical and qualitative identity, which applies to substances (but not to their qualities), has *no* application to experiences. If I have a splitting, throbbing headache in my temples, and you have a splitting, throbbing headache in your temples, then we *do* have the very same pain – *neither* numerically the same *nor* qualitatively the same, but just the same.[122] If Wittgenstein is right, then the conception of experiences as *identifiability-dependent particulars* is misconceived.

Strawson's rejection of Wittgenstein's account of first-person, present-tense psychological propositions is a fundamental disagreement. It ramifies further, since Strawson is similarly unsympathetic towards Wittgenstein's non-cognitive account of such propositions – namely, that where ignorance, doubt, wondering whether and so on are grammatically excluded, so too are knowledge and certainty. In Strawson's celebrated development of Grice's defence of the causal theory of perception, he drew upon Wittgensteinian apparatus, and put it to uses of his own. He greatly enriched the Gricean account by arguing that first-person descriptions of perceptual experiences of the (deliberately regimented) form 'It sensibly seems to me just as if I were perceiving a so-and-so' *presumptively imply* that one is perceiving a so-and-so, and that one believes one is. Indeed, it presumptively implies that there is a so-and-so, which one perceives. The subtleties of his development of this theme and of his ingenious defence of the causal theory need not concern us here. What is noteworthy, from our point of view, is that the relation of 'presumptive implication' is, at the very least, a cousin of Wittgenstein's concept of a criterion: that is, a logical relation that falls short of entailment, is defeasible, but in the absence of defeating conditions justifies certainty. Equally striking is the difference: namely, that Strawson, unlike Wittgenstein, holds that propositions of the form 'It sensibly seems to me just as if . . .' are (a) descriptions of sensible experiences, (b) are themselves known, and (c) constitute a priori evidence for propositions about material objects.[123] Here too there is a fundamental incompatibility between the Strawsonian and Wittgensteinian strategies.[124] For, on a Wittgensteinian view, (a) an utterance of the form 'It sensibly seems to me just as if . . .' is not what we *call* 'the description of a perceptual (sensible) experience'. That place in grammar is already occupied. No one would reply to the request to describe his experience of hearing Maria Callas sing Tosca by saying 'It (auditorily and visually) seemed to me just as if I were seeing and hearing Maria Callas singing Tosca'. (b) That it sensibly seems to me just as if . . . is not something I can be said to know, unless it is also something of which I might be ignorant or about which I might be mistaken, which I might doubt, find out or discover, something which might seem to me to be so yet not be so (but there is no use for the form of words 'It seems to me that it seems to me just as if . . .). (c) The role of such forms of words is not to constitute evidence, either for perceptual assertions such as 'I see a so-and-so' or for objective judge-ments about perceived objects, but typically to withhold or qualify a perceptual judgement. That I see the magnolia outside my window is not my evidence for there being a magnolia out there – I need no evidence, precisely because I can see it (seeing is a way of finding out, not evidence for things being as one sees them to be; evidence for there being a magnolia in the garden would be magnolia leaves in the drive). And that it seems to me just as if I were seeing . . . is not evidence for me that I am seeing . . . , though it may be evidence for another that I am hallucinating.

Other Oxford figures display similar traits. It would be possible to survey their work too, to trace the Wittgensteinian affinities and differences in Hampshire's *Thought and Action*, to uncover in detail the marks of Wittgenstein's and Waismann's impact in the writings of Hart, to scrutinize the work of the explicitly Wittgensteinian philosophers at Oxford (in particular Anscombe and, later, Kenny). Possible, but I think unnecessary. For the general picture of analytic philosophy at Oxford and of the manner in which Wittgenstein's philosophical ideas were received in Oxford is, I trust, clear. Some figures accepted much of what they understood and turned it to their own purposes. Some, like Austin and Grice, moved along their own trails, indifferent to Wittgenstein, sometimes parallel to him, sometimes tangen-tially. Others, like Ayer, argued extensively against Wittgenstein. Secondary figures at Oxford, some of whom have been mentioned *en passant*, assimilated a great deal, for Wittgenstein's ideas and Wittgensteinian ideas were extensively debated. (It must be remembered that throughout the period with which we are concerned there was extensive controversy about the interpretation of even the basic outline of his work.) There was often convergence with Wittgensteinian views, but some-times divergence. Sometimes the convergence was quite independent of Wittgenstein, at other times it resulted from Wittgenstein's influence. Sometimes the divergence was a conscious rejection of Wittgensteinian views; at other times it was the result of misinterpretation. So it is with intellectual influence, and so, by and large, it should be. The Cam flowed into the Isis, and mingled with its waters. If there were eddies of conflict, ripples of disagreement and even occasional weirs of antagonism, they were, on the whole, minor disturbances in the flow of the fructifying waters of analytic philosophy in its last great, connective phase. By the mid-1970s this was coming to an end. It is to the tale of how and why that happened that we must finally turn.

7

Post-positivism in the United States and Quine's Apostasy

1. The logical positivists in America

The impact of the logical positivist emigrés upon philosophy in the United States was considerable. It would be no exaggeration to say that it gave American philosophy its characteristic profile for the rest of the twentieth century. The preoccupation of many of the members of the Vienna Circle and affiliates with formal languages, and their use of the apparatus of formal logic in the service of philosophy, chimed well with current intellectual dispositions. The pragmatist tradition of Peirce, James and Dewey, with its instrumentalist conception of science, provided a healthy stock on which to graft logical empiricism, which, particularly in Carnap's work, already had a pragmatist bent. There were few philosophers of science in the United States prior to 1930, exceptions being Morris R. Cohen and A. C. Benjamin. There were, however, a number of distinguished philosopher-scientists who were concerned with the logic and methodology of their sciences: for example, the physicist Percy W. Bridgman and the psychologists E. G. Boring and S. S. Stevens at Harvard, J. B. Watson at Johns Hopkins and the physicist Victor F. Lenzen at Berkeley. Sympathy for specific strands in logical positivism was evident among the operationalists, led by Bridgman among the physicists, and among the behaviourist-cum-operationalist psychologists such as Boring, Stevens, E. C. Tolman, C. L. Hull and B. F. Skinner. Pragmatism, operationalism and behaviourism prepared the soil for the great growth of interest in the philosophy of science, in problems of induction and probability, and in various forms of physicalism in philosophical psychology, which was brought about by the emigration of so many members of the Vienna Circle and of the Berlin Society for Scientific Philosophy.

The first member of the Circle to visit the United States was Schlick, who spent a semester lecturing at Stanford in 1929, and another at Berkeley in 1931. His papers 'The Future of Philosophy' and 'A New Philosophy of Experience', both published in the United States in 1932, made some of the ideas of the Circle accessible to American audiences.

The first immigrant was Herbert Feigl, who spent nine months at Harvard in 1930–1 working with Bridgman on the foundations of physics. Together with his friend Albert Blumberg, he published 'Logical Positivism: A New Movement in European Philosophy' in the *Journal of Philosophy* (1931), which, in his words, 'started the ball rolling' as far as positivism in the United States was concerned.[1] He accepted the offer of a post at the University of Iowa in 1931, and settled in the

States. He moved to Minnesota in 1940, where he remained for the rest of his career. In 1946 Wilfrid Sellars was recruited to the faculty at Minnesota, and Feigl collaborated with him on various projects. Together they edited the influential anthology *Readings in Philosophical Analysis* (1949), which introduced American readers to many of the classics among the Circle's publications. Feigl and Sellars, together with May Broadbeck, John Hospers and Paul Meehl as co-editors, founded *Philosophical Studies*, originally as a counterpart to the British journal *Analysis*. In 1953, the Minnesota Center for Philosophy of Science was established, with Feigl as director. It published important papers in *Minnesota Studies in the Philosophy of Science*, among which Feigl's monograph 'The "Mental" and the "Physical"' (in vol. 2, 1958) attracted much attention.[2] The Minnesota Center invited visits from, and organized conferences of, leading scholars in the philosophy of science. Comparable centres were set up at the universities of Indiana and Pittsburgh, and, independently, in Boston (led by Robert S. Cohen) and Stanford (under Patrick Suppes).

Among American philosophers sympathetic to logical positivism in the 1930s were Charles Morris at Chicago and Ernest Nagel at Columbia. Both attended the Circle's International Congress of Philosophy in Prague in 1934, where Morris became acquainted with Carnap, whose interest in linguistic theory he shared. In 1936, he was instrumental in bringing Carnap to Chicago, and, in 1937, in obtaining a year's research post for Hempel. Later, he assisted in bringing Reichenbach to the United States. His *Signs, Language and Behaviour* (1947) formulated a theory of signs ('semiotic') in behavioural terms, distinguishing four different modes of signifying (the designative, appraisive, prescriptive and formative) and four basic uses of language (the informative, valuative, incitive and systematic). Nagel had studied under Dewey at Columbia and at City College under Morris Cohen, who fostered his interest in the philosophy of science. His later monumental *The Structure of Science* (1961) was a classic statement of positivist philosophy of science. In it he defended and elaborated Hempel's deductive-nomological account of the nature of scientific explanation, extending it to the biological sciences, arguing for the eliminability of forms of teleological explanation in biology, and developing Hempel's application of the 'covering law' model to historical explanation (see below). More generally, like all the logical empiricists, he denied the claim of hermeneutic philosophers that the human sciences are logically *sui generis* (e.g. that explanation of action in terms of reasons, intentions and motives is not logically homogeneous with explanation in the physical sciences).

The Vienna Circle and its associated groups were committed, as the 'Manifesto' had optimistically declared, to the 'shaping of economic and social life according to rational principles'. Some were liberals, others socialists or Marxists. As the Nazi menace in Europe grew, most of them fled.[3] The Vienna Circle ceased to exist; after the *Anschluss* its publications were prohibited because there had been Jews among its members and because the Ernst Mach Society was regarded as subversive.[4] In the following discussion, I shall limit myself to the philosophically most influential figures who escaped to the United States, and briefly recount their peregrinations in order to make clear their extensive influence in America, through both their teaching and their publications.

Hempel (b. 1905) fled Berlin in 1934 to Brussels. In 1937–8 he had a year's research post in Chicago, and early in 1939, he emigrated to the United States, where he taught first in New York, then at Yale (1948–55), from where he went to Princeton and later (1977) to Pittsburgh. From his Berlin days onwards, through his years in Belgium and his American career, he collaborated with his friend Paul Oppenheim (who also escaped from Europe). Together they wrote on the logic of non-quantitative ordering concepts, on confirmation theory and on scientific explanation. Hempel's main interests lay in these fields and in concept formation in the physical and social sciences.[5] He liberalized verificationism (as Carnap had done in the mid-1930s), and came to a more holistic conception of confirmation and cognitive significance than had characterized earlier sentential verificationism. His extensive writings on the logic of scientific explanation defended the 'deductive-nomological' or 'covering law' model. He wrote early and late upon historical explanation. His 'The Function of General Laws in History' (1942) extended the covering law model of explanation to history, and argued for methodological monism. This thoroughgoing empiricist conception of historical explanation dominated analytic reflection upon the subject until it was challenged by William Dray's *Laws and Explanation in History* (1957).

Reichenbach fled from Berlin in 1933 to Turkey, where he taught at the University of Istanbul until 1938, when he emigrated to the United States. He taught at UCLA until his death in 1953, becoming one of the leading philosophers of science in America. He published his *Philosophical Foundations of Quantum Mechanics* in 1944, *The Theory of Probability* in 1949, a revised edition of his 1935 book, and *The Rise of Scientific Philosophy* in 1951. In *Experience and Prediction* (1938), he defined his position in relation to orthodox logical positivism, rejecting phenomenalism in favour of a conventionalist form of realism about physical objects, as well as realism regarding unobservables in physical theory (which, in his view, are inferred, rather than constructed, entities). Like Carnap, he conceived of realism as a matter of the choice of a language; but, unlike Carnap, he thought of it as the choice of a language in which one can speak of things existing when unobserved, as opposed to a language in which one can speak of things only when observed by oneself.[6] The choice of a realist language is justified by 'normal language' and by our normal justifications of actions (e.g. taking out a life insurance policy). Impressions are neither evidence for the existence of objects, nor are they immediately given. Indeed, they are not directly observed at all, but are inferred entities. Impressions, as in dreams, are states of one's own nervous system. What we (corrigibly) observe are things; indeed, our immediate judgements about observables are not just corrigible, but also only probable, since any such judgement can be overturned by a future observation. He accepted verifiability as a criterion of meaningfulness, but held that probabilistic, rather than conclusive, verification is adequate. He construed causal laws as statistical and inductive inferences as probabilistic, involving estimates of the limit of a relative frequency in an infinite sequence. One posits that the limit of a given sequence approximates the relative frequency in the hitherto observed segment of the series. Induction, he argued, has a pragmatic justification.

Philipp Frank (1884–1966) left Prague in 1937, and accepted a post in the physics department at Harvard (1939–54), teaching primarily courses in the philosophy of science. He published a collection of his papers, *Between Philosophy and Physics*, in 1941. He contributed a monograph 'Foundations of Physics' (1946) to the *Foundations of the Unity Science* (vol. 1), and published *Philosophy of Science: The Link between Science and Philosophy* in 1957. Richard von Mises (1883–1953), like Reich-enbach, fled Berlin in 1933, and taught at the University of Istanbul from 1933 to 1939. In 1939 he managed to reach the United States, where he found a haven at Harvard, teaching mathematical physics and aerodynamics. He published *Positivism – A Study in Human Understanding* in 1951. Felix Kaufmann fled from Vienna, and was appointed to teach at the New School for Social Research in New York. His main English publication during the decade spent in the United States (he died in 1949) was his *Methodology of the Social Sciences* (1944), a completely new version of his 1934 book (see p. 282 n. 6). His work during the New York years was primarily in social theory.

Kurt Gödel (1906–78) left Vienna in 1939, and obtained an appointment at the Princeton Institute for Advanced Study, where he remained for the rest of his career. He published a proof of the consistency of the axiom of choice and con-tinuum hypothesis, and established an 'inner model' for set theory (the 'constructible universe L'). His 'Dialectica interpretation' of classical arithmetic in terms of prim-itive recursive functionals of higher type led to a new consistency proof for classical arithmetic. In his philosophical work (e.g. 'Russell's Mathematical Logic' (1944) and 'What is Cantor's Continuum Problem?' (1947)) he maintained an infinitistic viewpoint, propounding a realist, Platonist conception of mathematics.

Karl Menger (1902–85) left Vienna to become professor of mathematics at the University of Notre Dame, Indiana, in 1937. In 1948 he moved to the Illinois Institute of Technology in Chicago, where he taught until 1971, when he became an emeritus professor. Most of his work was in mathematics and, later, in econom-ics, although he wrote occasional papers on related philosophical themes.[7] Gustav Bergmann (1906–87) left Vienna for the United States in the same year, teaching first in New York, then succeeding Feigl in Iowa in 1940. He established there an idiosyncratic school of Platonist ontologists, who drew inspiration from, and con-tributed to the clarification of, the ontology and metaphysics of the *Tractatus*.

Alfred Tarski (1902–83) was invited to the Conference for the Unity of Science at Harvard in 1939, which was, in effect, the last pre-war gathering of the Vienna Circle in exile, organized by Morris and Neurath, who came from Holland. Woodger, Nagel, Morris and Quine pressed Tarski to come, and they raised funds for his visit. Once in the United States, a makeshift post was found for him at Harvard for 1939–40. This literally saved his life (his parents were murdered by the Nazis). In 1941–2, he accepted a post at Berkeley, where he taught for the rest of his career. Over the years, he established Berkeley as a world centre of mathematical logic. In 1958, he set up a graduate programme there, the Group in Logic and the Methodology of Science, designed to link philosophy, logic, mathematics and sci-ence. He gathered around him a group of leading logicians (e.g. Leon Henkin, John Addison, R. L. Vaught and Ralph MacKenzie of the older generation and Robert Solovay, Leo Harrington and Jack Silver of the younger). His work established model theory as a subject, and he made major contributions to set theory.

In 1940 Harvard was host to an extraordinary gathering of internationally famed philosophers. Russell was there giving the William James Lectures, Carnap was visiting professor on sabbatical from Chicago, Feigl was on sabbatical as a Rockefeller research fellow, Tarski was teaching there temporarily, I. A. Richards was a visitor, Quine and Morton White were members of the faculty, as were Frank and von

Mises, and Nelson Goodman had just finished his thesis 'A Study of Qualities' (later to become *The Structure of Appearances*), which was a further development of Carnap's *Logischer Aufbau*. The discussions which took place stimulated the decades-long controversy between Carnap and Quine on the nature of the analytic/synthetic distinction, Tarski, Quine and White lining up against Carnap.[8]

The influence of this group of European emigrés in America over the next two decades and more was considerable, particularly that of Carnap. He had left Prague in 1936, obtaining a chair at the University of Chicago, where he taught until 1952, when he moved to the Institute for Advanced Study at Princeton for two years, where he worked with John Kemeny on inductive logic – his major interest in his later years. On Reichenbach's death in 1954, he replaced him at UCLA, where he remained until his death in 1970.

Carnap's work falls into four phases. The first, culminating in the *Logischer Aufbau*, has been discussed. The second, briefly mentioned, culminated in *The Logical Syntax of Language* (1934). Here he tried to show two things. First, that the concepts of the theory of formal deductive logic, such as provability, derivability and logical independence, are purely syntactical. These concepts, he argued, depend only on the forms of sentences, not on their meanings, hence their definitions can be formulated in logical syntax. Secondly, that venerable philosophical controversies ostensibly about ontology concern no more than the question of whether a particular language form should or should not be used in a given domain – for example, in mathematics or science. When properly formulated, Carnap argued, controversies between intuitionists and classical mathematicians, or between realists and idealists, turn on the choice of a language. Any assertion that a particular language or logic is the correct one is misconceived. According to his principle of tolerance (or principle of the conventionality of linguistic forms), everyone is free to choose the rules of his language and hence his logic as he pleases. Hence, irresolvable debates concerning the correct logic, or realist and idealist ontologies, are replaced by resolvable questions concerning the syntactical properties of different languages and practical questions of their relative utility.

Under the influence of Tarski and his explication of truth, Carnap came to think that it is possible to talk in a metalanguage about the relation between expressions of an object language and the facts, given that the metalanguage contains the sentences of the object language or their translations. This change of view heralded Carnap's third phase – of semantics. Concepts previously treated purely syntactically, such as 'analytic', 'synthetic', 'extensionality', 'implication', 'equivalence', were now analysed in semantic terms. He explicated the concepts of extension and intension in terms of equivalence and L-equivalence, and invoked what he called 'the method of extension and intension' in analysing the meanings of linguistic expressions. He came to conceive of the task of philosophy not as logico-syntactical analysis, but rather as the semantic analysis of the meanings of linguistic expressions. His new outlook was developed in a series of three books: *Introduction to Semantics* (1942), *Formalization of Logic* (1943) and *Meaning and Necessity* (1947). Here he evolved his notion of L-truth in semantics, as an explication of Leibniz's concept of necessary truth and Kant's concept of analytic truth, and his notion of intensional isomorphism, as an explication of the concept of synonymy. These notions, he argued against Tarski and Quine, vindicated the Vienna Circle's distinction between factual and logical truth. Quine's ontological qualms about talk of abstract entities *praeter necessitatem* (in his 1948 paper 'On What There Is') were a stimulus for Carnap's best-known essay 'Empiricism, Semantics and Ontology' (1950). The question of whether classes, properties or numbers exist, Carnap argued, is a pseudo-question. It is not a theoretical question at all, but a 'framework' question concerning whether to adopt a language containing such expressions. It calls not for proofs of existence or ontological commitments, but for a decision, which turns not on any truth, but only on convenience, fruitfulness and simplicity of the resultant theory.

'Internal questions', such as 'Did King Arthur really live?' or 'Are unicorns real or imaginary?', are answerable by investigation. 'External' (or 'framework') questions are such as 'Do material objects exist?', 'Are there classes?', 'Do numbers exist?' These are raised only by philosophers. To be real in the scientific sense, Carnap argued, is simply to be an element in the chosen system or language. But the question of reality cannot intelligibly be raised about the system itself. We are free to choose a phenomenalist language, or a 'thing-language', as we please. If someone opts for the thing-language, we can say that he accepts the world of things. But that does not mean that he believes in the reality of the 'thing-world', for there is no such belief. It simply means that he has accepted certain rules for forming statements, for testing, accepting or rejecting them. The thesis of the reality of the thing-world cannot be formulated in the thing-language or in any other theoretical language. The efficiency of the thing-language is not evidence for the reality of the thing-world, but it does make it advisable to adopt this language rather than some other. Similar considerations apply to other seemingly ontological questions concerning the existence of propositions, classes, numbers or properties. It is merely a question of adopting a language in which certain kinds of expression are admitted. Two steps are essential. First, a general term, a predicate of higher level for the new kind of entities, must be introduced. This permits us to say of something that it belongs to this kind – for example, 'Red is a *property*', 'Five is a *number*'. Secondly, variables of the new type must be introduced into the language. The new entities are the values of these variables; the constants are substitutable for the variables. Having introduced these new forms into the language, it is possible to formulate genuine, internal questions, such as 'Is there a prime number which . . . ?' or 'Are there unicorns?' Questions of this kind may be empirical or logical. Accordingly, a true answer is either factually true or analytic.

The final phase of Carnap's work, which will not be discussed here, was largely concerned with probability and induction. It is noteworthy that his analysis of probability drew its inspiration in part from the *Tractatus*.

Carnap's influence in America was very great. After his death, Quine wrote:

> Carnap is a towering figure. I see him as the dominant figure in philosophy from the 1930s onward, as Russell had been in the decades before. Russell's well-earned glory went on mounting afterward, as the evidence of his historical importance continued to pile up; but the leader of the developments was Carnap. Some philosophers would assign this role rather to Wittgenstein; but many see the scene as I do.[9]

What is indisputable, as we shall see, is that Carnap's views were the primary stimulus for the development of the leading, and most influential, post-war American philosopher: namely, Quine. The rest of this chapter will be concerned with his philosophy.

2. Quine and Wittgenstein: similarity amidst differences

I shall dwell at length on Quine's philosophy for four reasons. First, the legacy of logical positivism in the United States was radically transmuted by him. Secondly, many of the *idées reçues* of contemporary American philosophy are derived from Quine, and are inimical to Wittgensteinian philosophy. If the turn away from Wittgenstein that has occurred in the last twenty years is to be understood, it is necessary that Quine's impact be appreciated.[10] Thirdly, his philosophy, if correct, brings analytic philosophy as depicted in this book to an end, for the conception that informs analytic philosophy (and has informed it since the 1920s) is inconsistent with that of Quine, who reverts to the earlier, Russellian phase of analytic philosophy which Wittgenstein criticized in the *Tractatus* (see pp. 29, 319 n. 23). This alone would justify a detailed comparison of Quine's philosophy with the later Wittgenstein's. But there is a further, fourth reason for close examination of Quine's thought. A first glance at the philosophies of Quine and Wittgenstein suggests an extensive convergence of views. Given that Quine's philosophy has been one of the main reasons for the turn away from Wittgenstein and analytic philosophy, the convergences, actual and merely apparent, as well as the deeper divergences call out for explanation.

They converge, at least superficially, with regard to the following points:

(i) The meanings of words are neither ideas in the mind nor objects (Platonic or otherwise) in reality. Both philosophers deny that the concept of meaning can be explained mentalistically – that is, by reference to mental acts of meaning or intending or by reference to mental images or ideas. Wittgenstein remarked in 1931 that the concept of meaning is now obsolete save for such expressions as 'means the same as' or 'has no meaning' (M 258; AWL 30). Quine wrote in 1948 that 'The useful ways in which people ordinarily talk about meanings boil down to two: the *having* of meanings, which is significance, and *sameness* of meaning, or synonymy. What is called *giving* the meaning of an utterance is simply the uttering of a synonym, couched ordinarily, in clearer language than the original. . . . But the explanatory value of special irreducible intermediary entities called meanings is surely illusory' (WTI 11f.).

(ii) One of the most famous Wittgensteinian dicta is 'Don't ask for the meaning, ask for the use'. Quine, in one of his relatively rare references to Wittgenstein, quotes it approvingly: 'Wittgenstein has stressed that the meaning of a word is to be sought in its use. This is where the empirical semanticist looks: to verbal behaviour. John Dewey was urging this point in 1925. "Meaning", he wrote, ". . . is primarily a property of behaviour." And just what property of behaviour might meaning then be? Well, we can take the behaviour, the use, and let the meaning go' (UPM 46).[11]

(iii) Quine denies the intelligibility of the analytic/synthetic distinction. Wittgenstein does not invoke it (save, very occasionally, to remark that if anything is a candidate for being synthetic a priori, it is mathematical propositions (RFM 246)). No more than Quine did he think that the analytic/synthetic distinction, whether in its Kantian, Fregean or Viennese form, was the instrument for elucidating the character of what are called 'necessary truths'. He did not think, as Kant and Frege (in different ways) did, that necessary truths can usefully be divided into those that are analytic and those that are synthetic a priori, or, as Carnap did, that all necessary truths are analytic. Part of the reason for the agreement between Wittgenstein and Quine on these negative points lies in their convergence with regard to the following point.

(iv) Both philosophers reject the Vienna Circle's view that logical truths are true by convention, or true in virtue of meanings. According to Quine, the idea that meanings of words, whether construed as ideas in the mind or as abstract entities, can determine truths or determine us to use words in a certain way is 'the myth of a museum in which the exhibits are meanings and the words are labels' (OR 27). According to Wittgenstein, to say, for example, that the truth of '$p = \sim \sim p$' *follows* from the meaning of negation is to be committed to the mythical *Bedeutungskörper* (meaning-body) conception of meaning, which he condemned (see pp. 48, 286 n. 50).

(v) Both deny that a natural language is a calculus with determinate rules which fix necessary and sufficient conditions for the application of all meaningful expressions in a language.

(vi) Both deny the reducibility of all propositions or sentences to a set of propositions or protocol sentences which are conclusively verifiable by reference to what is immediately given in experience.

(vii) Hence, both repudiate classical foundationalism in epistemology. Quine's stance is epitomized in the dictum that 'There is no First Philosophy'. Holism displaces foundationalism, and 'naturalized epistemology', drawing upon psychology, neurophysiology and physics, replaces the investigation of the justification of knowledge claims with causal explanations. Wittgenstein's private language arguments undermine classical foundationalism. He replaced it (in *On Certainty*) not with naturalized epistemology but with socialized epistemology.

(viii) They agree that language learning rests upon training. The mastery of a language is rooted in natural behavioural propensities and in the training a child receives in his acculturation. It does not presuppose thought, let alone innate knowledge.

(ix) They agree that language learning involves ostensive teaching, and that the mere ostensive gesture by itself does not suffice to determine the use of the word in question (RoR 44f.; OR 30f., 38f.)

(x) They agree that the way an expression was learnt, the manner of its introduction, as such, is irrelevant to its status and role. Quine argues that the conventional, legislative introduction of definitions or postulates 'is a passing trait, significant at the moving front of science but useless in classifying the sentences behind the lines. It is a trait of events and not of sentences' (CLT 112). Wittgenstein argues that 'the way we actually learn its meaning drops out of our future understanding of the symbol'; 'the history of how we came to know what [the colour-word 'green', e.g.] means is irrelevant' (LWL 23). 'The historical fact of the explanation is of no importance' (LWL 38). There is, he argued, 'no action at a distance in grammar', and what fixes the status of a proposition is its use, which may change over time or even from occasion to occasion of its employment.

(xi) Both invoke radical translation, the translation of the language of a wholly alien people, as a heuristic device to illuminate the concepts of language, meaning and understanding. Like Quine, Wittgenstein approached philosophical questions in this domain (and others) from 'an ethnological point of view'. He wrote: 'If we look at things from an ethnological point of view, does that mean we are saying that philosophy is ethnological? No, it only means that we are taking up a position right outside so as to be able to see things *more* objectively' (CV 37).[12] Hence he remarked, as Quine would, 'The common behaviour of mankind is the system of reference by means of which we interpret an unknown language' (PI §206).

(xii) Both recognize a problem of indeterminacy in the use of language and the interpretation of its use. Wittgenstein raises a problem of *apparent* radical indeterminacy in the applications of rules, since it seems that quite different courses of action can be made out to accord with a rule, given an appropriate interpretation. This leads to the paradox that there is no such thing as correctly or incorrectly following a rule (PI §201). That paradox must be defused, on pain of concluding absurdly that there is no correct or incorrect application of rules, and hence no such thing as a correct, meaningful use of language. For Quine, there is an apparent problem of radical indeterminacy of translation (both abroad and at home) and of radical indeterminacy or inscrutability of reference. This too must be defused, on pain of concluding absurdly that all reference to objects is nonsense (OR 48).

(xiii) At first blush, both approach questions of understanding behaviouristically. Quine holds that 'Semantics is vitiated by a pernicious mentalism as long as we regard a man's semantics as somehow determinate in his mind beyond what might be implicit in his dispositions to overt behaviour. It is the very facts about meaning, not the entities meant, that must be construed in terms of behaviour' (OR 27). Wittgenstein wrote: 'I conceive of understanding, in a sense, behaviouristically . . . What is behaviourist in my conception consists only in that I do not distinguish between "outer" and "inner". Because psychology does not concern me' (Vol. VI, 296f.; BT 284).

(xiv) They converge in their conception of truth, repudiating correspondence and coherence theories alike, and, relative to those theories, trivializing truth. However, Wittgenstein adopted a deflationary (Ramseian) account of truth, whereas Quine treats 'is true' as a disquotational device.[13]

(xv) A form of holism with regard to understanding a language is common to both. Quine remarks: 'It is of theoretical sentences such as "neutrinos lack mass", etc. above all that Wittgenstein's dictum holds true: "Understanding a sentence means understanding a language" (BB 5)', and adds in a footnote: 'Perhaps the doctrine of indeterminacy of translation will have little air of paradox for readers familiar with Wittgenstein's latter-day remarks on meaning' (WO 76f.).

(xvi) Both adopt holism with respect to the web of belief. They concur that the web consists of beliefs which are differently related to experience, some exposed to direct verification or falsification, others deeply embedded within the network. Wittgenstein wrote: 'All testing, all confirmation and disconfirmation of an hypothesis takes place within a system . . . The system is the element in which arguments have their life' (C §105). Again, 'A child learns to believe a host of things. I.e. it learns to act according to these beliefs. Bit by bit there forms a system of what is believed, and in that system some things stand unshakably fast and some are more or less liable to shift. What stands fast does so, not because it is intrinsically obvious or convincing; it is held fast by what lies around it' (C §144).

(xvii) Both agree that we hold mathematical statements immune to falsification. Quine's 'maxim of minimum mutilation' is one of the two guide-lines[14] of his holistic doctrine of accommodating the falsification of what he calls 'an observation categorical'[15] which is implied by a hypothesis in conjunction with other sentences of the theory. We need not reject the hypothesis, but may instead reject some of the other sentences. However, 'The maxim constrains us, in our choice of what sentences . . . to rescind, to safeguard any purely mathematical truth; for mathematics infiltrates all branches of our system of the world, and its disruption would reverberate intolerably' (TI 11). Similarly, Wittgenstein remarks that we should not ever *allow* anything to prove that we are wrong in saying $12 \times 12 = 144$ (LFM 291). We deposit mathematical propositions 'in the archives' (RFM 165), and they are thereby *withdrawn* from doubt (RFM 363). A proof shows one how one *can hold fast* to the proposition without running any risk of getting into conflict with experience (RFM 436). The 'hardness of the logical "must"' indicates our refusal to depart from a concept (RFM 238).

(xviii) Both reject *de re* necessity. Quine continues the previously quoted remark by saying: 'If asked why he spares mathematics, the scientist will perhaps say that its laws are necessarily true; but I think that we have here an explanation, rather, of mathematical necessity itself. It resides in our unstated policy of shielding mathematics by exercising our freedom to reject other beliefs instead.' So, too, Wittgenstein holds that the apparent inexorability of logic and mathematics is *our* inexorability in cleaving to them (RFM 37). What appear to be necessities in the world are merely the shadows cast by grammar.

Quine is widely held to be a paradigmatically systematic thinker. In so far as Quine's systematicity consists in his having discussed in detail all the above themes and having woven them into an apparently seamless web, then Wittgenstein is no less systematic, even though *his method of exposition* is 'unsystematic' – being aphoristic and often non-linear. For he too discussed all these themes in detail. But despite initial appearances, the tapestry he wove is profoundly different from Quine's. The negative points of convergence (*roughly* i, iii–vii, x, xiv and xviii) are genuine, although the reasons for them are often very different (especially iii, vii and xviii), and the conclusions drawn from the rejection of the doctrines in question are wholly different. The positive points, as we shall see, often mask profound disagreement (especially ii, xii and xv–xvii). Even where there is a degree of methodological agreement (xi and xiii), the employment of the methodology is altogether distinct, inasmuch as Wittgenstein's conception of language, unlike Quine's, is normative. The latter disagreement also infects the partial agreement over such points as (viii). For Quine, unlike Wittgenstein, does not a recognize a transition from mere training to teaching by way of explanations of meaning, to learning by asking for the meaning of terms (both in the form of questions such as 'What does "W" mean?' and in the form 'What is a W?') and being given rules for their use in the form of such explanations. Similarly, the agreement over ostensive teaching (ix) is superficial, for Quine does not conceive of ostensive definition as a rule for the use of a word, or of a sample as belonging to the method of representation and as constituting a standard for the correct application of the *definiendum*.

To show just how misleading the appearance of philosophical convergence is, we must first survey, as briefly as is compatible with fair representation, (a) the background to and (b) the main contours of Quine's philosophy.

3. Quine and logical empiricism: the end of analytic philosophy?

Quine (b. 1908) took his first degree at Oberlin College in mathematics (1926–30), and did his Ph.D. at Harvard, where he wrote a dissertation entitled 'The Logic of Sequences: A Generalization of *Principia Mathematica*'. A travelling scholarship enabled him to spend 1932–3 in Europe, where he dwelt in Vienna for five months, attending meetings of the Vienna Circle. Thence he went to Prague, where he was befriended by Carnap, attended his lectures, and read the first draft of *The Logical Syntax of Language* as it was being written. He spent six weeks in Warsaw, where he was befriended by Tarski. Much of his subsequent work was stimulated, both positively and negatively, by the logical empiricism of the Vienna Circle. In particular, Carnap was then and later the main stimulus for the development of Quine's philosophy. In his 'Homage to Carnap' (1970), Quine wrote:

> Carnap was my greatest teacher. I got to him in Prague 38 years ago, just a few months after I had finished my formal studies and received my Ph.D. I was very much his disciple for six years. In later years his views went on evolving and so did mine, in divergent ways. But even where we disagreed, he was still setting the theme; the line of my thought was largely determined by problems that I felt his position presented.[16]

Quine shared much common ground with Carnap and members of the Circle.

(i) Like them, he was and remained an empiricist, holding that all knowledge is derived from experience. Unlike them, he came to explicate (or, as he put it, 'to make an analytic tool of') the concept of experience in neither phenomenalist nor Carnapian physicalist terms, but rather in terms of stimulations of sense-receptors. The common-or-garden concept of experience, he came to think, is 'ill-suited for use as an instrument of philosophical clarification' (Res. 184f.).

(ii) Like the scientifically trained philosophers of the Circle, Quine held that the paradigm of knowledge is scientific knowledge. It is science and scientific theory that yield the best picture of the nature of reality. All understanding of reality is cut to the model of scientific understanding.

(iii) The Circle cleaved to the doctrine of the unity of science. Quine held *analogously* that all knowledge can be unified in a single system, the core of which is given by the master science – physics. For 'every change of any kind involves a change in physical microstates', and these are to be explained by physics. Physics gives us the fundamental description of reality, and all deep explanations of phenomena are physical explanations, for the fundamental laws of the universe are physical laws. Explanations in less fundamental sciences, though not reducible to physics, are at best local generalizations supervenient upon physical law.

(iv) Although Quine rejected the principle of verification, that 'the meaning of a statement is the method of confirming or infirming it' (TDE 37), he did not reject verificationism:

> The Vienna Circle espoused a verification theory of meaning but did not take it seriously enough. If we recognize with Peirce that the meaning of a sentence turns purely on what would count as evidence for its truth, and if we recognize with Duhem that theoretical sentences have their evidence not as single sentences but only as larger blocks of theory, then the indeterminacy of translation of theoretical sentences is the natural conclusion. And most sentences, apart from observation sentences, are theoretical. This conclusion, conversely, once it is embraced, seals the fate of any general notion of propositional meaning or, for that matter, state of affairs.
>   Should the unwelcomeness of the conclusion persuade us to abandon the verification theory of meaning? Certainly not. (EN 80f.)

(v) Quine shared the Circle's (general, though not uniform) distaste for 'abstract entities' and the nominalist preference for austere 'desert landscapes' (WTI 4). In a joint paper with Goodman in 1947, he wrote: 'We do not believe in abstract entities. No one supposes that abstract entities – classes, relations, properties, etc. – exist in space and time; but we mean more than this. We renounce them altogether.'[17] Although Quine came to 'accept' the existence of classes, functions and numbers, his philosophy is permeated with a preference for, though not a commitment to, nominalism. Abstract entities are to be admitted into one's ontology only in so far as they are required for respectable science and philosophy, and in so far as sharp extensional criteria of identity for them are forthcoming. He is therefore a qualified, economical realist, but an unqualified 'extensionalist' (Res. 182–4). Among what Quine thought of as illegitimate abstract entities are propositions, which he conceived of as the purported meanings of sentences.[18] Meanings – and indeed, 'intensions' of any kind – were banished from Quine's landscape as 'entities' wrongly posited by sundry theories.

Unlike the members of the Vienna Circle, Quine had a substantial American heritage, consisting of (a) pragmatism, derived from Dewey (and perhaps C. I. Lewis, who taught Quine at Harvard), and (b) behaviourism, derived from Watson, and behaviourist language theory, derived from Skinner.[19] He later came to accept Davidson's anomalous monism (or 'token physicalism' (PT 71)), conceding that Brentano was right about the irreducibility of intensional discourse, inasmuch as there are 'irreducibly mental . . . ways of grouping a lot of respectably physical perceptions as perceptions that p, and grouping a lot of respectably physical belief instances as the belief that p'. Nevertheless, even with this reluctant concession, he continued to argue that 'there is good reason not to try to weave it into our scientific theory of the world to make a more comprehensive system'. Early and late, he believed that 'in linguistics one has no choice but to be a behaviourist'. For 'Each of us learns his language by observing other people's verbal behaviour and having his own faltering behaviour observed and reinforced or corrected by others. We depend strictly on overt behaviour in observable situations' (PT 38). His behaviourism is the driving force behind his doctrine of the indeterminacy of translation (PT 37). It is also, as we shall see, the driving force behind his rejection of the analytic/synthetic distinction in so far as that rejection turns on the unavailability of behavioural criteria of synonymy which satisfy his construal of an untarnished behaviourist methodology.

Sharing some of the basic tenets of Viennese logical empiricism, Quine nevertheless rejected three of its fundamental doctrines in the name of a purified empiricism,
a verificationism revamped to the requirements of holism, and behaviourism.

(i) He rejected the intelligibility of the analytic/synthetic distinction, interpreted as
a distinction between truths that are grounded in meanings, independently of facts,
and truths that are grounded in empirical fact. Hence, too, he rejected the pivotal
positivist claim that so-called necessary truths are analytic – that is, true in virtue
of the meanings of their constituent expressions, or true by linguistic convention.[20]

(ii) He rejected the reductionism that had informed the early phases of Viennese
logical positivism – that is, the claim that all significant empirical sentences are
reducible to what is given in immediate experience. This conception had informed
the programme of logical construction apparently sanctioned by the *Tractatus* and
pursued (most notably by Carnap in *Der logische Aufbau der Welt*) in the wake of
Russell.

(iii) He repudiated sentential verificationism – that is, the claim that the unit of
empirical significance is the sentence, which is confirmed or disconfirmed in experience. Instead, Quine, like Duhem, defended a holistic conception of confirmation.[21]
Our statements about the external world face the tribunal of sense experience not
individually but as a corporate body.

These anti-positivist doctrines undermine the Vienna Circle's conception of philosophy, and not just that of the Circle, but of analytic philosophy in general. Of
course, it is not true that analytic philosophy in all its phases was committed either
to sentential verificationism or to reductionism. Nor was it necessarily committed
to upholding the analytic/synthetic distinction as traditionally conceived or as explicated by Carnap – Wittgenstein, as mentioned, was not so committed. (He distinguished, rather, between logical and grammatical truths on the one hand (which
are not to be assimilated) and empirical truths on the other (which are not uniform,
propositions of the *Weltbild* occupying a special position).) Nevertheless, a fundamental tenet of analytic philosophy, from its post-*Tractatus* phase onwards, was
that there is a sharp distinction between philosophy and science. Philosophy in the
analytic tradition from the 1920s onwards, whether or not it is conceived to be a
cognitive discipline, is conceived to be a priori and hence discontinuous with, and
methodologically distinct from, science.[22] Similarly, analytic philosophy in general
held that questions of meaning antecede questions of truth, and are separable from
empirical questions of fact. If Quine is right, then analytic philosophy was fundamentally mistaken. On Quine's view, philosophy is continuous with science (NK
126), and 'philosophy of science is philosophy enough'. In this respect Quine reverts to an older tradition, that of, for example, Herbert Spencer, Samuel Alexander and (with qualifications and inconsistencies) Russell in the 1910s. Contemporary
philosophers who follow Quine have, in this sense, abandoned analytic philosophy.[23] Or, to put the same point differently, if this conception is compatible with
what is now to be called 'analytic philosophy', then analytic philosophy has become
so syncretic as to lose all distinctive marks other than stylistic and thematic ones,
and has severed itself from its roots and trunk in the philosophical developments
that run from Moore and Russell through the early Wittgenstein and the Vienna
Circle, Cambridge analysis, the later Wittgenstein and Oxford analytic philosophy.
Quine's conception places him in stark opposition to Wittgenstein's twofold revolution in philosophy.

4. Quine's progress

(i) *Repudiation of the conventionalist doctrine of necessary truth.* The received view in the Vienna Circle was that all necessarily true propositions are analytic – that is, true in virtue of the meanings of their constituent terms, hence true in virtue of the conventions (definitions) assigning them meaning. Logical truths, as the *Tractatus* had apparently shown, are true in virtue of the definitions of the logical constants alone, and analytic truths are true in virtue of the definitions of their constituent non-logical terms and the laws of logic, since they are reducible to logical truths by the substitution of synonyms for words in accord with those definitions.[24]

Quine's main early argument turned on showing that to demonstrate that a sentence is analytic,[25] one must invoke the law of identity, which licenses substitution of *definiens* for *definienda*. Definitions are available only for transforming truths, not for founding them (TC 81). So if analytic or logical truths are to proceed from conventions, without being reduced merely to antecedent truths, they must proceed from conventions other than definitions. So, 'if logic is to proceed *mediately* from conventions, logic is needed for inferring logic from conventions' (TC 97). Moreover, conventions (so-called postulates), which allegedly generate truths rather than just transforming them, are introduced in a manner which makes free use of the very logical vocabulary of 'if', 'not', 'every', which one is attempting to circumscribe.[26] To this objection, the conventionalist might argue that the conventions governing the use of the primitive logical vocabulary are not introduced explicitly at all. We can adopt conventions through behaviour, without explicitly stating them, and can later formulate them verbally when a full language is at our disposal. On this view, verbal formulation is no more a prerequisite for the adoption of conventions than the writing of a grammar is a prerequisite of speech. Thus conceived, Quine conceded, conventions no longer involve us in a vicious regress, and this account, in his view, accords well with what we actually do. However,

> it is not clear wherein an adoption of the conventions, antecedently to their formulation, consists; such behaviour is difficult to distinguish from that in which the conventions are disregarded . . . In dropping the attributes of deliberateness and explicitness from the notion of linguistic convention we risk depriving the latter of any explanatory force and reducing it to an idle label. (TC 98–9)

Later he strengthened his objection:

> The distinction between the legislative and the discursive refers thus to the act, and not to its enduring consequences, in the case of postulation as in the case of definition. This is because we are taking the notion of truth by convention fairly literally and simple-mindedly, for lack of an intelligible alternative. So conceived, conventionality is a passing trait, significant at the moving front of science but useless in classifying the sentences behind the lines.
>
> Might we not still project a derivative trait upon the sentences themselves, thus speaking of a sentence as forever true by convention if its first adoption was by convention? No; this, if done seriously, involves us in the most unrewarding historical conjecture. Legislative postulation contributes truths which become integral to the corpus of truths; the artificiality of their origin does not linger as a localized quality. (CLT 112–13)

The supposed normative (legislative) character of the convention (postulate) is exhausted by the genesis of the allegedly analytic truth, and has no bearing on the nature of its truth or on its revisability in the face of recalcitrant experience. Hence Quine concluded: 'We may wonder what one adds [by saying that such truths are true by convention] to the bare statement that the truths of logic and mathematics are a priori, or to the still barer behaviouristic statement that they are firmly accepted, when [the conventionalist] characterizes them as true by convention in such a sense' (TC 99).

He deepened his criticism of the Vienna Circle's doctrine of necessary truth in his 'Carnap and Logical Truth'. He agreed that

> there can be no doubt that sheer verbal usage is in general a major determinant of truth. Even so factual a sentence as 'Brutus killed Caesar' owes its truth not only to the killing but equally to our using the component words as we do. Why then should a logically true sentence on the same topic, e.g. 'Brutus killed Caesar or did not kill Caesar', not be said to owe its truth *purely* to the fact that we use our words (in this case 'or' and 'not') as we do? – for it depends not at all for its truth upon the killing.
>
> The suggestion is not, of course, that the logically true sentence is a contingent truth about verbal usage; but rather that it is a sentence which, given the language, automatically becomes true, whereas 'Brutus killed Caesar', given the language, becomes true only contingently on the alleged killing. (CLT 101)

Against this conception, Quine argued that the linguistic doctrine of necessary truth explains nothing. We can say that 'Everything is self-identical' $((x)(x = x))$ depends for its truth on the usage of '=', or that it depends for its truth on the self-identity of its subject-matter: namely, everything. He repeated his general criticism: 'logical truths, being infinite in number, must be given by general conventions rather than singly; and logic is needed then to begin with, in the metatheory, in order to apply the general conventions to individual cases' (CLT 108).

His second criticism turned on his holism: a self-contained theory which confronts experience contains not merely hypotheses, but also portions of logic and mathematics. These confront experience as a whole, and there is no way to distinguish those hypotheses which confer truth by convention from those which do not (CLT 114f.). This criticism he deepened in 'Two Dogmas of Empiricism', which will be discussed below.

His third criticism turned on qualms about analyticity. He later wrote: '"Truth by Convention" . . . showed already the beginnings of my misgivings over analyticity: the seeds of my apostasy' (AQ 16). For the moment, let me merely quote the later remark from 'Carnap on Logical Truth': 'Analytic', Quine argued, 'means true by synonymy and logic, hence no doubt true by language and logic, and simply true by language *if* the linguistic doctrine of logical truth is right' (CLT 122). But the notions of 'true by language', 'synonymous' and 'analytic' are, in Quine's view, all equally questionable. We shall examine this shortly.

(ii) *Ontology and ontological commitment.* 'To be', Quine famously declared, 'is to be the value of a variable', or, prescinding from canonical notation, to be the referent of a pronoun in a subordinate clause such as 'There is something, such that it . . .'.[27] One is ontologically committed to the existence of those things which are required for the truth of beliefs expressible by sentences containing such pronominal reference. Neither proper names nor definite descriptions need involve one in any ontological commitments (e.g. in negative existential statements). For the former, Quine argued, are replaceable by verbs (hence 'Pegasus does not exist' = 'Nothing pegasizes'), and the latter are eliminable by Russellian paraphrase. In general, eliminative paraphrase relieves one of any undesired ontological commitment.

To say that some dogs are white commits one to the existence of dogs, but not of whiteness. With respect to the ontological problem of universals, Quine argued that we have no good reason to admit properties or relations into our ontology (unlike classes and numbers). To admit universals into one's ontology is tantamount to holding that, for example, red houses, red roses and red sunsets have something in common: namely, the attribute of redness, an entity named by the word 'redness' (WTI 10). However, one may admit that there are red things, but deny that *except as a popular and misleading manner of speaking*, they have anything in common. 'The words "houses", "roses", and "sunsets" are true of sundry individual entities which are houses and roses and sunsets, and the word "red" is true of each of the sundry individual entities which are red houses, red roses, red sunsets; but there is not, in addition, any entity whatever, individual or otherwise, which is named by the word "redness"' (WTI 10).

We are not, therefore, committed to the existence of universals. Are we, however, committed to the existence of physical objects?

> Considered relative to our surface irritations, which exhaust our clues to an external world, the molecules and their extraordinary ilk are thus much on a par with the most ordinary physical objects. The positing of those extraordinary things is just a vivid analogue of the positing or acknowledging of ordinary things: vivid in that the physicist audibly posits them for recognised reasons, whereas the hypothesis of ordinary things is shrouded in prehistory. Though of the archaic and unconscious hypothesis of ordinary physical objects we can no more speak of a motive than of motives for being human or mammalian, yet in point of function and survival value it and the hypothesis of molecules are alike. . . . A posit can be unavoidable except at the cost of other no less artificial expedients. Everything to which we concede existence is a posit from the standpoint of a description of the theory building process.' (WO 22)

Quine argued that we have confidence in our ontological commitment to physical objects for three reasons. First, terms for physical objects are among the first acquired in language learning. Second, they are the focus of interpersonal communication, inducing rapport which 'encourages confidence, however unconsciously, that one is making no mistake about his objects' (WO 234). Third, 'our terms for physical objects are commonly learned through fairly direct conditioning to stimulatory effects of the denoted objects. The empirical evidence for such physical objects, if not immediate, is at any rate less far-fetched and so less suspect than that for objects whose terms are learned only in deep context' (ibid.).[28] What then is the evidence? It is, as intimated above, our 'surface irritations'. 'Our very understanding of the physical world, fragmentary though that understanding be, . . . enables us to see how limited the evidence is on which that understanding is predicated. It is our understanding, such as it is, of what lies beyond our surfaces, that shows our evidence for that understanding to be limited to our surfaces' (SLS 216). Positing physical objects, in Quine's view, provides the best available explanation for the 'surface irritations' to our retinas, eardrums, nasal cavities and so on, which are the only evidence we have for the existence of such entities as physical objects. The objection to admitting physical objects comes from sense-data theories. Against such theories, Quine makes three points: (i) we cannot hope to make sense-data suffice to the exclusion of physical objects (for no phenomenalist reduction has been remotely successful); (ii) we don't need sense-data in addition to physical objects, in order to account for illusions and the like; (iii) we do not need to posit inter-mediary sensory objects of apprehension in order to account for our knowledge of physical objects themselves. The 'relevance of sensory stimulation to sentences about physical objects can as well (and better) be explored and explained in terms directly of the conditioning of such sentences or their parts to physical irritations of the subject's surfaces'. Whether we are well advised to admit or posit physical objects is a genuine question, and it is to be decided 'by considerations of systematic efficacy, utility for theory' (WO 237). 'In a contest for sheer systematic utility to science, the notion of physical object still leads the field' (WO 238).

How do things stand with respect to the mental? It is, Quine holds, a genuine question whether there are mental events and mental states. If there is any case for positing them, 'it must be just that the positing of them, like the positing of molecules, has some indirect systematic efficacy in the development of theory' (WO 264). On this, Quine, in *Word and Object*, had very definite views. If it is theoretically profitable to posit mental states and events underlying behaviour, surely as much can be achieved by positing merely correlative physiological states and events instead. The bodily states exist anyway, and there is no reason to add others. Introspection may be viewed simply as witnessing one's own bodily state, even though one is ignorant of the medical details (as when 'introspecting an acid stom-ach'). On the question of whether this form of physicalism is eliminative, repudi-ating the existence of the mental, or merely a theory (identity theory) of the mental, Quine suggested that the distinction is 'unreal' (WO 265). His later acceptance of anomalous monism made little difference to this vision. Each perception is a single occurrence in a particular brain, and is fully specifiable in neurological terms once the details are known (PT 70). Individual instances of beliefs and other propositional attitudes are neural realities (PT 71). But, 'As long as extensional science can pro-ceed autonomously and self-contained, with no gaps of causality that intensional intrusions could serve to close, the sound strategy is the linguistic dualism of anoma-lous monism' (PT 72).

From early in his career, Quine argued that acceptance of an ontology is similar to acceptance of a scientific theory, such as the system of physics. 'We adopt the simplest conceptual scheme into which the disordered fragments of raw experience can be fitted and arranged. . . . The considerations which determine a reasonable construction of any part of the conceptual scheme, for example the biological part or the physical part, are not different in kind from the considerations which deter-mine the construction of the whole' (WTI 16f.). Though he later abandoned talk of raw experiences in favour of 'triggering of sense-receptors', he did not change his view of the matter. 'Our talk of external things, our very notion of things, is just a conceptual apparatus that helps us to foresee and control the triggering of our sensory receptors in the light of previous triggering of our sensory receptors' (TTPT 1).

There is room for choice, and 'one chooses with a view to simplicity in one's overall system of the world' (TTPT 10). In general, in his view, all objects are theoretical. 'Even our primordial objects, bodies, are already theoretical – most conspicuously so when we look to their individuation over time. Whether we encounter the same apple the next time round, or only one like it, is settled if at all by inference from a network of hypotheses that we have internalized little by little in the course of acquiring the non-observational super-structure of our language' (TTPT 20).

Quine's conception of ontological commitment stands deliberately in stark contrast to Carnap's 'Empiricism, Semantics and Ontology'. He explicitly rejected Carnap's differentiation of internal from external questions. In his view, Carnap's distinction amounted to distinguishing category questions (e.g. 'Are there material objects?'), in which 'Are there so-and-so's?' purports to exhaust the range of a particular style of bound variables, from subclass questions (e.g. 'Are there do-dos?'), in which 'Are there so-and-so's?' does not. But, he argued, whether a question is a category question or a subclass question is a trivial consideration of whether one uses one style of variable for both physical objects and, say, classes, or two (CVO 130f.). Carnap, Quine argued, was evidently thinking of languages which contain fundamentally segregated styles of variables, so that styles of variable are so sealed off from one another that it is ungrammatical to use a variable of one style in place of that of another style. This, in turn, depends on accepting some version of Russell's theory of types, which, as Zermelo's set theory had (in Quine's view) shown, is dispensable. (This conception is diametrically opposed to Wittgenstein's; see n. 27.) Hence, where Carnap held that 'This stone is thinking about Vienna' is nonsense, Quine holds it to be simply false.[29]

(iii) *Repudiation of the analytic/synthetic distinction.* This is the theme of the best known of all Quine's essays, 'Two Dogmas of Empiricism' (1951), and became the leitmotif of much of his later writing. He denied that there is any distinction between truths that are grounded in meanings independently of fact (analytic truths) and truths that are synthetic, and he repudiated the intelligibility of empiricist reductionism (and hence the programme of logical construction as exemplified in Carnap's *Logischer Aufbau*). The case was argued on ground of Carnap's choosing, hence with the common premise that what are analytic, if anything, are type-sentences. Quine also took Carnap to be claiming that analytic truths, being necessary and impervious to falsification by experience, are therefore unrevisable in response to experience. But this was not Carnap's view: one can revise them all right, but revising them involves change of meaning.

Putative analytic statements (sentences) are either (i) logically true – for example, 'No unmarried man is married', which remains true under any reinterpretation of 'man' and 'unmarried' (a logical truth being characterized as a statement which is and remains true under all reinterpretations of its components other than the logical particles) – or (ii) such statements as 'No bachelor is married', which can be turned into a logical truth by substitution of the synonym 'unmarried man' for 'bachelor'. But that presupposes the concept of synonymy, which is as problematic as that of analyticity.[30] To say that (ii) reduces to (i) by definition is illegitimate, since it presupposes synonymy in usage (lexicographers being empirical linguists who report observed synonymy of terms on the basis of observed linguistic behaviour[31]). Interchangeability *salva veritate* is inadequate, since it guarantees only extensional equivalence, not cognitive synonymy. Invoking *necessary* coextensionality (e.g. that *necessarily* all and only bachelors are unmarried men) is illegitimate, since the concept of necessity is what we are trying to explain in terms of the concept of analyticity. In an extensional language, interchangeability *salva veritate* is no assurance of cognitive synonymy, since it guarantees only that, for example, 'All bachelors are unmarried' is true, as is 'All creatures with a heart have kidneys', not that it is analytically true. Carnap had suggested that the difficulty in separating analytic from synthetic statements in natural languages is due to their vagueness, which is remediable in an artificial language, in which one can explicate the philosophical concept of analyticity. This, too, Quine rejected, on the grounds that (a) Carnap's semantic rules explain only the concept of 'analytic for L', not the concept 'analytic', and (b) explaining that a statement is analytic if and only if it is true according to a semantic rule is inadequate, since the term 'semantic rule' is in equal need of explanation.[32]

The last move left to the defender of the analytic/synthetic distinction, according to Quine, is to appeal to the notion of verification: a statement is synthetic if and only if it can be verified or falsified by experience; it is analytic if and only if no experience can falsify it. Analytic statements, accordingly, are limiting cases of meaningful statements, which are confirmed no matter what (TDE 37). But this account presupposes a form of empiricist reductionism, according to which all sentences are reducible to protocol sentences, and the protocol sentences are verified or falsified individually by reference to immediate experience. The connection between the alleged analytic/synthetic distinction and verificationist reductionism is intimate: 'as long as it is taken to be significant in general to speak of the confirmation or infirmation of a statement, it seems significant to speak also of a limiting kind of statement which is vacuously confirmed, *ipso facto*, come what may; and such a statement is analytic' (TDE 41).

It was unfair to characterize Carnap's view of analytic truths as limiting cases of verifiable propositions, since he did not claim that analytic sentences are vacuously confirmed come what may (unless that is simply a misleading way of saying that they are not confirmed, and cannot be disconfirmed, by experience), but rather that they are true in virtue of the meanings of their constituent words antecedently to experience. However, it is true that Carnap was happy to talk of 'two kinds of truth', the one 'logical, necessary, based upon meaning', the other 'empirical, contingent, dependent upon the facts of the world',[33] whereas Quine insisted that 'truth is truth', and does not come in different kinds. The root of the matter, as I have already suggested, was that neither Carnap nor other members of the Vienna Circle who cleaved to the conventionalist doctrine of a priori truth faced up to the question of what the role of these vacuous (uninformative), so-called analytic truths is – and that was a crucial chink in their armour which Quine (unlike Wittgenstein) did not identify.

Against the verificationist conception of sentential confirmation, Quine proposed a holistic conception of confirmation. Our statements about the external world 'face the tribunal of sense not individually but only as a corporate body' (TDE 41). While agreeing that the truth of statements depends upon both language and extra-linguistic fact, Quine argued that it does not follow that there is a distin-guishable linguistic component and a factual component in the truth of any indi-vidual statement, let alone that there are limiting cases of statements whose truth depends only upon the linguistic component – that is, analytic ones. The truth of logical truths, which are not observation sentences confronting experience directly, but are deeply embedded in the web of our beliefs, depends upon the success or failure of the whole of science of which they are a part. Logic is a part of every theory, and is confirmed or disconfirmed by the truth of science as a whole. It does indeed 'confront experience', but indirectly and in company. That is not to say that logic is empirical, but rather that there is no distinction between what is empirical and what is a priori. In this sense, Quine's verificationism is more far-reaching than that of the Vienna Circle, inasmuch as he did not segregate logical (and so-called analytic) truths from confirmation of theories as a whole. 'Taken collectively, sci-ence has its double dependence upon language and experience; but this duality is not significantly traceable into the statements of science taken one by one' (TDE 42). Indeed, in taking the statement, rather than the term, as the unit of significance, as Frege urged, 'we have drawn our grid too finely. The unit of empirical significance is the whole of science' (ibid.).[34]

This exaggerated claim was untenable, and in his later writings Quine refined his position. 'Observation sentences' do indeed confront experience directly. These are sentences such as 'That is a rabbit', 'It is raining', and also 'Hydrogen sulphide is escaping' or 'The mixture is at 180 degrees' (TI 2), but not 'He is a bachelor', which is not observational. They are a subclass of 'occasion sentences' – that is, sentences that are true on some occasions, false on others (hence exclude such as 'All men are mortal') – the observationality of which consists in the fact that they would com-mand assent from any competent speaker on an occasion of appropriate stimulus, irrespective of any collateral information. 'An observation sentence is an occasion sentence that the members of the community can settle by direct observation to their joint satisfaction' (ibid.). It is 'the means of verbalizing the prediction that checks a theory. The requirement that it command a verdict outright is what makes it a final checkpoint' (PT 4f.). Observation sentences are thus the 'vehicle of scien-tific evidence' (PT 5). Furthermore, he ceased to claim that the whole of science confronts experience, admitting that 'some middle-sized scrap of theory usually will embody all the connections that are likely to affect our adjudication of a given sentence' (WO 13). Later, he elaborated further: 'A set or conjunction of sentences inclusive enough to imply synthetic observation categoricals without outside help will be called *testable*. Some unconjoined single sentences qualify as testable, notably the synthetic observation categoricals themselves. For the most part, however, a testable set or conjunction of sentences has to be pretty big, and such is the burden of holism. It is a question of critical mass' (TI 12).

In place of the Vienna Circle conception, Quine famously proposed the follow-ing picture:

> Total science is like a field of force whose boundary conditions are experience. A conflict with experience at the periphery occasions readjustments in the interior of the field. Truth values have to be redistributed over some of our statements. Reevaluation of some statements entails reevaluation of others, because of their logical interconnection – the logical laws being in turn simply certain further

statements of the system, certain further elements of the field. Having reevaluated one statement we must reevaluate some others, which may be statements logically connected with the first or may be statements of logical connections themselves. But the total field is so under-determined by its boundary conditions, experience, that there is much latitude of choice as to what statement to reevaluate in the light of any single contrary experience. No particular experiences are linked with any particular statements in the interior of the field, except indirectly through consid-erations of equilibrium affecting the field as a whole. (TDE 42f.)

(iv) *Radical translation: indeterminacy of translation and inscrutability of reference.* Quine's repudiation of the analytic/synthetic distinction involved a wholesale rejection of the very concept of meaning, to be replaced with a behaviourist ersatz. For in his view, the notion of meaning is acceptable only if there are available criteria of ident-ity for meanings. But that presupposes the intelligibility of the concept of syn-onymy, and hence of analyticity. However, his investigations of the concept of analyticity allegedly show it to be inextricably woven into a circle of equally sus-pect intensional notions. Hence he rejected the intelligibility of the common-or-garden question 'Does "x" mean the same as "y"?' Grice and Strawson objected that one could break into this circle of intensional notions by reference to the patent behavioural differences between not believing (e.g. that a three-year-old under-stands Russell's theory of types) and not understanding (e.g. that a three-year-old is an adult), between incredulity in the face of the implausible but intelligible and incomprehension in the face of a denial of a necessary truth (or affirmation of absurdity or self-contradiction).[35] This forced Quine to consider what exactly can be extracted from mere consideration of linguistic responses to circumstances, lan-guage being understood as 'the complex of present dispositions to verbal behaviour' (WO 27).

He construed the problem he set himself in his austere behaviourist terms – that is, as a matter of mapping 'surface irritations' or 'sensory stimulations' on to dis-positions to verbal behaviour, within the constraints of 'naturalised epistemology'. The

> human subject is accorded a certain experimentally controlled input – certain patterns of irradiation in assorted frequencies, for instance – and in the fullness of time the subject delivers as output a description of the three-dimensional external world and its history. The relation between its meagre input and the torrential output is a relation that we are prompted to study . . . in order to see how evid-ence relates to theory, and in what ways one's theory of nature transcends any available evidence. (EN 82f.)

The conclusion he aimed to establish is that the

> infinite totality of sentences of any given speaker's language can be so permuted, or mapped onto itself, that (a) the totality of the speaker's dispositions to verbal behaviour remains invariant, and yet (b) the mapping is no mere correlation of sentences with *equivalent* sentences . . . Sentences without number can diverge drastically from their respective correlates, yet the divergences can systematically so offset one another that the overall pattern of associations of sentences with one another and with non-verbal stimulation is preserved. The firmer the direct links of a sentence with non-verbal stimulation, of course, the less that sentence can diverge from its correlate under any such mapping. (WO 27)

To establish this conclusion, he adopted as a heuristic device consideration of the procedures of a field linguist engaged upon 'radical translation' – that is, translation from a wholly alien tongue as opposed to translation from a cognate language.[36] All the data the linguist has to go on 'are the forces that he sees impinging on the native's surfaces and the observable behaviour, vocal and otherwise, of the native' (WO 28). Observation sentences

> are the entering wedge into cognitive language for the translator as well as for the child on his native heath. Other utterances – greetings, commands, questions – will figure among the early acquisitions too, but the first declarative sentences to be mastered are bound to be observation sentences, and usually one word long. The linguist tries to match observation sentences of the jungle language with observation sentences of his own that have the same *stimulus meanings*. That is to say, assent to the two sentences should be prompted by the same stimulations; likewise dissent. (TI 2)

The linguist's first task is to hypothesize what counts as assent and dissent. Having done so, he can proceed to the translation of observation sentences. Meaning and synonymy being mere fictions, he makes do with a behaviourist ersatz. The 'affirmative stimulus meaning' of an observation sentence (for a given speaker) is the class of all the stimulations that would prompt the speaker's assent. This is accessible to the observant linguist. For sentences such as 'Red', 'Rabbit', 'The tide is out', the notion of stimulus meaning constitutes, Quine claims, a reasonable (though ersatz) notion of meaning (WO 44).

These speculations led Quine to dramatic consequences:

(a) *That radical translation is indeterminate*: that is, there will always be mutually incompatible possible translation manuals that fit the facts of the aliens' linguistic behaviour equally well, since theory is radically underdetermined by evidence.

> A manual of Jungle-to-English translation constitutes an inductive definition of a translation relation together with a claim that it correlates sentences compatibly with the behaviour of all concerned. The thesis of indeterminacy of translation is that these claims on the part of two manuals might both be true and yet the two translation relations might not be usable in alternation, from sentence to sentence, without issuing in incoherent sequences. Or, to put it in another way, the English sentences prescribed as translations of a given Jungle sentence by the two rival manuals might not be interchangeable in English contexts. (TI 5)

Observation sentences can be established by correlating utterances with stimulus conditions; truth-functions can be translated, since assent and dissent can be identified, and likewise conjunctive assent;[37] stimulus analytic sentences – that is, sentences which command assent, come what may – can be identified (but this does not distinguish 'There have been black dogs' from 'Bachelors are unmarried'); and stimulus synonymy (i.e. sameness of stimulus meaning) of native occasion sentences can be settled, but they can't be translated. On this basis, the linguist constructs *analytical hypotheses* for word – word translation. But sentences directly translatable by the independent evidence of similar stimulatory occasions are few, and underdetermine the analytical hypotheses on which the translation of all further sentences depends. Hence 'There can be no doubt that rival systems of analytical hypotheses can fit the totality of speech behaviour to perfection, and can fit the totality of dispositions to speech behaviour as well, and still specify mutually incompatible translations of countless sentences insusceptible of independent control' (WO 72).

> Quine admits that indeterminacy of translation is unlikely to intrude in practice, since the linguist assumes that the native's attitudes and ways of thinking are like his own, up to the point where there is contrary evidence. He accordingly imposes his own ontology and linguistic patterns on the native wherever compatible with the native's speech and other behaviour, unless a contrary course offers striking simplifications. . . . What the indeterminacy is meant to bring out is that the radical translator is bound to impose fully as much as he discovers. (TI 5)

The indeterminacy is not a matter of scepticism as to which of the two manuals is correct, but rather an anti-realist claim to the effect that there is 'no fact of the matter'.

(b) *Inscrutability or indeterminacy of reference*: translation of one-word observation sentences ('Gavagai' = 'Lo, a rabbit') does not suffice to determine the reference of the expression construed as a term. 'Gavagai' could just as well refer to rabbit, rabbit stage, rabbithood or undetached rabbit part. These cannot be differentiated by ostension (since to point to a rabbit could be to point to a rabbit stage, an undetached rabbit part, etc.), but only relative to the apparatus of expressions for identity and difference – that is, the native analogues of our articles, pronouns, singular and plural, copula and our identity predicate (WO 53). This whole apparatus is interdependent.

> If by analytical hypothesis we take 'is the same' as translation of some construction in the jungle language, we may proceed on that basis to question our informant about sameness of gavagais from occasion to occasion and so conclude that gavagais are rabbits and not stages. But if instead we take 'are stages of the same animal' as translation of that jungle construction, we will conclude from the same subsequent questioning of our informant that gavagais are rabbit stages. Both analytical hypotheses may be presumed possible. Both could doubtless be accommodated by compensatory variations in analytical hypotheses concerning other locutions, so as to conform equally to all independently discoverable translations of whole sentences and indeed all speech dispositions of all speakers concerned. And yet countless native sentences admitting no independent check . . . may be expected to receive radically unlike and incompatible English renderings under the two systems. (WO 72)

While we can have good evidence of stimulus synonymy of observation sentences between the jungle language and our own, there can be none for analytical hypotheses. 'The point is not that we cannot be sure whether the analytical hypothesis is right, but that there is not even, as there was in the case of "Gavagai", an objective matter to be right or wrong about' (WO 73).

Hence – *ontological relativity*: the choice of one translation of terms rather than another is relative to a chosen set of analytical hypotheses embedded in a preferred translation manual. Different translation manuals will deliver different ontological commitments. There is no objective fact of the matter concerning whether the natives are referring to rabbits, rabbit stages, rabbit parts or rabbithood. Of course, the field linguist would be sensible to equate the term 'gavagai' with 'rabbit', on the grounds that an enduring, relatively homogeneous whole is a likely reference for a short expression, but that is his own imposition settling what is objectively indeterminate (OR 34). Here the indeterminacy is not merely of meaning, but of reference. 'At the level of radical translation . . . extension itself goes inscrutable' (OR 35).

(c) *All linguistic understanding is a matter of translation, and radical translation begins at home.* In the *Investigations*, Wittgenstein wrote: 'But if you say: "How am I to know what he means, when I see nothing but the signs he gives?" then I say: "How is *he* to know what he means, when he has nothing but the signs either?"' (PI §504). That thought can be taken in two divergent directions, one followed by Quine, the other by Wittgenstein. Radical translation begins at home, Quine argued, for we need not, and do not always, equate another's English words with the same string of phonemes in our own mouths. Sometimes we recognize that another is using a word differently from the way we use it (e.g. 'cool', 'square', 'hopefully'), and we translate his word into a different string of phonemes in our own idiolect. Indeed, all understanding is translating.[38] 'Our usual domestic rule of translation is indeed the homophonic one, which simply carries each string of phonemes into itself', but we temper homophony with charity, construing another's word heterophonically if that makes his utterance less absurd (OR 46). But, as might be expected from reflection on radical translation, there is a vast range of sentences regarding which the homophonic method is indifferent. We can construe our neighbour's references to rabbits as really references to rabbit stages, and so forth. For we can reconcile alternative construals by 'cunningly readjusting our translations of his various connecting predicates so as to compensate for the switch of ontology', thus reproducing the inscrutability of reference at home. Indeed, inscrutability of reference can be applied to our own utterances too! For what goes for others goes for us too, and vice versa – and there is no fact of the matter (OR 47).

Of course, this, as Quine acknowledges, has absurd consequences. For not only does it imply that there is no difference between referring to a rabbit and referring to a rabbit stage, it also implies that there is no difference between a rabbit and a rabbit stage (OR 48). Ontological relativity is the means of extricating us from this absurdity. Reference becomes scrutable only with the aid of the apparatus of expressions of identity, difference, number and other logical particles. The network of these expressions constitutes, Quine claims, 'our frame of reference' or 'our background language'. Relative to our frame of reference, we can and do talk meaningfully about rabbits, rabbit stages and so forth. It is meaningless to ask absolutely whether our terms 'rabbit', 'rabbit stage', 'rabbit part' and the like really refer respectively to rabbits, rabbit stages, rabbit parts and so on, rather than to some ingeniously permuted denotations. We can ask this only relative to some background language, which gives the question relative sense. But if such questions of reference make sense only relative to a background language, then 'evidently questions of reference for the background language make sense in turn only relative to a further background language'. This alarming regress is brought to an end in practice by our 'acquiescing in our mother tongue and taking its words at face value' (OR 49). The upshot is that it makes no sense to say what the objects of a theory are, beyond saying how to interpret or reinterpret the theory in another theory (OR 50). Consequently,

Ontology is doubly relative. Specifying the universe of a theory makes sense only relative to some background theory, and only relative to some choice of a manual of translation of the one theory into the other. Commonly of course the back-ground theory will simply be a containing theory, and in this case no question of a manual of translation arises. But this is after all just a degenerate case of trans-lation still – the case where the rule of translation is the homophonic one. (OR 55)

5. Quine and Wittgenstein: differences beneath similarities

This sketch of the contour lines of Quine's philosophical system makes it evident that his vision is far removed from Wittgenstein's. So the convergences which we noted above, both positive and negative, stand in need of careful examination. In the following I shall draw out some of the deep differences. I should emphasize that, although my allegiance is obvious, I am not trying to *prove* the one right and the other wrong – that would be a task for an argumentative book in its own right. My purpose is to pin-point the differences and some of the reasons for them, to suggest some reasons for thinking that Wittgenstein is in the right, and to indicate the trajectory of the detailed arguments that would have to be settled to vindicate one vision rather than another.

Wittgenstein, as he himself wrote (see above, p. 85), made the transition from the question of truth to the question of meaning in 1929. Further, he came to view language not merely as representation or description, but, in a radical sense, instrumentally or functionally. We should look upon words as tools, and sentences as instruments. We should not be misled by forms of expression (or their transfor-mation into canonical notation), but focus upon their uses, their point and purpose in the stream of human life. In particular, the declarative form of a sentence and the ascribability of truth to what it expresses do not imply that its role is descriptive. Quine, one might say, made the transition from the question of meaning to the question of ontology. 'On What There Is' (1948) heralded more than forty years of investigations of ontology and its relation to scientific theory, ontological commit-ments and ontological relativity. The resultant differences between the two philoso-phers are profound, the transition to the question of meaning leading to the high road of analytic philosophy, the transition to the question of ontology leading to contemporary philosophical scientism.

(i) *Use.* Quine quotes the Wittgensteinian dictum 'Don't ask for the meaning, ask for the use' with approval, construing 'use' as mere behaviour, and concluding: 'Well, we can take the behaviour, the use, and let the meaning go' (see above, p. 189). But 'the use' of an expression, for Wittgenstein, signifies not merely behav-iour, but rule-governed behaviour or, more generally, behaviour subject to stand-ards of correctness. The use of a piece in a game – for example, a chess piece – is not merely the way in which people move it, but the way they move it when they move it correctly, in accord with the rules for its use. The use of an expression is the way it *is to be*, and normally *is*, used. In a passage in which he was addressing behaviourist conceptions of language, Wittgenstein wrote: 'If when language is first learnt, speech, as it were is connected up to action – i.e. the levers to the machine

– then the question arises, can these connections possibly break down? If they can't, then I have to accept any action as the right one; on the other hand, if they can, what criterion have I for their having broken down?' (PR 64). Language learning is indeed rooted in training, and such training is in some ways similar to setting up a causal mechanism by stimulus conditioning. It does not follow that in general 'the pronouncement of a word is now a stimulus, now a reaction' (PLP 113f.). Suppose we train a dog to behave in such-and-such a way in response to the stimulus of a sign '*p*'. Now contrast (a) the sign '*p*' means the same as the command to do so-and-so, and (b) the dog is so conditioned that the occurrence of the sign '*p*' brings about so-and-so. The behaviourist account of language reduces the explanation given in (a) to the description of a causal nexus given in (b). But (a) specifies a rule or convention for the use of the sign '*p*', an explanation within the network of rules of language, whereas (b) describes a causal mechanism. The truth of (b) is independent of the truth of (a), and the rule is independent of the reactions of the dog. A dog, no matter how well trained, may misbehave. But that what it does *is* misbehaviour is determined by reference to the stipulated convention of meaning. Otherwise, what meaning a sign has would always be a matter of a hypothesis about what reaction it will call forth, and its meaning would not be determinable in advance of the behavioural consequences of its use from occasion to occasion.[39]

The objection applies to Quine's behaviouristic conception no less than to Russell, Ogden and Richards, to whom it was addressed. Quine argues, correctly, that a learner has not only to learn a given word (e.g. 'red') phonetically, 'he has also to see the object; and in addition to this . . . to capture the relevance of the object' (OR 29). 'A child learns his first words and sentences by hearing and using them in the presence of appropriate stimuli' (EN 81). For the child 'is being trained by successive reinforcements and extinctions to say "red" on the right occasions and those only' (RoR 42). But what, on a pure behaviourist account, makes a stimulus 'appropriate', an object 'relevant', or an occasion 'right'? It is, to be sure, conformity with the use of the rest of the speech community into which he is being acculturated – but, of course, only in so far as their uses are correct, and not misuses.[40]

The vast majority of utterances of members of a speech-community doubtless employ the expressions of the language correctly, that being presupposed by their being members of a speech-community with a shared language. Hence any statistical sampling will collect what are predominantly correct instances of the use of the language. But it will not provide an adequate criterion for distinguishing correct uses from misuses (let alone for distinguishing correct literal from equally correct metaphorical, poetical or secondary uses). For *correct use* is not (or not *simply*) a statistical concept.[41] We distinguish between what *is* done and what is *to be* done. We draw a distinction between the statement that the chess king is to be moved one square at a time and the statement that chess-players move their king one square at a time. The use of an expression is not merely the verbal behaviour of users of the expression, but their verbal and other behaviour *in so far as it accords with the acknowledged rules for the correct employment of that expression*, rules which the users themselves acknowledge in their humdrum explanations of meaning and of what they mean and in their recognition of explanations by others of what certain expressions mean. These rules or conventions are not of course axioms or postulates of a formal system. Nor are they 'implicit rules' postulated by the field linguist. They are not 'mental entities'. Nor are they mere history, for their role is not exhausted in the original teaching of the expressions. Far from being 'explanatorily idle', as Quine suggested in his criticism of Carnap, they are explanatorily indispensable, since they determine the difference between correct and incorrect use, as well as the difference between sense and nonsense. They are exhibited in explanations of meaning (and of what one meant by an utterance), which are as accessible to observations of behaviour as are descriptive uses of declarative sentences.

These explanations include answers to questions such as 'What is a gavagai?' (and Wittgenstein's field linguist will fairly rapidly master the native technique of asking such simple questions). Such answers may take the form of ostensive definitions, many by reference to paradigmatic samples which are to be used as standards for the correct application of the *definiendum*.[42] They may take the form of synonyms (precise or rough and ready), or of exemplification ('Running is doing *this*', 'Hitting is *this*'), or of a series of examples (with a similarity rider) which are to be taken as a rule, or of paraphrase or contrastive paraphrase. (It can be presumed in our methodologically motivated ethnological thought-experiment that the native will be willing to *teach* Wittgenstein's field linguist, no less than he is willing to teach his own children.) The normative (i.e. rule-governed) *use* of words in sentences and the norms that are being complied with by speakers' applications of words are perfectly accessible – as accessible as the difference between showing how to use a measure and a judgement of the length of an object. The field linguist can come to identify the native judgements of lengths, say, by observing their measuring activities, and, hesitantly no doubt and presuming upon native tolerance, by participating in the measuring practices. He will come to identify what the natives *call* 'such-and-such a length' (a foot or a span) – that is, what their *standard* of measurement is – no less than he will come to identify their judgements that something is so-and-so many spans long. It is behaviour and participatory practice, not something arcane and mysterious, that give us access to standards of measurement (and analogously to standards of correct use of terms) no less than to judgements of measurement (to correct application of terms thus explained).

Quine and Wittgenstein agree that the genesis of an ability is irrelevant to its later characterization; how and whether one learnt the use of an expression does not matter, inasmuch as it is true that 'there is no action at a distance' in grammar. But Wittgenstein insists, and Quine denies (see above, p. 190), that rules, thus understood, play a constant role in the use of language – as standards of correct use, cited in explanations, appealed to in criticisms of use and in clarification of disagreements (to determine whether the disagreement is one in judgement or in definition), and employed in teaching. The relevance of teaching is not causal or genetic, but rather immanent: 'what matters is *what is given in the explanation*' (LWL 38, emphasis added). What is thus given is a rule, a standard, against which to judge the correctness of the application of an expression from case to case, and by reference to which we can generally distinguish disagreements in judgements from disagreements in definitions. (For detailed examination of Wittgenstein's conception of rules, of rules of grammar, of following rules, of the internal relation between a rule and what counts as compliance with a rule, and of the relation of rule and practice, see Volume 2, 'Rules and grammar', 'Accord with a rule', and 'Following rules, mastery of techniques and practices'.)

It is explanations of meaning that constitute standards for the correct use of their *explananda*, and what *counts* as a correct application of an expression is exhibited in the practice of its application (and the critical reactions, as well as the uncomprehending questions, that are forthcoming when an expression is misused). For communication by means of language to be possible, Wittgenstein argued, there must be agreement not only in judgements (as Quine holds), but also in definitions or explanations of meaning – in standards of correct use (cf. PI §242). There is an internal relation between an explanation of meaning (a definition or a rule for the use of an expression) and applications of that expression, and understanding an expression is grasping that relation – that is, grasping what counts as applying the expression correctly. For applying an expression in accordance with its explanation is one criterion of understanding. Another is explaining it correctly in context or, more minimally, assenting to another's correct explanation *as* an explanation of what one meant by an expression one used. In general, someone who cannot say what he means by the use of an expression *in some way* (by paraphrase, contrastive paraphrase, exemplification, ostension, etc.) will be said to be speaking without understanding what he is saying. And if what he means by it deviates significantly from what it means, he will be said to be misusing it. A third criterion of understanding is reacting *appropriately* in context to the use of an expression, and what counts as 'appropriate' is partly determined by what the expression means, as given by an acceptable explanation of its meaning.

It may well be that a child's early training in the use of language involves primarily one-word sentences, but surely not only observation sentences. Expressive sentences will be at least as important – for example, 'Hurts!', 'Good!' – as will ersatz imperatives – for example, 'Want!', 'Drink!', 'Apple!' And assent or dissent will be exhibited in responses to requests or demands no less than in responses to questions. However, he must rapidly progress beyond this to learn the use of terms, not by constructing analytical hypotheses (the child is no theorist or linguist), but by learning their use, mastering the technique of their application, including their combinatorial possibilities and impossibilities with other expressions. This is learnt not by theory construction, but by guided practice, subject to correction of error – which is not the same as conditioning and reinforcement. For what he learns includes, among other things, how to *justify* and give *reasons* for what he does by reference to the standards of correctness he learns, how to *criticize* and *correct* misuses, including his own. Once the child has learnt to ask 'What is that?', 'What is this called?' and 'What does "such-and-such" mean?', he has passed the stage of ostensive training, and moved on to the stage of being taught, by ostensive and other explanations, the use – the meaning – of words. He must learn, in a rudimentary way, no doubt, the differences, from case to case and context to context, between sense and nonsense. And nonsensical or ungrammatical forms of combination which he employs can be, and often are, corrected by parents and teachers.

It is evident that although Quine and Wittgenstein agree that in a sense all the field linguist and child have to go on in learning the language is behaviour, that agreement masks profound disagreement. I shall defer for a moment consideration of the differences between Quine's field linguist and Wittgenstein's (see pp. 218–23). Whereas Quine presents the child as being conditioned in the use of language, this conditioning being aided by the existence of innate responsive similarities and by induction, which is 'animal expectation or habit formation' (NK 125), Wittgenstein conceives of language learning as not just a matter of conditioned response. Although it rests on shared reactive propensities and discriminatory capacities, and begins with mere training, what are to be learnt are the techniques of a normative practice.[43] Those rule-governed techniques are learnt by engaging in the practice, subject to correction, guided by example and explanation.

From the point of view of a normative (rule-governed) conception of meaning and language such as Wittgenstein defends, a behaviourist conception like Quine's is simply no conception of meaning at all, not even an ersatz one.[44] Indeed, it is no conception of *language*, for a language stripped of normativity is no more language than chess stripped of its rules is a game.

(ii) *Meaning and synonymy*. Quine denies, rightly, that 'meanings' are 'entities'. He claims that at best we can talk of expressions having a meaning – that is, being significant – and of different expressions as having the same (or different) meaning. But we can speak of sameness of meaning, or synonymy, only if there are clear criteria of identity for meanings. He argues that none is forthcoming, since the concept of synonymy can be explained only by reference to equally problematic intensional notions like necessity, self-contradictoriness, definition, semantic rule, immunity to falsification by experience (unassailability, come what may) and a priority. It is important to note, however, that he does not take the concept of synonymy to be incoherent. 'The explicitly conventional introduction of novel notation for purposes of sheer abbreviation' is perfectly licit. 'Here the definiendum becomes synonymous with the definiens simply because it has been created expressly for the purpose of being synonymous with the definiens. *Here we have a really transparent case of synonymy created by definition*; would that all species of synonymy were as intelligible' (TDE 26, emphasis added). It is unclear whether we are to conclude that in such transparently intelligible cases, in which synonymy yields perspicuous criteria of identity, meanings *are* 'entities'.

If stipulation can produce synonyms, then there is such a thing as two expressions having the same meaning (rather than being merely 'stimulus synonymous'). There is certainly such a thing as two expressions *not* having the same meaning (e.g. 'ingenious' and 'ingenuous' or 'inimical' and 'inimitable'), and we can readily identify such differences in meaning. If so, why *cannot* there be unstipulated synonyms in use, as manifest in the explanations that competent speakers give of the use of terms (which is precisely what lexicographers often catalogue)? Maybe there are none; nevertheless, we understand what would *count* as a pair of synonymous expressions. Grice and Strawson liken Quine's position here to that of a man who claims to understand what it is for two things to fit together if they are specially made to fit together, but denies that it is intelligible that things not so made should fit together. Far from that being unintelligible, they further argue, synonymy by explicit convention is intelligible only if synonymy by usage is presupposed. There cannot be law where there is no custom, or rules where there are no practices.[45] To be able to stipulate that a novel expression is to mean the same as a previous one, one must already have a conception of synonymy. It may be that natural language so evolves as largely to exclude the kind of redundancy that is involved in the common existence of exact synonyms, but that is surely something to investigate, not to dismiss. If it be so, then we may find it useful, or indeed mandatory (as lexicographers do), to consider synonymy a matter of degree, context- and purpose-relative. But if so it be, that is a fact, not a defect.

Wittgenstein has no qualms about talking of the meaning of expressions. Meanings are indeed not 'entities'. To know the meaning of 'A', like to know the length of X, the age of Y or the price of Z, is not to be acquainted with an entity, but to know the answer to the question 'What does "A" mean?' ('What is the length of X, Y's age, or Z's price?'). The 'what' here is an interrogative pronoun, not a relative one. To say that 'A' has the same meaning as 'B' is not to say that there is some third thing which they both mean, but rather that 'A' means (the same as) 'B', that they are used in the same way, that an explanation of what 'A' means will also serve as an explanation of what 'B' means, and indeed that citing 'A' will serve as an answer to the question 'What does "B" mean?'[46] The meaning of an expression is determined by its use; it is given by what are accepted as explanations of meaning; it is what we understand when we understand or know what an expression means. And that is exhibited in the criteria of understanding – that is, correct use, giving correct explanations of what an expression means or of what one means by it (which conform with what it means), and in responding appropriately to its use by others. Expressions are synonymous if the explanation of what one means will also serve as a correct explanation of what the other means. To be sure, expressions are typically more or less synonymous, or synonymous in some contexts and not in others or for some purposes and not others; the matter of synonymy is indeed often context-dependent and purpose-relative:

> The question whether 'He can continue [the series 2, 4, 6, 8 . . .]' means the same as 'He knows the formula [$A_n = 2n$]' can be answered in several different ways: We can say 'They don't mean the same, i.e. they are not in general used as synonyms as, e.g., the phrases "I am well" and "I am in good health"'; or we may say '*Under certain circumstances* "He can continue . . ." means he knows the formula'. (BB 114f.)

Synonymy is not an all-or-nothing affair. For some purposes of describing spatial relations, 'on' and 'on top of' mean the same. 'The book is on the table' means the same as 'The book is on top of the table'. But 'Hillary is on Everest' does not mean the same as 'Hillary is on top of Everest'. The criterion of adequacy for a dictionary definition (if it is a specification of synonymy – as such definitions often are) is that the definiens should *standardly* be substitutable for the definiendum, but such specifications do not, and need not indefeasibly, license substitution. The demand for absolute, context-free, purpose-independent standards of synonymy is as absurd as the demand for completeness of definition or determinacy of sense (the exclusion not of vagueness, but of the very possibility of vagueness), prominent in Frege and the *Tractatus*.[47]

(iii) *Analyticity and necessary truth.* Quine takes so-called analytic truths to be true in exactly the same way as empirical propositions, and does not see them as having a different role from any other propositions embedded in the web of belief. Like Carnap, who never abandoned his conviction that, at least in a constructed language, one can sharply differentiate analytic truths from empirical ones, Quine never raises the question of the role of such truths as 'Red is darker than pink', 'Bachelors are unmarried', 'Either it is raining or it is not raining'. Truth is truth, and that's the end of the matter; and no one would deny that such statements are true.

From Wittgenstein's point of view, this is like saying that knowing is knowing, no matter if it is knowing that grass is green, that green is a colour, or that nothing can be red and green all over; or that believing is believing, no matter whether what is believed is that it will rain tomorrow, that $2 + 2 = 4$, that Goldbach's conjecture is true, that one should not steal, that one's name is N. N., that the world has existed for many years. It is not that 'true', 'know' or 'believe' are ambiguous (as are 'bank' or 'port' – ambiguity being coincidental, and unlikely to be preserved in translation into another language, save *per accidens*), but rather that we need to investigate, from case to case, what it is for one kind of proposition (e.g. '$2 + 2 = 4$') to be true, as opposed to another (e.g. 'Grass is green', 'Kindness is a virtue'), what counts as knowing one sort of proposition rather than another, what are the crucial differences between believing an empirical hypothesis and believing that Goldbach's conjecture is true, and so on. (See Volume 2, 'Grammar and Necessity', §4.)

Like Carnap, Quine takes it that analytic truths, if there were any, would be type-sentences, every token of which is analytic. Indeed, he assumes – wrongly, as we have seen – that Carnap and the Vienna Circle were committed to the view that if a sentence is analytic, its status canot be changed, whereas Carnap's view was that an analytic truth cannot be falsified by experience, but that we can 'abandon' it, cease to count it as such. However, to abandon it is to change the meaning of its constituent terms.

Wittgenstein, unlike the members of the Vienna Circle, did not explain so-called analytic truths by reference to type-sentences which are either (instances of) laws of logic or reducible to a law of logic by the substitution of synonyms for constituent expressions in accordance with definitions. Nor did he clarify the nature of so-called necessary truths by arguing that they are *consequences* of the meanings (definitions) of their constituent expressions. Indeed, Wittgenstein does not invoke the category of analytic truths in his later work. This may be partly due to a distaste for received jargon, partly to radical disagreement with the construal of such truths by the Vienna Circle and others, and partly to the fact that the concept of analyticity employed by his predecessors and contemporaries, no matter whether Kant, Frege or Carnap, does not cut along the distinction or distinctions that most concerned him, and hence, in his view, does not serve to explain or elucidate what it is for a proposition to be a 'necessary truth'. The Circle's account assimilated disparate linguistic phenomena: namely, logical truths, mathematical truths and analytic truths as traditionally conceived. Further, it proved powerless to illuminate such 'metaphysically necessary propositions' as 'Red is darker than pink', 'Red is more like pink than like blue', 'There is no transparent white'.

Whether a sentence expresses what we so misleadingly call 'a necessary truth' is a matter of what it is being used for, hence a feature of the use of token-sentences. Two tokens of the same type-sentence *may* be differently used, now to express a 'necessary truth', now to express an empirical proposition. 'War is war', for example, is rarely used as an instance of the law of identity, and 'What will be, will be' is not typically used to express a theorem of tense logic. 'This is red' may be used to make an empirical statement about the colour of the carpet, or used as a 'grammatical proposition' ('This (colour) is red'), which can indeed be taken as a 'necessary truth', although, like 'Red is a colour', it is in effect a rule for the use of the word 'red'. 'Acids turn litmus paper red' was once used to define acids – that is, as a grammatical proposition – but is no longer so used. Since criteria and symptoms in science often fluctuate, a proposition of physics may in one context be taken as an empirical law, and in another as a definition, depending on how it is employed in an argument. What Wittgenstein was adamant about was that no proposition could be used simultaneously to state an empirical truth and to express a grammatical rule, any more than a ruler can be used simultaneously as a measure and as an object measured ('measures' is irreflexive).

For Wittgenstein, the crucial question is: what is the use of so-called necessary or analytic truths? We say that the following are all true: '$2 \times 2 = 4$', 'Either it is hot or it is not hot', 'Red is a colour', 'Nothing can be red and green all over', and so on. But what is their point? What information are we conveying to anyone? What go under the name of necessary truths are expressed by the use of a mixed bag of kinds of sentences, and Wittgenstein does not impose uniformity upon them, but rather explains why we think of them as 'necessary' and what is meant by calling them so. He does not try to explain what 'makes them true' – a dubious question, since they are unconditionally true (not made true by anything). *A fortiori* he does not claim that they are made true by a convention. In the sense in which 'The sun is hot' is made true by the sun's being hot, then 'Red is a colour' or 'Either it is hot or it is not hot' are not made true by anything. Unlike members of the Vienna Circle, Wittgenstein never argued that any necessary truths are 'true in virtue of meanings', but condemned such a view as a mythology of meaning-bodies. Unlike Quine, he did not hold that the truth of statements (by which Quine meant sentences) depends upon both language and extra-linguistic fact; it is not sentences that are truth-bearers, any more than it is sentences that are supported by evidence, believed or doubted, feared or suspected, but rather what is said by their use. What it is that is said by the use of a sentence depends upon language, but whether what is thus said is true or false does not (save in the case of empirical assertions about language). Unlike Quine, he did not hold that what we call 'necessary truths' are simply those which we 'shield' from empirical disconfirmation by exercising our freedom to reject other beliefs instead (TI 11).

Truths of logic, he held, are vacuous (senseless, i.e. limiting cases of propositions with a sense). Despite the fact that they all say the same – namely, nothing – they nevertheless differ. For they are internally related to rules of inference, and different tautologies may be related to different rules of inference. Mathematical truths are rules which belong to a vast system of interconnected rules, the essential point and purpose of the system being the transformation of empirical propositions about the magnitudes or quantities of things, and the like. Analytic truths are rules in the guise of descriptions. 'Bachelors are unmarried men' is a grammatical proposition, an explanation of the meaning of the word 'bachelor', given in the material mode. It is a rule that licenses the inference from 'A is a bachelor' to 'A is unmarried'. Non-analytic necessary truths, such as 'Red is darker than pink', are similarly grammatical propositions, even though they are not transformable into logical truths by substitution of synonyms. Where Quine argued that '(x) $(x = x)$' can be said to depend for its truth upon the self-identity of everything, Wittgenstein held that there is no finer example of a useless proposition than 'A thing is identical with itself', it being comparable to 'Every coloured patch fits into its surrounding' (PI §216). The proposition '$a = a$' is a degenerate identity statement which says nothing (LFM 27, 283). 'An object is different from itself' is nonsense; so too is its negation. Although the law of identity seems to have fundamental significance, the proposition that this 'law' is nonsense has taken over its significance (BT 412).

Necessary truths are indeed unassailable. They persist unalterably, independently of all that happens – as the construction of a machine on paper does not break when the machine itself succumbs to external forces (RFM 74). Nothing is allowed to *falsify* them, but their 'necessity' is not explained merely by the fact that we refuse to abandon them; that, indeed, would not distinguish so-called necessary truths from truths of our world picture, such as 'The world has existed for many years', 'I was born of parents', 'I have never been to the stars'. What is marked by the 'must' of 'If it is red, then it must be coloured', 'If there are ten Xs in each of ten rows, then there must be a hundred', 'If it is red, then it must be darker than pink' is the normative role of such propositions as 'Red is a colour', 'Red is darker than pink', '$10 \times 10 = 100$'; they are rules, 'norms of representation' or 'norms of description'. 'Red is a colour' does not 'owe its truth' to red's being a colour in the sense in which 'Some dogs are white' owes its truth to the fact that some dogs are white (or to some dogs' being white). Its being true consists in its being an expression of a rule for the use of its constituent expressions 'red' and 'colour', as the truth of the proposition 'The chess king moves one square at a time' consists in its being the expression of a rule of chess. If we know that A is red and B is pink, we are entitled to infer without further observation that A is darker than B; if we know that there are ten Xs in each of ten rows, then we can infer without counting that there are a hundred Xs in all. If B turns out to be darker than A, then it was not pink, or A was not red, or one or the other has changed colour. If there are more or fewer than a hundred Xs, then there was a miscount, or some were added or removed. What we hold rigid is not a truth about the world, but a rule for describing how things are in the world.

It is true that we can, in certain cases, transform an empirical proposition into a rule or norm of representation by resolving to hold it rigid. (But 'The world has existed for many years', which we could not abandon without destroying the web of our beliefs, is nevertheless not a rule, since its role is not to determine concepts or inference rules.) It was an empirical discovery that acids are proton donors, but this proposition was transformed into a rule: a scientist no longer calls something 'an acid' unless it is a proton donor, and if it is a proton donor, then it is to be called 'an acid', even if it has no effect on litmus paper. The proposition that acids are proton donors (like '$25 \times 25 = 625$') has been 'withdrawn from being checked by experience, but now serves as a paradigm for judging experience' (cf. RFM 325). Though unassailable, so-called necessary truths are not immutable; we can, other things being equal, change them if we so please (with the above proviso concerning logic and appropriate qualifications when it comes to expressions that are so deeply embedded in our form of life as to be unalterable *by us*). *But if we change them, we also change the meanings of their constituent expressions* – here Carnap was right. If we abandon the proposition that red is a colour, we thereby change the meanings of 'red' and 'colour'; if we drop the law of double negation, we change the meaning of negation.

(iv) *Ostensive teaching and explanation.* The above characterization of the disagreement between Wittgenstein and Quine in the matter of analyticity and necessary truth makes it possible to deal briefly with an otherwise large and ramifying topic, the nature and role of ostensive teaching and definition. The depth of the difference between a causalist viewpoint and a normative one is strikingly evident here.

Quine takes ostension to be a matter of conditioning and induction (OR 31) – that is, learning to associate a given stimulus with an utterance. It depends upon a shared innate standard of similarity (NK 123). In the case of what he calls 'direct ostension', 'the term which is being ostensively explained is true of something that contains the ostended point [i.e. the point where the line of the pointing finger first meets an opaque surface]' (OR 39).[48] Wittgenstein similarly argues that ostension presupposes shared behavioural dispositions (e.g. to look in the direction of the pointing hand) and discriminatory capacities. But, unlike Quine, he distinguishes ostensive training (which he is willing to take behaviouristically) from ostensive definition or explanation. Of course, an ostensive definition sets up a connection between a word and a 'thing' (viz. a sample). But 'the connection doesn't consist in the hearing of words now having *this* effect, since the effect may actually be caused by the making of the convention. And it is the connection and not the effect which determines the meaning' (PG 190). An ostensive definition (the connection between word and sample) is an *explanation* of what a word means, and the explanation 'is not an empirical proposition and not a causal explanation, but a rule, a convention' (PG 68) for the use of the explanandum, a standard for its correct application, as is evident in cases in which the ostensive gesture, the utterance 'This', and the sample ostended can replace the definiendum in a sentence. Where a sample is employed, the sample is not an object of which the concept being explained is predicated, but rather *belongs to the method of representation.* It is the standard for the application of the term, not an instance of its application.

(v) *Revisability of beliefs.* Quine takes everything within the web of belief to be capable in principle of being relinquished, including logic and mathematics – even though we are least willing to relinquish these in the face of recalcitrant experience. He argued as follows:

> The totality of our so-called knowledge or beliefs, from the most casual matters of geography or history to the profoundest laws of atomic physics or even pure mathematics and logic, is a man-made fabric which impinges on experience only along the edges. . . . Any statement can be held true come what may, if we make drastic enough adjustments elsewhere in the system. Even a statement very close to the periphery can be held true in the face of recalcitrant experience by pleading hallucination or by amending certain statements of the kind called logical laws. Conversely, by the same token, no statement is immune to revision. (TDE 42f.)[49]

Similarly, he later claimed: 'In science all is tentative, all admits of revision – right down . . . to the law of the excluded middle' (SLS 232); 'mathematics . . . is best looked upon as an integral part of science, on a par with the physics, economics, etc., in which mathematics is said to receive its applications' (SLS 231), and 'Logic is in principle no less open to revision than quantum mechanics or the theory of relativity. . . . If revisions are seldom proposed that cut so deep as to touch logic, there is clear enough reason for that: the maxim of minimum mutilation' (PL 100). His invocation of the principle of minimum mutilation is wholly pragmatic, and does not rest on any discernment of a difference in function of mathematical and logical truths from any other truths ('truth is truth'). Castigating Carnap for putting grammar and logic on the same footing (*qua* analogues of formation and transformation rules in a formal deductive system), Quine wrote:

> We do better to abandon this analogy and think in terms rather of how a child actually acquires his language and all those truths and beliefs, of whatever kind, that he acquires along with it. The truths or beliefs thus acquired are not limited to logical truths, nor to mathematical truths, nor even to analytic truths, if we suppose some sense made of this last term. Among these truths and beliefs the logical truths are to be distinguished only by the fact . . . that all other sentences with the same grammatical structure are true too. (PL 101)

Wittgenstein agreed that we can envisage a language without the law of double negation. Nevertheless, fundamental propositions of logic, such as the law of non-contradiction, '$\sim (p \ \& \sim p)$', or the tautology '$p \ \& \ (p \supset q) \supset q$', are renounceable only at the cost of renouncing all thought and reasoning. For these tautologies are internally related to inference rules which are constitutive of what we call 'reasoning', 'arguing' and 'thinking'. And he takes propositions of mathematics as concept-forming rules, licensing inferences among empirical propositions. Moreover, he denies that even humdrum empirical propositions such as 'The world has existed for a long time' – that is, certain propositions of the *Weltbild* – can be revised or rejected. For their repudiation would tear apart the whole web of belief. It is these, not the propositions of mathematics and logic, that are so deeply embedded in the web of belief that they cannot be revised, even though they are not 'necessary truths'. And it is not such general propositions alone that we cannot relinquish. For could anyone (in normal circumstances) abandon the proposition that he had never been to the stars, or that his name is 'N.N.', or that he has two hands? Indeed, can one *decide* to abandon a belief at will, irrespective of compelling reasons? And would anything, in normal circumstances, count as a compelling reason for abandoning beliefs such as these?

However, propositions of logic are misconstrued as being akin to propositions of the *Weltbild* – that is, so deeply embedded in the web of belief as to be impossible to extricate without total mutilation. Rather, they are the correlates of the inference rules *that constitute the connecting links between the nodes of the web*. It is the logical relations between beliefs that make for the difference between a web of beliefs and a collection of beliefs; for to believe that all As are F is *ipso facto* to believe that this A is F, as it is to believe that there are no As which are not Fs. 'Abandonment' of the law of non-contradiction would not be, as Quine suggests, 'inconvenient'. Nor would it simply mean that we would score a poor ratio of successes to failures in our predictions. It would mean that the web of belief collapsed into a knotted tangle of incoherence. The role of the fundamental laws of logic is *toto caelo* different from that of the beliefs they connect within the web.[50] Indeed, one cannot be said to *believe* them as we believe empirical propositions; to believe that either it is raining or it is not raining is not to have any belief about the weather, and to believe the principle of bivalence is simply to determine the concept of a proposition as that which can be either true or false. (For detailed discussion of this contentious claim concerning believing a priori propositions, see Volume 2, 'Grammar and necessity', §4.)

(vi) *Understanding, interpreting, translating and indeterminacy.* Quine's thesis of indeterminacy of translation is rooted in empiricist qualms about the underdetermination of theory by evidence. Wittgenstein's explicit *paradox* of rule-following is, he argued, rooted in a misconception which turns on the underdetermination of a function by a fragment of its extension. This paradox is defused by the consequences of realizing that the relation between a rule and its extension is not akin to the relation between an empirical hypothesis and its evidence, since the relation is *internal*. A rule is not an explanatory hypothesis which explains the acts that constitute conformity with it. The instruction 'Observe a man's behaviour in the course of the day, and infer which of his acts were intentionally performed in conformity with rules given to him' is as absurd as 'Here is a husband, now tell me who is his wife'.[51] That a given activity (a game of chess, for example) is conducted according to such-and-such rules may indeed be a hypothesis or conjecture (of an observer who has not learned the game), but it is quite wrong to suppose that there is no 'fact of the matter' as to how chess is to be played. It would doubtless be exceedingly difficult to pick up the rules from mere observation of moves alone, independently of observations of the discussions and explanations of the game, but then no one has to; rather, we receive instruction and practice in playing the game.

Both Quine and Wittgenstein consider that reflection upon radical translation may be philosophically illuminating, and both approach radical translation behaviouristically – but each in a different sense. On Quine's official view, the problem set the field linguist is to map 'surface irritations' on to dispositions to verbal behaviour. What is to be studied is the relation between the 'meagre input' of 'certain patterns of irradiation in assorted frequencies, for instance', and the 'torrential output' (EN 83) of intricately structured talk of things (WO 26).[52] It is less than obvious that Quine cleaves to his rigorous behaviourism here, since behaviourism requires that behaviour be viewed as 'bare bodily movement', and speech as the emission of sounds, from which bare basis a translation is held to be derivable. The field linguist's point of access, according to Quine, is the one-word observation sentence, assent and dissent to which are allegedly identifiable inductively. But assent and dissent are intensional (as well as intentional) notions; a person assents not to a sentence, but to what is said by the use of a sentence – that is, to an assertion *that things are thus-and-so* – and assents *to what he understands* inasmuch as he *believes it to be true*.[53] The identification of assent and dissent therefore presupposes viewing the observed behaviour not as mere bodily movement, but intentionalistically[54] – and it is not obvious that Quine's austere behaviourism entitles him to this intentionalist stance.

Wittgenstein's 'behaviourist' approach to radical translation is unconnected with Watsonian or Skinnerian behaviourism. What is behaviourist about his conception of understanding is *only* that the distinction between the 'outer' and the 'inner' is irrelevant for him, since understanding is not a mental state, but akin to a capacity. The nature of the capacity and the degree to which it is possessed are to be seen in a person's behaviour, including his linguistic behaviour (see Volume 1, 'Understanding and ability'). Wittgenstein recognizes *ab initio* that the 'common behaviour of mankind' by reference to which we interpret an unknown language is behaviour intentionalistically conceived. When an explorer comes to a foreign land, he wrote, he can come to understand the native language 'only through its connections with the rest of the life of the natives. What we call "instructions", for example, or "orders", "questions", "answer", "describing", etc. is all bound up with very specific human actions and an order is only distinguishable as an order by means of the circumstances preceding or following // accompanying it//' (MS 165, 97f., quoted in Volume 2, p. 191). Hence, too, 'If a lion could talk, we could not understand him' (PI p. 223), not because his growls are unclear, but because his behavioural repertoire is so profoundly different from human behaviour, human expression, gesture and mien, and the forms of possible interaction we can engage in (even with a tame lion) are so limited. Our human 'form (or forms) of life' is not shared with lions. But 'speaking a language is part of a form of life'. 'It is a feature of our language that it springs up // it grows // out of the foundations of forms of life' (Vol. XV, 148; see Volume 2, 'Agreement in definitions, judgements and forms of life', §3). 'Instead of the unanalysable, specific, indefinable: the fact that we act in such-and-such ways, e.g. *punish* certain actions, *establish* the state of affairs thus-and-so, *give orders*, render accounts, describe colours, take an interest in others' feelings. What has to be accepted, the given – it might be said – are facts of living // forms of life' (RPP I §630, with a MS variant).

According to Quine, all understanding is translating. Understanding utterances of another in one's own language involves homophonic (and sometimes heterophonic) translation. To understand a language or conceptual scheme, to determine its ontological imports, is always to translate it into another language. 'It makes no sense to say what the objects of a theory are, beyond saying how to interpret or reinterpret that theory in another' (OR 50). 'Commonly of course the background theory will simply be a containing theory, and in this case no question of a manual of translation arises. But this is after all just a degenerate case of translation still – the case where the rule of translation is the homophonic one' (OR 55). For, as we have seen (above, p. 206), it only makes sense to ask what the references of terms are relative to a background language.

But understanding utterances is not the same as translating or interpreting (see Volume 4, 'Intentionality', §5(vi)). The former is akin to an ability, whereas the latter are typically activities one engages in (although there is a use of 'interpret' which is synonymous with *one* use of 'understand', as in 'He interpreted the order to mean . . .'; that is, he took it (understood it) to mean). Nor could Quine argue that all understanding *involves* translating. Translating is a matter of rendering the utterances of one language in another. Interpreting is a matter of clarifying utterances by means of more perspicuous paraphrases, especially in cases where an utterance admits of divergent readings (legal statutes, poetry) – it is *this* interpretation as opposed to *that* one (PG 47). Interpreting an utterance therefore presupposes understanding, where more than one way of understanding is on the cards, and interpretation weeds out the worse from the better way of understanding. If the speaker is still available, one is likely not to interpret his ambivalent utterance, but to ask him to explain what he meant – and he does not have to interpret his own words for himself. In cases where an utterance in one's own language is not understood at all, one neither translates it nor interprets it, but rather explains it. 'Homophonic translation' is no more translating than photographing a painting is a kind of painting, or giving money to oneself is charity.

Understanding utterances of one's own language is not exhibited by homophonic disquotation, this being neither necessary nor sufficient for understanding. A child exhibits understanding of the request 'Shut the door!' by shutting the door, not by engaging *sotto voce* in homophonic translation prior to shutting the door.[55] Someone who has mastered the device of disquotation may exhibit this skill without manifesting any understanding at all. The fact that misunderstanding is rectified by interpretation and lack of understanding (of a foreign tongue) by translation does not show that understanding ordinarily involves either.

Wittgenstein argues that 'any interpretation [of the expression of a rule in our own language] still hangs in the air along with what it interprets, and cannot give it any support' (PI §198). Not all understanding can consist in assigning interpretations. How I understand something is shown not only by the interpretation I give of it if asked, but in what I do in response, which shows what I call 'such-and-such'. In the case of an order, how I understand it is shown by what I do in compliance with it. Here 'He has interpreted it to mean . . .' just means 'He has understood it to mean . . .', not 'He has interpreted it to mean . . . , and now he has acted on that interpretattion'. For, if all understanding required an interpretation, this would indeed generate a regress, since he would now have to interpret the interpretation he gave. Moreover, it would follow that what was understood was not the order given, but only the interpretation of it (PG 47). An interpretation is given in signs, so the idea that every sentence stands in need of an interpretation amounts to claiming that no sentence can be understood without a rider. But this is absurd, since the rider would need an interpretation. We do sometimes interpret signs. But when asked what time it is, we do not; we react. We react, and our understanding is manifest in what we do (cf. PG 47). That a symbol can sometimes be further interpreted does not show that one does further interpret it. There is an internal relation between an order and what counts as compliance with it, as there is an internal relation between an assertion and what makes it true; and what one understands by an order or assertion is to be seen in one's behaviour, which manifests one's grasp thereof.

To be sure, Wittgenstein never considered Quine's theses of indeterminacy of translation and of inscrutability of reference. Nevertheless, some of his remarks and general strategies can be brought to bear upon the matter. In the first place, he would reject Quine's behaviourist methodology. For Quine, what are 'given' to the field linguist are surface irradiations and responses, which, to be strictly consistent, should be characterized in terms of bare bodily movements and emission of sounds (a limitation which, as we have seen, he fails to recognize). For Wittgenstein's field linguist, what are given are human forms of life, to be characterized intentionalistically. For Quine, the primary leverage to be employed by the linguist is prompting assent or dissent by one-word observation sentences in circumstances of appropriate stimulus. For Wittgenstein's linguist, it is participation in the alien form of life and practices, engaging in discourse aided by gesture and facial expression (and not merely prompting Yes/No answers from the native), requesting, ordering, thanking, expressing pleasure and dissatisfaction, warning and heeding warnings, commiserating with suffering and so on.

Three associated presuppositions might be questioned from a Wittgensteinian perspective. First is the assumption that there is no role in the process of translation for explanations of meaning (construed normatively) given by the native, in particular none for ostensive definition by reference to samples and their use. 'Someone coming into a strange country will sometimes learn the language of the inhabitants from ostensive definitions that they give him' (PI §32). That 'he will often have to *guess* the meaning of these definitions; and will guess sometimes right, sometimes wrong' (ibid.) does not mean that there is no fact of the matter regarding correct understanding of them. For what counts as understanding such an explanation is manifest in correct application, which is internally related to the explanation.

Secondly, Quine pays no attention to the grammar (and grammatical form) of expressions that are being translated (this is an aspect of his disregard of any distinction between nonsense and falsehood). His claim that the term 'gavagai' may indifferently signify 'rabbit', 'rabbit stage', 'undetached rabbit part' or 'rabbithood' is wrong. For the grammar of these expressions, their combinatorial possibilities in language, is wholly different. If the linguist succeeds in translating 'Hungry!' (a fairly early achievement, one would think[56]), then if gavagai (or a gavagai) is said to be hungry, he can be sure that 'gavagai' does not mean rabbithood or undetached rabbit part. A defender of Quine might respond that the native utterance might signify not 'This rabbit is hungry', but 'This undetached rabbit part is a part of a hungry animal'. It might – if it possessed the appropriate grammatical multiplicity. But if an expression might signify 'is a part of an ξ animal', then to be sure, it cannot, in another utterance, do service as the copula if such there be. An expression signifying a rabbit stage can only be interchangeable in translation with one signifying a rabbit if the grammar of phase-sortals is indistinguishable from the grammar of their corresponding sortal – which it patently is not. The supposition that all grammatical categories can be permuted in different translations compatibly with making *sense* rests on no argument, but only on Quine's bold assertion.

Finally, the use of language is embedded in the stream of human life. It is part of the endlessly differentiated pattern of human behaviour. The thought that there can be two or more equally acceptable translation manuals for a given language, and no fact of the matter in choosing between them, rested for Quine foursquare on the translatability (in terms of stimulus synonymy) of observation sentences (on the basis of identification of assent and dissent), the alleged indeterminacy of translation of standing sentences, the underdetermination of theory by evidence and the inscrutability of reference of terms in general. But the thought that the network of standing sentences is capable of divergent interpretation consistent with translation of observation sentences (including, *pace* Quine, expressive utterances and sentences containing indexicals) *and consistent with the intelligibilty of the associated human behaviour* is misconceived. Learning a language is no more learning a theory than is learning any other normative practice – for example, learning how to play a game. There are behavioural criteria for understanding words – that is, for having mastered the techniques of their use – no less than there are behavioural criteria for understanding the moves of pieces in a game of chess. It is striking (and no coincidence) that attempts by Quine's followers to defend his theses of indeterminacy of translation and inscrutability of reference take as examples not the natural languages of mankind, but one fragment or another of mathematics or logic which admits of sundry permutations or alternative projections into some other part thereof without affecting truth. It is evident that such examples do not exemplify radical translation at all, let alone indeterminacy of translation.

If understanding is not a matter of translating, and if 'homophonic translation' is no translation, then, to be sure, radical translation does not begin at home. It is, trivially, understanding that begins at home. Does one not understand one's own utterances? Is there no fact of the matter about what one is referring to when one uses words? A person normally knows what he means when he says 'N.N. is in the next room', knows whom he means, and can say whom he means if asked. Quine argues that the question of what our words refer to is meaningless save in relation to 'a background language' (above, p. 206). From Wittgenstein's perspective, taken one way, this is right; taken another, it is wrong. 'The meaning of a word is *its use in the language*' (PI §43, my emphasis), and a word *has* a meaning only as part of a language. Moreover, 'It is only in a language that I can mean something by something' (PI p. 18n.) Put hyperbolically, as Wittgenstein does (PI §199), 'To understand a sentence means to understand a language.' For the sentence is the minimal unit for making a move in a language-game. It is comparable to a move in chess, and a move is only a move in the context of a game. Hence one might say that what a word refers to is a question that can only be raised and answered in relation to its use in a sentence of the language to which it belongs. But this does not make the question of its reference relative – as the question of the reference of an indexical in a sentence is relative to the context of its utterance. What Quine means, however, is quite different from this, and has no justification. It was wrong to hold that 'If questions of reference of the sort we are considering make sense only relative to a background language, then evidently questions of reference for the background language make sense in turn only relative to a further background language' (OR 49). For all questions of reference arise only, and receive their answers only, with respect to the use of words in sentences of a language. It is misconceived to suppose that a metalinguistic question such as 'What does "rabbit" (as employed in an antecedent utterance) mean?' involves regress to a different language from the (English) utterance in which the word 'rabbit' occurred. (Talking about an English word in English does not involve two languages). So-called homophonic translation is 'a degenerate case of translation' (OR 55, quoted above, p. 207) only in the sense in which a point is a degenerate case of a conic section or in which a straight line always intersects a circle, sometimes in real, sometimes in complex, points. It is equally misconceived to suppose that one cannot ask for an explanation of what a word signifies save by so-called metalinguistic assent – 'What is a rabbit?' will do just as well. The supposition that there is a regress of different languages is as gratuitous as the relativity thesis. Quine's manner of extricating himself from the absurdity is 'That in practice we end the regress of background languages, in discussions of reference, by acquiescing in our mother tongue and taking its words at face value' (OR 49). The truth of the matter is that there is no regress, and the question of inscrutability of reference does not arise, precisely because we use our mother tongue, having mastered the technique of its use, and we normally take its words 'at face value', since they are not normally used meta- phorically or in a secondary sense, and we know, and can explain, what they mean. But that is not a conclusion Quine would wish to arrive at, or one to which his argument entitles him.

(vii) *Ontology*. Wittgenstein has no explicit general discussion of ontology, but his remarks on specific problems show how different his approach is from Quine's. Quine investigates what we are ontologically committed to by investigating our apparatus of quantification, and thinks that what actually exists is determined by logic, mathematics, physics and unified science. Wittgenstein, by contrast, investi- gates what is meant, from case to case, by attributions of existence in philosophi- cally problematic cases.

The difficulty posed by negative existential statements containing vacuous proper names is removed, in Wittgenstein's view, by pointing out that if one asserts, for example, that Moses did not exist, and is asked whom one meant, one would rightly reply by means of one or another definite description explaining whom one meant. This, he argued, does not imply that the proper name is equivalent in meaning to some definite description, or some determinate conjunction or disjunc- tion of descriptions, but rather that the name does not have a fixed, unequivocal use in all possible cases (PI §79). He had no objection to Russell's analysis of definite descriptions – it may sometimes serve to defuse confusion, although it may also mislead (PI §90).

He rejected the idea that red things have nothing in common in virtue of which we classify them as red. It is true that light red and dark red are not classified as shades of red in virtue of possession of a common property. But red houses, red roses and red sunsets trivially have a common property: namely, being red (cf. BB 130–5; PI §72). This does not mean that such houses, roses and sunsets, in addition to being red, possess a further entity – namely, redness – as a bicycle, in addition to having wheels, may or may not possess lights. To admit, in common parlance, that they have something in common does not, *pace* Quine, commit one to the existence of any 'entity' over and above the houses, roses and sunsets. The 'popular manner of speaking' (see above, p. 198) is not in the least misleading. To have something in common does not mean the same as having some thing in common.

Does admitting that red things have something in common commit one to the existence of properties or universals? It is correct to say that there is such a colour as red and such a property as redness or being red, as it is correct that there is no such colour as infra-red or ultraviolet. But all that amounts to is that 'red' is a colour-word the application of which is verified by looking, whereas 'infra-red' and 'ultraviolet' are not. To say that red is my favourite colour (hence that there is a colour I favour above all others), that red is darker than pink (hence that there is a colour darker than pink), or that something disturbs me about a certain painting, namely, the exaggerated redness of the sky, does not commit me to the existence of any dubious entities. There are criteria of identity for being red, as there are for being a metre long or a kilogram in weight, which are given by defining samples, but, of course, not criteria for numerical identity.[57] In short, 'we quite readily say that a particular colour exists; and that is as much as to say that something exists that has that colour' (PI §58). We must not let ourselves be misled by the use of the dubious term 'entity'.

Investigating whether there are properties or universals is altogether unlike investigating whether there are black holes or quarks or whether there is an intra-Mercurian planet. One may 'admit these into one's ontology' according to one's empirical observations and theories. But whether there are properties or universals is not answered by either observation or by theory, but by clarification of the use of the ordinary expression 'property' and the term of art 'universal'. Quine concedes that we say happily that some species are cross-fertile, and that some numbers are primes larger than a thousand. This, in his view, commits us to the existence of abstract entities. Wittgenstein, by contrast, repudiates such talk of abstract entities as misleading. So-called abstract entities are not kinds of things in an ontological zoo, side by side with concrete entities. To say that X is an abstract entity is just to say that the expression 'X' has the surface grammar of the name of an object or substance, although it is not such a name, but has a quite different use (RFM 262f.; see also Volume 2, 'Grammar and necessity', pp. 283f.). The idea that paraphrastic eliminability of an expression demonstrates the avoidability of any 'ontological commitment' is at best misleading. The fact, if it is a fact, that any reference to propositions can be paraphrased away does not show that there are not many propositions, such as X's theorem or Y's principle, not to mention stories or rumours, with which one is acquainted. But it does not follow that propositions are 'entities'. The fact that all reference to events can be paraphrased away does not show that one did not witness such-and-such an event this morning, let alone that there are no events (that nothing ever happens). One may happily agree that some species are cross-fertile, while denying that species are 'entities' – irrespective of the availability of paraphrastic elimination. For to say that there are species amounts to no more than saying that animals and plants are classifiable in a certain way. The term 'entity' envelops the ontological landscape in fog.

Quine suggested that the existence of physical objects is a 'posit', which is on a par with positing molecules, that such a posit or hypothesis rests on empirical evidence, that it is posited in the course of devising 'the simplest conceptual scheme into which the disordered fragments of raw experience can be fitted and arranged' (WTI 16f.) or in order to explain the 'physical irritations of the subject's surfaces'. The primary alternative to positing physical objects seemed to be, as Carnap had suggested, to posit sense-data – an alternative which, for various reasons, Quine rejected. But posit we must, since 'everything to which we concede existence is a posit from the standpoint of a description of the theory-building process', and 'we can never do better than occupy the standpoint of some theory or other' (WO 22).

Wittgenstein repudiated both Carnap's conception and the position defended by Quine. Contrary to Carnap, he did not think that there is a choice between adopting a 'thing-language' as opposed to a 'sense-datum language', for the so-called sense-datum language is but a fragment of language which is essentially parasitic upon our use of material object terms. One can no more construct a grammar of sense-data which is independent of the grammar of objects than one can talk of marrying money independently of the existence of the institution of marriage.

Wittgenstein agreed with Carnap that 'external questions' such as 'Do material objects exist?' are nonsense, that talk of *believing* in 'the existence of the external world' is nonsense, and that it is misconceived to argue that 'the efficiency of the thing-language is confirming evidence for the reality of the thing-world'. But he denied that there can be any question of *choosing* the 'thing-language'. *A fortiori* he denied that it makes sense to posit or hypothesize the existence of material things or of the 'external world'.

First, we hypothesize or posit the existence of something only relative to what is given, when there is a datum in need of explanation. A datum – that is, what is given – is not posited or hypothesized. It is what can safely (non-hypothetically, or non-conjecturally) be argued from, and does not need to be argued to. Quinean 'raw experience' is not given (save in the sense in which measles is given – i.e. it is something caused, rather than being something available as a premise in an argument),[58] and the character of our 'surface irritations' (itches and tickles apart) is a datum, at best, only to neurophysiologists. So the idea that we *posit* material objects in order to explain our own raw experiences or surface irritations is misconceived, even though it is true that our surface irritations are explained by reference to material objects.

Secondly, the thought that we have evidence for the existence of material objects is equally misguided. We may have evidence for the existence of the yeti, but we could not have evidence for the existence of material things in general. Neither 'raw experience' nor 'surface irradiations' are evidence for the existence of the external world. Of course, we know that something or someone is present inasmuch as we see them. But to see an object is not a 'raw experience'; although it involves 'surface irradiations', we are ignorant of them, and do not infer *that* we see or *what* we see from them.[59] Perceiving an object is not *evidence* for its existence (footprints are evidence for someone's having passed by, but seeing a person walking by is not one's evidence for his walking by, although one's report of having so seen the person may be someone else's hearsay evidence for it). Having evidence for the existence of particular material things (the existence of a newly discovered star) is not having evidence for the existence of the external world. The inference 'Here is my hand, so there are physical things' is like 'I see red, so there are colours' (C §57). All the consequence amounts to is that a hand is a physical thing, as red is a colour; but these are grammatical propositions, not ontological hypotheses.

Thirdly, the idea that we might have evidence for the existence of an external world presupposes that its existence is a hypothesis, which might be disconfirmed. That in turn would require that we be able to give an account of what would disconfirm this 'hypothesis', what would constitute evidence against it, what would settle the matter beyond doubt. Wittgenstein held that the sentence 'There are physical objects' is nonsense (C §35). For it is not an empirical proposition. If it were, then 'There seem to be physical objects' would make sense, and it would have to be possible to give an account of what it would be for there to seem to be physical objects yet not be any. 'A is a physical object' is a grammatical proposition which explains an aspect of the use of the terms 'A' and 'physical object'. It licenses such inferences as 'A is on the table, so there is a physical object on the table'. The concept of a physical object is not a theoretical concept at all; nor is it a concept on a par with concepts of particular kinds of material things. It is, rather, a logical concept, like colour, quantity and the like. That is why no such proposition as 'There are physical objects' can be formulated (C §36).[60]

Quine's claim that the existence of mental states and events *behind* physical behaviour are posits which it is ill-advised to make, and that we should rather rest satisfied with positing physiological states and events instead is a conception diametrically opposed to Wittgenstein's. Indeed, to a large extent, Quine's radical physicalism is rooted in the thought that it is the primary alternative to Cartesianism and the dualist conception of the 'inner'. Consequently, he in effect embraces one half of the Cartesian duality: namely, the dualist (mis)conception of the 'outer' (see Volume 3, 'Behaviour and behaviourism'). Wittgenstein, by contrast, makes a clean sweep, rejecting the whole picture of the 'inner' and the 'outer' as embodied in the Cartesian heritage.

Quine's treatment of the mental is cursory and dogmatic, and I shall compare it only cursorily with Wittgenstein's, whose general approach has been discussed above (pp. 130–5). Other people do indeed enjoy or suffer various mental states: for example, they may be in a state of depression or of good cheer, just as they may have a migraine. But, according to Wittgenstein, these no more lie *behind* their behaviour, than the joy, pain or anger in a person's voice lies behind his words. If one sees someone writhing in pain, it is not a hypothesis that he is in pain, let alone that his pain is hidden behind his behaviour, and is, advisedly or ill-advisedly, posited (PI p. 223). Pain behaviour, in appropriate circumstances, *manifests* pain. Manifestations of the 'inner' are *criteria*, not inductive evidence, for the inner. That such criteria are defeasible in certain circumstances does not imply that they are defeasible in all circumstances. It is not an *opinion* that our fellow human beings have experiences, are in one mental state or another (PI p. 178). A person can sometimes keep his thoughts to himself and suppress his feelings, and in some such cases one may say that they are hidden from others. But when he says what he thinks, vents his anger or expresses his delight, it cannot be said that what are manifest are mere words and movements, that the thought is hidden behind the words, the anger behind the furious words, or the delight behind the joyful face and mien.

Introspection may not be construed as witnessing one's own bodily state. To avow pain is not to report on any introspective observations, but to give expression to one's suffering. And where there is genuine introspection, as when one reflects upon one's past behaviour, one's previous reasons for action, the motives that move one, the considerations that might have inclined one to act differently, one is not 'introspecting one's physical states'. Many psychological concepts are not names of, or expressions for, mental states, processes or events at all (e.g. 'intends', 'means'); many others are hardly, if ever, used to signify such categories (e.g. 'knows', 'believes'); and those that are (e.g. 'is depressed', 'is anxious') nevertheless have expressive uses in the first-person present. 'I am so frightened (anxious, miserable)' is an expression of feeling, not a hypothesis or even (in numerous cases) a description. Their use in the first person is not 'based on introspection', let alone on 'introspecting one's physical or neural state', for they are not typically 'based on' anything, but give expression to (and sometimes report) something. Far from our uses of concepts of the mental involving ontological posits which are dispensable for respectable science, they are integral to, and constitutive of, human life – and, as such, a datum for worthy, scientific psychology. Eliminative physicalism (materialism), of which Quine was (perhaps inadvertently) a progenitor, eliminates the very subject-matter of psychology (see Volume 4, 'Methodology in philosophical psychology', §3).

I began this discussion with a survey of apparent convergences between Quine and Wittgenstein. Closer scrutiny, however, has shown the two philosophers to be as close, and as distant, as members of the far Right and the far Left in the horseshoe-shaped French National Assembly – one must travel through the whole spectrum of opinion to reach the one viewpoint from the other. The one is an exemplary 'hedgehog', a methodological monist, a defender of scientism in philosophy, a naturalizing epistemologist and propounder of an ontology guided by physics and canonical notation. The other is a paradigmatic 'fox', who viewed scientific method in philosophy as the worst source of misconceived metaphysics, a methodological pluralist appalled at the misguided idea that the only forms of knowledge and understanding are scientific, who socialized epistemology without naturalizing it, held the canonical notation of mathematical logic to have completely deformed the thinking of philosophers, and rejected the intelligibility of ontology as conceived by the philosophical tradition. But it was Quine's philosophy which, throughout the 1970s and 1980s, became a primary inspiration for the forms of American philosophy which progressively displaced the influence of Wittgenstein and Oxford analytical philosophy.

8

The Decline of Analytic
Philosophy

1. The critical backlash

The first chapter of this book opened with a quotation from Russell concerning Wittgenstein's influence upon twentieth-century analytic philosophy. It is therefore appropriate that the concluding chapter should commence with Russell's reactions to its development. Although he acknowledged that Wittgenstein had, in the opinion of many British philosophers, superseded him, he could see nothing in Wittgenstein's later writings other than 'a suave evasion of paradoxes'.[1] The doctrines of the last of the three schools of philosophy which Russell enumerated as having dominated the British philosophical scene, which he referred to as 'WII' (meaning Wittgenstein's later philosophy and the kinds of philosophy practised at Oxford after 1945), seemed to him an abnegation of intellectual responsibility. 'Its positive doctrines seem to me to be trivial', he wrote, 'and its negative doctrines unfounded. I have not found in Wittgenstein's *Philosophical Investigations* anything that seemed to me to be interesting and I do not understand why a whole school finds important wisdom in its pages' (ibid., p. 216). It is noteworthy – because characteristic of many unsympathetic and uncomprehending critics – that Russell rolled together not only the very diverse views of philosophers working in Oxford, but also Wittgenstein's ideas. Philosophers at Oxford and Wittgenstein were collectively characterized as a 'school', and a disagreement with any one of that large and diverse collection of writers was automatically held to condemn them all. Indeed, a mistake found in the arguments of any one of them was held to reflect upon all, and to damn whatever methods they employed in common.

What were Russell's objections? At a general level, they boil down to three. First and foremost, philosophy, as Russell understood it, was, like science, an attempt to understand the world. But, he complained, according to the adherents of WII, 'The desire to understand the world is . . . an outdated folly' (ibid., p. 219). Secondly, he claimed, Strawson and other Oxford philosophers 'are persuaded that common speech is good enough, not only for daily life, but also for philosophy. I, on the contrary, am persuaded that common speech is full of vagueness and inaccuracy, and that any attempt to be precise and accurate requires modification of common speech as regards vocabulary and as regards syntax. Everybody admits that physics and chemistry and medicine each require a language which is not that of everyday life. I fail to see why philosophy, alone, should be forbidden to make a similar approach towards precision and accuracy' (ibid., pp. 241–2). Thirdly,

Russell argued against Ryle that 'philosophy cannot be fruitful if divorced from empirical science. [The philosopher's] imagination should be impregnated with the scientific outlook and . . . he should feel that science has presented us with a new world, new concepts and new methods, not known in earlier times, but proved in experience to be fruitful where the older concepts and methods proved barren' (ibid., p. 254). It is only a dualistic prejudice which prevents us (and prevented Ryle) from locating mental occurrences in brains, in accordance with the latest deliverances of science.

Such objections were widespread, and clung both to 'Oxford' philosophy and to Wittgenstein's. As noted in chapter 6, and as was remarked by Warnock in 1976, the 'orthodoxy' prevailing in Oxford in the 1950s was actually at no time very much of an orthodoxy. 'It can only have been from a *very* great distance, or through glasses of highly imperfect focus, that everyone at the time looked much alike, like devotees of "school".'[2] But it was true that there was general agreement that philosophy is *not* continuous with the sciences, that philosophy does not contribute to the extension of our knowledge of the world, and that examination of the correct, ordinary use of the words, be they common or technical, involved in any philosophical investigation is an essential propaedeutic to that investigation. These commitments have been discussed in detail in previous chapters. It is true that they would be undermined *if* Quine's attack upon the analytic/synthetic distinction (a) were held to be successful in its own terms, which, as we have seen, is questionable; *and* (b) militated against Wittgenstein's different distinction between empirical and grammatical propositions, which, as we have seen, it does not.

Much of the philosophy done not only at Oxford, but in Britain in general, throughout the 1940s and most of the 1950s, was published in article form. Journals (and there were fewer of them) were more important then than they are today, and most philosophers actually read them. The fact that much philosophical writing took the form of 'vignettes', as it were, suggested, at least to some transatlantic eyes, a glorification of piecemeal work, an aversion – perhaps even a principled one – to systematicity or generality. Not too much should be made of this point, since, as we have seen, there were important books emerging from Oxford, not to mention Cambridge and elsewhere. Moreover, although to the impatient eye Wittgenstein's *Philosophical Investigations* gives the appearance of being unsystematic, it is, as has been amply demonstrated in the four volumes of *Analytical Commentary*, anything but unsystematic. It ranges over a very large number of topics (far greater than, for example, Quine's philosophy), weaving together endless complex conceptual connections with exemplary thoroughness. This is obscured by its *Bemerkungen* style of composition and by the distinctive character of its argumentation, which often leaves it to the reader to follow the trajectory of the thought expressed – but then, as Wittgenstein noted in his preface, he did not want his writing to spare other people the trouble of thinking. Nevertheless, it is interesting that some distinguished philosophers perceived post-war British analytic philosophy as lacking both generality and systematicity. Nelson Goodman wrote in 1958:

> the rejection of absolutistic justifications for system-building does not of itself constitute justification for the extremely asystematic character of typical current British analysis. Unwillingness to accept any postulates of geometry as absolute

or self-evident truths hardly diminishes the importance of the systematic development of geometries. Unwillingness to take any elements as metaphysical or epistemological ultimates does not make pointless all systematic constructions in philosophy. . . . Emphasis on spot-analysis is a natural reaction to a heavy-handed system building; but too little regard for system can lead us to run in circles or to overlook important likenesses while we are busy cataloguing subtle distinctions.[3]

It is true that philosophers in Oxford placed no faith in the kind of system-building Goodman had embarked upon in *The Structure of Appearance*. The objections to that enterprise of logical construction were indeed principled. Nevertheless, the accusation is unwarranted. First, its accuracy is questionable, even regarding the period prior to 1958 if 'systematicity' is taken to mean thoroughness, interconnectedness and generality of scope (as exemplified both in the *Investigations* and in such books as *The Concept of Mind* or *Introduction to Logical Theory*). Secondly, to the extent to which there was some truth in the accusation, the authors concerned were doing precisely what Russell, commonly held to be a paradigmatically systematic philosopher, had advocated fifty years earlier under the heading 'Scientific method in philosophy': namely, dividing 'traditional problems into a number of separate and less baffling questions', the maxim 'Divide and conquer' being the key to success here as elsewhere. 'Scientific philosophy' such as Russell recommended *ought* to be 'piecemeal and tentative like other sciences'.[4] Certainly the accusation of piecemeal work and lack of systematicity could hardly be directed at Oxford philosophers after 1959, in which year, as we have seen, Strawson published his celebrated *Individuals*, and Hampshire his *Thought and Action* (not to mention Hart's *Concept of Law*, which followed in 1961, and Austin's posthumous *How to do Things with Words* in 1962). What is true is that few philosophers at Oxford (unlike Cambridge) shared the widespread American post-positivist interest in the philosophy of science (the distinguished exception being Rom Harré), or conceived of philosophy as continuous with science. But Russell's remarks against Ryle were misguided. *Philosophy of science* cannot be divorced from empirical science, since it is concerned with modes of scientific explanation and theory construction, with the analysis of scientific concepts and their logical relations to observational concepts. Parts of philosophy of psychology and epistemology must deal with questions that arise out of scientific theory and its relation to non-theoretical descriptions of experience and its objects, for philosophical problems are generated by the appearance of conflict between the two kinds of description. But this was not denied by protagonists of WII, as is evident, for example, in Ryle's *Dilemmas* or Wittgenstein's criticisms of Köhler (see Volume 4, 'Methodology in philosophical psychology', §1).[5] Philosophy, *pace* Locke, is not the handmaiden of the sciences, but the tribunal of sense – in philosophy of science, as elsewhere.

However, 1959 was not only the year of these ambitious and ambitiously general works; it was also the year of the *cause célèbre* of Ernest Gellner's *Words and Things*, a polemical book directed indiscriminately against much of post-Russellian modern analytic philosophy. It was, indeed, a very bad book, and had it been reviewed briefly in *Mind*, and appropriately dismissed, it would doubtless have sunk without a trace. But Ryle, as editor of *Mind*, did not think that it merited a review. This provoked Russell, who had written a favourable introduction to Gellner's book, to open a vehement correspondence in the columns of *The Times*, which continued for many weeks.[6] It is doubtful whether the controversy had a significant effect upon professional British philosophers who had a clear idea of the issues involved, but it almost certainly damaged the public image of philosophy as practised in Oxford, and lent further currency to the idea that there was an Oxford 'school' of philosophy, which was committed to the examination of linguistic trivia, rather than pursuing the real business of philosophy.

The criticisms of the post-war phase of analytic philosophy were various, and came from diverse sources. I shall summarize the main general accusations, comment briefly upon those which have already been dealt with in chapter 6, and at greater length upon the others.

(i) *The neglect of metaphysics*. Price, already in 1945, had opened the methodological debate with an address to the Aristotelian Society entitled 'Clarity is not Enough' (PASS, 19 (1945)). His primary complaint was that contemporary 'clarifying philosophers' had neglected 'speculative metaphysics'. They did so, Price argued, because they believed that speculative metaphysicians are trying to do something impossible: namely, to establish conclusions about matters of fact by a priori argument. But, he claimed, this misrepresents their valid purpose, which is to produce alternative conceptual schemes to our ordinary one, alternative modes of conceptual arrangement by which the body of empirical data can be ordered. The choice between different systems of speculative metaphysics is not between the true and the false, but between the less good and the better, or between several things that are good, but good in different ways. So there is room not only for analysis and analytic clarity, but also for synopsis.

Price's conception was a second cousin to Carnap's replacement of traditional metaphysical controversy by consideration of the grounds for choosing one or another different 'languages' – for example, a phenomenalist or physicalist language – for various scientific and theoretical purposes, or classical as opposed to intuitionistic logic for mathematics. Price's conception of the true vocation of speculative metaphysics was to be echoed in Strawson's later notion (in *Individuals*) of revisionary metaphysics. There is nothing here against which post-war analytic philosophers need cavil, for the advocacy of connective and therapeutic analysis need not exclude revisionary metaphysics thus conceived. It should, however, be remarked that few (if any) traditional metaphysicians conceived of their endeavours thus. They did not see themselves as *merely* objecting to a notation, but rather as offering new insights into the nature of reality (see above, pp. 120f.). As Wittgenstein pointed out, the metaphysician 'sees a way of dividing the country different from the one used on the ordinary map. He feels tempted, say, to use the name "Devonshire" not for the county with its conventional boundary, but for a region differently bounded. He could express this by saying, "Isn't it absurd to make *this* a county, to draw the boundaries *here*?" But what he says is "The *real* Devonshire is this"' (BB 57). We could answer him, Wittgenstein continued, by saying 'What you want is only a new notation, and by a new notation no facts of geography are changed'. Price and Strawson would agree. But despite their agreement, not only do we lack examples of respectable, unconfused, revisionary metaphysics thus construed; we lack any clear conception of its philosophical point. The conceptual confusions and unclarities that bred the great metaphysical systems of the past would not be resolved or clarified by adopting a different language (Carnap), conceptual scheme (Strawson) or grammar (Wittgenstein), but only brushed under the carpet (just as Carnapian explication does not dissolve or resolve philosophical difficulties, but merely side-steps them). For different languages (in Carnap's sense), conceptual schemes or grammars (in Wittgenstein's sense) define different concepts, which cannot clarify existing ones (save as objects for comparison). A different grammar may be useful for specific practical (non-philosophical) purposes, but that is not what metaphysicians typically have in view. Einstein introduced a different grammar, and brought about a shift in the grammar, of space and time for purposes of relativity physics, abandoning the Newtonian concepts. But it would be misleading to characterize this as an exercise in metaphysics.[7] What could be claimed is that the philosophical invention of fragments of a different grammar (a different form of representation) for a given domain of discourse, such as colour ascriptions, may help to disabuse us of the misguided idea that our grammar is correct, that it faithfully mirrors the language-independent nature of things, or that it is the only possible one – at least for creatures such as us.

(ii) *The trivialization of philosophy*. This accusation, which featured in Russell's animadversions, was widespread. The examination of the use of words as a method of philosophical clarification was perceived as reducing all philosophical issues to mere verbal disputes, instead of pursuing a deeper, more systematic knowledge of reality. To a large extent the accusation has already been deflected by the detailed examination of post-war analytic philosophy in chapter 6. But it is perhaps worth surveying the ground again synoptically. One can distinguish here four different complaints against post-war connective analysis: first, that, according to this conception, the subject-matter of philosophy is ordinary language rather than the nature of things; secondly, that it held that the problems of philosophy arise exclusively from ordinary language or from the ordinary use of words; thirdly, that it invites investigations of language for their own sake, investigations that belong more properly to linguistic theory than philosophy; fourthly, that it encourages philosophical relativism, or 'flabby omnitolerance', the view that, as Wisdom was inclined to argue, almost every philosophy is really right, inasmuch as it brings out some kind of insight.

These accusations, in the light of chapter 6, can be dealt with as follows:

(a) In the sense in which the sciences have a subject-matter – that is, are first-order disciplines – philosophy has none. In the sense in which philosophy has a subject-matter, it is the problems of philosophy. These can best be characterized by examples of the peculiar kinds of conceptual questions with which the subject deals, and the manner in which it handles them. Questions about the nature of things in one sense are the province of the special sciences. In another, they are indeed philosophical questions. But then they are to be answered by a grammatical, linguistic investigation. For a philosophical question about the *nature* of X is as much about the word 'X' as is the question of how the word 'X' is used. In philosophy, the question 'What is the nature of . . . ?' actually asks for a word to be explained; only it makes us expect a wrong kind of answer (PI §370). For *essence* is expressed by grammar (PI §371), and it is grammar that tells us what kind of object anything is (PI §373). To claim that such grammatical clarification is a method, perhaps the primary (though not the only) method of philosophy (cf. PI §133), is not to claim that the subject-matter of philosophy is language, let alone ordinary language.

(b) It was indeed held that our language is one great source of philosophical problems. And it is also true that the problems which attracted most of the attention of philosophers in post-war Oxford were those that arise out of, or involve, the ordinary use of ordinary, non-technical language. But it was not held, either by Wittgenstein or by philosophers working in Oxford, that philosophical problems in the philosophy of logic, of mathematics or of science arise out of the use of ordinary language, but rather out of the use of technical language (see above, p. 160). Nor was it generally held, and certainly not by Wittgenstein, that entanglements in grammar are the sole source of the problems of philosophy. Other such sources are, according to Wittgenstein, the lure of the scientific model of explanation, illegitimately transposed to philosophy; the craving for generality in domains where specificity is all that is legitimate; the mesmerizing power and philosophically deforming influence of new discoveries, theories and inventions in science and mathematics, such as the predicate calculus, set theory, calculating machines, Freudian psychoanalysis and behaviourism; and the pursuit of justification beyond the point where justification makes sense. Nor was it generally held that the sole motivation for enquiry was philosophical paradox and puzzlement. The quest for understanding, for an overview of conceptual structures, and the concomitant diagnosis of illusion and of the craving for illusion, is no less important and legitimate.

(c) It is true that Austin in particular was happy to let his interests in language and its use lead him where they might. Though he evidently hoped that his theory of speech-acts would ultimately yield a philosophical harvest (which he did not live to reap), it would not have disturbed him unduly, I fancy, had the harvest been meagre, as long as his theory was true and illuminated the subject with which he dealt. He had, as we have seen, few *general* metaphilosophical commitments, and certainly did not hold that philosophy is no more than a branch of linguistics. But whatever may be true of Austin, it cannot be imputed undiscriminatingly to others engaged in analytic philosophy in Oxford and elsewhere from 1945 onwards.

(d) It is true that Wisdom tended towards a form of philosophical relativism. And so did Waismann, at least to some extent, in his later writings (see above, p. 165). But these views were propounded, certainly in Waismann's case, in opposition to Wittgenstein. And they found little if any support from other prominent philosophers in Oxford or Cambridge at the time. Forms of philosophical relativism should not, however, be confused with the correct claim that philosophical errors commonly reflect important truths, distorted or misconstrued.

(iii) *Sanctification of ordinary language and defective methodology.* Quotations taken out of context, and frequently misinterpreted, provided opponents of post-war analytic philosophy with objections to the method of examining the use of words as a means for, or at least a precondition of, resolving philosophical questions. First, Wittgenstein's remark that 'ordinary language is all right as it is' was often evoked to argue that 'ordinary language philosophers' were committed to the view that ordinary language cannot be improved upon, either in science or in drawing fine distinctions in philosophy. Similarly, Austin's remark that 'ordinary language ... embodies ... the inherited experience and acumen of many generations of men' was quoted to demonstrate a commitment to the idea that all the distinctions that are necessary for science or philosophy are already available in ordinary language. But, it was objected, it would be absurd to conduct sophisticated science or mathematics with no more than the linguistic resources of the common man. Secondly, the appeal to standard English (or to the idiom of Oxford dons) was held to be objectionable. (a) It gives English a status of privilege over other languages, which have different structures and idioms. And philosophical problems are not language-relative. (b) It gives unwarranted preference to idiolects or a local sociolect. Determining the ordinary use of expressions by reference to standard (Oxford) English presupposes that there are no alternative usages. Indeed, it is debatable whether there is all that much consensus over use even within a linguistic community.[8] (c) The manner in which descriptions of use are elicited is defective. The ordinary use of an expression is not to be discovered merely by reflection (which is no more than armchair linguistics), but requires socio-linguistic investigation.[9]

These objections, too, can be dealt with briefly in the light of previous discussions. Wittgenstein's remark merely reiterated what he said in the *Tractatus* (see above, p. 26) – hardly a paradigm of connective or therapeutic analysis, let alone of anything that might be called 'ordinary language philosophy'. It was endorsed in the *Investigations* §98 (cf. BB 28), since what it meant was merely that ordinary language is not *logically* faulty (*pace* Frege and Russell), and that it is not the task of philosophy to pursue the will-o'-the-wisp of an 'ideal language'. Being in good logical order is a condition of sense; a language which was not so would not be a language.[10] That remark involves no prohibition of linguistic innovation where and when necessary and fruitful for practical purposes (cf. PI §132) or the purposes of scientific theory. Moreover, Wittgenstein did not hesitate to introduce his own technical or quasi-technical terminology in philosophy (e.g. 'language-game', 'family resemblance concept', 'grammatical proposition'). Austin's remark, in context (see p. 174), was carefully qualified. *If* we are to proceed from ordinary language, which is *one* method, then we should be well advised to choose a subject in which ordinary language is rich and subtle in distinctions – hence his choice of the subject of excuses. But even here he did not suggest that such distinctions would be adequate 'if our interests are more extensive or intellectual than ordinary'. Moreover, as previously noted, Austin's typology of speech-acts is rich in novel technical terminology devised for the purpose of precise, fruitful classification.

Investigating the ordinary use of expressions, whether common or technical, in a given language does not give the language in question any privileged status over other languages: first, because it is the *use* of terms that is examined, a use that is to a large extent shared by terms in numerous other languages (see above, p. 161). Although the words we use are English words, and we assert whatever we assert *in* English, what is asserted is not English, nor yet German. To utter the English sentence 'Snow is white' is to assert that snow is white, which is precisely what is asserted by uttering the German sentence 'Schnee ist weiss'. What is asserted is no more language-relative than is truth; that snow is white is not 'true in English', but true *simpliciter*. A philosophical investigation of the concept of cause or of the objectivity or otherwise of colour ascriptions can be conducted in any language in which there are ergative verbs and colour-names in use. Marginal differences between languages may be irrelevant to the investigation. Descartes's and Locke's

Latin, French and English investigations of primary and secondary qualities, are all equally pertinent to the clarification of the problems involved, since the marginal differences in the use of, for example, the colour vocabulary are irrelevant. More substantial differences between languages may be significant, but not because they vitiate the account we give of *our* concept, as manifest in our use of a word or phrase. Rather, deviations between different languages may illuminate by drawing attention to alternative possibilities of concept formation. Such deviations may be useful objects of comparison, which help to highlight the use of words in our own language. It is noteworthy, however, that a philosopher need not investigate other natural languages. For he can, as Wittgenstein so often did, *invent* languages or fragments of languages for precisely this purpose (BB 28). A commitment to linguistic methods of connective analysis in no way renders philosophical problems more language-relative than they actually are. To be sure, certain philosophical questions and puzzles do not arise in all human languages. A language which employs either no copula or one which differs from the identity sign is unlikely to tempt one to confuse predication and identity, and a language which does not use the possessive pronoun in ascriptions of psychological predicates is unlikely to bring one to think of the mental as privately owned and inalienable.

Nor does careful description of the use of expressions as a method of resolving philosophical questions give unwarranted preference to any particular idiolect or sociolect, let alone presume that there are no alternative usages. Oxford philosophers such as Ryle, Austin and Hart were not concerned with a mere local sociolect, but with the concepts of, for example, voluntary and involuntary, excuse, justification and mitigation. These are common property, not Oxford Common Room property. Were they mistaken not to conduct polls concerning the use of these terms? Did the different accounts given by Ryle and Austin of the use of 'voluntary' and 'involuntary' show that usage is variable, and that social surveys are necessary? Describing the use of an expression in a language of which one is a competent speaker is not like describing the health of the community, which requires social surveys, but is rather akin to describing the rules of a common game which one plays day in day out, year in year out. One's description may be erroneous, for it is not easy to bring to mind all the various forms of licit grammatical structures and the differences and similarities with related but categorially distinct expressions, let alone the complex forms of context dependence of the use of expressions. Over and above the linguistic competence possessed by any normal speaker, a rich linguistic imagination is requisite, a sensitive ear and a high degree of linguistic self-consciousness. Certainly errors concerning usage occur in the writings of philosophers, but that is not the same as disagreements in usage, for they are rectified by reminders. (Ryle's response to Austin, one may presume, was not 'Well, that's how *I* use "voluntary" and "involuntary"', but rather 'Yes, you are right; that is how they are used'.) If, however, there *is* an interestingly different usage, that is merely further grist for the mill. As Austin pointed out:

> If our usages disagree, then you use 'X' where I use 'Y', or more probably (and more intriguingly) your conceptual system is different from mine, though very likely it is at least equally consistent and serviceable: in short, we can find out *why* we disagree – you choose to classify in one way and I in another. If the usage is loose, we can understand the temptation that leads to it, and the distinctions that

it blurs: if there are 'alternative' descriptions, then the situation can be described or can be 'structured' in two ways, or perhaps it is one where, for current purposes, the two alternatives come down to the same. A disagreement as to what we should say is not to be shied off, but to be pounced upon: for the explanation of it can hardly fail to be illuminating.[11]

It is unfortunate that Austin did not give examples of such differences of 'conceptual systems'. But, if we confine ourselves to legal theory, with which he was concerned in 'A Plea for Excuses', it would suffice to point to the very different ways in which legal theorists have construed the scope of such terms as 'duty', 'obligation', 'right' or 'power', from Bentham and Austin to Hohfeld, Hart, Joseph Raz, Alan White, Ronald Dworkin and beyond. Doubtless, some of these exemplify philosophical confusion. But it is equally evident that some are advocating different classifications and alternative modes of description.[12]

Wittgenstein's approach to these methodological questions was distinctively dialogical and dialectical, attuned to his therapeutic view of philosophy. The description of the use of an expression is subservient to the philosophical problem at hand. 'We are interested in language only insofar as it gives us trouble. I only describe the actual use of a word if this is necessary to remove some trouble we want to get rid of' (AWL 97). A philosophical problem is presented to one by one's own reflections or by someone else's (who may be present, or a long dead philosopher). What is so difficult, and what the other person cannot do, is to arrange the rules according to which he is using the relevant expressions step by step and in the right order, so that all questions are solved (WWK 183f.). A philosophical problem characteristically involves an entanglement in the rules for the use of an expression. Dialogue is the most natural form of philosophical investigation, a dialogue (actual or imaginary) between one who is caught in the web of language and one who guides the former, with his consent (hence the analogy with psychoanalysis), out of the endless traps that language sets us, to the 'correct logical point of view'. Hence,

> One of the most important tasks is to express all false trains of thought so characteristically that the reader says, 'Yes, that's exactly the way I meant it'. To trace the physiognomy of every error.
> Indeed, we can only convict someone else of a mistake if he acknowledges that this really is the expression of his feeling.// . . . if he (really) acknowledges this expression as the correct expression of his feelings.//
> For only if he acknowledges it as such, is it the correct expression. (Psychoanalysis.)
> What the other person acknowledges is the analogy I am proposing to him as the source of his thought. (BT 410)

Again, there is no need to conduct polls. All that is necessary is that the reader recognize the philosopher's characterization of the use of a given problematic expression as *his* use. Then disentanglement can proceed. And there is a presumption that the use in question, and the entanglement of rules, is common among those who are similarly ensnared in the net of grammar. That presumption is borne out by the fact that the great range of problems Wittgenstein addresses are articulated in forms familiar from the history of the subject, and exemplify confusions into which numerous philosophers, from Plato onwards, have fallen (even though Wittgenstein rarely mentions anyone by name.)

(iv) *The philistine defence of common sense*. It was sometimes held that post-war analytic philosophy was committed to a dogmatic, philistine defence of common sense against the deliverances of advanced science. To philosophers of Russellian persuasion, science had proved beyond cavil that material objects, such as lumps of rock, planks of wood and so on are not really solid; that objects around us are not really multi-coloured at all, but merely reflect light of various wavelengths which causes us to have 'ideas of colour' or 'subjective perceptions' of colour. That philosophy should be at odds with common sense is not something to be deplored; on the contrary, it is something to be demanded. For only thus will philosophy remain in tune with science. Indeed, as Russell had already remarked in 1918, 'the point of philosophy is to start with something so simple as not to seem worth stating, and to end with something so paradoxical that no one will believe it'.[13]

This accusation involves a multitude of misunderstandings and injustices, only some of which can be touched upon here. It is true that Moore defended 'common sense', and attempted to prove the independent existence of the material world. Important though his paper 'Proof of an External World' (1939) was, its importance did not lie either in the attempted 'proof' or in its success (for it is no proof). Its importance was twofold. First, it reminded philosophers that any philosophical claim such as that there does not exist a material, mind-independent world, or that nothing can be known with certainty, or that no one could ever have acted other than he did, or that everything that can be truly said to exist is material (or, as idealists contend, is mental), is to be rejected. But it was not part of Moore's view that *all* the deliverances of common sense (however they are to be circumscribed) are known to be true. Secondly, it picked out an array of propositions, such as that he was a human being, that he had never been far from the surface of the earth, that the world had existed for a long time, that he had two hands, and so forth, which have a very peculiar position and status within his noetic structure. The first point, as Moore himself recognized, is not the terminus of argument, but the beginning. Whether or not Moore's arguments are acceptable is indeed debatable. But that does not affect the correct point to which he was drawing attention. The second point lay fallow until Wittgenstein developed its implications in *On Certainty*. That book is anything but a dogmatic defence of common sense.

Wittgenstein, as remarked above (p. 83), did not think that there can be a common-sense answer to any philosophical problem. Nor, indeed, did he think that it is the task of philosophy to prove that there exists a material world, or that there are other people who have experiences, or that inductive reasoning is justified. Its task is to demonstrate the incoherence of the idealist's, solipsist's or inductive sceptic's claims. And a similar line of argument was pursued, with respect to specific topics, by von Wright, Ryle, Austin and Strawson (in a neo-Kantian mode), as well as by other post-war analytic philosophers. For common sense has nothing to say about the structure of our conceptual scheme, the character of our patterns of justification, the limits of justification and the bounds of sense. If some were guilty of a dogmatic defence of common sense, the leading figures of post-war analytic philosophy cannot be so accused.

As for the apparent conflict between the 'common sense' conception of the material world and the 'scientific' conception, the issue is not one of dogmatic common sense versus enlightened science. It is rather a matter of clarifying the conceptual connections between certain scientific descriptions and explanations of phenomena and the description of the data explained, hence a matter for philosophical investigation and argument. For it is far from obvious whether the *scientific conception of the world* (in contrast to the laws of nature discovered), as understood by (and inherited from) Galileo, Descartes, Boyle, Locke and Newton is (a) coherent and (b) in so far as it is coherent, incompatible with the truth of our ordinary descriptions of objects of our perceptual experiences as, for example, solid (as opposed to hollow, porous or penetrable without breakage or deformation) or coloured (as opposed to transparent and colourless).[14] To defend the view that solidity is compatible with being constituted of atoms in a lattice array, or that what we see when we gaze at the roses in the garden are coloured objects (and not merely the effects on us of retinal irradiation) is not a dogmatic defence of common sense, irrespective of whether it is successful or not.

(v) *The paradigm case argument.* In the immediate post-war period the so-called paradigm case argument enjoyed a brief, if controversial, vogue. The gist of the argument was stated by A. G. N. Flew:

> Crudely: if there is a word the meaning of which can be taught by reference to paradigm cases, then no argument whatever could prove that there are no cases whatever of whatever it is. Thus, since the meaning of 'of his own freewill' can be taught by reference to such paradigm cases as that in which a man, under no social pressure, marries a girl he wants to marry (how else could it be taught?): it cannot be right, on any grounds whatever to say that no one *ever* acts of his own freewill. For such cases as the paradigm, which must occur if the word is ever to be thus explained (and which certainly do occur), are not in that case specimens which might have been wrongly identified: to the extent that the meaning of the expression is given in terms of them, they are, by definition, what 'acting on one's own freewill' is.[15]

A similar argument had been propounded by Norman Malcolm, who claimed:

> In the case of all expressions the meaning of which must be *shown* and cannot be explained, as can the meaning of 'ghost', it follows, from the fact that they are ordinary expressions in the language, that there have been *many* situations of the kind which they describe; otherwise so many people could not have learned the correct use of the expressions. Whenever a philosophical paradox asserts, therefore, with regard to such an expression, that always when the expression is used the use of it produces a false statement, then to prove that the expression is an *ordinary* expression is completely to refute the paradox.[16]

This kind of argument was invoked by various writers to refute different forms of scepticism – about the existence of objects, free will or inductive reasoning. It did not take a single form, but at least in some forms it left hostages to fortune. To the extent to which the argument relies upon a conception of ostensive definition, and tries to draw anti-sceptical existential conclusions from the ostensive definability of a given expression, it is open to objection. First, one may explain an ostensively definable expression, wittingly or unwittingly, by reference to a sample which only apparently exemplifies the property in question. Or one may give an ostensive explanation by using a picture – for example, of a unicorn – but no one would try to prove the existence of unicorns from the fact that the use of 'unicorn' can be thus explained. Secondly, an ostensive definition by reference to a sample is misdescribed as 'showing the meaning' of the *definiendum*. Ostensive definition explains the meaning of a word, no less than an analytic definition does, but the ostended sample is not the meaning of a word, and from such an explanation of what a word means, no existential truths follow. Thirdly, an ostensive definition is not a true predication, but a rule for the use of a term; and one cannot derive an appropriate existential truth from such a rule.

To the extent that defenders of the paradigm case argument tried to derive existential truths from the fact that a given expression is, or must be, ostensively defined and learnt, it was indefensible. And it fails to clarify what is awry with the various forms of scepticism. But it should be stressed that one could hardly characterize post-war analytic philosophy by its commitment to any form of the paradigm case argument.

2. Criticisms of Wittgenstein

Wittgenstein was tarred with the same brush as the derided 'Ordinary Language Philosophy'. This was a double injustice. For much of the criticism of the philosophy emanating from Oxford was misplaced. Even when it was justly brought against a particular philosopher, it was not a charge that could be levelled at all philosophers; *a fortiori* it could not rightly be levelled at Wittgenstein without more ado. Ryle occasionally displayed a behaviourist drift (see above, p. 171), but that was no ground for lumping Ryle and Wittgenstein together as logical behaviourists. Nevertheless, the accusation stuck to Wittgenstein. So too did the claim that he was a crypto-verificationist, a claim made originally on the basis of a misinterpretation of his argument against the intelligibility of private ostensive definition, and later transmuted into the suggestion that he was, as the logical positivists were (wrongly) taken to be, an 'anti-realist'.

Since the *Investigations* was so difficult to fathom, and because the remaining writings, which shed much light on it, were unavoidably published piecemeal over many decades, misinterpretations of his thought were rife (see above, pp. 142f.). Moreover, the refutations of some of his followers' misinterpretations of his work were understandably thought to be refutations of Wittgenstein. In particular, Malcolm's *Dreaming* (1959) became a target for anti-Wittgensteinian polemics, it being thought that actual or supposed flaws in his argument were representative of errors in Wittgenstein's.[17] Similarly, I. A. Melden's *Free Action* (1961), which defended an inadequate form of 'the logical connection argument' to demonstrate the irreducibility of reasons to causes and of explanation in terms of reasons to a form of causal explanation, was held to demonstrate the untenability of Wittgenstein's position. It would be pointless to survey the multitude of misinterpretations of Wittgenstein's writings, or the attempted refutations of views imputed to him on the basis of such misinterpretations. Most of the significant ones have been discussed directly or by implication in the four volumes of the *Analytical Commentary*. What I shall do here is to confront six general, substantial kinds of attack on fundamental Wittgensteinian directions of thought. A detailed vindication of Wittgenstein's position and refutation of these attacks would require very lengthy treatment indeed, which in some cases has been given in the essays of the *Commentary*. Here I shall rest content with pointing out perspicuous errors and misinterpretations, and, regarding more complex issues, with starting hares rather than catching them, exploring profitable strategies that can be further pursued, rather than trying to settle the issues definitively.

(i) *The atheoretical conception, and purely descriptive method, of philosophy.* The greatest irritant to Wittgenstein's critics was his atheoretical conception of philosophy. (a) His view that philosophy should propound no theses – at least, none that can be controverted – was met with double scepticism. It was held to be 'probably the weakest part of his work'. Moreover, it was thought that his practice belies any such view, since it is 'quite easy to formulate theses which Wittgenstein advanced'.[18] (b) His claim that there can be no theories in philosophy was greeted with like scepticism. For all distinctions, it was argued, including philosophical ones, are rooted in some background theoretical understanding or frame of reference.[19] Indeed, Wittgenstein was held to have a theory of meaning[20] (viz. that the meaning of an expression is its use) which repudiated truth-conditional semantics in favour of an anti-realist theory of meaning rooted in the notion of assertion-conditions. (c) Alternatively, it was argued, he had 'a quite definite conception of what meaning consists in and, consequently, how it is to be characterized'.[21] But such a conception needs justification, not by reference to what is customarily said (which may be false or nonsensical – *vide* what pet lovers say of their cats or dogs), but by reference to what the 'conventions governing our use of language' (ibid., p. 165) require or entitle us to say. And for this is does not suffice to assemble reminders; rather, one needs some theoretical apparatus – in particular, an array of notions which can be claimed to suffice to characterize mastery of a language. This can be done, it was held, only by an explicit enquiry into the correct form which a theory of meaning for a natural language must take (ibid., p. 166).

Enough has already been said to indicate the trajectory of the reply.

(a) What may appear to be 'theses' in Wittgenstein's writings are either grammatical propositions or synopses thereof. They are not empirical theses. Nor do they claim to be metaphysical truths. They are, rather, expressions of rules ('conventions governing our use of language') for the use of their constituent expressions, sometimes expressed synoptically at a high level of generality.[22] Such apparent 'theses' are never invoked by Wittgenstein as premises in arguments, but occur as conclusions of extensive grammatical investigations. If they are controverted, then they can immediately be abandoned, and an investigation of the rules for the use of the relevant expressions recommenced in order to establish incontrovertibly how the protagonist is using the relevant expressions, what rules of use he is employing. Then the work of disentangling those rules can be resumed, in order to resolve philosophical puzzlement. This is not to understate the importance of apparent 'theses', but to characterize their status. They play an essential role in giving us a synoptic view of the grammar (in Wittgenstein's sense of the term) of a problematic domain of discourse, in bringing us to the point at which we know our way around in the network of the concepts we employ. It is precisely because of this that they must not feature as premises of argument; that they are not expressions of Wittgenstein's opinions (LFM 103); that, as he said, 'On all questions we discuss I have no opinion; and if I had, and it disagreed with one of your opinions, I would at once give it up for the sake of argument because it would be of no importance for our discussion. We constantly move in a realm *where we all have the same opinions*' (AWL 97; emphasis added). In philosophy, he held, 'we make our moves in the realm of the grammar of our ordinary language, and this grammar is already there. Thus we have already got everything and need not wait for the future' (WWK 183). There can be no *opinions* in grammar – any more than a skilled participant in a rule-governed practice has opinions about which rules he follows. But there may be different usages. Reminders of how we use expressions are necessary, for hasty characterization of the use of an expression is prone to overlook features of use. Certainly, attaining a synoptic view of our own use of expressions is difficult. Arranging the rules for the use of expressions in such a way as to dissolve or resolve philosophical problems needs both art and skill. But the grammatical propositions elicited, and their synopses, are not theses.

(b) Wittgenstein denied that there can be any theories in philosophy. Theory construction belongs to the domain of the empirical sciences, and characteristically involves hypothetico-deductive explanation of phenomena. But the network of grammar, as Wittgenstein employed this term, is flat. There are no 'surface rules' and 'deep rules', such that the deep rules have the status of hypotheses which explain the surface rules. Wittgenstein's contrast between surface and depth grammar (PI §664)[23] is the contrast between the immediate appearance of a word, its mode of occurrence in a given sentence, and the 'multitudinous paths leading off from it in every direction' – that is, the different transformations of which the sentence admits, the kinds of consequences it implies, the manner of its context dependence, its role in the language-game, the various combinatorial possibilities of the word and so forth. These are not 'hidden' from view, but visible to any speaker of the language who is willing to look around – at the common use of the expression in question. They are not hypotheses, but familiar truisms of which we need to be reminded. Hence the methods of philosophy are descriptive, and argumentative – when the descriptions are brought to bear upon the philosophical problems, and the entanglement in the rules is brought to light.

Of course, this does not mean that his investigations were conducted without any frame of reference. On the contrary. In one sense, the frame of reference is provided by the particular ramifications of the grammar of the problematic concept under scrutiny and by the character of the problems confronted. In another sense, his examination of the possibility of a 'private language', for example, has as its frame of reference a conception of language and of linguistic meaning, of explanation and understanding, that runs, implicitly or explicitly, through the dominant tradition of philosophy. But in neither sense is the frame of reference of Wittgenstein's investigations part of a theory which he espouses. The conceptual articulations that are examined ramify from the concept of ostensive explanation and sample, through the notion of a criterion of identity for the application of an expression, to the concept of sensation – its expressive use in first-person, present-tense utterances and the descriptive use of concepts of the inner in association with appropriate criteria in the third person, and the employment of epistemic verbs in connection with first- and third-person uses. But this far-reaching frame of reference does not make philosophical investigations akin to theory construction in the sciences.

Wittgenstein certainly propounded no 'theory of meaning', if that expression is to be construed along lines familiar from the philosophy of language that came into vogue in the 1970s and 1980s. He neither articulated a programme concerning the general form which a theory must take if it is to derive the meaning or truth-conditions of every well-formed sentence of the language from an array of metalinguistic axioms and formation and transformation rules; nor did he endeavour to execute any part of such a theory. Indeed, there is every reason to think that he would have viewed such a programme as deeply misconceived, rooted in a vision of language that is akin to the *Tractatus* conception of language as a calculus of rules (see below, pp. 267–71).[24] Nor did he propound anything that can justly be characterized as an 'anti-realist' theory of meaning, in pursuit of a similar programme focusing upon the notion of assertion-conditions.[25] He propounded no theory of meaning of any kind, and had good reasons for eschewing such a programme.

(c) To be sure, he had a conception of meaning. But what he saw as his task was not the articulation of a 'conception' in the sense of a set of beliefs, opinions, hypotheses and conjectures. Rather, his task was the *description* of the widely ramifying network of concepts associated with that of linguistic meaning. This he executed at great length and with unprecedented thoroughness. He traced the conceptual articulations that obtain between such concepts as the meaning of a word and of a sentence, meaning something by a word, meaning such-and-such by an utterance, meaning what one says. These in turn ramify into the network of concepts of explanations of meaning in all their diversity (e.g. of ostensive definition, of explanations of family resemblance concepts, of vague concepts, of proper names) and hence into the concept of a rule for the use of an expression and of the internal relation between the rules for the use of expressions (including explanations of meaning) and what count as applications of those rules. These concepts, like the former group, are interwoven with the concept of understanding (hence of ability and mastery of a technique) and of the behavioural criteria of understanding, misunderstanding and not understanding. This vast network ramifies still further – for example, into the opaque domain of 'experiencing the meaning of a word', with all its subtle complexities.[26] Side by side with the descriptive, constructive work, he lavished endless attention upon critical, destructive analysis, tracing the pernicious influence of the Augustinian picture of language through all its devious windings, destroying a multitude of philosophical conceptions and preconceptions (the conception of a distinction between sentence-radical and mood operator as a *sine qua non* for an account of sentence-meaning,[27] of the demand for determinacy of sense, of the predicate calculus as the depth grammar of any possible language, etc.) and demythologizing philosophical mysteries (of the 'harmony between language and reality', and hence of intentionality, of a 'private language' and of the associated misconceptions of understanding). This vast panorama is no theory of meaning, but it gives us an overview of the conceptual network which theorists of meaning misguidedly attempt to capture by way of axiomatic theory construction.

A quite different methodological question is whether the task of philosophy is always exhausted by careful descriptions of use and the employment of such descriptions in resolving philosophical problems. We have already examined Strawson's claim that the descriptive metaphysician may find that the discriminations we can make and the connections we can establish by a close examination of the actual use of words may be insufficiently general and far-reaching for his purposes (above, pp. 161, 175–9). Von Wright voiced a different qualm. Having abandoned his early view that task of philosophy is logical reconstruction, he came to see it as the explication of conceptual intuitions. Philosophers are characteristically interested in a network of concepts, which are, in different respects, problematic, unclear or in need of systematization. Having described elements of the network, we may find lacunae, or indeterminacies – strands that leave threads dangling. Our task can then be characterized as filling in such gaps in existing usage. Here we cannot consult usage, but only our own 'conceptual intuitions' about the expressions concerned – that is, about how and why we think the rules for their use can be fruitfully or illuminatingly extended. In so doing, the philosopher should not tamper with existing usage, since violation of usage would mean a distortion of the conceptual situation. His task of explicating his conceptual intuitions is a matter of invention or creation, and its touchstone is the light shed upon the problems at hand. In *The Varieties of Goodness*, von Wright exemplified this conception with great power and persuasiveness. Many of the expressions that belong to this ramifying network of normative, axiological and anthropological expressions are, he argued, words 'in search of a meaning' and of connections of meaning. The philosopher's role in the domain of ethics, political and legal philosophy, and aesthetics (in contradistinction to his role in 'theoretical philosophy', e.g. metaphysics and epistemology) is to *mould* or *shape* the meanings of problematic expressions.[28]

How is this conception related to Wittgenstein's? He emphasized, as we have seen, that philosophy should 'leave everything as it is', that it is not the task of philosophy to interfere *with the use of language* (PI §124). Its task is not to refine or complete the system of rules for the use of our words in unheard-of ways (PI §133). For our puzzles and difficulties stem from our lack of a surview of language as it is. In philosophical psychology, for example, we are tempted otherwise (see Volume 4, 'Methodology in philosophical psychology', §2). 'Mere description is so difficult because one believes that one needs to fill out the facts in order to understand them. It is as if one saw a screen with scattered colour-patches, and said: the way they are here, they are unintelligible; they only make sense when one completes them into a shape. – Whereas I want to say: here *is* the whole. (If you complete it you falsify it.)' (RPP I §257). This is *not* compatible with von Wright's conception. Nevertheless, two points are noteworthy. First, Wittgenstein wrote next to nothing after 1929 on ethics or value theory, and never wrote anything on political or legal philosophy. It is far from obvious how to extend his methodological principles to the domains of 'practical philosophy', or indeed whether they should be extended without modification. It could well be argued, as von Wright did, that these conceptual fields differ distinctively from those upon which Wittgenstein focused. To be sure, such a case has to be made out in detail. Secondly, it should be remarked that, from time to time, Wittgenstein himself suggested that there are problem areas within philosophy where the philosopher *should* sharpen blurred distinctions. 'Our investigation does not try to *find* the real, exact meaning of words; though we do often *give* words exact meanings in the course of our investigation' (Z §467). And again: 'The difficulty lies only in understanding how establishing a rule helps us. Why it calms us after we have been so profoundly // deeply // uneasy. Obviously what calms us is that we see a system which (sy̲s̲t̲e̲m̲a̲t̲i̲c̲a̲l̲l̲y̲) excludes those structures that have always made us uneasy, those we were unable to do anything with, and which we still thought we had to respect' (BT 416). Or, finally: 'if we wish to draw boundaries in the use of a word, in order to clear up philosophical paradoxes, then alongside the actual picture of the use (in which as it were the colours flow into one another without sharp boundaries) we may put another picture which is in certain ways like the first but is built up of colours with clear boundaries between them' (PG 76). This conception is never applied to a particular philosophical question; indeed, it is not even clear exactly what he had in mind.[29] But it demands precise clarification, and the scope of the methodological remarks, which apparently conflict with his dominant tendency, requires specification.

(ii) *Use and meaning*. Wittgenstein's association of the concept of meaning with that of use was part of his attack upon referential conceptions of meaning propounded under the sway of the Augustinian picture of language. Its negative implications involved repudiating the supposition that the meaning of a word is the object it stands for. The meaning of a word is neither an idea in the mind nor an object in reality, no matter whether concrete or abstract. It must be public and sharable, but this is not secured by assuming it to be an abstract object (as Frege did), such that different speakers can 'grasp' the numerically same 'sense' (by contrast with psychologistic accounts, according to which, as Frege rightly remonstrated, each speaker grasps a private 'idea', which is at best only qualitatively identical with another person's idea).[30] It is, rather, secured by associating meaning with use. However, as previously explained, this assumes its full significance only when the conceptual connections between use, meaning, meaning something, verification, grammatical rule, explanation of meaning, understanding and criteria of understanding and so on are fully articulated.

Many of the criticisms of Wittgenstein's later conception of the relation between meaning and use rested upon misunderstandings. For example, post-war speech-act theories of meaning, as exhibited, for example, in R. M. Hare's speech-act analysis of 'good'[31] or Austin's speech-act analysis of knowledge,[32] were held to be rooted in a conception of meaning as use, 'use' being construed as 'use to perform a specific type of speech act'. The defects which were found in such analyses were imputed to Wittgenstein's account. This was both inaccurate and misconceived. First, the notion of use as invoked by Wittgenstein applies to a far wider range of features of linguistic expressions and their employment than the character of the speech-act that is standardly performed by the utterance of a simple declarative sentence in which the given expression occurs. Nor does he ever equate the meaning of a word with the character of the speech-act or speech-acts that might be performed by the utterance of such a sentence. He did indeed emphasize that 'I have a pain' (unlike 'I had a pain' or 'He has a pain') is commonly employed as a substitute for a cry of pain, and is often an expression or manifestation (*Äusserung*) of pain. But it was no part of his argument that the word 'pain' signifies either a moan or a particular form of complaint, or that it has a different meaning in the first-person present tense from its meaning in other tenses or in the third person. The first–/third-person asymmetry is a distinctive feature of a single unified concept. Indeed, for better or worse, there is barely a mention of speech-act analysis in the whole of the Wittgenstein *œuvre*.[33] Secondly, there is no gainsaying that there often is a conceptual connection between an expression and a speech-act standardly performed by the utterance of a simple declarative sentence in which it occurs. That the word 'good' is a general adjective of commendation is no less a *part* of its grammar (in Wittgenstein's sense of the term) or of its use than the fact that it is an attributive adjective, just as it is partly constitutive of the meanings of the words 'poor', 'bad', 'wicked', 'evil' that they can be used to condemn or criticize.

Deeper criticisms came from other quarters. Grice's distinction between the meaning of an expression and its conversational implicatures can be brought to bear upon Wittgenstein's accounts of the meaning of various expressions in terms of use. For if Grice's argument is correct, then Wittgenstein attributed features of the use of expressions to their meaning, which are correctly ascribable not to their meaning but to pragmatic principles of discourse.[34] Grice argued that from the fact that it would be odd or inappropriate to use an expression in an utterance in certain situations which fail to satisfy a given (usually negative) condition, it does not follow that the satisfaction of that condition is a part of the meaning of the expression in question, is logically implied by, or presupposed by, its use. The fact that we would not *say* that *a* is *F* unless condition *C* were satisfied does not in itself show that it is not *true* that *a* is *F* even if it is not the case that *C*. So, for example, the fact (if it is a fact) that we would not say that someone's action was voluntary unless what he did was wrong does not show that it is part of the meaning of 'voluntary' (as opposed to being part of its use) that what is voluntary is faulty. Similarly, he argued, the fact that, when confronted with a red rose under normal conditions, we would not say 'It looks as if it is red to me (or 'to A')' does not show that the latter proposition is not true. Grice examined three groups of examples in all of which, he argued, the conflation of meaning with use had led to mistaken accounts of the meanings of certain expressions: (i) accounts of specific concepts, such as Ryle's account of 'voluntary', Wittgenstein's account of 'I know I am in pain' (as well as 'He knows he is in pain') and his claim that not all seeing is 'seeing something as . . .', claims that 'looks as if . . .' applies only in cases of doubt, that one can be said to try only if difficulty in execution is in view, and the general Austinian principle 'no modification without aberration'; (ii) accounts of the alleged divergence between the meaning of the sentential connectives in natural language and their truth-functional counterparts in the logical calculus; (iii) speech-act analyses of 'good', 'know' and 'true', according to which the meaning of 'good' is characterized by the fact that such sentences as 'This is good' are used to commend, the meaning of 'know' by the fact that 'I know that . . .' is used to guarantee, and the meaning of 'true' by the fact that 'It is true that *p*' is used to endorse. The inappropriateness of utterance in specimen circumstances, which is held to confirm the proferred analyses in these kinds of cases, is, Grice argued, to be ascribed not to the meaning of the relevant expression, but rather to such principles of discourse as: not to assert the obvious – for example, if it is generally true that one always tries to do whatever one does, then it is pointless, because obvious, to say that someone tried to *V* when they *V*'d; or: not to utter a weaker statement when one is in position to utter a stronger one – for example, not to say 'My wife is either in Oxford or in London' when one knows perfectly well that she is in Oxford; or: to a co-operative principle of discourse – namely, that one should make one's conversational contribution such as is required by the accepted purpose or direction of the exchange. Violating such pragmatic maxims of discourse does not result in saying something false, truth-valueless or nonsensical, but rather in various forms of redundancy or misleadingness.

It is not to the present purpose to examine the details of Grice's subtle and detailed account of the various forms of conversational maxims.[35] What is relevant here is whether Grice's strictures establish a case against Wittgenstein's account of the relation between meaning and use; in particular, whether, in his analyses, he wrongly allocated to meaning features of the use of expressions that properly belong to pragmatic principles of conversation. It should be noted that the three groups of examples to be examined are, according to Wittgenstein, dissimilar. The first involves a nonsensical utterance, the second a falsehood and the third truth-valuelessness.

(a) *The use of 'I know'.* A crucial element in Wittgenstein's philosophy of language, of psychology and epistemology is his argument that 'I know that I have a pain' and similar locutions with respect to other psychological expressions (such as 'I know what I want, believe, intend, imagine') do not make genuine knowledge claims. Rather, they are either emphatic assertions to the effect that I really have a pain, want, believe, intend or imagine something, or (in philosophical contexts) philosophers' nonsense (see Volume 3, 'Avowals and descriptions'). A Gricean attack upon this account would argue that it confuses meaning with use, that while it would be pointless to say 'I know that I am in pain' or 'He knows that he is in pain', since this is something anyone knows when they are in pain, it is nevertheless true in appropriate circumstances. But there would only be a point in asserting such a sentence if there were some further condition the satisfaction of which would, for example, provide some reason for thinking that the person in question might not know that he is in pain.

The criticism would be misconceived. First, Wittgenstein did not argue that there is *any* condition which must be satisfied for an epistemic use (i.e. use to make a knowledge claim) of 'I know I have a pain' or 'He knows he has a pain'. His argument was not that its use presupposes the satisfaction of a condition which, if not fulfilled, renders the utterance either false or truth-valueless. Rather, he argued that, construed as philosophers have typically construed 'I know I have a pain' (viz. as a claim to knowledge, which is typically held to be privileged and indubitable), it is unconditionally *nonsense*; however, it does have a respectable (non-epistemic) use: namely, as an emphatic assertion that I am in pain (and there are other uses one might add, e.g. as a concessive remark to someone who tiresomely keeps on telling one that one is in pain). Secondly, were Grice's criticism correct, then 'I don't know whether I am in pain' would normally have to be false, for its standard falsity is what supposedly renders the utterance 'I know I am in pain' pointless, because too obvious to be worth saying. But, according to Wittgenstein, it too is nonsense, not false. So whether Wittgenstein is right or not, *his* argument does not turn on confusing meaning with conversational conditions of use. For his claim is that there are *no* conversational conditions for the (epistemic) use of 'I know that I am in pain' or 'He knows that he is in pain'. Thirdly, the application of Grice's argument assimilates 'I know I am in pain' to such utterances as 'I am breathing'. The latter, or indeed its third-person counterpart, would indeed only be uttered in circumstances in which there is, or might be supposed to be, some reason for thinking that the person in question is not breathing. But the assimilation is unwarranted. For one can readily specify such circumstances, but one cannot specify circumstances in which the putative knowledge claim 'I know that I have a pain' has any point. Indeed, Wittgenstein's reasons for excluding it as nonsensical (as invoked by philosophers) have nothing to do with circumstance dependence or non-satisfaction of required presuppositions of use, but rather with the absence of the requisite conceptual connections with doubt, certainty, recognition, evidence, finding out and the like. (But rejecting Grice's criticism does not imply that Wittgenstein's case does not require elaboration, refinement and careful qualification.)

(b) *Trying*. Grice faulted Wittgenstein's description of the grammar of 'trying to *V*' as requiring the satisfaction of a further condition over and above *V*ing (in contexts in which the agent did indeed *V*): namely, that *V*ing needs, or is thought by the agent (or, Grice adds, by the speaker or his addressee) to need, some effort. On Grice's construal, we would not *say* that someone who *V*s also tries to *V*, but that is again because we would not say the obvious, and we would not want to be misleading. It would be misleading, because it would conversationally imply that the person had to, or thought he had to, make an effort, that condition being what gives a point to the assertion that he tried. But the non-satisfaction of that condition does not imply that the statement is not true. For whenever one *V*s, one tries to *V*.

However, if Wittgenstein's view is correct, this account is misconceived. For Wittgenstein argues that in the absence of actual or supposed impediments or difficulties, it is *false*, not truth-valueless, that if an agent *V*s he also *tries* to *V*. For some *V*ings, '*A V*'d effortlessly, without even trying' makes perfectly good sense. 'I saw A *V*', 'I saw A trying to *V*', and 'I saw A trying to *V* successfully' are quite different statements, *with different criteria for their assertion*. 'I saw A catch a bus' does not imply that I saw him trying to catch a bus; the latter would be true if I saw him running for it, not if I simply saw him stepping leisurely into the stationary vehicle. There are specific criteria for trying to *V*, which involve such features as effort or anticipated effort, recognition by the agent of impediments or difficulties and so on. These are partly constitutive of the *meaning* of 'try'. They apply both when the agent tries and succeeds in *V*ing and when he tries but fails, and these criteria are not satisfied in the overwhelming range of cases of *V*ing *simpliciter*.[36] (For detailed argument, see Volume 4, 'Willing and the nature of voluntary action', §6.)

(c) *Recognizing*. Similar Gricean arguments might be brought against Wittgenstein's description of the grammar of 'recognize'. To be sure, a Gricean argument would run, we do not *say* that we recognize the familiar. But that is not because it is false, but because it is too obviously true to be worth saying. However, Wittgenstein did not argue that in the normal case it is false that I recognize familiar objects, but rather that it is truth-valueless (presumably because 'recognize', unlike 'try', is an achievement verb, the negation of which implies that one did not know the identity of the person or object encountered). When I greet my family at the breakfast table each morning, I neither recognize nor fail to recognize my wife and children. There are distinctive behavioural criteria for recognizing, as there are for failing to recognize, none of which is satisfied in normal encounters with the familiar. True, no one would normally say 'When I breakfasted with my wife this morning, I recognized her'. But that is not because it is too obvious to be worth saying (for a detailed account of recognition, see Volume 4, 'Memory and recognition', §5). The onus is now upon the Gricean to explain what *he* takes to be the criteria for recognizing such that every case of seeing the familiar satisfies those criteria.

A more careful examination of the relation between meaning and use and a comprehensive survey of Wittgenstein's account of that relation was given by B. Rundle.[37] He pointed out that Wittgenstein hesitated between claiming that the meaning of an expression is to be identified with its use and claiming more circumspectly that the meaning of a word is determined by its use. On the one hand, we find such emphatic remarks as 'The use of a word in the language is its meaning' (PG 60) and 'A meaning of a word is a kind of employment of it' (C §61). On the other hand, we find more qualified claims, such as 'isn't the meaning of the word ['cube'] also determined by this use?' (PI §139); 'Not every *use*, you want to say, is a meaning' (LW I §289); 'Suppose we take the meaning of a word to be *the way it is used*. To use the phrase "the meaning of a word" as equivalent to "use of a word" has the advantage, among other things, of showing us something about the queer philosophical case where we talk of an object corresponding to the word' (AWL 44); and '*use of a word* comprises a large part of what is meant by "the meaning of a word"' (AWL 48). Wittgenstein's hesitations appear to turn primarily upon the fact that our criteria of identity of use, on the one hand, and of meaning, on the other, are not sharp, and the area of indeterminacy differs. It is not always clear whether we should say that a given word has one meaning or two closely related meanings; and equally, it is not always clear whether two words have the same or different meaning (synonymy, as argued (p. 212), not being an all-or-nothing affair). Wittgenstein himself was inclined to say, for example, that 'walk' and 'walks' mean exactly the same thing – they mean *this* – and we would demonstrate walking (LW I §274), but (presumably) their use differs. In a language which had two different words for negation 'X' and 'Y', where reiteration in the one case constitutes affirmation and in the other constitutes emphatic negation, the question whether 'X' means the same as 'Y' in sentences *without any reiteration* can be answered *differently* with equal justification (PI §556). The considerations that are brought to bear upon questions of identity of use in penumbral cases are not necessarily the same considerations that bear upon questions of identity of meaning in such cases. Marginal differences in use (and in the rules for the use) of a pair of expressions do not always justify claiming that there is a difference in meaning; it depends upon whether the difference in use is *important*, and that is a context- and purpose-relative consideration. (If, in some country, chess were so played that before moving the queen, one had to rotate the piece three times, no one would say that this was a different game, or that it was chess with 'a queen' in a different sense.)

Rundle points out that the expressions 'use of a word' and 'meaning of a word' are not themselves used in the same way. This seems correct, but one must take care not to blur the distinction between use (a normative notion which stands in contrast to misuse) and usage. As Wittgenstein employs the term 'use', it is, at least typically, employed normatively. To the extent that the notion of use is identified with that of meaning, it is the manner in which the expression is *to be* used (which is given by an explanation of meaning) that is equated with the meaning of the expression. Rundle suggests that we may say that the use of indexicals in certain contexts requires the accompaniment of a deictic gesture, but not that the meaning of an indexical does. The expression 'the use of "X"', he contends, is not substitutable in all contexts for 'the meaning of "X"'. For we ask '*What* does "X" mean?', but '*How* is "X" used?' (But note that the example has shifted from noun to verb.) Moreover, there are expressions in a language which might be said to have a use but no meaning: for example, 'Abracadabra' or 'Tally-ho'. It is unclear whether certain differences of 'tone' or 'atmosphere' (to use Wittgenstein's phrase) are to be allocated to meaning or to use: for example, the difference between 'over' and 'o'er' or 'horse' and 'steed' (cf. LW I §726, in which his example is 'Sabel' and 'Säbel'). It is not obvious, *pace* Wittgenstein, that it is correct (or useful) to speak of personal names as having a meaning (other than in the sense in which 'Peter' means 'rock'), but we do explain the use of such a name in a sentence, in the sense that we explain whose name it is – that is, to whom reference is being made. And there are numerous expressions in the language, most obviously prepositions and various sentential connectives and modifiers ('perhaps', 'however') which sit uneasily in juxtaposition with 'means' but not with 'use'. It is difficult to judge what weight to give to these considerations. But nothing of note is lost by retreating to Wittgenstein's more cautious position, insisting that although not every feature of use is necessarily a feature of meaning, it is the use that determines the meaning of an expression, and every difference of meaning is a difference of use.

(iii) *Verificationism.* The accusation that Wittgenstein was committed to some form of verificationism arose, as noted above, through a misinterpretation of his argument against the possibility of private ostensive definition. That this is misconceived is evident from the detailed account of that argument given in Volume 3 ('Private ostensive definition'). Nevertheless, the accusation that he was a crypto-verificationist hung on, associated with the misconceived claim that he, like the logical positivists, was an 'anti-realist'. The details of his brief adoption and subsequent abandonment of verificationism were spelt out in chapter 3. But it is worth stating explicitly why his *later* philosophy is not to be so characterized. First, he did not claim that the meaning of a proposition or sentence is given by its method of verification, but only that in *some* cases saying how a proposition is verified is a *contribution* to describing its grammar. Secondly, he did not claim that verifiability is a necessary condition of meaningfulness. First-person, present-tense psychological propositions *have no verification*, but they are certainly meaningful. So are imperative, interrogative and optative sentences. Thirdly, he insisted that nothing could be more misleading than to think that a proof in mathematics is equipollent with the verification of an empirical proposition (to be sure, the logical positivists did not think this; but if one misrepresents them as 'anti-realists', it seems as if they should have done). Fourthly, he never argued that there are not perfectly intelligible verification-transcendent empirical propositions (e.g. Julius Caesar's thoughts the night before his death, my own thoughts at 2 p.m. on 15 March 1985, whether a brontosaurus crossed this spot at such-and-such a time in the afternoon so-and-so many millions of years ago). That innocuous claim is not to be confused with the claim that there can be no proof-transcendent mathematical truths (other than postulates). Fifthly, it is true that Wittgenstein denied that Russell's hypothesis that the world was created five minutes ago, or that the supposition that there is a white rabbit between two chairs whenever no observations or verifications are being carried out, makes sense (AWL 26). But this is not because he held that the meaning of a sentence is its method of verification, but rather because these pseudo-propositions are so made that nothing *could* count as evidence for or against them (unlike the trivially verification-transcendent propositions). They look as if they are meaningful, and have the surface grammar of ordinary verifiable propositions, 'But they are otiose, like wheels in a watch which have no function although they do not look to be useless' (ibid.). Sixthly, it is true that Wittgenstein would have rejected the alleged moral of science-fiction tales about 'super-Spartans' who never express pain, but are born with an innate knowledge of language, including 'pain', and experience pain and know that they do so, without ever manifesting it, and without ever ascribing pain to others.[38] This is supposed to show the intelligibility of possessing the concept of pain in circumstances in which it is severed from any connection with behavioural manifestations of pain. But Wittgenstein's grounds for rejecting the tale would not turn on the principle of verification; they would turn on the requirement that the possibility of criterionless application of the word 'pain' to oneself (even in thought) demands recognition of the behavioural criteria for ascribing pain to others. Innate knowledge of a language which includes the term 'pain' implies innate knowledge of the criteria for third-person ascriptions of pain, whether or not there is any occasion for ascribing pain to others. Otherwise there is no reason to suppose that by 'pain' the super-Spartans, as described in this tale, mean what we mean by 'pain'. That requirement is supported not by the principle of verification, but by the unintelligibility of private ostensive definition as constituting the standard for the correct application of the word 'pain' in one's own case.

(iv) *The heteronomy of grammar according to metaphysical realism in semantics.* A quite different challenge to Wittgenstein's approach to meaning emerged in the 1960s and 1970s, associated with the writings of Saul Kripke and Hilary Putnam. It is a leitmotif of Wittgenstein's reflections on meaning that the meaning of an expression is given by what are accepted as correct explanations of meaning, which constitute rules for the use of the expressions explained. Rules for the use of expressions are not true or false, and are not answerable to reality for their correctness (an aspect of what he called 'the arbitrariness of grammar' or 'the autonomy of language'). In stark opposition to this, scientific realists argued that scientific discoveries about the inner constitution of the items belonging to the extension of a 'natural kind' term (viz. names of kinds of stuffs or of species) may reveal its real meaning. The meaning of a natural kind term involves four features: a syntactic marker (in the case of 'water', for example, *mass noun, concrete*), a semantic marker (*natural kind, liquid*), a stereotype (*colourless, transparent, tasteless, thirst-quenching, etc.*) and an extension (H_2O). The first three are features of the use of a term, and are aspects of a normal speaker's linguistic competence. They do not, however, determine that facet of the meaning of an expression which is held to be constituted by its extension. That is, as it were, up to nature, and is to be discovered by scientific investigation.[39] The connection between the use of an expression, which a competent speaker has mastered, and its actual meaning, which incorporates its extension, is determined by a 'rigid' referential component and a paradigm. This is effected by an ostensive definition, the indexical of which rigidly attaches to a paradigmatic instance belonging to the extension of the term. The kind is then defined as consisting of all individuals (or partitioned quantities of stuff) that bear an appropriate 'sameness relation' to the sample, that relation being a matter of having the same inner constitution or 'real essence'. The micro-structural features of any member of a natural kind belong to it of 'metaphysical necessity', and are discovered a posteriori.[40]

This account has striking consequences. (a) The extension of a natural kind term is determined not by its intension, nominal essence or sense, but by the possibly unknown 'sameness relation' between the micro-structural properties of the paradigm and items belonging to the extension. (b) Expressions in different languages may share the same syntactic and semantic markers and the same stereotype, yet mean something quite different. Hence a liquid (on an imagined planet called 'twin Earth') with all the properties of water save being constituted of XYZ rather than H_2O, despite being called 'water' (by twin-Earthians), would not actually be water. (c) Conversely, expressions which do not share the same stereotype may nevertheless turn out to have the same extension or real essence. For example, a substance with atomic number 79, which possessed none of the overt properties of gold, would none the less be gold (and if so, then the stereotype of gold was wrong). (d) Scientific discovery can show that what Wittgenstein would take to be a 'grammatical proposition', and others would take to be 'analytic', is actually false. (It is, e.g. held to be intelligible that cats might not be animals.) (e) Mastery of the use of an expression falls short of knowing what it really means. Indeed, a linguistic community may use an expression for millennia without finding out what it really means, and without realizing that they do not know what it really means. (f) The ultimate arbiter of what natural kind terms mean is empirical science. It is not that scientific discoveries lead to changes in the meanings of the relevant terms, but rather that they reveal what those terms, unbeknownst to their users, have always meant. For what water or gold, a tiger or a lily, really are, *and* what these expressions really *mean*, is determined by nature. (g) The notion of 'metaphysical necessity', though unexplained, is apparently reinstated, leading, as was remarked by an enthusiast, to 'the resurgence of metaphysics as an important branch of philosophical study'.[41]

If this account were true, it would spell ruin for Wittgenstein's philosophy. However, the scientific realist semantics is gravely flawed.[42] First, it is questionable whether, were we to discover a liquid (on 'twin Earth') which shared all the properties of water except for being constituted of XYZ rather than H_2O, we would have to say that it is not water, since water is necessarily H_2O. We would only have to say that *if* we had accepted that being so constituted was definitive of water (part of its intension, nominal essence or the explanation of its use). But since we accept that 'heavy water' – D_2O, composed of deuterium (an isotope of hydrogen with twice the atomic weight) and oxygen – is a kind of water, it would be open to us to view XYZ as a further kind of water. Moreover, since symptoms and criteria characteristically fluctuate in science, it would always be open to us to view the chemical composition of water as a symptom rather than a criterion, *if* such an extraordinary discovery were made. Finally, science fiction, if not thought through, makes for poor philosophy. Were it discovered that a substance might be identical in all its properties and powers with water, yet differently constituted, then the whole of our chemical theory would collapse, and with it the very reasons we have for ascribing importance (let alone criterial status) to the molecular constitution of substances.[43]

Secondly, it is confused to suppose that we can bridge the gap between stereotype and extension by means of an ostensive definition that picks out a standard member of the extension, and define a given substance as anything which has a 'sameness relation', construed in terms of inner constitution, to the item pointed at. If the natural kind term (e.g. 'water') were introduced thus, then the mode of introduction would be no explanation of meaning. For in advance of discovering the inner constitution of water, no one is given any guidance in applying the term by this mode of introducing it. What seems to be an ostensive definition is not one, and the quantity of water pointed at is no sample. For a sample employed in an ostensive definition is an object for comparison, which provides a standard for the application of the definiendum. But here, no perceptible, *usable* feature of the putative sample is relevant to the use of the term. So the putative sample provides *no* guidance for the use of the definiendum, and can make no contribution to explaining what it means. Of course, we might take a sample of stuff, subject it to chemical analysis, and denominate anything with the discovered micro-structure 'water' – but that is no ostensive definition. Without such analysis there is no definition, and with analysis there is a definition, but not one in which a sample plays any essential role. *A fortiori* the supposition that pre-scientific societies, in using so-called natural kind terms, were (or should have been) explicitly or implicitly committed to such explanations, is erroneous. A promissory note on an as yet non-existent bank is no currency.

Thirdly, there is little reason to suppose that science can cash the promissory note anyway. For the kinds distinguished by science commonly do not correspond to the extensions of terms in common language. As Dupré has shown, biological taxonomy diverges, for good reasons, from our common categories (which are none the worse for the divergence, since their purposes are often quite different). No one would be persuaded to call onions or garlic a kind of lily, but they belong to the *Liliaceae*. We would not characterize a vulture as a kind of hawk, or a butterfly as a kind of moth.

Fourthly, the scientific realist's account holds that we can determine the extension of a natural kind term by reference to a theoretical 'sameness relation' to a paradigm. It is anything but obvious how to select a paradigm and a microstructural 'sameness relation' that will pick out, for example, the 290,000 recognized species of beetle. Nor is there any good reason for supposing that there is one.

It should be evident that the purposes of common-or-garden classification are very different from those of science. We do indeed have compelling reasons for not calling onions and garlic 'lilies', and good reasons for not classifying together daisies, cacti and oak-trees (angiosperms), while excluding pine-trees. Equally, it should be no surprise that the term 'tree' has no place in scientific taxonomy.

A scientific realist might respond with the claim: so much the worse for all pre-scientific classification. Rather than objecting to this, one might pay out more rope. For the supposition underlying the scientific realist's argument is that scientific classification yields absolute, purpose-independent, precise categories, determined by the natural order of things. But this too is illusion. Morphological criteria often quarrel with evolutionary criteria, and neither uniformly deliver determinate answers. Assigning organisms to species is no less purpose-relative, variable and partly arbitrary than common-or-garden classification. There are many different ways of classifying the products of evolutionary processes, and whether one way or another is the most fruitful depends upon specific purposes and the peculiarities of the organisms in question. It is no coincidence that many of the examples given in defence of scientific realism are derived from momentary reflection upon chemistry, and in particular upon the periodic table of elements, on the assumption that chemical elements are definable by atomic number, from which essential property all their law-governed behaviour flows. However, the fruitfulness of this typology is exceptional in science. Moreover, it is rarely remarked that different isotopes count as the same element, despite having different atomic weights, and that, as Dupré points out, ions of a given element (e.g. ferrous ions and ferric ions) have the same atomic number (as iron), yet have very different properties and conform to very different laws. But there are good reasons for not classifying iron atoms, ferrous ions and ferric ions as three different natural kinds.[44]

There is no ground here for rejecting Wittgenstein's account of meaning or his argument for the autonomy of grammar. The meaning of an expression is what is given by an explanation of its meaning, by the rules for its use. It is what someone knows when he knows what an expression means, what he understands when he understands an expression. It is not determined by the extension of a term. Indeed, the extension of an expression is not a feature of its meaning, but is determined by its meaning in conjunction with the facts. In so far as water is necessarily H_2O or gold necessarily has atomic number 79, that is not because of *de re* metaphysical necessities in nature, but because we have incorporated these empirical discoveries into our definitions of these terms (at least within scientific discourse[45]). There is 'no action at a distance in grammar', and future discoveries of science cannot tell us what an expression really means, although they may lead to partial change in meaning.[46]

(v) *Wittgenstein and logical behaviourism.* As remarked above, there was, and remains, a persistent tendency to classify Wittgenstein's philosophical psychology as a form of logical behaviourism on the grounds that he held that there was a conceptual connection between inner states and their behavioural manifestation.[47] This was held to be justified on the grounds that the term 'behaviourism' in psychology applies equally to such radical behaviourists as Watson and Skinner and to moderate methodological behaviourists such as C. L. Hull. The application of the term to philosophy, it was argued, is analogical, and there is no good reason to restrict it to reductionist views. It suffices that a philosopher argue that there is *some* sort of logical connection between behaviour and the mental.

This rationale is unsatisfactory. It is true that behaviourism in psychology can range from the extreme view that consciousness, mental states and so on are fictions, to moderate views, which are committed only to the methodological constraint that empirical psychology is most fruitfully to be pursued by confining itself to observable behaviour (in contradistinction to Wundt's introspectionist methods). However, the point of applying the term 'logical behaviourism' in philosophy is to pick out not a methodological thesis, but a logical one. And there is good reason to construe the doctrine more narrowly than the modest claim that there is some logical relation between the inner and the outer, and to restrict it to such reductive claims as were made, for example, by Carnap in 'Psychology in Physical Language' (in *Erkenntnis*, 3 (1932–3)). Logical behaviourism is the view that statements ostensibly about mental states, events and the like are actually about behaviour and dispositions to behave; that mental states, events and so forth are logical constructions out of behaviour and behavioural dispositions. To take the wider construal would be to commit oneself, *mutatis mutandis*, to characterizing, for example, Grice's and Strawson's defence of the causal theory of perception as a form of '(logical) ideal-ism' or phenomenalism, since they hold that there is a logical connection between statements about subjective perceptions and statements about material objects.

Wittgenstein emphatically denied that he was defending any form of behaviour-ism (PI §§304–8; see Exg.). There could be no greater difference, he insisted, than pain-behaviour accompanied by pain, and pain-behaviour without any pain. He did not deny that there are inner processes, but only that the picture of an inner process gives a correct idea of the use of, for example, the verb 'to remember', which does not signify an inner process. Unlike Watson, he did not claim that everything except human behaviour is a fiction, but rather that it is a *grammatical fiction* that we know that we are in pain by introspective scrutiny of a mental object, and that we know what the word 'pain' means by associating it with, or giving it an ostensive definition by reference to, a private object (see MS 124, 5f., quoted in Exg. §307). Unlike Carnap, he insisted that 'it is not our job to reduce anything to anything', for, as Butler had nicely remarked, 'everything is what it is and not another thing'. To be sure, there are negative affinities between the logical behaviourists' and Wittgenstein's philosophical psychology (see Volume 3, 'Behaviour and behaviour-ism', §3), in that both are opposed to the dualist conception of the relation between the inner and the outer. But Wittgenstein, unlike Carnap, explored the grammar of the expression or manifestation of the inner. These 'utterances' (*Äusserungen*) are *also* forms of behaviour, but they are uses of language, and are not *about* behaviour (PI p. 179; RPP I §287). He was critical of the logical behaviourists' misconception of behaviour as 'bare bodily movement', insisting that behaviour is infused with, and only properly describable in terms of, the inner (see Volume 3, 'Behaviour and behaviourism', §4). Indeed, he rejected the whole picture of the 'inner' and the 'outer'. His argument that there must be behavioural criteria for what we call 'the inner' was not an attempt to *preserve* that venerable picture by devising a new logical relation between two distinct domains, the one mere bodily behaviour and the other consisting of ethereal objects, events and processes in the mind. On the contrary, he aimed to extirpate that very conception.

There are indeed logical connections between (crudely speaking) the mental and its outer manifestation. We would have no use for our expressions for the 'inner' if they were not bound up with behavioural criteria (LPE 286). The groundless first-person, present-tense use of psychological verbs makes sense only because it is bound up with, and partly constitutive of, the behavioural criteria for third-person ascriptions (a person's expression of pain, e.g., is a criterion for his being in pain). Were that not so, we would need an inner criterion of identity in the first-person case (PI §§258, 288), which would have to be supplied by a private ostensive definition – which is unintelligible (PI §§258, 261, 265). The 'inner' is verified by reference to the 'outer', and doubts about the inner – for example, over dissimulation – are settled by more evidence consisting of the outer. But the inner is not reducible to the outer; pain is not the same as pain-behaviour. To be sure, a sincere avowal is itself a form of behaviour. The utterance 'It hurts' or 'I have a pain' is a behavioural manifestation of pain, but it is not about pain-behaviour. A criterion for the inner does not entail the inner. It is typically defeasible. And inner states, events and processes may often occur without *any* outward manifestation (but what can happen some of the time may be unintelligible if thought of as happening all of the time). Similarly, in cases of dissimulation, behaviour may occur without the correlative inner state and so on. The speaker who expresses his pain in an utterance does not *know* it to be true on the grounds of his behaviour, as others do, or on any other grounds, since he cannot be said either to know or to be ignorant of its truth. It is groundlessly uttered, and not verified by the speaker either by reference to his behaviour or by reference to 'introspection'. Furthermore, it would be misconceived to think that most of our psychological verbs signify mental objects, states, events or processes. So to think involves, *inter alia*, a fundamental distortion of the meaning of intentional verbs (e.g. 'believe', 'think', 'remember', 'want', 'intend', 'mean'). Finally, the grammar of expressions (manifestations) of the inner is not the grammar of names of objects, nor yet the grammar of correlation of two distinct domains, or even that of a single domain of behaviour. Here, as elsewhere, Wittgenstein undercut received dichotomies and options, eschewing both dualism and behaviourism, mentalism and physicalism.

(vi) *Full-blooded conventionalism.* An accusation commonly levelled against Wittgenstein's account of necessary truths, originating in Dummett's review of the *Remarks on the Foundations of Mathematics*,[48] is that he defended an extreme, and extremely implausible, form of conventionalism. Dummett associated what he called 'moderate conventionalism' with the Vienna Circle's doctrine that necessary truths are true in virtue of conventions of meaning. The axioms of a formal system were held to be meaning rules, and the theorems were held to be consequences of these conventions, which we, unlike an infinite intellect, have to work out. This conception, Dummett claimed, is flawed, for it leaves unexplained how the stipulated conventions can have (necessary) consequences. Having laid down the initial conventions, it seems that we then have no choice but to accept the consequent theorems, and this necessity seems forced upon us, rather than being merely a convention (ibid., p. 425). Wittgenstein, on Dummett's construal, avoided this difficulty by adopting an extreme form of conventionalism. The logical necessity of any necessary truth is, on this conception, always a 'direct expression of a linguistic convention'. That a proposition is necessary always consists in our having expressly *decided* to treat the proposition in question as unassailable, that decision not being forced upon us, but rather being optional (ibid., pp. 425f.).

Against this, Dummett argued that a mathematical proof seems to drive us along willy-nilly until we arrive at the theorem (ibid., p. 426), which we then *must* accept *if* we are 'to remain faithful to the meanings of the expressions' as laid down in the axioms. But, on this interpretation, Wittgenstein held that at each step in reasoning we are free to choose to accept or reject the proof. There is nothing in our formulation of the axioms and rules of inference which forces us to accept the proof. *If* we accept the proof, *then* we confer necessity upon the theorem, and will count nothing as telling against it. But in so doing, we are making a new decision (ibid., p. 427). This seems a form of 'Bolshevism in mathematics' (LFM 67).[49] After all, a machine can follow the explicitly formulated rule for generating the series of even natural numbers. Whence does a human being gain a freedom of choice in this matter which a machine does not have (Dummett's review, p. 428)? According to Wittgenstein, Dummett claimed, a proof has the effect of *persuading* us to count a certain form of words as unassailably true, or to exclude a certain form of words from our language. But 'it seems unclear how the proof accomplishes this remarkable feat' (ibid., 430). It is natural to think that given a proof, we have no choice but to accept it if we are to remain faithful to the understanding we already have of its constituent expressions. Could someone familiar only with counting, who was then introduced to the practice of adding, reject the proposition that $7 + 5 = 12$ consistently with his antecedent understanding of number-words and of counting? Introducing such a person to the concept of addition is not merely getting him to adopt a new criterion of miscounting (i.e. if he counts first 5 boys, then 7 girls, and then counts 13 children, the proposition that $7 + 5 = 12$ provides a new criterion for a miscount), but rather showing him something to which he is already committed if he wishes to remain faithful to the concepts he *already* has. However, Wittgenstein holds that he could have rejected the proof without doing any more violence to his concepts than by accepting it. And it is 'extraordinarily difficult to take this idea seriously when we think of some particular actual proof' (ibid.). We want to say, Dummett contends, that we do not know what it would be like for someone who, by ordinary criteria, already understood the concepts employed to reject the proof. It is part of the meaning of 'true' that if a statement is true, there is something in virtue of which it is true (ibid., p. 433). But Wittgenstein seems to hold that it is up to us to *decide* to regard any statement we please as being necessarily true. In so doing, we partly determine the meaning of its constituent expressions. Since we are free to assign what sense we please to words, we have a right to lay down as necessarily true any statement we wish (ibid., p. 434). But this, Dummett objected, seems mistaken, since we must remain faithful to the meanings already assigned to the constituent terms. If Wittgenstein were right, communication would break down, for the decision to count a particular form of statement as necessarily true affects not only the meaning of statements of that form, but of many others too (ibid., p. 435). One may reject Platonism (realism) in mathematics (conceived of as a thesis about the objectivity of truth), without rejecting the objectivity of proof (ibid., p. 445).

More recently Dummett has added two further criticisms.[50] (a) It is part of Wittgenstein's argument that a proof provides us with a new criterion for the application of its constituent expressions. For example, the proof that the intersection of a plane with a cylinder is an ellipse gives us a new criterion for something's being elliptical. But, Dummett argues, this is a platitude if construed as compatible with assuming that it will always agree with the old criteria, when these are correctly applied in accordance with our original standards for their correct application. And it is absurd if construed as incompatible. That is, whenever we judge, by the old criteria, that this is a cylinder and this a plane, and, applying the new criterion, judge their intersection to be an ellipse, we should have been justified by the old criterion in declaring it to be an ellipse, even though, had we not learnt the theorem, we might not have noticed that it was, or even, as the result of some mistake, have judged it not to be one. The force of the proof is precisely to unfold the implicit commitment in the existing concepts to the new criterion. (b) Wittgenstein distinguishes calculation from experiment simply by reference to the fact that we resolve to treat the result of a calculation (once done and checked) as a criterion for having done the calculation correctly. So if we never do a given calculation, there *is* no correct result, no determinate result which we should get were we to perform the calculation correctly according to our criteria of correctness, and even God cannot be said to know the result. This, Dummett remonstrates rightly, is implausible. Suppose the calculation to be an ordinary addition. One of the rules of the computation procedure is that if one of the two final digits is 7 and the other 8, you write 5 in the digits column and carry 1 to the tens column. To maintain that there is no determinately correct result, one must either say that until someone has done it, it is not determinate what would count as writing down 5 and carrying 1, or that although the outcome of each application of one of the rules is determinate, it is not determinate what would be the outcome of a large but finite number of such applications. Both these alternatives are absurd.

It is true that the position being criticized here is difficult to take seriously, and that the conclusions derived are in some cases absurd. But the position is not Wittgenstein's, and the absurd conclusions are not his.

The key to understanding Wittgenstein's account of mathematical propositions is given by the following ideas of his.[51] (a) Mathematical propositions are *rules*. (b) The fundamental role of mathematics is to license the transformation of empirical propositions about quantities, magnitudes, spatial relations and so forth of things. For 'it is essential to mathematics that its signs are also employed in *mufti*' (RFM 257).[52] This is not to say, of course, that there are no parts of mathematics which have no application at all, or other parts that are only indirectly connected with application. There are; but they are essentially interwoven with the body of mathematics the fundamental role of which is to provide norms of representation.[53] (c) Just as 'a logical proof of a proposition that has sense and a proof *in* logic must be two entirely different things' (TLP 6.1263) – that is, that proof *by* logic is *toto caelo* different from proof *in* logic – so, too, proof *by* mathematics (e.g. in engineering) is wholly different from proof *in* mathematics. (d) A mathematical proposition is a rule, but unless it is an axiom, it is 'not simply stipulated but produced according to a rule' (RFM 228). And here we must distinguish between producing a mathematical proposition within a well-established *proof system* (e.g. doing a new computation, which is typically just 'homework' (PR 187) and *extending* a proof system by an extension of mathematics. (e) Proofs that extend mathematics create new internal relations, modifying existing concepts by linking them with concepts with which they were hitherto unconnected. Mathematics is *concept formation*; the propositions of mathematics determine the mathematical concepts they invoke.

These five points are highly controversial. But they must be kept constantly in view if one is to have any grasp of Wittgenstein's discussions in the philosophy of mathematics. Certainly, they require detailed elaboration, elucidation and development (in particular, the distinction between 'homework' and extensions of mathematics). I shall not undertake this here. All I wish to establish is that the accusations brought against Wittgenstein in Dummett's influential review misconstrue his arguments and miss their target. Wittgenstein did not adopt the absurd doctrine which Dummett characterizes as 'full-blooded conventionalism', although it is true that his conception *is* radical, and goes against the grain of received reflections, by mathematicians and philosophers alike, on the nature of mathematics.

Certainly we say of the rule for generating the series of even natural numbers that the steps are determined by the formula. This can mean one of two things: first, that this rule, unlike the formula $y > x^2 + 1$ or $y = x^2 \pm 1$, has only one correct answer for any given value of x; second, that people are so educated in the use of such a formula that they all work out the same value for y for any given value of x (RFM 35). It seems that something is missing in this account, for we want to say not that people so educated will write down such-and-such, but further that they *have* to do so. A machine can be programmed to write down the series, and it 'has no choice in the matter' – so surely we have no greater freedom of choice when faced with mathematical necessity (Dummett's review, p. 428)? That is muddled: 'a machine has no choice' does not mean the same as 'I have no choice'. The machine does not follow a rule, and it cannot be said to understand (nor yet to fail to understand or misunderstand) what it does. There is no such thing as a machine *choosing* to do something in the sense in which a human being can (any more than it can *refuse* to do something or do something reluctantly or willingly). And a human being, asked to follow the rule '+2', cannot say, as he reaches '1000' that he 'has no choice' but to write '1002' as the next step. For he does have a choice: he can write '1004', or '10', or just stop writing. (He might say that he had no choice if he was being threatened with a gun!) Of course, if he writes '1004', he will be said to have made a mistake, since the rule for generating the series of even natural numbers is indeed a rule which uniquely determines a number for every value, and the number that comes after 1000 is not 1004.

That, it might be replied, is not the point. Rather, if one really follows the rule, one *must* get such-and-such a result. Wittgenstein's response was that if this is not 'the somewhat hysterical way of putting things that you get in university talk' (RFM 430), then it merely says that getting *this* result is our criterion for having correctly followed *this* rule (RFM 317). The rule and the result are internally related. To say that one *must* get this result is not to say that one *will* inevitably get this result, but rather that if one does not, then one will not have followed the rule. One may still object: at any rate, one has no choice if one wishes to remain in accord with the rule (if one wishes to 'remain faithful to the meanings of the relevant terms'). But the question of whether *this* step is to be *called* 'accord' is itself given by a rule, and so too is the question of whether writing *that* is to count as doing the same as previously or doing something different (RFM 79). What this shows is that the *must* does not signify a form of compulsion (necessitation), but is the expression of a convention. If one does not infer thus-and-so, then 'we shan't *call it* "continuing the series" and presumably not "inference"' (RFM 80, emphasis added). It is a rule (convention) that getting *this* result is to be called 'continuing the series', and getting any other result is not. Rules cannot compel us as the circuitry of a calculating machine 'compels it' to write thus-and-so. But it is true that rules of mathematics can be said to compel us no less than rules of law – that is, in the sense that if we fail to follow them, we will get into trouble, be punished and so forth (RFM 81). And it is also true that we say such things as 'If you grant *this* and *this*, then you must grant *this!*' We compel people to admit things thus, just as we compel someone to go over there by an imperious gesture.

The bare truth of the matter is that once one has understood a rule, one is bound in one's *judgement* about what is in accord with the rule and what not (RFM 328f.). What Wittgenstein was doing in making these observations was *demystifying* the confusions embedded in talk of logical compulsion. He was not arguing that 'logical compulsion' is a kind of psychological compulsion. Rather, what we misleadingly call 'logical compulsion' is not a species of compulsion at all. We are prone to think of it as a form of 'super-compulsion', even stronger than causal necessity. But that is a confusion. It is no more a super-compulsion than the 'inexorability of the law' is a kind of super-inexorability, which, unlike judges, who sometimes show clemency, always punishes transgression (RFM 82).

When we are operating *within* a proof system (and we might conceive of the rules of elementary computation as such a system), then we may indeed say that, e.g., '$25 \times 25 = 625$' follows *necessarily* (LFM 241); but we must not confuse the necessity *within* the system with the putative necessity *of* the system. For it means nothing to say that the system as a whole is necessary. But within this proof system, there is only one correct answer to such a computation. Otherwise 'necessarily' is pleonastic, adding nothing to 'it follows' (within this system). Each computation derives a rule, *in accord with a system for the derivation of such rules.* Suppose one undertakes a computation never done before. Is one then free to accept or reject the result as one pleases? That would indeed be 'Bolshevism in mathematics'. If we are concerned with a proof within a well-established proof system, then 'If anyone *doesn't* acknowledge it, doesn't go by it as a demonstration, then he has parted company with us even before anything is said' (RFM 60). It does not matter whether the computation is one that has been done before or a new computation. The practice of multiplication is such that we are not willing to recognize an equation (rule) as a result within the system unless it can be obtained in a certain rule-governed way. 'For instance, we do not accept the rule that $1500 \times 169 = 18$; we should not call that a multiplication. The way in which it can be got we accept or acknowledge as a *proof* of it' (LFM 106). The system generates an infinite number of rules, but the technique of generation is accepted. And it is of crucial importance that there is general agreement about its results. Consequently, it would be absurd to say of a calculation (within such a proof system) that had never been done before that there is no determinate result which we should get were we to perform the calculation correctly according to our criteria of correctness.

However, suppose that there is a community with a practice of elementary computation. Suppose, further, that its members start making enormous multiplications with numerals with a thousand digits, and suppose that, beyond a certain point, different people get different results, and that there is *no way* of preventing this deviation, no matter how often they check their results, both synchronically and diachronically. What would be 'the right result'? Would anyone have found it? Would there be a right result? (It is no use saying that the right result is the result *we* would get. Suppose that we are they.) Here, Wittgenstein suggests, we should say that this has ceased to be a calculation (LFM 101). They might say that Mr So-and-so (the best calculator in the community) has arrived at a certain result, and adopt that as the result. *That* is a decision.[54] And *in this kind of case*, one could indeed say that God didn't know more than any one else what the result of the calculation was. There is nothing to stop them from postulating that Mr So-and-so's result is right, so that in future, children will have to copy it out as the result. *Then* it is right. 'Here there is nothing for a higher intelligence to know – except what future generations will do'; that is, whether and when they will transform the result of *an experiment* (e.g. Mr So-and-so's calculation) into a rule. But *in* mathematics, 'we know as much as God does' (LFM 103f.) – if we do our 'homework'.

Matters differ, however, when we are not operating within a proof system, but extending a system. In a community familiar only with the practice of counting (perhaps only to 20, more than 20 being simply 'many'), the introduction of the practice of addition is an extension of mathematics. Here, prior to the introduction of rules for addition, the result of counting is 'an experiment', and if today someone counts first 5 boys, then 7 girls, and then 12 children, and tomorrow he counts first 5 boys, then 7 girls, and then 13 children, there is nothing in what he has done (relative to the concepts available to him) that shows that he has made a mistake. Maybe yesterday one child slipped out while he was counting the group as a whole; or today a child slipped in. The only criterion for a miscount is that the 'experiment' has produced divergent results – that is, that two counts of the same unchanging group differ. So if he recognizes that there are no new faces in the class today, he will argue correctly that there cannot be both no more than 12 children and no less than 13 children in the class. So he must have miscounted, and will recount to make sure. But once the technique of addition is introduced, then there is a new criterion, a *mathematical criterion,* for having miscounted, where previously the only criterion for a miscount was divergence of counts together with no perceptible difference in the group. In this case, '5 + 7 = 12' provides a criterion for no child's having entered or left. If there are 5 boys and 7 girls, then there *are* 12 children (this is *now* merely an alternative description). So if counting the group as a whole yields 13, and none have entered, then there was a miscount. But the new mathematical criterion was not implicit in the simple counting practice or in the concepts of numbers. For those concepts are not our concepts. It is not part of what is meant by '12' in this primitive practice that it is the very same number as '7 + 5', '8 + 4', '9 + 3' and so on, for these expressions are as yet quite meaningless. Adding the arithmetical operations changes the concept of number no less than introducing signed integers to someone familiar only with natural numbers changes his concept of number. It was no more implicit in the mere practice of counting that 7 + 5 = 12 than it was implicit that 7 − 12 = −5, or that −3 × −4 = 12.[55]

So, too, with the example of the geometrical theorem. The proof that the intersection of a cylinder with a plane is an ellipse gives us a new criterion for something's being elliptical. Suppose that prior to the proof, the concept of an ellipse was determined simply as that of a closed curve in a plane such that the sum of the distances of any point on the curve from the two foci is constant. Suppose, too, that antecedently to the proof the only way to determine whether a given form on a plane (in reality) was elliptical is by measurement. After the proof, one can determine that a form is elliptical if it is produced by the intersection of a cylinder with the plane. Must the new criterion always agree with the old one? Obviously it must agree with the characterization of an ellipse as a closed curve in a plane and so forth. But must it agree with the measurements made? No, of course not – no more that $7 + 5 = 12$ must agree with counting 'experiments'. What the proof does is to establish a new pattern of internal relations. The proof provides *a new criterion for mismeasurement*. If one has ensured that what one has is a cylinder, and that the curve is in a plane, and one then measures the sums of the distances of a range of points from the foci and does *not* get constant quantities, *then* one has mismeasured. (Conversely, if after checking again and again, one can find no mismeasure, then the curve is not in a plane, or the intersecting figure is not a cylinder.) But it was not part of the antecedent concept of an ellipse that it is the intersection of a cylinder and a plane. Prior to acceptance of the proof, there was no rule for the use of the expression 'ellipse' which said that it can be replaced (in appropriate contexts) by the expression 'the shape formed by the intersection of a cylinder with a plane'. The force of the proof is not 'to unfold the implicit commitment in the existing concepts to the new criterion'. Rather, what one has effected by means of the proof is an extension of the concept of an ellipse by connecting it up with, and hence forming a new internal relation with, the concept of a cylinder. Now suppose that there were other accepted theorems about an ellipse, hence other ways to determine that a shape in an actual plane is elliptical apart from direct measurement of the shape. Then the new theorem is constructed. Is it to be assumed ('platitudinously') that it will always agree with the antecedent geometrical criteria when these are correctly applied? Certainly it will agree – but that is no *assumption*, and not obviously platitudinous. The whole point of constructing a proof is precisely to ensure agreement between the different, evolving criteria for something's being an ellipse, by weaving them together in a pattern of new internal relations. Otherwise one might just as well make a stipulation.

Did Wittgenstein hold that when we are dealing with proofs that extend mathematics, then 'anything goes', – that we are free to accept or reject proofs as we please? Did he argue that in mathematics it is up to us to decide (or refuse) to regard any statement we please as being necessarily true (thus disregarding the alleged fact that it is part of the meaning of 'true' that if a statement is true, there is something in virtue of which it is true)? That would be a travesty of his arguments.

A systematic and perspicuous account of Wittgenstein's later views on proof in mathematics has yet to be written (and any such account would have to take care not to amalgamate uncritically writings from the early 1930s and later writings). All that I can do here is to show that the above criticisms do not touch their target, and to indicate the direction and point of Wittgenstein's argument. It is, at best, misleading to say that if any statement is true, then there is something in virtue of which it is true (Dummett's review, p. 433). One may say that the statement that it is now raining is true in virtue of the fact that it is raining (look out of the window and see!). But all that amounts to are the rules that 'It is true that p' = 'It is a fact that p', and 'The proposition that p' = 'The proposition made true by the fact that p' for any empirical proposition. One could not say that it is true that red is darker than pink in virtue of the fact that red is darker than pink, for that red is darker than pink is not a fact but a grammatical proposition. It is a rule for the use of the constituent words, and there is no question of looking to see; for if one 'saw' anything different, one would not be seeing red or seeing pink, or one would not know what the proposition meant. Nor could one say that it is true in virtue of a convention, for it is not true *in virtue* of a convention, it *is* (the expression of) a convention. To say that it is true *is* just to confirm that it is a norm of representation. In the sense in which one can say that the proposition that it is raining is made true by the fact that it is raining, the only kind of proposition that can be made true by a convention is a proposition of the form 'There is a convention that . . .'. Similarly, it is true that $\sim \sim p = p$, but one cannot say that it is true in virtue of the fact that it is so; nor can one say that it is true in virtue of the meaning we have given to '$\sim$'. For, as we have seen, the rule of double negation does not *follow* from the truth-tabular explanation of negation, but is itself a further rule for the use of '$\sim$', which determines its meaning.

If we follow Wittgenstein thus far, then clearly we will not say that if a mathematical proposition is true, then there must be something in virtue of which it is true. For that is misleading, suggesting, as it does, that mathematical propositions are answerable to a mathematical reality in the manner in which empirical propositions are answerable to empirical reality.[56] To this it may be replied that a mathematical proposition is true in virtue of its proof (mathematical reality is not to be found but constructed). But this too is misleading, for there is no mathematical reality, either to be found *or* to be constructed; both these conceptions, according to Wittgenstein, are misguided. But it is correct that if we have proved a mathematical proposition, then we may say that it is true, or assert it – which amounts to the same thing (LFM 188).

A true mathematical proposition does not stand to a false one as a true empirical proposition stands to a false one. A true mathematical proposition – for example, that $12 \times 12 = 144$ – corresponds to a licit transformation of empirical propositions – for example, that there are 12 bags each containing 12 marbles, *so* there are 144 marbles. But a false mathematical proposition – for example, $12 \times 12 = 51$ – corresponds to an illicit transformation of empirical propositions (e.g., . . . , so there are 51 marbles). One might indeed say that a 'false mathematical proposition' is not a proposition of mathematics at all, for it does not have the role of propositions of mathematics.[57] A mathematical proposition shows us what it makes sense to say (RFM 164). The role of mathematics is *normative*. To prove that a certain mathematical proposition is true is just to prove that proposition, and to prove a mathematical proposition is just to prove that *it is* (henceforth) a proposition of mathematics; that is, that it is thereby incorporated as *a rule* within a vast system of interconnected rules.

To this one may object that mathematical propositions are necessary truths. We do indeed so characterize them. But the moot question is what we mean by so doing. According to Wittgenstein, what it means is that they are rules, the fundamental corpus of which are norms of representation for the transformation of empirical propositions. It is not *the rules* that are necessary – for there is no such thing as a '(logically) necessary rule'. Rather, to call them 'necessary truths' is a misleading way of characterizing their role as norms of representation. What is true is that in empirical reasoning, when we have recourse to mathematics, we argue that if, for example, there are 12 bags each with 12 marbles, then there *must* be 144 marbles altogether. Hence:

> Let us remember that in mathematics we are convinced of *grammatical* proposi-
> tions; so the expression, the result, of our being convinced is that we *accept a rule.*
>   . . . even if the proved proposition seems to point to a reality outside itself, still
> it is only the expression of acceptance of a new measure (of reality).
>   Thus we take the constructability (provability) of this symbol (that is, of the
> mathematical proposition) as a sign that we are to transform symbols in such and
> such a way. (RFM 162f.)

Does it follow that Wittgenstein thought that every mathematical proposition is
always a 'direct expression of a linguistic convention', which we expressly *decide* to
treat as 'unassailable'? The question already rests on a misunderstanding. For it
conflates two distinct claims: (a) that mathematical propositions are rules (conventions), and (b) that every mathematical proposition is a *direct* (underived) expression
of a rule – an 'optional decision'. Every mathematical proposition is indeed the
expression of a rule. But unless it is an axiom, it is a rule that has been derived
from other rules, *in accord* with rules. The upshot of a proof can indeed be said to
be that one has 'won through to a *decision*' (RFM 163). But the decision is not to
believe a hitherto unknown truth, but rather *to use the proved proposition as a norm
of representation.*

> I go through the proof and say: 'Yes, this is how it *must* be; I must fix the use
> of my language in *this* way.'
>   I want to say that the *must* corresponds to a track which I lay down in language.
> (RFM 165f.)

What is unassailable is not akin to an empirical proposition which describes phenomena; rather, it is a *rule* for describing phenomena. Is the decision to accept the
result of the proof as a norm of representation optional or arbitrary? Wittgenstein
remarked:

> There could be no mathematical investigation if there were nothing by which our
> procedure was guided in one way rather than another, and nothing by which our
> results could be checked to see whether they are right or wrong. If anyone makes
> a discovery[58] in arithmetic, he can give reasons in support of it, convincing to
> anyone who knows arithmetic; and he can give reasons showing that anything else
> would be wrong. But this does not mean that the character of arithmetic and the
> way in which it develops is determined by the properties of numbers. (RR 115)

Is the decision not forced upon us? Surely, merely to concede that there are *reasons*
for accepting the proof is not enough. For do we not *have* to accept it, if we are to
'remain faithful to the meanings of the expressions as laid down in the axioms'?
Unless we are speaking merely of 'homework' within a proof system, that too
would be wrong. A proof introduces a new concept, puts a new paradigm among
the paradigms of language. It changes the grammar of our language, and with it our
concepts. It does so by making new connections, and thereby creating the concept
of those connections. But *it does not establish that they are there; they do not exist until
it makes them* (RFM 165f.).[59]

It is tempting to think that the antecedent rules lead this way, even if no one has
followed the route before; that our pre-existing concepts already committed us to
just these connections, even though no one realized it. 'Here one sees the mathematical machine, which driven by itself, obeys only mathematical laws and not

physical ones' (RFM 249). For one is inclined to think that if a proof *can* be constructed, then, in some sense, it is already there in the realm of mathematics, awaiting discovery or implicit in our existing concepts, requiring only to be unfolded. For we are tempted to hold that 'What in the ordinary world we call a possibility is in the geometrical [mathematical] world a reality' (LFM 144). But this is mystification.

A proof that extends mathematics creates a new concept by creating (or being) a new sign, or by giving the proposition which is its result a new place (RFM 173). A proof is not so much the discovery of a *truth*, but the determination of a new internal relation. To believe that the concepts involved 'contain' these internal relations in advance of a proof is to believe in a kind of mythology. For there is no more to a concept than the rules for the application of an expression, and there is no such thing as 'hidden rules' for the use of an expression which await discovery. (We are inclined to think otherwise, partly because we conflate proofs within a proof system, such as elementary computation, with proofs that extend the system.) But it would be absurd to think that the concepts of angle, trisection, compass and rule are such as to *contain* within themselves the proof that one cannot trisect an angle with compass and rule, which proof is effected algebraically by reference to whether a certain cubic equation is soluble entirely by means of square roots (PLP 398–400).

A *great* deal more needs to be said about Wittgenstein's philosophy of mathematics, about his elucidation of the concept of proof, about the distinction between proofs within a system and proofs that extend the system (doubtless, there is no sharp dividing line here, but a continuum – and that is problematic), and about the crucial role of analogy in proof. But enough has been said to make it evident that characterizing his philosophy of mathematics as an extremely implausible form of 'full-blooded conventionalism', refutable by mere consideration of a few examples of elementary computation, is a deep misconstrual of his thought.

3. The aftermath

Writing in 1976 on the period during which Ryle edited *Mind*, Warnock remarked: 'if the twenty-five years or so before 1948 were years in which the face of philosophy changed very greatly, what about the years since then? . . . if I had to take a stand, it would be on the proposition that at least no very radical mutation is discernible.'[60] This was the last time in which any such thing could have been written. The centre of gravity of philosophy was shifting, geographically, thematically and methodologically. A decade later, not one, but numerous, mutations had occurred.

By the mid-1970s Oxford's sun was setting. Most of the figures who had led the post-war revolution in analytic philosophy had either died or retired, or had already made their major contributions to their subject. The principal sabbatical traffic (and 'brain drain') across the Atlantic was no longer to Oxford, but from Oxford to Harvard, Princeton, Cornell, Berkeley, etc. The motivation was not only, although it was also, economic. The centre of Anglophone philosophy became the United

States. There were more philosophers teaching there than the sum of philosophers in the whole history of the subject. There was no 'school' of American philosophy, or indeed a single major university department that led the field as, first, Cambridge and, later, Oxford had done in Britain. Nevertheless, the philosophical tradition there was, as is evident from chapter 7, very different. To be sure, Wittgenstein's influence continued for some years more, both under the aegis of his ex-pupils and through the writings and teaching of a second generation who had not been taught by him (e.g. Rogers Albritton, Stanley Cavell and Burton Dreben). And Grice continued his work at Berkeley, where John Searle further developed ideas originating with Austin (and Grice). However, the impact of ex-members or affiliates of the Vienna Circle and, in particular, Quine's influence steered philosophy into new channels. It was primarily they and their pupils who moulded the shape of philosophy in the United States over the next decades. To a large extent, the 'scientific world-view' was transformed into a *scientistic* world-view.

In the first quarter of the century, the astonishing developments in physics, the triumph of Darwinism, the achievements of Freud, and the advances in social theory could indeed give the younger generation faith that science held the key to intellectual and social progress, that the future lay with scientific rationality, and that it was the task of philosophy, rearmed with the new logic, to side with the future, eradicate irrational, pre-scientific modes of thought, extirpate metaphysical mystery-mongering, and reconstruct the edifice of human knowledge in the spirit of science. Half a century, and two world wars later, that future was there to be seen (and it did not work all that well). What had triumphed in society was not so much the rationality of science, but scientific technology, which swept all before it. Although science could no longer be thought to ensure social progress and human felicity, in its own sphere it was invincible, unlocking the secrets of the microcosm and macrocosm alike, revealing the origins of life, and uncovering the mysteries of DNA. Its success bred intellectual complacency. The proper sphere of science, it seemed, was the whole sphere of human knowledge. What *can* be understood, *must* be understood in the manner – and, indeed, the footsteps – of science. Philosophy, too, is a quest for such understanding – for explanation at the most general, all-encompassing level. Hence it seemed, as Russell had remarked, that a condition for respectable philosophy is that the philosopher's imagination be impregnated with the scientific outlook, and that his work be an extension of science.

With the impact of post-positivism in the United States, that condition was readily satisfied there. A different paradigm or related set of paradigms came to dominate the subject. Quine's arguments against the analystic/synthetic distinction were widely accepted, even by those who did not share his sympathy for behaviourism, and did not, it seems, notice the extent to which Quine's arguments depended not only upon his holism, which Carnap shared, but also upon the acceptance of a behaviourist methodology. This fostered the belief that philosophy, *pace* Wittgenstein and Oxford, *is* continuous with science. It is concerned, no less than science, with theory construction, albeit at a higher level of generality, and in some cases at least (e.g. in philosophical psychology) at a more speculative level (anticipating future scientific discoveries about the structure and operations of the brain). Like science, its goal is to add to human knowledge about reality. For the paradigm of understanding is given by scientific understanding of the phenomena of nature, and the paradigm of secure knowledge in any domain whatever, is scientific theory. Since every conceptual scheme seemed (as Quine argued) unavoidably theoretical, involving ontological commitments, ordinary language is merely the traditional pre-scientific conceptual scheme of a culture, useful for the mundane purposes for which it evolved, but committed to a host of misconceived pre-scientific theories. Embedded in ordinary language is a pre-scientific physics (as is evident, it seems, from our talk of the sun's setting and rising, from our use of the colour vocabulary and so forth) and a pre-scientific psychology (as is apparent in our talk of the mind, of mental states and processes). Philosophical theorizing need therefore pay no more attention to the ordinary use of ordinary expressions than does physics or scientific psychology.

With such preconceptions, shared by many American philosophers, analytic philosophy, as it has been depicted throughout this book, lost its impetus. In each of its great phases, it had been driven by a revolutionary fervour – to sweep away the confusions and mystification of the past, and bring philosophy into the light. By the 1970s, that fervour had dissipated. Science and the scientific spirit of investigation no longer needed defending, but only following, for it was triumphant. Few realized that it might itself contain the seeds of metaphysical nonsense, that it could breed dogmatism and conceptual confusion no less pernicious than its now vanquished adversaries (the pronouncements of religion upon scientific matters, rationalist metaphysics, prejudice, moribund tradition, alleged common knowledge). Few worried that it might give rise to scientistic thought – that is, modes of thought that emulate the forms of scientific theories, the jargon and formalization of respectable science, without the constraints of systematic data collecting, quantitative methods and experimental testing. On the contrary, many leading American philosophers enthusiastically welcomed the ideas that philosophy, like science, is concerned with constructing theories and that its methods should approximate those of the sciences. The thought that understanding in the humanities (*Geisteswissenschaften*), in history, parts of psychology, economics and the social sciences, might *not* conform to the model of understanding in the physical sciences was rejected by mainstream Anglophone philosophy (in conformity with the logical positivist doctrines of Hempel, Nagel, Feigl, etc.), although the hermeneutic tradition flourished on the Continent, and analytical hermeneutics[61] was developing under Wittgensteinian influence at the hands of such philosophers as Dray, Kenny, Charles Taylor, Winch and von Wright. Similarly, under the influence of Quine (and against the doctrines of logical positivism), the idea that philosophical understanding is *sui generis* was rejected. The stream which had originated in Cambridge in the late 1890s, flowing vigorously there between the wars, broadening to a great river in the Vienna of the 1930s and in Oxford after the war, reached a broad plain and broke into numerous tributaries and rivulets, some of which became dissipated in marshlands. Boundary lines blurred, and the linguistic turn which philosophy had taken in the 1920s and 1930s gradually slipped from sight as the waters spread over the plain.

The kind of philosophy of language that had been fostered by Wittgenstein and cultivated in Oxford was brushed aside as unsystematic, as non-scientific 'ordinary language philosophy', lacking any firm theoretical foundations. In its place, a variety of enterprises emerged, which aimed to fill the apparent vacuum – possible world semantics, Montague semantics, and, what was destined to be most influential in Britain, the systematic Davidsonian project of constructing a general theory of meaning for a natural language.[62] Analytic philosophy of mind in the Wittgensteinian and Rylean tradition was similarly eschewed, and was replaced by a variety of scientistic investigations inspired, on the one hand, by neuro-scientific discoveries and advances in computer science and artificial intelligence and, on the other, by the new linguistics of Chomsky's school. Hence, after a brief flurry of central state materialism,[63] functionalism enjoyed a short spell of popularity, succeeded by anomalous monism, varieties of so-called cognitive science, and the emergence of 'neurophilosophical' eliminative materialism and connectionism. Analytic descriptive metaphysics, as advocated by Strawson, was replaced by scientific-realist metaphysics, inspired by the conception of rigid designation introduced by Kripke and the consequent idea that there are a posteriori necessary truths awaiting discovery by science.

By the mid-1980s, Anglophone philosophy had lost any distinctive marks. Although analytic methods continued to be used in some quarters, much of the work done in the last decade can be called 'analytic philosophy' only in so far as its headwaters can rightly be so called. The tale of its manifold rivulets does not belong to this book, for it does not concern Wittgenstein's place in twentieth-century analytic philosophy. What remains to be done is to try to delve a little deeper into the question of why Wittgenstein's influence waned and connective analytical philosophy declined. Such a venture is bound to be highly speculative, and doubtless a clearer picture will emerge with the passing of time. The following remarks are offered as no more than tentative.

In the opening pages of this book, I suggested that the kinds of philosophy that displaced analytic philosophy in its post-war phase manifested the triumph not of the *Tractatus*, but of the *spirit* of the *Tractatus* over the spirit of the *Investigations*. This can be exhibited both in the large and in the small. A salient feature of the *Tractatus* vision was the thought that *depth* analysis could reveal hitherto unknown, undreamt-of structures, the deep structure of language, of thought and of the world. Mankind possesses the ability to construct languages capable of expressing every sense, without having any idea how each word has meaning or what its meaning is. Indeed, language disguises thought, and it is not possible to infer from its surface what the underlying forms are (TLP 4.002). These are to be uncovered by analysis. The key to such analysis lay in the new logic, invented by Frege and Russell. The predicate calculus, doubtless with further modifications and improvements, would deliver the essential, hidden forms of thought and language. For a language is a calculus of rules. The hidden rules of the calculus of language are comprehensive and definite. They ensure that the logical requirement of determinacy of sense is satisfied. For any combination of signs, they determine unequivocally whether it makes sense and what sense it makes. It is of the essence of a proposition that it should be able to communicate a *new* sense to us (TLP 4.03), that we can understand indefinitely many sentences which we have never heard before. The *Tractatus* purported to explain this 'creative power of language' (as it later became known) by reference to our knowledge of the meanings of a stock of primitive words, their essential forms, and the combinatorial rules of logical syntax, which we unknowingly operate in thought and speech. The sense of a sentence is a function of the meanings of its constituent expressions and their forms. All entailments are the result of truth-functional combination. Apparent non-extensional contexts are reducible to extensional ones. If anyone utters a sentence and means or understands it, he is operating a calculus according to definite rules (PI §81), even though he may not be conscious of so doing.[64] This vision, repudiated root and stock in the *Investigations*, was revived in transmuted form in the last quarter of the century.

How did this reversion to a model of thought which had been rejected in mid-century with good reason take place? Against a background of (i) the growth of scientism and (ii) the acceptance of continuity between philosophy and science, it can perhaps be partly explained by reference to four further factors:[65] (a) the emergence, in the wake of Quine's work, of new kinds of philosophy of language; (b) the simultaneous development of the new theoretical linguistics at the hands of Chomsky and his followers, which seemed to complement the work in philosophy of language; (c) the computer revolution, which inclined philosophers, scientists and psychologists to construe the operations of the mind and the workings of the brain on the model of computers; and (d) advances in neurophysiological psychology, which, at a highly speculative level, seemed to invite an attempted synthesis of theoretical linguistics, philosophy of language, artificial intelligence and cybernetics, psychology and philosophy of mind – a trend culminating in the invention of a new subject, representational 'cognitive science'. Each of these, in different ways, fostered complementary features of thought which can be said to be 'in the spirit of the *Tractatus*', even though often vulgarized.

Of the philosophies of language which displaced Wittgenstein's (as well as more detailed[66] and more general[67] forms of) descriptive philosophy of language, the most influential was Donald Davidson's. He advocated the project of constructing a philosophical theory of meaning for a natural language, and pursued it systematically in a large number of carefully crafted papers.[68] In one of his early papers he declared his goal thus:

> I dream of a theory that makes the transition from the ordinary idiom to canonical notation purely mechanical, and a canonical notation rich enough to capture, in its dull and explicit way, every difference and connection legitimately considered the business of a theory of meaning. The point of a canonical notation so conceived is not to improve on something left vague and defective in natural language, but to help elicit in a perspicuous and general form the understanding of logical grammar we all have that constitutes (part of) our grasp of our native tongue.[69]

In a manner not unlike the *Tractatus* conception, he held that

> a satisfactory theory of meaning must give an account of how the meanings of sentences depend upon the meanings of words. Unless such an account can be supplied for a particular language, . . . there would be no explaining the fact that we can learn the language: no explaining the fact that, on mastering a finite vocabulary and a finitely stated set of rules, we are prepared to produce and understand any of a potential infinity of sentences.[70]

Davidson had been educated on a diet of positivist works.[71] The greatest influence upon him was Quine, whose rejection of the analytic/synthetic distinction he accepted, as he did Quine's holism, although he rejected Quine's behaviourism, his preoccupation with 'surface irritations', and his repudiation of any intelligible conception of meaning other than 'stimulus-meaning'. Quine invoked radical translation as a heuristic device to demonstrate that, *pace* Grice and Strawson, there are no respectably observational ways of establishing synonymy. His investigation led to the conclusion of indeterminacy of translation and inscrutability of reference, and to the desired view that radical translation does not begin at the fringes of the jungle, but at home – hence synonymy is no more available in our own mother tongue than in translation from alien languages. *All* understanding is translating, and is subject to the same constraints. Davidson argued similarly that all understanding is *interpreting* (and that interpretation is essentially translation). Davidson's project, characterized very generally, was to clarify the principles whereby we might construct a general theory of meaning for a natural language which will be capable of delivering the meaning of any arbitrary sentence of the language from an array of 'axioms' (definitions) and formation and transformation rules, in the form of a Tarskian T-sentence specifying in a metalanguage the truth-conditions of the sentence in the object language.

The inspiration for Davidson's programme was not the *Tractatus*. But the spirit informing the programme was that of the *Tractatus*.[72] Like Wittgenstein in the *Tractatus*, Davidson argued that concealed beneath the forms of ordinary speech lies the complex apparatus of the predicate calculus with identity, enriched in various ways (e.g. by quantification over events) to accommodate all legitimate inferences recognized in normal speech. Surface grammatical forms conceal underlying logical forms, as, for example, the form of an action-describing sentence incorporating an adverbial modification ('A shut the door quickly') conceals the presence of a quantifier, logical connectives and a verbal noun ('There was a shutting of the door, and it was done by A, and it was quick'). Logical form is the form of a sentence as represented, preferably in canonical notation, by depth grammar, which will make perspicuous all logical relations. Though not conceived as a reflection of the logico-metaphysical forms of things, nevertheless logical form makes clear our ontological commitments, and can be employed to prove that ontological commitments are justified by theory. Hence, for example, quantification over events, together with adequate criteria of identity for events, proves that events exist.[73] All entailments are determined by the inner complexity of sentences in depth grammar. Appearances notwithstanding, the deep structure of a language is extensional. The meaning of a sentence is given by its truth-conditions (although the concept of a truth-condition has been stretched, following Tarski, to accommodate talk of truth-conditions of atomic sentences). A language is a calculus of signs. The metalinguistic theory of the language should account for the meaning or truth-conditions of every sentence of the language by analysing it as composed, in truth-relevant ways, of elements drawn from a finite stock, thus explaining how a language is learnable, and how learning a language equips one to understand a potential infinity of sentences.[74] Speakers of a language use a system or a theory of meaning for the language, in terms of which they interpret the utterances of another. Such a system can be thought of as a machine which, when fed an arbitrary utterance, produces an interpretation. A model for such a machine is a Tarskian theory of truth, which provides a recursive characterization of the truth-conditions of all possible utterances of the speaker through an analysis of utterances in terms of sentences made up from the finite vocabulary and the finite stock of modes of composition. That is not to say that speakers have explicit knowledge of such a theory, but rather that the theory is a model of the interpreter's (listener's) linguistic competence, and *some mechanism in the interpreter must correspond to the theory*.[75]

A different development, extraneous to philosophy, which, in a similar way exhibits something of the spirit of the *Tractatus*, was the emergence of a new form of theoretical linguistics at the hands of Chomsky and his followers. Indeed, the similarity between the allegedly empirical science of theoretical linguistics and philosophical theories of meaning seemed to provide confirmation of the intelligibility and point of the endeavour.[76] Although restricted initially to syntax, in due course Chomskian linguistic theory came to embrace semantics too, and, like the Davidsonian project, it aimed to produce a theory of meaning for a language. Like philosophical theorists of meaning, Chomsky took the fact that we can understand (and utter) sentences we have never heard before to be a deep problem, which can be answered only by reference to hidden mechanisms and complex theories allegedly 'cognized' (unconsciously known) by every speaker. The human 'language faculty' was held to be a component of the 'mind/brain', which incorporates a wide variety of grammatical principles 'as a matter of biological necessity'. These principles collectively constitute the 'universal grammar' of all human languages, and are 'part of the fixed structure of the mind/brain', innately cognized of 'biological necessity', although buried deep within the unconscious.[77] Presented with utterances, the child's language faculty has to determine the grammar of the particular language with which it is confronted, which is necessarily 'parametrized' within the scope of universal grammar. This being accomplished, a language – that is, a computational system that 'provides structured representations of linguistic expressions' which determine their sound and meaning – 'grows' in the mind/brain. The grammar of a natural language is 'the set of rules and principles that determine the normal use of language', but these too are not 'consciously known' (but only 'cognized') by ordinary speakers. Indeed, it would be 'miraculous' if a speaker could become conscious of them.[78] Understanding an utterance is a computational process in which the mind/brain 'must determine its phonetic form and its words and then use the principles of universal grammar and the values of the parameters to project a structured representation of this expression and determine how its parts are associated'. This representation is a 'mental representation' which is 'visible to the mechanisms of the mind'. The computations involved may be fairly intricate, 'but since they rely on principles of universal grammar that are part of the fixed structure of the mind/ brain, it is fair to suppose that they take place virtually instantaneously and of course with no conscious awareness and beyond the level of possible introspection'.[79]

That Chomsky's conception of the deep structure of language bears analogies to the *Tractatus* conception of the hidden forms of the logical syntax of all possible languages is evident. The grammatical rules and the patterns of grammatical transformation which Chomsky's linguistics claimed to uncover were no less 'hidden' than those postulated by the *Tractatus*. The philosophical psychology presupposed by the *Tractatus* was undeveloped, and barely brought into view. Not so in the case of Chomsky. And the psychological assumptions that accompanied his linguistics gave birth to an a priori speculative psychology that was conceived as contributing to the emergent subject of cognitive science. Among his followers, some, such as J. A. Fodor, argued that language acquisition demands not merely innate knowledge of principles of universal grammar, but also an innate language of thought. Here, too, one can discern an affinity with one strand in the *Tractatus* conception: namely, that 'thinking too is a kind of language' (NB 82); that a thought is a kind of proposition, with thought-constituents that have the same sort of relation to reality as words (R 37); that a thought has a logical structure that enables it to picture reality no less than a sentence, so that 'A thinks that p' has the same form as '"p" says that p' (TLP 5.542; for a discussion of the *Tractatus* conception of thought, see Volume 3, 'Thinking: the soul of language', §1). The fact that Wittgenstein had demolished his earlier conception with powerful and as yet unrefuted arguments went unnoticed (as far as arguments against the intelligibility of a 'language of thought' were concerned), misinterpreted (as far as his examination of rules and rule-following was concerned), or misunderstood (as far as the private language arguments were concerned).[80]

Chomsky's linguistic theory swept through university departments of linguistics in the 1960s and 1970s. With the demise of behaviourist theories of language, it gave contemporary theoretical linguistics a new lease of life and a mission hitherto undreamt of: namely, not merely to study human languages, their forms and structure, but to penetrate the 'deep mysteries' of the human mind. It was significant that Chomskian grammar lent itself to computerization, that the picture painted of the operations of what was denominated 'the mind/brain' was indeed of a biological computer, and that the theory captured the imagination of so many scholars at the very time at which computer science and technology matured. It was a historical coincidence that this advance in technology occurred simultaneously with the rise of the new theoretical linguistics, but it is plausible to conjecture that this coincidence played a role in the demise of analytic philosophy as previously conceived, and stimulated the emergence of very different philosophies of language and, associated with them, equally different forms of philosophy of psychology. For the growth of computer science exercised an irresistible fascination. Where our ancestors had pictured themselves in the image of God, it was now tempting to picture ourselves in the image of our machines. And a double irony ensued. The gods were conceived as creating us in their image, whereas we created them in ours. We invented machines to do automatically what we do thoughtfully, and then proceeded to conceive of ourselves on the model of our automata.[81] It was difficult to resist the idea that computers can think, or, if the current generation of computers cannot quite do so yet, that at any rate the next generation will. Hence it was equally difficult to resist the temptation of conceiving of the hidden operations of the mind and (or) the brain on the model of our machines. Cognitive science was born. Behaviourism was rejected. So too was Cartesian dualism, often to be replaced by brain/body dualism. Wittgenstein, like Ryle, was thought to be a logical behaviourist – and dismissed accordingly. *Mutatis mutandis* the mind must either be identical with the brain or, alternatively, stand to the brain as the software to the hardware of a computer.

It was equally coincidental that during the 1960s and 1970s there was a dramatic breakthrough in neurophysiological psychology. Technological advances made possible investigations of the brain with a precision hitherto undreamt of, and the results, especially in the study of vision, were dramatic. Functional localization had long been known, but the degree of structural organization of the 'visual' striate cortex, demonstrated by the brilliant experimental work of D. H. Hubel and T. N. Wiesel came as a dramatic surprise. The fact that one can map certain features in the visual field on to the firings of systematically organized arrays of cells in the hyper-columns of the striate cortex encouraged misleading talk of 'maps' in the brain. That in turn released a flood of confused metaphors. Arrays of firing brain cells were held to *represent* features in the visual field, to encode and process *information* (and 'information' in the information-theoretic sense was readily conflated with 'information' in the semantic sense), which would enable brain cells, for example, to *assign colours* to surfaces. Nerve-cells were held to 'use the same inductive logic as the detective', and to use information derived therefrom in order 'to build up higher perceptual concepts'.[82] The brain was held to ask and answer questions, to interpret and understand messages,[83] construct hypotheses and make inferences.[84] The homunculus fallacy of ascribing predicates to parts of a being which it only makes sense to ascribe to the creature as a whole ran rife (see Volume 3, 'Men, minds and machines'). The impact upon the philosophy of psychology and newly emerging cognitive science was profound, turning the subject away from analytic philosophy of mind, and transforming it into speculative science if not, indeed, scientism.

By the last decade of the century, the tradition of connective analytical philosophy had waned. Wittgenstein scholarship flourished, and a minority of philosophers continued to work in the Wittgensteinian tradition, but mainstream Anglophone philosophy had moved off in quite different directions. What, from Wittgenstein's perspective, were diseases of the intellect, to many of which he himself had suc-cumbed as a young man and which he had laboured long to extirpate, broke out afresh in mutated, virulent forms. From the perspective of his therapeutic concep-tion of the philosopher's activity, this was, perhaps, to be expected, given the cultural and intellectual pressures of the times. Medicine is not rendered obsolete by the discovery of a cure for a current disease, if one knows that the virus that causes it is prone to mutate. And there is no limit to the forms of confusion into which we may fall when reflecting upon our concepts of mind and body, perception and its objects, thought and language, consciousness and self-consciousness, mathemat-ics and logic. Each new intellectual advance, such as the invention of non-Euclidean geometries, of new logical calculi, of Gödel's incompleteness theorem, of intui-tionistic mathematics and so forth, illuminates new domains of thought, but also casts long shadows across our conceptual scheme. New theories and discoveries in science, such as relativity theory, quantum mechanics, molecular biology and neurophysiological psychology reverberate throughout our intellectual framework, shaking elements loose from their scaffolding, introducing new concepts the articu-lations of which with pre-existing concepts and conceptual structures cannot easily be apprehended. Advances in technology, such as computer science and cybernet-ics, mesmerize us, and lead us astray. The elucidatory task of philosophy never ends.

Wittgenstein's legacy was a new vision and new methods. He provided a vision – for those who no longer accept assurances that philosophy is really at last on the brink of producing the philosophical knowledge which it has repeatedly promised to deliver for the last two and a half thousand years. His bequest is a vision of philosophy as the pursuit not of knowledge but of understanding. The task of philosophy is not to add to the sum of human knowledge, but to enable us to attain a clear understanding of what is already known. He provided new methods – for those who, like him, are not concerned with the construction of new buildings, but rather crave a perspicuous view of possible buildings, clarity as an end in itself (CV 7). His bequest is an array of methods for disentangling the conceptual confusions that are the business of philosophy, for curing us of the diseases of the intellect to which we are all prone. Practised with skill, they can lead us to a correct logical point of view (TLP 4.1213), from which to see the world aright (TLP 6.54). The resultant understanding is the only prize that philosophy can offer. To achieve it in the ever changing stream of human history is a goal towards which each generation must strive afresh. Whether, and when, philosophy will turn back to Wittgenstein's methods, and properly assimilate his great insights, I cannot venture to guess. But I should like to believe that what he wrote of others can be applied to him too: 'The works of great masters are suns which rise and set around us. The time will come for every great work that is now in the descendant to rise again' (CV 15).

Notes

Chapter 1   The Background

1   Bertrand Russell, *My Philosophical Development* (Allen and Unwin, London, 1959), p. 216.

2   Quine wrote that he had been more influenced by Carnap than by any other philosopher (W. V. Quine, 'Carnap's Positivistic Travail', *Fundamenta Scientiae*, 5 (1984), p. 333). Of course, he came to disagree profoundly with Carnap, but it is noteworthy that much of this disagreement was anticipated *within* the Circle by Neurath (see D. Koppelberg, 'Why and How to Naturalize Epistemology', in *Perspectives on Quine*, ed. R. Barrett and R. Gibson (Blackwell, Oxford and Cambridge, Mass., 1990), pp. 200–11). For detailed discussion of Quine's philosophy, see ch. 7 below.

3   Although the terms 'analysis', 'logical analysis' and 'conceptual analysis' were widely used more or less from the inception of the analytic movement to characterize the methods of philosophy advocated, the name 'analytic philosophy', as von Wright has pointed out ('Analytic Philosophy: A Historico-Critical Survey', in *The Tree of Knowledge and Other Essays* (Brill, Leiden, 1993), p. 41, n. 35) entered currency as the name of a philosophical movement surprisingly late. It was used during the 1930s (e.g. in E. Nagel's 'Impressions and Appraisals of Analytic Philosophy in Europe', *Journal of Philosophy*, 33 (1936)), but does not seem to have caught on. Von Wright conjectures that when it did catch on, it did so partly through the post-war writings of Arthur Pap, who published his *Elements of Analytic Philosophy* (Macmillan, New York) in 1949, *Analytische Erkenntnistheorie, Kritische Übersicht über die neueste Entwicklung in USA und England* (Springer Verlag, Vienna) in 1955, and *Semantics and Necessary Truth: An Inquiry into the Foundations of Analytic Philosophy* (Yale University Press, New Haven and London) in 1958. Certainly it is striking that the two most influential post-war anthologies of writings in analytic philosophy, *Readings in Philosophical Analysis*, ed. H. Feigl and W. Sellars (Appleton-Century-Crofts, New York, 1948) in the United States and *Logic and Language*, ed. A. G. N. Flew (Blackwell, Oxford, 1951) in Britain, did not invoke the term 'analytic philosophy' in either their titles or their introductions. W. B. Gallie published a paper entitled 'The Limitations of Analytical Philosophy' in *Analysis*, 9 (1949), and others followed suit. By the late 1950s the name had taken root. The famous Anglo-French Royaumont colloquium of 1959 was entitled *La Philosophie analytique*. Blackwell's purported successor to Flew's successful anthology was *Analytic Philosophy*, ed. R. J. Butler (Blackwell, Oxford, 1962), and later in the 1960s Bernard Williams and Alan Montefiore published their anthology *British Analytic Philosophy* (Routledge and Kegan Paul, London, 1966), which was designed to survey the methods of contemporary British, especially Oxford, philosophy.

4   I owe the term 'connective analysis' to P. F. Strawson's *Analysis and Metaphysics:*
      An Introduction to Philosophy (Oxford University Press, Oxford, 1992), ch. 2. The
      term 'analysis' in this context (as Strawson points out) can be misleading. For what
      was undertaken was not the decomposition of anything into its components, but
      rather the elucidation of concepts. Philosophers of this persuasion referred to their
      mode of philosophizing as 'analytic' and to their activities as 'conceptual analysis',
      and saw their investigations as heirs to the forms of analysis practised by the
      previous generation.
5   G. E. Moore (1873–1958) read, first, classics and then for the Moral Sciences
      Tripos at Trinity College, Cambridge (1892–6). He wrote a fellowship disserta-
      tion on Kant's ethics, on the basis of which he was elected to a six-year fellowship
      (1898–1904), during which time he published his pivotal papers against the Abso-
      lute Idealists, as well as his *Principia Ethica*. In 1911 he returned to Trinity to
      succeed J. N. Keynes as university lecturer in moral sciences, a post he held until
      1925, when he succeeded James Ward in the Chair of Mental Philosophy and
      Logic. He was editor of *Mind* from 1921 until 1947. He retired from his chair in
      1939.
6   Bertrand Russell (1872–1970) read for the mathematics Tripos and Moral Sciences
      Tripos at Trinity College, Cambridge, between 1890 and 1894. His Fellowship
      dissertation was entitled 'The Foundations of Geometry', and was subsequently
      published as *An Essay on the Foundations of Geometry*. He was a fellow of Trinity
      from 1895 to 1901. During the following decade, without a university post, he
      completed, first, his *Principles of Mathematics* (1903), then his great collaborative
      three-volume work with A. N. Whitehead, *Principia Mathematica* (1910–13). He
      returned to Trinity as lecturer in philosophy in 1910, a post he held until his
      dismissal in 1916 on account of his pacifist activities. He held no further university
      post until he moved to the United States in 1938, where he taught at the Univer-
      sity of Chicago, UCLA, Harvard (1940) and the Barnes Foundation (1941–3). In
      1944, he returned, again as a Fellow, to Trinity.
7   I am indebted for the following account to both John Passmore's masterly ency-
      clopaedic work *A Hundred Years of Philosophy* (Penguin, Harmondsworth, 1968)
      and A. M. Quinton's illuminating paper 'Absolute Idealism', repr. in his *Thoughts*
      and Thinkers (Duckworth, London, 1982), pp. 186–206.
8   Thus J. H. Muirhead, writing in 1924, in 'Past and Present in Contemporary
      Philosophy', in *Contemporary British Philosophy*, 1st Ser., ed. Muirhead (Allen and
      Unwin, London, 1924), p. 323. Muirhead's owl did indeed take flight after dusk.
9   The observation is James's, quoted by Passmore in *A Hundred Years of Philosophy*,
      p. 56.
10   J. E. McTaggart (1866–1925) read for the Moral Sciences Tripos at Trinity Col-
      lege, Cambridge (1884–8). He was elected to a Fellowship at Trinity in 1891, and
      was a lecturer in philosophy from 1897 until his retirement in 1923.
11   In a letter to Desmond MacCarthy, in August 1898, he wrote: 'I am pleased to
      believe that this is the most Platonic system of modern times' (see T. Baldwin,
      G. E. Moore (Routledge, London and New York, 1990), p. 40.
12   He wrote to MacCarthy: 'I have arrived at a perfectly staggering doctrine . . . An
      existent is nothing but a proposition: nothing *is* but concepts. There is my philoso-
      phy' (ibid., p. 41).
13   See G. E. Moore, 'A Reply to my Critics', in *The Philosophy of G. E. Moore*, ed.
      P. A. Schilpp (Northwestern University Press, Evanston, Ill., and Chicago, 1942),
      pp. 660–7.
14   This is the ancestor of later distinctions between knowing 'by practice how to

operate with concepts' and being able to 'state the logical regulations governing their use' (Ryle), and between 'tacit knowledge' and 'explicit knowledge' of a theory of meaning for a language (Dummett).

15   G. E. Moore, 'Is Existence a Predicate?', PASS, 15 (1936), pp. 175–88.

16   This book, published, at John Wisdom's instigation, only in 1953, consists of the twenty lectures which Moore delivered in the winter of 1910–11. Chapters 1–10, in unpublished form, are acknowledged by Russell in his preface to *The Problems of Philosophy* (1912) as giving him 'valuable assistance' as regards the relations of sense-data to physical objects. It is also evident that Moore's conception of philosophy stimulated Russell's somewhat different conception in the final two chapters of his book.

17   There is a striking resemblance between Moore's 'description of the most important things we know to be in the Universe' and Strawson's much later account of the basic particulars of any conceptual scheme which we can render intelligible to ourselves (see P. F. Strawson, *Individuals, an Essay in Descriptive Metaphysics* (Methuen, London, 1959). The equally striking differences are a measure of the transformation of analytic philosophy between 1910 and 1959. For a discussion of Strawson, see pp. 175–82.

18   He was later to write: 'I felt [the new philosophy] as a great liberation, as if I had escaped from a hot-house on to a wind-swept headland. I hated the stuffiness involved in supposing that space and time were only in my mind. I liked the starry heavens better than the moral law, and couldn't bear Kant's view that the one I liked best was only a subjective figment. In the first exuberance of liberation, I became a naïve realist and rejoiced in the thought that grass is really green' (Russell, *My Philosophical Development*, p. 61). However, there was a difference between Russell's preoccupations and Moore's (ibid., p. 54). Moore's primary interest lay in the rejection of idealism, whereas, despite the above passionate reaction, Russell's was in the rejection of monism (although, as he pointed out, the two were closely connected through the doctrine of internal relations). There was an even more pronounced difference in their philosophical temperament. Moore had no doubts about many important things which he took himself to know with certainty. His was a quest not for certainty, but for the analysis of things which he was convinced we do know with certainty. Russell, by contrast, was made in the Cartesian mould. His aim was to set knowledge on the firm foundations of certainty: first, mathematical knowledge, which he attempted to erect on the foundations of pure logic alone (rather than resting satisfied with the Peano axioms), and subsequently (in so far as is possible) empirical knowledge of mind and matter. Hence he approved of the Cartesian method of doubt. We do not know in advance where methodical doubt will lead us, and there is no reason to suppose that it will leave intact the humdrum certainties which Moore cited.

19   Russell examined the matter in detail in ch. 26 of his *Principles of Mathematics*.

20   I am grateful to Ray Monk for pointing this out to me.

21   Russell, *My Philosophical Development*, pp. 35f.

22   Russell, *The Autobiography of Bertrand Russell, 1872–1914* (Allen and Unwin, London, 1967), pp. 67f.

23   See Russell, *Portraits from Memory and Other Essays* (Allen and Unwin, London, 1956), p. 24. The next major mathematical influence on Russell occurred in 1900, 'the most important year in my intellectual life', as he later wrote ('My Mental Development', in *The Philosophy of Bertrand Russell*, ed. P. A. Schilpp (Library of Living Philosophers, Inc., Evanston, Ill., 1946), p. 12), when he encountered Peano at the International Congress of Philosophy in Paris. He described this

meeting as 'a turning point in my intellectual life'. While reading the works of Peano, he wrote, 'it became clear to me that his notation afforded an instrument of logical analysis such as I had been seeking for years' (*Autobiography 1872–1914*, p. 144). The encounter with Peano and his ideas transformed Russell's work on *The Principles of Mathematics*, most of which was drafted or rewritten over the following five months.

It is noteworthy that in the concluding chapter of his *History of Western Philosophy* (1946), on 'The Philosophy of Logical Analysis', Russell attributes the origin of what *he* understood by 'analytic philosophy' to 'the achievements of mathematicians who set to work to purge their subject of fallacies and slipshod reasoning' (p. 857).

24   Russell, *My Philosophical Development*, pp. 14f. In his preface to *Our Knowledge of the External World*, Russell generously characterized the writings of Frege as 'the first complete example' of 'the logical-analytic method in philosophy'. It is indeed true that Frege's philosophy of mathematics can be so characterized. However, Russell's conception of analysis evolved independently of Frege's, and the application of the 'analytic method' (as Russell understood it) to philosophy in general (in particular to epistemology, ontology and metaphysics) was the work of Russell (and Moore).

25   He later wrote: 'The definition of number to which I was led . . . had been formulated by Frege sixteen years earlier, but I did not know this until a year or so after I had rediscovered it' (*My Philosophical Development*, p. 70). The *Principles* was originally intended to be the first volume of a two-volume work, the second of which was to be written in collaboration with Whitehead. As it turned out, the second volume was never written, its place being taken by the far more sophisticated three-volume *Principia Mathematica*.

26   The matter is illuminatingly discussed in P. Hylton, *Russell, Idealism and the Emergence of Analytic Philosophy* (Clarendon Press, Oxford, 1990), ch. 6.

27   Poincaré, who disliked mathematical logic and had accused it of barrenness, exclaimed gleefully: 'It is no longer sterile, it begets contradiction.' Whitehead, to whom Russell communicated the startling news, failed to console him by quoting Browning's *The Lost Leader*: 'never glad confident morning again'.

28   Gottlob Frege (1848–1925) studied mathematics at Jena and Göttingen universities (1869–73), completing his doctoral dissertation 'On a Geometrical Representation of Imaginary Figures in a Plane' in 1873. His *Habilitationsschrift* 'Methods of Calculation based upon an Amplification of the Concept of Magnitude' was on mathematical analysis, and contained the seeds of his subsequent generalization of the mathematical theory of functions to logic. He became a *Privatdozent* at Jena in 1874, where he taught for the rest of his career. His three pivotal works were *Conceptual Notation* (1879), *The Foundations of Arithmetic* (1884) and his two-volume *The Basic Laws of Arithmetic* (1893, 1903). He retired in 1918, but continued writing until his death.

29   For more detail on Russell's conception of philosophy, see Volume 1, 'The nature of philosophy', §1; for his views on logic and logical truths, see Volume 2, 'Grammar and necessity', §5; for some of his views on language, see Volume 1, 'Augustine's picture of language: *das Wesen der Sprache*', §5.

30   For more detailed discussion, see Volume 4, 'A note on negation', and Volume 1, 'Augustine's picture of language', §4; for a comprehensive examination of Frege and Wittgenstein's early criticisms of his philosophy of logic, see G. P. Baker, *Wittgenstein, Frege and the Vienna Circle* (Blackwell, Oxford, 1988), pp. 1–166, to which I am much indebted.

31   B. Russell, *Philosophical Essays* (Longmans and Green, London, 1910), ch. 7.
32   In such cases, he argued, understanding is not a multiple relation, but a dual relation between the person and a pure form. For the logical proposition, unlike 'Socrates preceded Plato', has no constituents.
33   B. Russell, 'On Scientific Method in Philosophy', repr. in *Collected Papers*, vol. 8 (Allen and Unwin, London, 1986), pp. 65f.
34   G. Frege, 'Sources of Knowledge of Mathematics and the Mathematical Natural Sciences', in his *Posthumous Writings* (Blackwell, Oxford, 1979), p. 273, and 'Numbers and Arithmetic', ibid., pp. 279f.
35   He was probably thinking here of Frege's Axiom V, which was the source of the set-theoretic paradox.
36   See also G. Frege, 'Boole's Logical Calculus and the Concept-script', in *Posthumous Writings*, p. 18; 'Introduction to Logic', ibid., p. 194n; 'Sources of Knowledge of Mathematics and the Mathematical Natural Sciences', ibid., p. 272; and BLA i. §§17f.
37   Frege, 'Logic', in *Posthumous Writings*, p. 128.
38   G. Frege, 'Function and Concept', repr. in his *Collected Papers* (Blackwell, Oxford and New York, 1984), p. 156.
39   Frege, 'Logic', p. 6.
40   'Logic', in *Posthumous Writings*, p. 143; 'Sources of Knowledge in Mathematics and the mathematical natural Sciences', p. 270; *Philosophical and Mathematical Correspondence* (Blackwell, Oxford, 1980), p. 68.
41   Frege, letter to Husserl dated 30 Oct.–1 Nov. 1906, in *Philosophical and Mathematical Correspondence*, pp. 67f.
42   G. Frege, 'Logical Generality', in *Posthumous Writings*, p. 259.
43   G. Frege, 'Number', in *Posthumous Writings*, p. 266.
44   For a more detailed investigation of Frege's attitude to language and its relation to thought, see G. P. Baker and P. M. S. Hacker, *Frege: Logical Excavations* (Blackwell, Oxford, and Oxford University Press, New York, 1984), ch. 3, and *idem*, 'Dummett's Frege or Through a Looking-glass Darkly', *Mind*, 92 (1983), pp. 239–46.
45   B. Russell, 'The Philosophy of Logical Atomism' (1918), repr. in *Collected Papers*, vol. 8, p. 205.
46   Ibid., p. 176.

Chapter 2   The Achievement of the *Tractatus*

1   Erwin Panofsky, *Problems from Titian, Mostly Iconographic* (New York University Press, New York, 1969), p. 18.
2   The analogy holds, as we shall see, for the second stage of Wittgenstein's work, viz. the *Investigations*. One might even say that *On Certainty* stands to the rest of the corpus as the Rondanini Pietà stands to the rest of Michelangelo's sculpture – an unfinished fragment, unlike all that precedes it. It is not, perhaps, 'inaccessible to all', but it is the beginning of a foray into epistemology which promises to revolutionize that branch of philosophy no less than Wittgenstein's previous work revolutionized the philosophy of logic, of language, of mathematics and philosophical psychology. How this new interest might have developed, however, is, and will remain, unfathomable.
3   Unlike Frege, however, he did not think of propositions, thoughts or senses of expressions as denizens of a 'third realm' of abstract entities, or of numbers as abstract objects.
4   For a detailed account of the character and limitations of Frege's anti-psychologism, see G. P. Baker and P. M. S. Hacker, 'Frege's Anti-psychologism', in *Perspectives*

on Psychologism, ed. M. A. Notturno (Brill, Leiden, 1989), pp. 75–127. Frege was by no means the first to object to psychologism in post-Kantian thought on the Continent. He was anticipated by Krug, Bolzano and Lotze. Similarly, the Absolute Idealists were not alone in the nineteenth century in objecting to psychologism in the British tradition (not only among classical empiricists, but also in the contemporary work of Hamilton and Boole), for Jevons and Spencer sided against psychologism in logic, arguing rightly that it compromised the objectivity of logic and mathematics.

5 G. Frege, 'Logic', in *Posthumous Writings* (Blackwell, Oxford, 1979), p. 145.
6 Ibid., p. 128.
7 L. Wittgenstein, *Letters to C. K. Ogden*, ed. G. H. von Wright (Blackwell, Oxford, and Routledge and Kegan Paul, London and Boston, 1973), p. 50.
8 He was later to change his view on the *nature* of the good order in natural language, but not his criticism of Frege and Russell.
9 B. Russell, 'Meinong's Theory of Complexes and Assumptions', repr. in *The Collected Papers of Bertrand Russell*, vol. 4: *Foundations of Logic 1903–5* (Routledge, London and New York, 1994), p. 473.
10 Wittgenstein was later to relinquish the thesis of bipolarity, arguing instead that the concept of a proposition is a family resemblance concept. The members of the family include such diverse cousins as propositions of arithmetic, theorems of geometry, ethical and aesthetic propositions, scientific generalizations, laws of nature, empirical descriptions, historical propositions, avowals of experience, fictional propositions, theological propositions, propositions of the 'world picture', etc. These display a multitude of overlapping similarities and differences. Bipolarity applies only to a subclass of propositions. Nevertheless, he continued to insist upon an internal relation between the concept of a proposition and the concepts of truth and falsity (PI §136). And his criticisms of his predecessors hold independently of his own conception of the bipolarity of the proposition in the *Tractatus*.
11 However, unlike Husserl's *Logical Investigations* (1900–1), which conforms even more closely to the Augustinian paradigm, the *Tractatus* rejected the referential conception of meaning for logical constants.
12 He was later to defend the *autonomy* of language and grammar and to deny that a language is answerable to reality for its structure (see pp. 79–81, and, in more detail, Volume 4, 'The arbitrariness of grammar and the bounds of sense').
13 That relations are objects according to the *Tractatus* has been disputed; see below, ch. 4, n. 43.
14 It has been suggested that the *Tractatus* was also realist in a further sense: viz., that it propounded a form of realism, as opposed to anti-realism, in its account of meaning. This is both anachronistic and confused. Realism in semantics is identified with truth-conditional theories of meaning, and is contrasted with notional theories of meaning associated with assertion-conditions. However, in the sense currently understood, the *Tractatus* did not espouse a truth-conditional account of meaning. For although it did indeed argue that the sense of a molecular proposition is given by its truth-conditions, it did not argue (and given the conception of truth-conditions in the book, it would have been absurd to argue) that the sense of an elementary proposition is given by its truth-conditions. An elementary proposition, according to the *Tractatus*, does not have any *truth-conditions*. (See pp. 52f., and in more detail, P. M. S. Hacker, *Insight and Illusion – Themes in the Philosophy of Wittgenstein* rev. edn (Clarendon Press, Oxford, 1986), pp. 61–4, 322–35; and G. P. Baker and P. M. S. Hacker, *Language, Sense and Nonsense* (Blackwell, Oxford, 1984), chs 5–6.)

15   That there was a form of idealism in the *Tractatus* has been argued in Volume 3, 'Behaviour and behaviourism', §2, 'I and myself', §1, and 'The world of consciousness', §1, but it was not a form of 'dogmatic' or 'problematic' idealism. I referred to it in Volume 3 as 'transcendental solipsism'. For a detailed account of his early solipsism, see Hacker, *Insight and Illusion*, ch. 4. Further evidence for this suggestion is to be found in a letter of Russell's and in a coded passage in the pre-*Tractatus* notebooks (see B. F. McGuinness, *Wittgenstein, A Life: Young Ludwig (1889–1921)* (Duckworth, London, 1988), pp. 106, 225). See also Frege's letter to Wittgenstein, dated 3 April 1920.

16   See G. E. M. Anscombe, *An Introduction to Wittgenstein's* Tractatus, 4th edn (Hutchinson University Library, London, 1971), p. 78.

17   Wittgenstein later withdrew his claim that rules of inference are superfluous, without, however, reverting to the position of Frege and Russell. Rules of inference, he later argued, are rules of grammar, and are not independent of the meanings of the constituent expressions between which entailment holds (see Volume 2, 'Grammar and necessity', §5, and G. P. Baker, *Wittgenstein, Frege and the Vienna Circle* (Blackwell, Oxford, 1988), pp. 130–5).

18   This is a little understood feature of the *Tractatus*, which is commonly credited with introducing truth-table definitions of the logical connectives and the truth-tabular decision procedure for the propositional calculus. This is quite mistaken, as Wittgenstein himself later pointed out. His innovation, he later said, was to use truth-tables as *symbols for molecular propositions* (LFM 177). They are in effect an alternative notation to Russell's truth-functional notation, enabling one to dispense altogether with the logical connectives (LWL 52; AWL 135f.). The motivation was wholly philosophical: to show the essential difference between a proposition of logic and a description of a state of affairs, and to make clear that logical propositions have nothing to do with self-evidence.

19   Wittgenstein argued that the sense of a universal generalization is a function of *the senses* of the elementary propositions of the common form involved, since the understanding of the generalization depends on understanding the corresponding elementary propositions. Since '$(x)fx$' entails 'fa', he explained universal quantification as the simultaneous assertion of all propositions of the form 'Φx'. It was crucial to his account of the quantifiers as operations, and hence to their topic neutrality, that elementary propositions be logically independent. When he later relinquished the independence thesis, he also had to abandon the idea of T/F notation as a generally valid notation for the display of tautologies. He also had to abandon his account of the quantifiers (a consideration wholly independent of the availability of a decision procedure for the predicate calculus, which had never been his concern). He relinquished the commitment to their topic neutrality, arguing instead that there are as many different kinds of generality as there are different forms of singular propositions, that 'there are as many different "alls" as there are different "ones"' (PG 269).

20   Every proposition of logic, Wittgenstein argued, can be rewritten in the form of a *modus ponens* (TLP 6.1264). This does not fit the tautology '$p \vee \sim p$', although it is true that in T/F notation there is no difference between '$p \vee \sim p$' and '$p \supset p$'. Perhaps he meant that '$p \supset p$' can be rewritten in the form '$p \mathbin{\&} (p \supset p) \supset p$'.

21   For a detailed description of his later views, see Volume 2, 'Grammar and necessity', and Baker, *Wittgenstein, Frege and the Vienna Circle*, ch. 4.

22   There was something misleading, however, about this doctrine. For analysis would reveal structures with which we are *unfamiliar*: e.g. that generalizations consist of infinite logical sums or products, or that propositions ascribing to a particular a

determinate of a determinable must contain real numbers (as he argued briefly in 1929) in order to budget for degrees of qualities. This can hardly be denied to be new knowledge!

23   Anthony Kenny, following Dummett (*Origins of Analytic Philosophy* (Duckworth, London, 1993), p. 5), has argued that the 'linguistic turn' is to be dated to Frege's *The Foundations of Arithmetic* of 1884, 'when Frege decided that the way to investigate the nature of number was to analyse sentences in which numerals occur' (A. J. P. Kenny, *Frege* (Penguin, Harmondsworth, 1995), p. 211). However, if the principle that the way to investigate the nature of X is to analyse sentences in which 'X' occurs signals the linguistic turn in philosophy, then the turn is to be dated to Bentham's *Chrestomathia* of 1816. Bentham's form of the context principle rightly stressed that the sentence is, as Wittgenstein was later to argue (PI §49), the minimal move in a language-game:

> But by anything less than an entire proposition, i.e. the import of an entire proposition, no communication can take place. In language, therefore, the *integer* to be looked for is an entire proposition – that which logicians mean by the term logical proposition. Of this integer, no one part of speech, not even that which is most significant, is anything more than a fragment; and, in this respect, in the many-worded appellative, *part of speech*, the word *part* is instructive. By it, an intimation to look out for the integer of which it is the part may be considered as conveyed. A word is to a *proposition* what a *letter* is to a word. (*Chrestomathia*, appendix No. IX, 'Hints towards the Composition of an Elementary Treatise on Universal Grammar', in *The Works of Jeremy Bentham*, ed. J. Bowring. (Tait, Edinburgh, 1843), vol. 8, p. 188)

Like Frege, Bentham thought that certain kinds of names have a meaning, even though they do not stand for any idea. Unlike Frege, his interest was in names of what he called 'fictitious entities' (e.g. 'obligation', 'a right'), and his concern was to show not that they signify abstract entities in a 'third realm', but rather that they have a meaning – contribute to the meaning of the sentence in which they occur – even though they do not stand for anything. This is to be demonstrated by means of *paraphrasis* – i.e. 'that sort of exposition which may be afforded by transmuting into a proposition, having for its subject some real entity, a proposition which has not for its subject anything other than a fictitious entity' (*Essay on Logic*, in *Works*, vol. 8, p. 246). Thus the term 'obligation' is to be explained by embedding it in a sentence (an operation Bentham denominated 'phraseoplerosis'), and then 'exhibiting another [sentence] which shall present exactly the same import' but without containing the problematic expression in question. Note that in the paraphrastic elimination of names of fictitious entities, it should not 'for a moment so much as be supposed that . . . the reality of the object is to be denied in any sense in which in ordinary language the reality of it is assumed' (*Chrestomathia*, appendix No. IV, 'Essay on Nomenclature and Classification', section XX, in *Works*, vol. 8, p. 126). Although the context principle, whether in its Benthamite or in its Fregean form, is of great importance, its introduction does not warrant the appellation 'the linguistic turn in philosophy'. But one might say that Bentham, like Frege, was one of the many precursors of twentieth-century analytic philosophy.

Chapter 3   The Impact of the *Tractatus*: The Vienna Circle

1   Established for, and held by, the great physicist Ernst Mach from 1895 to 1901, and subsequently occupied (1902–6) by the equally distinguished physicist Ludwig Boltzmann.

2   Friedrich Waismann (1896–1959) was born in Vienna. He read mathematics and

physics at the University of Vienna, where he was taught by Hahn and Schlick. He began his career as a teacher of mathematics, subsequently becoming an unofficial assistant to Schlick. It was through Schlick that he met Wittgenstein and became involved in the doomed project of *Logik, Sprache, Philosophie* (see p. 41). He represented Wittgenstein's point of view at the international conferences organized by members of the Circle and their affiliates in Prague in 1929 and Königsberg in 1930. His main publication from his Viennese days was *Introduction to Mathematical Thinking* (1936, tr. 1951), a lucid exposition of a Wittgensteinian philosophy of mathematics. For his subsequent career in Oxford, see pp. 153, 163–8.

3   Herbert Feigl (1902–88) was born in Reichenberg in the Sudetenland, read physics and physical chemistry in Munich, but left for Vienna in 1922 in order to study under Schlick. He wrote his doctorate on 'Chance and Law: An Epistemological Investigation of Induction and Probability in the Natural Sciences'. It was, apparently, at his and his friend Friedrich Waismann's instigation that Schlick was induced to form the discussion group that grew into the Circle. In 1929 he published *Theorie und Erfahrung in der Physik*. For his later career in the United States, see pp. 183f.

4   Hans Hahn (1879–1934) belonged to the 'Ur-Kreis' that had been formed in his student days at the University of Vienna (see n. 7 below). A distinguished mathematician, he had a lively interest in philosophy and scientific methodology. He taught at the University of Czernowitz before the war, and later, having been invalided out of the army, at Bonn. In 1921 he accepted appointment to a chair in mathematics at Vienna. It was through his influence that Schlick was offered the professorship the following year, and he was also instrumental in electing Carnap to an instructorship in 1926. In his obituary, Philipp Frank remarked of his old friend that he 'may be regarded as the real founder of the Vienna Circle'. Prior to Carnap's arrival, it was Hahn more than anyone else who directed the interest of the Circle towards modern logic.

5   Otto Neurath (1882–1945) studied mathematics at the University of Vienna (where Frank and Hahn were fellow students) and economics in Berlin. He was one of the prime moving spirits of the Circle, indefatigable in organizing congresses, arranging for publications, and fostering extensive foreign contacts. His own major interests were in sociology and social theory, economic and social planning, and educational method (particularly visual and diagrammatic methods). Passionately opposed to metaphysics, he advocated a behaviourist social theory. It was he who induced Carnap's 'physicalist turn' in the early 1930s. He was the main advocate of the 'unity of science' characteristic of the Circle and the primary organizer of the project of the *International Encyclopaedia of Unified Science* (see p. 59).

6   Felix Kaufmann (1895–1949) studied in Vienna under Hans Kelsen, receiving a doctorate in law in 1920 and in philosophy in 1922. He became a *Privatdozent* in the law faculty there. His early writings were in legal philosophy, where he tempered Kelsen's Kantianism with Husserl's phenomenological epistemology. He was a regular attender of the meetings of the Circle, with no less interest in the philosophy of mathematics than in the philosophy of law and the social sciences. In 1930, he published *Das Unendliche in der Mathematik und seine Ausschaltung* (tr. Paul Foulkes in *The Infinite in Mathematics*, ed. Brian McGuinness (Reidel, Dordrecht, 1978)). In 1934, he published his *Methodenlehre der Sozialwissenschaften*, which bears more of a phenomenological impress than that of positivist philosophy of social science (as exemplified by Neurath, e.g.). For his later years in the United States, see p. 186.

7   The pre-war 'Ur-Kreis', later referred to affectionately as 'prehistoric', included most notably Philipp Frank, Hans Hahn, Richard von Mises and Otto Neurath.

They met in an old Viennese coffee-house on Thursday evenings for discussions about the philosophy of science (see H. Feigl, 'The *Wiener Kreis* in America' (1969), repr. in *Herbert Feigl: Inquiries and Provocations, Selected Writings 1929–1974*, ed. Robert S. Cohen (Reidel, Dordrecht, 1981), p. 58.

8 The name originated simultaneously in Scandinavia, with Eino Kaila's *Der logistische Neopositivismus* (1930) and Ake Petzäl's *Logistischer Positivismus* (1931) (see G. H. von Wright, 'Analytic Philosophy – a Historico-Critical Survey', in *The Tree of Knowledge and Other Essays* (Brill, Leiden, 1993), p. 34), and in the United States with Albert Blumberg's and Herbert Feigl's 'Logical Positivism: A New Movement in European Philosophy', *Journal of Philosophy*, 28 (1931), pp. 281–96. It was disliked by some members of the Circle, since it misleadingly suggested a connection with Comte's nineteenth-century positivism. To that extent, the alternative name 'logical empiricism' was preferable, suggesting, correctly, a synthesis of Machian and classical empiricism with the new logic, replacing psychological analysis by logical analysis.

9 Rudolf Carnap (1891–1970) was born in Ronsdorf in Germany. He studied philosophy, mathematics and physics at Jena (where he attended three courses given by Frege) and Freiburg. After serving in the war, he wrote his doctorate on space (1921). He became friends with Reichenbach, who introduced him to Schlick in 1924. Schlick offered him an instructorship in Vienna in 1926. Throughout the mid-1920s he worked on his first major book *Der logische Aufbau der Welt* (1928). From 1931 to 1935 he held the chair of natural philosophy at the German university in Prague. His second major work was *The Logical Syntax of Language* (1934). He emigrated to the United States in 1936. For his later work and career, see pp. 187–9.

10 Hans Reichenbach (1891–1953) was born in Hamburg. He studied at the universities of Berlin, Munich and Göttingen, obtaining his doctorate from the University of Erlangen with a dissertation on probability, a theme which was to preoccupy him for the rest of his life. Though never a member of the Circle, his close friendship with Carnap and attendance at the frequent congresses kept him in touch with developments in Vienna. For his later career in the United States, see p. 185.

11 Russell anticipated them in *Our Knowledge of the External World* (1914), 'Lectures on Logical Atomism' (1918), and *Analysis of Mind* (1921), but he had reservations with respect to empiricism which they did not share (as is evident, *inter alia*, in his later paper 'The Limits of Empiricism', PAS, 26 (1935–6), pp. 131–50).

12 Feigl wrote: 'The spirit of enlightenment, the spirit of Galileo, of Hume, and of the French Encyclopedists is fully alive again in the contemporary encyclopedists of a unified science' ('Logical Empiricism' (1943), repr. in *Readings in Philosophical Analysis*, ed. H. Feigl and W. Sellars (Appleton-Century-Crofts, New York, 1948), p. 5).

13 *The Scientific Conception of the World: the Vienna Circle* (Reidel, Dordrecht, 1973), p. 8. Subsequent references in the text to this pamphlet will be flagged 'Manifesto'; for its origin, see p. 41.

14 R. Carnap, *The Logical Structure of the World*, tr. R. A. George (Routledge and Kegan Paul, London, 1967), p. xviii. *Der logische Aufbau* was published in 1928, and the preface is dated May of that year.

15 In his 1929 introduction to the projected volume by Waismann (see p. 41), which is printed in F. Waismann, *Logik, Sprache, Philosophie*, ed. G. P. Baker and B. F. McGuinness (Reclam, Stuttgart, 1976), pp. 11–23. The above quotation is taken from pp. 20, 21.

16   Reported by von Wright, 'Analytic Philosophy, a historico-critical survey', p. 34.
17   The record of the discussions from Dec. 1929 to Dec. 1931 is F. Waismann's
      WWK.
18   J. Jörgensen, *The Development of Logical Empiricism*, repr. in *Foundations of the Unity
      of Science*, vol. 2, ed. O. Neurath, R. Carnap and C. Morris (University of Chi-
      cago Press, Chicago, 1970), pp. 868 and 874. Carnap concurred: 'In the Vienna
      Circle, a large part of Ludwig Wittgenstein's *Tractatus Logico-Philosophicus* was read
      aloud and discussed sentence by sentence. . . . Wittgenstein's book exerted a strong
      influence upon our Circle' ('Intellectual Autobiography', in *The Philosophy of Rudolf
      Carnap*, ed. P. A. Schilpp (Open Court, LaSalle, Ill., 1963), p. 24.
19   V. Kraft, *The Vienna Circle: The Origin of Neo-positivism – a Chapter in the History
      of Recent Philosophy* (1953; Greenwood Press, New York, 1969), p. 16.
20   Reported by K. Menger in his introduction to H. Hahn, *Philosophical Papers* (Reidel,
      Dordrecht, 1980), p. xii.
21   Carnap, 'Intellectual Autobiography', p. 24.
22   A. J. Ayer, *Language, Truth and Logic*, preface to 1st edn (Penguin, Harmondsworth,
      1971), p. 41; originally published by Gollancz, London, 1936.
23   For the curious and sad history of this work, which ultimately saw the light of day
      only posthumously (in a very different form from that originally envisaged) as *The
      Principles of Linguistic Philosophy*, ed. R. Harré (Macmillan, London, 1965), and in
      Logik, Sprache, Philosophie, see G. P. Baker, '*Verehrung und Verkehrung*: Waismann
      and Wittgenstein', in *Wittgenstein: Sources and Perspectives*, ed. G. C. Luckhardt
      (Cornell University Press, Ithaca, NY, 1979), pp. 243–85, as well as his preface to
      G. P. Baker, ed., *Wittgenstein and Waismann: Dictations and Preparatory Studies for
      'Logic, Language and Philosophy'* (Routledge, London and New York, forthcoming).
24   Schlick's preface to *Logik, Sprache, Philosophie*, p. 23.
25   This was the dominant conception shared by the classical empiricists, and clearly
      articulated by Hume. A variant upon it was revived by nineteenth-century Ger-
      man psychologism, which Frege criticized. As previously pointed out, the young
      Wittgenstein accepted Frege's anti-psychologism, with the deleterious consequence
      that crucial *philosophical* issues were swept under the carpet.
26   The main proponent of this view was, as we have seen, Russell. He wrote that
      philosophy 'is essentially one with science, differing from the special sciences only
      by the generality of its problems', and that the new philosophy 'conceives that all
      knowledge is scientific knowledge, to be ascertained and proved by the methods
      of science' (*Sceptical Essays* (Allen and Unwin, London, 1928), p. 71). To be sure,
      the latter claim was consonant with the view of the *Tractatus* and that of members
      of the Circle. But Russell never embraced the non-cognitive conception of phi-
      losophy, conceiving of philosophical knowledge as part of 'science'.
27   Including both speculative and transcendent metaphysics, such as the philosophies
      of Hegel, Bradley and Heidegger, and the Kantian conception of metaphysics as
      engaged in eliciting the synthetic a priori truths that are allegedly presupposed
      by the possibility of (conceptualized) experience. Although, as we have seen, the
      Tractatus was itself a metaphysical treatise, one of its salient doctrines was the
      ineffability of metaphysical truths; any attempt to say what can only be shown by
      language must result in transgressing the bounds of sense. Hence part of the pro-
      gramme for future philosophy was to curb once and for all the metaphysical
      impulse.
28   See, e.g., the extensive debates on the nature of analysis in *Analysis*, founded in
      1933, and the symposia on philosophy and analysis in the *Proceedings of the Aristo-
      telian Society*: e.g. S. Stebbing, 'The Method of Analysis in Metaphysics', PAS, 33

(1932–3), pp. 65–94; and 'Some Puzzles about Analysis', PAS, 39 (1938–9), pp. 69–84; M. Black, 'Philosophical Analysis', PAS, 33 (1932–3), pp. 237–58; M. Black, John Wisdom and M. Cornforth, 'Is Analysis a Useful Method in Philosophy', PASS, 13 (1934), pp. 53–118; A. E. Duncan-Jones and A. J. Ayer, 'Does Philosophy Analyse Common-Sense', PASS, 15 (1937), pp. 139–76. The debate about what philosophers ought to be doing far outstripped the doing, so much so that when Ryle, in 1946, was asked by Paton to contribute a volume to the new Hutchinson series, he decided 'that what the subject and the clients of the subject needed was not any more lapidary statements to colleagues of what philosophy was and wasn't, but a full scale application of these lapidary ideas to some integral and comprehensive philosophers' tangle. The thing to be done was to *show working* the thing we had been telling each other was the only thing that would work. Not a treatise on Method, but a treatise *with* a method – a philosophical treatise with a meta-philosophical moral' (G. Ryle, 'Paper read to the Oxford Philosophical Society 500th Meeting, 1968', in his *Aspects of Mind*, ed. R. Meyer (Blackwell, Oxford, 1993), pp. 104f.). Hence *Concept of Mind*.

29 M. Schlick, 'The Turning Point in Philosophy', *Erkenntnis*, 1 (1930–1), pp. 1–11, repr. in *Logical Positivism*, ed. A. J. Ayer (Free Press, Glencoe, Ill., 1959), p. 54.

30 M. Schlick, 'The Future of Philosophy', repr. in his *Gesammelte Aufsätze* (Georg Olms Verlag, Hildesheim, 1969), p. 131.

31 R. Carnap, 'The Elimination of Metaphysics through the Logical Analysis of Language', *Erkenntnis*, 2 (1931–2), pp. 219–41, repr. in *Logical Positivism*, ed. Ayer, p. 77.

32 R. Carnap, *The Logical Syntax of Language* (Routledge and Kegan Paul, London, 1937), p. 279.

33 Later, Ayer was to introduce the new conception of philosophy into Britain with the following remark: 'The philosopher is not in a position to furnish speculative truths, which would, as it were, compete with the hypotheses of science, nor yet to pass a priori judgements upon the validity of scientific theories, but his function is to clarify the propositions of science, by exhibiting their logical relationships, and by defining the symbols which occur in them' (*Language, Truth and Logic*, p. 42).

34 Kraft, *Vienna Circle*, pp. 26f. Again, it must be stressed that 'propositions of science' included not only the propositions of science *stricto sensu*, but the whole range of empirical propositions.

35 The *Tractatus* had argued that these are ineffable necessary truths about the nature of any possible language. It is less clear whether the Circle would have accepted, let alone insisted upon, this necessitarian claim. But its members did accept these theses in the form specified.

36 W. E. Johnson, *Logic* (Cambridge University Press, Cambridge, 1921), pt. I, ch. 7, §7.

37 Carnap, 'Intellectual Autobiography', p. 24.

38 Letter from Wittgenstein to Waismann, July 1929, about the Manifesto; quoted in M. Nedo and M. Ranchetti, *Wittgenstein, sein Leben in Bildern und Texten* (Suhrkamp, Frankfurt, 1983), p. 243.

39 O. Neurath, 'Sociology and Physicalism', *Erkenntnis*, 2 (1931–2), pp. 393–431, repr. in translation in *Logical Positivism*, ed. Ayer, p. 284.

40 For a detailed discussion of the historical background and development of the Circle's conventionalism, see G. P. Baker, *Wittgenstein, Frege and the Vienna Circle* (Blackwell, Oxford, 1988), pt. II.

41 It is by no means obvious, e.g., whether there is any such thing as an implicitly

defined *concept* without any 'interpretation', a pure form without any content. Even if one adopts the *Tractatus* view of formal concepts as variables, a variable is the common form of its range of values. In the absence of a stipulated range of values, it is nothing.

42   For a detailed account of Schlick's early conventionalism, see Baker, *Wittgenstein, Frege and the Vienna Circle*, pp. 187–206.

43   H. Hahn, 'The Significance of the Scientific World View, Especially for Mathematics and Physics', *Erkenntnis*, 1 (1930–1), pp. 96–105, repr. in Hahn, *Philosophical Papers*, pp. 21, 24.

44   Schlick, 'Form and Content, an Introduction to Philosophical Thinking', in *Gesammelte Aufsätze*, p. 223.

45   Carnap, 'Intellectual Autobiography', p. 24.

46   Carnap, 'The Old and the New Logic', *Erkenntnis*, 1 (1930–1), pp. 12–26, repr. in *Logical Positivism*, ed. Ayer, pp. 141f.

47   F. Waismann, 'Das Wesen der Logik', unpublished lecture, 1930.

48   H. Hahn, 'Logic, Mathematics and Knowledge of Nature', the second volume of the series *Einheitswissenschaft* (1933), the first four sections of which are reprinted in translation in *Logical Positivism*, ed. Ayer, p. 159. See also Ayer, *Language, Truth and Logic*, ch. 4. It is interesting to note that Russell too came to this belief. His philosophical development, in respect of mathematics and logic, was, as he put it, 'a gradual retreat from Pythagoras', forced in part by his encounter with Wittgenstein. Like members of the Circle, however, he mistakenly took Wittgenstein in the *Tractatus* to have argued that mathematical propositions are tautologies. In *My Philosophical Development* (Allen and Unwin, London, 1959), he wrote: 'I have come to believe, though very reluctantly, that [mathematics] consists of tautologies. I fear that to a mind of sufficient intellectual power, the whole of mathematics would appear trivial, as trivial as the statement that a four-footed animal is an animal' (pp. 211f.).

49   Hahn, 'Logic, Mathematics and Knowledge of Nature', pp. 158f. Carnap held that the difference between tautologies and arithmetical propositions was insignificant (see his 'Intellectual Autobiography', p. 47).

50   The analogy with a meaning-body is explained in PLP 234ff., PG 54, PI §138 and §559. If we misconceive the meaning of an expression as something *attached* to it (as the (Fregean) sense of an expression is often said to be), then it is as if each expression were akin to a geometrical solid – e.g. a square, prism, or pyramid – made of glass, and invisible save for one painted surface. The visible forms that can be produced by different combinations will be determined, as it were, by the combinatorial possibilities of the invisible solids behind the painted faces. This is a vivid representation of the conception of the meanings of expressions as *determining* which combinations they can enter into, what meaning the resultant combinations will have, and what follows from any given combination. Accordingly, one will misconceive the rules for the use of expressions as *describing* the combinatorial possibilities of 'meaning-bodies'. Against this picture, Wittgenstein argued that the meaning of an expression is no more 'attached' to it than the value of £5 is attached to a £5 note. Its meaning does not determine its combinatorial possibilities and consequences, but rather is *constituted* thereby.

51   Menger worked with Brouwer as a privaatdocent in Amsterdam from 1925 to 1927, and it was he who first adopted what he called 'a policy of logical tolerance' towards alternative logical calculi. He was appointed to the Chair in Geometry at the University of Vienna in 1927, and attended meetings of the Circle for the next decade.

52 The following discussion is derived from P. M. S. Hacker, *Insight and Illusion: Themes in the Philosophy of Wittgenstein*, rev. edn (Clarendon Press, Oxford, 1986), pp. 134–45.

53 In his 1957 addendum to his 1930–1 paper 'The Old and the New Logic', he wrote of ' "The principle of verifiability", first pronounced by Wittgenstein' (see *Logical Positivism*, ed. Ayer, p. 146).

54 B. von Juhos, 'The Methodological Symmetry of Verification and Falsification', in his *Selected Papers on Epistemology and Physics*, ed. G. Frey (Reidel, Dordrecht, 1976), pp. 134ff.

55 V. Kraft, *Vienna Circle*, pp. 31 and 197, n. 29.

56 Reported in D. A. T. Gasking and A. C. Jackson, 'Wittgenstein as Teacher', repr. in *Ludwig Wittgenstein: The Man and his Philosophy*, ed. K. T. Fann (Dell Publishing Co., New York, 1967), p. 54.

57 F. Waismann, 'A Logical Analysis of the Concept of Probability', *Erkenntnis*, 1 (1930–1), pp. 228–48; repr. in translation in his *Philosophical Papers*, ed. B. F. McGuinness (Reidel, Dordrecht, 1977), p. 5.

58 M. Schlick, 'Meaning and Verification', *Philosophical Review*, 45 (1936), pp. 339–69, repr. in his *Gesammelte Aufsätze*, p. 341. Rather curiously, Schlick connected this idea with the Wittgensteinian claim that philosophy is not a doctrine or theory but an activity. One must realize, he wrote, that 'philosophical activities can never be replaced and expressed by a set of propositions. The discovery of the meaning of any proposition must ultimately be achieved by some act, some immediate procedure, for instance, as the showing of yellow; it cannot be given in a proposition. Philosophy, the "pursuit of meaning", therefore cannot possibly consist of propositions; it cannot be a science. The pursuit of meaning consequently is nothing but a sort of mental activity' ('The Future of Philosophy', in *Gesammelte Aufsätze*, pp. 129f.). This was far removed from what Wittgenstein had in mind when he claimed that

> Philosophy is not a body of doctrine but an activity.
> A philosophical work consists essentially of elucidations.
> Philosophy does not result in 'philosophical propositions', but rather in the clarification of propositions. (TLP 4.112)

He did not mean that a philosophical work consists of ostensive definitions. Nor did his claim that philosophical truths can only be shown, not said, have anything to do with ostensive definitions.

59 Carnap, 'Elimination of Metaphysics Through Logical Analysis of Language', in *Logical Positivism*, ed. Ayer, p. 63.

60 Schlick, 'Meaning and Verification', in *Gesammelte Aufsätze*, p. 340. He added: 'If the preceding remarks about meaning are as correct as I am convinced they are, this will, to a large measure, be due to conversations with Wittgenstein which have greatly influenced my own views about this matter.'

61 One might say that they are indeed incompatible *now*, but that they were not incompatible *then* – for in the intervening decades the *concepts* have shifted.

62 The inspiration for this conception came from M. A. E. Dummett, who wrote:

> A verificationist theory of meaning differs radically from the account of meaning as given in terms of truth-conditions implicit in Frege's work and explicit in Wittgenstein's *Tractatus*. On a theory of the latter kind, the crucial notions for the theory of meaning are those of truth and falsity: we know the meaning of a sentence when we know what has to be the case for that sentence to be true. A verificationist account takes as central to the theory of meaning the entirely

different account of that by which we can recognize a sentence to be conclusively
shown to be true or to be conclusively shown to be false: we know the meaning
of a sentence when we are able to recognize it as conclusively verified or as
conclusively falsified whenever one or the other of these conditions obtains.
('The Significance of Quine's Indeterminacy Thesis', repr. in Dummett, *Truth
and Other Enigmas* (Duckworth, London, 1978), p. 379)

63   For a detailed account of the evolution of truth-conditional semantics and the
successive changes in the concept of a truth-condition, see G. P. Baker and P. M.
S. Hacker, *Language, Sense and Nonsense* (Blackwell, Oxford, 1984), ch. 4. For a
discussion of whether the *Tractatus* can be deemed a realist philosophy, see Hacker,
Insight and Illusion, rev. edn, pp. 62–5.

64   The *Tractatus* held that 'the meaning of simple signs must be explained to us if we
are to understand them' (TLP 4.026). This was conceived to be done by 'elucidations'
or 'clarifications' (*Erläuterungen*), which 'are propositions that contain the primitive
signs. So they can only be understood if the meanings of those signs are already
known' (TLP 3.263). In *Insight and Illusion* (rev. edn, pp. 75–7), I suggested that
his thought here was similar to Russell's in *Principia* *1: viz., that 'The primitive
ideas are *explained* by means of descriptions intended to point out to the reader
what is meant; but the explanations do not constitute definitions, because they
really involve the ideas they explain' (PM 91). A *Tractatus* elucidation, it seems,
was a bipolar proposition of the form 'This is *A*'. In a sense, it is an ostensive
definition misconstrued as a bipolar empirical proposition.

65   One of the reasons why the currently popular formulations in a neo-Tarskian
idiom are unsatisfactory is because they apply the predicate 'true' to *sentences*, viz.
' "*p*" is true iff *p*'. But it is no more *sentences* that are true or false than it is sentences
that are believed, disbelieved, proved or refuted, well-supported or disconfirmed.
We do not believe (disbelieve, prove, refute, support, disconfirm) sentences (a
well-supported sentence is presumably a well-propped-up inscription), but only
what can be asserted by their use. Yet we usually hope that *what* we believe is true;
we try to confirm or disconfirm what we believe to be true and to find adequate
support for what we believe. What we suspect or fear may be true, but we do not
suspect or fear sentences. What is true or false is also what is certain or doubtful,
convincing or implausible, credible or incredible, conjectured or discredited. But
these are not properties of sentences at all, or at least not in the same sense (an
incredible sentence might be one written in letters a mile high, a doubtful sentence
one of questionable grammaticality). Sentences may be English or French sentences, but the truths which they are used to express are not English or French
truths, let alone true *in* English or *in* French; just as what is said by an English or
French sentence, which may be exaggerated, cannot be exaggerated *in* English or
French. (See Baker and Hacker, *Language, Sense and Nonsense*, pp. 182–90.)

     Tarski's account of truth for a formal language seemed to Carnap to liberate
philosophy from restrictions which the *Tractatus* had placed upon what can be said,
in particular from the idea that nothing can be said about the relation of signs to
reality. This, however, was confused, arguably misconstruing the claims of the
Tractatus as well as accepting from Tarski the misguided idea that truth is a
metalinguistic property of sentences.

66   For a detailed account of Wittgenstein's conception of a hypothesis, see F. Waismann,
'Hypotheses', repr. in his *Philosophical Papers*, pp. 38–59.

67   M. Schlick, 'Positivism and Realism', *Erkenntnis*, 3 (1932–3), pp. 1–31, repr. in
translation in *Logical Positivism*, ed. Ayer, p. 88.

68   Schlick, 'Meaning and Verification', in *Gesammelte Aufsätze*, p. 341.

69 The term 'logical construction' here is not used in Russell's sense, but to signify the 'hypothesis' a priori determined by symptoms, which stand to it as cuts through a curve to the equation for the curve.

70 The *Aufbau* was published in 1928, a year before the Manifesto, but was begun in 1922, before Carnap had come into contact with the Vienna Circle. Originally its title was to be *Konstitutionssystem der Begriffe*, the final title being adopted on Schlick's suggestion.

71 Carnap, *Logical Structure of the World*, §§61–4.

72 R. Carnap, 'Logical Foundations of the Unity of Science', in *Foundations of the Unity of Science*, ed. Neurath et al., vol. 1 (3rd impression, 1971), p. 52.

73 Carnap, *Logical Syntax of Language*, §17.

74 Letter from Neurath to Waismann, dated 4 Aug. 1939, quoted by Baker, *'Verehrung und Verkehrung*: Waismann and Wittgenstein', p. 261.

75 See G. H. von Wright, 'Wittgenstein and the Twentieth Century', repr. in his *Tree of Knowledge*, p. 88, and 'The Myth of Progress', ibid., pp. 208f., to which I am much indebted.

76 Carnap, *Logical Structure of the World*, preface to 1st edn, pp. xvif.

Chapter 4   The Inter-war Years: Cambridge and Oxford

1 W. E. Johnson (1858–1931) read mathematics and later psychology at King's College, Cambridge. He was appointed to a university lectureship in Moral Sciences in 1896, teaching primarily psychology until the logician J. N. Keynes became University Registrar in 1911, after which Johnson lectured on logic. His main publication was his three-volume *Logic* (1921–4). A fourth volume on probability was planned, on which Johnson had long worked. After his death, Braithwaite extracted from his notes three articles, which were published in *Mind* in 1932.

2 Charles Dunbar Broad (1887–1971) read for the Natural Sciences Tripos and Moral Sciences Tripos at Trinity College, Cambridge (1906–10). In 1911 he was awarded a Prize Fellowship at Trinity (his essay was the basis for his first published book *Perception and Reality* (1914)). Instead of staying at Trinity, Broad chose to go to the University of St Andrews as assistant to G. F. Stout. In 1920 he was elected to the chair at Bristol University. He returned to Cambridge in 1923, and was elected Knightsbridge Professor of Moral Philosophy in 1933, a post he occupied until his retirement in 1953. His major works, apart from his commentary on McTaggart, were *Five Types of Ethical Theory* (1920), *Scientific Thought* (1923) and *The Mind and its Place in Nature* (1925).

3 C. D. Broad, 'Critical and Speculative Philosophy', in *Contemporary British Philosophy*, 1st ser., ed. J. H. Muirhead, (Allen and Unwin, London, 1924), p. 78.

4 'Si Russell savait, si Moore pouvait', he remarked apropos Russell's production of a different philosophical system every few years, and Moore's inability to produce one at all (ibid., p. 79).

5 Only the first two are mentioned in Broad's 'Critical and Speculative Philosophy'. All three are itemized in Lee's discussion of Broad's philosophy with Wittgenstein, and are derived from Lee's notes of Broad's lectures on 'Elements of Philosophy' in 1931. On the Principle of the Extreme Case, Wittgenstein conceded that it is advantageous to point out such cases in order to highlight ambiguities, but warned against trying to work out a theory which will incorporate both the normal and the extreme cases. He rejected Broad's Principle of Pickwickian Senses – it is the very last thing philosophy should do, for philosophy endeavours to clarify the ordinary meanings of terms that give rise to confusions, and only further confusions can

result from employing these very terms in a Pickwickian sense. He approved of the Transcendental Method, whereby one starts with what we know to be so, and examines the validity of what we suppose we know (LWL 73f.).

6 R. B. Braithwaite, 'Philosophy', in *University Studies*, ed. H. Wright (Nicholson and Watson, Cambridge, 1933), p. 1.

7 B. Russell, *The Autobiography of Bertrand Russell, 1914–44*, vol. 2 (Allen and Unwin, London, 1968), p. 57.

8 B. Russell, 'The Philosophy of Logical Atomism', in *The Collected Papers of Bertrand Russell*, vol. 8 (Allen and Unwin, London, 1986), p. 160.

9 B. Russell, *Introduction to Mathematical Philosophy* (Allen and Unwin, London, 1919), p. 205n.

10 So much so that Wittgenstein rejected it and wrote to Russell: 'When I actually saw the German translation of the Introduction, I couldn't bring myself to let it be printed with my work. All the refinement of your English style was, obviously, lost in translation and what remained was superficiality and misunderstanding' (R 47). Consequently Reclam refused to publish the book.

11 In the introduction to the second edition of *The Principles of Mathematics* (1937), he wrote: 'Logical constants, therefore, if we are to be able to say anything definite about them, must be treated as part of language, not as part of what language speaks about. In this way, logic becomes much more linguistic than I believed it to be at the time when I wrote the "Principles". It will still be true that no constants except logical constants occur in the verbal or symbolic expression of logical propositions, but it will not be true that these logical constants are names of objects, as "Socrates" is intended to be' (PrM, 2nd edn, pp. xi–xii). He continued, however, to think that logical propositions are perfectly general: 'no proposition of logic can mention any particular object. The statement "If Socrates is a man and all men are mortal, then Socrates is mortal" is not a proposition of logic; the logical proposition of which the above is a particular case is: "If x has the property of ϕ, and whatever has the property ϕ has the property ψ, then x has the property ψ, whatever x, ϕ, ψ may be"' (ibid., p. xi).

12 He wrote: 'I am much indebted to my friend Wittgenstein in this matter [of his view of the most important issues in philosophy]. I do not accept all his doctrines, but my debt to him will be obvious to those who read his book' (B. Russell, 'Logical Atomism', in *Contemporary British Philosophy*, 1st ser., ed. Muirhead, p. 371).

13 C. D. Broad, *Mind and its Place in Nature* (Kegan Paul, Trench, Trubner and Co., London, 1925), p. vii. Wittgenstein later remarked to Drury: 'Broad was quite right when he said of the *Tractatus* that it was highly syncopated. Every sentence in the *Tractatus* should be read as the heading of a chapter, needing further exposition. My present style is quite different; I am trying to avoid that error' (see M. O'C. Drury, 'Conversations with Wittgenstein', in *Recollections of Wittgenstein*, ed. R. Rhees (Oxford University Press, Oxford, 1984), p. 159). Despite Broad's dislike of Wittgenstein, when it came to the latter's application for Moore's chair in Cambridge in 1939, Broad remarked that to deny Wittgenstein the chair in philosophy would be like denying Einstein a chair in physics.

14 Frank Plumpton Ramsey (1903–1930) read mathematics at Trinity College, Cambridge (1920–3). He was elected to a Fellowship at King's College, Cambridge, in 1924, and was appointed university lecturer in mathematics in 1926. He made major contributions to the debate on the foundations of mathematics, to mathematics and economics, and was the originator of the subjective theory of probability.

15 F. P. Ramsey, 'Foundations of Mathematics', repr. in *Foundations: Essays in Philoso-*

phy, Logic, Mathematics and Economics, ed. D. H. Mellors (Routledge and Kegan Paul, London, 1978), p. 152.

16   Braithwaite, 'Philosophy', p. 20.

17   Ramsey, 'Facts and Propositions', repr. in *Foundations*, ed. Mellors, p. 57.

18   The idea that general propositions are not genuine propositions at all, but rules for generating propositions, was suggested by Hermann Weyl in his 1921 paper 'Über die neue Grundlagenkrise der Mathematik', *Mathematische Zeitschrift*, 10 (1921), pp. 39–79, which Ramsey read (see F. P. Ramsey, *Notes on Philosophy, Probabilty and Mathematics*, ed. M. C. Galavotti (Bibliopolis, Naples, 1991), p. 198n). What Weyl called 'Anweisung auf Urteile', Ramsey dubbed 'variable hypotheticals': 'Variable hypotheticals are not judgements but rules for judging "If I meet a ϕ, I shall regard it as a ψ". This cannot be *negated* but it can be *disagreed* with by anyone who does not adopt it' (Ramsey, 'General Propositions and Causality' (1929), repr. in *Foundations*, ed. Mellors, p. 137). Finite generalizations (e.g. 'All days of the week . . .'), he argued, are equivalent to conjunctions, but open generalizations (e.g. 'All men are mortal') are rules for judging.

19   Ramsey, 'Facts and Propositions', p. 44. I am indebted to Erich Ammereller and Laurence Goldstein for pointing out to me that the *Tractatus* was not committed to a correspondence theory of truth.

20   Richard Bevan Braithwaite (1900–90) read for the Mathematics and Moral Sciences Tripos at King's College, Cambridge, and was elected to a Fellowship at King's in 1924. He was appointed to a university lectureship (1928–34), and subsequently became Sidgwick Lecturer in Moral Science (1934–53). In 1953 he succeeded Broad as Knightsbridge Professor of Moral Philosophy. (See further below, n. 33.)

21   Braithwaite, 'Philosophy', p. 3.

22   This is misleading. Moore did not advocate an uncritical acceptance of common sense, and he did not think that common sense was infallible. But he did think that many propositions affirmed by common sense are known with certainty to be true, and are also incompatible with much that philosophers have said on the relevant subjects.

23   Braithwaite, 'Philosophy', p. 5.

24   Ibid., p. 23.

25   In his only published piece of writing between 1930 and his death, Wittgenstein wrote a letter to *Mind* in 1933, remonstrating against Braithwaite's misrepresentation of his views in the latter's essay 'Philosophy' in *University Studies*. It is true that in saying that tautologies are statements of how language is to be used, Braithwaite misrepresented Wittgenstein's view of tautologies. Apart from this flaw, Braithwaite roughly (perhaps too roughly) delineated Wittgenstein's principle of verification and his methodological solipsism, both of which he had propounded in his lectures in 1929–31. However, by the time Braithwaite published his article, Wittgenstein had abandoned both these positions.

26   Wisdom remained in Cambridge from 1934 until 1968. For those who were not privileged to attend Wittgenstein's classes, Wisdom's articles in the 1930s and 1940s 'were an indispensable source of information about the work of Wittgenstein' (R. Bambrough, ed., *Wisdom, Twelve Essays* (Blackwell, Oxford, 1974), p. vii). For his subsequent career, see p. 145.

27   It is noteworthy that Schlick delivered his lectures 'Form and Content' in London in 1932.

28   Norman Malcolm (1911–90) completed his first degree at the University of Nebraska, where his teacher was O. K. Bouwsma. He went to Harvard for graduate work, and came to Cambridge on a Harvard University Fellowship to study with

Moore, who had agreed to supervise his Ph.D. work. He remained in Cambridge from 1938 to early 1940, and was befriended by Wittgenstein, whose lectures he attended. After the war, he spent another year, 1946–7, in Cambridge, again attending Wittgenstein's classes. See further, pp. 146f.

29 N. Malcolm, 'Moore and Ordinary Language', in *The Philosophy of G. E. Moore*, ed. P. A. Schilpp (Northwestern University, Evanston, Ill., and Chicago, 1942), p. 349.

30 This conforms with the claim in the *Tractatus* (2.0251) that space, time and colour (being coloured) are forms of objects. In the *Proto-Tractatus* he had remarked, a little more perspicuously, that 'Space and time are forms of objects. In the same way colour (being coloured) is a form of visual objects' (PTLP 2.0251–2).

31 In the *Tractatus* he had thought that determinate exclusion, on analysis, would reveal 'that the colour R contains all degrees of R and none of B and that the colour B contains all degrees of B and none of R' (RLF 168f.), thus displaying exclusion as a case of formal contradiction. Already in Vol. I (MS 105), 36ff. he realized that this would not work. In PR ch. 8 he gave a detailed argument explaining why (see P. M. S. Hacker, *Insight and Illusion, Themes in the Philosophy of Wittgenstein*, rev. edn (Clarendon Press, Oxford, 1986), pp. 108–12).

32 Alice Ambrose (b. 1906) read for her first degree at Millikin University, and did her Master's and Ph.D. degrees at the University of Wisconsin (1932). She was in Cambridge from 1932 to 1935, supervised by Moore and attending Wittgenstein's lectures, and obtained her Ph.D. from Cambridge in 1938. From 1937 she taught at Smith College in the United States. Her *Wittgenstein's Lectures, Cambridge 1932–1935*, compiled from her and Margaret Macdonald's lecture notes and including notes of informal discussions with Wittgenstein as well as a selection from the so-called Yellow Book, provides an invaluable picture of the evolution of his thought during these years. His influence upon her subsequent philosophy was paramount. In 1966 she wrote:

> His original insights into the nature of philosophical problems and theories have been for me an intellectual compass. What he taught us seemed to me then, as it does now, revolutionary and vastly promising for a subject whose problems, as time has shown, have no exits. There can be no doubt that his conception of philosophy lights up the labyrinth of language in which the philosopher wanders. His conception gives us a perspective in which the intractability of philosophical controversies finds an explanation and which promises the dissolution of the problems. . . . The view that philosophical positions are verbal structures with a false scientific façade is destructive of the treasured illusion that philosophers are in search of truth. But it compensates in full by improving our understanding of a time-honoured intellectual phenomenon. (*Essays in Analysis* (Allen and Unwin, London, 1966), Preface)

(See further pp. 147f.)

33 Braithwaite subsequently ploughed his own furrow, primarily in the fields of the philosophy of science, induction, probability and games theory, which he applied *inter alia* to moral philosophy. However, in his preface to his *Scientific Explanation* (Cambridge University Press, Cambridge, 1953), he wrote: 'I should not be philosophizing in the way I do had it not been my good fortune to have sat at the feet, in Cambridge, of G. E. Moore and of Ludwig Wittgenstein.' Mary Hesse reports 'his passionate declaration, in Senate–House debate [in the 1960s] on the criteria for a Ph.D., that only Wittgenstein in this century could be said to have made an original contribution to philosophy' (see PBA, 82 (1992), p. 370).

34 R. L. Goodstein (1912–85) read mathematics at Magdalen College, Cambridge, subsequently doing research there with Littlewood on transfinite numbers. He

attended Wittgenstein's lectures between 1931 and 1935. He taught mathematics at the University of Reading (1935–47), and was subsequently Professor of Mathematics at University College, Leicester (1948–77). He was the first person whose main interests were in mathematical logic to hold a chair in a British University. Most of his philosophical essays are published in his *Essays in the Philosophy of Mathematics* (Leicester University Press, Leicester, 1965). See further, p. 148.

35   A. Duncan-Jones became the first editor of the journal *Analysis*, founded in 1933 in collaboration with Stebbing, C. A. Mace and Gilbert Ryle. Its declared purpose was to publish 'short articles on limited and precisely defined philosophical questions about the elucidation of known facts, instead of long, very general and abstract metaphysical speculations about possible facts or about the world as a whole'. When Margaret Macdonald, who succeeded Duncan-Jones as editor, published a selection of articles from the journal in 1954 as *Philosophy and Analysis* (Blackwell, Oxford, 1954), she used as her epigram the quotation from the *Tractatus* 'The object of philosophy is the logical clarification of thoughts'.

36   G. A. Paul's paper 'Is There a Problem about Sense-data?' (PASS, 15 (1936)), is the *locus classicus* for an early (broadly Wittgensteinian) critical rejection of sense-datum theories of perception propounded by Russell, Moore, Broad, Price and Ayer in the inter-war years.

37   Rush Rhees (1905–89) was an American who had studied philosophy at Rochester University (1922–4) and then at Edinburgh, where his teachers were N. Kemp Smith and John Anderson. From 1928 to 1932, he was an assistant lecturer at Manchester, where J. L. Stocks held the chair. He spent 1932–3 in Innsbruck, working with Alfred Kastil, a Brentano scholar. In 1933, he registered as a doctoral student at Cambridge, where he was supervised by Moore. It was here that he first met Wittgenstein, and attended his lectures. He became one of Wittgenstein's closest friends and disciples (and on Wittgenstein's death was appointed one of his literary executors, together with Anscombe and von Wright). In 1937 he returned to Manchester as a temporary replacement for Stocks, and in 1940 went to Swansea, where he taught until his retirement in 1966 (see further, pp. 145f.).

38   Georg Henrik von Wright (b. 1916) came to Cambridge in early 1939, having completed a first degree at Helsingfors University under the supervision of Eino Kaila, who was championing logical positivism in Finland. Consequently, he was well versed in the writings of 'the new philosophy' of Russell, Wittgenstein (i.e. the *Tractatus*) and members of the Vienna Circle. For his doctorate, he wrote a dissertation on the justification of induction (published as *The Logical Problem of Induction*). He decided to go to Cambridge because of its 'impressive living tradition in inductive logic', of which Broad and Braithwaite were members. In Cambridge he attended Wittgenstein's lectures on the foundations of mathematics (now splendidly edited by Cora Diamond from the notes taken by R. G. Bosanquet, Norman Malcolm, Rush Rhees and Yorick Smythies). 'The strongest impression a man ever made on me', he wrote in his diary at the time. Wittgenstein's impact, he wrote in 1972–3 in his 'Intellectual Autobiography' for *The Philosophy of Georg Henrik von Wright*, ed. P. A. Schilpp and L. E. Hahn (Open Court, La Salle, Ill., 1989) 'was to shake me up', calling into question the basic principles of Carnapian logical positivism (in *Logical Syntax*), which he had imbibed under the influence of Kaila. He returned to Cambridge only in 1947, and attended Wittgenstein's final Cambridge lectures on the philosophy of psychology (see p. 138). His fine 'Biographical Sketch' is published together with Malcolm's *Ludwig Wittgenstein: A Memoir* (Oxford University Press, Oxford, 1958). For further details of his career, see pp. 143–5.

294   *Notes to pp. 77–83*

39   G. Ryle, 'Ludwig Wittgenstein', *Analysis*, 12 (1951), repr. in his *Collected Papers*, vol. 1 (Hutchinson, London, 1971), p. 249.
40   But it is still important that T/F notation shows the dispensability of the connectives in those cases where the propositions are independent, and supports the criticism of Frege and Russell that the logical constants are not names. Moreover, once severed from the idea of the essence of the elementary proposition, it does point in the right direction for the elucidation of the character of the propositions of logic.
41   See NB 62; TLP 2.01, 2.03–2.032, 2.1–2.15, 3.14–3.21, 4.2211, 5.542. For discussion see P. M. S. Hacker, 'Laying the Ghost of the *Tractatus*', repr. in *Ludwig Wittgenstein: Critical Assessments*, ed. Stuart Shanker (Croom Helm, London, 1986), vol. 1, pp. 76–91.
42   See B. Rundle, *Grammar in Philosophy* (Clarendon Press, Oxford, 1979), pp. 339–48, for an illuminating discussion of this issue.
43   There has been extensive controversy over the characterization of the objects of the *Tractatus*, and many commentators have suggested that Wittgenstein did not know what kinds of things objects might turn out to be, but only that there had to be such logical atoms if representation was to be possible. This is a misstatement of the correct point that a *logico-philosophical* treatise should not deal with the application of logic: 'The *application* of logic decides what elementary propositions there are. What belongs to its application, logic cannot anticipate' (TLP 5.557). 'Some Remarks on Logical Form' was his only attempt to deal with the application of logic. Others, on the basis of a misinterpretation of TLP 3.1432 ('Instead of, "The complex sign '*aRb*' says that *a* stands to *b* in the relation R", we ought to put, "that '*a*' stands to '*b*' in a certain relation says *that aRb*"'), have argued that relations are not objects, and that no names of relations would occur in an ideal notation. The point of Wittgenstein's remark is not to suggest that relation-names disappear on analysis, but rather that the proposition is a fact (TLP 3.1432 is subordinate to 3.142 – 'Only facts can express a sense' – and 3.143 – 'Although a propositional sign is a fact, this is obscured by the usual form of expression in writing or print'). What represents in the sign *aRb* is the fact that '*a*' flanks 'R' on its left, and '*b*' flanks it on its right (in speech the representing fact would be the fact of the temporal ordering of the names). The matter has been discussed in the *Analytical Commentary* (see, e.g. Exg. §§50, 104). Definitive refutation of such views is provided by Wittgenstein's own explanation to Desmond Lee of TLP 2.01 ('An atomic fact is a combination of objects (entities, things)'): 'Objects etc. is here used for such things as a colour, a point in visual space etc. . . . . "Objects" also include relations; a proposition is not two things connected by a relation. "Thing" and "relation" are on the same level. The objects hang as it were in a chain' (LWL 120). See, for a more comprehensive discussion, Hacker, *Insight and Illusion*, rev. edn, pp. 65–72.
44   Of course, one can pin a name written on a name-plate on to an object, but what makes it a name of the object is its use and the way in which it is explained. Being pinned on to the object does not make it a name (a label saying 'Shake well' is not the name of the object on which it is stuck), and *meaning* by the name *this* object is not a better kind of connection.
45   Or states of affairs. For present purposes the distinction does not matter.
46   And Strawson was later to argue that he had distorted the use of definite descriptions in his paraphrastic account; see P. F. Strawson, 'On Referring', *Mind*, 59 (1950).
47   It was only in the last year and a half of his life that Wittgenstein focused sharply

upon Moore's defence of common sense, and what he then unfolded was a picture of epistemology far removed from anything Moore ever dreamt of, and indeed from the whole tradition of epistemology (see *On Certainty*).

48   He remarked to von Wright: 'Why should philosophy in the age of airplanes and automobiles be the same (thing) as in the age when people travelled by coach or on foot?' Yet, von Wright observes, he thought of his own activity as the legitimate heir to the search for truth which, since the days of the ancient Greeks, had been cultivated under the name 'philosophy' (see G. H. von Wright, 'Intellectual Autobiography', p. 42).

49   It is noteworthy that of the forty-five numbered sections on the nature of philosophy in the *Investigations*, §§89–133, fifteen are derived from the 'Big Typescript'. The chapter on philosophy there, derived from MSS completed in 1930–1, already represents the transformation in his conception of the subject.

50   This part of his later philosophy has been the least influential and the least understood. There are various reasons for this, quite apart from the fact that the philosophy of mathematics is not a subject of widespread interest among philosophers. First, his philosophy of mathematics is arguably the most revolutionary of all his revolutionary philosophical work. The imaginative leap necessary to free oneself from received conceptions in this domain and to apprehend that Wittgenstein was trying to undermine the presuppositions of logicism, formalism and intuitionism alike has evidently proved difficult. For there has been a persistent temptation to locate his philosophical reflections on the existing map of possibilities, and to misclassify his views as a form of strict finitism or an extreme existentialist form of constructivism, anti-realism or 'full-blooded conventionalism'. Secondly, the difficulty of grasping his radical conception was undoubtedly exacerbated by the piecemeal, and often heavily edited, publication of his mathematical writings. Thirdly, the most influential reviews of the *Remarks on the Foundations of Mathematics* displayed profound misunderstandings of Wittgenstein's philosophy of mathematics, and they unfortunately moulded the approach of most philosophers who grappled with this most difficult of texts over the next decades (see pp. 139f.).

 Some indication of the trajectory of Wittgenstein's thought was given in Volume 2, 'Grammar and necessity'. Since the influence of his philosophy of mathematics on the development of analytic philosophy has been negligible, I shall not discuss this subject further here, save to show that the accusation that he embraced an absurd form of so-called full-blooded conventionalism is misconceived (see pp. 255–64).

51   Alice Ambrose, H. M. S. Coxeter, R. L. Goodstein, Margaret Masterman and Francis Skinner.

52   Not so in Vienna, where communication with Waismann and Schlick continued sporadically (and extensive dictations were given), and his ideas were duly relayed to members of the Circle.

53   'Wittgenstein's Notes for Lectures on "Private Experience" and "Sense Data"' were first published in the *Philosophical Review*, 77 (1968), pp. 275–320, in an edited version by R. Rhees. They are derived from MSS 148, 149, 151. A much revised and expanded version has since been published in L. Wittgenstein, *Philosophical Occasions 1912–51*, ed. J. C. Klagge and A. Nordmann (Hackett, Indianapolis and Cambridge, 1993), pp. 202–88. Rhees's notes of the lectures Wittgenstein delivered on these subjects from mid-February until June 1936 were published in the journal *Philosophical Investigations*, 7 (1984), pp. 1–45 and 101–40, and reprinted in Klagge and Nordmann, eds.

54   See Volume 2, 'Two fruits upon one tree', for a discussion of the problems this

poses and the conclusions that can be drawn from the fact that it was even possible to envisage such different fruits growing from the same stock.

55 Passmore notes that when Wittgenstein's later ideas finally reached Oxford, they 'were grafted on to an Aristotelian-philological stock; the stock has influenced the resultant fruits which, amongst other things, are considerably drier and cooler than their Cambridge counterparts' (*One Hundred Years of Philosophy* (Penguin, Harmondsworth, 1968), p. 441).

56 H. A. Prichard (1871–1947) read Literae Humaniores at New College, was a Fellow of Hertford (1895–8) and subsequently of Trinity (1898–1924). He was elected to the new White's Chair in Moral Philosophy (1928–37). The only book he published during his lifetime was *Kant's Theory of Knowledge* (1909), in which he defended a Cook-Wilsonian epistemology. His much more important book *Moral Obligation*, a collection of his papers and lectures, was published posthumously in 1949, as was his collection of papers on epistemology, *Knowledge and Perception* (1950).

57 It was amusingly said of Joseph that in his formidable tutorial teaching he was dedicated to the Socratic art of midwifery: he sought to bring forth error and strangle it at birth.

58 J. D. Mabbott, *Oxford Memories* (Thornton's, Oxford, 1986), p. 73.

59 An exception was F. C. S. Schiller (1864–1937), a disciple of William James. Schiller had studied at Balliol College and Cornell University before becoming a Fellow of Corpus Christi College (1897–1935). He had international links and an international reputation among pragmatists, but his influence in Oxford was negligible.

60 J. D. Mabbott (1898–1988) read Greats (the second part of the Literae Humaniores course) at St John's, where he was taught by J. L. Stocks. After a brief period at Bangor, he returned to St John's as a tutor in philosophy (1924), where he remained for the rest of his days, subsequently becoming President of the College. He was a member of the 'Wee Teas' (see p. 90 and n. 64). After the Second World War, he was, together with Ryle, the progenitor of the B.Phil. degree, which was a major contributory factor in making Oxford a great international centre for postgraduate philosophical studies. His writings were largely in political philosophy, *The State and the Citizen* (1947) being his best-known work.

61 Gilbert Ryle (1900–76) read Literae Humaniores and then Philosophy, Politics and Economics at Queen's (1919–24), where he was tutored by Paton (whom he described as 'an unfanatical Crocean – the main alternative to being a Cook-Wilsonian' (G. Ryle, 'Autobiographical', in *Ryle: A Collection of Critical Essays*, ed. O. P. Wood and G. Pitcher (Doubleday, New York, 1970), p. 2). He became a Student of Christchurch (1925–45), and was later elected to the Waynflete Chair in Metaphysics (1945–67). For discussion of his work and its relation to Wittgenstein's, see pp. 168–72.

62 Ryle, 'Autobiographical', p. 4.

63 A. J. Ayer, who succeeded Price in the Wykham Chair of Logic, wrote in his inaugural lecture (1960): 'In the sombre philosophical climate of the Oxford of that time, here was a bold attempt to let in air and light: a theory of perception in which the principles of British empiricism were developed with a rigour and attention to detail which they had in that context never received' ('Philosophy and Language', repr. in Ayer, *The Concept of a Person and Other Essays* (Macmillan, London, 1964), p. 1). Isaiah Berlin was similarly impressed by Price: 'The most admired philosopher of the thirties in Oxford was, I should say, Henry Price, whose lucid, ingenious and beautifully elegant lectures fascinated his audiences,

and were largely responsible for putting problems of perception in the centre of Oxford philosophical attention at this time' ('Austin and the Early Beginnings of Oxford Philosophy', in *Essays on J. L. Austin*, ed. Berlin et al. (Clarendon Press, Oxford, 1973), p. 2). Nevertheless, Price's writings, unlike Ryle's, belong to an 'intermediate' generation, uncomfortable in the world of their pre-war teachers, and not at home in the emerging linguistic style of analytical philosophy. His approach to problems of perception and of thinking (in his later book *Thinking and Experience* (1953)) was phenomenological rather than by way of linguistic analysis.

64 A breakaway group of the Scottish Free Church in the nineteenth century was dubbed 'The Wee Frees'. The Wee Teas were disbanded only in 1966, by which time, they thought 'the fires of revolt might have burnt low' (Mabbott, *Oxford Memories*, p. 78).

65 Ryle, 'Autobiographical', p. 6.

66 H. J. Paton, in his essay 'Fifty Years of Philosophy' (in *Contemporary British Philosophy*, 3rd ser., ed. H. D. Lewis (Allen and Unwin, London, 1956), pp. 335–54), remarked of the prevalent anti-psychologism: 'As to psychology, every hackle was up at the mere mention of its name . . . and the prevailing attitude was mirrored in the well-known story of the examinee who finished a not too impressive answer by saying, "Here Logic ends and Piscology and Error begin"' (p. 345).

67 G. Ryle, Introduction to *Collected Papers*, vol. 2 (Hutchinson, London, 1971), p. vii.

68 G. Ryle, 'Paper read to the Oxford Philosophical Society 500th Meeting', in *Ryle: Aspects of Mind*, ed. R. Meyer (Blackwell, Oxford, 1993), p. 106.

69 Ryle, 'Autobiographical', p. 5.

70 I am unable to discern how close their friendship was. Ryle referred to Wittgenstein, both in discussion and in print, as 'my friend' (and when criticizing him, he would preface his comments by 'although a genius and my friend'), an epithet not used lightly by men of his generation. Certainly they went on walks and walking holidays together. Ryle attended meetings of the Cambridge Moral Sciences Club, which Wittgenstein dominated. And he was one of the first in Oxford to read the *Blue Book*, in the 1930s. Wittgenstein's influence upon Ryle was very considerable; it was amusing to learn from Isaiah Berlin that when he asked Ryle in the 1950s whether Wittgenstein had had an influence upon his thinking, Ryle replied (in typical Rylean manner) 'Influence? – None at all. I learnt a great deal from him.' During the war, when Naomi Wilkinson, a cousin of Ryle's, asked Wittgenstein how many people understood his philosophy, he replied 'Two – and one of them is Gilbert Ryle' (see R. Monk, *Ludwig Wittgenstein: The Duty of Genius* (Jonathan Cape, London, 1990), p. 436). In 1949, Wittgenstein read at least part of Ryle's *Concept of Mind* (see p. 169).

71 At the Royaumont colloquium in 1958 Ryle remarked: 'It is certain that when I wrote "Systematically Misleading Expressions" I was still under the direct influence of the notion of an "ideal language" – a doctrine according to which there were a certain number of logical forms which one could somehow dig up by scratching away at the earth which covered them. I no longer think, especially not today, that this is a good method. I do not regret having travelled that road, but I am happy to have left it behind me' ('Discussion of Urmson's "The History of Analysis"', repr. in *The Linguistic Turn*, ed. R. Rorty (University of Chicago Press, Chicago and London, 1970), p. 305). The change in his views seems to have occurred in the late 1930s.

72 A. G. N. Flew, ed. *Logic and Language*, 1st ser. (Blackwell, Oxford, 1951), introduction, p. 5.

73   G. Ryle, 'Categories', repr. in his *Collected Papers*, vol. 2, p. 181.

74   As was pointed out in P. F. Strawson's 'Categories', in *Ryle: A Collection of Critical Essays*, ed. Wood and Pitcher, p. 187n. In this paper, Strawson sharpened Ryle's notion of a category. A categorial predicate, he argued, is a predicate which (a) is a priori acceptable for at least some individuals under all adequately identifying designations of that individual; (b) is either a priori acceptable or a priori rejectable for any individual whatever under all adequately identifying designations of that individual. A predicate is category-mismatched to an individual if and only if it implies a categorial predicate which is a priori rejectable for all adequately identifying designations of that individual.

75   Ryle himself being the exception. He wrote the first English review of Heidegger's book in *Mind*, 38 (1928). He characterized it as 'a big advance in the application of the "Phenomenological Method"', adding that he suspected it to be an advance towards disaster.

76   A. J. Ayer, *Part of My Life* (Oxford University Press, Oxford, 1978), p. 119.

77   Isaiah Berlin (b. 1909) read Literae Humaniores and Philosophy, Politics and Economics at Corpus Christi College, and was elected to a Prize Fellowship at All Souls in 1932. He was a Fellow of New College from 1938 until 1950, when he returned to All Souls. In the 1940s, as a result of a conversation during the war with the Harvard logician H. M. Sheffer, he abandoned philosophy for the history of social and political ideas. He was elected to the Chichele Chair of Social and Political Theory (1957–67), subsequently becoming the first President of Wolfson College.

78   See Berlin, 'Austin and the Early Beginnings of Oxford Philosophy', p. 3.

79   Ayer, *Part of My Life*, p. 120.

80   Among the regular attenders at this time were Schlick, Neurath, Waismann, Menger, Hahn, Gödel and Quine, who, like Ayer, was a visitor for six months.

81   Whitehead wrote: 'I can't imagine a greater blessing for English philosophical learning than the rise in Oxford of a vigorous young school of Logical Positivists. The assigning of the proper scope to their method, the discussion of the new problems which it raises or of the new light which it throws on old problems will revivify and reconstruct the presentation of the topics of philosophical thought which the new doctrine fails adequately to deal with. It will rescue the philosophy of the twentieth century from repeating its complete failure in the nineteenth century, when science and history overwhelmed it' (Ayer, *Part of My Life*, p. 163).

82   Paton wrote: 'Perhaps the flutter was only a mild one, but I should hesitate to say in print some of the things said about him at the time. Whoever may have failed in the art of communication, he certainly did not. He exposed the nature of Logical Positivism, if I may so express myself, in all its naked horror, and he did so with a plausibility of John Stuart Mill at his best' ('Fifty Years of Philosophy', p. 346). Mabbott described it as bringing a blast of fresh air to Oxford (*Oxford Memories*, p. 78). Grice reminisced that 'Oxford was rudely aroused from its semi-peaceful semi-slumbers by the barrage of Viennese bombshells hurled at it by A. J. Ayer, at that time the *enfant terrible* of Oxford philosophy' (H. P. Grice, 'Reply to Richards', in *Philosophical Grounds of Rationality*, ed. R. E. Grandy and R. Warner (Clarendon Press, Oxford, 1986), p. 48). Like Ryle, Grice had doubts: 'Many people, including myself, were greatly interested by the methods, theses, and problems which were on display, and some were, at least momentarily, inspired by what they saw and heard. For my part, my reservations were never laid to rest; the crudities and dogmatisms seemed too pervasive.'

83   John Langshaw Austin (1911–60) read Literae Humaniores at Balliol (1929–33), was elected to a Prize Fellowship at All Souls in 1933, and to a Fellowship at Magdalen in 1935. For further discussion of his career, see pp. 150–2, 172–5.

84   See Berlin, 'Austin and the Early Beginnings of Oxford Philosophy', p. 8.

85   Ibid., pp. 11f. He adds: 'the intellectual freshness and force, both of Austin and of Ayer, were such that although they were in a state of almost constant collision – Ayer like an irresistible missile, Austin like an immovable obstacle – the result was not a stalemate, but the most interesting, free, and lively discussions of philosophy that I have ever known' (p. 16).

86   It may well be that Austin's interest in speech-acts originates in Prichard's discussion of promising ('The Obligation to Keep a Promise', repr. In Prichard, *Moral Obligation* (Clarendon Press, Oxford, 1949), pp. 169–79).

87   Paton, 'Fifty Years of Philosophy', p. 350.

88   W. C. Kneale (1906–90) read Literae Humaniores at Brasenose (1923–7), and after a period of teaching at Aberdeen and Newcastle, became a Fellow of Exeter College (1933–60). He succeeded Austin in the White's Chair in Moral Philosophy (1960–6). (See further, p. 153.)

89   Grice, 'Reply to Richards', p. 48.

Chapter 5   The Achievement of the *Investigations*

1   In addition, *On Certainty* constitutes a fragment of a fresh departure into the field of epistemology. I do not mean that there are not extensive writings on epistemological themes in earlier works from which one could readily reconstruct 'Wittgenstein's epistemology'. But *On Certainty* is unique in concentrating upon this subject, and moves in a different direction from earlier reflections, even though there are anticipations.

2   It is perhaps noteworthy that among the papers he left was a folder on which was written 'The Philosophy of Psychology'. This folder contained the carbon copy of TS 227 (the final copy of the *Investigations*), but whether that was what it *originally* contained is impossible to say. Regardless, it seems to me highly improbable that the huge quantity of material which Wittgenstein wrote on the philosophy of psychology in his post-war phase was not intended to form, or would not have evolved into, a separate work.

    His decision to abandon his work on the philosophy of mathematics was taken in 1944 when he was staying with Rhees in Swansea, and seems to have coincided with the decision to continue the draft of the *Investigations* with the material on the private language, rather than with that on the philosophy of mathematics, as originally planned (see Volume 2, 'Two fruits upon one tree'). In the spring of 1944, when Wisdom sent Wittgenstein a short biographical entry about him for a biographical dictionary, Wittgenstein added to Wisdom's entry the sentence 'Wittgenstein's chief contribution has been in the philosophy of mathematics'. Two or three months later, when Wittgenstein was working on the remarks on the private language arguments as the sequel to PI §§1–189, Rhees asked him: 'What about your work on mathematics?' Wittgenstein answered with a wave of the hand: 'Oh, someone else can do that' (R. Monk, *Ludwig Wittgenstein: The Duty of Genius* (Jonathan Cape, London, 1990), p. 467). It is noteworthy, however, that as late as 1949 he wrote: 'I want to call the enquiries into mathematics that belong to my Philosophical Investigations "Beginnings of Mathematics"' (MS 169, 37). It therefore seems plausible to suppose that the work that had originally been envisaged as a continuation of *Investigations* §§1–189 was now conceived as a further book. Whether Wittgenstein saw *himself* as the one who would complete it, or whether this was a task he preferred to leave to his literary executors is another question.

3 He told Malcolm that he really thought that in the *Tractatus* he had provided a perfected account of a view that is the *only* alternative to the viewpoint of his later work (see N. Malcolm, *Ludwig Wittgenstein – A Memoir*, 2nd edn (Oxford University Press, Oxford, 1984), p. 58.

4 I. Berlin, 'The Hedgehog and the Fox', repr. in his *Russian Thinkers* (Hogarth Press, London, 1978), pp. 22–81.

5 He remarked: 'Hegel seems to me to be always wanting to say that things which look different are really the same. Whereas my interest is in showing that things which look the same are really different' (M. O'C. Drury, 'Conversations with Wittgenstein', repr. in *Ludwig Wittgenststein: Personal Recollections*, ed. R. Rhees (Blackwell, Oxford, 1981), p. 171).

6 G. H. von Wright, 'A Biographical Sketch', in Malcolm, *Ludwig Wittgenstein – A Memoir*, p. 14.

7 The link between verificationism and intuitionistic mathematics, on the one hand, and the repudiation of the law of excluded middle, on the other, were alien to the logical positivists. Verificationism, as propounded by members of the Vienna Circle, was firmly connected with the classical logical calculus of *Principia* and the *Tractatus*.

8 F. P. Ramsey, 'Universals', repr. in his *Foundations, Essays in Philosophy, Logic, Mathematics and Economics*, ed. D. H. Mellor (Routledge and Kegan Paul, London, 1978), pp. 20f.

9 One might add a sixth: viz. the implied conception of epistemology. For if Wittgenstein is right about the salient features of these five domains, then much of traditional epistemology is in ruins. As noted above, Wittgenstein repudiated any form of foundationalism in epistemology. He repudiated all traditional strategies that seek to *demonstrate* (e.g. by analogy or by inference to the best explanation) that we can and do know other people's mental states, etc. He argued that scepticism is not to be refuted or answered; rather, we should show that it is nonsense, that it transgresses the bounds of sense. However, since epistemological issues are not in the foreground of the *Investigations* (with the exception of the discussion of induction), I have refrained from discussing this in detail.

10 See G. P. Baker and P. M. S. Hacker, *Language, Sense and Nonsense* (Blackwell, Oxford, 1984), ch. 9, §4.

11 For detailed criticism of the theoretical linguists' idea that speaking a language is a matter of following rules which are innate or 'buried deep in the unconscious mind' but not explicitly known by or used by speakers of the language, and which can be discovered by linguists, see ibid., chs 5–9.

12 For detailed discussion of these matters, see ibid., chs 6–7. For Grice's defence of the correspondence between the logical operators of the calculus and their natural language counterparts, see pp. 154, 322 n. 37.

13 Wittgenstein rarely pursues what I have here called 'connective analysis' in a systematic way in consecutive remarks (an exception is his discussion of psychological concepts in *Zettel* §§472ff.). His preference in practice was for therapeutic analysis, on the one hand, and, connected with it, the production of the *erlösende Wort* (the redeeming or magical word), which will break the hold of a picture that holds one captive, on the other. Nevertheless, as is evident from essays in the volumes of *Analytical Commentary*, one can often assemble his numerous remarks on specific concepts (e.g. sensation, thinking, imagining, intending, meaning something) to

yield a perspicuous representation of the grammar of the relevant concept, which can, without distortion, be characterized as a form of 'connective analysis'. But it is noteworthy that he rarely gathered his own material together in this way.

14   In the case at hand, Wittgenstein was concerned with the concept of the infinite and its use in the calculus of arithmetic.

15   If one is tempted on think otherwise, one might reflect on Siamese twins who both complain of a pain at the point of juncture (PI §253; see Exg.). If they both have a pain in the head with the same phenomenal characteristics, the location of the pain cannot be picked out as differentiating A's pain from B's pain. Of course, what we call 'having a pain in the same place' just is having a pain in corresponding locations. The grammar of pain location is quite different from the grammar of the location of objects.

16   Of course, that is not to deny that a great deal was achieved by way of clarification of our concepts and eradication of conceptual confusions. If one compares the philosophical quest for ordering our concepts to arranging the books in a library (BB 44), and achievement in philosophy to separating books which appear to belong together but do not, while juxtaposing books which actually belong together, then much of the endeavour of the past has rightly sorted some of the 'books' – but often put them on the wrong shelf. And, to stretch Wittgenstein's simile, the catalogue of the 'books' has typically been placed among the books themselves.

17   As Ramsey remarked, 'If you can't say it, you can't say it – and you can't whistle it either.'

18   In a simile which is echoed in Ryle's later talk of the logical geography of concepts, Wittgenstein observed: 'One difficulty with philosophy is that we lack a synoptic view. We encounter the kind of difficulty we should have with the geography of a country for which we had no map, or else a map of isolated bits. This country we are talking about is language and the geography its grammar. We can walk about the country quite well, but when forced to make a map, we go wrong' (AWL 43).

19   B. Russell, *My Philosophical Development* (Allen and Unwin, London, 1959), pp. 210f., quoting from his early article 'The Study of Mathematics' (1907). Russell characterized his development from the early years of the century as a gradual retreat from such Pythagorean mysticism. 'All this', he wrote in 1959, 'though I still remember the pleasure of believing it, has come to seem to me largely nonsense, partly for technical reasons and partly from a change in my general outlook upon the world. Mathematics has ceased to seem to me non-human in its subject matter. I have come to believe, though very reluctantly, that it consists of tautologies. . . . I think that the timelessness of mathematics has none of the sublimity that it once seemed to me to have, but consists merely in the fact that the pure mathematician is not talking about time. I cannot any longer find any mystical satisfaction in the contemplation of mathematical truth' (ibid., pp. 211f.).

20   In his lectures he remarked that one could say that aesthetic explanation is not causal. Like certain psychoanalytic explanations, characteristic aesthetic explanation must command the assent of the person who demands it (LA 18). He must see connections of which he was previously unaware *as* connections. It does not follow, of course, that there is no room whatever for causal explanation in the resolution of aesthetic questions. Rather, the characteristic forms of aesthetic explanation are not hypothetical, but descriptive; they point out formal, not causal, connections.

21   Again, one need not deny the relevance of *any* form of causal, hypothetical explanation in anthropology in order to accept Wittgenstein's arguments against Frazer.
In the case of Frazer's attempted explanations of the ritual murder of the *Rex
Nemorensis*, Wittgenstein held it to be misguided to try to explain the practice by
reference to a flimsy historical hypothesis concerning false beliefs that gave rise to
magic, conceived as proto-science. For the hermeneutical questions which Frazer
raised are not answered by his aetiological hypotheses, but would be answered by
a perspicuous arrangement of the kinds of facts Frazer so painstakingly assembled
(see P. M. S. Hacker, 'Developmental Hypotheses and Perspicuous Representations',
Iyyun: The Jerusalem Philosophical Quarterly, 41 (1992), pp. 277–99).

22   Wittgenstein wrote nothing on political or legal philosophy, and next to nothing,
apart from the backward-looking 'Lecture on Ethics' (1929), on moral philosophy.
It is not clear whether his strictures apply in the same way to these domains of
philosophical reflection (see p. 243).

23   In the following I have drawn freely on the more extensive discussion of this theme
in P. M. S. Hacker, *Insight and Illusion: Themes in the Philosophy of Wittgenstein*
(Clarendon Press, Oxford, 1986), rev. edn, ch. 7, §3.

24   This does not mean that he despised metaphysics, as some members of the Vienna
Circle did. He remarked to Drury that he regarded some of the great metaphysical
systems of the past as among the noblest productions of the human mind. But,
he added, 'For some people it would require an heroic effort to give up this sort
of writing' (see Drury, 'Conversations with Wittgenstein', p. 120). That 'heroic
effort' is precisely what is needed by those who are tempted by the mysteries of
Platonism in mathematics (such as Frege), the wonders of mental substances (such
as Descartes), the vision of logic as the mirror of the logical structure of the world
(such as the author of the *Tractatus*). It involves abandoning certain combinations
of words as senseless (e.g. 'abstract objects', 'immaterial substance', 'constituents
of facts'), and that itself may necessitate a painful resignation (BT 406).
    Wittgenstein's admiration for the great metaphysical systems of the past, cou-
pled with his vehement repudiation of the scientistic metaphysics of his day, may
be explained by the fact that the historical contexts in which Plato, Descartes or
Kant wrote were so different – hence their endeavours must be viewed differently,
and their results, though unacceptable, evaluated differently. It may also be that he
admired the dedicated striving of classical metaphysicians for a *Weltanschauungs-
philosophie*, while viewing modern scientistic metaphysics as crude and vulgar.

25   How this claim bears upon the enterprise of 'descriptive metaphysics' introduced
by P. F. Strawson's *Individuals* (Methuen, London, 1959) is discussed later (see
pp. 176f.).

26   In his 'official writings', Wittgenstein had next to nothing to say about 'transcendent metaphysics', which seeks to prove the existence of God or the immortality of
the soul. From his 'occasional writings' (e.g. *Culture and Value*) and reported conversations, it is evident that he thought that the attempt to *prove* such things is
absurd, involving a profound misunderstanding of religious belief and of the role
of assertions concerning God, the soul or the afterlife in the forms of life of
religious believers. The conception which he advocated has been highly influential
among some writers on philosophical theology, and hotly contested by others.

27   The primary interest of such propositions stemmed from the fact that they are
neither empirical nor analytic, i.e. reducible to explicit definitions and the laws of
logic. Hence they seemed (to Husserl, e.g.) to vindicate the category of synthetic
a priori truths.

28   That is not to say that the adoption of a new notation is always a triviality. In

certain circumstances, it may be momentous (as in the case of the adoption of decimal notation or arabic numerals in arithmetic, or talk of unconscious motivation in psychology). But that is not typically the case in metaphysical speculation.

29 It is interesting that, but for the fact that Moore had already used this famous quotation from Butler as the motto for *Principia Ethica*, Wittgenstein would have liked to use it for the *Investigations* (see G. Kreisel, 'The Motto of "Philosophical Investigations" and the Philosophy of Proofs and Rules', *Grazer Philosophische Studien*, 6 (1978), pp. 15ff.).

30 Russell, *My Philosophical Development*, p. 117.

31 Wittgenstein, contrary to what has sometimes been said of him, had no objection to Cantor's new calculus with transfinite cardinals, but only to his interpretation of its significance – e.g., to the idea that he had discovered a new and wonderful domain of mathematical entities. In response to Hilbert's remark that no one was going to turn mathematicians out of Cantor's paradise, Wittgenstein said, 'I wouldn't dream of trying to drive anyone out of this paradise. I would try to do something quite different: I would try to show you that it is not a paradise – so that you'll leave of your own accord. I would say, "You're welcome to this; just look about you"' (LFM 103).

32 As Wolfgang Köhler had done in his book *Gestalt Psychology*, against which this remark was directed (see Volume 4, 'Methodology in philosophical psychology', §1).

33 Here, in the sciences, by contrast with philosophy, the conceptual confusions arise not when language is like an engine idling (PI §132), but when it is doing work – badly.

34 This paragraph has been taken from P. M. S. Hacker, *Appearance and Reality: A Philosophical Investigation into Perception and Perceptual Qualities* (Blackwell, Oxford, 1987), pp. 51f.

35 Wittgenstein sometimes seems to take the more extreme line of identifying the two (perhaps in PI §43; LFM 192), which is ill-advised. Elsewhere he is more cautious, arguing that use *determines* meaning (PI §139), that the use of a word may teach us its meaning (PI pp. 212, 220), and examines cases in which a difference in use is not tantamount to a difference in meaning (LW I §§279–304; LW II, p. 2). See pp. 248f.

36 An ostensive definition by reference to a sample is best viewed as akin to a substitution rule in which the *definiens* (the indexical 'this', the gesture of pointing, and the sample pointed at) constitute a partly 'concrete' symbol. So, e.g., instead of saying 'The curtains are red', one can equally well say 'The curtains are *this colour* ↗' (pointing at a sample of red).

37 See M. O'C. Drury, 'Some Notes on Conversations with Wittgenstein', in *Ludwig Wittgenstein: Personal Recollections*, ed-Rhees, p. 94.

Chapter 6   Wittgenstein's Impact upon Post-war Analytic Philosophy

1 Save for his contribution to R. T. Grant and E. B. Reeve, *Observations on the General Effects of Injury in Man with Special Reference to Wound Shock*, Medical Research Council Special Report Series, no. 277 (HMSO, London, 1951). Although not mentioned by name, his hand is evident in the general discussion of the concept of shock, in which the fluctuation between criteria and symptoms of shock is identified as a primary source of unclarity. (See Volume 3, 'Criteria', §2.)

2 Elizabeth Anscombe (b. 1919) read Literae Humaniores at St Hugh's College, Oxford (1937–41), before going to Newnham College, Cambridge, as a research student (1942–6). She returned to Oxford as a Junior Research Fellow of Somerville

(1946–52), where she remained until her election to Wittgenstein's old chair in Cambridge (1970), in succession to Wisdom. For further details of her career, see p. 145.

3   P. T. Geach (b. 1916) read Literae Humaniores at Balliol before the war, and studied at Cambridge between 1945 and 1951. He taught at the University of Birmingham from 1951 until 1966, when he was elected to a chair at the University of Leeds, where he taught until his retirement in 1981.

4   S. E. Toulmin (b. 1922) obtained his Ph.D. at Cambridge in 1948, and was elected to a Fellowship at King's College in 1947. He lectured in the philosophy of science at Oxford (1949–55), before taking up a chair at the University of Leeds (1955–9). Between 1960 and 1964 he was director of the Nuffield Foundation Unit for the History of Ideas, subsequently emigrating to the United States, where he taught at Brandeis, Michigan State and Chicago.

5   P. F. Strawson, 'Review of Wittgenstein's *Philosophical Investigations*', *Mind*, 63 (1954), p. 70. There were some serious misinterpretations in Strawson's otherwise outstanding review. These turned largely on the matter of privacy: of naming, recognizing, identifying and reporting sensations in one's own case, of criteria for sensation and their employment. They were corrected by Malcolm in his review of the *Investigations* in *Philosophical Review*, 63 (1954).

6   'An Interview with Professor Sir Peter Strawson', by E. Pivcevic, *Cogito*, 1989, p. 7.

7   G. Ryle, 'Ludwig Wittgenstein', *Analysis*, 12 (1951), repr. in his *Collected Papers* (Hutchinson, London, 1971), vol. 1. The quotations are taken from the latter publication, pp. 249 and 256–7.

8   G. Ryle, 'Review of Ludwig Wittgenstein: *Remarks on the Foundations of Mathematics*', repr. in his *Collected Papers*, vol. 1, p. 267.

9   B. Russell, 'Some Replies to Criticism', in *My Philosophical Development* (Allen and Unwin, London, 1959), pp. 216–17.

10   A. R. Anderson, 'Mathematics and the Language Game', *Review of Metaphysics*, 11 (1958), pp. 457–8.

11   Part I of the *Remarks on the Foundations of Mathematics* was as polished as the 1938 version of the *Investigations*, for which it was designed as the continuation, and that version was twice offered to Cambridge University Press for publication.

12   M. A. E. Dummett, 'Wittgenstein's Philosophy of Mathematics', *Philosophical Review*, 68 (1959), p. 324. It is noteworthy that the 'errors' of which Wittgenstein is accused turn out to be not mistakes in the mathematics, but philosophical arguments with which his critics disagree (and sometimes simply misunderstand). In an interview with Joachim Schulte in 1987, Dummett explained how he wrote this influential review:

> I in fact reviewed the *Remarks on the Foundations of Mathematics* when it first came out. I felt simultaneously stimulated and frustrated by the book. I'll tell you the experience that I had: I had tried to write this review in the usual way, with the book beside me and looking up passages in it, and I found that I couldn't do it. I couldn't get a grip on Wittgenstein's thought to determine just what he was saying. When I tried to summarise his views and quote bits in illustration, I found it all crumbling in my fingers. So I put the book away and deliberately thought no more about the review for about three months. Then, with my now impaired memory of the book, I wrote the review – deliberately without opening the book again; because then some themes came into sharp focus which I know would grow hazy once more as soon as I opened the book again. Finally I inserted some references. (Michael Dummett, *Origins of Analytical Philosophy* (Duckworth, London, 1993), pp. 173f.)

For criticism of this unfortunately influential review, see pp. 255–64.

13   P. Bernays, 'Comments on Ludwig Wittgenstein's *Remarks on the Foundations of Mathematics*', *Ratio*, 2 (1959); the quotations are from pp. 14 and 6 respectively.

14   For a discussion, see S. G. Shanker, 'Introduction: The Portals of Discovery', in his *Ludwig Wittgenstein: Critical Assessments* (Croom Helm, London, 1986), vol. 3, pp. 1–25. One might imagine a similarly uncomprehending review of the *Investigations* remarking that Wittgenstein writes as though natural languages existed solely for the purposes of asking builders to pass slabs, blocks and beams and of ascribing colours to objects by the use of indexicals. It is also noteworthy that the title Wittgenstein envisaged for the book he contemplated compiling from his voluminous writings, which was conceived to be complementary to the *Investigations*, was 'Beginning Mathematics' (see p. 299 n. 2).

15   Waismann's *Einführung in das mathematische Denken* (1936), translated as *Introduction to Mathematical Thinking* (1951), which was much influenced by Wittgenstein's work in the philosophy of mathematics in the early 1930s, seems to have made very little impact. Similarly, Ambrose's early articles, of which Wittgenstein disapproved, attracted relatively little attention (see n. 16), and covered only a limited range of his later concerns. A. G. D. Watson's paper, of which Wittgenstein approved, 'Mathematics and its Foundations', *Mind*, 47 (1938), pp. 440–51, on, *inter alia*, Gödel's incompleteness theorem, seems to have gone unnoticed.

16   By, e.g., A. Ambrose, *Essays in Analysis* (Allen and Unwin, London, 1966), chs 1–5 (papers written between 1937 and 1965) and numerous other papers in various collections; R. L. Goodstein, 'Wittgenstein's Philosophy of Mathematics', in *Ludwig Wittgenstein: Philosophy and Language*, ed. A. Ambrose and M. Lazerowitz (Allen and Unwin, London, 1972), pp. 271–86; G. P. Baker and P. M. S. Hacker, Volume 2 of the *Analytical Commentary*, 'Grammar and Necessity' (1985), and S. G. Shanker, both in his essays in the collection cited in n. 14 and his *Wittgenstein and the Turning Point in the Philosophy of Mathematics* (Croom Helm, London, 1987).

17   See G. P. Baker, *Wittgenstein, Frege and the Vienna Circle* (Blackwell, Oxford, 1988).

18   These three works have not been published, but copies of the typescripts have been deposited in the libraries of Trinity College, Cambridge, the Bodleian and Cornell University. The appendices to these volumes include lists correlating remarks of the various TS drafts of the *Investigations* with the final version, and correlating the numbered remarks of the *Investigations* with their *final* occurrence in the manuscripts.

19   See G. H. von Wright, *Wittgenstein* (Blackwell, Oxford, 1982), and *The Tree of Knowledge and Other Essays* (Brill, Leiden, 1993), chs 1, 2, 5.

20   G. H. von Wright, 'Intellectual Autobiography', in *The Philosophy of Georg Henrik von Wright*, ed. P. A. Schilpp and L. E. Hahn (Open Court, La Salle, Ill., 1989), p. 16.

21   Nevertheless, it is noteworthy that von Wright's enterprise is foreshadowed by one of the very few remarks on axiology in Wittgenstein's later writings: 'it could be said that the use of the word "good" (in an ethical sense) is a combination of a very large number of inter-related games, each of them as it were a facet of the use. What makes a single concept here is precisely the relationship between these facets' (PG 77).

22   Other important milestones on this road are his 'Freedom and Determination' (*Acta Philosophica Fennica*, 31 (1980), pp. 4–88) and his Tanner Lectures, 'Of Human Freedom' (*The Tanner Lectures on Human Values*, vol. 6, ed. S. M. McMurrin (Cambridge University Press, Cambridge, 1985), pp. 109–70.

23 See his 'Cause and Effect: Intuitive Awareness', repr. in *Ludwig Wittgenstein: Philosophical Occasions 1912–1951*, ed. J. Klagge and A. Nordmann (Hackett, Indianapolis, 1993), pp. 370–426.

24 See Ayer's account of the rift between himself and Wittgenstein in his autobiography *Part of My Life* (Oxford University Press, Oxford, 1978), pp. 304–6. Wittgenstein's anger is manifest in a note he wrote at the time. Some philosophers, he remarked, make much of the keys they have stolen (Ayer, Wisdom), but it does not matter; they cannot open any locks with them.

25 His later works are *Paradox and Discovery* (1965), a collection of his later papers, and *Proof and Explanation* (1990), his lectures at the University of Virginia in 1956–7, edited by S. Barker.

26 The only books he published were collections of papers, *Discussions of Wittgenstein* (Routledge and Kegan Paul, London, 1970) and *Without Answers* (Blackwell, Oxford, 1969). He left behind a voluminous *Nachlass*, currently being edited by D. Z. Phillips. One volume, shortly to be published, is entitled *Religion and Philosophy*; another, still in preparation, bears the provisional title 'The Reality of Discourse'.

27 G. Ryle, 'Paper read to the Oxford Philosophical Society 500th Meeting, 1968', in Ryle, *Aspects of Mind*, ed. R. Meyer (Blackwell, Oxford, 1993), p. 104.

28 Exceptions being his contributions to an Aristotelian Society symposium 'The Problem of Guilt' (PASS, 21 (1947)) and to *The Revolution in Philosophy*, ed. Ryle et al. (Macmillan, London, 1956), entitled 'G. E. Moore: Analysis, Common Usage and Common Sense'. His pre-war paper 'Is There a Problem about Sense Data?' continued to be most influential.

29 Preface to his collection of papers *Language and Philosophy* (Cornell University Press, Ithaca, NY, 1949). These remarks characterize his methods throughout his later works too. Though Black wrote numerous essays, which were duly published in collected papers, he never managed to bring his work together in a comprehensive book.

30 Repr. in his *Thought and Knowledge* (Cornell University Press, Ithaca, NY, 1977), pp. 159–69.

31 Repr. in *Investigating Psychology: Sciences of the Mind after Wittgenstein*, ed. J. Hyman (Routledge, London, 1991), pp. 27–47.

32 See G. H. von Wright's memorial address 'Norman Malcolm', *Philosophical Investigations*, 15 (1992), p. 221.

33 O. K. Bouwsma (1898–1978) taught philosophy at the University of Nebraska from 1928 to 1966 and at the University of Texas at Austin from 1966 to 1976. Initially much influenced by Moore, his encounters with Wittgenstein transformed his ideas. He was the first American philosopher to give the John Locke Lectures in Oxford (1950–1), during which sojourn he renewed his acquaintance with Wittgenstein. His record of their meetings is *Wittgenstein, Conversations 1949–1951*, ed. J. L. Craft and R. T. Hustwit (Hackett, Indianapolis, 1986).

34 See Bouwsma's review of the *Blue Book*, repr. in his *Philosophical Essays* (University of Nebraska Press, Lincoln and London, 1965), pp. 175–201 and his posthumously published essay 'A Difference between Ryle and Wittgenstein', in *Toward a New Sensibility: Essays of O. K. Bouwsma*, ed. J. L. Craft and R. T. Hustwit (University of Nebraska Press, Lincoln and London, 1982), pp. 17–32. Ryle's reply to the latter, reprinted in his posthumously published papers *On Thinking*, ed. K. Kolenda (Blackwell, Oxford, 1979), pp. 131–2, rightly remonstrated against this interpretation. 'The clang of Wittgenstein's metal against the metals of Frege, Russell, Ramsey, Brouwer, Moore, and the author of the *Tractatus* is here soothed

to a bedside murmur,' he wrote (p. 132), objecting angrily to Bouwsma's claim that there are neither arguments nor refutations or rectifications in the *Investigations*. Wittgenstein's wearisome interrogatives (like 'I remember having meant *him*. Am I remembering a process or state? – When did it begin, what was its course, etc.?' (PI §661)) are, Ryle retorted, commonly 'the rhetorically barbed conclusions of *reductio ad absurdum* arguments'. That the meaning of a name is its bearer is refuted by argument; that the privacy imputed to sensations is incoherent is a confusion or battery of confusions rectified by argument. To Bouwsma's claim that Wittgenstein 'sought to bring relief, control, calm, quiet, peace, release, a certain power', Ryle spluttered indignantly, 'Well! – what of the Wittgenstein who got us interested, fascinated, excited, shocked? He electrified us. Whom did he ever tranquillize?' (p. 131).

35   Such interpretations, as noted, infuriated Wittgenstein, and did considerable harm to the cause of the dissemination of his philosophy. For a discussion of how far the psychoanalytic analogy goes, see Exg. §255 and, more generally, Volume 1, 'The nature of philosophy'.

36   See esp. his *Constructive Formalism: Essays on the Foundations of Mathematics* (University College, Leicester, 1951), preface, pp. 9f.

37   Goodstein, 'Wittgenstein's Philosophy of Mathematics'. It is noteworthy, given Geach's frequently quoted story that Wittgenstein related to him that when he first met Frege, 'He wiped the floor with me' (G. E. M. Anscombe and P. T. Geach, *Three Philosophers* (Blackwell, Oxford, 1967), p. 130), that Goodstein was told of the same episode fifteen years earlier in a more extended version. Samuel Alexander, professor of philosophy at Manchester when Wittgenstein was working there on aeronautics, told Wittgenstein that Frege was the greatest living philosopher, 'and so Wittgenstein wrote to Frege to arrange a meeting. Frege invited him to tea, and after tea they had a discussion in which (in Wittgenstein's own words) Frege wiped the floor with him. Wittgenstein returned to England very disheartened, but a year later he sought another interview with Frege and this time "he wiped the floor with Frege, and though they met for tea many times after they never discussed philosophy again"' (ibid., p. 272). Geach has remarked on this that what he heard about Frege from Wittgenstein's own lips makes him confident that *this* anecdote is spurious (*Wittgenstein's Lectures on Philosophical Psychology 1946–47*, ed. P. T. Geach (Harvester Wheatsheaf, Hemel Hempstead, 1988), p. xiv). The second meeting with Frege is probably the one about which Wittgenstein wrote to Russell on 26 December 1912: 'I had a long discussion with Frege about our Theory of Symbolism of which, I think, he roughly understood the general outline. He said he would think the matter over' (R 7).

38   It would be interesting to know who first employed the term 'Ordinary Language Philosophy' as a label. It was not used, as far as I know, by the leading figures in Oxford, such as Ryle, Austin and Strawson. The label does not originate with, but may arise from, Norman Malcolm's 1942 essay 'Moore and Ordinary Language', in *The Philosophy of G. E. Moore*, ed. P. A. Schilpp (Northwestern University, Evanston, Ill., and Chicago, 1942). Malcolm concluded the paper with the remark 'Moore's greatest historical role consists in the fact that he has been perhaps the first philosopher to sense that any philosophical statement which violates ordinary language is false, and consistently to defend ordinary language against its philosophical violators.' (Moore did not altogether agree with this characterization of his work.) The paper gave rise to considerable debate after the war. But it is noteworthy that neither Chisholm, in his criticism 'Philosophers and Ordinary Language' (*Philosophical Review*, 60 (1951), pp. 317–28), nor

Malcolm, in his reply and partial recantation (*Philosophical Review*, 60 (1951), pp. 329–40), used the label 'Ordinary Language Philosophy'. By the mid-1950s, however, the term had become common. Benson Mates, in his 1958 paper 'On the Verification of Statements about Ordinary Language' (repr. in *Philosophy and Linguistics*, ed. C. Lyas (Macmillan, London, 1971)) refers to 'the so-called "ordinary language" philosophers' (p. 121).

39   Ayer, *Part of My Life*, p. 294. Ryle, by contrast, wrote: 'After we got back to Oxford in the middle 1940s, the philosophical atmosphere did not smell very different from what it had been five or six years before. But it was different in some ways' ('Paper read to the Oxford Philosophical Society 500th Meeting, 1968', p. 104). The differences Ryle noted were: (i) Wittgenstein's influence via Paul and Waismann; (ii) Austin's influence; (iii) the growing, if still amateur, competence in formal logic.

40   Strawson, 'Interview', p. 6.

41   George Pitcher later wrote that at Harvard in 1955 'we all looked upon Oxford as a leading centre of philosophy, and many of us viewed it as *the* place in the world where exciting new work was being done in our subject' ('Austin: A Personal Memoir', in *Essays on J. L. Austin*, ed. I. Berlin et al. (Clarendon Press, Oxford, 1973), p. 17). For the first post-war quarter of a century almost every major American philosopher visited Oxford on sabbatical.

42   G. J. Warnock, 'John Langshaw Austin, a Biographical Sketch', repr. in *Symposium on J. L. Austin*, ed. K. T. Fann (Routledge and Kegan Paul, London, 1969), p. 10.

43   G. Ryle, 'Philosophical Arguments', repr. in his *Collected Papers*, vol. 2, p. 201.

44   See Ryle, *Collected Papers*, vol. 2, and his *On Thinking*, published after his death.

45   Curiously, no record seems to have survived of what he thought of this work. The only recorded observation I have come across is an expression of puzzlement at Frege's demand that a definition of number should tell us that Julius Caesar is *not* a number (see G. J. Warnock, 'Saturday Mornings', in *Essays on J. L. Austin*, ed. Berlin et al., p. 36), a qualm he shared with Wittgenstein.

46   Warnock reports that Austin was inclined to read a book (in the 'Saturday Mornings' at any rate) 'by taking the sentences *one at a time*, thoroughly settling the sense (or hash) of each before proceeding to the next one. . . . most writers, some more than others, often say things, whether wittingly or not, that are only fully intelligible in the light of other things they have not yet said. This did not greatly matter in the case of Aristotle, with the whole of whose text Austin was perfectly familiar, and the rest of us decently so. But the *Investigations*, I think, did not come up looking their best in this relentless light' (ibid., p. 37). Austin is reported by more than one person as having expressed disdain, if not, indeed, contempt, for Wittgenstein.

47   Herbert Hart remarked to R. S. Summers many years later that he probably knew more about the rules of baseball than anyone alive, his brief having been the rules of that game. This, to be sure, was a case of knowledge by description rather than by acquaintance.

48   Ryle, 'Paper read to the Oxford Philosophical Society 500th Meeting', pp. 104f.

49   Paul Grice, 'Reply to Richards', in *Philosophical Grounds of Rationality*, ed. R. E. Grandy and R. Warner (Clarendon Press, Oxford, 1986), p. 50.

50   Ibid., p. 51. Grice, like many of the others, never abandoned this modest commitment. Austin, Grice recounted, communicated a vision of ordinary language as a purposive instrument

whose intricacies and distinctions are not idle, but rather marvellously and subtly fitted to serve the multiplicity of our needs and desires in communication. . . . When put to work, this conception of ordinary language seemed to offer fresh and manageable approaches to philosophical ideas and problems . . . When properly regulated and directed, 'linguistic botanizing' seems to me to provide a valuable initiation to the philosophical treatment of a concept, particularly if what is under examination (and it is arguable that this should always be the case) is a family of different but related concepts. Indeed, I will go further, and proclaim it as my belief that linguistic botanizing is indispensable, at a certain stage, in a philosophical enquiry, and that it is lamentable that this lesson has been forgotten, or has never been learned. (Ibid., p. 57)

Other accusations levelled against 'Oxford philosophy' or 'Oxford ordinary language philosophy' will be examined below (see ch. 8, §1).

51 Ayer's dignified and temperate reply, 'Has Austin Refuted the Sense-datum Theory?', repr. in his *Metaphysics and Common Sense* (Macmillan, London, 1969), pp. 126–48, made it clear that Austin's assault was far from watertight. Nevertheless, together with Ryle's writings on perception and Wittgenstein's private language arguments and anti-foundationalism, it served to extirpate this philosophical disease for a generation, after which it re-emerged in mutated form.

52 G. Ryle, 'Review of "Symposium on J. L. Austin" ', repr. in his *Collected Papers*, vol. 1, p. 273.

53 On the concluding page of the book Austin remarks: 'I have purposely not embroiled the general theory with philosophical problems . . . ; this should not be taken to imply that I am unaware of them. . . . The real fun comes when we begin to apply it to philosophy.' Unfortunately, he did not live to show where he thought the real fun would lie.

54 Ryle, 'Autobiographical', in *Ryle: A Collection of Critical Essays*, ed. O. P. Wood and G. Pitcher (Doubleday, New York, 1970), p. 14. He pointed out that his chief interests in linguistic matters were breaches of logical syntax, in particular its trouble-makers and paradox-generators, while Austin's were in communicative dictions.

An examiner might pose two questions:
  1) Why cannot a traveller reach London gradually?
  2) Why is 'I warn you . . . ' the beginning of a warning, but 'I insult you . . . '
not the beginning of an insult?
On six days out of seven Question 1 would be Ryle's favourite; Question 2, Austin's. Each of us would think – wrongly – that there is not much real meat in the unfavoured question. But their meats are of such entirely disparate kinds that the epithet 'linguistic' would apply in totally different ways 1) to the answer sketch 'Adverbs like "gradually" won't go with verbs like "reach" for the following reason . . .'; 2) to the answer sketch 'To insult is to say to someone else pejorative things with such-and-such an intention, while to warn is to say . . .'. Anti-nonsense rules govern impartially sayings of all types. 'Reach gradually' will not do in questions, commands, counsels, requests, warnings, complaints, promises, insults or apologies, any more than it will do in statements. Epimenides can tease us in any grammatical mood. To an enquiry into categorial requirements, references to differences of saying-types are irrelevant; to an enquiry into differences between saying-types, references to category-requirements are irrelevant. Infelicities and absurdities are not even congeners. (Ibid., p. 15)

55 Other works of the period were von Wright's *The Logical Problem of Induction* (1941) and *A Treatise on Induction and Probability* (1951), D. C. Williams's *The Ground of Induction* (1947) and Braithwaite's *Scientific Explanation* (1953).

56   Waismann's lectures in Cambridge utilized materials from *Logik, Sprache, Philosophie*; i.e. ideas derived from Wittgenstein's philosophy in the early 1930s. At the same time Wittgenstein was propounding his substantially different contemporaneous ideas in his Cambridge classes, and found it intolerable that his earlier (often rejected) thoughts were being given currency in the same university by another.

57   Indeed, in the concluding sentence of his *Part of My Life*, he wrote: 'What I have achieved is for others to estimate, but if I could be thought even to have played Horatio to Russell's Hamlet, I should consider it glory enough' (p. 312).

58   In P. F. Strawson, *Freedom and Resentment and Other Essays* (Methuen, London, 1974), pp. 66–84.

59   In *Perception and Identity, Essays Presented to A. J. Ayer*, ed. G. F. Macdonald (Macmillan, London, 1979), pp. 41–60.

60   In *Philosophical Grounds of Rationality*, ed. Grandy and Warner, pp. 229–42.

61   Cf. PI p. 178: 'My attitude towards him is an attitude towards a soul. I am not of the *opinion* that he has a soul.' Interestingly, in an earlier draft of this remark, Wittgenstein wrote 'is an attitude towards a person'.

62   Hart had studied Literae Humaniores at New College (1926–9), before going to the Chancery Bar. After the war, his former tutor, A. H. Smith, by then Warden of the College, wished to lure him back to philosophy, believing that he would be 'a real bulwark' against the new 'radical empiricism'. This belief proved to be wrong. Hart became a leading figure in post-war Oxford legal, moral and political theory, although, to be sure, his work would be mischaracterized as 'radical empiricism'.

63   Stevenson had attended Wittgenstein's classes in Cambridge in the early 1930s. However, there is little trace of this in his book. He told me that he had turned to ethics in order to distance himself from Wittgenstein's influence. Wittgenstein did not think much of *Ethics and Language*.

64   H. J. Paton, 'Fifty Years of Philosophy', in *Contemporary British Philosophy*, 3rd ser., ed. H. D. Lewis (Allen and Unwin, London, 1956), pp. 350f.

65   The title of a volume of essays published in 1963, critical of the 'linguistic turn' in philosophy, edited by H. D. Lewis. It is noteworthy that contributors included such Oxford figures as Price, Kneale, Hampshire, Hardie and Ayer. For a discussion of the title paper by Price, see ch. 8, §1(i).

66   G. Ryle, 'Ordinary Language', repr. in his *Philosophical Papers*, vol. 2, pp. 301–18.

67   Unless what was in question was an investigation of metaphor.

68   For Carnap's account of explication, see his *Logical Foundations of Probability* (University of Chicago Press, Chicago, 1950), ch. 1; for a criticism of this conception, see P. F. Strawson, 'Carnap's Views on Constructed Systems versus Natural Languages in Analytic Philosophy', in *The Philosophy of Rudolf Carnap*, ed. P. A. Schilpp (Open Court, LaSalle, Ill., 1963), pp. 503–18. In Strawson's view, Carnapian explication replaces a puzzle-generating concept in natural language by a 'rationally reconstructed' one in a formal (or formalized) scientific system, at the cost of sweeping the original conceptual puzzle under the carpet, rather than resolving it. If one is puzzled by the fact that it may be warmer today than yesterday even though the temperature is lower, one is hardly relieved of one's puzzlement by being told to abandon the sensory concept of warmth in favour of the scientific explication of the concept of warmth by that of temperature or mean kinetic energy.

It is interesting to note that Quine argued that Wittgenstein's view that the task of philosophy is not to solve problems, but to dissolve them by showing that there were really none there, 'aptly fits explication'. For, 'when explication banishes a problem it does so by showing it to be in an important sense unreal; viz., in the sense of proceeding from needless usages' (W. V. Quine, *Word and Object* (MIT Press, Cambridge, Mass., 1960), p. 260). It is indeed true that explication banishes a problem; what it does not do is dissolve it. As Avishai Margalit nicely remarked to me, if one wants to know how birds fly, it does not help to be shown how to build an aeroplane.

69   By the 1970s, Grice, then in California, had come to think differently. He said to me, when we met again in Michigan in 1974, that he now thought that in philosophy, 'if you can't put it into symbols, it isn't worth saying'. A few days later, back in Oxford, I told Strawson of Grice's remark. He smiled wryly, and said, 'Oh no! If you *can* put it into symbols, then it isn't worth saying.' Grice later issued a partial recantation, resulting from 'a growing apprehension that philosophy is all too often being squeezed out of operation by technology; to borrow words from Ramsey, that apparatus which began life as a system of devices to combat *woolliness* has now become an instrument of *scholasticism*' ('Reply to Richards', p. 61).

70   J. L. Austin, 'A Plea for Excuses', repr. in his *Philosophical Papers* (Clarendon Press, Oxford, 1961), pp. 129f.

71   P. F. Strawson, *Individuals* (Methuen, London, 1959), pp. 9f.

72   S. Hampshire, *Thought and Action* (Chatto and Windus, London, 1959), p. 253.

73   Ryle, 'Ordinary Language', p. 317.

74   G. H. von Wright, 'Analytic Philosophy: A Historico-critical Survey', in his *Tree of Knowledge*, p. 38.

75   Strawson, 'Interview', p. 7.

76   M. A. E. Dummett, 'Reckonings: Wittgenstein on Mathematics', *Encounter*, 50/3 (1978), pp. 63f.

77   Ryle's 'Systematically Misleading Expressions', Findlay's 'Time: A Treatment of Some Puzzles', Margaret Macdonald's 'The Philosopher's Use of Analogy' and 'The Language of Political Theory', Paul's 'Is There a Problem about Sense-data?', Waismann's 'Verifiability' and Wisdom's 'Gods'. Findlay's paper was written in 1941, before he dissociated himself from Wittgensteinian philosophy. In the prefatory note, Findlay wrote: 'It will be obvious that the basic ideas of this paper derive from Wittgenstein.'

78   A. G. N. Flew, introduction to *Logic and Language*, 1st ser. (Blackwell, Oxford, 1951), p. 10. It is noteworthy that Flew's sequel, *Logic and Language*, 2nd ser. (Blackwell, Oxford, 1953), included papers by Ryle, Waismann and Gasking, as well as a paper by Moore, and also essays from the new Oxford generation, viz. Austin, Pears, Warnock and Urmson.

79   G. J. Warnock, *English Philosophy since 1900* (Oxford University Press, London, 1958), p. 62.

80   J. O. Urmson, 'Discussion of Urmson's "The History of Analysis" at the Royaumont Colloquium', repr. in *The Linguistic Turn: Recent Essays in Philosophical Method*, ed. R. Rorty (University of Chicago Press, Chicago, 1967), p. 305.

81   Recounted by Professor R. S. Summers in conversation.

82   A remark he made to me in 1964.

83   There had been an equally abortive attempt to publish the book in English before the war. Margaret Paul (Ramsey's sister) translated the text of *Logik, Sprache, Philosophie*, which was typeset for publication by Routledge and Kegan Paul in 1939. For unknown reasons, the plan was abandoned. *The Principles of Linguistic*

Philosophy (1965) was derived from Waismann's extensively corrected galley proofs of this projected pre-war publication. *Logik, Sprache, Philosophie* (1976) was later reconstructed from Waismann's drafts for the earlier projected German publication.

84 Although, as Hampshire now recollects, Anscombe's *Intention*, published a couple of years later, made a greater impact. Nevertheless, Waismann was interested in these themes, and had written extensively on the related subjects of voluntary action and of the contrast between reason and motive, on the one hand, and cause, on the other. His writings on these topics have since been published, edited by J. Schulte, under the title *Wille und Motiv* (Reclam, Stuttgart, 1983).

85 Whether so much as to justify Berlin's description of him (in conversation) as 'Waismann's disciple', I do not know. Hampshire (also in conversation) has compared Waismann's influence upon Hart to Wisdom's early influence upon Austin. Wisdom's articles 'Logical Constructions' (see p. 72) helped Austin break free from the Cook-Wilsonian heritage in the 1930s, and Waismann alerted Hart to the limitations of analytic definition, to vagueness and 'open texture', to defeasibility, etc.

86 A term is vague if there is, in the practice of its application, significant disagreement about its applicability in conformity with what are recognized as correct explanations of it. Such disagreements, irresolvable within the practice of explaining the term, may produce agreement that there are borderline cases of its application. Open texture is not vagueness, but lack of determinacy of sense – i.e. the *possibility* of there being irresolvable disagreements in judgements about the applicability of a term. Determinacy of sense is therefore the impossibility of vagueness, and its opposite is not vagueness but the mere *possibility* of vagueness – which is what Waismann called 'open texture'. For more detailed discussion, see Volume 1, 'Vagueness and determinacy of sense', §§4–7, and Exg. §80.

87 F. Waismann, 'Language Strata', repr. in his *How I See Philosophy* (Macmillan, London, 1968), p. 98.

88 Understandably, given the personal bitterness he felt towards Wittgenstein, both regarding the sorry history of *Logik, Sprache, Philosophie* and with respect to Wittgenstein's failure to support him in Cambridge. He referred to Wittgenstein as 'the greatest disappointment of my life', and accused him of 'complete obscurantism'. In his notebook of 1948, he wrote: 'Wittgenstein – der führende Denker unserer Zeit (nämlich der ins Falsche führende)' ('Wittgenstein – the leading thinker of our time (namely, he who leads into error'). See Wolfgang Grassl's introduction to his edition of Waismann's *Lectures on the Philosophy of Mathematics* (Rodopi, Amsterdam, 1982), p. 10.

89 F. Waismann, 'How I See Philosophy', repr. in his *How I See Philosophy*, p. 32.

90 Since this conception was propounded deliberately *in opposition* to Wittgenstein, it is striking to find it being currently revived *and attributed to* Wittgenstein, by, e.g., G. P. Baker, in '*Philosophical Investigations* Section 122: Neglected Aspects', in *Wittgenstein's Philosophical Investigations: Text and Context*, ed. R. L. Arrington and H.-J. Glock (Routledge, London and New York, 1991), pp. 35–68, and in 'Philosophy – Eidos or Simulacrum', in *Philosophy in Britain Today*, ed. S. G. Shanker (Croom Helm, London, 1986). For criticism of this interpretation, see H.-J. Glock, '*Philosophical Investigations* §128: "Theses in Philosophy" and Undogmatic Procedure', in *Wittgenstein's Philosophical Investigations*, ed. Glock and Arrington, pp. 69–88.

91 E.g. in telling us that physics reveals that there are really no solid objects, or that all propositions about sense experience are vague, or that all phenomena are in flux (BB 46).

92 Published in his *Philosophical Papers*, ed. B. F. McGuinness (Reidel, Dordrecht, 1977), pp. 150–65, and written sometime after 1953.

93 F. Waismann, 'Discovering, Creating, Inventing', in his *Lectures on the Philosophy of Mathematics*, pp. 29–34. This conception of the mathematician as a Dr Frankenstein, and of his creation as autonomous, apparently fell upon ready ears, since it is echoed in Dummett's review of the *Remarks on the Foundations of Mathematics* (repr. in *Wittgenstein: The Philosophical Investigations, A Collection of Critical Essays*, ed. G. Pitcher (Doubleday, New York, 1966), p. 447). In opposition to Wittgenstein, Dummett proposed an alternative picture betwixt Platonism and constructivism, a picture of 'objects springing into being in response to our probing. We do not *make* the objects but must accept them as we find them (this corresponds to the proof imposing itself on us); but they were not already there for our statements to be true or false of before we carried out the investigation which brought them into being.'

94 Ryle, 'Autobiographical', p. 11. In characterizing Wittgenstein as a 'monoglot', Ryle was castigating him for his lack of interest in the work of other philosophers.

95 Ryle, 'Discussion of Urmson's "History of Analysis" at Royaumont, 1961', p. 305.

96 J. L. Austin, 'Intelligent Behaviour: A Critical Review of *The Concept of Mind*', repr. in *Ryle: A Collection of Critical Essays*, ed. Woods and Pitcher, p. 48.

97 In *Dilemmas* (Cambridge University Press, Cambridge, 1954), p. 9, Ryle wrote:

> This idiom [of categories] can be helpful as a familiar mnemonic with some beneficial associations. It can also be an impediment, if credited with the virtues of a skeleton-key. I think it is worth while to take some pains with this word 'category', but not for the usual reason, namely that there exists an exact, professional way of using it, in which like a skeleton-key, it will turn all our locks for us; but rather for the unusual reason that there is an inexact, amateurish way of using it in which, like a coal-hammer, it will make a satisfactory knocking noise on doors which we want opened to us. It gives the answers to none of our questions but it can be made to arouse people to the answers in a properly brusque way.

98 In an unpublished version of Bouwsma's notes on conversations with Wittgenstein. The remark was excised in the published version.

Although before the war Wittgenstein spoke highly of Ryle, there was a rift between the two men after the war, one reason for which was Ryle's warm review of Popper's *The Open Society and its Enemies* (1945) in *Mind*, 56 (April 1947). Wittgenstein presumably found Popper's conception of social engineering crude and his conception of social institutions vulgar and superficial (interestingly, Rhees, partly in response to Wittgenstein's urging, wrote a scathing article on Popper's 'social engineering', in *Mind*, 56 (October 1947). Wittgenstein may also have been infuriated by Popper's extensive comments on him in the footnotes of *The Open Society*, some of which he doubtless found offensive (e.g. 'reinforced dogmatism', 'naïve', 'inviting every kind of metaphysical nonsense to pose as deeply significant'), others of which display great crudity (e.g. 'using the word "know" in the ordinary sense, we can, of course, never know what another person is feeling. We can only make hypotheses about it. This solves the so-called problem' (*The Open Society and its Enemies* (Routledge and Kegan Paul, London, 1962), vol. 2, pp. 351f.)). Wittgenstein may have felt that Ryle should have defended him in print, rather than allowing others to treat him, as he complained bitterly, as '*vogelfrei*', i.e. an outlaw at whom everyone may take a pot-shot with impunity. He also accused Ryle, as he accused most of his pupils who wrote anything, of 'borrowing other men's ideas' (see Bouwsma, *Wittgenstein: Conversations 1949–1951*, p. 50).

99   Not that Wittgenstein invokes it all that much either!

100 See *Dilemmas*, ch. 4, and 'Pleasure', PASS, 28 (1954).

101 A. M. Quinton, 'Ryle on Perception', in *Ryle: A Collection of Critical Essays*, ed. Wood and Pitcher, p. 134.

102 See also A. R. White, *The Philosophy of Mind* (Random House, New York, 1967), ch. 6.

103 White, whose work has not had the influence it merits, was the most skilful developer of Rylean and, to a lesser degree, Wittgensteinian ideas in philosophical psychology. His early work *Attention* (1964) was a thorough, refined development of Ryle's remarks on 'heed concepts' (see *Concept of Mind*, pp. 135–49), viz. attending, noticing, awareness, consciousness, realization, care, etc. His later *The Nature of Knowledge* (1982) was an equally exhaustive investigation of the concepts of knowledge, knowing how and knowing that, the objects of knowledge, and the relation of knowledge to belief. If anyone surpassed Austin in subtlety and refinement in the discrimination of grammatical differences, it was White. His linguistic imagination was, I think, unparalleled, and he applied it with great finesse to a wide range of problems. In the last decade of his life he also worked on jurisprudential problems pertaining to action, intention, voluntariness, negligence and recklessness (*Grounds of Liability, an Introduction to the Philosophy of Law* (1985) and *Misleading Cases* (1991).

104 See J. F. M. Hunter, 'Believing', in *Midwest Studies*, 5 (1980), pp. 246–8.

105 Examples of such incautious moments are: 'The radical objection to the theory that minds must know what they are about, because mental happenings are by definition conscious, or metaphorically self-luminous, is that there are no such happenings' (p. 161), and 'To talk of a person's mind is not to talk of a repository which is permitted to house objects that something called "the physical world" is forbidden to house; it is to talk of the person's abilities, liabilities and inclinations to do and undergo certain sorts of things, and of the doing and undergoing of these things in the ordinary world' (p. 199). Both remarks are partly true, partly false. Certainly minds do not 'know what they are about', people do; and if Wittgenstein is right, it is wrong to conceive of a person's ability to say that he is or is not in pain as an instance of *knowing* anything. But it was, at best, misleading to say that there 'are no such happenings'. Similarly, the mind is not a repository, and pains, twinges and tickles are not 'in the mind'; moreover, to say that a thought crossed one's mind or that one had something in mind is indeed not to describe events or objects in a private repository, but just to say that one thought of something or meant something. But it was wrong to claim that *all* talk of a person's mind is talk of abilities, liabilities and inclinations to do or undergo things.

106 Both Strawson, orally, and Grice, in print ('Reply to Richards', p. 51), attest to this remark. Austin particularly admired Moore's 'Is Existence a Predicate?' Grice, too, was wholly unimpressed by Wittgenstein.

107 Von Wright, 'Analytical Philosophy: A Historico-Critical Survey', p. 39. Von Wright characterizes Austin's philosophy as 'a new form of scholasticism', hence the allusion to Duns Scotus.

108 See Grice, 'Reply to Richards', p. 57. Similarly, Rom Harré relates that when he took a draft of his B.Phil. thesis to show Austin, Austin opened the file at the page of contents, and proceeded to spend the next three hours discussing the differences between 'contents', 'list', 'index', 'table', etc. Harré recollects 'experiencing a Zen-like illumination, which rapidly faded on the way back from Corpus to Univ.'.

109 Hence, having found 'a good site for *field work* in philosophy', viz. one in which ordinary language is rich and subtle, as it is in the matter of excuses, and in which the field has not been too much trodden into bogs or tracks by traditional philosophy, 'we should be able to unfreeze, to loosen up and get going on agreeing about discoveries, however small, and on agreeing about how to reach agreement' ('A Plea for Excuses', p. 131). In a footnote Austin added 'All of which was seen and claimed by Socrates, when he first betook himself to the way of Words'.

110 Indeed, Harré recollects Austin once comparing the number of ways of using words to the number of species of insects (i.e. in the millions).

111 J. L. Austin, 'Ifs and Cans', in *Philosophical Papers*, p. 180.

112 B. Russell, *The Problems of Philosophy* (Oxford University Press, London, 1967), p. 90.

113 The term 'conceptual scheme' was already used by Quine in his essay 'On What There Is' (repr. in his *From a Logical Point of View* (Harvard University Press, Cambridge, Mass., 1953) in 1948 (if not earlier). He has recounted that he inherited the phrase through L. J. Henderson from Pareto, employing it as a nontechnical term; he could, he said, just as well have spoken of a language (see W. V. O. Quine, *Theories and Things* (Harvard University Press, Cambridge, Mass., 1981), p. 41). It is noteworthy, however, that a conceptual scheme, according to Quine, is also a theory replete with ontological commitments.

114 Ch. 2 of *Individuals* explores a non-spatial 'sound-world', only to conclude that, in such a world, identifying reference to particulars and a distinction between experience and what it is experience of is possible only on condition of the existence of structural *analogues* of space, location and movement, persistent particulars and subjects of experience.

115 It could be argued, however, that Strawson, in his striving for generality, pays insufficient attention to the fluidity of the concept of experience and the conceptual diversity it subsumes.

116 P. F. Strawson, *Skepticism and Naturalism: Some Varieties* (Methuen, London, 1985), p. 23.

117 P. F. Strawson, *The Bounds of Sense* (Methuen, London, 1966), p. 43. Once the Kantian Copernican revolution is rejected, the category of synthetic a prior is determined only as a residuum of propositions which are a priori but not analytic, and is in no way explained.

118 Ibid., p. 29. Our size, e.g. conditions a large part of our way of talking and thinking, but we do not 'feel it to be non-contingent'.

119 Cf. Strawson, *Individuals*, pp. 22, 29.

120 It would involve too long a digression to recount the complex, many-pronged attack that Wittgenstein mounts on scepticism. Briefly, he forces the sceptic into a self-destructive defence of the intelligibility of a private language. He denies the intelligibility of the sceptic's doubts about the existence of material objects, for doubts about existence make sense only within a language-game. The sentence 'There are physical objects' is either nonsense or a grammatical proposition, and not the expression of an empirical hypothesis which might be false and for which it could make sense to adduce evidence. Our language-games, he argues, begin with certainty, and that is not due to human weakness or folly, but is an essential part of learning the practice of judging. He insists that the logical possibility of a doubt is not a reason for doubting, and argues that reasons for doubt presuppose the intelligibility of reasons against it, hence that doubt presupposes the possibility of certainty. More important, he stressed that we *are* certain of many things, that some such certainties constitute part of our world picture. Their falsity would

imply not a mistake, but chaos, which would engulf not merely all certainties, but also the very language we speak, the language with which the sceptic voices his qualms.

121   In *The Bounds of Sense* (p. 165), Strawson concedes the criterionlessness of self-ascription of current or recalled experience. This concession alone, however, does not suffice to remedy what seem, to a Wittgensteinian eye, to be the flaws in his account in *Individuals*. For the possibility, the legitimacy, of such criterionless employment of these concepts, their use without a justification but with right (PI §289), calls for further elucidation.

122   See further, ch. 5, n. 15.

123   Wittgenstein toyed with this move in the *Blue Book* (p. 51), though never again (save in the problematic PI §354, which was drafted in 1933; see Exg.). Arguably, he had good reasons for rejecting it (see Volume 3, 'Criteria').

124   For one possible way in which a Wittgensteinian strategy might be developed here, see P. M. S. Hacker, *Appearance and Reality* (Blackwell, Oxford and Cambridge, Mass., 1987), ch. 6, §§3–4.

Chapter 7   Post-positivism in the United States and Quine's Apostasy

1   H. Feigl, 'The *Wiener Kreis* in America' (1969), repr. in *Herbert Feigl: Inquiries and Provocations, Selected Writings 1929–1974*, ed. Robert S. Cohen (Reidel, Dordrecht, 1981), p. 71.

2   In it he defended a form of identity theory, arguing that we have direct experience of 'raw feels', which, as a matter of fact, are identical with neurophysiological states or events. Ascription of such experiences to others is analogical. The barbaric 'raw feels' derives from E. C. Tolman's *Purposive Behaviour in Man and Animals* (1932).

3   Kraft and von Juhos remained in Vienna and survived the war. Other affiliates who did not escape in time were killed. Kurt Grelling (1886–1943), who was a member of the Berlin circle, was murdered by the Nazis, as were some of the Lvov–Warsaw group, such as Janina Hosiasson-Lindenbaum (1899–1941), Adolf Lindenbaum (d. 1941) and Mordechaj Wajsberg (d. 1942?).

4   V. Kraft, *The Vienna Circle: The Origin of Neo-positivism* (Greenwood Press, New York, 1953), pp. 8f.

5   His contribution to *Foundations of the Unity of Science*, ed. O. Neurath, R. Carnap and C. Morris (University of Chicago Press, Chicago, 1970), the publication which in effect was all that came of the grand project for an encyclopaedia of unified science, was the monograph 'Fundamentals of Concept Formation in Empirical Science' (1952).

6   This was in effect, a 'realist' dichotomy analogous to the difference between Berkeleian idealism with and without God.

7   These were brought together in his *Selected Papers in Logic and Foundations, Didactics, Economics* (Reidel, Dordrecht, 1979).

8   In his 'Two Dogmas of Empiricism' (1951), Quine acknowledges 'a large and indeterminate debt to Tarski and others'. It is interesting that in a letter to Morton White in 1944, Tarski expressed many of the ideas that have since become familiar from Quine's 'Two Dogmas'. White had asked Tarski for his reactions to Felix Kaufmann's remark in his *Methodology of the Social Sciences* (p. 66) that the meaning of 'true' as applied to analytic propositions is essentially different from its meaning when applied to synthetic propositions. Tarski responded that this depends on how one defines '*A* means in *B* something different than in *C*', adding: 'I must say that I simply don't know what such a phrase means. I imagine a useful definition

of meaning in contexts like "*B* and *C* (i.e. two sentences or expressions) have the same meaning", "the meaning of *B*" etc. But "the meaning of *A* in *B* is different from that of *A* in *C*" – this seems to me too involved.' Whether sentences like 'Everything coloured is extended' are necessary, he added, depends on how one defines 'necessary sentence' and on the language involved. Logical and mathematical truths, as Mill had argued, do not differ in their origin from empirical truths, Tarski continued. More important:

> I think that I am ready to reject certain logical premisses (axioms) in exactly the same circumstances in which I am ready to reject empirical premisses (e.g. physical hypotheses). . . . We reject certain hypotheses or scientific theories if we notice either their inner inconsistency, or their disagreement with experience . . . No such experience can logically compel us to reject the theory: too many additional hypotheses (regarding the 'initial conditions', circumstances of the experiment, instruments used) are always involved. We can practically always save the theory by means of additional hypotheses. . . . Axioms of logic are of so general a nature that they are rarely affected by such experiences in special domains. However, I don't see here any difference 'of principle'; I can imagine that certain new experiences of a very fundamental nature may make us inclined to change just some axioms of logic. And certain new developments in quantum mechanics seem clearly to indicate this possibility. (Morton White, 'A Philosophical Letter of Alfred Tarski', *Journal of Philosophy*, 84 (1987), pp. 28–32)

9   W. V. Quine, 'Homage to Carnap', repr. in *Dear Carnap, Dear Van*, ed. R. Creath (University of California Press, Berkeley, 1990), p. 463.
10 To be sure, interest in Wittgenstein did not evaporate in the 1970s and 1980s. Wittgenstein studies were, and continue to be, pursued. Interest in Wittgenstein was maintained at Harvard (even after it had waned at Cornell) through Burton Dreben and Stanley Cavell, and was transmitted to the younger generation. Richard Rorty harnessed Wittgenstein to postmodernist concerns, and Saul Kripke, preceded by Robert Fogelin, generated a lively debate (based on a misinterpretation of Wittgenstein's writings) about following rules. Nevertheless, it is true that philosophy in the United States turned away from the Wittgensteinian paradigm, both in mainstream philosophy of language and in the philosophy of mind (see pp. 270–2). In due course, this affected philosophy in Britain and elsewhere.
    It is striking that the contemporary American philosophers who do profess a Wittgensteinian influence, unlike the earlier generation of his American pupils and their circles, show a marked tendency to graft Wittgenstein's ideas on to American pragmatism, and some attempt to synthesize his ideas with Quine's. Whether either of these can be done coherently is a question worth pursuing.
11 Quine's references to Wittgenstein are few and sometimes, as here, betray little understanding. Wittgenstein did not suggest, as Dewey did, that meaning is a property of behaviour (see pp. 207–11). Dewey's conception of meaning was behaviourist, 'use' being construed as behavioural effect. Congenial though this is to Quine, it is far removed from Wittgenstein's normative conception of use. Elsewhere (OR 27) Quine suggests that Dewey's claim that language presupposes the existence of an organized social group from which speakers have acquired their speech habits is a rejection of the possibility of a private language in Wittgenstein's sense. This is mistaken, since Wittgenstein is not concerned with the social genesis of a language. A private language in his sense (a language the individual words of which refer to the speaker's immediate private sensations, which can be known only by him) might be thought to be acquired only in social interaction, as Augustine intimated (cf. PI §1), and as any Lockean might have claimed. Similarly,

Quine suggests that Wittgenstein's conception of philosophy as dissolving philosophical problems by showing that there were none really there is satisfied by
Carnapian explication (WO 260). This, as pointed out (p. 310 n. 68), is the con-
verse of the truth.

12   See also Rhees's notes to the 'Lecture on Ethics' (*Philosophical Review*, 74 (1965),
p. 25).

13   Ramsey's account is not disquotational. In his view, truth is ascribed primarily to
propositions, not sentences. Hence he claims not that '"*p*" is true' = '*p*', but rather
that 'It is true that *p*' = '*p*' ('Facts and Propositions', repr. in *F. P. Ramsey: Foundations – Essays in Philosophy, Logic, Mathematics and Economics*, ed. D. H. Mellor
(Routledge and Kegan Paul, London, 1978), pp. 44f.). Wittgenstein, although he
asserted in the *Philosophical Investigations* that '*p*' is true = *p* (PI §136), had argued
in the *Grammar* that 'the quotation marks in the sentence '"*p*" is true" are simply
superfluous', since '"'*p*' is true" can only be understood if one understands the
grammar of the sign "*p*" as a propositional sign, not if "*p*" is simply the name of
the shape of a particular ink mark' (PG 124). Like Ramsey, he had no qualms about
propositional quantification, agreeing with him that 'What he says is true' = 'Things
are as he says' (PG 123); i.e. 'For all *p*, if he says that *p*, then *p*'. His adoption of
a deflationary account of truth antedates Ramsey's (NB 9; TLP 4.062); see above
pp. 71, 291 n. 19.

14   The other is the maxim of simplicity of theory.

15   A statement of the form 'Whenever *p*, *q*', which is compounded of observation
sentences. It specifies a generality to the effect that the circumstances described in
the one observation sentence are invariably accompanied by those described in the
other (PT 10).

16   Quine, 'Homage to Carnap', p. 464.

17   N. Goodman and W. V. Quine, 'Steps Towards a Constructive Nominalism', repr.
in Goodman, *Problems and Projects* (Bobbs-Merrill, Indianapolis, 1972), p. 173.

18   This is rather surprising, since most philosophers who cast propositions in the role
of truth-bearers do not make the mistake of characterizing them as meanings of
sentences. What is true (or false) is also what is believed, assumed or claimed to
be true, but it makes no sense to believe, assume or claim the meaning of a sentence to be true. What is believed may be implausible, exaggerated or inaccurate,
but the meaning of a sentence cannot be any of these.

19   In his autobiography *The Time of My Life* (MIT Press, Cambridge, Mass., 1985)
Quine recounts that he read Watson as an undergraduate at Oberlin College (p.
59). He first met B. F. Skinner when he was elected a Junior Fellow of the Harvard
Society of Fellows in 1933. It has been wrongly assumed, he writes, 'that I imbibed my behaviourism from Fred [Skinner]; I lately learned from his autobiography that in fact my exposure to John B. Watson slightly antedated his. It was
particularly in language theory, rather, that Fred opened doors for me. My linguistic interest had run to etymological detail; he put me on to Bloomfield and Jesperson
and gave me a first American edition of John Horne Tooke' (p. 110).

20   But it is noteworthy that having ejected the Carnapian conception of analyticity
through the front door, he later let in by the back door its explication in austerely
Quinean behaviourist terms via the concept of the analyticity of an 'observational
categorical', which is analytic if the affirmative stimulus meaning of the consequent is included in that of the antecedent, as in 'If there are three sticks, then there
are two sticks' or 'If it is a robin, then it is a bird'. Quine's 'analyticity of an
observational categorical' is, as he notes, reminiscent of Kant's conception of
analyticity (a judgement whose subject contains the predicate) (TI 10). This is a

striking volte-face, since in 'Two Dogmas' Quine had summarily rejected Kant's account of analyticity as mere metaphor. The account given in 'Three Indeterminacies' might even be said to be an explication of Kant's distinction. Carnap, one suspects, would have smiled!

21 Like Duhem, but also different, for Duhem's holism was confined to scientific theory, and it was not part of his philosophy that, as Quine put it, 'most sentences, apart from observation sentences, are theoretical' (EN 80, quoted on p. 194). Duhem stated as a fundamental principle that 'An experiment in physics is the precise observation of phenomena accompanied by an *interpretation* of those phenomena; this interpretation substitutes for the concrete data really gathered by observation abstract and symbolic representations which correspond to them by virtue of the theories admitted by the observer' (*The Aim and Structure of Physical Theory*, tr. P. P. Wiener (Princeton University Press, Princeton, 1954), p. 147). An example of the kind of statement he had in mind is: the electromotive force of a certain gas battery increases by so and so many volts when the pressure is increased by so many atmospheres. It is a statement to which 'we cannot attribute any meaning . . . without recourse to the most varied and advanced theories of physics' (p. 148). What Duhem conceived of as theoretical terms, viz. 'electromotive force', 'voltage' and 'atmospheric pressure', are much more limited than what Quine conceives to be so, for Duhem did not count common or garden names of material objects as theoretical. Equally, for Duhem, what faces the tribunal of experiment as a corporate body is a physical theory, not (as for Quine) our humdrum statements about the 'external world' (including past-tense statements, predictions and mundane generalizations). Finally, Duhem did not confine what he called 'observation' within the narrow compass of Quinean 'observation sentences'. He wrote: 'The characteristics which so clearly distinguish the experiment in physics from common experience, by introducing into the former, as an essential element, a theoretical element excluded from the latter, also mark the results arrived at by these two sorts of experience' (p. 147). The results of an experiment in physics 'are abstract propositions to which you can attach no meaning if you do not know the physical theories admitted by the author' (p. 148).

Consequently, there is no such thing as 'the Quine–Duhem thesis', for Duhem would never have agreed to Quine's extreme holism. It should be noted, however, that Quine's holism was not *derived* from Duhem (see 'Comment on Koppelberg' in *Perspectives on Quine*, ed. Barrett and Gibson, p. 212), although he wrongly attributed to Duhem the general view that our statements about the external world face the tribunal of sense experience only as a corporate body (TDE 41n.).

22 Even in its Russellian phase, philosophy, though construed as cognitive and continuous with science, was committed to, indeed limited to, reductive and constructive analysis – and this too is repudiated by Quine.

23 Inasmuch as Quine harks back to the early Russellian phase of analytic philosophy, one might argue that he continues the analytic tradition into yet another phase, marrying a Russellian conception of philosophy with the American pragmatist tradition. That would be misleading, although by no means incoherent or wrong *simpliciter*. One cannot swim back in the stream of history. The river bed of analytic philosophy was decisively shifted by the *Tractatus*, and shifted in a direction inimical to Russell's conception of philosophy, which had no further influence upon the analytic movement. By the time Quine's major work was published in 1960, it was not continuous with mainstream analytic philosophy as it had flowed for the previous forty years. Although Quine reverts to a roughly Russellian conception of philosophy, he does not accept the salient feature which gives Russell

his place as one of the two founders of twentieth-century analytic philosophy, viz.
his conception of analysis, manifest first in his logicism, then in his reductionism
regarding both mind and matter.

24 This does not apply, as we have seen, to such problematic necessary truths as are
exemplified by determinate exclusion. Here Carnap would rely on stipulated 'meaning postulates' (see *Meaning and Necessity*, enlarged edn (University of Chicago
Press, Chicago, 1956)) to exclude by fiat such combinations as 'Ra & Ga' in the
case of 'red' and 'green', as Wittgenstein had suggested in 'Some Remarks on
Logical Form' in 1929, and later repudiated. It is striking that a flaw which led
Wittgenstein to a complete revolution, overturning his first philosophy, led Carnap
merely to a minor revamping presumed to leave everything else intact.

25 Quine, like Tarski, Carnap, and a host of others, takes sentences to be the
basic truth-bearers. This is anything but trivial, and is highly debatable. See ch. 3,
n. 65.

26 E.g. 'No matter what x may be, no matter what y may be, no matter what z may
be, if x and z are true [statements], and z is the result of putting x for "p" and y
for "q" in "If p then q" then y is to be true' (TC 96f.).

27 This, as Wittgenstein pointed out (LFM 268), is more problematic than it appears.
This form of words is derived from ordinary language, as when we say that there
is a circle in the square, such that it is blue. But if we say that there is something
in the square, such that *it* is circular and it is blue, what is the *something* which is
circular and to which we refer by means of the pronoun? There are no criteria of
identity for 'somethings', and there are no 'bare particulars' to bear properties. Of
course, we can say 'There is a geometrical figure in the square, such that it is
circular and it is blue'; but then we cannot say 'There is something in the square
such that it is a geometrical figure, and it is circular and it is blue'. In a formal
system, where a domain of quantification is carefully specified, this may be
unproblematic. It is not so, in Wittgenstein's view, if the domain of quantification
ranges over categorially distinct things (PG 202–7). Moreover, it is highly problematic when one prescinds from canonical notation. (One can ask whether *that* is
a circle or an ellipse, but not whether *that* is a circle or a hat. What one means by
the word 'that', Wittgenstein argued, must be independent of what one asserts
about it.) Quine's criterion for a speaker's ontological commitments cannot, as he
himself realized, be confined to canonical notation.

28 This seems to suggest that our 'positing' of molecules 'and their extraordinary ilk'
is, after all, not on a par with our 'positing' ordinary physical objects.

29 Carnap's concept of a category, Quine contended, is obscure; formal logic needs
no such strictures on negation and complement of a class that limit them to things
belonging to the same category as that to which a given predicate applies; and
considerable theoretical simplifications are to be gained by lifting such prohibitions
(SLT 153). However, Quine did not confront the question of what counts as
understanding such nonsense as 'The number two turned green and married the
square root of −1'. But it needs to be confronted, since understanding is presupposed by the judgement that such a statement is, as Quine would have it, false.
Theoretical simplification is doubtless a desideratum, but it cannot transform gib-
berish into good sense without specifying what sense it is to make.

30 There is something puzzling about demanding an explanation of what 'analytic'
means and then repudiating any attempt to explain what it means on the grounds
that any such explanation must involve the concept of synonymy, i.e. 'means the
same as'. For, to explain what an expression means is paradigmatically, of course,
to explain that it means the same as some other expression, or to paraphrase a

phrase or sentence in which it occurs in terms of another phrase or sentence in which it does not occur, but which means the same. (See H.-J Glock, 'Wittgenstein vs. Quine on Logical Necessity', in *Wittgenstein and Contemporary Philosophy*, ed. S. Teghrarian (Thoemmes Press, Bristol, 1994), pp. 191–3, to which I am much indebted, as I am to its author for innumerable conversations on Quine and Wittgenstein over many years.)

31   This too is puzzling, for lexicography is a well-entrenched practice. Whatever philosophical problems may attach to the concept of meaning and sameness of meaning, one can hardly claim that to explain what 'analytic' means by invoking the notion of 'meaning the same as' is explaining *obscurum per obscurius*, since the concept of 'meaning the same as' has a perfectly well accepted use, and, unlike 'analytic', is not a technical term of art. As Grice and Strawson objected (see 'In Defense of a Dogma' (1956), repr. in H. P. Grice, *Studies in the Way of Words* (Harvard University Press, Cambridge, Mass., and London, 1989), p. 200), it is difficult to believe that whenever one says that 'bachelor' means the same as 'unmarried man', but that 'renate', though it applies to everything to which 'cordate' applies, does not mean the same, one is talking nonsense.

32   Carnap, unsurprisingly, was incredulous. His account of analyticity, he remonstrated, was intended as an explication of the philosophical concept of analyticity as applied to ordinary language, which is indeed imprecise, since expressions in ordinary language do not have sharply defined meanings. Quine had argued that he did not know whether 'Everything green is extended' is analytic or not, and he attributed his uncertainty to the unclarity of the term 'analytic' (TDE 32). Carnap objected that the unclarity was due not to the term 'analytic', but to the fact that it is unclear in ordinary language whether the term 'green' is applicable to a single spatio-temporal point, where a point is construed as lacking extension, since ordinary language does not talk of points thus construed. (Grice and Strawson strengthened Carnap's point in noting that the same uncertainty attaches to the question of whether it is true that everything green is extended – and Quine could hardly complain that the term 'true' is irremediably unclear.) In a constructed language, one lays down meaning postulates in order to ensure clarity. Hence, if it is a meaning postulate that 'G' ('green') is inapplicable to spatio-temporal points, then '$(x) (Ux \supset \sim Gx)$' is analytic in L, and so is '$(x) (Gx \supset Ex)$' (where 'U' signifies 'unextended' and 'E' 'extended'). 'Analytic in L', Carnap argued, signifies sentences whose truth depends on their meanings alone, and is thus independent of the contingency of facts, or 'true in virtue of meanings'. Of course, it does not follow that such statements cannot be revoked; the same sentence can be analytic in one system and synthetic in another. An analytic truth is unrevisable only in the sense that it remains analytically true as long as the language rules are not changed. (He might have added that it is anything but obvious what it would be to revise one's belief that bachelors are unmarried, without changing the use (or meaning) of the expression.) The attribution of truth to synthetic sentences may be changed in the light of experience, even though the logical structure of the language does not change. 'The analytic/synthetic distinction can be drawn always and only with respect to a language system, i.e. a language organised according to explicitly formulated rules, not with respect to a historically given natural language' (Carnap, 'Quine on Analyticity', in *Dear Carnap, Dear Van*, pp. 427–32).

33   R. Carnap, 'Meaning Postulates', repr. in his *Meaning and Necessity*, p. 222. Carnap's claim should not be conflated with Kaufmann's (see n. 8 above) that the word 'true' has two different meanings. According to Carnap, the difference in kind turns on the difference in truth-grounds. According to Kaufmann, to say of an

analytic proposition that it is true is to say something different from saying of an empirical proposition that it is true. *Pace* Tarski and Quine, there is something right about both claims, although 'seen through a glass darkly'.

34   It is striking, as Daniel Isaacson has noted ('Carnap, Quine and Logical Truth', in *Subjectivity and Science*, ed. D. Bell and Wilhelm Vossenkuhl (Akademie Verlag, Berlin, 1993), pp. 114–16), that Quine's argument turns on pitting a variant of Duhemian holism against Carnap (for present purposes we may disregard the Quinean distortion of Duhem's claims for physics (see n. 21 above)). But Carnap accepted (a version of) Duhemian holism:

> If a sentence which is an L-consequence of certain P-primitive sentences contradicts a sentence which has been stated as a protocol sentence, then some change must be made in the system. For instance, the P-rules can be altered in such a way that those particular primitive sentences are no longer valid; or the protocol sentences can be taken as non-valid; or again the L-rules which have been used in the deduction can also be changed. There are no established rules for the kind of change which must be made.
>
> There is in the strict sense no refutation (falsification) of an hypothesis; for even when it proves to be L-incompatible with certain protocol sentences, there always exists the possibility of maintaining the hypothesis and renouncing acknowledgement of the protocol sentences. . . . Thus *the test applies, at bottom, not to a single hypothesis but to the whole system of physics as a system of hypotheses* (Duhem, Poincaré).
>
> No rule of the physical language is definitive; all rules are laid down with the reservation that they may be altered as soon as it seems expedient to do so. This applies not only to the P-rules but also to the L-rules, including those of mathematics. In this respect, there are only differences in degree; certain rules are more difficult to renounce than others. (*The Logical Syntax of Language* (Routledge and Kegan Paul, London, 1937), p. 318)

Isaacson points out that Carnap accepted holism, without renouncing, but, rather, insisting on, the validity of the analytic/synthetic distinction. Analyticity is relative to pragmatic constraints on theory; we can relinquish any kind of statement in the face of experience, but to relinquish L-valid truths is different from relinquishing empirical truths. The former, but not the latter, involve change of meaning. The one involves admitting falsehood, the other change of concepts, as pointed out by Grice and Strawson. Carnap's principle of tolerance implied that one can adopt any logic one pleases, if it makes our science more successful, and that is something with which Quine agreed.

I am indebted to Dr Isaacson for numerous discussions about Quine.

35   Grice and Strawson, 'In Defense of a Dogma', pp. 204f.

36   Side by side with this excursus into armchair anthropology, Quine engages in armchair learning theory. It is striking that so many American critics of Wittgenstein and Oxford analytic philosophy (castigated as 'ordinary language philosophy') have accused its proponents of 'armchair linguistics', whereas few have accused Quine of what is patently armchair learning theory and armchair anthropology. The accusation levelled at Wittgenstein and Oxford analytic philosophy was unwarranted (see pp. 233–7), but it is not easy to see how Quine can be justified in his a priori description of the methodology of field linguists engaged upon radical translation, or in his a priori characterization of language learning. His interpretation of the constraints of a behaviourist methodology is arguably far too narrow (see pp. 207–11, 218–21).

37   It is by no means obvious that the identifiability of negation and conjunction suffice to yield a translation of sentential connectives such as 'if . . . , then . . .'. If

Strawson is right about the deviation of the truth-functional connectives of the logical calculus from the sentential connectives of natural languages, then 'If . . . , then . . .' is not, in the requisite sense, truth-functional, and is not used in the same way as, and does not mean the same as, 'Not both not . . . and . . .'. (See P. F. Strawson, '"If" and "⊃"', in *Philosophical Grounds of Rationality*, ed. R. E. Grandy and R. Warner (Clarendon Press, Oxford, 1986), pp. 229–42.) The argument against the truth-functional analysis, and against the Gricean attempt to explain away apparent differences between the natural language sentential connectives and the truth-functional logical connectives by reference to pragmatic conversational conventions, is pursued further in O. Hanfling, *The Bent and Genius of our Tongue: Philosophy and Ordinary Language* (forthcoming). It is anything but obvious, Hanfling points out, that, as Quine suggests, we can learn 'that an alternation is implied by its components, with the very learning of the word "or"' (RoR 80). If someone has asserted, or assented to, the utterance 'Mummy is at home', it is more than merely improbable that he will then also assent to the question 'So either Mummy is at home or dead?' No matter whether adult or child, he is likely to respond with incomprehension. And if the query is: 'So Mummy is either at home or out shopping?', the correct reply would be dissent: 'No, I just told you that she is at home.'

38 See H.-J. Glock, 'The Indispensability of Translation in Quine and Davidson', in PQ, 43 (1993), pp. 194–209, for a critical discussion of the matter.

39 For more detailed discussion of Wittgenstein's objections to behaviourist accounts of meaning, see Volume 3, 'Behaviour and behaviourism', §§2–3, from which the remarks made here are derived.

40 See S. Shanker, 'The Conflict between Wittgenstein and Quine on the Nature of Language and Cognition and its Implications for Constraint Theory', forthcoming in *Wittgenstein and Quine*, ed. R. Arrington and H.-J. Glock (Routledge, London, 1996).

41 If it were, then, *inter alia*, there would be no deferring to experts to explain the use of technical and quasi-technical terms; appeal to socio-linguistic surveys would suffice.

42 Quine makes room for ostensive instruction, but interprets it causally rather than normatively, thus failing to distinguish ostensive training from ostensive teaching, ostensive definition and explanation of meaning (see p. 216).

43 It should be noted that not everything that is not normative (rule-governed) is conditioning. Innumerable purposive activities, skills and techniques – e.g. how to whistle tunes or tell jokes – are neither normative or theory-constructing activities nor a matter of stimulus/response conditioning. They are typically open-ended and 'plastic', adaptable to indefinitely many circumstances.

44 Quine's concept of stimulus meaning is allegedly an ersatz behaviourist concept of meaning, trimmed to the demands of rigorous science. The affirmative stimulus meaning of an observation sentence (for a speaker) is the class of all stimulations that would prompt the speaker's assent, stimulations being taken as the impact of radiation, etc. on his sense-receptors. This, Quine claims, '*is a reasonable notion of meaning*' for such observation sentences as 'Rabbit' and 'The tide is out' (WO 44). But 'stimulus meaning' is not a technical term which is related to, and a refinement (or explication) of, our ordinary notion of meaning. Rather, it is a notion of meaning that has broken all connection with what we understand by 'meaning'. This will not disturb Quine, but may give pause to those who are less cavalier about our workaday concepts and their refinement for specialized purposes. (i) It violates the grammar of 'meaning', for some stimulus meanings are larger than

others (since some classes are larger than others), some stimulus meanings include members which are exclusively sound-waves (e.g. the stimulus meaning of 'Noise!'), and some stimulus meanings consist exclusively of painful stimuli (e.g. 'Hurts', 'Stings', 'Burns'). But the meaning of a one-word sentence cannot intelligibly be said to be larger than that of another; the meaning of the exclamation 'Noise!' (or of the sentence 'There is a noise') cannot be said to include sound-waves among its members; and the meaning of 'Hurts!' or 'Stings!' does not include members that are painful or pleasurable stimuli, since the meaning of an expression is not a class of anything. On the other hand, the meanings of some sentences are hard to grasp, difficult to explain, and impossible to render precisely in French; but classes of stimulations that prompt assent are neither easy nor difficult to grasp, cannot – in the relevant sense – be explained (since there is nothing in the semantic dimension to explain), and there is no rendering classes of stimuli in French. (ii) It provides no standard by reference to which the use of an expression can be said to be correct or incorrect. The class of stimuli (construed in terms of surface irritations) that prompt one's assent to 'Gavagai', not to mention those that prompt another's assent, is not only inaccessible (since, scientists apart, few speakers know anything about the character of surface irritations and their description), but no standard of correct use. (iii) It bears no connection to understanding an expression. For to understand an expression is to have mastered the technique of its use, and that is a normative skill, not a conditioned response.

If this is correct, it is far from obvious why Quine's notion should be characterized as a concept of *meaning* (even an ersatz one) at all. Saccharine is ersatz sugar, but something that is neither sweet nor water-soluble is not.

45   Grice and Strawson, 'In Defense of a Dogma', p. 207.
46   For an illuminating discussion of the confusions involved in supposing that our humdrum talk of the meanings of linguistic expressions commits us to an 'ontology of meanings', see B. Rundle, *Grammar in Philosophy* (Clarendon Press, Oxford, 1979), pp. 377–83.
47   For more extensive discussion, see G. P. Baker and P. M. S. Hacker, *Language, Sense and Nonsense* (Blackwell, Oxford, 1984), pp. 211–18.
48   Yet it is noteworthy that one can ostensively define directions of the compass. And one can ostensively define smells and sounds by reference to samples, even though one does not, strictly speaking, point at an object (see Volume 1, 'Ostensive definition and its ramifications', §2).
49   Even the law of non-contradiction has the same status as all else. It is just that 'without it we would be left making mutually contrary predictions indiscriminately, thus scoring a poor ratio of successes over failures' ('Comment on Quinton', in *Perspectives on Quine*, ed. Barrett and Gibson, p. 309).
50   See A. M. Quinton, *The Nature of Things* (Routledge and Kegan Paul, London, 1973), pp. 216f., and his 'Doing without Meaning' in *Perspectives on Quine*, ed. Barrett and Gibson, p. 307, and Glock, 'Wittgenstein vs. Quine on Logical Necessity', pp. 216–20.
51   For detailed argument, see G. P. Baker and P. M. S. Hacker, *Scepticism, Rules and Language* (Blackwell, Oxford, 1984), pp. 92f.
52   It is curious that Quine should think the input 'meagre'. What would it be like if it were richer? Even more 'irradiations', incessant noise and flashing of lights? In *Word and Object*, he wrote: 'We have been reflecting in a general way on how surface irritations generate, through language, one's knowledge of the world. . . . The voluminous and intricately structured talk that comes out bears little evident correspondence to the past and present barrage of non-verbal stimulation; yet it is

to such stimulation that we must look for whatever empirical content there must be' (WO 26). This is equally curious. If the 'input' is to be described in terms of surface irritations, then the 'output' should be described in terms of bare physical movements and the generation of sound-waves. If the output is to be described in terms of structured talk (and human action), then the input should be described in terms of what is perceived, the visible and audible, etc. environment, including the voluminous and intricately structured talk of our fellow human beings.

53 Assent to a sentence, according to Quine, is passing a *verdict* on its truth, which may be *mistaken*. The subject is held to *believe* what is uttered (UPM 48). The observation sentences which are the 'entering wedge in the learning of language' are vehicles of scientific *evidence*, verbalizing the predictions which *check* scientific theories (PT 4f.). Consequently, the concept of assent which he deploys is intimately interwoven with epistemic and intensional concepts. Invoking the principle of charity as a pragmatic guide-line for translation makes this evident.

54 The primacy of behaviour viewed intentionalistically is a leitmotif of G. H. von Wright's extensive writings on the explanation of human action, from *Explanation and Understanding* (1971) onwards.

55 For detailed discussion, see Baker and Hacker, *Language, Sense and Nonsense*, ch. 8.

56 And one regarding which it would be difficult to argue, given the associated behaviour, that there is no fact of the matter about the translation of the term, no less than the one-word sentence.

57 Nor for qualitative identity either, since the colours, lengths or weights of things that have the same colour, length or weight are neither numerically nor qualitatively identical; it is the numerically distinct objects that share these properties that may be qualitatively identical.

58 It is opaque what Quine means by 'raw experience'. If it is something preconceptual (as Kant supposed intuitions to be), then it is no datum from which one can argue. If it *is* a datum, then, it seems, it is given in terms of concepts which are not ontologically relative. Moreover, it is then given in terms that presuppose the existence of things in general which are not raw experiences, e.g. that it seems to one just as if one were perceiving such-and-such a thing. And if it is thus given, then it is not posited. Nor is it part of any theory.

59 To be sure, some 'surface irritations' may be the grounds for an inference. A thump on the back may be grounds for thinking that someone has hit me, as a tickling sensation may be grounds for thinking that an insect is crawling on my neck.

60 He adds that this is no answer to the scepticism of the idealist or the assurances of the realist. But one could say that the assertion that there are physical objects, or its denial, is a misfiring attempt to express something which cannot be thus expressed (C §37).

Chapter 8   The Decline of Analytic Philosophy

1 B. Russell, *My Philosophical Development* (Allen and Unwin, London, 1959), p. 214.

2 G. J. Warnock, 'Gilbert Ryle's Editorship', *Mind*, 85 (1976), p. 51.

3 N. Goodman, 'Review of Urmson's *Philosophical Analysis*', repr. in his *Problems and Projects* (Bobbs-Merrill, Indianapolis, 1972), p. 44.

4 B. Russell, 'On Scientific Method in Philosophy', repr. in *The Collected Papers of Bertrand Russell* (Allen and Unwin, London, 1986), vol. 8, p. 66.

5 Russell's assertion that it is dualist prejudice that prevents us from locating mental occurrences in brains is wrong. It is, rather, that saying that the pangs of dispriz'd love occur in one's brain, that one's stomach-ache is located in one's head, or that

one's decision to go to London took place in one's cranium, transgress the bounds of sense. (See Volume 3, 'Privacy', §1, for a discussion of the grammar of the location of pain; 'Thinking: methodological muddles and categorial confusions', §4, for a discussion of the grammar of the location of thoughts and thinking; and 'Men, minds and machines', §§1 and 4, for a general discussion of the fallacy of ascribing a predicate to parts of a being which applies licitly only to the creature as a whole.) No sense has been assigned to such forms of words. Of course, we could assign sense to them – but we must first do so. Were we to do so, it would not be because scientific discoveries have shown that our existing grammar is false, and the new grammar is true to the facts. For there is no such thing as a *false* grammar. The form of an expression, e.g. 'He has a pain in his stomach', cannot say something false 'even when that proposition *faute de mieux* asserted something true' (PI §402 and Exg.). Moreover, the new idiom would still have to distinguish between having a stomach-ache in one's brain and having a headache in one's brain.

6   For an amusing, popular account of the matter, see Ved Mehta, *The Fly and the Fly-bottle* (Weidenfeld and Nicolson, London, 1963).

7   For more detail, see P. M. S. Hacker, *Insight and Illusion: Themes in the Philosophy of Wittgenstein*, rev. edn (Clarendon Press, Oxford, 1986), pp. 193–206, from which my discussion is derived.

8   Indeed, since there were conflicting accounts of what was alleged to be ordinary use by Oxford philosophers, Ryle arguing that 'voluntary' and 'involuntary' apply only to actions that ought not to be done, and Austin holding that 'we may join the army or make a gift voluntarily, we may hiccup or make a small gesture involuntarily' ('A Plea for Excuses', in his *Philosophical Papers*, ed. J. O. Urmson and G. J. Warnock (Clarendon Press, Oxford, 1961), p. 139), it was remarked: 'If agreement about usage cannot be reached within so restricted a sample as the class of Oxford Professors of Philosophy, what are the prospects when the sample is enlarged' (Benson Mates, 'On the Verification of Statements about Ordinary Language' (1958), repr. in *Philosophy and Linguistics*, ed. C. Lyas (Macmillan, London, 1971), p. 125).

9   Mates, 'On the Verification of Statements about Ordinary Language', held that assertions about what the ordinary use of an expression is are empirical claims, verifiable by extensional or intensional methods of socio-linguistic investigation. The extensional method involves observing how a representative sample of speakers use the expression and extracting from the data what is common to all cases. The intensional method involves asking a sample of speakers how they use an expression, and confronting them, in Socratic manner, with counter-examples and borderline cases until they settle upon a definition or account. Both, Mates, claimed, are equally scientific, but may yield conflicting results.

10 Of course, Wittgenstein's conception of what *counts* as being in 'good logical order' changed between the *Tractatus* and the *Investigations*, but that does not affect the validity of his remark.

11 Austin, 'A Plea for Excuses', p. 132.

12 Grice took a different line on these methodological questions (see 'Postwar Oxford Philosophy', in his *Studies in the Way of Words* (Harvard University Press, Cambridge, Mass., and London, 1989), p. 175). One is providing, he argued, a conceptual analysis of one's own use. This one may do correctly or incorrectly, and if one does it incorrectly, one's error will duly be pointed out by others who share the same language. Certainly there is a presumption of sameness of use, for the expressions typically in question are commonly used in the same way by members

of a particular speech-community. But there is no need to conduct a poll. For if there are alternative uses, that does not matter. The philosophical puzzle with which one is dealing is a puzzle which arises in connection with one's own use, and its resolution by reference to one's analysis will be of value to whoever uses the relevant expression in the same way – which in the vast majority of cases will include all who are puzzled by the problem.

One must be careful not to underplay the extent to which the description of use in connective analysis is intended to be (a) common (shared) use and (b) pivotal to a common philosophical problem at hand. Grice's methodological individualism arguably distorts the practice of philosophy.

13 B. Russell, 'The Philosophy of Logical Atomism', repr. in *Collected Papers*, vol. 8, p. 172.

14 For arguments in favour of their compatibility, see P. M. S. Hacker, *Appearance and Reality, a Philosophical Investigation into Perception and Perceptual Qualities* (Blackwell, Oxford, 1987).

15 A. G. N. Flew, 'Philosophy and Language', in *Essays in Conceptual Analysis*, ed. Flew (Macmillan, London, 1956), p. 19.

16 N. Malcolm, 'Moore and Ordinary Language', in *The Philosophy of G. E. Moore*, ed. P. A. Schilpp (Open Court, La Salle, Ill., 1942), p. 361.

17 See, e.g., C. S. Chihara and J. A. Fodor, 'Operationalism and Ordinary Language: A Critique of Wittgenstein', repr. in *Wittgenstein, The Philosophical Investigations – A Collection of Critical Essays*, ed. G. Pitcher (Doubleday, New York, 1966), pp. 384–419.

18 M. A. E. Dummett, 'Oxford Philosophy' (1960), repr. in his *Truth and Other Enigmas* (Duckworth, London, 1978), p. 434.

19 B. Williams, 'The Spell of Linguistic Philosophy: Dialogue with Bernard Williams', in B. Magee et al., *Men of Ideas, Some Creators of Contemporary Philosophy* (British Broadcasting Corporation, London, 1978), pp. 144f.

20 Dummett, 'Oxford Philosophy', p. 436.

21 M. A. E. Dummett, *Origins of Analytic Philosophy* (Duckworth, London, 1993), pp. 164f.

22 Thus, e.g., the proposition that 'inner processes' stand in need of outward criteria (mentioned only in irony to disabuse one of the idea that belief is an inner process or state – see Exg. §580) is a grammatical proposition that gives us a synoptic view of the rules for the use of a host of psychological expressions. Extensive argument has been deployed in order to show that the use of such expressions is bound up with behavioural criteria for their third-person ascription, in the absence of which, the first-person, criterionless use collapses into incoherence.

23 As noted (Exg. §664), the metaphor of surface and depth is not a happy one, being more suited to the *Tractatus* conception of language than to that of the *Investigations*. The *Tractatus* conception of analysis calls out for such a geological metaphor, but the *Investigations* demands a topographical one.

24 For detailed substantiation of this view, see G. P. Baker and P. M. S. Hacker, *Language, Sense and Nonsense* (Blackwell, Oxford, 1984).

25 For detailed explanation of why Wittgenstein cannot be characterized as an 'anti-realist', see Hacker, *Insight and Illusion*, pp. 322–35.

26 For an illuminating discussion, see Stephen Mulhall, *On Being in the World: Wittgenstein and Heidegger on Seeing Aspects* (Routledge, London and New York, 1990).

27 Critics of Wittgenstein who also defend the enterprise of constructing a theory of meaning for a natural language based on the concept of a truth-condition often express bewilderment at Wittgenstein's repudiation of a distinction between

sentence-radical and force-operator (see e.g. M. A. E. Dummett, 'Frege and Wittgenstein' in *Perspectives on the Philosophy of Wittgenstein*, ed. I. Block (Blackwell, Oxford, 1981), pp. 40f.). It is true that *if* one is to explain word-meaning in terms of the contribution of a word to the truth-conditions of any sentence in which it can occur, then every sentence in which it can occur must be conceived of as having truth-conditions. This forces the theorist to argue that imperative sentences and sentence-questions must have truth-conditions, which in turn forces upon them the view that such sentences 'contain' a truth-value-bearing component, i.e. a sentence-radical. This is precisely what Wittgenstein denied, for any attempt to make out such a case results in absurdity (see Exg. §22 and p. 11n, and Volume 1, 'The uses of sentences'; for detailed refutation of the truth-conditional theorist's manœuvre, see Baker and Hacker, *Language, Sense and Nonsense*, chs 2–3). An explanation of the meaning of a word must be indifferent to whether that word occurs in a declarative, imperative or interrogative sentence, and its meaning cannot in general be characterized as its contribution to the truth-conditions of any sentence in which it can occur, since it can occur meaningfully in indefinitely many sentences which cannot be said to have any truth-conditions or to contain a truth-value-bearing component.

28 G. H. von Wright, *The Varieties of Goodness* (Routledge and Kegan Paul, London, 1963), pp. 4–6; *idem*, 'Intellectual Autobiography', in *The Philosophy of G. H. von Wright*, ed. P. A. Schilpp and L. E. Hahn (Open Court, La Salle, Ill., 1989), pp. 47–53.

29 The only example that comes to mind is the suggestion that to dissipate Hegelian confusions arising out of the use of 'is', one might recommend its replacement by two different signs, viz. '=' and '∈' (PLP 35f.).

30 One of the many questionable consequences of Frege's account is that his reification of sense commits him to the view that different speakers grasp the numerically same sense, in contradistinction to ideas, which are allegedly such that no two people can have the numerically same idea. This in turn commits him to the impossible task of having to explain what it would be for different speakers to grasp numerically distinct but qualitatively identical senses. If A and B both understand an expression '*s*', then they can be said to 'grasp the same sense' (i.e. to know what '*s*' means); but the sense they both 'grasp' is neither numerically nor qualitatively the same, it is just the same. Frege was mistaken in accepting the view that 'ideas' are 'privately owned', that one man cannot have another man's idea – *if* that means that two people cannot have the very same idea: not numerically the same, nor qualitatively the same, but just the same. The distinction between numerical and qualitative identity, which applies to substances, applies neither to ideas nor to senses or meanings of expressions. (For discussion of the confusions of the 'private ownership' of ideas and sensations, see Volume 3, 'Privacy', §2, and Exg. §253; for criticisms of Frege's conception of thoughts, see G. P. Baker and P. M. S. Hacker, *Frege: Logical Excavations* (Blackwell, Oxford, and Oxford University Press, New York, 1984), pp. 353–61.

31 R. M. Hare, *The Language of Morals* (Oxford University Press, Oxford, 1952).

32 J. L. Austin, 'Other Minds', repr. in his *Philosophical Papers*, pp. 44–84.

33 Rare exceptions are Vol. XII, 172 and MS 124, 232, which point out that 'I greet you' and 'I thank you' are not statements, but greetings and thanks respectively (see Exg. §489).

34 Grice developed this form of analysis in various papers, beginning with 'The Causal Theory of Perception' (PASS, 1961) and culminating in the 'Prolegomena' to *Studies in the Way of Words*, in which all the relevant papers are collected.

35   See H.-J. Glock, 'Abusing Use', forthcoming in *Dialectica,* and in more detail O.
      Hanfling, *The Bent and Genius of our Tongue: Philosophy and Ordinary Language*
      (forthcoming). For a systematic examination of the use of sentential connectives in
      natural language, see B. Rundle, *Grammar in Philosophy* (Clarendon Press, Oxford,
      1979).

36   Of course, there are criteria for trying which are satisfied only when the agent
      fails, and which turn not on what the agent did (he might, on another occasion do
      exactly the same and be said to have V'd without trying) but on the circumstances
      of the act. If I wave to a friend to attract his attention, I do not normally try. But
      if, as I raise my hand, a passing bus occludes me from his view, then I tried to
      attract his attention, but failed.

37   B. Rundle, *Wittgenstein and Contemporary Philosophy of Language* (Blackwell, Ox-
      ford, 1990), ch. 1.

38   See H. Putnam, 'Brains and Behaviour', in *Analytical Philosophy*, 2nd ser., ed. R. J.
      Butler (Blackwell, Oxford, 1968), pp. 1–19.

39   This Putnamian account is a contemporary modification of the Lockean distinction
      between nominal and real essence, which, *pace* Locke, holds the real essence of X
      to be a feature of the meaning of 'X'. Kripke's rather different account will not be
      discussed here.

40   H. Putnam, 'The Meaning of "Meaning"', repr. in his *Mind, Language and Reality*
      (Cambridge University Press, Cambridge, 1975), pp. 215–71.

41   S. P. Schwartz, ed., *Naming, Necessity and Natural Kinds* (Cornell University Press,
      Ithaca, NY, and London, 1977), pp. 34f.

42   For detailed criticism, informed by extensive knowledge of scientific classification,
      see J. Dupré, *The Disorder of Things – Metaphysical Foundations of the Disunity of
      Science* (Harvard University Press, Cambridge, Mass., and London, 1993), chs 1–
      3. For criticism of the attendant science fiction (which I have bypassed), see O.
      Hanfling, 'Scientific Realism and Ordinary Language', *Philosophical Investigations*, 7
      (1984), pp. 187–205.

43   If X, Y and Z are elements, what are their atomic numbers? How can they be
      accommodated in the periodic table of elements? There is no 'room' for them
      compatible with our knowledge of chemistry. What valencies might they have,
      and what is the form of the chemical bonding into which they enter in the com-
      pound XYZ? What are the properties of pure X (Y and Z), which are such that
      twin Earth is overtly indistinguishable from Earth? Does XYZ have the same
      weight as H_2O? If so, how is that possible, given the rest of our knowledge of
      chemistry and of chemical elements? If not, then it cannot behave in the same way
      as H_2O. If X, Y and Z are not elements, but 'XYZ' merely abbreviates a 'long and
      complicated formula' (as Putnam suggests), how is it possible, compatibly with
      established chemical theory, that it have the same overt properties (freezing and
      boiling points, weight, etc.) as H_2O?

44   See J. Dupré, 'The Disunity of Science', *Mind*, 92 (1983), pp. 326f.

45   But not into ordinary parlance in any straightforward fashion. To ask for a glass
      of water is not to ask for a glass of H_2O, since the latter, unlike the stuff that comes
      out of the tap, can readily cause death if drunk in quantity, and is deadly if infused
      directly into the veins.

46   Putnam has tried to adduce persuasive examples to bolster his claim that scientific
      discovery does *not* bring about a change in meaning, but, rather, reveals the true
      meaning of a customary expression. In Newtonian physics, he points out, mo-
      mentum was defined as 'mass times velocity', and was found to be conserved in
      elastic collision. To maintain momentum as a conserved quantity, the theory of

relativity revised the identification of momentum with rest mass times velocity. But, Putnam argued, this cannot be construed as revising the meaning of the term 'momentum', for that would imply that scientists are now talking about something different. 'But no, we are still talking about the same good old momentum – the magnitude that is conserved in elastic collisions' (H. Putnam, *Representation and Reality* (MIT Press, Cambridge, Mass., 1988), p. 11). This is confused. Prior to Einstein, the meaning of 'momentum' oscillated between 'mass times velocity' and 'whatever quantity is conserved in elastic collision', either of which could be taken as defining it. Since they seemed invariably to coincide, there was no need to decide which was a criterion and which a symptom. With the discovery that rest mass times velocity is not strictly conserved in elastic collision, it became reasonable to define momentum as what is conserved in elastic collision, not as mass times velocity. And this was, indeed, a change in the meaning of momentum, a change from a meaning that was allowed harmlessly to oscillate between two distinct but apparently coincident conditions to a meaning that is not. Putnam's example exemplifies the importance of Wittgenstein's remark 'The fluctuation in grammar between criteria and symptoms makes it look as if there were nothing at all but symptoms' (PI §354). For

> nothing is more common than for the meaning of an expression to oscillate, for a phenomenon to be regarded sometimes as a symptom, sometimes as a criterion, of a state of affairs. And mostly in such a case the shift of meaning is not noted. In science it is usual to make phenomena that allow of exact measurement into the defining criteria for an expression; and then one is inclined to think that now the proper meaning has been *found*. Innumerable confusions have arisen in this way. (Z §438)

(See H.-J. Glock, 'Wittgenstein vs. Quine on Logical Necessity', in *Wittgenstein and Contemporary Philosophy*, ed. S. Teghrarian (Thoemmes Press, Bristol, 1994), pp. 205–8.)

47   E.g. Chihara and Fodor, in 'Operationalism and Ordinary Language', and Putnam, 'Brains and Behaviour'.
48   M. A. E. Dummett, 'Wittgenstein's Philosophy of Mathematics' (1959), repr. in *Wittgenstein, The Philosophical Investigations*, ed. Pitcher, pp. 420–47; subsequently referred to as 'Dummett's review'.
49   My allusion is to Ramsey's accusation against Brouwer and Weyl that they introduced 'Bolshevism' into mathematics – i.e. disrupted mathematics. Turing, as Wittgenstein noted (LFM 67), thought much the same of what Wittgenstein was doing, although in fact the very last thing Wittgenstein wanted to do was to interfere with *the mathematics* of mathematicians, only with what they had to say about what they were doing or had done.
50   M. A. E. Dummett, 'Wittgenstein on Necessity: Some Reflections', in his *The Seas of Language* (Clarendon Press, Oxford, 1993), pp. 446–61.
51   For a much more extensive account, though still woefully incomplete, see Volume 2, 'Grammar and necessity'.
52   Wittgenstein already remarked in the *Tractatus* that 'in real life a mathematical proposition is never what we want. Rather, we make use of mathematical propositions *only* in inferences from propositions that do not belong to mathematics to others that likewise do not belong to mathematics' (TLP 6.211).
53   The statement that π lies between two rationals amounts to the following in application: that if one measures the circumference of a circle and says that it is $d\pi$, then every *rational* measure will be inexact, will be either too much or too little.

But, Wittgenstein conceded, most of the mathematics of the continuum has no such direct application to physical things. The roots of the development of mathematical systems lie in their practical purpose, in the sense that without it the work of systematizing mathematics would never have got started. But the further elaboration of mathematics may be concerned to achieve greater 'elegance', simplicity and uniformity between different deductions. This in turn may lead to the development of new branches of mathematics without reference to any possible application at all, to the construction of systems of 'empty connections'. For some of these an application may subsequently be found, sometimes in an unexpected way. Sometimes an application may be found for a new branch of mathematics, not directly to physical phenomena, but rather to the process of doing mathematics itself – which may be extremely useful in giving an account of certain mathematical procedures. But in some cases it may be that no application will ever be found (RR 132).

54 Nor would it make any difference if they had computers. For to accept *whatever* a computer produced as *the* result, irrespective of the fact that members of the speech-community could not arrive at agreement in calculations, is likewise a decision.

55 For more detailed examination of Dummett's example, see Volume 2, 'Grammar and necessity', pp. 320–2, whence the above argument is derived.

56 For some of Wittgenstein's objections to this realist, Platonist conception of a mathematical reality, see Volume 2, 'Grammar and necessity'.

57 That does not mean that it cannot have a role *within* mathematics, e.g. in *reductio* proofs.

58 Wittgenstein may well have used the term 'discovery' here, in a casual conversation, but he was generally opposed to the misleading picture of 'mathematical discovery' (see Volume 2, 'Grammar and necessity', pp. 295–303).

59 Wittgenstein cautiously prefaces this remark with 'One would like to say'. How much of a qualification this is meant to be is unclear to me.

60 Warnock, 'Gilbert Ryle's Editorship', *Mind*, 1976, p. 52.

61 For the distinction between dialectical and analytical hermeneutics, see G. H. von Wright, *Explanation and Understanding* (Routledge and Kegan Paul, London, 1971), pp. 29f. and 181f.

62 It is striking that Quine had relatively little impact in Britain, perhaps because his major contribution to the subject occurred in the 1950s and 1960s, when the native tradition was still flourishing and powerful. By contrast, Davidson, whose most influential work was done two decades later, became the primary influence upon philosophy of language and philosophy of psychology in Britain in the 1970s and 1980s.

63 Central state materialism emerged (in its contemporary form) in order to plug what seemed to materialist-minded philosophers a gap in Ryle's thinking in *The Concept of Mind*. Noticing (unlike those who accused Ryle of behaviourism) that Ryle did not try to reduce sensations to behaviour and dispositions to behave, it appeared to them that the 'ghost in the machine' had not been fully exorcized. Hence early central state materialists, U. T. Place and J. J. C. Smart, initially argued only that sensations are contingently identical with states of the central nervous system. But before long David Armstrong, in his *A Materialist Theory of the Mind* (Routledge and Kegan Paul, London, 1968), extended the identity theory to the whole domain of the mental, abandoning altogether the Rylean insights into the conceptual complexity, diversity and distinctiveness of our mental vocabulary. In effect, such materialist doctrines reverted to classical empiricist conceptions of the *causal structure* of the mental and its relation to behaviour, differing from them

primarily in identifying the mental with the neural. Accordingly, causation is not merely the cement of the universe; it is also the glue of the mind. The result can with some justice be characterized, as previously remarked, as 'brain/body dualism'. Functionalism, which succeeded central state materialism, did not differ in this respect.

64   There is a noteworthy similarity here between the *Tractatus* and de Saussure's conception of 'langue' as an abstract system of rules underlying 'parole'.

65   I disregard here such platitudinous, but not unimportant, features as the fact that a new generation had come on-stage, that many of the protagonists of connective analytic philosophy had either died or retired (had Austin lived longer, the development of philosophy in Oxford might well have been different), that the conception of connective analysis that was transmitted to the younger generation was grossly distorted by widespread misinterpretation, and that, as we have seen, Wittgenstein was conceived, especially in the United States, as an 'ordinary language philosopher', and was accordingly assimilated to the distorting composite picture of 'Oxford philosophy'.

66   Here one might cite Rundle's masterly *Grammar in Philosophy*.

67   E.g. Strawson's *Subject and Predicate in Logic and Grammar* (Methuen, London, 1974), as well as his numerous papers, some of which are collected in his *Logico-linguistic Papers* (Methuen, London, 1971).

68   See D. Davidson, *Inquiries into Truth and Interpretation* (Clarendon Press, Oxford, 1984).

69   D. Davidson, 'The Logical Form of Action Sentences', in *The Logic of Decision and Action*, ed. N. Rescher (University of Pittsburgh Press, Pittsburgh, 1967), p. 115.

70   D. Davidson, 'Truth and Meaning' (1967), repr. in his *Inquiries into Truth and Interpretation*, p. 17.

71   He remarked that he got through graduate school at Harvard by reading Feigl and Sellars ('Hempel on Explaining Action', repr. in D. Davidson, *Essays on Actions and Events* (Clarendon Press, Oxford, 1982), p. 261). Hempel was a major influence upon his conception of explanation of action, and Tarski upon his conception of truth and of meaning as given by specification of truth-conditions.

72   This was noted by S. Kripke, *Wittgenstein on Rules and Private Language* (Blackwell, Oxford, 1982), p. 71, n. 60; by Baker and Hacker, *Language, Sense and Nonsense*, pp. 4–11, 45–6 and ch. 9; and by J. C. C. Smart in his 'How to Turn the *Tractatus* Wittgenstein into (Almost) Donald Davidson', in *Truth and Interpretation, Perspectives on the Philosophy of Donald Davidson*, ed. E. LePore (Blackwell, Oxford and New York, 1986), pp. 92–100.

73   But it is misconceived to argue that events *exist*; objects exist, whereas events happen, occur or take place. It is questionable whether it even makes sense to *prove* that there are events, inasmuch as it makes no sense to question or doubt whether anything ever happens. See P. M. S. Hacker, 'Events, Ontology and Grammar', *Philosophy*, 57 (1982), pp. 477–86, and 'Events and Objects in Space and Time', *Mind*, 91 (1982), pp. 1–19.

74   For criticism of the interpretation of the question of how it is possible to understand sentences never heard before, and of the methods of answering it that became popular throughout the 1970s, see Baker and Hacker, *Language, Sense and Nonsense*, ch. 9.

75   D. Davidson, 'A Nice Derangement of Epitaphs', in *Truth and Interpretation*, ed. LePore, pp. 437f.

76   This was explicitly acknowledged by Davidson: 'Philosophers of a logical bent have tended to start where the theory was [viz. the formal semantics of logical

calculi] and work out towards the complications of natural language. Contemporary linguists, with an aim that cannot easily be seen to be different, start with the ordinary and work towards a general theory. If either party is successful, there must be a meeting' ('Truth and Meaning', p. 30).

77 The similarity with the *Tractatus* conception of a single, uniform logical syntax of all possible languages is obvious. So too are the differences, the one being held to have species-specific biological roots, the other to have metaphysical foundations.

78 N. Chomsky, *Rules and Representations* (Blackwell, Oxford, 1980), p. 70.

79 N. Chomsky, *Language and Problems of Knowledge* (MIT Press, Cambridge, Mass., 1988). The fragments quoted are taken from pp. 55, 60, 78, 81, 90, 136. For a detailed anatomization of errors, see P. M. S. Hacker, 'Chomsky's Problems', *Language and Communication*, 10 (1990), pp. 127–48.

80 Very briefly, he argued that if thought were a language, it would make sense for a person to raise the question of what he meant by what he thought or by a constituent of his thought; but it makes no sense to think that N.N. is in New York, and to wonder what one means thereby, or to wonder who one means by 'N.N.' (see Volume 3, 'Thinking: the soul of language', pp. 314f., 330f.). Similarly, he held that it is senseless to conceive of a person *following* rules with which he is unacquainted, for to follow a rule is to use or be willing to use a rule as a standard for correct behaviour, a reason for acting and a ground for criticism. It must be possible for one to cite the rule as a justification or to acknowledge it as the rule one is following, and to refer to the rule in an explanation (see Volume 2, 'Accord with a rule' and 'Following rules, mastery of techniques and practices'). The fact that a certain behaviour *can* be mapped on to a notional rule does not constitute a reason for thinking that there is any such rule or that anyone has been following it. To follow a rule, one must know what *counts* as acting in accordance with the rule, and guide one's conduct accordingly. For detailed discussion of the role attributed to hidden rules in contemporary linguistic theory, see Baker and Hacker, *Language, Sense and Nonsense*, chs 7–9.

81 See Baker and Hacker, *Frege: Logical Excavations*, p. 26.

82 See, e.g., C. G. Phillips, S. Zeki and H. B. Barlow, 'Localization of Function in the Cerebral Cortex, Past, Present and Future', *Brain*, 107 (1984), p. 338.

83 See J. Z. Young, *Programs of the Brain* (Oxford University Press, Oxford, 1978), pp. 126f. For a critical examination of these and kindred ideas, see P. M. S. Hacker, 'Languages, Minds and Brains', in *Mindwaves*, ed. C. Blakemore and S. Greenfield (Blackwell, Oxford, 1987), pp. 485–505.

84 The prime defender of this conception is R. L. Gregory. See, e.g., his paper 'The Confounded Eye', in *Illusion in Nature and Art*, ed. R. L. Gregory and E. H. Gombrich (Duckworth, London, 1973), and 'Perceptions as Hypotheses', *Philosophical Transactions of the Royal Society*, B, 290 (1980). For a critical examination, see P. M. S. Hacker, 'R. L. Gregory's Theory of Perception', *Iyyun: The Jerusalem Philosophical Quarterly*, 40 (1991), pp. 289–314.

Index

Index